The Hidden Jesus

In this remarkable book Dr Michael D Magee peels off the pious accretions and interpretative wrappings added by the earliest gentile bishops to the story of the exploits of Jesus to make the gospels acceptable to the Romans and the basis of a universal religion. The truth is peculiarly transparent in the bible, although two thousand years of conditioning and the invention of spurious translations of Greek words to suit Christian belief in the so-called New Testament Greek have succeeded in blinding even the most critical of scholars. The gentile bishops of the embryonic religion were faced with travellers tales from Palestine that Jesus was not what the church wanted. This oral tradition was strong because Jews were already widespread in the Empire and after the defeat of their rebellion in the Jewish War and their dispersion in 70 AD many more arrived from Palestine. Pericopes, individual stories about Jesus, kept coming to the bishops and when they did not match their preferred image of a saintly Son of God, had to be "corrected". The bishops had to say to their flocks, "Ho, Ho, Theophilus, how silly you are. It was not quite like that. No, this is what really happened." Then they would change a few subjects and objects and retell the tale such that a core remained but the sense favoured the view they were propagating rather than the truth. It still happens today. There never was a gate in Jerusalem called The Eye of a Needle but it was invented by clerics to allow the rich to be saved when the plain sense of Jesus's aside was that it was *impossible* for the rich to be saved. Dr Magee explains parables and the healing miracles, and such difficulties as the cursing of the fig tree, the meaning of Nazarene, the cleansing of the temple, the release of Barabbas, Peter's triple denial, the tribute money and the Gadarene swine.

This book is a tour de force. For honest reasoning people, though not those who are irrational or emotionally dependent on the traditional image of Jesus, gospel stories will never be the same again—they now make sense. Oddly, the message of many modern Christians is upheld—that God is not an external supernatural entity ready to interfere with the world at a whim or a prayer. Jesus believed an external God *was* ready to intervene—he was forsaken or rather mistaken—but Christians have made the same mistake ever since, teaching people to blame devils instead of facing up to their own responsibility for their actions. Our gods and devils are within us and there we must seek and come to terms with them.

By the same author from AskWhy! Publications:

Who Lies Sleeping?
The Dinosaur Heritage and the Extinction of Man

ISBN 0-9521913-0-X

The Mystery of Barabbas:
Exploring the Origins of a Pagan Religion

ISBN 0-9521913-1-8

The Hidden Jesus

The Secret Testament Revealed

Michael D Magee

AskWhy! Publications Selwyn
Frome England

For
Shirlie Spence Griffiths

First published in Great Britain 1997
by AskWhy! Publications
Selwyn 41 The Butts, Frome
Somerset BA11 4AB
ISBN 0-9521913-2-6

Typeset by Avonset, Bath

Printed in Great Britain by

Hillman Printers (Frome) Ltd, Somerset

CONTENTS

Acknowledgements

Extracts from the Authorized Version of the Bible (The King James Bible), the rights in which are invested in the Crown, are reproduced by permission of the Crown's Patentee, Cambridge University Press.

The most accessible source of English translations of the scrolls is Geza Vermes's *The Dead Sea Scrolls in English* published by Penguin. Vermes himself observes that translators are apt to be too free in their renderings or too literal and he claims to avoid falling between the two stools. However, it is all a matter of taste and, for me, Vermes is slightly too refined. Though arguably easier to follow, his translation loses the biblical impression given by the use of the word *and* as a punctuation mark which another scholar is careful to preserve. Nevertheless I lean on Vermes though occasionally taking liberties by preferring a word or a passage from elsewhere.

The provincial boundaries and caravan routes in the map follow those of the map of Palestine in New Testament Times by Thomas Nelson and Sons in Peake's Commentary.

THE PALESTINE OF JESUS

SEEKING THE HIDDEN JESUS

Belief or Examination

Belief

In the western world, most of us are brought up as Christians. Christianity distinguishes itself from other monotheistic religions in its devotion to a divine being who, it is claimed, appeared at a known time and place in history and whose life and teachings are accurately known because they were recorded by people alive at the time.

Christianity teaches that its founder, Jesus of Nazareth, fulfilled the prophecies of the Old Testament, the holy scriptures of the Jews, which narrate the unfolding of God's plan for his chosen people, originally the Jews but, from the advent of Jesus, the whole human race. Jesus was the Christ, the Messiah, the saviour promised by God, a divine being, one of the Trinity of God the Father, God the Son and God the Holy Ghost. As the Son of God, he was incarnated on earth, was crucified to atone for the sins of humanity, was resurrected as proof of his divinity and ascended into heaven. Because humanity's sins have been forgiven by the sacrifice of the Son of God, salvation and eternal life await for those who believe it—those who have faith.

The principal form of Christian worship is the mass or holy communion in which worshippers achieve communion with God by consuming consecrated wine and bread which miraculously is the blood and body of the crucified god. The holy book of Christianity, the Bible, consists of a version of the scriptures of the Jewish religion added to which are four gospels describing the ministry of Jesus on earth, the Acts of the Apostles (mainly of Paul, the evangelist), letters of some of the apostles of Christ, again mainly Paul, and an apocalypse.

The gospels describe the human sacrifice of the incarnate God and include a core of teaching broadly expressed as love thy neighbour. Christianity has several holy days—the principal ones being the supposed anniversaries of Jesus's death, resurrection and birth—and has adopted Sunday as its sabbath.

These are the essentials of Christianity, a religion which today holds the hearts and minds of over a thousand million people—many in the most advanced countries of the world. Christians, even in these cultured societies, really believe that Jesus was the absolute god who came to earth as a man, and this is a fact of history. But is it?

Many other gods were thought by their devotees to have been historical people who wandered around doing good deeds—Orpheus and Hercules, for example— yet most people do not now believe they existed. Why do we consider worshippers of Hercules to be insane but worshippers of Jesus inspired? The clergy teach that

11

all gods are myths other than their own but what makes the Christian god an exception to the rule? Who could believe a book published today that abounded in miracles? If the holy book of another religion had miracles comparable to those in the gospels, would a Christian believe it? Why are events as remarkable as miracles recorded only in some gospels and not in others? If anyone today claimed to be a Son of God, we should consider them to be deluded or a charlatan, and our skepticism would be justified. Yet because we are brought up to it, we accept it without question of a man whose followers proclaimed him a god around 2000 years ago.

Even St Augustine admitted: *I should not believe in the gospels if I had not the authority of the church for so doing.* A saint he may be but his argument is circular, for he admits without this special authority, it would not be possible to believe the gospels, yet, if the gospel story is not to be believed, what special authority has the church? If the gospels were not the foundation of our own religion we would find them preposterous and would not comprehend how anyone could believe such nonsense. And, if our faith is greater than St Augustine's and we do not need the authority of the church to accept the gospels as God-given truth, how do we explain the many contradictions in them? Why is God so confusing—or confused?

Can we be sure the Son of God of the gospels is not an illusion or a fraud? Could we be gullible dupes whose ethical base is a confidence trick? For Christians such questions are impertinent. Christianity is genuine. It is the only genuine religion. All others are heathen. Pagan! Christians have sufficient proof—their belief! Celsus, an early critic of Christianity, said the Christians do not examine but believe. Is it credible that highly educated, worldly people today will not examine but simply believe? It is credible! They *do*—just believe!

These difficulties arise because Christian beliefs are built upon the fallible testimony of men, but they include the belief that the original testimonies, fallible as they are, are the infallible testimony of God. Some Christians seeking rationality, struggling with the knowledge that men wrote the accounts they revere, resolve their doubts by claiming they were inspired by God, or by an aspect of Him—the Holy Ghost. Though written by men they are still infallible. The Bible is the holy book. The gospels can be nothing other than true: they are the gospel truth—the word of God himself.

Examination

Those a little more skeptical might wonder why God leaves the reporting of His incarnation on earth to disciples who are terminally stupid and succeed in botching up the story, when He could have rendered it accurately himself during His sojourn here. Or, He could have sent an angel to reveal it inscribed on tablets of gold. Why didn't He do something obviously infallible and save a lot of trouble?

Evidently He chose not to, and a Christian would say we cannot be expected to understand. Yet, according to Genesis, God made us in His own image, endowing us with brains. It would be unreasonable to believe He does not expect us to use them. Quite the reverse. Having given us brains He must expect us to use them, and, if necessary, uncover false doctrine. The Christian scholar, Sir Edwyn Hoskyns, pleads that the basis of Christianity demands historical and critical study—its piety depends upon it. If Christian faith rests upon a particular event in history, those who refuse to investigate it honestly must betray a lack of that faith, for they dare not risk discovering they are mistaken!

Perhaps the origins of Christianity are not what they seem. Perhaps cautionary tales that circulated among oppressed and ignorant people came to be believed. Could Roman slaves and housewives be expected to understand what motivated the Jewish nation in its plight?—that Jesus was not what the church is now compelled to teach, lest it should destroy its own foundation?

It is hard to be dispassionate about the Bible when we have been taught to revere it all our lives, and our systems of beliefs seem to depend upon it. The gospels have such authority in our society that most people, practising Christians or otherwise—like St Augustine—believe that they are absolutely or essentially true. But rational people must want to examine the origins of their beliefs and show that they are well founded. They must be sufficiently curious to wish to examine the relevant Christian texts to justify and confirm their views. They must be willing to look at the books of the New Testament in their human and historical context, accepting that, if God inspired their composition, it would shine through. Equally, if it does not, they must be willing to accept the Christian holy books are merely the work of men wilfully or misguidedly duping their fellows. Would God want us to believe it if it were not true?

Pilate said: *What is truth*? Whatever we accept as the truth of Christian origins, there is sure to be a deeper truth waiting to be discovered. Why should anyone fear it? My purpose here is to offer the Christian story from the viewpoint of a skeptic— to show that it is possible to interpret the facts offered to us by the early Christian writers in a non-mystical, non-supernatural way, and thereby recover from the Christian gospels the remnants of historical truth.

But the gospels themselves offer serious problems to any rational interpretation.

Which Gospel?

The Gospels

As rational people we might wish to discover what we can about the origin of Christianity from the evidence, but not much evidence remains other than the works long ago categorized by Christian bishops as canonical, which is to say those which they deemed acceptable for general consumption. Most evidence deemed unacceptable has been destroyed. Not simply lost, decayed or despoiled by the ravages of time but destroyed by the Christians themselves! Anything that has not been destroyed has been savaged by early Christian editors until it is difficult to know what was original and what has been interpolated or re-written.

Most Christians who are not theologians do not realize this. They do not realize that the gospels were not written as accurate records for the archives but purely to persuade people to believe. They were not written as historical documents but to recruit converts, just as modern holiday brochures are written to persuade people to spend their money. Like the exaggerated colours of the brochures, gospel stories could be mainly hype, and gentle Jesus simply a glossy picture to attract new punters!

Nor are the earliest Christian records those which appear first in the New Testament, the gospels, but some of Paul's epistles. The earliest of Paul's epistles may have been written only a few decades after the crucifixion, in about 52 AD. But Paul's letters tell us almost nothing about Jesus, the person. Indeed the absence of detail about the life of the founder of Christianity by his most important apostle seems astonishing.

Paul can say very little about Jesus:

- he was a Jew of the line of David—Paul knew of no divine impregnation—and was the first of many children;

- he started the tradition of the Eucharist;

- he was crucified;

- he rose from the dead on the third day;

- he appeared to various people after his resurrection, including a multitude;

- he had died before Paul was converted and Paul never met him.

Paul overcame the last impediment by claiming a superior way of knowing Jesus—supernaturally! Paul apparently was a medium. From time to time he would fall into a trance and have visions of the risen Jesus telling him where the chosen apostles were going wrong!

Paul uses very little of the life or teaching of Jesus because he did not know it and thought it irrelevant anyway. Paul was preaching his own message. For Paul a belief in the risen Christ was all that was needed for salvation. Whatever Jesus thought while he lived simply did not matter to Paul, and Paul could not know what was attributed by the church to Christ later. These are the reasons why much of the teaching of Jesus seems mysterious, and even contradict Christianity as it has come to us via Paul. If you believe in the risen Christ, you are saved so what does it matter what Jesus taught?

Nor do Paul's epistles refer to written accounts of the life of Jesus. If they existed, it is inconceivable that Paul would never have quoted from them when it suited him. We can safely conclude that the gospels did not exist in documentary form when Paul wrote his letters. Paul's epistles were written around 50–60 AD whereas the earliest narrative gospels are from around 60–90 AD. Paul had no gospels but at some stage the gospel writers or editors discovered Paul. They could make use of

Paul's teaching and also incorporate the theory and practice of the church as it had evolved in the years following the death of Jesus.

Why was it not until about 30 years after the traditional date of Jesus's death in 33 AD that the earliest written accounts of his mission appeared?

The Jewish disciples of Jesus, the Nazarenes, considered the second coming—in Greek, parousia—and the end of the world as imminent and regarded it as a pointless exercise to record the events of Jesus's life. For the same reason the apostles—preachers not writers—practised an oral tradition rather than any written one. Being Jewish, the apostles' teachings initially were transmitted orally in Aramaic, the Jewish vernacular of the time, a semitic language related to Hebrew and Arabic. The dominant themes of the early church were the passion, the resurrection and the impending return of the messiah. Whatever the apostles knew about these, they would have told. They would have been less interested in events preceding the week of the passion. Nor would they have been too concerned about any peripheral teaching of the fledgling god. The first Christians were not expecting to have to teach teachers.

Only as time passed and the second coming did not arrive did those who retained their faith decide to write down details of the passion, and then other details of Christ's life and thought. The original oral tradition of the Nazarenes became a written tradition. Accounts in the form we now have them were years later still. By then the stories had been told many times, the tellers of the stories, missionaries, had dispersed to many lands, and the stories had become stylized and idealized.

The first Christian missionaries, the evangelists and those who preceded them—a church already existed at Rome when Paul arrived there—had founded many Christian churches in the Roman Empire. These different churches produced different holy books. After the Roman destruction of Jerusalem in 70 AD no single church had any special seniority. Some, like the church of Alexandria in Egypt, consisted largely of Jewish Christians who felt better able to understand the teachings of a Jew than the essentially gentile congregations of other churches like that at Rome where the Jewish War had left a bad impression and local Christians were keen to play down the Jewish origins of their religion.

These different congregations saw Jesus in different ways. Jewish converts who did not revert to Judaism, were interested in the thought of Jesus, essentially Jesus the rabbi, and therefore keen on his sayings. The gentile churches including those set up by Paul were interested in the dying and resurrected god and had little interest in Jesus's life otherwise. Others saw parallels between Jesus and Orpheus or Adonis and it became expedient to write in appropriate stories and parables.

Some Christian historians think different followers of Jesus specialized in different aspects of Jesus's ministry. One collected parables, another miracles, another passion narratives, and so on. Evidence of this is taken to be the prologue of Luke in which he refers to a number of writers who have established the facts of the religion as handed down by the original eyewitnesses. Luke is admitting he had earlier sources—earlier gospels—but, because they were omitted from the canon, they have since been lost, though fragments are discovered from time to time. It seems likely, however, that if these were systematic collections of any sort then they preceded Jesus. They would have been collections of messianic scriptural prophecies and testimonia which the gospel writers indiscriminately applied to Jesus.

The results of the divers sources and interests of the writers were a number of variant accounts which at first circulated separately in particular communities. Among them were the four gospels or their prototypes which the church later defined as being authoritative but which were evidently not accepted by Christian writers until after 140 AD to judge by citations by early churchmen. The acceptance of the four gospels by the church does not mean they were the most original or the most accurate accounts. It means they were the ones that best suited the growth of the church in its Roman milieu.

For these reasons the four canonical gospels are not reliable. Unauthentic elements were incorporated into them. For example, the personal views of the evangelists were written into the gospels because the translator or scribe had no way of knowing whether something was true or the evangelist's opinion. They were heavily and clumsily edited by their authors and by later theologians who felt they could be improved in this or that small way. Some gospels, like Luke, are not at all in their original form. They contain anachronisms—confusing Nazarene beliefs with what the church at a later date wanted converts to believe. Matthew 16:18–19, on the role of Peter when Jesus says: *upon this rock I will build my church*, notes a later concern of the church not a concern of Jesus, who believed the world was about to be renewed under the direct rule of God. But no single editor ever had the authority to rewrite all the holy texts to eliminate contradictions. That was to be a boon for the church, allowing it to do as it wished, always able to quote some bit of scripture in justification, but it is also a boon for the inquirer because ad hoc editing leaves inconsistencies that can be revealing.

Why, you might ask, are we so fussy about the reliability of the New Testament books? Our oldest copies of Herodotus and Thucydides are only hundreds of years old yet we do not question the accuracy of their every word. And there are many more manuscripts and fragments of manuscripts of the gospels preserved from long ago than of any other book. Surely such fussiness is unwarranted.

The answer is that Herodotus and Thucydides are not the sacred books of millions of people who believe they are the true word of God. The copyists of Herodotus and Thucydides had little reason to alter them, whereas the copyists of the New Testament texts had every reason to alter the holy books to suit church politics and to match its changing dogmata. Deliberate alterations were made to the gospels within only a few years of their being written. Earlier drafts of the gospels are now lost and lost versions could explain some of the puzzles of the connexions between the gospels. But even the completed versions were altered in parts by later editors and copyists.

Still, the gospels were written successively and the evolution of theology can be seen from gospel to gospel, Jesus growing, for example, from the modest son of man of Mark into the fully fledged god cast in the eastern saviour mould of John. Jesus's own message of a personal repentance from sin to join the elect of God and secure entry into the coming kingdom was replaced by Paul's innovations, redemption from original sin by irrational faith mediated by the power and ritual of the church. The paraphernalia and dogmas of the church were constructed in imitation of rival religions or through political necessity not from any prescriptions of Jesus. When christologically advanced concepts appear in the gospels they were probably inserted by a later editor.

The skeptic therefore takes the view that anything in the Christian scriptures which seems inappropriate or contradicts church doctrine is likely to be a remnant of the original tradition that has escaped editorial correction. An inquirer will examine the culture of first century Palestine and will believe the gospel account when it agrees with the culture of Palestine at that time. Otherwise he will doubt it just as he would doubt the authenticity of a Roman bicycle pump.

The Gospel of John

Christians might believe that in the gospels they have independent accounts of the ministry of Jesus. One observer, they might argue, could have been mistaken but could four? Regrettably examination of the texts tends to explode this argument. One expects different accounts of the same events to tell broadly the same story, but when the common material extends to the same word order, vocabulary and grammatical peculiarities one begins to suspect copying. The four gospel writers are not independent witnesses.

The one which does seem to be independent of the others in large measure is the last in the New Testament and the last one completed. The first three gospels, Matthew, Mark and Luke are called the synoptic gospels because they tell essentially the same story—they have the same viewpoint. John is quite different from the other three, omitting—apparently deliberately—much of their content. The author seemed to feel another full account could serve no purpose but that there was scope for refinements—doctrinal clarifications and additional material to answer criticisms. The author of John was writing a work to complement the synoptics.

The high prestige of John for Christians partly comes from Paul's description of John in Galatians 2:9 as one of the pillar apostles, the others being Peter and James, but it is unlikely that John the apostle wrote it. Very little, if any, of the New Testament is written by people who knew the Son of God in person. Despite its own claims, the signs are that it was written late, so long after the events it records that the apostle John must certainly have been dead. John could have been written as early as 100 AD or some say, certainly mistakenly, as late as 160 AD. It is not mentioned by Papias or Marcion writing about 140 AD and Justin Martyr only quotes from it tentatively in 163–167 AD as if he knew his readers would not regard it as authoritative. Not until the third century did it become generally accepted.

John propagates a well developed theological outlook, its parts being linked together as a uniform whole to a much greater extent than the other gospels. It is more than the set of pericopes—units of oral tradition—that can be seen in the synoptic gospels. John is more didactic, philosophical and theological than the synoptics. It is mainly discourse rather than narrative, and depicts Jesus as giving lengthy disquisitions rather than the homely sayings and parables of the other gospels. These long connected discourses suggest the source was a programme of sermons, possibly derived from originals by the evangelist, which were worked up by authorities in one of the regional churches.

The history of the church is of doctrine becoming more and more elaborate not of it being simplified. Furthermore the evolution of Jesus from man to messiah to divinity to equality with the Almighty places John late in the timescale—advanced elements would not be lost once established so it could not have preceded the synoptics. As it adds at a late date much that is not in the other gospels and is overlaid with later theology, it can only be used as a secondary source.

The material peculiar to John is the miracle at Cana, Nicodemus, the Samaritan woman, healing a cripple and a blind man in Jerusalem, raising Lazarus, washing the feet of the disciples, the farewell discourses, parts of the passion and the prologue. We must treat these additions with skepticism not least because Matthew and particularly Luke obviously made determined attempts to pull together every particular of tradition they could find, and yet never heard of such an astonishing event as the raising of Lazarus. In John this was so amazing a miracle it was the reason for Jesus being crucified, so it could hardly have been forgotten by those interviewed by Matthew and Luke.

Unlike the synoptics Jesus's messiahdom is recognized very early (Jn 1:14). Yet in John 6:15, when the multitude want to make Jesus king, he refuses to accept, taking measures to evade the crowd. The cleansing of the temple and the anointing are in a different setting and order from the other gospels and there is little verbal agreement with them. But John is very free with the rendering of his Old Testament quotations and it is possible that he was equally free with his rendering of the bits of the synoptic gospels he chose to use. The title Son of man is less used than in the synoptics—Son of God is favoured.

Besides these, John's chronology has been mixed up, either by him for doctrinal reasons or by editors, or perhaps by accident—some pages look as though they have been interchanged for no clear reason. In several places in John transpositions would improve the flow of the text. The raising of Lazarus from the dead is the immediate cause of Jesus's arrest not the cleansing of the temple, which occurs near the start of the gospel, but some scholars think John 2.13b–25 has been misplaced and should really be after the raising of Lazarus thus restoring the cleansing of the temple to its proper place. Possibly an editor attempted to answer the criticism that Jesus's behaviour in the temple was an act of banditry and redolent of rebellion by deliberately moving it earlier in the story.

The date of the last supper in the synoptics and John differ. In the synoptics it is a Passover meal but in John it is one day before. This difference might be due to the

Nazarenes' use of a different calendar, the solar calendar of the Essenes prescribed in Jubilees not the lunar one of Jerusalem. Or perhaps the synoptics used the reckoning of Jews in the diaspora in which the Passover was fixed not varying according to the phase of the moon. But even this puzzle, which John creates, looks less like calendrical confusion than that John thought it suited God's purpose to depict Jesus as the paschal lamb—simply altering the chronology to have him crucified on the day when the lambs were being sacrificed in readiness for the Passover. Some scholars take all John's references to time to be symbolic.

John is the most hostile of the three to the Jews, but it has more in common with Jewish mysticism than with Rabbinism. The author of John also allegedly wrote the Revelation of St John the Divine between 69 and 93 AD, which, being an apocalypse, is in the style of the Essenes. It was always controversial, Marcion rejected it, Jerome as late as 420 AD rejected it, but Justin Martyr accepted it and gradually it became accepted universally. It is difficult for the modern mind to understand how such mumbo-jumbo continues to be included in the Christian canon but, since no one now has the authority to change God's Bible, it is easier to ignore it, or leave it to fundamentalists, who love it! Historically it is valuable, being largely Essene.

Since the discovery of the Qumran scrolls—dubbed the Dead Sea Scrolls from the proximity of the site to the Dead Sea—about fifty years ago in the Judaean wilderness, we now realize the gospel of John also has Essene features and vocabulary. Concepts like light and truth, previously thought to be Hellenistic, are found in the scrolls as is the contrast of light against darkness. There are parallels with the Hermetica of Hermes Trimegistus in Egypt in the second and third centuries AD and some common imagery in the work of Philo of Alexandria such as the metaphors for God of light, fountain and shepherd. Philo also uses the concept of the Logos.

John might contain therefore some elements of genuine Nazarene tradition, treated from a different perspective from the other three gospels—but, being the last and the most highly developed in its thinking, John remains historically the least reliable of the gospels. John still has to be treated with the most caution, and especially where it reports remarkable incidents that no one else ever heard of.

The Synoptic Problem

Matthew, Mark and Luke are earlier than John but are not at all independent. Indeed in some respects they are so similar they create a problem of their own, called by scholars, the synoptic problem. The problem is to explain the following facts.

- These three gospels have much common material. Matthew covers 90% of Mark! These two have 250 verses in common, many containing the same words and phrases. Only seven short passages of Mark fail to appear in Matthew. Luke contains almost 50% of Mark but misses out the whole chunk

19

of Mark 6:45 to 8:26. Only four passages of Mark, about 30 verses, are not covered in either Matthew or Luke.

- In about half of the material common to all three, the grammar and phraseology and even unusual vocabulary are often the same. Compare for example the following three passages from the synoptic gospels.

> ...and as he was walking in the temple, there come to him the chief priests, and the scribes, and the elders, and they said unto him, By what authority doest thou these things? or who gave thee this authority to do these things? And Jesus said unto them, I will ask of you one question, and answer me, and I will tell you by what authority I do these things. The baptism of John, was it from heaven, or from men? answer me. And they reasoned with themselves, saying, If we shall say, From heaven; he will say, Why then did ye not believe him? But if we should say, Of men; they feared the people: for all verily held John to be a prophet. And they answered Jesus and say, We know not. And Jesus saith unto them, Neither tell I you by what authority I do these things.

> (Mark 11:27–33)

> And when he was come into the temple, the chief Priests and the elders of the people came unto him as he was teaching, and said, By what authority doest thou these things? and who gave thee this authority? And Jesus answered and said unto them, I also will ask you one question, which if ye tell me, I likewise will tell you by what authority I do these things. The baptism of John, whence was it? from heaven, or of men? And they reasoned with themselves, saying, If we shall say, From heaven; he will say unto us, Why did ye not then believe him? But if we shall say, Of men; we fear the multitude; for all hold John as a prophet. And they answered Jesus, and said, We know not. And he also said unto them, Neither tell I you by what authority I do these things.

> (Matthew 21:23–27)

> ...as he was teaching the people in the temple, and preaching the gospel, there came upon him the Chief Priests and the scribes with the elders, and they spake, saying unto him, Tell us: By what authority doest thou these things? or who is he that gave thee this authority? And he answered and said unto them, I will also ask you one question; and tell me: The baptism of John, was it from heaven, or of men? And they reasoned with themselves, saying, If we shall say, From heaven; he will say, Why did ye not believe him? But if we shall say, Of men; all the people will stone us: for they be persuaded that John was a prophet. And they answered, that they knew not whence it was. And Jesus said unto them, Neither tell I you by what authority I do these things.

> (Luke 20:1–8)

These passages are effectively identical. Not only are they from the same source they are copied almost unaltered.

- Matthew and Mark often agree when Luke differs and Luke and Mark sometimes agree when Matthew differs but in each case the order of the common material is nearly always the same. There is also a body of material in Matthew and Luke but not in Mark, mostly the teachings of Jesus with little narrative and no passion. Again the similarity often extends to wording but Matthew and Luke rarely agree when Mark differs.

- On the other hand there are parts where the same events in Matthew and Luke are given different settings and different vocabulary is used, as in the healing of the centurion's servant (Mt 8:5ff; Lk 7:1ff).

- Matthew and Luke often include doublets, accounts of apparently the same event with slight differences. Each of these two gospels also have aspects peculiar to themselves: Luke's travel narrative is largely his own (9:51–18:14) whereas Matthew groups his material into five themes.

As long ago as 1778 G E Lessing attempted to solve the synoptic problem by proposing that the gospels were different translations of an original Aramaic gospel—the story of Jesus told by his companions and early Jewish followers. But the best explanation is that two of the gospel writers used the work of the other, and, where they used it, they copied it virtually word for word. Since Matthew and Luke between them contain almost the whole of Mark, we can deduce that Mark was the original gospel and the other gospel writers had sight of it before they completed their own versions. The reasons are as follows.

- We have seen that, in the sections common to all three synoptic gospels, passages are constructed too similarly to be independent.

- Mark's order is followed in both Matthew and Luke. The differences in Matthew are because Matthew has consciously grouped his material into five themes yet this order is not reflected in Luke or Mark. Since only seven short passages of Mark do not appear in Matthew, evidently Matthew had Mark to work from and incorporated nearly all of it into his own account. We saw that Luke covers almost half of Mark, usually retaining the same order.

- Matthew and Luke are more concise than Mark. Mark has six verses to describe how Jesus healed in crowds by driving out the unclean spirits (Mk 3:7–12). In Matthew only two verses are required and in Luke only three (Mt 12:15–16 and Lk 6:17–19). They also usually improve Mark's style by omitting unusual words and unwieldy grammatical constructions. These are signs that Mark has been edited in Matthew and Luke.

- Though Mark is more verbose he is often less precise, as when he calls Herod a king in Mk 6:14 although, as Matthew and Luke correctly state, he was only a tetrarch (Mt 14:1 Lk 9:7). Mark has been corrected in Matthew and Luke so must have come first.

- As the gospels became aimed at an increasingly gentile audience editors would be expected to eliminate Aramaic words. Mark has more Aramaic words in the sayings of Jesus than Matthew and Luke. Also Mark was not writing for Jews because he explains Jewish customs like handwashing (Mk 7:3–4) and defines the Aramaic words and phrases he uses—unless it is expedient not to.

- Mark is more honest in his accounts, showing Jesus with human emotions and even some foibles. Mark says Jesus could do no mighty work in Nazareth (Mk 6:5), Matthew says not many (Mt 13:58) and Luke omits it. In the stilling of the storm Mark is definite in his wording, *Do you still have no faith?* compared with Luke's, *Where is your faith?* and Matthew's, *You of little faith* (Mk 4:40 Mt 8:26 Lk 8:25). Humanity fades in later editions as the man receded and the god advanced.

Modern biblical analysts do not doubt that the similarities between the synoptic gospels must imply common sources, but was it a single one? Many scholars postulate two written sources for Matthew and Luke—Mark and a source labelled by scholars Q. Thus the doublets mentioned above can be explained as accounts from both Q and Mark that differed sufficiently for Matthew or Luke to want to include both.

Luke and Matthew were not named as the authors of their gospels until Irenaeus did so in 180 AD. Such late assignments cast doubt on their validity.

Matthew

Though sophisticated Christians today prefer John, Matthew was considered the most important of the gospels for almost the whole history of the church. It was placed first in the canon because of the regard in which it was held.

Matthew is the most Jewish of the gospels and probably reflects most strongly the ambience of the Jerusalem Church. Jewish customs and words are not explained as they are in Mark and, in that sense it seems to anticipate a Jewish readership. Some see this strong Jewish flavour as proof of its authenticity. Others dislike it as signs of the work of Judaizers, a mythical breed of early Jewish Christians who tried to deny the innovations introduce by the Son and revert to good old Mosaic Jewishness. Despite Judaizers and its Jewish tone, it propagates the Hellenized view of the Christ—that conditioned by Greek culture— rather than the Jewish view of the messiah. It does not use as many Aramaisms as does Mark and most of his quotations are from the Septuagint, the Greek version of the scriptures, both of which could point to the source of the original draft of Matthew being a city like Alexandria or Antioch where Jewish communities had long been Hellenized. There are thematic indications that Matthew is Essenic in nature, and so it is not unreasonable to believe that Matthew did have its origin in one of these cities. Nazarenes, escaping the troubles in Palestine after the crucifixion, dispersed to various centres where their brothers the Essenes had strong communities. Many of the survivors of the fall of Jerusalem had settled in Alexandria because of its proximity and its large Jewish population—a third of its population of three million—or Antioch where an early church was established possibly based on an existing Essene community. But as time went by with no sign of the kingdom appearing, Jewish Christians were reverting to orthodox Judaism. Attempts were made to stem the ebbing of the tide in vain. Even in these largely Jewish cities, the gentile theology of Paul began to dominate, and Jesus had to become divine—but in Matthew it was Jews who recognized it—the disciples not the Roman.

Its strong emphasis on the leadership of Peter (in Matthew, Peter is granted special authority) suggests it arose in a Jewish milieu where Peter was revered, Antioch being the place of choice. It seems odd that Matthew, a Jewish composition, should lean so heavily upon Mark, a gentile composition, as it obviously does. The explanation can only be that Mark carried great authority, and that authority traditionally is that Mark is largely the Gospel of Peter, Peter having related the core of it to Mark. Matthew could forgive Mark his clumsy style, Latinisms and other foibles because he was passing on the words of the man who had been Jesus's minder.

Matthew is the only gospel to mention a church (Mt 16:18; 18:17), certainly late interpolations—other late influences appear in the concluding passages (Mt 28:18–20)—though it might be based on the word used by the Essenes, often translated congregation. The author seems not to be defying or negating the Jewish religion but rather is showing here is a thoroughly Jewish faith of a firmly established church. Matthew is a polemic with the rabbis of the synagogues—a polemic which continues the polemic of the Essenes with the Pharisees. His purpose is exactly that of the sectarians of Qumran—he is stating categorically that only the elect, formerly the Essenes but now the Christians, will enter the kingdom of God.

Matthew is more carefully constructed than the other gospels. It has many similarities with the Damascus Rule of the scrolls. Though not being quite so obviously a manual of rules, there are rules in it—most notably in the sermon on the mount. And, like the Damascus Rule, it gives some history of the foundation of the movement and some exhortations or discourses—in Matthew they end with the formula, ...*and it came to pass when Jesus had ended these sayings*—each being devoted to a topic: the sermon on the mount, a missionary discourse, a parable discourse, a church discourse, and an eschatological discourse, thus serving as a vade mecum for members, as the Damascus Rule did.

Matthew is keen to show Jesus—who is a parallel figure to Moses—as the fulfilment of Old Testament prophecy. His approach is akin to the pesher method of commentating on scripture favoured by the Qumran community whereby current events are interpreted as prophesied by the scriptures. Matthew has five scriptural references in the birth narrative to show that prophecy was fulfilled in Jesus. Matthew's use of these quotations is rarely precise. He does just what the sectarians of Qumran did—change the quotation subtly to suit his purpose.

An aim of Matthew seems to have been to answer criticisms and to do so he concocts unlikely explanations. The reluctance of John the Baptist to baptize Jesus and the guards at the tomb serve to explain respectively that John the Baptist recognized Jesus as superior and that the disciples could not have stolen the body. Similarly narratives of Peter walking on water, Judas bargaining for silver and Pilate washing his hands serve respectively to boost Peter, damn the Jews as money-grabbing traitors and absolve Romans of any responsibility for torturing a god.

The infancy narrative seems to answer charges of Jesus's illegitimacy. The flight to Egypt and subsequent return parallels Moses and the children of Israel's sojourn there in the scriptures, but Jesus's family return to Nazareth, instead of Bethlehem, providing an explanation for Jesus's title—the Nazarene. Some wiseacres in the Empire might have remembered that the Nazarenes were a group of Jewish revolutionaries so an innocent explanation of the title was needed. In like fashion, modern apologists, embarrassed by Jesus so plainly stating that to be rich is to be a sinner, have invented a narrow gate in the walls of Jerusalem called the Needle's Eye. There is no historical evidence for any such gate. Jesus's metaphor is paralleled several times in the Jewish Talmud which also has large animals attempting to do incredible things serving as visual images of the impossible.

Scholars have long recognized that Matthew had at hand a collection of citations written in Aramaic because he punctuates his narrative at various points with the formula, *this happened in order to fulfil what was said by the prophet...* This collection they called the Logia. Such collections existed in the Jewish world, for example in one of the Qumran testimonia documents in which three sections consist of quotations of messianic prophecies and the fourth is from the apocryphal Psalms of Jonah. Their use suggests the author was a member of a sect like the Essenes. According to the biblical scholar, Donald Guthrie, if Matthew belonged to a group which, like the men of Qumran were devoted to such exegesis, it is easy to see how many of the texts would spring naturally to his mind when he was writing the narrative. In Matthew the Logia is combined with Mark's account to create a richer synthesis than Mark alone. But since it was not completed until around 100 AD, the apostle Matthew cannot have had any part in the final editing. Additions continued to be made for another 100 years.

A church Father, Papias allegedly affirmed that Matthew collected oracles or sayings—the Logia—which were translated by others as best they could. He says the Logia was a collection of Jesus's sayings compiled by Matthew for the use of Christian teachers—it was indeed a manual. The version used by the gospel writers was probably a good Greek translation of the original Aramaic. Scholars consider it was assembled 25–30 years before the gospels and some clergymen believe it might actually have been collected in Jesus's lifetime. Much of it seems to have been in practical form, and, because its allusions are often rural, believers consider they give an insight into Jesus's character.

Now we can see that the Logia preceded Jesus, deriving from a collection of Essene liturgy, prayers, testimonia, maxims and orders, probably arranged in five parts to reflect the five books of the Pentateuch, inspiring Matthew's fivefold arrangement, and apparently an early catechism or manual of discipleship. Its rural character arose because the Essenes were farmers and herdsmen. The source called Q is essentially the Logia but Luke evidently left out much of it as being too Jewish—emphasis on the fulfilment of the law, remarks about the lost sheep of the house of Israel, some sayings and testimonia, and perhaps some anti-Pharisaic material. Matthew's apocalypse is much longer than Mark's and eschatology also shows in the parables of the tares and the talents suggesting a pronounced Essene influence.

There is much in Matthew to value though it is not a Greek translation of the Aramaic Gospel of the Nazarenes. If Matthew belonged to a community of Nazarenes then even his collection of oracles will be of interest in understanding them although they might not help us greatly in settling the narrative sequence.

Luke

The gospel of Luke also is not independent. Luke is thought to have been a doctor, the companion of Paul on his travels. So, he was neither an eyewitness of the events he describes nor the secretary of one, as was Mark—Paul only met Jesus in his imagination. If Luke was the companion of Paul, the two did not communicate a great deal because Luke does not seem to use Paul's epistles or understand Jesus in quite the Pauline way.

Luke evidently was an educated man whose Greek was good, though not classical (writers of literary Greek always copied the classical style) and who, by his own account, did some research before writing. The prologue to Luke's gospel says he used the works of a number of writers who had recorded the memories of the original disciples of Jesus. By the time he put it all together, Christians had long abandoned the idea of an early parousia. Luke was well versed in the Septuagint. He also wrote Acts, both his books being written for gentiles.

Luke arguably had knowledge of Antiquities of the Jews written in 93 AD by the Jewish historian, Josephus, and Acts is usually dated at about 100 AD, but some consider it could have been much earlier. Acts ends tantalizingly with Paul awaiting trial in Rome in around 64 AD suggesting to some theologians that the work was written about then. But Paul's fate might not have been what the early church wanted to record, and the narrative in Acts might have been left deliberately unfinished. Though the events of Acts follow those of Luke, Acts—or parts of it—was probably drafted first. Luke would have written down first what he was familiar with—the history of his companion, Paul, so parts of Acts might be quite early but the gospel much later. The Acts of the Apostles was probably written by Luke in part as early as 64 AD. Luke himself or editors then tampered with it considerably.

Luke has much to say about the conversion of gentiles and gentiles are often painted in a good light. He is evidently a gentile writing for gentiles, but he is one who seems quite well versed in Essene ways of thinking. He shows every indication of being either an Essene proselyte of Stephen's Hellenistic wing of the Nazarenes, or a godfearer who had stood for a long time at the edge of the Essene movement, longing to join but not having the courage to be circumcised and grateful for Stephen's revisions of the law allowing gentiles to be admitted into a form of Judaism. He shows his Nazarene influence in his desire that people should repent, repentance being a central theme of Luke, but—like Stephen—he extends repentance beyond the Jews to everyone, and thus helps to universalize the narrow sectarianism of the Essenes. So there are dangers in accepting Luke as a primary source but indications that he was familiar with pre-crucifixion Essenism. Providing that care is taken to resist Luke's universalistic desire, evidence about the Nazarene mission can be gleaned from his gospel.

Luke uses Mark, that is plain, but is much less deferential towards it than Matthew. He renders some of the passages in Mark much more freely, as indeed he seems to with all his material, and omits quite a lot. Other curiosities of Luke are that it gives unusual prominence to the role of women and that the travel narrative gives little indication of an itinerary. Luke refers to Jesus as the Lord on 14 occasions— Mark and Matthew never do (except in the fictional dialogue of demons or angels) indicating that in Luke the split from Nazarene teaching was essentially complete.

Luke was often much freer with his material than one would expect of an editor— he was more a re-writer. Parts of Luke seem to be taken from both Mark and Matthew. Some scholars think that Luke used Mark and Matthew but regarded Matthew as only a secondary source much of which he rewrote. However most scholars believe that the material common to Matthew and Luke but absent in Mark came from the source Q which Luke as well as Matthew had before him as he wrote.

Comparison of the three synoptic gospels allows the missing source Q to be crudely reconstructed. If it were a collection of sayings, it ought to contain no narrative yet it seems to include the healing of the centurion's servant which Guthrie considers mystifying. Parts of the two accounts of the centurion's servant differ considerably, which might be explained if there were yet more sources besides Mark and Q. Other parts of Luke are similar to accounts in other gospels but are also different enough to suggest another source (Lk 24:1–12). These additional sources are called M and L. The narrative material independent of Mark could have been common to M and L leaving Q a collection of pure sayings. The additional source for Luke, L, comprises parables, isolated sayings and narrative material.

It must be remembered that some of the Logia might not have been used in either Matthew or Luke and is lost altogether, and some might have been used by one gospel writer but not the other so that M and L both are partly Logia—like the strongly Jewish material of Matthew omitted by Luke. The few sayings of Jesus in Paul's epistles, which we have seen pre-date the gospels, stem from Q—roughly the version of Matthew—suggesting it was the earliest Christian text. There is evidence for Q also in the non-canonical Gospel of Thomas.

Naturally the problem is enormously complicated by later editing when copyists tried to harmonize the gospels or improve them for the sake of doctrine, and indeed by the possibility of there having been earlier editions, now lost, but in circulation before the ultimately accepted versions. Vincent Taylor, a professor of New Testament language and literature, convinces us that Luke combined Q and L to give a proto-Luke which he later combined with Mark when he came across that gospel. He reasons thus.

- Luke omits half of Mark suggesting he had other material he preferred.

- Luke's passion narrative contains only 20% of Mark also suggesting Luke had another source. When Mark's material is subtracted a continuous narrative remains. Luke changes Mark's order unusually often (12 instances between 22:14 and 24:11).

- The same seems to apply to Luke 21 (the eschatological discourse) where verses 20–34 at least are non-Marcan but with insertions from Mark.

- Q material is often combined with L material but never with material from Mark which appears in distinct blocks suggesting it was added afterwards.

- In the main narrative of the ministry there are blocks of material from Mark alternating with other material. When the material from Mark is extracted a reasonably continuous story remains.

- The proto-Luke text lacked Galilaean material, miracles and kingdom parables. These were inserted from Mark.

- Different words are used in the Greek for those rigidly adhering to the law: grammateus in the parts from Mark but nomikos in the other parts.

The dating in Luke 3:1 was the start of proto-Luke. The birth narrative was added later. Possibly Luke originally wrote proto-Luke-Acts together as one book with no knowledge of Mark's gospel. Later he came across it and added into proto-Luke what he thought was useful. An editor at some stage split off Acts as a different book and subsequently it was blown hither and thither by the zephyrs and whirlwinds of early church politics.

It seems then that there were two primary gospel sources but the authors of Matthew and Luke had additional material. The source of the gospel narrative was Mark. The second source was an unknown book of gospel sayings, labelled Q, which was known as the Logia.

The Jerusalem Church must have had a gospel and written it down in Aramaic as the Gospel of the Nazarenes. We know from Jerome this was still used by the Nazarene sect of Arabia in the fourth century. The Quran speaks of the Gospel, in the singular, which must have been the gospel of the Nazarenes evidently still existing in Arabia at the time of Muhammed in the seventh century and revered by local Christians. It was written in Aramaic. Ibn Ishaq, the first biographer of Muhammed, tells us in the eighth century that the Abyssinians, who were Christians, followed the same gospel as the Christians of Arabia but were circumcised, revered what was claimed to be the Ark of the Covenant and kept the laws of the Torah including the food taboos.

Some critics believe that a Nazarene Gospel existed even before Jesus and that his followers applied it to him after Jesus's crucifixion—a distinct possibility if the Nazarenes were inspired by Essenes. Ancient scholars identified the Nazarene Gospel with a version of Matthew and, if this is true, it probably contained little narrative. Essentially it would have been Q, a collection of sayings and testimonia of the type found at Qumran. Paul, who probably had this among the books he carried with him, would have been content with it since he ignored any stories about Jesus's life as irrelevant to the spiritual person wearing the body.

In the post-War years Robert Graves and Joshua Podro tried, by combining classical and Jewish scholarship, to restore this Nazarene Gospel rather fancifully. They rashly accepted all of the gospels as equally true, each relating genuine Nazarene tradition, and, together with bits of other books whether canonical like Acts or non-canonical like the Recognitions of Clementine, tried to restore the original as a rearranged and reinterpreted combination of them all!

My objective also is to try to retrieve the true events of the gospel but I shall be less rash. I do not accept the gospels as equally valid. The fourth gospel, John, seems to stem from a different tradition from the other three especially in its account of the last week in Jerusalem but is too late to be of primary interest. Matthew, Mark and Luke are not independent. Matthew and Luke are mostly based on Mark and Q but Q, though earlier, seems to be a collection of wise sayings with little or no narrative so can add relatively little to the story I seek to uncover which is largely narrative.

What is left is Mark's gospel.

The Gospel of Mark

Mark is theologically the most primitive of the gospels. Evidently it was the earliest one written down, though it is not the most Palestinian—that is Matthew.

Mark is, according to Eusebius (writing around the beginning of the third century but quoting Papias who wrote about 130 AD), the interpreter and companion of Peter in his later travels. Perhaps Mark translated lessons given in Aramaic by Peter for the Greek speakers in the audience. At any rate Papias says he recorded in no particular order the old man's memories of the acts and sayings of Jesus. Mark was therefore not first hand. He had not known Jesus, but from Peter's sermons and anecdotes he was able to write his gospel shortly after Peter's death in about 64 AD.

Clerics think the passages in Mark related in the third person plural were Peter's own words. Some of the adjacent material seems so closely related to it that, sensibly, it too should be included with that thought to have been Peter's. The rest of the material in Mark seems to be in well arranged blocks or pericopes suggesting already collected pre-Marcan material. Inasmuch as Peter must have followed the Nazarene tradition in his sermons and the other material, being very early, can hardly have lost much of its original content, Mark should be closest to the true story of the Nazarenes.

Difficulties with the testimony of Papias are that Peter has no special significance in Mark's book and Mark's theology is Hellenized like Paul's. Matthew, the singularly Jewish gospel, uses Mark lending some credence to the view that Mark must have been based on the testimony of an authoritative Jewish figure—Peter—and possibly Peter emulated Jesus in his modesty, feeling little need to play up his own role. When Paul's influence waxed the gospel would have been edited to suit his outlook. It seems to have assumed a shape close to the present one by about 90 AD.

Mark had been written down in no particular order but later was tampered with by editorial additions and rearrangements. In the version which we now have there is a broad chronology leading from Galilee to Jerusalem, and then to the events leading to the crucifixion, but individual episodes cannot be assumed to be in the correct order. It gives a description of the work and movements of the Nazarene band but its true meaning has been thinly disguised to anyone who cared to believe other than the Christian gloss.

Significantly, since Mark's is considered the earliest gospel, the last twelve verses are not original—these last verses cannot be the recollections of Peter. Peter's story ends with the message of a young man in a white robe (the garment of the fully initiated Essene) sitting in Jesus's tomb that Jesus is risen and gone ahead of them to Galilee. Whereupon the disciples fled in fear and said nothing to anyone. No appearances! No ascension! A later editor, considering the ending inappropriate, added the last twelve verses in which Jesus appeared all over the place and then rose into heaven to be received at the right hand of God. How many Christians realize that all these essential notions of their religion are absent from the earliest version of Jesus's life? The editors of the Revised Standard Version are honest enough to relegate these verses to a footnote.

Mark writes in colloquial Greek not the more refined classical Greek of an educated man. He includes Latinisms suggesting the influence of Rome (Marcus was a very common Roman name at that time). He seemed unfamiliar with the country of Palestine or common Jewish customs, scholars giving the following examples:

- Dalmanutha referred to in 8:10 does not exist by that name, though it seems to be the same as Magdala of Matthew 15:39 properly rendered Magadan;

- in Mark 5:1 the country of the Gerasenes extends to the Sea of Galilee but Gerasene is really some forty miles from the lake, behind the mountains in what is now Jordan and then was the country of the ten Greek cities called Decapolis;

- he describes the town of Bethsaida in 8:26 as a village;

- he invents Jewish proceedings;

- he confuses references to the Herodian family in 6:17;

- he thought the appearance of Jesus before the High Priest was a trial not the committal hearing that it was;

- he thought a wife could divorce a husband contrary to Jewish law in 10:12.

29

Though some of these anomalies can be explained, it seems Mark either was not a Jew or, if he was, was so thoroughly Hellenized he retained few traces of his Jewish roots. He could have been a gentile, judging from his name and his Latinisms, possibly a Roman Christian convert with no direct experience of Palestine, and writing in Rome for a gentile readership.

Mark tries to flatter the Romans and denigrate the Jews because it was composed when Jewish nationalism was a nuisance in the Empire and he wanted the Christians distanced from the Jews. The missionaries were trying to get converts among the gentiles of the Roman Empire so the Romans in the story had to be blameless. There are several signs of this.

- Paul and the authors of Matthew and Luke accept the descent of Jesus from David but Mark ignores it dissociating Jesus from any claims to the throne of Israel.

- He calls the disciple, Simon, a Cananaean to avoid the word Zealot.

- He relates the story of the tribute money such as to acknowledge Caesar's authority not reject it.

- He puts the responsibility of the death of Jesus on the Jews and relieves Pilate of it by inventing the custom of releasing a prisoner, a custom which is otherwise unknown and most unlikely.

- The divinity of Jesus is first recognized in Mark by a Roman.

- He inserts the passage attributed to Jesus that a prophet is not without honour except in his own country and among his own kin to indicate that Jesus acknowledged his rejection by his family and countrymen. But it rests uneasily with his brother James and thereafter his nephew succeeding him as the head of the Nazarenes.

- He runs down the apostles appointed by Jesus—they are stupid, weak, argumentative, vain, treacherous, cowardly—all part of the process of dissociating the Son of God from the Jews.

Writing a couple of decades later when Jewish nationalism had ceased to be an issue, Luke has no need to be as cautious. Roman distaste for the Jews had faded and Josephus had published his Jewish War as a warning to potential hotheads in Palestine. Jews were no longer a threat and poor and illiterate Christian converts would not have understood references to them.

Mark includes as part of chapter 13 what was originally an Essene explanation of the signs of the coming kingdom now garbled with a Christian prophecy of God's punishment of the Jews inserted after the fall of Jerusalem.

Mark was not a companion of Jesus, possibly not an inhabitant of Palestine and possibly not a Jew. His gospel includes garbled bits of Essene and later material, is confused in its geography and sociology and has a false ending. Nevertheless, if Mark's should be accepted as the most authoritative rather than the least of the gospels. It is this gospel that should be the central reference for anyone reconstructing the true events at the foundation of Christianity. The other two synoptics are obviously later but have much of the original tradition and can be used to supplement deductions from Mark. John is much too late to be anything but secondary. Nothing that occurs only in John can be trusted unless it can somehow be traced to Mark or to the Essene tradition.

Mark's is the first gospel to be recorded. It was considered accurate enough by two more gospel writers to be reproduced by them in large measure and, if Mark really wrote down what Peter said, as church tradition has it, then it should contain the essence of the Aramaic oral tradition, the story of the Nazarenes as perceived by Peter. Peter was an old man addressing Greek and Latin speakers in Aramaic. He probably told a truth that could not be told directly to the audience and was therefore attenuated by Mark and the bishops in translation. When travellers' tales came in from the orient adding a nugget to the story here or there, they also had to be retold for popular consumption. The essence of the truth is there but distorted. This book corrects it for the astigmatism introduced in the first century by the leaders of the infant church who had to blur the truth or lose their growing status.

The Premise of this Book

To follow this commentary on Mark, readers need to know my premise and some information missing from the gospels to persuade them that this premise has some foundation. With this foreknowledge the commentary should make enough sense for readers to judge whether the analysis of the gospel and its tentative reconstruction are valid.

The key premise is that Jesus Christ, the God of the Christians, was an Essene. The information missing from the gospels is who the Essenes were, how they related to the other Jewish sects which do appear in the gospels, why Jesus seemed not to be even an orthodox Essene and what it all had to do with the Roman occupying forces.

The synopsis which follows should give preliminary answers to these questions enabling the reader to see the point of the preparatory material and understand the subsequent commentary.

Jesus was an devout Jew—he stoutly defended the law of Moses as the gospels illogically admit. Most Jews yearned for their gentile enemies—especially the Romans who ruled them—to be overcome so that they could be ruled as a theocracy—a kingdom of God. They believed that God had promised them a messiah, a great king who would drive out the gentiles allowing the promised kingdom to begin, as an extension of heaven, on earth.

One sect of the Jews believed this so strongly that they had separated themselves from the ungodly to prepare the way for the messiah and begin to create the kingdom of heaven on earth—they were the Essenes. Their community they considered to be perfectly holy, and their members had to behave as perfectly holy people, to be a foundation of the heavenly kingdom. But they believed that the kingdom of God could not encompass the world until the men of perfect holiness detected the signs of the times which announced the acceptable day of the Lord— the day of vengeance of God—when God would avenge the wrongs done to His people. When the time was right there would be a cosmic battle in which the forces of darkness and evil would be overcome by God's miraculous intervention. The duty of the Essenes was to watch for the signs and lead out the saints, those who were perfectly holy, against the forces of darkness—the Romans and their allies, sinful Jewish collaborators.

When the signs indicated that God was ready to create His kingdom on earth, most Jews, being children of Israel, the chosen people of God, would revert from sinfulness to godliness—they were the simple of Ephraim, Jews who had been misled by their pragmatic and collaborating leaders—the Pharisees. But though Essenes had the secrets of discerning the signs of the times, it was not a perfect art because heaven had not yet arrived, and the Essenes had to send out leaders with the mission of converting the simple of Ephraim. The success of these missionaries would itself be an important sign of the coming kingdom.

The men sent on this essential mission were senior figures in the Essene hierarchy. Jesus was such a man and so was John the Baptist. They had to urge the simple of Ephraim to prepare for the coming kingdom. Jesus was the nasi, the prince of Israel, a leader in the Davidic mould who would convert sinful Jews and assert the authority of God's righteous. Only *the righteous* could enter the kingdom so sinful Jews had to repent sincerely, ritually purify themselves through baptism and prepare for the coming battle. In his acts of conversion, the nasi was metaphorically casting out evil spirits, making the blind see and healing the sick. Those who were thus purified could enter the kingdom and were the soldiers in the messianic army. The nasi represented the messiah but could make no claim to be him, the appointment being God's alone at the end time.

If the nasi were successful then the kingdom was nigh, and if the sum of the signs were such that the acceptable day of the Lord was imminent then the forces of light would engage the forces of darkness, precipitating the cosmic battle for the kingdom. Then one like unto the Son of man, who the prophet Daniel told would come on a cloud from God—the archangel Michael with a heavenly host riding out of the Mount of Olives as it cleaved east and west—would arrive to institute the kingdom. Essenes felt that God only helped those who help themselves and the kingdom of God had to be won by the righteous taking on their enemies, then God would intervene with a miracle.

Jesus was appointed nasi by John the Baptist. After initial successes recruiting the simple, the authorities caught on and hounded them, the Nazarenes were seen as a liability, many followers asked Jesus and his generals to leave them alone and they had to flee from Antipas's soldiers to Phoenicia.

Jesus hid, then ventured back into Antipas's country. He was still certain the signs were correct but had come to believe that God wanted him to to capture Jerusalem and the temple and that to inaugurate the kingdom of God he was required to play the role of the messiah, Melchizedek. Then God would intervene with a miracle.

His disciples crowned him Melchizedek—he was transfigured! His band proceeded to Jerusalem with Jews travelling for the coming Passover. No one could address him by any title that might draw attention to the spies of the authorities. Outside the city the Nazarenes overcame the inadequate Jerusalem garrison and Jesus purposely revealed himself by fulfilling the prophesy of Zechariah—entering the city on a foal of an ass—and controlled the temple. The defeated Roman garrison in the Antonia barracks withdrew to await reinforcements from Caesarea.

Pilate's troops counter attacked after a few days, killed the Galilaeans in the temple, battered the Tower of Siloam where some were holding out and recaptured the city. Still there was no miracle. Jesus and his generals in hiding took a last supper together—an Essene messianic meal. Jesus, convinced that he had done all that God required and that a miracle was still in the offing, said he expected to be eating his next meal in the coming kingdom. His men remained armed. The next day was the Passover, a likely occasion for a miracle. They went to the Mount of Olives where, according to prophecy, the miracle would take place and Jesus urged his men to keep watchful—not for the enemy but for God's intervention.

It did not occur. A body of the temple guard arrived instead. Jesus had been proven a false prophet and had to suffer the appropriate fate prescribed in Zechariah—he had to die as the worthless shepherd.

JESUS THE ESSENE

Philosophies of the Jews

Jewish sects

The gospels show Jesus as an independent healer and preacher fervently opposed by the Pharisees, a sect of pious Jews. However, the Pharisees were not the only sect of the Jewish religion, and a proper understanding of Jesus and the gospel stories requires an awareness of the Jewish sects and Jesus's relationship to them.

Jews had split into the four philosophies of the Jews described by Josephus—the Pharisees, the Sadducees, the Essenes and the Zealots. As God's chosen people pious Jews were set on obeying His commandments to the letter. But the commandments were not always clear or applicable to changed circumstances. They had to be interpreted and with it came disagreement and sectarianism. The Pharisees and the Sadducees we meet in the gospels but we do not meet the Essenes or the Zealots, a curious omission because these last two were as important as the other two, and they must have been a major influence on the lives of people living in small towns and villages such as those preferred by Jesus and his disciples. Nor do the writers of epistles in the New Testament mention the Essenes. They might as well have not existed, but we know they did from Josephus, Pliny and Philo.

Now that we can add to these classic authors the evidence of the excavations at Qumran and the Dead Sea Scrolls, a clear understanding of the Essenes and their connexion with Christianity is beginning to emerge. The four philosophies were religious, but equally important to understanding them was their political dimension—their attitude to the Roman invaders and their Greek culture. Jews did not distinguish religion from politics because their state was a theocracy—it was to be ruled by God through His priesthood—but the Romans had usurped God's position.

Josephus and the gospel writers were cagey, having to humour the Romans, so they were less than truthful. The scrolls are also not transparent being couched in arcane codes and interpretations to hide their true objectives lest the invader should ever get hold of them. Even the early Christians sought to defend their religion by censorship to hide its original anti-Roman nature and so alter or omit vital facts.

The Pharisees

Pharisees were far from being the jealous hypocrites of the gospels. It is true that Pharisee sages thought of themselves as heirs to the prophets but they claimed no prophetic abilities themselves—prophecy had ceased with the biblical prophets and would start again only with the age of the messiah. Their point was the prophets came from the people and, like them but unlike the hereditary and wealthy priesthood, Pharisees came on merit from all levels of Jewish society including the poorest. Like Jesus the carpenter of the Bible, most had to develop a practical skill with which to earn a living and only a few were wealthy.

Pharisees left the sacerdotal role to the Sadducees, considering priests merely to be functionaries of the temple with no authority to speak on the law or religion. They reserved this role for themselves. They were admired for their fairness as judges of the law, their legal knowledge and the originality of their religious interpretation. Though they practised temple worship, the centre of their lives was the synagogue.

Pharisees were progressive whilst the Sadducees were conservative. They accepted the Torah as inspired by God but, unlike the Sadducees, were not fundamentalists. They believed that the oral law, carefully recorded by the scribes, was more immediate, pertinent and vibrant than the ancient laws. Their justification was: the Torah is not in heaven—whatever is not in heaven could not be perfect—so it had to be interpreted. But with the end of prophecy, God might express His will through anyone—everyone's views on interpretation had to be considered. This effort of reasoning was good for the soul and necessary to the finding of truth: according to the effort is the reward. When a decision was made, it was not divine but human and therefore fallible—rejected views might later prove correct and were recorded by scribes to be available for reconsideration. Pharisees were democratic.

Pharisees did not punish dissenters unless they refused to abide by the majority decision, and even then punishment was merely a period of ostracism. This was just as well because the Pharisees were far from a homogeneous body, as the disputes between the rabbis Hillel and Shammai in the century before the crucifixion testify. Different views on the messiah could be, and were, voiced perfectly acceptably, including the one that there could be no messiah because he had already appeared as the virtuous king, Hezekiah.

What then was the reason for Jesus's bitterness toward the Pharisees? Most of them were pragmatists, who believed hostility to the invader was futile, though there were more nationalistic factions. Most would not advocate dissension, being unwilling to risk reprisals against Israel by organizing against Rome. And though Pharisees rarely actively collaborated like the Sadducees, in earlier times they had invited foreign powers into Israel to quell civil war which they considered the greater evil. Indeed they distrusted Jewish princes having suffered at their hands in the previous century. For Jesus this was hypocrisy. They had betrayed God by inviting gentiles into God's land and condoned their continued presence as rulers. That was why he opposed them, and they him.

The Sadducees

The Sadducees were wealthy families, mainly of priests, who collaborated openly, fearful of losing their riches and social position if there were any sedition. The priesthood originally comprised a caste notionally descended from Aaron, Moses's brother, according to the ancient Jewish legends which the returning Babylonian exiles had rewritten. But under the Greek kings, the priestly line was broken and the Chief Priests established as agents of foreign rule. And so they remained under the Romans. An Egyptian had assumed the role of High Priest under Herod the Great, and his descendants constituted the priestly family of the Boethusians in the rabbinical literature. They might have been the Herodians of Mark and Matthew, Herod having rebuilt the Jerusalem temple, the source of their influence. The Roman governor appointed the High Priest making his selection from the priestly families. Romans thought that control of the temple would control the people, but the separation of the sacerdotal and the teaching functions in the Jewish religion is one reason why it has survived. Destruction of the ceremonial centre never affected the religion as a whole.

Sadducees were fundamentalists needing no interpretation of the Bible and therefore no scholars. Atonement through temple ritual was sufficient. The priests serviced the temple financed by supposedly voluntary tithes that were often extorted. Many Jews were distressed because the administrators of the temple were corrupt, but tolerated it as God's will. Not so the Essenes. To judge by the Dead Sea Scrolls, they were training a pure priesthood in waiting ready to replace the unclean upstarts in the temple.

A final difference between Sadducees and Pharisees was that the Sadducees denied the resurrection of the dead while the Pharisees accepted it. In the New Testament Jesus takes the view of his enemies, the Pharisees, but the Essenes too believed in resurrection to judge by the scroll fragments.

Jesus and the Essenes hated the Sadducees because they openly collaborated with the Romans and because they had gained riches by extortion—riches were ill-gotten by wicked people who gathered where they had not sowed. Sadducees pretended to be God's servants while robbing Him and His children of their birthright.

Zealots

Josephus first mentions the Zealots as the fighters against the Romans in the Jewish rebellion of 66–73 AD. Zealots were of major significance in Palestine during the whole of the period of the gospels so the single reference to them in Luke (Simon, the Zealot) looks suspicious. For Josephus, Zealots became gangsters, killing for personal gain, killing Jews rather than gentiles and fighting amongst each other. It transposed, like the Mafia, from a liberation movement into gangs of criminals.

Zealots became robbers. In John, Barabbas—who we shall identify as Jesus the Nazarene—is described as a robber and the other gospels tell us he was an insurrectionist. Plainly Barabbas was a Zealot.

The Essenes

Pliny tells us that the Essenes lived on the western shore of the Dead Sea. They were a solitary people who renounced women and money, but maintained their numbers by enrolling those driven by the vicissitudes of fortune and weariness of life. Oddly, nowhere in the Dead Sea discoveries are the curators of the scrolls called Essenes but, since the Qumran caves and ruins are just where Pliny said they were, there is no doubt who they are.

In the Dead Sea Scrolls they know themselves variously as the the righteous, the elect, the poor, the holy or the saints, the keepers of the covenant, the new covenanters, the remnant of Israel, the perfect of the way and the sons of light. Their priestly caste had the name, the sons of Zadok. Zadok, in Jewish legend, was the noble priest of David and Solomon suggesting they claimed historic credentials, but the sons of Zadok were really the priests of Ezekiel's ideal temple (Ezek 40:46ff)—they were ideal priests, God's own priesthood building the kingdom of God on earth.

In his two famous books, the Jewish War and the Antiquities of the Jews, Josephus agreed that the Essenes, all Jews by birth, did not marry though they were not against marriage in principle—they realized it was necessary for the continuation of mankind—but propagated the sect by adopting other people's children. Another order of Essenes accepted marriage though maintaining strict rules about intercourse. There were about 4000 Essenes altogether, constituting a closely knit brotherhood with similarities to the Pythagoreans, devotees of Orpheus. They regarded pleasure as evil and disciplined themselves in continence and self control. They wore white garments just as did the priests.

In the Quran the followers of Jesus—the Nasrani—were called the people in white. The Manichaeans who derived from the Mandaeans—or Nasoraeans—followers of John the Baptist were called white robes. All took their habit of wearing white from their ultimate founders, the Essenes, who called themselves Lebanon, which means white, because they habitually wore sparklingly white robes of fine linen.

Essenes renounced riches (they were the poor) and kept no servants, ministering to one another, eating only the simplest food and wearing their clothes and shoes to shreds. They held their goods in common yielding their possessions to the order when they joined and contributing all their earnings. Failure to do this was a grave dishonesty and was severely punished. In return they received all that they needed. Guardians directed their daily lives leaving them able to do only two things of their own free will, assist those in need and to show mercy—the pre-eminent characteristics of the Nazarenes of the gospels.

They settled in all towns in Palestine living apart in organized communities based on a centre where they congregated for meals. When travelling, they never needed to carry anything with them except weapons to protect themselves against robbers because wherever they lived someone was appointed to look after visitors—they offered hospitality to any visiting brother Essene. There was no commerce between them, everything being given willingly to brothers who had need, once the guardian approved.

Their first act in the morning, before dawn, was to pray as if in supplication for the sun's rising. They took to their tasks until the fifth hour (11 am) whereupon they returned, clothed themselves in delicate white raiments, bathed in cold water and assembled in a room into which only the initiates were allowed for a sacred meal. Following grace said by the priest they partook of bread and a single type of food and concluded with another prayer in praise of God as the provider of the food. They then changed back into their working clothes and resumed their labours until the evening. Sweating through exertion was not considered impure and they would not sanitize themselves by using fragrant oil as a cosmetic—oil was a defilement used other than functionally, for medicine or cooking. Philo adds they never used the weather as an excuse not to work and each day they returned from work rejoicing, as if it had been a great pleasure. Then they repeated the cleansing ritual in preparation for the evening meal after the same manner. Conversation at the meal was orderly, each speaking in turn, otherwise silence prevailed, and they ate and drank only what they needed thus maintaining their perpetual sobriety.

Having sworn the solemn ritual oaths of their initiation they were bound then no longer to swear oaths believing that those who were untruthful were condemned by God. Thus they were faithful, peaceful and restrained. They spent much time studying the writings of the ancients, the scriptures, taking from them what was good for their body and soul including medicinal knowledge based on roots and stones.

To be admitted, a proselyte had to first live in the manner of an Essene for a year to prove he was capable of it. Then he was baptized but was still not admitted to the order—he had to continue to live in their fashion for two more years to prove his worthiness. It was at this stage that he took solemn oaths to become a full member and participated in the sacred meal. He had to swear piety toward God, justice toward men, not to harm anyone of his own accord or at the command of another, to hate the wicked and assist the righteous, to show faith to all men especially those in authority but not to abuse his own authority or try to outshine others in garments or other finery, to love truth and reprove those who lie, not to steal or covet, not to conceal from others in the sect nor divulge their doctrines to others on pain of death, to pass on the rules to proselytes just as he received them, and to preserve the books of the sect and the names of the angels.

Having discovered the scrolls after almost 2000 years we know they successfully preserved their books, but the names of the angels? The scrolls show us that they were a secretive community. Evidently the allusion is to the mysteries which they were taught and had to keep.

Their judgements were just, not being passed by a court of less than a hundred, and usually permanent. If anyone was guilty of sin he was cast out eating only grass since he could accept no succour from anyone without the permission of the guardian and thus he wasted away to die of starvation. Excommunication therefore meant death because no Essene would forgo his vows even though excommunicated. In practice the community accepted them again when they felt they had been punished enough. They obeyed their elders and accepted majority decisions.

Josephus writes that, after God, they revered most the name of their legislator, it being a capital offence to blaspheme him. They avoided spitting in public and were stricter than other Jews in observing the sabbath, preparing all their food on the day before and not even defaecating on the sabbath. On workdays they carried with them a small hatchet to dig a pit as a latrine which they refilled when they had finished. While in the act of defaecating they wrapped themselves with their white robe so that they did not offend, not simply other people because their toilets were well away from habitation, but the divine rays of light. Afterwards they washed themselves thoroughly.

The full members were split into four classes. Seniors considered junior members to be as unclean as a gentile and had to undergo purification if they touched one.

Their regular and simple lifestyle and diet made them long lived, often living to over a hundred years old.

They believed in an immortal soul locked in a corruptible body. The body was a prison for the soul which rejoiced when freed of it. This sounds like a contradiction of the Pharisaic, and early Christian ideas, of resurrection—the resurrection of the physical body but some scroll fragments use the bones passage of Ezekiel to signify resurrection, seeming to imply physical resurrection.

The Essene view sounds contradictory but we cannot assume that it seemed so to them. Essenes believed that the righteous would be resurrected in the kingdom of God on the third day of the kingdom (Hosea 6:2). Essenes were to be resurrected into an ideal world because they were God's perfect. Everything would seem as it was, but things would be perfect—the kingdom would be on earth but it would be free of sin. Since sin and corruption were synonymous, the kingdom was free of corruption. They would live for ever in incorruptible bodies—bodies such as those they had always lived in but rendered free of corruption by God, their reward for being righteous.

The significance of the Christian myth of the resurrection of Jesus is that it proved the kingdom of God had arrived. Modern Christians believe in a spiritual resurrection of the soul in heaven rather than a physical resurrection of the body, but the point about the Essene kingdom of God was that it was a coming together of heaven and earth—the physical body was resurrected on earth, but only when it had become part of heaven.

For the Essenes, heaven had no storms, snow or intense heat but was refreshed by a cool breeze always blowing gently from the ocean. Hell was a dark and stormy pit full of torments. These were inducements to men to be good in life for fear of being punished after death. Unlike other Jewish sects they did not offer sacrifices at the temple, indeed were excluded from it contradicting Josephus's statement that they were favoured by Herod. Some Essenes foretold the future and were rarely wrong.

Another account of the Essenes by Philo of Alexandria broadly matches Josephus's. Only mature men were admitted and Essenes lived all over Judaea but Philo adds that they preferred to live in villages not towns. The sick and elderly were cared for—the scrolls tell us that the infirm and the sick were already spiritually saved under the guardianship of the angels of holiness.

Philo tells us Essenes were farmers, shepherds, cowherds, beekeepers, artisans and craftsmen, but they did not make weapons, would not engage in commerce and were no sailors. They avoided towns because of the contagion of evils rife within them, living instead in country villages. They rejected slavery, believing brotherhood to be the natural relationship of men but that it had been spoiled by covetousness. Though they studied they were interested in morals not philosophy.

Though Josephus and Philo give the impression Essenes were pacifist adherents of the law, Josephus belies it when he says that in the war with the Romans they were above pain and could not be broken though they were racked and twisted, burnt and broke. If they were pacifist why did the Romans need to torture them? Though they were tortured, they did not shed a tear, indeed laughed at their tormentors rather than blaspheme their legislator or eat forbidden food, and gloried in death rather than the misery of life. They sounded tough.

Much of the account of the Essenes by Josephus has been remarkably confirmed by the discovery in the Judaean wilderness of the Dead Sea Scrolls, nothing less than the library of the Essenes, comprising 600 documents including parts of every book of the Hebrew Bible except the book of Esther. The pots in which the scrolls had been stored were of a type unknown in Palestine but of a recognized Egyptian pattern suggesting a link with Egypt, the home of the Therapeutae, with whom Philo had associated the Essenes. Nearby was a ruin which proved to be the monastic headquarters of the Judaean Essenes during the life of Jesus.

Essene Life and Beliefs

The New Covenant

Among the complete scrolls found by the Dead Sea were four books of regulations for Essene communities: the Community Rule, the Damascus Rule, the War Scroll and the Rule of the Congregation. The Damascus Rule refers to marriage and children and to other affiliated communities in Palestine, showing that the Qumran Community was not the only Essene settlement, just as Josephus said. Each different rule book provided for different circumstances and therefore differed in some ways from others but the underlying common values remained and they are plainly rules for a single organization.

Books like the Community Rule, formerly unknown in Jewish literature, were common in Christian communities of the early centuries as exemplified by the Didache. This cannot be coincidence and adds to the proof that Christianity stemmed from one particular type of Judaism, the Essenes, and not Judaism in general. The Qumran books reveal the tap root of Christianity in Palestine.

The Dead Sea Scrolls are clear that the purpose of the Essenes was to keep themselves spiritually and ritually pure because they were expecting the apocalypse when God would endow a messiah to purge and judge the world. Josephus said the Essenes rejected the temple as unclean and offered their sacrifices by themselves. The communities of the Essenes were the true Israel and the priesthood they maintained in the wilderness, the true Zadokite priesthood. Not that they could have restored the hereditary line of priests but they expected to restore purity in sacerdotal practice. They objected to the debasement of the temple and the venality of the Sadducees. They scorned the illegal priests of Jerusalem, and had rejected them to adopt a largely frugal and monastic life uncorrupted by the scandal of pollution and collaboration.

Some of the scrolls found near the Dead Sea are the rules of a Jewish sect living at the time described in the gospels but never mentioned in them. These scrolls prove them to be the Essenes described by classical writers—Jewish nationalists and proto-Christians.

They were opposed to foreign invaders, and their expected war between good and evil was largely a conflict between the Jews and the gentiles. Despite Philo and Josephus, they were not peace-loving monks. Hyppolytus, writing about 230 AD, maintains that Zealots were a branch of the Essenes.

The Essenes saw the history of the chosen people as a series of God's covenants with respectively Noah, Abraham, Moses and Joshua. In the covenant God made with Abraham, if a male Jew was circumcised at eight days old, then he became one of the chosen, and this was considered sufficient by most Jews. The sect of the scrolls however was exclusive. They believed, following God's announcement in Jeremiah 31:31,33 in a new covenant between God and the remnant of Israel that was righteous.

Behold, the days come, saith the Lord, that I will make a new covenant with the house of Israel, and with the house of Judah. But this shall be the covenant that I will make with the house of Israel; After those days, saith the Lord, I will put my law in their inward parts, and write it in their hearts; and will be their God, and they shall be my people.

Only the Essenes were writing the law in their hearts and only they—the remnant of Israel—were God's people. It was with the remnant of Israel that God made his new covenant—it excluded all but those who, after the age of twenty, undertook the solemn vows of the sect not to depart from any command of God. Most Jews were not righteous and were excluded but herein lies the distinction of the Nazarenes from the Essenes. Nazarenes were Essenes who regarded the new covenant as the saviour of the old covenant of Abraham. The Essenes kept perfect so that they could bring back into the flock the lost sheep of the house of Israel in the last days before the end time when God would right the wrongs of the world.

The new covenant seems to have been founded by Jews in exile. The Damascus Rule tells us it was with those who had gone out of the land of Judah into the land of Damascus that God established his covenant with Israel forever, revealing to them the hidden things in which all Israel had strayed, where all Israel—meaning the whole nation—is deliberately distinguished from Israel—meaning the remnant who were pure enough and observant enough, the sectarians themselves. The new covenanters had returned from exile in about 160 BC expecting the purity of the temple to be restored by the Maccabees, the rebellious family of Jewish nationalists. When it was not, they decided to withdraw into the wilderness, to set up a pure people ready for the judgement of God.

The story is told in the Damascus Rule. A group of Jews went with their righteous teacher to a place in the wilderness to uphold the law. The Community Rule, following Isaiah, commands:

THEY SHALL BE SEPARATED FROM THE MIDST OF THE GATHERINGS OF THE MEN OF WRONGS TO GO TO THE WILDERNESS TO PREPARE THERE THE WAY OF THE LORD, AS IT IS WRITTEN: IN THE WILDERNESS PREPARE THE WAY OF THE LORD; MAKE STRAIGHT IN THE DESERT A HIGH WAY FOR GOD. THIS IS THE STUDY OF THE LAW, AS HE COMMANDED THEM THROUGH MOSES TO DO ALL THAT HAS BEEN REVEALED FROM AGE TO AGE, AND, BY HIS HOLY SPIRIT, AS THE PROPHETS REVEALED.

God's covenant with Israel in the desert brought down by Moses had been replaced by the new covenant with God's elect in the desert, because of the backsliding of the children. The military preparations the children of Israel made to enter the promised land were now being made by God's elect to enter the kingdom of God. Many Qumran sectarian documents are aggressive in their phraseology and content. When Josephus wrote that the Essenes were pacifists, it must have been for Roman consumption. He himself tells us of a John the Essene who was a general in the Jewish war. God's soldiers had to be pure, whence the Essene's celibate regime, baptism and exemplary lifestyle.

All men were formed at birth with fixed amounts of good and ill in their dispositions. Only perfectly good people would be saved at the judgement day— evil people would be scourged for eternity. The Essenes could assay the degree of goodness of a person from his characteristics, but all was not lost for those who were not born perfectly good. All men had free will to be good despite their disposition at birth and could benefit from the grace of God. Even men born evil could submit themselves humbly to the precepts of God, and through self-discipline offer their souls for salvation, but the final decision was God's.

Like Paul, the sectaries made salvation depend ultimately on the grace of God, but the sectaries saw a clear role for works. For them a life devoted to achieving perfection—or alternatively sincere repentance of sins—was a necessary condition for salvation, but it was not sufficient because God had the final say. But God was not whimsical, he was just—so Essenes believed that their own righteous deeds submitted humbly to God could gain them salvation. What they did not know was how God considered their various iniquities in coming to His judgement, and this uncertainty kept them constantly striving for humility and perfect holiness in all respects.

The Master

The monks of the headquarters at Qumran were the men of perfect holiness also known as saints, the word used of Christians by Paul in his epistles and often in Revelation. The practical head of the monastery and of the movement as a whole was the Mebaqqer, the Guardian or Bishop, also called the Master (Maskil). There was also a bursar and a titular head, nominally above the Mebaqqer. Each of the camps of village Essenes had a Mebaqqer as well. Jesus was called master in the gospels and Judas was the bursar of the Nazarenes, showing that they organized on Essene lines.

The Master or Mebaqqer was a righteous teacher. The Community Rule, an instruction manual for the Master, directs him to teach the saints the ways of perfection and it agrees remarkably with Josephus. The Master had to instruct the community in the dualistic theology of the Essenes and show them how to interpret the scriptures correctly, not just the law but the prophets also, and to act in judgement over infringements of the rules.

> THE MASTER SHALL TEACH THE SAINTS TO SEEK GOD WITH A WHOLE HEART AND SOUL, AND DO WHAT IS GOOD AND RIGHT BEFORE HIM AS HE COMMANDED THROUGH MOSES AND THROUGH ALL HIS SERVANTS, THE PROPHETS: TO LOVE ALL THAT HE HAS CHOSEN AND HATE ALL THAT HE HAS REJECTED; TO PUT AWAY ALL EVIL AND HOLD FAST TO ALL GOOD; TO PRACTISE TRUTH, RIGHTEOUSNESS AND JUSTICE UPON EARTH; TO WALK NO LONGER IN THE STUBBORNNESS OF A WICKED HEART AND EYES OF FORNICATION, DOING ALL EVIL; TO BRING ALL THOSE THAT HAVE OFFERED THEMSELVES TO DO GOD'S PRECEPTS INTO A COVENANT OF LOVINGKINDNESS; TO BE JOINED TO GOD'S SCHEME OF THINGS AND TO WALK BEFORE HIM PERFECTLY ACCORDING TO ALL THE THINGS THAT HAVE BEEN REVEALED OF THE APPOINTED TIMES OF THEIR TESTIMONIES; TO LOVE ALL THE SONS OF LIGHT, EACH ACCORDING TO HIS LOT IN GOD'S SCHEME OF THINGS, AND TO HATE ALL THE SONS OF DARKNESS, EACH ACCORDING TO HIS GUILT IN THE VENGEANCE OF GOD.

In the Damascus Rule the Master instructs everyone in the congregation, examines them in counsel with the assembly to assess and grade them and inscribes them each year in their rank. The Damascus Rule specifically orders: *He shall not rebuke the men of the pit nor dispute with them*, meaning those outside the community, especially the wealthy—the Sadducees—and orders him not to give them any doctrine:

> HE SHALL CONCEAL THE TEACHING OF THE LAW FROM MEN OF DECEIT, BUT SHALL IMPART A KNOWLEDGE OF TRUTH AND RIGHTEOUS JUDGEMENT TO THOSE WHO HAVE CHOSEN THE WAY.

These restrictions are qualified by the Master's song of blessing to God which contains the line: *I will not grapple with the men of perdition until the day of vengeance*, evidently permitting disputation on that day if no other. The scenes in the gospels of Jesus disputing with Sadducees and Pharisees are false except those in the temple after he has captured it. Jesus then thought the day of vengeance had come and that he was allowed to tell the men of the pit what he thought of them. Previous disputes featured in the gospels arose within the Nazarene community, with Jesus in his role as Master instructing novitiates, except those where he taught in parables which were intended to enlighten those who had ears to hear but, as Mark says, conceal doctrine from others, and so must have been spoken in public.

The Master is the one who had to keep God's appointed times and watch for the signs of the coming visitation by God:

> HE SHALL BE ZEALOUS FOR GOD'S APPOINTED TIME FOR HIS DAY OF VENGEANCE... HE SHALL CONSTANTLY WATCH FOR THE JUDGEMENT OF GOD.

The sectaries took literally God's prescription in Joshua 1:8:

> This book of the law shall not depart out of thy mouth; but thou shalt meditate therein day and night, that thou mayest observe to do according to all that is written therein.

The oft mentioned Book of Meditations of the scroll texts is revealed as the books of Moses, the Pentateuch or Torah. The Essenes had to recite from the book of the law continuously, by day and by night. To keep the recitations going by night, the congregation had to watch together in a rosta for a third of every night of the year, and the Master had to lead prayers:

> AT DAWN AND AT DUSK AND AT THE VARIOUS WATCHES OF THE NIGHT AND THE DAYS OF THE NEW MOON.

And, finally:

> HE SHALL PERFORM THE WILL OF GOD IN ALL HIS WORKS AND SHALL FREELY DELIGHT IN OUGHT THAT BEFALLS HIM.

Jesus warned that the day of vengeance was nigh. When he decided it had arrived he entered Jerusalem as a king. He watched and prayed throughout the night for God's judgement in the Garden of Gethsemane. At the end he admitted he was a failed prophet and stoically accepted his fate.

Essene Monastic Life

Essenes were to be admitted to the Community only after a lengthy procedure, but evidently Jesus, and before him John the Baptist, had decided there was not enough time for a probation period because of the imminence of God's visitation. Normally initiation was at least three years but the day of vengeance could happen at any time, such were the portents. So Jesus would have started his ministry believing that the kingdom was due within three years.

When admitted fully into the new covenant, the priests blessed the elect with a prayer for God to preserve the new sectaries from evil. All priestly blessings were concluded with calls of Amen, Aramaic for quite so or truly or verily, as it is often translated in the gospels. The curses of Satan and apostates by the Levites which followed were similarly concluded with cries of Amen, Amen. In John's gospel Jesus is depicted idiosyncratically saying: Verily, Verily, just as the Essene litany required. It seems probable that this litany was observed each year at the annual renewal of the covenant.

Those who were saved were those who held fast to the community's rules, followed the law, listened to the righteous teacher and confessed before God.

The various rules of the community prescribe punishments for infringements of the rules. Essenes were to be truthful, righteous and just that they might do as Jeremiah had commanded—seek God with their entire heart and soul. The Community Rule declares that the men of perfect holiness, each with his neighbour, shall walk according to these rules. They had to practise what was good and what was just, love one another, and share with each other their knowledge, powers and possessions. Not one word of the law of Moses could be transgressed—Jesus said not one jot or tittle (Mt 5:18). The punishment was expulsion and shunning by every member unless the transgression was inadvertent when the member could be readmitted after two years.

They had to live, eat and pray together and own only limited personal possessions, everything else being held by the community under the control of a custodian of property. This reflects Nazarene practice as we know from Acts. Lying in matters of property such as concealment of personal possessions was punished by partial expulsion for a year and a cut in rations. But in Acts 5:1–10 two converts are apparently killed for doing this, showing that their true crime was far worse. Expulsion was the punishment for rebelling against the leadership of the community or for slandering them. The Community Rule has:

WHOEVER HAS SLANDERED THE CONGREGATION SHALL RETURN NO MORE. WHOEVER HAS MURMURED AGAINST THE AUTHORITY OF THE COMMUNITY SHALL BE EXPELLED AND SHALL NOT RETURN.

Expulsion was death as far as the sectaries were concerned. Their oath was to do only what their Mebaqqer permitted. A conscientious Essene would die if expelled. The deaths in Acts however are quick ones, carried out by God in the presence of Peter—in short, by Peter! The two in Acts probably committed treason, betraying the sect to the authorities for money. Neither the Essenes nor the Nazarenes could have had any legal powers of execution. That is not to say that they would not have killed, but they would only have done it according to the rule of God as they perceived it. The scrolls state that no one was allowed to condemn a fellow according to the law of the gentiles—the punishment being death. Ananias and Sapphira must have tried to betray the community to the gentiles and this is why Peter struck them down.

Monastic Essenes had to bathe daily in holy water and eat each day a sacred meal of bread and wine. They were to keep meticulously the appointed times of the solar calendar prescribed in the Book of Jubilees. They had to maintain total self-control—members were fined if they showed anger toward each other (unless it was ritualized). No one was allowed to be ill-tempered or stubbornly obtuse and could not bear malice from one day to the next. Disagreements between the sectaries were to be expressed truthfully and openly, and heard humbly and charitably. If a disagreement were serious then the plaintiff had to publicly rebuke his tormentor before he could take his complaint before the full congregation to be judged. To indicate correct procedure the Damascus Rule quotes Leviticus 19:18 and 19:17:

> You shall not take vengeance against the children of your people, nor bear rancour against them... You shall rebuke your companion and not be burdened by sin because of him.

Jesus teaches the same (Mt 18:15–17).

The monks had to organize themselves in a strict hierarchy of members and speak only in order, keeping silent when others were speaking and respecting the wishes of the majority. They had to follow liturgy precisely.

Above we saw the Community Rule's instruction that members had to swear to hate the Sons of darkness for all eternity. Rich people were regarded as deceitful and wicked, and the Essenes were to keep apart from ungodly and wicked men whom they were obliged to hate with everlasting hatred. The Damascus Rule specifies that:

> THEY SHOULD SEPARATE FROM THE SONS OF THE PIT AND SHALL KEEP AWAY FROM THE UNCLEAN RICHES OF WICKEDNESS ACQUIRED BY VOW OR ANATHEMA OR FROM TEMPLE TREASURE; THEY SHALL NOT ROB THE POOR OF HIS PEOPLE, MAKE OF WIDOWS THEIR PREY AND OF THE FATHERLESS THEIR VICTIM... THEY SHALL LOVE EACH MAN HIS BROTHER AS HIMSELF AND SUCCOUR THE POOR, THE NEEDY AND THE STRANGER.

They were to love their brother Essenes as themselves but not all men—most of them they hated as wicked. Riches are wicked, the poor are venerated, widows should not be robbed of their mites nor orphans exploited. The language is very much the language of Jesus, but Christians in setting up a universal religion, omitted the qualifications—a brother was not any man. The pit is one of the three snares of Belial discussed below and represents riches, so the sons of the pit are the wealthy—mainly Sadducees. The poor are subtly distinguished from the poor of His people. The poor is a name for themselves, whereas the poor of His people are the poor of the children of Israel—God's children. In the final sentence the poor, the needy and the stranger all stand for fellow Essenes, brothers who they have to love as themselves.

The Community Rule also emphasizes separation from the wicked, citing Exodus 23:7: *Keep thou far from a false thing.* The verse continues: *and the innocent and righteous slay thou not, for I will not justify the wicked.* Isaiah 2:22 is also quoted: *Cease ye from man, whose breathe is in his nostrils; for wherein is he to be accounted of.* This is in a passage in which God is saying what punishments he will mete out to wicked men. Yet Essenes were not to take it upon themselves to punish the ungodly. That was God's job and, in the Community Rule, the blessing of God, which the Master has to recite at the various watches, says:

I WILL PAY NO MAN THE REWARD OF EVIL; I WILL PURSUE HIM WITH GOODNESS. FOR JUDGEMENT OF ALL THE LIVING IS WITH GOD AND IT IS HE WHO WILL RENDER TO MAN HIS REWARD.

In practice this is stronger than turning the other cheek. It was not for men to punish anyone who had wronged them for it is up to God alone to punish; but nor was the recommended course as indifferent as simply turning another cheek—pursuit with goodness was needed. Hatred of the ungodly was required but no one could judge another man with a view to handing out punishment. He had to pursue him with goodness.

All this sounds odd in the light of the War Scroll and many other texts but it was a command which applied only until God set about purging the world of the wicked on the day of vengeance when the perfect would become agents of God's vengeance, and it was a rule which would not have applied to gentiles in any case— it applied only to Jews. The gentiles had to be driven from the land irrespective of individual personal qualities. The net effect was that initiates of the Essene order had to hate the wicked but could do nothing about it until God indicated the appointed time.

The temple of Herod with its unclean Sadducaic priests was disregarded by the sectaries living in separation in the monastery at Qumran, though the village Essenes still used the Jerusalem temple in the normal way. The Community Rule commands that:

THE MEN OF THE COMMUNITY SHALL BE SET APART AS A HOUSE OF HOLINESS FOR AARON AND THOSE WHO WALK IN PERFECTION SHALL BE JOINED AS A HOLY OF HOLIES AND AS A HOUSE OF COMMUNITY FOR ISRAEL. THE COUNCIL OF THE COMMUNITY WILL BE ESTABLISHED IN THE TRUTH AS AN ETERNAL PLANTING—A HOLY HOUSE FOR ISRAEL AND A FOUNDATION OF THE HOLY OF HOLIES FOR AARON. IT SHALL BE A WITNESS TO TRUTH AT THE JUDGEMENT, WHEN THE ELECT, BY GOD'S WILL, SHALL ATONE FOR THE LAND AND PAY TO THE WICKED THEIR RECOMPENSE.

Note here that the elect were to atone for the land, and pay the wicked their recompense at the judgement day. Atoning for the land refers to the occupation of Judaea by the gentiles, and of other Jewish lands by the puppet Herodians, who were all to receive retribution. Essenes were not just pacifist monks as Josephus implied.

A house for Aaron is, of course, a temple, Aaron being Moses's brother and priest of Israel who might enter the holy of holies. Since the community was a temple and the temple was the most substantial building in the land, the sectaries were fond of solid architectural metaphors like: *It shall be the tested wall; the precious cornerstone; its foundation will not shake or become displaced.* In the Master's song blessing God of the Community Rule we find:

HE HAS JOINED THEIR ASSEMBLY TO THE SONS OF HEAVEN, TO BE A COUNCIL FOR THE COMMUNITY, A FOUNDATION FOR THE BUILDING OF HOLINESS, AND ETERNAL PLANTATION THROUGHOUT ALL AGES TO COME.

47

Evidently the new covenanters considered themselves to be joined to heaven already—the foundation of heaven on earth: God's bridgehead for the coming kingdom.

Daniel tells us that there is a god that revealeth secrets, who maketh known what is to come to pass. In the dream of Nebuchadnezzar, a *stone* destroys the four great kingdoms of the dream. Later in Daniel the four kings are replaced by the saints of the Most High, an Essene name for themselves, who take the kingdom and possess it *for ever, even for ever and ever*. The everlasting kingdom therefore replaces the earlier four earthly kingdoms and must therefore be on earth. Essenes expected heaven and earth to unite to form a perfect and incorruptible earth.

The Qumran Community regarded itself as a living temple, an image found in John 2:21: *He spake of the temple of his body*, and used by Paul (1 Cor 3:16–17). In 1 Peter 2:5 the Christian church was to be a spiritual temple in which spiritual sacrifices are made. Each believer is described as a *living stone* in this spiritual temple and the chief corner stone is Jesus (Eph 2:20), the whole growing to become a living temple to the Lord—purely Essene.

If the community council was a holy of holies for Aaron and a temple for Israel, it seems that the council at Qumran was an alternative temple for all Essenes. The monastic Essenes did not live in the buildings of Qumran but in caves nearby and a tented city which would have provided for a transient as well as a permanent population. The Essenes of the villages had cause to visit as pilgrims.

The Essenes aimed to be perfect. Yet they could not be sanctimonious about it. An absolute requirement was to be meek and humble. Their hymns and writings reminded them constantly that they were wicked and sinners, that they had disobeyed God and strayed from his precepts. They were unworthy and must try constantly to be perfect—by the grace of God they would succeed. The Community Rule orders: *None of the saints shall lean upon works of vanity*, and, as if to counter any grand ideas the sectaries might get from hearing the Master's blessing of God several times a day the Master goes on to say:

> I BELONG TO WICKED MANKIND, TO THE COMPANY OF UNGODLY FLESH. MANKIND HAS NO WAY, SINCE JUDGEMENT IS WITH GOD AND PERFECTION OF WAY IS OUT OF HIS HAND. ALL THINGS COME TO PASS BY HIS KNOWLEDGE AND HE ESTABLISHES THINGS BY HIS DESIGN AND WITHOUT HIM NOTHING IS DONE.

If they showed any such failings, they fell down the rankings at their yearly assessment and might be expelled altogether. These requirements of humility are the origin of the humble and gentle Jesus, meek and mild. For those who tried with all their heart, God was bountifully merciful. Note that in the preface of John we find: *All things were made by him; and without him was not any thing made that was made* (Jn 1:3), an identical sentiment to the final sentence above. The author of the fourth gospel is using an Essene song without even mentioning the Essenes—unless they were the Nazarenes.

Furthermore in Numbers 12:3: *the man Moses was very meek, above all the men which were upon the face of the earth.* For the Essenes Moses was the priest, prince and prophet, the first messiah sent by God—and they were sure that the expected messiah could be no less. Thus all Essenes had to be meek toward each other—but not toward the men of darkness.

Essenes vowed to be zealous for the law *until there shall come the prophet and the messiahs of Aaron and Israel,* apparently suggesting that three people were expected, the prophet, the priestly messiah and the princely messiah. In fact, they expected one man to embody all three roles like Moses.

Village Essenes

For a village Essene matters were less rigid but many requirements were the same as those for the monastic order. The children of any Jew (those who had entered the covenant granted to all Israel forever) could become an Essene by swearing an oath on their reaching twenty—the age of enrolment. Before then nothing of the statutes was to be revealed to them. Particular rules for village Essenes were given in the Damascus Rule and the Rule of the Congregation, or the Messianic Rule as Vermes has renamed it.

- Members had to cleave to the laws of Moses;

- the Mebaqqer of the camp or village community was its head, its teacher and its director; he allowed commerce with the impure and the imperfect but had absolute power over it, permitting no casual contacts;

- temple sacrifice was permitted and demanded absolute ritual purity;

- full maturity was reached according to the Rule of the Congregation only at the age of 30;

- observance of the sabbath was strict, the rule expressly forbidding the picking and eating of fruits from the fields;

- members were not allowed to bear witness in the courts of the gentiles—the Romans. The punishment was death.

Note that village Essenes brought up in an Essene community were not considered mature until the age of thirty, the age at which Jesus was baptized. No Jewish priest was allowed to enter office until he was thirty years old and the Essenes were a priestly sect.

Village Essenes owned their own property, instead of holding their goods in common, paying a sum of two days' wages a month to a fund to provide for orphans, the old and needy, and widows.

The Damascus Rule requires that the village Mebaqqer *love his people as a father loves his children and shall carry them in all their distress like a shepherd his sheep*—two metaphors, children and sheep, used by Jesus for his followers tumbling out of one scroll sentence. He had to ensure that there was no friendly contact with those outside the sect, the sons of the pit. The Mebaqqer would allow commerce but not friendship. Transactions must have been very abrupt and matter-of-fact.

Precedence and the Annual Renewal

The Essene organization was arranged to reflect the nation of Israel (whence the distinction between Israel and all Israel in the scrolls) having casts of priests, Levites, lay people and converts—the four ranks of membership spoken of by Josephus. Lay Essenes were divided into twelve tribes, Israel historically having been split into twelve tribes. The priesthood regarded themselves as the perfect priests of Ezekiel's heavenly temple, sons of Zadok, the keepers of the covenant. If ten or more Essenes met then a priest had to be present and the priest said grace at the common meals. In the village situation, if there were no priest available, a Levite could be substituted when the ten gathered.

The Community Rule prescribes a council of twelve men and three priests, without being absolutely clear whether the three are included in or excluded from the twelve, or whether the Mebaqqer is himself included or stands above the other members:

> THERE SHALL BE IN THE COUNCIL OF THE COMMUNITY TWELVE MEN, AND THERE SHALL BE THREE PRIESTS WHO ARE PERFECT IN ALL THAT HAS BEEN REVEALED OF THE WHOLE LAW. THEY SHALL PRACTISE TRUTH AND RIGHTEOUSNESS AND JUSTICE AND LOVINGKINDNESS AND WALKING HUMBLY EACH WITH HIS NEIGHBOUR; PRESERVE FAITHFULNESS IN THE LAND WITH STEADFASTNESS AND MEEKNESS; ATONE FOR SIN BY THE PRACTICE OF JUSTICE AND BY SUFFERING THE SORROWS OF AFFLICTION; WALK WITH ALL BY THE STANDARD OF TRUTH AND BY THE RULE OF THE TIME.

Interestingly in Micah 5:5 fifteen leaders are prescribed to assist the messiah in defeating the gentiles but it consists of seven shepherds and eight principal men. A scroll fragment clarifies the constitution of the council of the community—it also refers to a council of fifteen men. This will have been the Nazarene set up too, Jesus having twelve apostles, the gospel writers not knowing or admitting that there were three additional priests. Yet when the Jerusalem Church is founded Paul says three apostles are special, the pillar apostles—Peter, James and John. In the gospels more than twelve apostles are mentioned, and in Acts 1:20–26 an apostle is appointed to replace the dead Judas, proving that the apostles were not peerless but were fulfilling an office and could be replaced. The War Rule indirectly supports an apparent Council membership of sixteen, including the messianic leader. It says the prince of the congregation has inscribed on his battle shield, his own name, the names Israel, Levi and Aaron and the names of the twelve tribes—sixteen names reflecting the full Council.

Note that Essenes were to be perfectly versed in the law, truth, righteousness, justice, lovingkindness and humility, and be ready to suffer the sorrows of affliction.

Hierarchy was strictly enforced. Each year all the camps—the village communities—assembled probably at Qumran for the feast of the renewal of the covenant, the principle holy day of the year, to renew the covenant and to allow initiates to be regraded. At the renewal sectaries pledged themselves anew to the principles of the sect and confessed their sins. A priest learned in the Book of Meditation or a Levite ruled each ten Essenes. Priests, Levites, the men of Israel and the proselytes were enrolled by name and were inscribed by name in order. Then the Master, the leader of the monastic community, questioned everyone on all matters to assess their progress and regrade them, according to the perfection of their spirit. All of the sectaries had their progress checked and their rank for the following year recorded. No one could alter their registered rank except by being re-graded and registered in a new rank at the renewal.

Evidently the Master was also Mebaqqer of all the camps, the leader of the organization at large because he presided over this annual gathering, and carried out the spiritual examination of the sectaries. The priest who called the gathering—the titular head of the organization—had to be between 30 and 60 and the Mebaqqer had to be between 30 and 50. In Luke Jesus was about 30 at his baptism and in John it is observed that Jesus was not yet 50—he had to be under 50 if he were to be the Master or Mebaqqer of all the Nazarene camps.

The annual convention at Qumran probably explains the animal remains found there and the graves of a few women and children. The animal remains, once thought to have been remains of sacrifices, are now thought to be remains of the meals provided for the faithful. The women and children buried there were unfortunate enough to have died during the holy celebrations.

The renewal feast occurred at Pentecost, the chief of the agricultural festivals which were held every 50 days (whence pentecontads from the Greek for fiftieth). The Pentecost of the Essenes was the feast of the new wheat, the Jewish feast of weeks, held about the beginning of June. Unfortunately the parts of the Damascus Rule describing this have been lost or exist only in fragments. In the gospels it is depicted as the feeding of the five thousand—the feeding was spiritual.

The Damascus Rule tells that they assembled in their ranks, the priests, then the Levites and after them:

> ALL THE PEOPLE ONE AFTER ANOTHER IN THEIR THOUSANDS, HUNDREDS, FIFTIES AND TENS, THAT EVERY ISRAELITE MAY KNOW HIS PLACE IN THE COMMUNITY OF GOD.

This description of the ranks, which follows Exodus 18:25, is reminiscent of that used in the mass feedings of Mark's gospel (6:39–40) but which gets edited down or out in the others:

> And he commanded them to make all sit down by companies upon the green grass. And they sat down in ranks, by hundreds, and by fifties.

Essene rankings were evidently extremely strictly enforced but they must have been quite dynamic because the obedience of the ordinances needed to maintain a ranking was also strict. The Essene had to be truthful, humble, loving, kind and merciful to his fellows. If anyone strayed in these qualities he would be downgraded in rank. Thus we can be sure that there was no room at all for ambition or pride in the ranks of the Essenes. If a priest were sanctimonious or boorish he would be reduced to the ranks, or expelled.

One scroll fragment is an excommunication test. According to this fragment, the purpose of Pentecost was not the Christian one of celebrating the descent of the holy spirit, but to curse those who depart from the law. Evidently those suspected of transgressing had to undergo a ritual purification. This is exactly what James required of Paul at his final Pentecostal visit to Jerusalem to prove that he was still walking in the way and keeping the law. Paul believed and taught that the curse of departing from the law had been lifted by Jesus having been hung on a tree, a debasing punishment.

After the regrading, the Master would have given an exhortation, an example of which is provided in the Damascus Rule. Matthew's sermon on the mount is an evangelical attempt at recording the speech.

The number of people saved in Revelation is 144,000. They are plainly Essenes, and indeed monastic ones, for they were not defiled with women—they were virgins. The War Scroll refers to groupings of myriads—ten thousands. The Essenes could never have been so numerous that there were divisions of myriads because Philo tells us there were only 4000 all together. Scholars reckon that there could never have been more than 200 Essenes in permanent occupation at Qumran. The conclusion is that they were providing for bigger numbers than they ever achieved, but numbers they expected to achieve in the last days.

The men of perfect holiness in the desert will have attracted lay support from quite early in their existence and it is possible that pious converts of the simple of Ephraim—Jews who had been led astray by the smooth things of the Pharisees—became village Essenes. The Commentary on Nahum explains that the ranks of the sectaries would be expanded, prior to the battle with the sons of darkness, by the conversion of the simple of Ephraim. As the kingdom drew nigh the numbers of such converts were expected to explode as the new covenant attracted back to the fold the lost sheep of the house of Israel. The Rule of the Congregation is written specifically for all the congregation of Israel that will join the community in the last days. The phrase, all the congregation of Israel, implies that many Jews were expected to return to the fold by the end time. Rankings of myriads would then have been justified.

The Kingdom of God

God's Visitation

Jewish eschatology is the idea that God, having created the world, has been faced with various evil forces trying to subvert his purpose. At some point he will intervene decisively on the side of good, overthrow the evil forces in a cosmic battle and inaugurate a kingdom on earth true to his original purpose—the kingdom of God.

The Qumran Community was an apocalyptic sect. They were expecting the end of the world. When this happened those who had been true to God's commandments, His chosen ones or the elect, would be resurrected into God's presence to enjoy a messianic banquet and blissful eternal life. The Qumran library proves that apocalypticism was an ample movement in Judaism, not merely a fringe interest. It arose with the death of classical Jewish prophecy when the Israelites were carried off to Babylon, soon to become absorbed into the empire of the Persians. Apocalypticism seems to owe a great deal to Persia and the influence of Persian religion on Judaism stems partly from the apocalyptic writers.

In Persian religion the devil, called by the Essenes Belial, and his angels rose out of the abyss to attack the good spirit and the angels of light. Neither good nor evil was victorious and the battle between good and evil continues, but eventually Belial will be defeated. God will send a deliverer, the saoshyant, to herald the end of evil and a new age. The Jewish messianic ideal of a saviour was Persian. There follows a day of the Lord and trial by ordeal for mankind when the earth will be flooded with molten metal which burns up the wicked but is like warm milk for the righteous. Micah 1:4 says: the mountains shall be molten. A thanksgiving hymn in the Hymn Scroll describes it in detail. The earth would be levelled into a great plain just as it is in Isaiah 40. Finally Belial will be cast back into the abyss and mankind will ascend to the realm of light to dwell with God.

Essenes believed that all men walk in two spirits appointed by God, the spirits of truth and falsehood. The scrolls speak of good and evil, light and dark, the way of darkness and the way of light, the spirit of darkness and the spirit of light, the children of darkness and the children of light, truth is light but falsehood is darkness. The teacher of righteousness is opposed by Belial, the demon of evil. The way of good leads to salvation, the way of evil leads to torment. God has set an everlasting hatred between the two spirits and the cosmic balance is equal until the final age.

All of this was prescribed in God's design. Everything that ever happened had its appointed time. God knew the years of their comings and the length and exact duration of their times for all ages to come throughout eternity, says the Damascus Rule. They were fatalists. That is why they thought it essential to keep accurate dates and times. At the end time the Essenes expected a visitation by God and his holy angels to punish the wicked and to save the righteous. They hoped to be able to work out God's plan so as to predict God's visitation. These expectations are recorded in the Community Rule:

> BUT GOD, IN THE MYSTERIES OF HIS UNDERSTANDING AND IN HIS GLORIOUS WISDOM, HAS ORDAINED A TIME FOR THE RUIN OF DECEIT AND IN THE APPOINTED TIME OF THE VISITATION HE WILL DESTROY IT FOREVER. THEN INTO THE WORLD FOREVER SHALL COME TRUTH; FOR, AS DECREED, IT HAS WALLOWED IN THE WAYS OF WICKEDNESS IN THE DOMINION OF DECEIT UNTIL THE APPOINTED TIME OF JUDGEMENT.

> THEN GOD WILL REFINE IN HIS TRUTH ALL A MAN'S DEEDS, AND WILL PURIFY FOR HIMSELF A MAN'S BODY, CONSUMING EVERY SPIRIT OF DECEIT HIDDEN IN HIS FLESH, AND CLEANSING HIM WITH THE HOLY SPIRIT FROM ALL WICKED DEEDS. AND HE WILL SPRINKLE UPON HIM A SPIRIT OF TRUTH, LIKE HOLY WATER CLEANSING HIM FROM ALL ABOMINATIONS OF DECEIT AND IMPURE HABITS, TO MAKE HE WHO IS UPRIGHT PERCEIVE THE KNOWLEDGE OF THE MOST HIGH AND THE WISDOM OF THE SONS OF HEAVEN, TO SHOW THOSE WHOSE WAY IS PERFECT, FOR WHOM GOD HAS CHOSEN AN EVERLASTING COVENANT, THAT THEIRS IS ALL THE GLORY OF ADAM. AND THERE SHALL BE NO DECEIT, TO THE SHAME OF ALL WORKS OF LIES.

AT THE VISITATION, FOR ALL WHO WALK BY THE SPIRIT OF TRUTH: HEALING AND ABUNDANCE OF PEACE IN LENGTH OF DAYS AND FRUITFULNESS; EVERLASTING BLESSINGS AND EVERLASTING JOY IN A LIFE WITHOUT END; A CROWN OF GLORY AND RAIMENT OF MAJESTY IN EVERLASTING LIGHT.

AT THE VISITATION, FOR ALL WHO WALK BY THE SPIRIT OF DECEIT: ABUNDANCE OF AFFLICTIONS BY THE DESTROYING ANGELS; EVERLASTING DAMNATION IN THE WRATH OF THE VENGEANCE OF GOD AND EVERLASTING TORMENT AND EVERLASTING DESTRUCTION IN DISGRACE AND DISHONOUR IN THE FIRE OF DARK PLACES. AND FOR ALL TIME THEIR GENERATIONS WILL BE IN SORROWFUL MOURNING AND BITTER MISERY, IN DISASTERS OF DARKNESS UNTIL THEY ARE DESTROYED, WITH NO REMNANT OR ANY THAT ESCAPE.

God's prophets had written down the signs of the appointed time of the visitation, the end time. As the possessors of the holy spirit, the Essenes had the power to understand these writings. They scoured the scriptures for these signs, indications that the wicked would be destroyed and they, God's elect upon earth, would be chosen to rule. They wrote pesharim or interpretations of the scriptures in terms of the events of the last days, and they found the signs were appearing. To see the signs the interpreter—the pesharist—would used puns, word association, variant readings, and re-readings of a scriptural text to extract its hidden meaning. Fragments of a letter in the Qumran caves describe how the end time can be foreseen by a particular concatenation of events. They discovered they were already in the last days!

The Essenes expected the kingdom of God to come only after a cosmic war between the heavenly hosts led by the archangel Michael and the forces of darkness led by Belial, the devil. The battle is even and only God's intervention allows Belial's defeat. Jesus's temptation symbolizes this battle.

The importance of the Essenes in New Testament studies is that they, like Jesus, were convinced that the end time was nigh. The devout were being oppressed by falsehood. God's visitation was imminent. God would soon intervene on their behalf.

With the visitation of God, Armageddon would begin. A cosmic battle would be fought between the forces of light and good and the forces of darkness and evil; between truth and lies; between God and Belial. Mankind would be purged of deceit and individual humans would be judged on the balance of the spirits within them. By then there would be no repentance or pardon. In life, evil deeds could only be cancelled out by good deeds, and judgement was on this balance (the message of the Epistle of James the Just, the brother of Jesus). The people of Israel had to return to the law never to turn back if they were to be judged as righteous or just at the day of judgement. Good men would be saved and the wicked condemned. Belial would be cast down and the kingdom of God would dawn.

The Commentary on Habakkuk predicts that, at God's appointed time, the last priests of Jerusalem who had amassed a fortune from donations to the temple, particularly from diaspora Jews, would be destroyed by the Kittim, meaning the Romans. It says that the Jewish enemies of the Essenes were the wicked of Ephraim and Manasseh, meaning the Pharisees and the Sadducees.

Describing the punishment of the wicked, the Damascus Rule summarizes Essene expectations regarding the visitation in the form of these pesharim. It furnishes the pesher of Zechariah 13:7 as:

THE HUMBLE OF THE FLOCK ARE THOSE WHO WATCH FOR HIM. THEY SHALL BE SAVED WHEREAS THE OTHERS SHALL BE DELIVERED UP TO THE SWORD WHEN THE MESSIAH OF AARON AND ISRAEL SHALL COME, AS IT CAME TO PASS AT THE FORMER VISITATION CONCERNING WHICH GOD SAID BY THE HAND OF EZEKIEL: THEY SHALL PUT A MARK ON THE FOREHEADS OF THOSE WHO SIGH AND DECRY ABOMINATIONS. BUT THE OTHERS WERE DELIVERED UP TO THE AVENGING SWORD OF THE COVENANT.

The humble of the flock and those who watch are again references to the Essenes. In the Garden of Gethsemane Jesus kept urging his disciples to watch and does so elsewhere in the gospels. Watchers for the kingdom or Zophim were Essenes. The former visitation was that celebrated at the Jewish feast of Passover when, on the eve of the escape from bondage in Egypt, God visited death on the firstborn of those who were not identified by a covenant of lambs blood on the lintel of each home. Ezekiel describes the return of the angels of death to punish the apostate Jews of Jerusalem. Either the Essenes believed this to have been true history or they believed that Ezekiel prescribed the proper means of identification—the righteous were marked, not with blood but with the mark of the cross made in water on their foreheads so that it could be seen by God and His seven avenging angels but not by men. The reference is to Ezekiel 9:4, the prophet's vision of the destruction of the sinners of Jerusalem—those not marked. The sprinkling of water mentioned in the quotation above from the Community Rule probably means the making of this sign. The same is the practice of the clergymen when baptizing.

The sword of the covenant is an expression that recalls Jesus saying in Matthew: *I come not to send peace but a sword*. He obviously meant the sword of the covenant. The sword of God is a phrase met in the War Scroll where it is a sword of war. In this quotation from the Damascus Rule it is plainly the sword of judgement. The sword of war is necessary to initiate the kingdom of Israel on earth which then brings the sword of judgement and finally peace. Thus the people of God, the Jews, will make everyone to rest from the sword so there will be peace on earth. The origin of this sword metaphor—and that of the refiner's fire—is Genesis 3:24 where God leaves a sword of flame to prevent fallen man from re-entering the Garden of Eden. The righteous have to run the gauntlet of the sword of fire to prove, being free of sin, they are worthy of re-entering the Garden of Eden, which is—the kingdom of God.

The Essenes were God's new covenant perpetually ready to face the sword of flame, to join battle against the forces of evil—spiritually and ritually pure through repentance and baptism. They practised the messianic meal every evening. They had the holy spirit with them. Their reward, according to the Damascus Rule, was everlasting life: *Those who hold fast to it are destined to live forever and all the glory of Adam shall be theirs.* Elsewhere it quotes Deuteronomy 7:9: *God keepeth covenant and mercy with them that love Him and keep his commandments to a thousand generations*, as proof that all who walk in perfect holiness according to His Covenant shall live forever—the meaning to an Essene of, to a thousand generations. Those not of the covenant could have their sins forgiven by God (with sincere repentance) until the age is completed but thereafter there is no more forgiveness.

The Qumran literature frequently refers to the community as the poor, the meek and the downtrodden which, in the scrolls, seem to be used interchangeably. The scrolls have hymns to the poor. This name the Essenes gave to themselves was a reaction to the cultural imperialism of the Greeks—Hellenization. Judaea had historically been a poor country and Jerusalem a refuge for the poor, but under Greek influence many Jews discovered a talent for commerce and developed a taste for wealth. So even before the Abomination of Desolation when the Greeks violated the Jewish temple with a statue of Zeus, Ben Sira could complain that the citizens of Jerusalem thought poverty disgraceful. Evidently the disgust of the Essenes for the Greek way of life included a disgust for the love of money that was concomitant with it.

Can it be coincidence that the poor was a name of the followers of James in the Jerusalem Church (Gal 2:10 and Jas 2:3–5)? Paul claims the only condition James imposed upon him in his missions to the gentiles was to remember the poor. He is reminding him to send money not for any poor but for *the poor*, the Nazarenes, who, after the defeated uprising, had a lot of widows to support (Acts 6:1–6).

The meek was also one of the community's names for itself. Jesus said: *blessed are the meek for they shall inherit the earth*, an exact expression of the community's beliefs about itself for, when God created His kingdom on earth, the elect would inherit it. In one scroll fragment God visits the meek and calls the righteous by name and God's spirit hovers over the meek announcing to them glad tidings. Other fragments contain references to making the blind see, raising up the downtrodden and resurrecting the dead. The pious are glorified on the throne of the everlasting kingdom, and the righteous are promised resurrection.

In his Ecclesiastical History written in the fourth century, Eusebius describes a deviant Christian sect, the Ebionites, who held the brother of Jesus, James the Just, in special regard. They refused to accept that Jesus was divine but thought of him as an ordinary man, naturally conceived and notable for his righteousness but having no divine aspects. They did not accept that faith was sufficient to save and were therefore careful to observe the law in addition—they evinced great zeal to observe the literal sense of the law. They had no regard at all for Paul.

Eusebius thought their name came from their low and mean opinions of Christ, Ebionites is, in Hebrew, Ebionim meaning The Poor. They were the remnants of the

Jerusalem Church of James the Just perpetuating the name used by the Nazarenes, the Essenes and James himself.

Aramaic quite commonly uses as nouns adjectives like poor, pious, holy, just, righteous and meek but what the Greeks translating the words of the evangelists did not know was that the words they used when they said: the poor, the holy or the righteous meant the Essenes and not the poor, holy or righteous in general. Though there must be occasions in the New Testament when these words have been used in a general sense, perhaps by a later editor, in their original use they refer to the Essenes.

The Star Prophecy

The Damascus Rule gives a pesher on Amos 9:11. The pesher, which does not obviously relate to the scriptural quotation, is an arcane confirmation of the prophecy of the star of Numbers 24:17:

> There shall come a star out of Jacob, and a sceptre shall rise out of Israel, and shall smite the corners of Moab, and destroy all the children of Sheth.

This particular scriptural text is one of those that the community were particularly fond of and it occurs in several Qumran sources. Following a quotation of this star prophecy in the War Scroll, the author explains what then would happen, referring to the sectaries by their name of the poor:

> BY THE HAND OF THE POOR WHOM YOU HAVE REDEEMED BY YOUR POWER AND THE PEACE OF YOUR MIGHTY WONDERS... BY THE HAND OF THE POOR AND THOSE BENT IN THE DUST, YOU WILL DELIVER THE ENEMIES OF ALL THE LANDS AND HUMBLE THE MIGHTY OF THE PEOPLES TO BRING UPON THEIR HEADS THE REWARD OF THE WICKED AND JUSTIFY THE JUDGEMENT OF YOUR TRUTH ON ALL THE SONS OF MEN.

The poor were to conquer all the enemies of Israel. The Essenes were preparing for a holy war. Note that, if son of man was a messianic title as the theologians believe, the judgement here would be of lots of messiahs! It means nothing more than man, and sons of men simply means men.

The star prophecy is the true source of the mysterious star of Bethlehem in Matthew. It was not a conjunction of planets, a comet or a supernova but simply a metaphor of the star, meaning the messiah of David, come to free Israel and conquer the world of the flesh. A related scroll fragment ends with an explanation of Jacob's blessing on Judah (Gen 49:10):

> The sceptre shall not pass from Judah, nor the staff from between his feet until the coming of Shiloh to whom the people will gather.

The scroll writer's interpretation is that the sceptre is sovereignty and the staff is the covenant of the kingdom given to the branch of David in perpetuity because he kept the law with the men of the community! Shiloh is the messiah of righteousness and is the same as the branch of David. The sceptre and the star are embodied in the same man, the nasi, the prince of the congregation who shall smite all the children of Seth, the enemies of Israel—Numbers 24:17 specifies them as Moabites and Edomites, signifying gentiles. The staff is the law which has to be followed until he who pours out righteousness is resurrected at the end time. Thus the messiah of righteousness and he who pours out righteousness are the same—the branch of David. Nowhere in the scriptures is Shiloh used as a messianic name except here and modern scholars have sought other meanings, but for the Essenes its interpretation was plain. Though the messianic leader, the nasi, will smite Israel's enemies, here he seems not to be the messiah himself—though in Daniel 9:25 the messiah is identified as the prince (nasi).

The star prophecy, supported by other messianic readings, was the key to the persistent troubles in Palestine in the intertestamental period. The uprising in 132 AD was evidently grounded in the same prophecy because the leader of the uprising, one bar Kosiba was renamed bar Kochba, the son of the star, a pun—the words having almost the same pronunciation. Interestingly a papyrus, found at Murabba'at near Qumran, describes bar Kosiba as prince of Israel—nasi. So bar Kosiba, was both nasi and messiah as in Daniel.

The prophet, priest and prince represented originally by Moses, Aaron and David, in the scrolls were to be paralleled by three messiahs. The Essenes seemed to believe their founder, the righteous teacher, was the prophet—the priest and prince were still expected. The priestly messiah was higher in rank than their princely messiah. The righteous teacher was also a priest—all senior Essenes were priests anyway—and his enemy was the wicked priest.

Often the messiahs were considered to be embodied in one person as in Psalms 45:7 where the meaning of, *anointed... above thy fellows*, implies that the messiah had higher qualities than anyone else anointed—prophets, priests or princes—and so must have had the qualities of all. The Damascus Rule describes a messiah of Aaron and David and the root of planting out of Aaron and Israel, apparently one messiah out of the two lineages of Aaron and Israel. The one is both priest and prince—the Melchizedek, the prince of righteousness, the name used for Jesus as the supreme priest in the Epistle to the Hebrews! Fragmentary material at Qumran tell us that the Melchizedek is the judge on the day of atonement, but elsewhere the judge is the archangel Michael, the heavenly prince of light, who would lead the heavenly hosts in a cosmic battle against the forces of darkness. In the Apocrypha, the judge is the Son of God, the messiah. The implication is that the messiah was conceived of as an aspect of the archangel Michael, and the earthly prince and the heavenly prince would unite when heaven united with earth in the kingdom yielding the judge—Melchizedek.

The descriptions of the two figures in Revelation convince us that they are the same. In Revelation 10:1–4 an angel is described which descended from heaven with a rainbow on his head and clothed in a cloud. His face was like the sun and his feet were like pillars of fire. In Revelation 1:13–16 one like unto a son of man is described as clothed in a garment completely down to his feet, whose countenance was as the sun, whose eyes were as fire and whose feet were like fine brass, as if they burned in a furnace. His voice roared as the sound of many waters while the angel's voice roared like a lion. These entities are so similar that they must be the same. For the early Christians, the one like unto the son of man was an angel—the archangel Michael, matching Essene beliefs.

Gentiles

Essenes hated gentiles. The Damascus Rule forbids a man to shed the blood of a gentile for riches or gain, implying he could do so for other reasons, presumably religious or political. The writer of one fragment urges his readers not to give their inheritance to foreigners for they will come to dwell among you and become your masters. Another fragment includes the sentence: *The Lord is ruler... to Him alone belongs sovereignty*, which recalls Josephus who wrote of the followers of Judas of Galilee founder of the Zealots: *They call no man Lord but God*, allowing no recognition of rulers other than God and proving that they must have opposed Roman rule in Judaea.

A High Priest, Joezar, son of Boethus, the Egyptian that Herod made priest, had persuaded the Jews to pay tax to Rome which the Herodians collected. This was not popular, nor were tax collectors. Josephus explains in the Jewish War that the acceptance of unclean foreign gifts, which was an innovation introduced by the Boethusians, helped spark the War. The Zealots were so incensed by foreign gifts to the temple that they wanted them banned. It was the eventual refusal of the junior priests to offer foreign sacrifices that helped trigger the war.

The attitude of the Qumran community exactly matched this. The community was not anti–temple but it was anti–the polluted temple. It was zealous for a pure temple and that was an important symbol of Jewish nationalism. The temple was at least in part polluted by foreigners and their unclean contributions presented in skins of animals which had been sacrificed to idols. These problems are unlikely to have applied at the earlier period of the Maccabees implying that they pertained to the time of Jesus. Dogs were also banned from the temple as unclean flesh eaters. The elect referred to gentiles as dogs, metaphors for their opponents along with the deaf and the blind. Herodians were equally foreign as collaborators and in the war the rebels torched their palaces and those of the Boethusian High Priests.

The Qumran use of the word fornication is also relevant to the question of foreigners. It was applied to those who married outside Jewry. The essential aim was to keep Israel, a holy people, separate from others. The command in the Community Rule was to separate themselves to prepare a way in the wilderness. Thus another theme arose—how to recognize purity and separateness. Separateness extended to crops in the field and fibres in a cloth—no mixing was allowed in either. In the Damascus Rule the separateness of pure and impure in the temple is considered inadequate because: *they sleep with women during their periods and they marry their nieces*. Who are they? Those who sleep with women during their periods are the gentiles because Jews considered this grossly impure. Those who marry their nieces are, of course, the Herodians for whom marriage of nieces was common. The temple was therefore itself grossly impure.

Jesus had nothing to do with foreigners. He was interested only in Jews. Even the Syro-Phoenician woman only won him over through her humbleness. Several of Jesus's remarks show disdain if not hatred for foreigners. Jesus in saying love your enemies spoke to Jews and knew they understood him to mean only Jews. He wanted Jews to love each other so that God's kingdom could begin. Partly this involved uniting them against the foreigner because God helped only those who help themselves. It was necessary to atone for the land, to rid the land of the pollution of the foreigner to bring in the kingdom of God.

The Last Battle

The War Scroll, which is markedly apocalyptic, explains that the day of vengeance will include the total defeat of the gentiles, notably the Kittim (Romans). It anticipates a battle between the Kittim, the sons of darkness and the sons of light, the familiar expression for the members of the community. At the appointed time the War Scroll explains there will be a preliminary battle between the righteous and the armies of the Kittim allied with the ungodly of the covenant in some specific place now lost because of scroll damage. Then the exiles of the desert would move to Jerusalem for the final battle of the first week of years. Following victory over the Romans, the temple would be cleansed and correct temple worship would be restored. There seems to be no role for the leader of the elect except simply to lead out his forces—which is perhaps reason to believe that having done so he is transformed into another protagonist. Beyond that victory is assured by God.

> ON THE DAY WHEN THE KITTIM FALL THERE SHALL BE BATTLE AND TERRIBLE CARNAGE BEFORE THE GOD OF ISRAEL, FOR THAT SHALL BE THE DAY APPOINTED FROM ANCIENT TIMES FOR THE BATTLE OF THE DESTRUCTION OF THE SONS OF DARKNESS. AT THAT TIME THE ASSEMBLY OF GODS AND THE HOSTS OF MEN SHALL BATTLE WITH THE COMPANY OF DARKNESS AMID THE SHOUTS OF A MIGHTY MULTITUDE AND THE CLAMOUR OF GODS AND MEN TO MAKE MANIFEST THE MIGHT OF GOD. AND IT SHALL BE A TIME OF GREAT TRIBULATION FOR THE PEOPLE WHICH GOD SHALL REDEEM; OF ALL ITS AFFLICTIONS NONE SHALL BE AS THIS, FROM ITS SUDDEN BEGINNING UNTIL ITS END IN ETERNAL REDEMPTION.

On the first day the Essenes had to pitch their camp before the king of the Romans. The officers spoke to all those ready for battle, strengthening the resolve of the brave and making those lacking courage withdraw. In the victory hymn of the War Scroll, God has to stiffen the resolve of the Essene army:

> HE HAS TAUGHT WAR TO THE HAND OF THE FEEBLE AND STEADIED THE TREMBLING KNEE; HE HAS BRACED THE BACK OF THE SMITTEN. HE HAS GIVEN AUTHORITY OVER THE HARD OF HEART TO THE POOR IN SPIRIT.

Note here the use of the same curious expression—the poor in spirit—that Jesus the Nazarene uses in the sermon on the mount (Mt 5:3) but which has never before been found in any ancient work and was long thought to have been a mistranslation. It is not a negative concept as we might think. It does not mean the dispirited, or people of poor spirit. For Essenes it is wholly positive, meaning those having the spirit of poorness—those who appreciate the blessings of a state of poverty and humility and and live accordingly.

They believed Moses had taught them what to do when battle drew nigh. The priest appointed for the day of vengeance had to rise and address God, saying: *Thou art in the midst of us, a mighty God and terrible, causing all our enemies to flee before us.* Then he had to turn to the armies of the elect and give a stirring address to his soldiers. He begins: *Hear, O Israel! You draw near to battle this day against your enemies. Do not fear. Do not let your hearts be afraid. Your God goes with you to fight for you against your enemies that He may deliver you.* And he ends: *The hosts of conquering angels gird themselves for battle and prepare for the day of vengeance. For the God of Israel has called out the sword against all nations, and He will do mighty deeds by the saints of His people.*

The saints of His people are, of course, the Essenes. It is not hard to imagine how such sentiments could stir passionate but ill-armed men to great deeds. Further sorties followed, each accompanied by a stirring speech by the priest. The battle continues for the first week of years in seven sorties. Then, having secured victory in the land, for another 33 years the elect fight and conquer all the gentile races of earth.

While the righteous pitted themselves against the ungodly on earth the heavens would be echoing to a mighty conflict between the archangel Michael, the prince of light, and Belial, the prince of darkness, and their hosts of gods (angels and demons). The battle hymn of the War Scroll tells the priest again to make a speech to the sons of light. It refers to a spiritual kingdom led by the archangel Michael and an earthly kingdom of Israel led by the nasi. The battle is indecisive because the forces of good and evil are evenly matched and victory is given to the righteous and the angels only through God's intervention.

In Daniel 2:44 the prophet says that God will set up a kingdom which will last forever. The battle hymn in the War Scroll tells us that the outcome the Essenes were expecting was the establishment of everlasting dominion to Israel, God's earthly kingdom. The Community Rule, quoted above, explains the reward for the righteous as everlasting joy in life without end, a crown of glory and a raiment of majesty in unending light, a continuation of life in the midst of all flesh—in other words on earth. The punishment for sinners was: eternal torment and endless disgrace together with shameful extinction in the fire of the dark regions.

Other scroll fragments also speak of a kingdom ruled by a messiah, the Son of God or the Son of the Most High, whose rule will be an everlasting rule but nonetheless an earthly one. Compare this with Luke 1:32–35:

> He will be great and will be called the son of the Most High; and the Lord God will give him the Throne of his father David. And he shall reign over the house of Jacob forever, and of his kingdom there shall be no end.

Luke has told us that he who receives the throne of David is the Son of the Most High but at this point he breaks the flow of the argument by inserting a conversation between Mary and an angel before returning to conclude: *for that reason the holy child will be called the Son of God.* Omitting the misleading interjection, Luke says that the ruler of the House of Jacob, an eternal kingdom, is a Son of God, as he is in the scrolls, and he will judge the earth (2 Esdras 7) bringing peace by subjugating all other kingdoms and peoples.

Christian theologians used to believe that the anticipation of God's kingdom to come was uniquely Jesus's message. Now we see it was hundreds of years old, had come out of Persia with the exiles and had been perpetuated by the Essenes.

The Nazarenes

The Call to All Israel in the Last Days

Scroll scholar, Yigael Yadin, thought that Jesus was the leader of a schismatic faction of the Essenes, an Essene who advocated revision of the Community Rule. It is not so. There does seem to be a distinction between the Essenes and the Nazarenes—the Nazarenes seem less exclusive—but the philosophy of the Nazarenes was Essene philosophy. The Essenes recognized that in the last days all Israel must be told of the coming visitation and have the chance to repent and enter the kingdom. The Essenes allowed for the recruitment to the elect of the simple of Ephraim, those who had been misled by the Pharisees who seek smooth things, as described in the Nahum Pesher:

> THIS CONCERNS THOSE WHO SEEK SMOOTH THINGS, WHOSE EVIL DEEDS SHALL BE UNCOVERED TO ALL ISRAEL AT THE END TIME... THE SIMPLE SHALL SUPPORT THEIR COUNSEL NO MORE... MANY SHALL UNDERSTAND THEIR INIQUITY AND TREAT THEM WITH CONTEMPT BECAUSE OF THEIR GUILTY PRESUMPTION. WHEN THE GLORY OF JUDAH SHALL ARISE, THE SIMPLE OF EPHRAIM SHALL FLEE FROM THEIR ASSEMBLY. THEY SHALL ABANDON THOSE WHO LEAD THEM ASTRAY AND SHALL JOIN ISRAEL.

Besides pointing to the expectation that all Israel will join Israel at the end time, this passage illustrates that the Essenes had contempt for the Pharisees as well as the unclean Sadducees. The Essenes disdained them because they presumed to do God's will in building walls around the law and taking easy options in placating the foreign oppressors rather than aiming to evict them.

The Rule of the Congregation also orders that in the last days:

> ALL THE CONGREGATION OF ISRAEL SHALL JOIN THE COMMUNITY TO WALK ACCORDING TO THE LAW OF THE SONS OF ZADOK THE PRIESTS AND THE MEN OF THE COVENANT... THEY SHALL SUMMON THEM ALL.

When the whole congregation of Israel had been summoned—women and children too—they had the statutes of the covenant read into their ears that they may no longer stray, implying that there was no time for the usual three years of initiation—simply being told the rules would have to suffice as long as the simple had sincerely repented. Thus, at the end time all Israel would be called to enrol into the elect.

The Essenes evidently had the same idea as John the Baptist and Jesus—to warn all Jews that their time was nearly up, and that they should repent if they wanted to enter the kingdom. Neither Essenes nor John the Baptist or Jesus regarded anyone of the congregation of Israel as irredeemably lost to Belial, but note that their message was addressed only to Jews—all Israel or the congregation of Israel—the Jews were God's chosen people and they alone were called, not foreigners.

The duty of the elect was to try to take as many of the chosen as possible into the coming battle for the kingdom. Jews were needed as soldiers of the sons of light, and any Jew could have a favourable outcome in the kingdom of God no matter what sins they had committed as long as they sincerely repented. The Essenes were no longer exclusive at the end time. The new covenant made with the elect was a covenant to ensure there were enough righteous Jews to preserve the old covenant and ensure that the chosen people had the chance to repent and enter God's kingdom.

This suggests the following Essene practices at the end time. When the diviners of the signs considered the end time was nigh, a nasi was sent out into the community to test the mettle of the simple of Ephraim. He told them of the imminence of the kingdom and called them to repentance. This safeguarded the Essenes as a whole while allowing God to show whether the auguries were correct or not. John the Baptist was one—Jesus was his heir—the nasi, the prince, the leader of a vanguard whose duty was to mobilize the rank and file. Accordingly his converts were called Nazarenes—followers of the nasi. This explains why the followers of John the Baptist were also called Nazarenes. The nasi might not be the messiah, that depended upon God. He was simply the leader of the congregation of Israel in the last days, but the semitic root nsr, meaning protector or saviour, suggests that by god's will he would become the messiah. The sectaries identified the two because the nasi played the role of the messiah at the messianic meal of the men of repute.

AND WHEN THEY SHALL GATHER FOR THE COMMON TABLE, TO EAT AND TO DRINK NEW WINE, WHEN THE COMMON TABLE SHALL BE SET FOR EATING AND THE NEW WINE POURED FOR DRINKING, LET NO MAN EXTEND HIS HAND OVER THE FIRST FRUITS OF BREAD AND WINE BEFORE THE PRIEST, FOR IT IS HE WHO SHALL BLESS THE FIRST FRUITS OF BREAD AND WINE, AND SHALL BE THE FIRST TO EXTEND HIS HAND OVER THE BREAD. THEREAFTER, THE MESSIAH OF ISRAEL SHALL EXTEND HIS HAND OVER THE BREAD.

This is the procedure followed in the gospels for the mass feedings and the last supper. The Essenes felt that when their predictions proved correct the nasi would be transfigured into the messiah. As the kingdom arrived, men would be transformed into angels and the first would be the nasi who would become the archangel Michael.

The literature of Qumran describes a messianic elite who had chosen to follow Isaiah 40:3: to make a straight way in the wilderness for our God. They lived in desert camps waiting to be joined by a heavenly host of angels to engage in a holy war against their enemies. They were preparing themselves for the last days by living a life of extreme purity. They sought the way of perfect righteousness and the way in which the law works. Acts 9:2 calls members of the early church the followers of the way!

The Meaning of Nazarene

Jesus is described as of Nazareth in Galilee—Mark's attempt to explain the description of Jesus in the Greek as Nazarene, a word of unknown meaning because there was no place called Nazareth attested by anyone other than translators of the

New Testament. He took it from the local name for Galilee which is Gennesaret and had to make the change because the Nazarenes were known by some Romans as Palestinian rebels. If the town Nazareth existed at that time, it was so insignificant that it could never have been used as a helpful description. People would have said: Jesus of where? Nazarene was obviously a word which people understood. The best that can be done is to leave it as Jesus the Nazarene—whatever a Nazarene was, it was not someone from Nazareth.

Let us look at the semantics of the word Nazarene more closely. The Hebrew alphabet was purely consonantal except for some consonants which partly expressed vowels just as our w and y do. In writing no vowels were used. Even in English vowels are often unimportant. They can vary widely in the spoken word but its sense is understood from the use and context. In Yorkshire we use a full, rounded u sound but most English regard it as vulgar and reduce it to an e sound. A woman orders better in a restaurant and the waiter brings her butter. A man describing a cricket match says: He gave it some bit, but we know he is not talking about a horse. The woman wants to be recognized as upper class and the man is probably South African. Vowels vary a great deal with dialect but the speakers can still be understood.

By omitting vowels, written Hebrew could be understood without distracting regional variations of representing vowels. Only later, when no one was actually speaking Hebrew in everyday life, was it felt important to put in vowels because, without them, no one in the synagogue would have had any idea how to pronounce it. So in the 6th century AD Jewish scholars introduced vowels by copying the pronunciation of a related language, Syriac.

Hebrew in the intertestamental years was not dead but dying, being replaced by Aramaic. By the time of the gospels Aramaic was the language of Palestine but influenced by the older language. Thus nothing can be deduced with confidence from supposed variations in vowel sounds in Hebrew. Even consonants, like the sibilants, s, sh, ts, ch, dj, tz and z, were in flux. Hebrew had five sibilants but their properties were variable, even becoming d or t. Moreover even ancient roots showed such changes suggesting they had occurred long ago in some instances. All of this needs to be remembered when the origins and meanings of puzzling New Testament words like Nazarene are sought.

The word nazar is to separate or to consecrate and sometimes to abstain from. All of these definitions are superlatively applied to the Essenes. To separate is the use of the word in Leviticus 15:31 where the children of Israel were told to separate themselves from uncleanness caused by menstrual and sexual discharges. The noun nazir literally means one who is separated or consecrated but also means a prince, in the sense of being consecrated into that office and being distinct and distinctive—though the concept of prince for nazir might be derived from the related word nizer which has the clear connotation of crown. Priests had to separate from all pollution and were, of course, consecrated. The Essenes were a priestly sect who also chose to be separate from other Jews. It seems the Essenes also called themselves princes.

The noun nazir occurs most frequently in the scriptures referring to the Nazirites who were spiritual role models, dedicated men and women holy unto the Lord. The vow of the Nazirite could be temporary or permanent, but the only people the Bible tells us were lifelong Nazarites were Samson, Samuel, and John the Baptist.

Practical details of the Nazirite vow of separation is recorded in Numbers 6:1–21, where the Nazirite is described as abstaining from products of the grape, allowing his hair to grow, and avoiding the ritual pollution of a dead body. If a Nazirite accidentally defiled himself, he had to ritually purify himself and begin the full period of consecration over again. The Nazirite was consecrated to God and his long hair was symbolic of it. We know from Luke that John the Baptist was a Nazirite, one dedicated to God who did not drink wine. We are not told explicitly that John wore his hair long but he is identified with Elijah and the Old Testament describes him as hairy. Also a Nazirite was Jesus's brother, James, who became leader after the crucifixion. It is unlikely that Jesus was not. It seems Nazarenes were Nazirites.

The Essenes considered themselves in the same category. Since the Essenes wrote of their use of new wine or unfermented grape juice at their messianic meal, it seems they were not Nazirites according to the scriptures though they regarded themselves as separated and consecrated to God. They will have seen a contradiction in the fruit of the grape being forbidden to holy men yet wine being served at the messianic banquet in God's kingdom and deduced that God had forbidden only fermented grape products, the wine of the messianic banquet in God's kingdom being new wine. Essene references to wine should be read as new wine and the same is probably true of the gospels. (Indeed there is reason to think that new wine was really water!) Jesus was not a wine bibber. Relevant here is the meaning of nazir as an unpruned or undressed vine. In Leviticus 25:5 and 11 the vine (nazir) was to be unpruned during sabbatical and jubilee years and left to grow naturally. In Jeremiah 6:9 the remnant of Israel, a name of the Essenes, is likened to a vine, while Jesus in John 15:1 referred to himself as the true vine, meaning the natural, undressed vine, the nazir.

The noun nezer means separation, consecration and a crown. In Exodus 29:6, explained in Exodus 28:36–38, nezer is an engraved gold plate which a priest wore over his forehead to mark him as a consecrated person. According to Numbers 6:7 and 9 the Nazirite also wears his nezer unto God upon his head. His nezer was his uncut hair. The word nizer is used of a royal crown in several places including Zechariah 9:16 where God, smiting the enemies of Israel, saves his flock who shall be as the stones of a nizer (crown) over His land. Psalms 89:39 and 132:18 both replete with Essene imagery and language, use nizer.

All of these words in nzr seem to come from a primitive root nadar to vow to give something to God. Indeed a vow in the scriptures is a promise to God, not to men. The vow implies a promised gift or sacrifice. The noun neder thus means a vow or a votive offering, either the vow, or that offered to mark the vow. A neder is an offering for God to grant zeal for the law, and He only accepted it when the offerer had no sin in his heart. Essenes tried to be perfect and zealous for the law, never made oaths to men and regarded their vows to God as inviolable.

There is a common word in the scriptures which means to lift up, to bear or carry or support, and to take or take away. It is nasa. It is used especially of bearing the guilt or punishment of sin. He shall bear his iniquity occurs frequently in the scriptures. Sin can be forgiven of those that bear it when it is taken up and carried away. Jesus was reputed to blaspheme by forgiving sins. It is possible that the Essenes had this power because one scroll fragment speaks of a holy man forgiving the king's sins to cure him of an ulcer.

The word nasa yields nasi—one lifted up, an elected chief, a captain, a leader, a ruler, a prince, a king. A nasi is an official who has been lifted up, that is chosen or called, as in Numbers 1:16 where the sentence, these are the ones chosen (or called), occurs. The ones chosen are the elect, the Essenes. Solomon is a nasi and so are any rulers of God's people and leaders of the congregation. Though the gospels never refer to Jesus as the prince, we find repeatedly in John Jesus being described as lifted up. Thus in John 3:14—*even so must this Son of man be lifted up*. John is trying to maintain that the title nasi simply meant lifted up not prince of Israel.

In the Damascus Rule we find that God called all the captives of Israel *princes* because they were lost and wanted to find Him (a pun on the word *masa*) and were men of repute or renown. The captives of Israel were the priests of the Essene sect, the sons of Zadok. Evidently Essene priests were called princes—they were the heirs of Melchizedek. In the Qumran literature the Hebrew word nasi is used frequently to mean a messianic leader, the prince of the many or the prince of Israel, apparently one of the head priests of the remnant of Israel. The nasi seemed to play the role of the messiah at the sacred meal of the council of the community. Significantly, in Ezekiel, nasi is constantly used for the coming Davidic prince, the messiah. A plural noun *nesiim* means clouds or vapours, enabling the nasi to come in the nesiim reminding us of Daniel. But logically it means princes so is the messiah coming not on the clouds but with the princes—the saints and angels of the heavenly host? Nasi could be the specific origin of the gospel term Nazarene. The Nazarenes were those who followed the messianic leader, the nasi, and were either Essenes or their converts.

Now, besides being separated and princes, the Essenes were keepers of the covenant and watchers for the kingdom, to use their own names. Here is another Hebrew word similar to Nazarene—nasar, which means to watch, to keep and to protect. The Arabic word from the same root has become nazara, to keep in view. The Arabs still call Christians the Nasrani. Watchers or noserim were employed to guard anything valuable, like a vineyard, and a watch tower would usually be built for them. The Qumran monastery had a watchtower. In Jeremiah 31:6 and 2 Kings 17:9 and 18:8, God is a keeper or watchman over his vineyard, Israel. The children of Israel have to keep the covenant and God's commandments in return for His lovingkindness. The Essenes considered that only they kept this bargain properly by protecting His covenant with the people of Israel and watching for the signs of the arrival of God's kingdom. The Essenes were also guardians of certain mysteries or secrets and significantly nasar is used in this same sense. In Isaiah 48:6 nasar refers to hidden things not revealed by God, the hidden things which the Essenes sought in the scriptures and believed they had found, according to the scrolls. Nazarenes kept the hidden things of God—the secrets or mysteries of God. Paul in Romans, 1 Corinthians and Ephesians speaks of the revealing of divine mysteries through the holy spirit. Isaiah 49:6 calls those of Israel gathered to Him in the end days the preserved or protected of Israel—the word for preserved is nasar, and promises (Isaiah 49:8) a covenant of the people that shall *raise up* the land.

Nasar itself comes from an older root natar used in farming contexts of those who keep or guard vineyards, but is also used in the sense of keeping one's anger or wrath, bearing malice or a grudge. In Leviticus 19:18, a favourite of Jesus (Mt 19:19; Mk 12:31), Israel is commanded: *Thou shall not take vengeance nor bear any grudge (natar) toward the children of your people, but you shall love your neighbour as yourself.* But God keeps wrath (natar) for his enemies (Nah 1:2). The Essenes believed in brotherhood towards the children of Israel but wrath towards their enemies, the gentiles.

Epiphanius tells us that besides Nazarenes the early Christians were known as Jessaeans. David, the great king of the Jews, the model of the warrior messiah, was the son of Jesse. So it seems that the Jessaeans were simply followers of Jesus because he was the heir of David (before he became the son of a virgin). The truth is slightly more extended. The identification Jessaeans comes from Isaiah 11:1 which records: *And there shall come forth a rod out of the stem of Jesse, and a branch shall grow out of its roots*

A Roman centurion typical of the period of the gospel events. He carries the vitis or vine shoot as a symbol of his authority. But for the Nazarenes only the nasi was the true vine.

and bear fruit, a quotation much revered by the writers of the scrolls and by Christians, referring to a descendant of David who realizes all that God has promised to David (2 Samuel 7:1ff). The branch is an alternative name for the messiah. The word neser, vocalized netzer, means a branch—it is equivalent to the word Nazarene. This is surely what was spoken by the prophets when we read in Matthew 2:23: *and came and dwelt in a city named Nazareth: that it might be fulfilled what is spoken by the prophets, that he should be called a Nazarene.* This reference in Matthew to the prophets has puzzled scholars because they have no explicit mention of a Nazarene; Nazareth—in the Christian sense of a place—was not mentioned in the scriptures because it did not exist or was totally insignificant. The reference, recognizable to messianic Jews, is to Isaiah's neser—the branch of the stem of Jesse—which gives us both Nazarenes and Jessaeans.

As if to explain that the followers of the branch, the Nazarenes, are the Essenes, neser is used also in Isaiah 60:21: *Thy people also shall be all righteous, they shall inherit the land forever; the branch of my planting, the work of my hands, that I may be glorified. The little one shall become a thousand and the small one a strong nation.* The Essenes would clearly have seen this as a reference to themselves and their duty to recover the land and make the people righteous. The many were given the name of the branch, who they hope to emulate and perhaps invoke. It also shows that the followers of the branch, the Nazarenes, had the duty of building up a strong nation. To do this they had to redeem the men of the land, the simple of Ephraim and the sinners.

Thus Nazarenes appear to be a branch of the Essenes to which Jesus and John the Baptist both belonged. Within twenty years of the crucifixion they were being called Christians. Nazarenes thought the end had come and wanted to convert the whole of Israel before the day of vengeance. The apostle, Paul, extended the elect of God further still—to the foreigner. He wanted to give all men the chance to join God's elect and enter God's kingdom, even gentiles. Paul identified with the Essenes because they had split from the Jerusalem temple. The Essenes contrasted themselves with the temple hierarchy in the Damascus Rule. Quoting Proverbs 15:8 it says: *The sacrifice of the wicked is an abomination to the Lord but the prayer of the righteous is his delight,* which reminds us of Jesus's discussion with the Pharisee (Mk 12:28–34). For the Essenes in the last days the split with the temple was of no further consequence. They were God's elect and the dawn of the kingdom was nigh when the wicked and their polluted temple would be destroyed. The kingdom never came but the temple was destroyed by the Romans leaving the two traditions: the Pharisaic and the Essene. The one became Judaism and the other became Christianity.

Pre-Christian Nazarenes

A century ago William B Smith argued that there was a sect of Nazarenes in existence before the followers of Jesus. It now seems he was correct. Epiphanius in Heresies spoke of two types of Nazarenes. One seemed to be a sect from Beroe in Syria who were a type of Christian using a gospel related to Matthew's—this might have been the Logia, not the gospel we know today. A similar account occurs in his book, On Heretical Fables, by Theodoret, bishop of Cyrrhus beyond Antioch, who wrote: *The Nazarenes are Jews who know Christ as a just man and use a gospel called According to Peter.* The expression *a just man* denotes an Essene saint. The others were pre-Christian Nazarenes. Both sects had similar characteristics and were identifiable with the Ebionites, the poor—a name of the Essenes. It was also the name of the members of the Jerusalem Church but that was because they inherited the name from their founders, the Essenes.

However, Hyppolytus tells us of a sect which dates back to remote antiquity called the Naasseni, and he kindly preserves one of their hymns. It begins mournfully chanting about a lost soul, groaning and weeping in suffering, trying to find God but unable to escape from a labyrinth beyond the kingdom of light. Looking on, Jesus appeals to his father, saying: Send me for his salvation that I might descend with the seals in my hands, that I might traverse the aeons, that I might make known the secrets, that I might reveal unto him the essence of God, and announce unto him the mystery of the holy life which is wisdom. This is considered Gnostic but its language resonates with that of the scrolls.

There is also tentative evidence from the traditions of the Carmelite monks. The order was founded by Berthold, a French Catholic priest who offered himself as a hostage to God during the crusades in exchange for a victory in battle. The battle won, to seek what God might want of him, he decided to go to Mount Carmel, where Elijah and Elisha, the prophets, had meditated. He was astonished to find a small colony of Orthodox monks already established there. They told him they had, centuries before, succeeded a school of Jewish Christian monks who had themselves succeeded a tribe of Jewish hermits who had worshipped on the mountain since before the time of Jesus—indeed to the time of Elijah himself! The only Jewish monks we know of are the Essenes of Qumran, whom we have associated with the name Nazarene, and many of whom would have become the first Jewish Christians. It seems likely that the Essenes or Nazarenes had a monastic community on Mount Carmel because of its association with the prophet Elijah as well as the one now recognized at Qumran.

The Nazarenes were indeed a pre-Christian sect identifiable with the Essenes.

MARK'S GOSPEL ANALYSED

Preamble

In reconstructing the events leading to Jesus's death we follow the gospel of Mark. We want to build on the earliest tradition and the one most free of later Christian accretions. The other gospels are of less value the later they are but they can help when they clearly relate to episodes in Mark. Matthew and Luke and less so John can be used to flesh out the shorter but more original account of Mark. In accepting assistance from these other gospels we can feel more assured when there is a clear Essene reference, and less assured when the references are traceable to the gentile church.

Tradition is that Mark took Peter down in no particular order and yet the arrangement of Mark does seem to be ordered. An examination of Mark shows that there is a broad sequence of events which could hardly be altered. That broad sequence can be used and the individual items of the tradition, or pericopes as they are called, can then be themselves examined to find whether there is any better way of fitting them into the outline. Without a general theory that is difficult but given a hypothesis along the right lines the pericopes can be fitted together like a jigsaw puzzle. Some pieces are missing and some have been bent but a reasonable picture emerges. Of course it must be true that some sayings Jesus used in his eschatological speeches were used more than once so there is no fixed context. Some of these can be perceived in the gospels dotted here and there. We must try to see more closely the relevance of such scattered sayings to the general argument and place them accordingly.

Many of the miracles are complete misunderstandings of the mystical language or code used by the Nazarenes. Others could have arisen as metaphors of sayings or titles of the messiah. The healing of a blind man was probably code but used as a metaphor of the light of the world. The withering of a fig tree is a metaphor of the destruction by God of the enemies of Israel but was taken to be a metaphor of the destruction by God of Israel implying that Christianity had superseded Judaism.

The four gospels are anti-Jewish. The gospels and *Acts* arose in an atmosphere of racism that New Testament scholars are aware of but say nothing about. They were written to disassociate Jesus from the Jewish cause at a time when Jews were looked upon unfavourably by most citizens of Rome. Yet since they were based on a Palestinian tradition elements of it still emerge from the deliberate obfuscation of the New Testament. They aim to disassociate Christianity from its Jewish origins and remove any hints that it was anti-Roman. Jesus and his followers are depicted as harmless healers and preachers. Since the gospels were completed and widely circulated only after the Jewish War, the purpose of the bowdlerizing was clear— Jewish nationalists were unpopular. The result is the bizarre story of the passion in which a monster like Pilate is an angel and respectable religious sects like the Pharisees are demonic. Furthermore, with the dispersion of the Jerusalem Nazarenes, the heresies of Paul had no one to oppose them and found new favour among the godfearers of the Empire. The Hellenists took over and were able to dictate policy. Mark wrote the first and most factual gospel with these two objectives in mind to provide a new authority after the destruction of the Jerusalem Church.

The first details of the new gentile religion that were put together were the details of Jesus's suffering or passion, to use the technical term. E Trocme believes that Mark was originally in two main sections. Chapters 1–13 told the mission story and it was added to the passion narrative of chpaters 14 and 15, which was either from an older written source or from an oral source so often repeated that it had already become stylized. This idea does not contradict the tradition that Peter was the original prime source. Gentiles were mainly interested in the dead and resurrected god, and the passion must have formed the central part of missionary preaching in the first few decades. That is not to say that an apostle like Peter would not tell other parts of the story, but these would have been most often related to close associates in private company. Mark was apparently the first to combine the private recollections of Peter with the public ministry centred on the passion. Vincent Taylor believes that Mark's passion narratives themselves stem from two sources: a narrative form from a gentile source, and a semitic collection of self contained narratives. The gentile source has to be treated with suspicion. It comprises: Mark 14:1–2; 10–11; 17–21; 26–31; 43–46; 55–64; 15:1; 3–5; 15; 21–24; 29–33; 34–37; 39; 16:9–20. One or two other doubtful passages have been given here the benefit of the doubt.

We adopt the procedure of trawling through Mark's gospel noting each event and assessing its authenticity and place in the story, checking where appropriate the parallel accounts in other gospels. First, though, what of the introductory events in the other two synoptics—the birth narratives? Can any Nazarene tradition be found among them?

Birth Narratives

Nothing certain is known about Jesus's birth, childhood and early manhood. Mark and the last gospel have no narratives of Jesus's birth and upbringing. They begin the history with Jesus heralded and baptized by John the Baptist. The implication of the omission of the birth stories from the final gospel might be that its author did not accept them. Since they were also omitted from the first gospel, either Mark did not know about them or he also did not accept them. These observations alone seem sufficient to treat them with distrust. Matthew and Luke both have birth narratives but each has a different story. In Matthew Jesus's parents came from Bethlehem in Judaea but on returning from Egypt they settled in Nazareth in Galilee. In Luke they lived in Nazareth and go to Bethlehem to be taxed. In Mark Jesus is simply of Nazareth and Bethlehem is not mentioned.

By introducing the village of Bethlehem Luke and Matthew connect Jesus as messiah with David the warrior king whose home town this was. There is nothing else in the gospels to associate Jesus with Bethlehem. In Luke 1:26 Nazareth is a city! But Nazareth was probably not even a village—it did not exist until Christianity became the official religion of the Empire in the fourth century AD when noble Romans on pilgrimage to the Holy Land were horrified to find Nazareth did not exist and named an obscure site in a suitable location Nazareth to fit the story.

The birth stories in Matthew and Luke differ widely and each contradicts its thesis that Jesus's mother was a virgin by giving a genealogy to show that Joseph was descended from David, an irrelevancy if Joseph was not Jesus's natural father. The editors of both gospels see a problem and try to avoid it: in Luke by inserting *as people thought* to show Jesus was not really Joseph's son and in Matthew by slyly separating Joseph from his son by inserting, after Joseph: *the husband of Mary, of whom was begotten Jesus*. Thus some Christian commentators claim that Jesus was of the house of David through his mother's lineage, but if the intention was to imply that Mary was begetting Jesus then the person inserting the story was either ignorant or depended on the ignorance of his readers, for only men could beget according to Jewish convention. If not then the genealogies of Joseph are doubly spurious.

Luke's genealogy appears in an odd place (Lk 3.23), when Jesus begins his ministry at 30 years of age not at his birth, but the birth narrative of the first two chapters of Luke is in a style and language distinctive from the rest of Luke. It is Greek with a strong flavour of Hebrew as opposed to the normal Greek of the rest. It is as if someone today deliberately wrote in biblical English. Theologians claim it is a deliberate stylistic device to give continuity with the Old Testament. However, the elaborate dating given in Luke at the start of Jesus's ministry (Lk 3:1) suggests that the original gospel started here and the birth narrative in its peculiar style was added. The genealogy therefore originally came near the start of the gospel, where it would be expected, but associated with Jesus's baptism on his thirtieth birthday. It shows that Jesus was a king after the fashion of the Pharaohs who were reborn at their thirtieth birthday and, indeed, Essene practice was to consider people mature only at their thirtieth birthday. We know from the Damascus Rule that the Essenes kept lists of the *Sons of Zadok, the elect of Israel, according to their generations*. These lists will have offered a source for the genealogies of Matthew and Luke.

The original idea of tracing Jesus's lineage through Joseph to David to fulfil messianic prophecy was spoiled when the idea of making Jesus divine through a virgin birth was tacked on. The virgin birth can safely be dismissed as a fabrication of the gentile church, invented years after the event, to prove Jesus's divinity. It is not mentioned in the mystical work, the Revelation of St John the Divine, nor in the epistles and indeed Paul writes unequivocally that Jesus was of the seed of David according to the flesh. Neither Luke nor Matthew refers to the birth story again and despite kings, gifts, shepherds, heavenly hosts and what have you, Jesus's mother later on was unaware that her son had been designated a king. Luke in 2:19

acknowledges the problem, pretending that Mary kept it to herself. Both Luke and Matthew refer to Joseph in the main narrative as the father of Jesus just as the Ebionites accepted Joseph as the natural father. Our primary source, Mark, does not mention Joseph at all, and nor does the apostle to the gentiles, Paul. Interestingly in Matthew 1:19 Joseph is called a just man which is code for an Essene.

An attempt was made in Matthew 1:22–23 to justify the virgin birth story by referring to *Isaiah* 7:14 where is written: *Behold a virgin shall conceive and bear a son, and they shall call his name Emmanuel.* Though Matthew interprets this as a messianic prophecy it is not—it is part of a warning *Isaiah* is giving regarding events of that time—and indeed it is absurd even in the gospel because Matthew's angel has just directed Joseph to call the child *Jesus,* not *Emmanuel!* Nevertheless, Matthew's reading of it as a messianic prophecy is just what Essene pesharists did. Matthew even uses the pesharist's formula, *which being interpreted is.* In their books of commentaries Essenes would take parts of the scriptures and reinterpret them in ways that suited them. That Christians freely did the same indicates their common roots—and they still happily call Jesus *Emmanuel* though that was never his name.

The word translated *virgin*—in the original Hebrew, *almah*—means an immature girl who had not yet started to menstruate. Young girls were betrothed to their future husbands until they could legally marry at the age of twelve and a half—menstruation usually started later. A married virgin could therefore conceive—in Joel 1:8 a virgin's husband is mentioned. Mary was described as betrothed to Joseph implying that she was a minor under the age of twelve and a half—Joseph might have broken the law by having sex with a minor, and pretended he was surprised at the outcome to protect himself. Matthew 1:25 is at pains to refute any such thought by stating that Joseph *knew her not* till she brought forth her first born son—the euphemism *knowing her* meaning having sex with her. In any event the virgin Mary could have given birth—but no miracle was involved.

The name Mary appears in the earliest gospel, Mark's, only in five verses and one of the occurrences, referring only to Mary Magdalene, is in the twelve bogus verses added at the end. In none of the remaining four verses naming Mary are we told explicitly that she is the mother of Jesus. The closest is Mark 6:3:

> Is not this the carpenter, the son of Mary, the brother of James, and Joses, and of Juda, and Simon? and are not his sisters here with us? And they were offended at him.

where we have to assume that the carpenter mentioned is Jesus though we have no prior knowledge from this gospel that Jesus *is* a carpenter.

In the remaining three verses (Mk 15:40; 15:47; 16:1) the writer seems to want to avoid describing Mary as the mother of Jesus for otherwise why does he not say so clearly.

> There were also women looking on afar off: among whom was Mary Magdalene, and Mary the mother of James the less and of Joses, and Salome.

> And Mary Magdalene and Mary the mother of Joses beheld where he was laid.

73

> And when the sabbath was past, Mary Magdalene, and Mary the mother of James, and Salome, had bought sweet spices, that they might come and anoint him.

And yet in these last three verses where a Mary is mentioned, her sons have the same names as some of the brothers of Jesus, and James the brother of Jesus is identified with James the Less (meaning that he was small in stature), the son of Alphaeus. Now Mark 6:3 and the end of 6:4 are inserted by the gentile church to divorce Jesus from his Jewish family. The editor who added these lines possibly took his cue from the later verses, assuming that Jesus's mother must have been called Mary. Gods and those akin to gods commonly have mothers called Mary or a cognate name. Adonis was born of Myrrha, Hermes of Maia, Cyrus of Mariana or Mandane, Joshua of Miriam, Buddha of Maya and Khrishna of Maritala. Since Moses, the first messiah, was born of Miriam, Jesus the final one also had to be.

As an Essene Jesus was quite likely to have been surrendered to the order as a babe consecrated to God. His mother probably had no role to play in the gospel events and she and several other women were added in the earliest days of the gentile church as a sop to its mainly female congregations.

In Matthew Jesus was born at home in a house in Bethlehem; in Luke he was born in a stable usually depicted as a cave. The cave at Bethlehem said to be the birthplace of Jesus was, the Christian father Jerome tells us, actually a rock shrine to the god Tammuz (Adonis—Lord) whose symbol was a cross. The Christians took over a pagan sacred site as they did many times over, and adopted the cave, a common symbol of pagan religions. Apollo, Cybele, Demeter, Hercules, Hermes, Ion, Mithras and Poseidon were all adored in caves. Hermes and Dionysus were wrapped in swaddling clothes and laid in mangers.

In Matthew three wise men bearing gifts of gold, frankincense and myrrh arrive having followed a star from the east. This reads like pure fairy tale but it probably contains some genuine Nazarene tradition. Matthew mentions the word east three times in nine verses, and curiously it is the same word translated *dayspring* in Luke 1:78 which also means *a branch*! Now this might seem coincidental but *the star* referred to is a metaphorical use of the messianic scriptural citation Numbers 24:17. Since the reference to *a branch* is also messianic, the coincidence is beginning not to look accidental.

Matthew records (Mt 2:10): *When they saw the star they rejoiced with exceeding great joy.* This verse makes much more sense if in *the star* they recognize a man of destiny rather than a twinkle in the sky. The first part of Matthew 2:11 has been inserted, for without it the wise men rejoice with exceeding great joy then fall down and worship him—all very natural if *the star* is human. Essenes were organized such that there were twelve leaders and three priests. It seems from the clues remaining that the three wise men are really three Zadokite priests, the leadership of the Essenes. In reality they were present to participate in the crowning ceremony, the baptism in the gospels, but have been moved back thirty years in Matthew to appear at the actual birth rather than the ritual rebirth of the baptism.

It seems then that a call on the lines of, *Where is he that is born prince of Israel? for he is the star, and he is the branch*, was part of the coronation ceremony. Matthew immediately records that Herod heard of this and was troubled. Herod was the paranoid Idumaean king of the Jews who murdered half of his sons, young princes he suspected of plotting against him. When Augustus Caesar heard of Herod condemning his son Antipater, he remarked: *It is better to be Herod's pig than his son.* If Herod had discovered that part of an Essene ritual involved crowning a prince, he would have been outraged. Now Josephus says that Herod and the Essenes were on good terms but that is belied by the fact that the Essene centre at Qumran was deserted during most of Herod's reign. If Matthew 2:1–18 is anything to go by, Herod did not get on with the Essenes.

Instead of wise men Luke 2:8–21 has lowly shepherds, who had been *watching their flock*, coming a–visiting, notified by angels of the birth of God. Christian imagery usually has both! In fact the metaphor of a shepherd is one of those that the Essenes were fond of—which is why it appears so often in Christianity. The Essenes, among many other things, called themselves *the watchers for the kingdom*. Thus the Master in the Community Rule is commanded to watch always for the judgement of God. We have noted that the Damascus Document interprets Zechariah 13:7—a very important passage for Essenes and Christians—by applying the metaphors *the humble of the flock* and *those who watch for him* to the Essenes themselves. Luke has used the same metaphor of the watchers and their flock, the children of Israel, and dramatized it into the birth story. One scroll fragment, discussing the expected visitation, even uses the same terms as Luke: *the holy spirit, the meek, glad tidings, the messiah shepherds the holy ones* and *commands the heavens and the earth including the heavenly host.*

The heavenly host in Luke 2:14 are calling for the kingdom of God when they sing: *Glory to God in the highest; on earth peace, good will towards men.* Though a desirable sentiment the offer of goodwill to all men is not meant. The proper translation of the best manuscripts is given as: *on earth peace to men in whom He is well pleased.* The men in whom God is well pleased are the Essenes, His righteous, to whom glory and peace come in His kingdom, because those who *walk by the spirit of truth shall receive abundance of peace and everlasting joy in a life without end.*

Next Luke 2:22–38 has Mary and Joseph—described as the parents thus acknowledging Joseph as the father (in short, a passage preceding the invention of the virgin birth)—present at the temple for Mary's ritual purification after childbirth. There an unknown man described as *just* and *devout, waiting for the consolation of Israel*, and *having the holy spirit upon him* chants his Nunc Dimittis before Jesus. These words denote him as an Essene. The word translated *devout* is peculiar to Luke and might be his translation of *Nazirite*. The clergy have always denied any connexion with the Nazirites, perhaps because they did not like others besides Jesus in the story consecrated to God, and because the word is remarkably similar to Nazarene, suggesting that the latter might have had nothing to do with Nazareth. So Luke or an editor avoids it. *Waiting for the consolation of Israel* meant he was waiting for the messiah and therefore the kingdom.

The word *Lord* beginning the song in Luke 2:29 is a mistranslation—it should be *Master*, immediately showing its Essene origins and that it is the departing Master recognizing the new Master. The song is litany from the coronation or transference ceremony of the nasi. Luke being a gentile has altered verse 2:32. Originally, following *Isaiah* 9:2, it will have read, *a light to lighten the darkness*, meaning the sins of the people, but Luke had a good knowledge of the scriptures and knew that Israel was *the light of the gentiles* (Isa 49:6) and merely substituted this here. Anna the prophetess is one of Luke's female additions to placate the church's female congregations.

The Year of Jesus's Birth

When was Jesus born? Dionysus Exiguus, a sixth century monk, calculated the year of Herod's death and assumed it was also the year of Jesus's birth. Unfortunately his calculation was four years out and so our calendar has been ever since. Herod's death is now recorded as 4 BC rather than 1 AD as it would have been if the monk were correct.

In any case was he right to assume Jesus was born in the same year that Herod died? Matthew 2:13–18 says Joseph learnt in a dream that Herod would kill the baby and so took off to Egypt just in time to miss the massacre of the innocents of Bethlehem by Herod, only returning after Herod had died. Josephus, who records all the crimes of Herod, does not mention this atrocity. Nor does Luke who has a reputation among theologians as a good historian. Nevertheless the story places the nativity in the reign of Herod the Great, 37 to 4 BC, and so Jesus was born sometime before 4 BC.

If Matthew was written in Alexandria in Egypt, his birth narrative is merely a little touch to humour the large Jewish population of the city, suggesting that the Son of God was sheltered in Egypt, presumably by Egyptian Jews. The story itself is the same as that of Abraham who Nimrod attempted to murder by killing all the infants in the land, the Jewish first born in Egypt who were threatened by the Pharaoh to eliminate Moses, and Hadad, who fled to Egypt when Joab tried to account for him by killing all the men of Edom. Suetonius says that the Roman Senate tried to get rid of the baby Octavius, (the Emperor Augustus) in the same way. Matthew wants to show Jesus as the equal of Moses and so exalts him by giving him an equal history.

The element of truth in the story is probably that at this time Herod suppressed the Essenes. Now Josephus says the Essenes were favoured by Herod because one of them, Menehem, had accurately prophesied that Herod would be king. They were allowed not to make an oath of fealty to him unlike all other Jews except Pharisees. Essenes would not, of course, recognize any Lord but God and, short of butchering them all, Herod perhaps had no choice. Josephus relates this tale immediately before he describes Herod's reconstruction of the temple in 19 AD even though the event itself occurred twenty years before—even before Herod became king. The association of the favouring of the Essenes with the construction of the temple implies that Herod sought the Essenes' support in his project which was initially unpopular.

The help he might have needed was an army of priests trained as masons to build the sacred inner buildings, the holy of holies and its approach. Bribed with the promise that the Zadokites would be established as the accepted priesthood, it seems the Essenes agreed only later to find they had been tricked. Assembling the materials must have taken a year or so, the construction of the inner buildings took eighteen months and the outer cloisters another eight years, but the surrounding porticoes and the immense platform supporting the temple courts took many more years to build. The Essenes might have been fobbed off with Herod's excuses for not instating them during the eight year period but surely for no longer and so they could have fallen out of favour between about 15 and 8 BC.

Luke 2:1–7 tells us Caesar Augustus decreed a taxation and associates the birth with the necessary census. Matthew has no record of there being a census and no census in the reign of Augustus is known in Judaea near the supposed year of Jesus's birth, though there certainly was one about 6 or 7 AD conducted by Quirinius, Legate of Syria, putting Jesus's birth date at least ten years later than Matthew. Such a late date means either that Jesus was crucified at the age of 30 in the year that Pilate was recalled, or that he was younger than 30 when he died. If the length of his ministry in John is correct, Jesus must then have been only around 25 when he started his ministry. And, if the census was that of 6 AD it is not clear why Jesus's family had to be assessed for tax by the Romans when Quirinius taxed Judaea since they lived in Galilee and Galilee was not ruled by the Romans but by the puppet king Herod Antipas. Furthermore Roman custom was to register people for a census at their place of residence not at their place of birth which would impose absurd burdens on people who had established themselves elsewhere, and many enterprising Jews had done this even in those distant times.

Christian apologists try to explain all this by asserting without sure foundation there was another census ten or fourteen years earlier—from Augustus, Romans carried out a census every fourteen years in their dominions—and indeed Herod could have agreed to a census when the Jews were persuaded to pay tribute to Rome. This takes us again to about 8 BC by which time the Essenes had fallen out of favour with Herod, and Jesus's family was fleeing to Egypt in Matthew. It is also about the time that Qumran began to be reoccupied after several decades of desertion. Indeed Egypt might have been Essene code for Qumran. It all ties together but there is no evidence for the earlier census. Why, for example, doesn't Matthew mention it? And why was there no rebellion when the earlier taxation was imposed as there was for the later one? The Essenes would certainly have been opposed to it.

We have to admit that there is no solid evidence about when Jesus was born, though it was before 4 BC when Herod died.

The story in Luke of the boy Jesus remaining in the temple when his parents spent three days looking for him contains no elements of Nazarene tradition, except that

Jesus might have been intensively coached by the Essene priesthood. No Jewish boy would have been so rude to his parents as to say: *Why are you looking for me? You ought to know I'd be about God's business!* Such lack of respect for parents, then or now, is quite un-Jewish. Since Mary and Joseph did not understand this reply, the circus of the nativity must have been nonsense and, indeed the composition of this passage preceded the nativity as the use of the word *parents* shows. An editor of Luke realizes it and pretends (Lk 2:51) that Mary was keeping her knowledge of Jesus's destiny a secret. The final verse (Lk 2:52) of this section indicates that Jesus was a Nazirite—he was *in favour with God*, a scribal formula meaning he had been dedicated to God, which was why he was being coached by sages.

The Preface

Mark 1:1

1:1 The beginning of the gospel of Jesus Christ, the Son of God;

The Preface

The author of Mark leaves no doubt at the beginning that he is telling about a Son of God, suitably impressing his readers, without explaining that a Son of God to a Jew meant a king or a priest not the product of a god's procreative prowess as it was for the Greeks. Elsewhere Mark explains Jewish concepts when he wants to. Here he appears deliberately not to, but some ancient manuscripts omit the phrase suggesting it might have been an editor's early improvement to the original.

Jesus is the Greek form of the Hebrew word Joshua, itself short for Jehosua, which means *saviour of God*, *God of salvation* or *God saves*, the root being *yesha*. It is the same name as *Isaiah* but with the root words for God and salvation swapped around. Hosea, meaning salvation, was the original name of Joshua. It is properly written Osea. The Aramaic for *save us* is *osanna* the cry of the multitude when Jesus entered Jerusalem as a king. Epiphanius speaks of the Ossenes, a Jewish sect by the Dead Sea, obviously the Essenes since vowels are fluid in Semitic languages. Essene in Hebrew is Osim, *the saviours*. The name Jesus is clearly linked semantically with the word Essene. The Quran's name for Jesus is Essa or Issa from the same word, Osea. It is likely that the Osim were the followers of *the saviour*, Jesus, and that Jesus or Joshua was a title.

H Raschke forty years ago proposed that the Essenes deliberately used the susceptibility of Aramaic and Hebrew to punning to deliver double meanings and thereby conceal real meanings. It is surely true. God's elect were evidently keen on punning as we have seen from their interpretation of scripture and their adoption of the word Nazarene with its multiple roots. Essene is apparently similar. Besides its plain reference of *salvation* it has several other meanings. Osh means *a foundation* and they considered themselves *the foundation of heaven on earth*; esh meant *a flame* or *fire* while *isseh* meant an *offering by fire* and they believed that the earth would be offered for purification in a refiner's fire, representing judgement; *hesed* meant *holiness, lovingkindness* or *piety* and *the hasidim* were *the holy ones* or *the saints*; finally they were interested in healing people of their spiritual ills and, in Aramaic, a healer or doctor was *assaya*.

Some scroll fragments are striking for their emphasis on salvation. We find *the children of salvation* and *the salvation of His works*. Yesha is a common Qumran word and its importance in the context of Christian origins has not been acknowledged by the Qumran experts. It appears in the Damascus Rule: *they would see His salvation*, effectively: *they would see Jesus*.

Zechariah 3:1–10 suggests that the name Joshua might have been a priestly title. It relates the appointment of the High Priest, Joshua, and proves to be very important in the testament of Mark. This Joshua was the High Priest who with Zerubbabel and the remnant of the people (Hag 1:12ff) rebuilt and reconsecrated the temple on the return from exile. Joshua was the son of Jehozadak, a man who never left captivity in Babylon and whose name literally means *God is righteous*, but might be a contraction of *Joshua the priest* (zadok) or *Joshua the righteous* or *just* (zaddik). All of it chimes sweetly with all we know about Essene tradition. Conceivably here are links with the foundation of the new covenant. Sure enough we find in the Community Rule that the priests bless *the God of salvation* (bless Joshua or Jesus) while the initiates call out Amen, Amen.

Christ is the Greek word used to translate the Hebrew *messiah* but the two words have come to mean something different. Because Christ is the divine title of Jesus the Christian God, people tend to think it has always been a divine title. It has not. The Jewish messiah was a saviour prince.

This is how the legend arose. Palestine was not the rural idyll of Renan's Life of Jesus. It was politically and socially unstable, being at the crossroads between Asia and Africa. When the Babylonians under Nebuchadnezzar conquered Palestine in about 600 BC, they used it as a source of slaves and skilled labour and many Jews were carried away captive to Babylon. They were allowed to return when Babylon in its turn was defeated by the Persians under their king, Cyrus, in 538 BC. Under the umbrella of the Persians, the former exiles built a new temple in Jerusalem and set up a theocracy in Judah— the holy people were to be ruled by God through his recognized priesthood. For the next few hundred years Jewish sages rewrote and reinterpreted Jewish legend creating the scriptures, known to us as the Old Testament. Then the Greeks took control of Palestine from 332 BC and sought to impose a common Hellenic religion.

God's own people, the Jews, felt violated and dreamed of a saviour, a warrior they called the messiah who would free them from their enemies and institute a kingdom of God on earth in which the Jews, as *the chosen people*, would be the elite. The messiah is described in Daniel written about 160 BC during the period of Greek oppression. In Daniel 7:13–14 he was a superman to whom God gave a kingdom, that all the peoples, nations, and languages, should serve him: *His dominion is an everlasting dominion, which shall not pass away, and his kingdom that which shall not be destroyed.* The messianic kingdom of the Jews would last forever and all other kingdoms on earth would be its vassals.

Spurred by such dreams, the Jews began a period of rebellion. The family of the Maccabees successfully rose against their Greek masters and set up a Jewish state for a short time but the kingdom divided again and fell under Roman domination first under Pompey and then under the client monarch, Herod the Great, who reigned as a tyrant for 33 years. Herod was an Idumaean who adopted the Jewish religion and rebuilt the temple. He was a good soldier and a competent king, providing work for his poverty stricken subjects through huge building projects, but he was cruel and immoral and remained unpopular with the Jews.

Judaea was not unimportant for the Romans for it commanded vital trade routes from east to west and the strategic isthmus between Africa and Asia. Parthia to the east was the only power to rival Rome at this time and had a large Jewish population. Jewish intransigence could not be tolerated

When Herod died in 4 BC, a period of rebellion and repression began, culminating in the destruction of Jerusalem by the Romans in 70 AD. In 6 AD the Romans instituted direct rule over the southernmost part of Palestine, Judaea, replacing one of Herod's sons, Archelaus, who was as cruel as his father but less competent. The sages who had compiled the Old Testament, fresh from the years of exile under the Babylonians, had written in Deuteronomy 17:15 that Jews had to be ruled by a Jew and not by any foreigner. This was the Royalty Law. Such a law is easier to write than to enforce and the Jews had grudgingly submitted to foreign domination for hundreds of years—but the Romans were particularly hated. A succession of Roman prefects and procurators were put in charge of Judaea to quell the discontent of the population.

The political position of the Jews under the Romans seemed hopeless. Most Jews felt they had suffered enough. Popular Jewish hopes were still of their warrior king, born in the image of and of the line of, king David, their messiah who would save his people—free them from the oppressor. The messiah was not a god or an aspect of God, but was entirely human, though backed by the supernatural might of God. Judaism was monotheistic—it had only one God and it was a heresy for Jews to think otherwise. In truth Jews were henotheistic. Their god was the Most High—so called because he was the highest god. He accepted angels and demons as lesser gods, his heavenly subjects, but a human who claimed to be a god, no! Even their messiah could not be regarded as divine. A Jew proclaiming a messianic claimant a god at the time of Jesus would have been stoned for blasphemy, but it was no blasphemy to claim to be a messiah, a man.

According to the Psalms of Solomon, written in the first century BC, to establish the kingdom, the messiah would gather the Jewish nation together to purge Jerusalem from nations that trample her down and shatter unrighteous rulers. All nations would be in fear of him. The Jews would be righteous, a holy people, and neither visitor nor stranger would remain amongst them any more—they did not love gentiles. The messiah would shepherd the flock of the Lord faithfully and righteously and would suffer none among them to stumble in their pasture. They would be sons of God. He would judge peoples and nations in the wisdom of his righteousness and would have the heathen nations to serve under his yoke. Note that the messiah's flock would all be sons of God!

The idea of a saviour messiah ignited the torch of Jewish nationalism for several centuries. Throughout New Testament times rioting and insurrection were commonplace in Judaea fueled by these messianic hopes. When Pontius Pilate was the prefect of Judaea, uprisings had been occurring regularly for over twenty years and would continue to occur even beyond the destruction of Jerusalem forty years in the future. Leaders of varying degrees of credibility were to step forward, from the death of Herod to the defeat of Bar Kosiba, claiming to be the messiah of God, as the Jews yearned for an end to the trials and indignities of Roman rule. Each led an unsuccessful revolt and died.

Jews had incessantly been humiliated by foreign rulers for centuries with only the Maccabees providing any hope. Submission had got them nowhere. A deliverer had become a fervent belief. A mendicant pacifist preaching goodwill to all men, including the Roman oppressor, was not the Jews' best idea of a leader to free them from their enemies. Yet in the midst of this turmoil the gospels tell us that God sent as His messiah a gentle wandering holy man who was maliciously picked on by jealous priests, unfairly turned over to the Romans as a pretender to the throne of Judaea and unjustly tortured to death on a cross.

Later we shall find that Jesus also had the nickname Barabbas.

Mark 1:1 Restored

The beginning of the gospel of Jesus, which is God's saviour, whom they called Barabbas, which is the son of my father, for he was the Son of God, the messiah, a prince of Israel.

John comes Baptizing

Mark 1:2 – 1:8

1:2 As it is written in the prophets, Behold, I send my messenger before thy face, which shall prepare thy way before thee. 1:3 The voice of one crying in the wilderness, Prepare ye the way of the Lord, make his paths straight. 1:4 John did baptize in the wilderness, and preach the baptism of repentance for the remission of sins. 1:5 And there went out unto him all the land of Judaea, and they of Jerusalem, and were all baptized of him in the river of Jordan, confessing their sins. 1:6 And John was clothed with camel's hair, and with a girdle of a skin about his loins; and he did eat locusts and wild honey; 1:7 And preached, saying, There cometh one mightier than I after me, the latchet of whose shoes I am not worthy to stoop down and unloose. 1:8 I indeed have baptized you with water: but he shall baptize you with the Holy Ghost.

John comes Baptizing

Mark begins his gospel by introducing John the Baptist, who lives in the wilderness, the rocky desert between Qumran, the monastery of the Essenes, and Jerusalem. He lives on wild honey and on locusts—possibly the insects, which Essenes were allowed to eat as long as they had been treated by fire or water, but probably the carob bean, the food of repentance of rabbinic tradition. John is calling for repentance in readiness for the day of the Lord, and many people respond. Not literally everybody could have done, as the gospel states, but the Nazarenes, the branch of the Essenes to whom John and Jesus belonged, hoped everybody would respond—literally—since they believed their duty was to secure all Israel for the coming kingdom.

Because Mark is writing for gentiles, he rarely uses Old Testament quotations which would have meant nothing to early gentile converts to Christianity. His purpose in quoting the scriptures here is to establish John the Baptist as merely the forerunner of Jesus and nothing more. When Mark was writing his gospel, some people—mainly diaspora Jews—believed it was John the Baptist who was the messiah. Mark wants to show plainly that they were wrong, by John's own admission.

The first Old Testament quotation is from Malachi 3:1. The quotation is subtly changed however. In the scriptures, God said, *before me*, meaning that the messenger preceded God's visitation on the day of judgement. Mark wanted the messenger to precede the messiah, Jesus, who in turn preceded judgement day. Such changes are characteristic of Essene methods of exegesis which had obviously influenced Mark. If the scriptures did not say quite what suited them for interpretation Essenes seemed to have no qualms about changing them. The Habakkuk Commentary contains many examples.

The context of the quotation in Malachi is that the messenger is the messiah himself sent to purify the world like a refiner's fire, the metaphor John himself uses when he is describing he that cometh. In the final verses of Malachi (4:5) God promises to send Elijah, the prophet, before the great and terrible day of the Lord and so

Mark identifies John with Elijah, whence the description of the leather girdle about his loins in verse 6 which parallels Elijah's leather girdle in 2 Kings 1:8, and the camel hair of John which makes him hairy like Elijah. Evidently, the last verse does not give a true description of John but a description of Elijah to make the prophetic point, though John would have had long hair because he was a Nazirite. In the fourth gospel John the Baptist denies that he is Elijah, a recognition by the church that Jesus had not heralded the judgement day—it had still not arrived after almost a century—and therefore that John the Baptist could not have heralded it either. The judgement day now was not due until Jesus returned—his parousia.

The second Old Testament quotation is from Isaiah 40:3, the prophet whose name means saviour, as does Jesus, and who is especially revered by the Essenes. The Community Rule uses exactly the same quotation from Isaiah: *they shall be separated from the midst of the gatherings of the men of wrongs to go to the wilderness to prepare there the way of the Lord, as it is written: In the wilderness prepare the way of the Lord; make straight in the desert a high way for God.* Unlike the gospels however, which pretend that the Mosaic law has been revoked by Jesus, the Community Rule unmistakably identifies the straight high way as the law: *This is the study of the law, as he commanded them through Moses to do all that has been revealed from age to age, and, by his holy spirit, as the prophets revealed.* Note that, like Christians, the Essenes were fond of invoking the holy spirit, or the Spirit of Holiness as scroll scholars often translate it to make it sound different.

The voice of one crying in the wilderness, prepare ye the way is a deliberate mistranslation. It puts the voice in the wilderness when the correct meaning is, *The voice of one crying: in the wilderness prepare ye the way.* This is how the Essenes read it and this is what they attempted to do, setting up their monastery at Qumran, and preparing the way for the nasi. When the clergy had control of book production they repunctuated the expression even in the Septuagint because for them the way was no longer to be prepared in the wilderness but anywhere that Christians happened to be.

The two quotations are run together in a way characteristic of the Essenes. Mark gives John the role of the messenger of God prophesied in Malachi and in Isaiah but not the role of messiah. Mark knew that John the Baptist was a significant man in his own right and could have said more about him here (he does later) and his followers were offering a rival to Jesus, but here he deliberately plays him down, treating him solely as the forerunner of Jesus.

A Baptism of Repentance

John is preaching a baptism of repentance as did the Essenes. Baptism was a special rite to the Jews, a ritual purification for a soldier before going to battle in which, of course, he might die. It was an oath of allegiance, a sacramentum, and is still so called by the church. The Essene Community Rule prescribed washing in water for those who had repented: *They shall not enter the water to partake of the pure meal of the saints, for they shall not be cleansed unless they turn from their wickedness—* for all who transgress his word are unclean. Everyone—all Israel—had transgressed, in allowing the foreigner to rule. Even a potential messiah, to the Jews a man—with supernatural powers maybe—but not a god, had to be washed clean of this sin by baptism.

For the elect of the Qumran community, it was a cleansing of the body, the soul having already been purified by righteousness. In the Community Rule the sectaries were rendered pure by sincere repentance and acceptance of the precepts of God. Without them, no amount of physical cleansing would work; with them, the initiate was cleansed by the holy spirit enabling him to accept the sprinkling of purifying water and the cleansing of sanctified water which prepared him to walk perfectly in the ways of God in the covenant of the everlasting community.

Purification had to be done in clean water and sufficient of it to completely cover a man as the Community Rule makes clear. It could not be effected by washing from a vessel, Essenes believed in total immersion but the implication of the sprinkling of holy water is that a priest, in this case John, would have conducted some appropriate ceremony to accompany the ritual cleansing. Ezekiel 9:4 describes the procedure when, in his vision, the righteous of Israel were spared from the wrath of God's six avenging angels—they had been marked with water on their foreheads. Clergymen to this day use exactly the same ritual—the sign of the cross is made in water on the forehead. We can deduce with some confidence that the Essenes and the Nazarenes, before Christianity was invented, baptized converts with the mark of the cross.

John announces that a mightier one, who would baptize not with water but with the holy spirit, is to follow him. Matthew 3:11 adds *and with fire* referring back to the refiner's fire of Malachi 3:2. Judgement would be a pleasant experience only for the righteous (Mal 4:1–3):

> When the day cometh it burneth as a furnace, and all the proud and all that work wickedness shall be stubble, and the day that cometh shall burn them up... but ye that fear my name shall gambol as calves of the stall and ye shall tread down the wicked, for they shall be ashes under the souls of your feet.

John's message was that the day of judgement was due and all of Israel should prepare for it. John was not specifying any particular person as the messiah, the mightier one, but simply teaching Jewish received wisdom that a messiah would arrive to bring judgement.

In Luke 3:9 and Matthew 3:10 the message is expressed as a different parable: *Every tree which bringeth not forth good fruit will be hewn down, and cast into the fire.* It was up to every Jew who was not righteous to look to his own salvation by repentance and baptism, lest he be baptized with fire. Note that John the Baptist, like Jesus, spoke in parables. He illustrated his meaning with analogies or allegories that would not have been meaningful to a gentile unfamiliar with messianism.

Note also the expression, *O generation of vipers*, which appears three times in Matthew and also in Luke, though sometimes *generation* is rendered *offspring*. Though serpents are often mentioned in the scriptures, vipers occur quite rarely. The word appears in Matthew and Luke as often as it appears in the whole of the Old Testament. The metaphor seems to relate to tongues, particularly lying tongues, and the poison which they metaphorically administer. In the Epistle of James 3:8 the tongue is described as a restless evil full of deadly poison. One of the smaller scroll fragments is very reminiscent of James's epistle in form and content. It uses the imagery of tongues and vipers to attack lying adversaries just as James and the Damascus Rule do and calls for restraint and patience. The origin is one of the four scriptural citations of vipers in Job 20:16, where it is said of the wicked: *the viper's tongue shall slay him*. The Damascus Rule rails against the Pharisees, saying: *They open their mouth with a blaspheming tongue against the laws of the covenant of God* and, quoting in an altered form, typically Essene, another of the four scriptural references to vipers—Isaiah 59:5, *their eggs are vipers' eggs*. Those who are born of vipers' eggs are the generation or offspring of vipers. *O generation of vipers* looks like an Essene phrase. It is used by both John the Baptist (Mt 3:7; Lk 3:7) and Jesus (Mt 12:34; 23:33) showing it was a cult expression.

Matthew 3:9 and Luke 3:8 also have here a telling reference to God being able of these stones to raise up children unto Abraham. John is warning the multitude not to take refuge in the fact that they are of the old covenant of God with Abraham, being his seed. He is concerned that they have not remained righteous, thus dissolving the old covenant. If God merely wanted the seed of Abraham he could make them out of stones. We have a play on words. The word banim means children or, if male, sons and abanim means stones. Josephus in his autobiography tells us of one Banus, an Essene who lived in the desert rather like the John the Baptist of the gospels. If Banus read his name as the son and he was a disciple of John the Baptist who called himself Enosh, meaning man, then he, like Jesus, was a Son of man! In fact Banus must have been a successor of Jesus as nasi of the orthodox Essenes after the Jerusalem Church separated from them.

Luke 3:1–18 adds more information to suggest that John was an Essene. In Luke 3:11 John the Baptist urges people to hold everything in common like the Essenes, saying: *He who has two coats, let him share with him who has none; and he who has food, let him do likewise.* The Essene monks had to give all their goods to the community, as did the Nazarenes in the Acts of the Apostles. Yet he indicates that he is willing to accept repentance from publicans and soldiers, both of whom served the interests of the oppressors. Though this latter seems to be contrary to an Essene position, it takes the position of the Nazarenes—Essenes who, on the eve of the day of judgement, are willing to accept sincere repentance from any Jew on the grounds that they are all God's chosen and must be given the chance to be saved at the judgement and to fight in God's army against the forces of evil.

This idea appears in the Rule of the Congregation which is for the many of Israel in the last days when they shall join the community. The Essene scribes used the word Israel both to mean themselves, the pure Israel, and to mean the nation at large, all Israel. But if Israel is joining the community then the Israel referred to is all Israel because the community is the Essene community—that of the pure Israel. Essenes believed that all Israel should be given the chance to join the perfect of Israel in the last days. That is exactly what John the Baptist and Jesus after him were doing. They were offering all Jews the chance to repent and rejoin the chosen of God—those who would be saved in the coming holocaust. In Luke 3:12,14 publicans and soldiers come to John asking him what they should do to be saved. The answer is the same for all Jews—sincerely repent and receive baptism—but the trivial answers in Luke are nonsensical, the work of the gentile church when the return on a cloud had receded.

Note that John was baptizing on the river Jordan at a place called Bethabara, according to John's gospel, or later at a place called Aenon near Salim. Though both are boldly marked on maps of the Holy Land, both are unknown places though Bethabara appears to be across the Jordan in Peraea about five miles from the Dead Sea. Yet according to Mark and Matthew, John was in the wilderness of Judaea. Luke avoids the problem by saying he was in all the country about Jordan, thus covering all possibilities. Actually, there is a traditional baptizing site at the mouth of a wadi not far from the Essene centre at Qumran. Later however John was captured by Herod Antipas so he must have been in Peraea. None of these places are more than about twenty miles from Qumran, and indeed most can be seen to the north of the elevated promontory on which Qumran is sited.

John the Baptist has too many similarities with the Essenes to be coincidence. The obvious difference was that John is depicted as a solitary ascetic not a member of a community. Plainly though this is not true. John the Baptist had disciples as all four gospels tell us and Acts further explains that his disciples had spread far and wide. Christian baptism was rivalled by the baptism of John (Acts 19:3).

The Year of John's Appearance

Note that Matthew's Gospel associates John's initial appearance with the return of Joseph and Mary from Egypt (*in those days*). Since the holy family had fled from Herod and returned when he died, those days must have been soon after 4 BC. The apocryphal Gospel of the Twelve Apostles says that John came baptizing in the days of Herod, king of Judaea. Herod, king of Judaea must have meant Herod Archelaus, son of Herod the Great, who ruled Judaea from 4 BC until 6 AD as a minor king, an ethnarch. Mandaean tradition is the same.

Luke seriously contradicts these, apparently giving the date when the word of God came to John extremely precisely, writing (Lk 3:1–2): *Now in the fifteenth year of the reign of Tiberius Caesar, Pontius Pilate being governor of Judaea, and Herod being tetrarch of Galilee, and his brother Philip tetrarch of Ituraea and of the region of Trachonitis, and Lysanias the tetrarch of Abilene, Annas and Caiaphas being the high priests, the word of God came unto John the son of Zacharias in the wilderness.* Naming all of these rulers, secular and religious, seems to make the dating extremely precise but really it is spurious. The only measure of time given is in relation to the reign of Tiberius. No time is given in relation to the reigns of the others, and all we can be sure of, if the whole passage is not bogus, is that all of these people were in power at the time referred to—except Annas.

Tiberius succeeded Augustus on 19 August in 14 AD and so Luke is giving the year as 28 or 29 AD depending upon whether the remainder of 14 AD counted as year one of Tiberius. The Romans usually counted as a year part years within a calendar year, so that 14 AD probably was year one of Tiberius. Indeed Tiberius was a joint regent with Augustus from 11 AD and the regency year might have been included as years of Tiberius, in which case Luke is giving the year 25 AD as the start of John's mission. Theologians put the start of Jesus's ministry in 28/29 AD and its end in 29 AD if it lasted one year as the synoptics suggest or 33 AD if it lasted three or four as the fourth gospel suggests. Note that in Luke John the Baptist was jailed by Herod Antipas almost as soon as he started his ministry which seems unlikely.

Annas was a powerful figure who ceased to be High Priest in 15 AD but remained influential. He was deposed by the prefect preceding Pilate, Gratus, who introduced the practice of replacing the High Priest annually to limit his power (John 11:49). If Annas was the High Priest Luke is giving a date before 15 AD but then Pilate cannot have been prefect—Josephus gives 26 AD as the year of Pilate's appointment. Possibly Luke was fooled, by Pilate being the prefect at the time of the crucifixion, into thinking that he was there all along when really Gratus was prefect at the start.

If Pilate was appointed in 18 AD in the fifth year of Tiberius and that is the time to which Luke refers, all of these rulers were already in post—accepting Annas as an eminence gris behind Caiaphas—including the mysterious Lysanius who received the tetrachy of Abilene in 14 AD. The exact specification of the year of Tiberius in Luke has either been copied in error or deliberately changed. Where we now see in the Greek pentakaidekato, meaning fifteenth, originally it read pempto meaning fifth. Early manuscripts might also have used Greek numbers rather than written ordinals for brevity of copying, in which case the change was simply from the letter epsilon to the letter omikron. The changes in the numbers and in the name of the prefect were made because changes were made to Josephus to take the year of the crucifixion away from the year 21 AD which is when the Acts of Pilate put it. Clergymen could therefore claim that the Acta Pilati were forgeries.

But these changes do not bring us into the reign of any Herod of Judaea. The reason is that Luke is telling us the year that Jesus was baptized not the year that John began his ministry. In that year *the word of God*—meaning Jesus (he is called the word explicitly in John 1:1,14)—*came unto John in the wilderness.* Luke must mean this because he makes no further reference to Jesus being baptized—in Luke 3:21 Jesus is already baptized. When Jesus came to be baptized, John the Baptist must have been baptizing for many years, as the other sources maintain—and he must have been at least 60 years old and more likely nearer

70 when he was murdered. The earlier story in Luke that Jesus and John were the same age, like most of the birth narratives, was an invention, or perhaps a misunderstanding—they were both baptized at the same age, 30 (but a generation apart).

In the gospels Jesus has the highest praise for John but the authors render it as faint praise, praising him merely as the forerunner of the messiah. Great though they say he is, the gospels play John the Baptist down to a compere for the main act. Nonetheless they admit that John heralded not just the messiah but a whole period of violence: *In the days of the Baptist and until now the kingdom of heaven has suffered violence, and the men of violence take it by force.*

Zacharias—Luke 1:5–80

Luke tells us more about the background of John the Baptist. Zacharias is an elderly priest whose wife Elisabeth is childless. While offering incense in the temple, an angel appears to him telling him: *thy prayer is heard.* Prayer is singular so the old man had prayed there and then—clergymen tell us for a child. But Luke 1:6 adds the details that Zacharias and his wife are both righteous before God, walking in all the commandments and ordinances of the Lord, blameless—they were Essenes! We can be sure that Zacharias's humility before God was such that he would not have prayed for personal benefit—a son—which would have been selfish. He prayed for a deliverer for Israel—a Son of God.

The further detail that Zacharias is burning incense not offering a sacrifice confirms that the old man was an Essene. According to the Community Rule, the Essene was to forgo the flesh of holocausts and the fat of sacrifice because a prayer was the acceptable savour of the righteous, and perfection the proper offering to God. Earlier in the same book of rules we are told that the council of the community with everlasting knowledge of the covenant of the just, shall be a most holy dwelling for Aaron—in short a temple—and shall offer up a sweet savour. The conclusion from these passages is that the Essenes preferred incense and prayer to animal sacrifice. Evidently the council of the community would meet and offer up fragrance and prayer to God as a living temple of perfection. That the first Christians had the same beliefs is confirmed in Revelation 8:3–4 which speaks of an angel with a golden censer and much incense: *that he should offer it with the prayers of all saints upon the golden altar which was before the throne. And the smoke of the incense, which came with the prayers of the saints, ascended up before God.* Offering prayers and a sweet savour instead of sacrifices is purely Essene.

The angel (Lk 1:15) commands Zacharias to call his son John which means the mercy of God and that:

> He shall be great in the sight of the Lord, and shall drink neither wine nor strong drink, and he shall be filled with the holy ghost even from his mother's womb.

He is telling Zacharias that John must be consecrated to God from birth. Such men, like Samson and Samuel, were Nazirites—all Essenes were Nazirites. The angel also promises (Lk 1:17) that John shall:

> turn the hearts of the fathers to the children and the disobedient to the wisdom of the just, to make ready a people prepared for the Lord,

a passage that declares John to be a Nazarene, an Essene dedicated to converting the impious Jews to righteousness. *The just* is code for the Essenes—it is the same word as righteous.

In Luke 1:18–20, Zacharias doesn't believe the messenger and is told that he would remain dumb until the prophecy was fulfilled. The angel expressly says he would be struck dumb, *because thou believest not my words*. This is an instance proving that afflictions are meant to signify doubts, disbelief, poor faith, opposition and apostasy. Once the words had been fulfilled Zacharias would have no choice but to believe, and then his dumbness would be cured.

At this point Luke 1:31–35 sends an angel to announce the birth of Jesus to Mary, which he does in purely Essenic messianic language, as we noted above, plainly declaring that Jesus would be a son of David, and a son of God, meaning a king. For all that Luke recounts the virgin birth, in verse 1:28 he unequivocally states that the angel came in unto her which means he had sex with her. As a consequence Mary was troubled, as she would have had cause to be.

However the Quran, which seems to preserve elements of the tradition of the original Jerusalem Church, confirms the annunciation of Mary described in Luke but calls Mary a siddiqah (5:17), a zaddik, one of the righteous, and the elect of God amongst women (3:42). She is a female Essene. Like the Essenes the Quran refers to Abraham and Joseph as being of the righteous. The Quran adds that Mary was, like John, a Nazirite vowed before birth to the service of God (3:33–37) who Zacharias sponsored to enter the temple. And in Luke 1:36 Mary and Elizabeth are cousins so that Mary, like Elizabeth, was a Levite which the Quran also confirms. The inference from this is that Mary held a ritual position in the birth of Jesus— she was a ritualized mother for the rebirth of the nasi and the annunciation by the angel was exactly that—an announcement of the ceremonial conception. The angel's intercourse with Mary when he came in unto her was a ritual formality merely describing his announcement.

Then Mary goes to meet Elisabeth and sings, or in some old manuscripts Elisabeth sings (Lk 1:46–55), the Magnificat—an Essene song of praise to God similar to many in the sectarian scrolls.

> My soul doth magnify the Lord, And my spirit hath rejoiced in God my Saviour. For he hath regarded the low estate of his handmaiden: for, behold, from henceforth all generations shall call me blessed. For he that is mighty hath done to me great things; and holy is his name. And his mercy is on them that fear him from generation to generation. He hath shewed strength with his arm; he hath scattered the proud in the imagination of their hearts. He hath put down the mighty from their seats, and exalted them of low degree. He hath filled the hungry with good things; and the rich he hath sent empty

> away. He hath holpen his servant Israel, in remembrance of his mercy; As he
> spake to our fathers, to Abraham, and to his seed for ever.

This song has God doing all the things the Essenes expected Him and His messiah
to do for Israel: put down the mighty, exalt those of low degree, feed the hungry
and send the rich away empty. This is obviously a song of the poor, the Ebionim—
the Essenes. Elisabeth then gives birth and they name the son John whereupon
Zacharias is relieved of his dumbness—his disbelief—the prophecy has come true
so he must now believe it.

Another song, the Benedictus, by Zacharias follows (Lk 1:68–79).

> Blessed be the Lord God of Israel; for he hath visited and redeemed his people,
> And hath raised up an horn of salvation for us in the house of his servant David;
> As he spake by the mouth of his holy prophets, which have been since the world
> began: That we should be saved from our enemies, and from the hand of all that
> hate us; To perform the mercy promised to our fathers, and to remember his holy
> covenant; the oath which he sware to our father Abraham, That he would grant
> unto us, that we being delivered out of the hand of our enemies might serve him
> without fear, In holiness and righteousness before him, all the days of our life.
> And thou, child, shalt be called the prophet of the Highest: for thou shalt go
> before the face of the Lord to prepare his ways; To give knowledge of salvation
> unto his people by the remission of their sins, Through the tender mercy of our
> God; whereby the dayspring from on high hath visited us, To give light to them
> that sit in darkness and in the shadow of death, to guide our feet into the way of
> peace.

It is an extract of Essene liturgy, apparently part of the ceremony of ordination of
the nasi described in the baptism of Jesus. Many Essene words appear: visitation,
redemption or deliverance or salvation from enemies, covenant, righteousness,
preparing His ways, remission of sins, light and darkness, and death meaning
everlasting death—those in darkness, the sinners, are in the shadow of death
because they will not enter God's everlasting kingdom.

If further proof is needed it is the use of the word which in the Septuagint translates
branch, but here is rendered *dayspring*. The word is *semah* which, in the messianic
sense in which it is used here, is synonymous with neser, and it appears as such in
Zechariah 6:12 which describes another part of the coronation ceremony. Nasi and
neser are both understood in the word Nazarene. Looked at this way, it can be seen
that the Magnificat must have been the nasi's response upon being crowned or
ordained.

The word *child* has probably been added to chime with Luke's context, but *children*
in the gospels is commonly used to mean God's chosen people. It also seems that
the Essenes as *the righteous* believed that they had been present at the creation.
Certainly God's prophets were righteous ones and the reference to *the holy
prophets, which have been since the world began* might mean the Essenes
themselves, there being no other Jewish or Christian tradition that the prophets were
present at the creation. Peter uses the same expression in Acts 3:21 when he begins
to persuade people that Jesus was the messiah and was to come again. Revelation,
an essentially Essene work, brackets saints and prophets several times. Perhaps

Essenes regarded themselves as prophets, hardly surprisingly in view of their belief that they understood the secrets of God's appointed times.

Various thanksgiving hymns in the scrolls contain phrases remarkably similar to those in the Magnificat and the Benedictus. Since the gospels are translations from Aramaic oral tradition into Greek thence into English, the originals could well have been the same. Compare the following with those in the Lucan songs above.

> BLESSED BE THE GOD OF ISRAEL WHO STORETH MERCY FOR THOSE OF HIS COVENANT, AND KEEPETH THE APPOINTED TIMES OF HIS SALVATION FOR THE PEOPLE HE HATH REDEEMED.

> Blessed be the Lord God of Israel; for he hath visited and redeemed his people,

> THOU HAST RAISED THE FALLEN BY THY STRENGTH, BUT HAST CUT DOWN THE GREAT IN HEIGHT.

> He hath put down the mighty from their seats, and exalted them of low degree.

> BLESSED ART THOU, O LORD, FOR IT IS THOU WHO HAST DONE THESE THINGS.

> For he that is mighty hath done to me great things;

> ILLUMINED WITH PERFECT LIGHT FOREVER, WITH NO MORE DARKNESS, FOR UNENDING SEASONS OF JOY AND UNNUMBERED AGES OF PEACE.

> To give light to them that sit in darkness and in the shadow of death, to guide our feet into the way of peace.

> BLESSED BE THY NAME, O GOD OF MERCIES, WHO HAS KEPT THE COVENANT WITH OUR FATHERS.

> To perform the mercy promised to our fathers, and to remember his holy covenant;

> HE HAS LIFTED UP IN JUDGEMENT THE FEARFUL OF HEART AND HAS OPENED THE MOUTH OF THE DUMB THAT THEY MIGHT PRAISE THE GREAT WORKS OF GOD.

Amazingly here the mouths of the dumb are being opened to praise the great works of God, precisely as Zacharias does, but not in the song—in Luke's narrative! Luke has dramatized a verse of an Essene hymn. Perhaps it has happened elsewhere in the gospels. Those who praise the works of God are not stricken but those who deny the works of God are dumb. Again we have confirmation that physical afflictions for Essenes represent states of disbelief.

The truth in Luke's story of Zacharias and John is that Zacharias was the predecessor of John as nasi. Zacharias ordains John and later John ordains Jesus. Luke indicates this by the exact parallel between the birth stories of John and Jesus. He is saying they both were appointed in the same way—because they both had the same job. John would have uttered the same words at the baptism of Jesus that Zacharias said at his. Zacharias would have announced, *Thou art my beloved son*, at the coronation ceremony. In verse 76 Luke has changed the original *Son of the Highest* to *prophet of the highest* because theologians had reserved the title Son for Jesus, and indeed Luke's angel had announced in 1:32 that Jesus would be the *Son of the Highest*. In the original litany it was used of each nasi, and so both of them were Sons of the Highest in succession. John was the ritual son not the natural son

91

of Zacharias, which explains why an old man with an elderly wife could have a child. Zacharias is just a Greek form of Zechariah, the prophet Jesus deliberately fulfils when he enters Jerusalem on an ass, approaching the climax of the story.

From Luke 1:5 we know John the Baptist came from a priestly family. In the Hebrew and Arabic versions of Josephus, John the Baptist is called the High Priest. Since he could not have been the High Priest of the Jerusalem temple a position reserved at that time for a few aristocratic priestly families, the opponents of the regime must have had an alternative hierarchy with their leaders paralleling those in Jerusalem. The centre of the alternative organization was Qumran and John must have been a High Priest of the alternative priesthood. Essene practice spelled out in the Damascus Document was that senior positions had to be given up at 60 years of age because God ordained in the Book of Jubilees that a man's understanding would depart even before his days are completed. The Master had to retire at 50 and could not be appointed until he was thirty, explaining the two ages mentioned in connexion with Jesus. Jesus might have been crowned as successor to John when the latter was nearing 50, and John succeeded Zacharias when he was 50. The most senior position in the Essene order, though largely a titular position, seems not to have been the Master but the High Priest who called the annual festival of the renewal of the covenant. After the baptism of Jesus as nasi, John the Baptist might have become the High Priest, which would explain why he was able to question Jesus's progress in Matthew 11:2–3.

Luke concludes this section (Lk 1:80): *And the child grew, and waxed strong in spirit, and was in the deserts until the day of his shewing unto Israel.* What is meant by, *the child... was in the deserts*, other than that he was brought up at Qumran. The Qumran community took in waifs, strays and orphans according to the classical writers. One of the thanksgiving hymns in the Hymn Scroll appears to confirm this having: *Thou wilt care for me; for my father knew me not and my mother abandoned me to thee.* Thus Elisabeth is a pious invention of Luke. He humours the women of the early church who were 80 to 90 per cent of its gentile congregations. Elisabeth is modelled on Abraham's wife Sarah.

And John the Baptist was in the deserts until *the day of his shewing unto Israel.* The expression implies a deliberate coming out or debut in some important role that he had been prepared for. The role was the nasi and the preparation was by the Essenes.

Mark 1:2 – 1:8 Restored

Even as it is written in the prophets: *The voice of one crying: in the wilderness prepare ye the way of the Lord, make straight a high way in the desert for our God. For the glory of God shall be revealed and all flesh shall see it together. The Lord saith: Behold, I send my messenger, which shall prepare my way before me, and the Lord whom ye seek shall suddenly come to His temple.* John appeared baptizing and preaching a baptism of repentance for the remission of sins, saying: *Ye shall not enter the water to be cleansed unless ye turn from thy wickedness, obeying the law, as He commanded you through Moses to do by His holy spirit; for all who transgress His word are unclean.* John was the nasi, which is prince of the congregation, the Master of the Nazarenes, the successor of the nasi Zacharias, but, being humble, called himself Enosh, which is man; and he was great in the sight of the Lord drinking neither wine nor strong drink for he was also nazir, which is consecrated to God. He went before God to make ready a righteous people ready for the day of the Lord. And multitudes from Judaea and from Jerusalem went out to him and were baptized in the river Jordan, confessing their sins. And John announced: *After me one who is mightier than me will come, and I am not fit to stoop and untie the latchet of his sandals. I have baptized you with water but he will baptize you with the holy spirit for it is written: Who may abide the day of His coming? For he is like a refiner's fire. And I will come near to you in judgement. When the day cometh it burneth as a furnace, and all the proud and all that work wickedness shall be stubble, and the day that cometh shall burn them up; but ye that fear my name shall gambol as calves of the stall and ye shall tread down the wicked, for they shall be ashes under the souls of your feet.* Being interpreted, the angel Michael cometh to judge the world.

The Baptism of Jesus

Mark 1:9 – 1:11

1:9 And it came to pass in those days, that Jesus came from Nazareth of Galilee, and was baptized of John in Jordan. 1:10 And straightway coming up out of the water, he saw the heavens opened, and the Spirit like a dove descending upon him: 1:11 And there came a voice from heaven, saying, Thou art my beloved Son, in whom I am well pleased.

The Baptism of Jesus

Jesus arrives for baptism and is acknowledged by a spirit and a voice from heaven as the Son of God but if, as Christians believe, Jesus was already a god, a perfect being, why should he need to undergo baptism for remission of sins? The true explanation—that Jesus was being crowned the nasi as successor to John the Baptist—is much more coherent.

The first gospel written, Mark, does not tell us that John the Baptist recognizes Jesus as the messiah. Matthew introduces it (Mt 3:14) and it is strengthened in John. We can take it that John the Baptist did not recognize Jesus as a messiah, especially since later he has to send a message from prison (Mt 11:2–3) asking whether it is true, but when he baptized Jesus he did crown him a prince or a priest because a voice acknowledges him as a Son of God.

The word used in the gospels *beloved* equates to *only begotten* in Old Testament usage. Thus in Genesis 22:2, God says to Abraham: *Take your son, your only son, your beloved, even Isaac*. In Psalms 2:7 we have: *The Lord said unto me: Thou art my son; this day have I begotten thee*, the implied birth signifying an adoption. This formula is ancient. One of the inscriptions of Rameses the Great records the hidden god, Amun-Ra, addressing the Pharaoh with the same words: *I am thy father. I have begotten thee like a god*. The Pharaoh replies: *I am thy son. Thou hast given me the authority of a god*—unless he is an extremely precocious codling, he is being crowned not being born! The author of Psalms, Jews believed, was David the king and it is he who God is adopting.

That the poem (Ps 2:6–12) was part of the old coronation liturgy is clear when it is read in full. The king is expected to be a great warrior and conquerer of the enemies of the Jews:

> I have set my king upon my holy hill of Zion. I will tell thee of the decree: The Lord said unto me, Thou art my son; This day have I begotten thee. Ask of me and I will give thee the nations for thine inheritance, and the uttermost parts of the earth for thy possession. Thou shalt break them with a rod of iron; thou shalt dash them in pieces like a potter's vessel.

The Ebionites, the remnant of the Jerusalem Church which took to the desert after the destruction of Jerusalem by the Romans, had their own gospel. It is now lost but Epiphanius regarded it as heretical and in his book, Against Heresies, he has preserved parts of it in his quotations. The Ebionites had both formulae in their gospel explicitly: *Thou art my beloved Son, in thee I am well pleased*, and: *This day I have begotten thee*. It is at this point that Luke, in his gospel, inserts the genealogy because the baptism was considered a rebirth.

In John 3:1–21 Jesus teaches the councillor, Nicodemus, and his speech ends in purely Essene phraseology:

> Men loved darkness rather than light because their deeds were evil. For every one that doeth evil hateth the light, neither cometh to the light, lest his deeds should be reproved. But he that doeth truth cometh to the light, that his deeds be made manifest.

It shows John contains genuine tradition. At the beginning of the section, we find (Jn 3:4) Jesus saying: *Except a man be born again, he cannot see the kingdom of God*. When Nicodemus asks how this can be, Jesus explains: *Except a man be born of the water and the spirit, he cannot enter the kingdom of God*. The water is baptism and the spirit is sincere repentance—together they are a ritual rebirth into righteousness.

The baptism by John was his coronation of Jesus as the prince of Israel—the king of the Jews. He becomes a Son of God by adoption—the rebirth is ritual. In the messianic Psalms of Solomon, the nations are to be broken and dashed to pieces. This Son of God was not meant to suffer silently to bring salvation to the world. He was to initiate the Jewish conquest of the world.

Isaiah 11:2 has: *The spirit of the Lord would settle on him*, the origin of the imagery at Jesus's baptism. The scrolls have the same but expressed even more explicitly: *The holy spirit settled on His messiah.* Here the spirit of the Lord becomes the holy spirit and the recipient of it, His messiah, is explicit. God would decide whether the man appointed or elected nasi would become the messiah. An element of ancient Middle Eastern coronation ceremonies is the descent of a bird, normally a hawk, but changed here into a spirit like a dove by Mark because he wanted to symbolize that Jesus signaled *a renewal* of the world (Genesis 8:11). The Community Rule refers to *a renewal* at the appointed end, confirming that the world was not destroyed but was renewed as it was after the flood. An interesting speculation is that the Essenes who had given up sacrifices in favour of prayer might on special occasions have retained as a symbolic sacrifice, the release of doves acknowledging the righteousness of Noah and the purification of the world in peace. Leviticus 12:6,8 prescribes the sacrifice of turtle-doves for purification of an unclean woman. As we shall see later the land of Israel was personified as an unclean woman and the doves might have been symbolic of the purging of the land of the pollution by the stranger. The dove mentioned in the gospels might have been so released. Furthermore in 2 Esdras 5:26 Israel is a dove, so the freeing of a dove symbolically liberated Israel. Only Jesus saw the heavens open and the spirit descend; no one else did. Mark admits that no one but the man he considered to be a God saw this miracle.

In Isaiah 42:1; 44:2 the word used instead of *only* is *chosen* which in the Greek is the same word as *elect.* The messiah was known also as the chosen one as he was in Enoch 45:3, a book favoured by the Essenes, and as Jesus is called in Luke 23:35. Since *chosen* means *elect* the messiah was also the *elect one* matching the name of the Essenes—the elect—and completing the link with Enoch. Much of the book called Second Isaiah where these expressions are found speaks of a suffering servant identified with Israel as a whole but possibly referring specifically to the Essene Righteous Teacher. Second Isaiah is a late addition to the original book and in these passages the chosen one is the servant. But the Greek for a servant *pais* can also be rendered *son*, so the identity of the various coronation formulae is complete.

Jesus's Appearance

Luke says Jesus was about 30 when his ministry began. This might be a prophetic harmony with king David who was about 30 when he started his career, or might signify that as an Essene he had reached the minimum age of responsibility. About 30 seems quite a good age for a fighting man, a revolutionary leader, but rather young for a sage. Even John might be taken to imply that Jesus was middle aged (Jn 8:57), a curious observation to make about a thirty year old, though one which tells us the Jews at the time associated wisdom with age. But it was really an observation that Jesus, as the Mebaqqer of all the Camps—the Master—had to be under 50.

What did Jesus look like? There are no descriptions of him in the gospels but descriptions must have been written of him—when the Sanhedrin issued its warrant for his arrest as John describes (Jn 11:57) and when Pilate submitted his account of the trial. Each of these would contain the name, charge and description of the criminal.

The Christian image of Jesus is derived from a forgery issued to counter the publication of the Acta Pilati, the Acts of Pilate, which proved that Jesus was a bandit, justly executed under Roman law. This forgery is called the Letter of Lentulus, Lentulus being a Roman of higher rank than Pilate to discredit the latter. Lentulus describes Jesus as a man of classical European beauty. He has light (red, in early pictures, like king David), curly, shoulder-length hair, blue eyes, a ruddy complexion unblemished by spots or marks, a faultless nose and mouth, and a short divided beard; he has a grave demeanour. This has been the Jesus of Christian art ever since, though earlier imagery had been pagan—Jesus was a beardless youth like Attis or Orpheus.

This forgery describes Jesus as tall, but that is belied by the measure of his height which is given as 15 palms and a half, not more than five feet two inches if a palm is understood to be four inches—it was probably three! St Ephraim in his Gospel Commentaries writes: *God came down to us in small stature.* Both Tertullian and Celsus described Jesus as short and of mean appearance. The apocryphal Acts of John says Jesus was a man of small stature and Jesus's twin brother is described as small in the Syrian Acts of Thomas. If Luke 19:3 is to be taken literally, Zacchaeus sought to see Jesus who he was, *and could not for the crowd, because he was little of stature.* For Christians this ambiguity means that Zacchaeus was little of stature when it could mean Jesus was. And Jesus calls himself *but little in the kingdom of God* (Lk 7:28) meaning the least significant but punning on his small height. The Slavonic Text of Josephus's the Jewish War pictures Jesus not as fair, handsome, tall and upright, and in the prime of life but as a bent, short, possibly hunchbacked, older man with beetling brows and a dark skin.

Was Jesus Unmarried? If he was, it was unusual for Jews at that time, but Moses had stopped living with his wife to undertake his prophetic role and the rabbis deduced that prophecy and marriage were incompatible. However the age of prophecy was over and it was the duty of all Jews to procreate—some first century rabbis compared celibacy to murder. The Hasidim had mixed views. Some, like Honi and Hanina were married but others accepted that abstinence led to holiness.

Soldiers in campaign and those taking part in worship had to abstain from intercourse. The wilderness Essenes, who regarded themselves as soldiers preparing for the terminal battle, did segregate themselves from the opposite sex in their pursuit of holiness. As a soldier of God Jesus would have chosen chastity but he seems to have had little in common with Essene asceticism because he had the specific task of converting the sinners of Israel before the coming battle—for him, it was a duty to mix with the impure that they might become pure. The provision needed for widows in Acts of the Apostles 6:1–6 shows that Nazarenes in general married like the village Essenes of the Damascus Document.

Mark 1:9 – 1:11 Restored

Now it came to pass in those days that a man of repute, a Nazarene, being thirty years old, was baptized by John in the Jordan, and Zadokite priests came from Damascus by the Dead Sea. One was the Angel of the Lord and one was the Satan and John was Joshua, the High Priest. And the Angel spake: *Be silent, all ye flesh, before the Lord, for he is raised up out of his holy habitation.* And the Zadokites asked: *Where is he who shall be the prince of the congregation, a sceptre who shall smite all the children of Seth, for it is written: a star shall come out of Jacob and a sceptre shall rise out of Israel.* And straightway the Nazarene rose up from the water. And the Angel said: *Saith the Lord of hosts: If thou wilt walk in my ways, and if thou wilt keep my charge, then thou shalt also judge my house, and shalt also keep my courts, and I will give thee places to walk among these that stand by. Hear now, behold, I bring forth my servant the branch; and I will remove the iniquity of that land in one day.* And Joshua, the High Priest spake: *Saith the Lord of Hosts: I have set my king upon my holy hill of Zion. Thou art my son. This day have I begotten thee. Ask of me and I will give thee the nations for thine inheritance, and the uttermost parts of the earth for thy possession. Thou shalt break them with a rod of iron. Thou shalt dash them in pieces like a potter's vessel. Thou shalt be called the Son of the Highest, for thou shalt go before the face of the Lord to prepare his ways, to give knowledge of salvation unto his people by the remission of their sins, through the tender mercy of our God, whereby the branch from on high hath visited us, to give light to them that sit in darkness and in the shadow of death, to guide our feet into the way of peace.* Joshua, the High Priest, sprinkled him with water, making the sign of the cross on his forehead so that he would be among the saved, as in the previous visitation. They named him Joshua, the salvation of God, which is Jesus. And Joshua, the High Priest, spake unto Jesus: *The Lord saith: Behold, I have caused thine iniquity to pass from thee, and I will clothe thee in pure apparel.* And they gave him holy objects and clothed him in clean white garments, and the spirit of the Lord settled on him. And Joshua said unto Jesus: *Master, now lettest thou thy servant depart in peace, according to thy word, for mine eyes hath seen salvation which thou hast prepared before the face of the people, a light to lighten the darkness and the glory of thy people Israel.* And Jesus replied saying: *My soul doth magnify the Lord, And my spirit hath rejoiced in God my saviour. For he hath regarded the low estate of His servant: and from henceforth all generations shall bless Him. For He that is mighty hath done great things; and holy is His name. And His mercy is on them that fear Him from generation to generation. He hath shewed strength with His arm; He hath scattered the proud in the imagination of their hearts. He hath put down the mighty from their seats, and exalted them of low degree. He hath filled the hungry with good things; and the rich He hath sent empty away. He hath holpen His servant Israel, in* remembrance of His mercy, as He spake to our fathers, to Abraham, and to his seed for ever. And Jesus blessed God, saying: *Blessed be the Lord God of Israel; for He hath visited and redeemed His people, And hath raised up an horn of salvation for us in the house of His servant David, as He spake by the mouth of His holy prophets which have been since the world began, that we should be saved from our enemies, and from the hand of all that hate us, to perform the mercy promised to our fathers, and to remember His holy covenant, the oath which he sware to our father Abraham, that He would grant unto us that we, being delivered out of the hand of our enemies, might serve Him without fear, in holiness and righteousness before Him, all the days of our life.*

The Temptation

Mark 1:12 – 1:13

1:12 And immediately the spirit driveth him into the wilderness. 1:13 And he was there in the wilderness forty days, tempted of Satan; and was with the wild beasts; and the angels ministered unto him.

The Temptation

The story of the temptation in Mark serves to establish Jesus as a great leader, superior even to Moses. And the offer of the kingship of the world by the devil in Luke and Matthew was intended by gentile Christians as a rebuttal of the idea that Jesus was a messiah in the Jewish mould who would become a world ruler—that is what the devil offered him and he refused it. But was it pure invention?

In Mark, these two terse and cryptic verses are all we get about the temptation of Jesus, eased by the ministrations of angels—surely the Essenes of Qumran who lived in the wilderness, considering themselves the foundation of heaven on earth and therefore akin to the angels. The Greek word translated as tempt has a wider scope of meaning centred on the idea of a test or a trial of strength. The writer is really saying that, in the trial of strength with Satan, Jesus had begun the battle for the kingdom.

What we have is an almost complete abridgement of the Essene belief that the kingdom of God is inaugurated by the cosmic battle with Satan. In the War Scroll we have a full account of this cosmic battle. The fortunes of the battle switch from one side to the other. Finally God brings down Satan and all his army in everlasting destruction. The War Scroll, like this pericope, begins with several references to the desert or the wilderness where the battle occurs. The gospel writer avoids a long distraction and simply hints at it, but the conjunction of a struggle between God's agent and Satan, ministrations by angels and the period of forty days hint strongly at the original. Beasts always signify the gentile enemies of Israel in these allegories. The principal beast was Rome and the Revelation of St John the Divine uses the same imagery.

The battle in the War Scroll was to be 40 years long not forty days but the change is no problem, the Old Testament and Essene texts often referring to a week of years (seven years) in which a year is equated with a day. The forty arises because David the king reigned for forty years, seven years over Judah and 33 years over all Israel and Judah (2 Samuel 5:4–5). The same division of years appears in the War Scroll.

The temptation ceremony would not have lasted for forty days but it seems was followed by a forty day fast.

The coronation of a priest described in Zechariah 3 describes how the acting priest rebukes someone taking the role of the devil. The enrolment ceremonies of the Essenes involved long chanted cursing of the devil and his cohorts. It seems that a ritualized form of the defeat of Belial was part of much Essene ceremonial. Mark has used the ritual abusing of the devil as a reason for bringing in his couple of verses about the temptation. As we shall see the form of it arises again in the transfiguration where Jesus rebukes Peter in his role as Satan. In the description of the temptation in Matthew 4:10 and Luke 4:8 we get an identical rebuke confirming that it was associated with a coronation. Conceivably the mocking by the soldiers after Jesus's trial could be a misplaced example of what happened here physically. The nasi had been crowned a king but had to remain the humblest of all to retain his position and so had to suffer this mockery without complaint.

The details of the temptations in Matthew 4:3–11 and Luke 4:3–13 might be parts of the coronation ritual. What they seem to have in common is Jesus's answers which are all from Deuteronomy where the preacher is reminding the children of Israel not to be carried away by the realization of God's promise of the entry into Canaan. The Israelites had been wandering in the desert for forty years but were now to enter the promised land. The correspondence with the forty days temptation and the forty years of warfare preceding the entry into the kingdom of heaven is plain. The people had to keep the commandments if they were to inherit the land and, now that the goal was almost achieved, God could still humble them (Deut 8:1–2). So it seems that, in a ritual call and response litany, the Satan figure nominally offered the nasi temptations to cancel entry into the kingdom. Of course, the nasi knew his lines and gave the correct responses.

Luke 4:13 implies that the ceremony was repeated at different seasons. The Essenes were obsessed with times and calendars because they were sure that through them they could understand God's mysteries. The scrolls show that they had hymns and rituals for different times of day and seasons, meaning monthly, quarterly and annually. The rules pertaining to the Master in the Community Rule makes it clear that he has duties to fulfil at these times and seasons. The word season is explicitly used repeatedly especially at the beginning of the Song of the Master. Possibly the temptation ritual had to be followed at the start of each major season—all a part of keeping the Master humble.

The Testaments of the Twelve Patriarchs—thought to have been an early Christian work but of a form now known from the Dead Sea Scrolls and so likely originally to have been an Essene work of the intertestamental period—in the Testament of Napthali, gives a closely similar idea to Mark 1:12–13: *If you do good, my children, both men and angels shall bless you, and the devil shall flee from you and the wild beasts shall fear you and the Lord shall love you.* Possibly Mark took his imagery from this source, though the Christianized version might be dependent on Mark.

It is significant—in the light of Josephus saying that the followers of Judas of Galilee held God to be their only ruler and Lord—that Jesus's reply to the offer of the nations of the world, quoting from Deuteronomy 6:13 and 10:20 was: *Thou shalt worship the Lord thy God, and Him only shalt thou serve.* It is exactly what the Galilaeans of Judas believed. They refused to serve the Roman oppressors. The Galilaeans of Jesus seem to have been the same cult of zealous Essenes. Now if this is true, every reference to Galilee in Mark is called into question. The stories coming out of Palestine to the gentiles of Rome were stories of a band of Galilaeans and Galilaean bands were known as guerillas fighting against the Romans. The bishops had to find an excuse and fortunately it was easy—they said Jesus was a Galilaean because he came from Galilee not because he was a bandit. In their movements around Palestine the Nazarenes subsequently must have spent time in Galilee but it is unlikely that they were mostly natives of that province.

Mark 1:12 – 1:13 Restored

And the Satan tested him with promises of finery and glory. And they all called out: *The Lord bless Jesus, the salvation of God, and all the men of the lot of God who walked perfectly in his ways*; and they all called: *Truly, Truly.* And they called out: *The Lord rebuke thee Satan, and all the men of the lot of Satan for their wickedness and the darkness of their deeds; yea, the Lord that hath chosen Jerusalem rebuke thee Satan, for is not this brand now plucked out of the fire?* And they all called: *Truly, Truly.* And he was tested by the Satan that he should stumble on the path to the kingdom of God. But Jesus was not tempted, rejecting all that Satan offered. And he said: *Get thee behind me, Satan; for it is written, Thou shalt worship the Lord thy God, and Him only shall thou serve.* And when the devil had ended all the temptation, he departed from him for a season. Immediately the spirit driveth him into the wilderness; for the battle for the kingdom would be forty years and for every year a day and a night he fell down before the Lord in the wilderness lest Belial should triumph and the Lord look upon the stubbornness of His people, or on their wickedness, or sin, and destroy them. And the Lord hearkened to him that His people should enter the kingdom which He had promised. And the Angel and God's elect ministered to him.

Jesus begins his Ministry

Mark 1:14 – 1:15

1:14 Now after that John was handed over, Jesus came into Galilee, preaching the gospel of the kingdom of God, 1:15 And saying, The time is fulfilled, and the kingdom of God is at hand: repent ye, and believe the gospel.

Jesus begins his Ministry

Jesus did not automatically become the nasi on his baptism. Matthew and Mark imply Jesus did not succeed John, as the leader of the Nazarenes, until John was handed over or cast into prison by Herod. Only then did he begin spreading the gospel. In Acts 10:37 Peter addressing Cornelius also implies that Jesus only began his ministry after John the Baptist was imprisoned. Jesus was the prince in waiting, crowned in preparation for John to stand down. The ultimate fate of John the Baptist is not told until later but since he has no further role in the story it could be concluded here—and so we do in our reconstruction.

As successor to John, Jesus takes up the same message. Note it is the *same* message—Jesus had not changed it. It was exactly that of John the Baptist— the same task—not the new one of God's messiah. He makes no claim to be the messiah but simply continues John's call to the simple of Ephraim— they should repent in preparation for the coming kingdom—the time had come, the kingdom of God was near, repentance was needed. God's kingdom was on earth, though it would have been cleansed and renewed by God's holy fire. It would be presided over by the messiah. His lieutenants would be *the righteous* of the children of Israel—if they had died before the triumph, resurrected on the third day (Hosea 6:2). Faith was not sufficient to enter the kingdom as theologians later believed—Jews who wanted to be amongst *the righteous* had to repent. Salvation was the gift of God but it had to be earned by righteousness or sincere repentance.

The kingdom of God is near sounds pretty innocuous to us but to the Jews it was a call to arms. They expected God's reign to be initiated by the messiah liberating the chosen people from foreign yoke. God would intervene but he only helped those who helped themselves.

No mention is made in Mark of baptizing, yet baptism was required of those who sincerely repented—a ritual cleansing to accompany the spiritual cleansing of repentance. Mark's omission of baptism is deliberate. Christians wanted to distinguish themselves from the followers of the Baptist, who were still active when Mark wrote, as Acts proves. So they mostly deleted baptism from the story, just as they disguised or deleted all occurrences of the Essene sacred meal until the last supper, to give a romanticized and spurious account of its origin. However we learn from John 3:26 and 4:1 that Jesus and John were both baptizing at the same time. John the Baptist takes the news that Jesus was successful as proof that he was indeed God's choice and it was time for John to step down (decrease)—all men come to him (Jn 3:26) and Jesus made and baptized more disciples than John, an excuse for John to deny he is the messiah. Later (Jn 4:2) an editor saw a problem in John's account of the Son of God behaving like John the Baptist and inserts a parenthesis that it was the disciples who baptized!

Note the phrase, *the time is fulfilled*, which implies that whoever was judging the nature of the time has reason to believe something was about to happen. The Essenes spent a great deal of energy in keeping time precisely and in seeking clues to God's intentions by comparing the scriptures with current events. The scrolls speak of the end time as does Daniel 12:4 and 12:9. If there were other apocalyptic sects at the time of Jesus besides the Essenes, it is odd that we should never have heard of them, and if they were so small what resources could they offer to the divining of times. The Essenes apparently had a well developed school at Qumran and a widespread organization. Only they had the resources. The conclusion must be that Jesus and John the Baptist, his predecessor, were Essenes.

The Greek translated, *is at hand,* is rendered by some scholars as, *has arrived,* which suggests that like, *the time is fulfilled*, the Nazarenes read signs which unmistakably proclaimed the kingdom in such a way that there was no stepping back. For Mark the temptation had started the cosmic battle which would terminate in the everlasting kingdom.

Galilaeans

John was baptizing by the mouth of the Jordan and was held in prison in the fortress of Machaerus to the east of the Dead Sea but Jesus begins his ministry in Galilee. At this time, Galilee was ruled by a tetrarch, a Roman title for a minor king— Antipas (4 BC–39 AD), a son of Herod the Great—but Judaea had been ruled directly from Rome under a prefect, a Roman governor, since 6 AD, when Antipas's brother, Archelaus, ruler of Judaea, was banished to Gaul. Galilee was wealthy and well populated with industrious people though many had been turned off their land to become day labourers—the source of several parables—and resentment was high.

The regional accent of Galilaeans was strong and their gutturals almost disappeared making it difficult to distinguish certain words. Lazarus (Lazar) is the Galilaean dialect pronunciation of Eleazar. In Matthew 26:73 Peter is recognized by his accent as being a follower of Jesus, but since this scene is fictional, so too is the focus on Peter's accent. It is part of the pretence that Jesus's Galilaeans came from Galilee. No doubt some did, but that is not why they are Galilaeans! Almost every reference to Galilee in the gospels is false. They all stem from Mark's gospel and were introduced to hide the truth that Jesus was an active opponent of the Romans. He was a Galilaean because his philosophy was that of Judas of Galilee, the outlaw.

Josephus in Antiquities of the Jews describes the philosophy founded by Judas of Galilee as the fourth sect of Jewish philosophy but does not give it a name, merely saying it accepted Pharisaic notions and that its sectaries accepted only God as their

Lord. As it was the philosophy of Judas of Galilee and his followers, the Rev. Matthew Black writing in Peake's Commentary on the Bible calls its adherents, Galilaeans. Judas was a learned man whose motives like Jesus's were religious and not merely malice or greed. Judas and his Galilaeans called for an uprising, breaking into Herod's arsenal in 4 BC.

When Roman rule was declared in Judaea in 6 AD after the banishment of Archelaus, Quirinius, the legate of the Roman province of Syria which included Judaea, carried out a census to assess the population for taxes. Since the followers of Judas believed the only master of the Jews was God, it was improper to pay taxes to a gentile and it was improper to acknowledge false gods—the Emperors were beginning to claim divinity. Furthermore the law of Moses forbade not only foreign rulers, it forbade numbering the people. For some this was the final straw. Judas of Galilee and a mystery man called Sadduc combined to resist the numbering of the people by the Romans and formed a religious and political movement of fanatical nationalists. They urged the Jews to rebel and not to pay taxes to Rome, and *men received what they said with pleasure, and the nation was infected with this doctrine to a violent degree such that one violent war came after another.* Since the Essenes called themselves the sons of Zadok, this association of a Galilaean and Sadduc (a variant spelling of Zadok) in founding of the Fourth Philosophy links the Galilaeans with the Essenes.

Galilaeans had an inviolable attachment to liberty, holding God to be their only ruler and Lord, and refusing to call any man Lord even though threatened with death or torture. Jesus would not be tempted by Satan, saying: *Thou shalt worship the Lord thy God and Him only shalt thou serve*—just what Galilaeans believed. The Galilaeans believed they had to formulate plans for successful exploits and tirelessly pursue them or God would not help them—in short God only helped those who were united and showed initiative, boldness and persistence. Josephus tells us Galilaeans endured pain with resolution and were ready to suffer any manner of death and—just like the poor ones—they put honour before wealth. In all of this Josephus is describing a sect not a nation. Other early writers are quite specific. Hegesippus lists Galilaeans alongside Sadducees, Pharisees, Samaritans and Essenes, listing the Galilaeans with the Essenes, the Hemerobaptists and the Masbotheans as all being baptizing sects. Justin of Samaria also lists the Galilaeans as a Jewish sect.

By proclaiming the kingdom of God, John the Baptist and Jesus were proclaiming an end to foreign rule—an uprising—just as Judas the Galilaean had. Naturally this would not have been to the Romans' liking so Jesus had to take care about his claims. Jesus, according to Mark, consistently denied that he was himself the messiah and indeed sought to silence those who said otherwise. Clergymen say this is the messianic secret—Jesus, for some reason unknown to theologians wanted to keep his messiahship secret. If Jesus really was the messiah as the clergy claim then he was lying when he denied it and covered it up. The Christian theory of the messianic secret makes God, in His aspect of the Son, into a liar. It must be far more convincing, and more acceptable, to believe that Jesus, at this stage of his ministry, either was not yet the messiah or did not realize

103

that he was the messiah, and would have wanted to keep his activities secret anyway because his aim was to prepare the way for a Jewish king—an enemy of the Roman state. Charismatic itinerant preachers were not unknown at the time. Under the guise of such a man Jesus could call upon people to prepare for the uprising while claiming to be no threat to Rome. There was not the contradiction here that there might seem to us. To the Jews politics and religion were at one. The nasi was a political leader, a prince, and a religious leader, a priest or prophet. Jesus could use the guise of prophet though in reality a prince.

In John 7:41 the Jerusalem crowd whisper among themselves: *Surely the messiah is not to come from Galilee*? If the tradition here is genuine it must have been: *is not a Galilaean?* When Nicodemus, a Pharisee, defends Jesus to the Chief Priests and Pharisees, they say: *Are you a Galilaean too? Prophets do not come from Galilee* (Jn 7:52). The meaning of the question was: *Are you an opponent of the Romans*? An editor added the assertion about the prophets not coming from Galilee to pretend that *Galilaean* in the question meant, *from Galilee*, rather than a rebel. The gospels pretend throughout that Jesus is from Galilee when he was really a Galilaean—an outlaw like Judas of Galilee.

Scholars regard the Galilaeans as Zealots. In the Jewish War, when Josephus tells us that Judas of Galilee was a teacher of a peculiar sect of his own, he proceeds to describe at length the Essenes, implying that the Galilaeans were a branch of the Essenes. Elsewhere he maintains they held the notions of the Pharisees, but it seems unlikely because Pharisees had traditionally preferred to accomomodate the foreigner rather than fight them. Hyppolytus confirms the Zealots as Essenes. The word from which we get Pharisee means, *separated*, a description which would apply perfectly to the Essenes. So it is conceivable that Josephus wrote in Aramaic, *the notions of the separated ones*, meaning the Essenes but his amanuensis mistook him to mean the Pharisees. His description of Judas's ally, Sadduc, as a Pharisee in the same chapter seems to repeat the error.

Despite the decline of the Zealots into banditry, Judas of Galilee and his family continued to be respected, for later we find his sons also leading rebellions against Roman rule. Tiberius Julius Alexander, a Romanized Jew, procurator of Judaea from 46–48 AD and the nephew of Philo of Alexandria, crucified two of them, Jacob and Simon. A third son, Menehem, captured the stronghold of Masada from the Romans but subsequently died in faction fighting among the rebels. Eleazar, a nephew of Menehem, with only a few hundred Zealots, held Masada against the Romans for three years after the fall of Jerusalem in 70 AD.

That Essene texts were found among the Zealot debris in the ruins of the fortress of Masada is evidence that Zealots were Essenes even if all Essenes were not Zealots. The classical authors have misled us into believing that Essenes were pacifists because they would not serve as soldiers—they would not fight in *any* war. But if they had decided a war was a just war called by God against the men of darkness—a holy war—they would fight with unrestrained ferocity and the bravery possessed of all those who believe that dying for God means eternal life.

Letters written by bar Kosiba in 135 AD found at Murabba'at, about 12 miles from Qumran, complain about the lack of support he is getting from the Galilaeans and yet he warns one of his generals: *not to wrong any of the Galilaeans who are with you.* Why should Galilaeans be specifically mentioned among the rebels by the Dead Sea unless they were freedom fighters, a type of Zealot—a type that evidently did not wholeheartedly support bar Kosiba? These Galilaeans—like the Galilaeans of the gospels—were not necessarily from Galilee but people who supported the aims of Judas, the Galilaean. They supported Bar Kosiba's stand against the Romans but could not accept Bar Kosiba as the messiah because they recognized Jesus as their messiah.

Another letter from the same source speaks of the purchase of a heifer. It seems bizarre that a rebel group, sought by twelve legions of Roman soldiers, should be entering into commercial contracts and sending letters to seal them when, as the letter says, the gentiles were so close. These were desperate men hiding in the wilderness from the conquering legions. The letters are obviously not what they seem but are coded messages. Moreover, the letter was written in Hebrew, a language which was already dead in everyday use and only preserved for religious purposes. In short, the letter was doubly coded—disguised as a bill of sale and written in a dead language that the gentiles would not know. A heifer, from Numbers, represented the covenant, and the sense is perhaps that of an apology for failing to render needed assistance to those of the covenant. The point however is that these anti-Roman rebels used ways of encrypting their messages. The Nazarenes did the same.

Jesus's ministry was to all Jews, so he could have been operative in any of the Jewish countries of Palestine, Judaea, Galilee and Iturea. In Acts 10:37 Peter tells us that Jesus preached throughout Judaea not only in Galilee: *That word, I say, ye know, which was published throughout all Judaea, and began from Galilee, after the baptism which John preached.* It seems Jesus escaped to the north because Herod was busy rounding up troublemakers in the south— Matthew says so: *Now when Jesus had heard that John was cast into prison, he departed into Galilee*—but he would have been safer still in Judaea, outside of Herod's jurisdiction, intimating that the escape to Galilee might be false. In John, Jesus recruits disciples immediately after his baptism, and therefore in the region of the Dead Sea not in Galilee. He goes to Galilee after a few days. We are told that the disciples come from towns in Galilee to cover the fact that they are Galilaeans.

If the references to Galilee and Galilaeans in the gospels mean the province of Galilee it is strange that Galilaean cities are hardly mentioned. Sepphoris, the main city in Galilee, is *never* mentioned in the gospels even though it was only four miles from Nazareth. If Nazareth existed it must have been so small that it would have been only natural to refer to the rearest large town to indicate its locality—no one ever did. Tiberias is hardly mentioned even though it was a magnificent new town built in honour of the reigning Emperor. The town that is

105

mentioned is Capernaum, a custom post which was little more than a village. Indeed Josephus, who as a general in the Jewish army fighting in Galilee ought to know, does not even describe it as a village but merely as a highly fertilizing spring. Luke calls Nazareth a city but Mark calls a city, Bethsaida, a village. In Greek there is no word for a town, so that intermediate sized habitations had to be judged as either villages or cities, but the confusion suggests that these places are not places in Galilee.

On the face of it Jesus and his disciples moved around villages. They were barjonim—outsiders or even outlaws. They studiously avoided towns except Jerusalem. Whatever later Christianity has tried to say about Jesus having a message for gentiles, the truth is that he pointedly avoided them. Gentiles and their allies, Hellenized Jews, lived in towns—most Pharisees and Sadducees lived in towns. Josephus writes that the Pharisees were influential in the cities, leading one to infer that they had little influence in the countryside. The Pharisee Party had little support in Galilee suggesting again that the clashes between Jesus and Pharisees in Galilee are false. Either they did not occur or they did not occur in Galilee. Pharisees in conflict with Jesus are twice described as visitors to Galilee in Mark, as if to forestall any criticism. The countryside was the place of the Essenes (though some did live in towns, and among gentiles, and the community provided strict rules for them—the Damascus Rule).

Mark 1:14 – 1:15 Restored

Now Herod the tetrarch feared John as a disturber of the multitudes, which counted him a prophet and were ready to do anything he should advise, and went out to lay hold on him, and would have him killed. He took him and bound him, and held him in prison in the fortress of Machaerus. But Herod feared John knowing he was a righteous one and an holy one for he was an Essene, and kept him safe. And when he heard him, he heard him gladly. And this is what became of John. Herod sought to divorce his wife, the daughter of the king of Petra, that he might marry a niece, his brother Philip's wife, Herodias. And John said unto him: *It is not lawful that a man should marry his niece, nor even the mother of his brother's children; yet thou wouldst uncover her nakedness though she hath four children, thy brother's.* And when he heard him Herod was sore perplexed, and Herodias had a quarrel against him; and Herod resolved to rid himself of John. And a day came that Herod on his birthday, made a supper to his lords, high captains, and chief estates of Galilee, for he was at war with the king of Petra who would avenge the wrong done to his daughter, and he said unto Herodias: *Whatsoever thou shalt ask of me, I will give it thee.* And straightway she came in with haste unto the king, saying: *I will that thou give me by and by the head of John the Baptist.* And the king sent an executioner, and commanded his head to be brought for Herodias's sake. And he went and beheaded him in the prison, and brought his head unto Herod. And he gave it to Herodias in a charger. And when his disciples heard of it, they came and took up his corpse, and laid it in a tomb. After that John was handed over in Peraea, Jesus took up his mantle that had fallen from him, and he came thence into Galilee, by the sea that he might baptize, preaching the gospel of the kingdom of God. saying: the time is now come; the kingdom of God is at hand; hear this gospel; repent and be saved by God's mercy.

Fishers of Men

Mark 1:16 – 1:20

1:16 Now as he walked by the sea of Galilee, he saw Simon and Andrew his brother casting a net into the sea: for they were fishers. 1:17 And Jesus said unto them, Come ye after me, and I will make you to become fishers of men. 1:18 And straightway they forsook their nets, and followed him. 1:19 And when he had gone a little farther thence, he saw James the son of Zebedee, and John his brother, who also were in the ship mending their nets. 1:20 And straightway he called them: and they left their father Zebedee in the ship with the hired servants, and went after him.

Fishers of Men

Jesus has to start to assemble God's army. Here he gathers disciples who apparently were fishermen, hardly surprising by the Sea of Galilee, you might think, but references to Galilee are not to be trusted. The phrase by the sea of Galilee in verse 1:16 reads very strangely in the Greek and is considered by many scholars to be an addition, whether by Mark or an editor is unknown. Nearly all of the little stories called pericopes which make up Mark have no indications of time or place other than what is required internally by the story and when they otherwise appear they have been added by the author to provide a spurious connexion with a previous passage. Here the indication of by the sea of Galilee looks particularly odd and has evidently been added because the men being recruited were supposedly fishermen. Since this is probably a misunderstanding, deliberate or otherwise by Mark, the recruitment might well have happened elsewhere. Again a reference to Galilee is probably false.

The code used by Mark should be read here, especially since the gospel explicitly says: I will make you fishers of men. The disciples were never fishermen but all were fishers of men whatever their jobs beforehand.

The imagery of people caught in a pit, a net or snare is common in the scriptures. The net is most often a fowler's net—fish nets are less commonly used in this context—but the meaning is the same. In Ezekiel 32:3 and Jeremiah 16:15–16, God fishes for those he wishes to judge that He might bring them into His land:

Thus saith the Lord God; I will therefore spread out my net over thee with a company of many people; and they shall bring thee up in my net.

And I will bring them again into their land that I gave unto their fathers. Behold, I will send for many fishers, saith the Lord, and they shall fish them.

The people of Israel were already caught in the net of the oppressor. We find in Habakkuk 1:14–17 a little diatribe against colonialism using the simile of the people captured by foreigners as the fishes of the sea caught in a net:

> And makest men as the fishes of the sea, as the creeping things, that have no ruler over them? They take up all of them with the angle, they catch them in their net, and gather them in their drag: therefore they rejoice and are glad. Therefore they sacrifice unto their net, and burn incense unto their drag; because by them their portion is fat, and their meat plenteous. Shall they therefore empty their net, and not spare continually to slay the nations?

One of the scrolls is a commentary on Habakkuk. The oppressor, who in the original work was the Chaldaeans, becomes the Kittim, the imperial Romans, according to professor G R Driver, because they sacrificed to their standards and worshipped their weapons of war—the soldiers of republican Rome had never had the idea of worshipping their standards. The sign that the Essenes took to inaugurate the end time might well have been the imperial standards that Pilate allowed the legions to bring into Jerusalem, especially if they were taken into the temple. Pious Jews of all denominations would have seen this as an Abomination of Desolation, the signal which started the Maccabaean uprising, and which in Daniel was a sign of the end.

Jesus was a Galilaean but not necessarily from Galilee. It means his views were those of Judas of Galilee, he would not accept foreign rule for God's people. He did not recruit fishermen but fisher of men, those who would bring about the judgement day.

In Ecclesiastes 9:12 the sufferings of the people in an evil time are compared to fish caught in an evil net—the evil net of Belial of the scrolls:

> For man also knoweth not his time: as the fishes that are taken in an evil net, and as the birds that are caught in the snare; so are the sons of men snared in an evil time, when it falleth suddenly upon them.

The net in Essene code means profanation of the temple but the Essenes considered that the temple was profaned partly at least by the gentiles—the court of the gentiles and the polluted gifts which came from Jews of the Diaspora.

Looked at this way the disciples were called fishermen because Jesus had selected them as fishers of men. They were God's fishermen saving the chosen people from the nets of the foreigner because the day of judgement was nigh. Luke dramatizes the fishing at this point (Lk 5:6) with an account of the miracle of the huge draught of fish representing all the children of Israel who would be saved from evil and foreign oppression—it was no miracle but part of Jesus's apocalyptic speech, signifying the expected success of the mission of winning over the simple of Ephraim. Matthew's parable about a dragnet, which exactly illustrates the point here, is left until much later (Mt 13:47–50):

> The kingdom of heaven is like unto a net, that was cast into the sea, and gathered of every kind, which, when it was full, they drew to shore, and sat down, and gathered the good into vessels, but cast the bad away. So shall it be at the end of the world: the angels shall come forth, and sever the wicked from among the just, And shall cast them into the furnace of fire: there shall be wailing and gnashing of teeth.

It occurs also in John but after the crucifixion in a gentile Christian context. In John 21:11 the number of fish caught is recorded precisely as 153, not because anyone bothered to count them but because that was the supposed number of nations in the world to a gentile (to a Jew it was seventy). John is saying allegorically that the Christians would convert the whole world not only the Jews.

Jesus's fishers were always metaphorical ones.

There is a passage in Ezekiel's vision of the temple where the prophet describes (Ezek 47:1–10) a wondrous stream of water flowing from the alter of the perfect temple eastward into the Dead Sea and as it flowed toward the Dead Sea it got deeper and deeper. The waters of this river were healing waters which eventually entered the Dead Sea and restored it to life—resurrected it!

> And every thing that liveth, which moveth, whithersoever the rivers shall come, shall live: and there shall be a very great multitude of fish, because these waters shall come thither: for they shall be healed; and every thing shall live whither the river cometh. And the fishers shall stand upon it from Engedi even unto Eneglaim; they shall be a place to spread forth nets; their fish shall be according to their kinds, as the fish of the great sea, exceeding many.

A river flowing east from Jerusalem would enter the Dead Sea at Qumran. The two places mentioned in the vision seem to denote the coast of the Dead Sea along which the Essenes had their wilderness settlements. Engedi, the spring of the kid, is in the south, a few miles north of the natural fortress of Masada where the Zealots held out against the Romans, and Eneglaim, the spring of the heifers—an unidentified place—seems to be near the mouth of the Jordan. Besides the coincidence that the stream flows out in Essene country, it is a stream of healing waters which would revive the Dead Sea, and the Essenes were great believers in the purifying power of water. Since they identified spiritual purification with physical healing in their metaphors, their baptismal waters have exactly the powers of Ezekiel's magical river.

Engedi and Ain Feshka, close to Qumran, are both oases at the edge of the Dead Sea with bubbling fresh water supporting colonies of croaking frogs in season and even palm trees. It seems possible that the Essenes saw these springs as the first trickles of Ezekiel's magical river.

The Essenes considered themselves the perfect priests, the Sons of Zadok, of Ezekiel's perfect temple, and it seems that they identified themselves also with Ezekiel's fishers of the magical waters. Sure enough in the scroll of the Thanksgiving Hymns we find, referring to the quotations above: *Thou hast caused me to dwell with the many fishers who spread a net upon the face of the waters.* The hymn writer goes on to tell us that he dwells with the fishers because God put him there for justice and to confirm the counsel of truth in his heart and the water of the covenant for those who seek it. The fishers are the Essenes!

The hired servants of Zebedee are mentioned to show that even wealthy people were willing to give up their material wealth to follow Jesus in his campaign for the kingdom of God. In our restoration we omit the mention of the ship as an unwarranted extension of the metaphor.

In calling people from their work to be disciples, Jesus was effectively calling on them to strike. Since the day of God's vengeance was due, work had no further purpose to them, though we can be sure that their employers would have been displeased as wealthy employers always are when those who are not slaves exercise their right as freemen not to work. The first Christians were expecting the judgement day to be soon but, displaying his cynicism, Paul the apostle rebuked those (2 Thes 3:10–12) who believed they could give up work to wait for the coming of the Lord—if 2 Thessalonians is to be attributed to Paul.

Mark 1:16 – 1:20 Restored

And many heard, and Jesus spake unto them saying: *As the fishes that are caught in an evil net even so are the sons of men snared in an evil time. But, saith the Lord: I shall send for many fishers, and they shall fish them and I will bring them again unto their land that I gave unto their fathers. If thou wilt, follow me and thou shalt be fishers of men. For the day of judgement is like a net cast into the sea which drew in fishes of every kind, clean and unclean. The fisher gathered the clean into baskets but cast away the unclean. In like wise shall the wicked be separated from the righteous in the end time. For the prophet Enoch said: The Most High will deliver the evil ones to His angels for punishment for they have oppressed His children but the righteous and elect shall be saved. Cast ye nets on the wrong side and ye will gather in empty but cast ye nets on the right side and ye will gather in full, for every nation on earth will yield to the good net.* And they were astounded by his teaching, for he taught them with authority; and only a king's word hath authority. And he saw Simon and Andrew his brother, and Jesus said unto each of them: *Wilt thou repent and be a fisher of men?* And they followed him and were baptized. And he saw James the son of Zebedee, and John his brother; and Jesus said unto each of them: *Wilt thou repent and be a fisher of men?* And they left their father Zebedee with the hired servants, and went after him and were baptized.

The Unclean Spirit

Mark 1:21 – 1:28

1:21 And they went into Capernaum; and straightway on the sabbath day he entered into the synagogue, and taught. 1:22 And they were astonished at his doctrine: for he taught them as one that had authority, and not as the scribes. 1:23 And there was in their synagogue a man with an unclean spirit; and he cried out, 1:24 Saying, Let us alone; what have we to do with thee, thou Jesus of Nazareth? art thou come to destroy us? I know thee who thou art, the Holy One of God. 1:25 And Jesus rebuked him, saying, Hold thy peace, and come out of him. 1:26 And when the unclean spirit had torn him, and cried with a loud voice, he came out of him. 1:27 And they were all amazed, insomuch that they questioned among themselves, saying, What thing is this? what new doctrine is this? for with authority commandeth he even the unclean spirits, and they do obey him. 1:28 And immediately his fame spread abroad throughout all the region round about Galilee.

The Unclean Spirit

In the synagogue at Capernaum Jesus astonishes his audiences by his authority, a word which can also be translated as power. This is one of the more subtle clues to Jesus's kingship in the gospels. We get the impression it means he knew what he was talking about but reference to Ecclesiastes 8:4 gives the true meaning:

the king's word hath authority; and who may say unto him, What doest thou?

Authority or power is code for a king.

An excitable man realizing that Jesus was claiming to be a king and fearing reprisals by the Romans and their puppets calls out: *We know what you mean. You are saying you are God's holy one. Do you want to destroy us? Leave us alone! We want nothing to do with you!*

Christian commentators tell us that the unclean spirit was a demon—a demon speaking perfectly sensible Aramaic in a synagogue! Can anyone today give credence to such a scene? The man was not a demon or possessed by one—he had simply inferred that Jesus meant to face up to the occupying forces and, disapproving of it strongly, remonstrated with Jesus. He wanted no further retribution from the Romans. He used the plural, *Let us alone*, not meaning that there were many unclean spirits but that he spoke for the many Jews who realized the power of Rome and feared the consequences of resistance. Unclean spirit is code for an opponent of the Nazarenes. Sticklers for precise translation should note that the Greek translated, *unclean*, could better be translated as *malicious* or *spiteful*.

Jesus, according to Mark, exorcises the devil. In reality, because the Nazarenes were not ready to have their aims declared openly in case the Romans or Herod should hear of it, Jesus rebuked the man, sternly ordering him to shut up: *Hold thy peace*. In Luke 4:35 the devil throws the man down in their midst—not the disciples but

111

the devil, according to Luke! The unclean spirit tearing him eventually came out with a loud cry. The Greek implies strong emotions like terror and fear for life—scream of fear would be a more accurate translation. The man feared the blows of the disciples who had knocked him down and shut him up with a beating. Luke sees all of this is too obvious in Mark and hastens to add: *and hurt him not.*

The Nazarenes would not have been troubled at manhandling a man they understood to have an unclean spirit. In the War Scroll we find:

> CURSED BE SATAN FOR HIS SINFUL PURPOSE AND MAY HE BE CAST OUT FOR HIS WICKED RULE. CURSED BE ALL THE SPIRITS OF HIS COMPANY FOR THEIR UNGODLY PURPOSE AND MAY THEY BE CAST OUT FOR ALL THEIR SERVICE OF UNCLEANNESS. TRULY THEY ARE THE COMPANY OF DARKNESS, BUT THE COMPANY OF GOD IS ONE OF ETERNAL LIGHT.

Those with unclean spirits were of the company of darkness and had to be cast out. The Damascus Rule specifies that every man who preaches apostasy under the sway of the spirits of Satan shall be judged according to the law for those possessed by a ghost or a familiar spirit. Leviticus 20:27 orders that a man or woman possessed by a spirit shall surely be put to death. The Damascus Rule also quotes Nahum 1:2:

> God is jealous, and the Lord revengeth; the Lord revengeth, and is furious; the Lord will take vengeance on his adversaries, and he reserveth wrath for his enemies.

These were sufficient reason for the Nazarenes to take a firm line with such opponents. The kingdom might be at stake. They could hardly murder people in the streets without raising a hue and cry—eventually raised anyway—but they could hand out admonitory beatings. For them the cosmic battle for the kingdom had started. The crowd were amazed at the urgency of Jesus's teaching of the coming kingdom and his assertiveness in silencing his opponents.

This incident of the unclean spirit demonstrates correct interpretation. Taken literally it seems that Jesus's aim was to assist the mentally and physically sick—though it seems horribly arbitrary a priviledged few should be cured while many more were left to suffer. Accepting that Jesus was an Essene, it is easy to be misled by Josephus who records the Essenes' searches for cures by investigations into roots and stones and by using drugs from plants. They had a reputation as healers, but they were interested in the well-being not mainly of the body but of the soul. Now in Luke 13:32, we find Jesus explaining his strategy: *Today and tomorrow I shall be casting out devils and working cures; on the third day I shall reach my goal.* The third day of God's kingdom was when the heavenly built temple descended to earth and *the righteous* were resurrected to reign over the saved (Hosea 6:2). Jesus obviously wasn't curing people of physical sickness believing the heavenly kingdom had a ban on the diseased. He was curing them of moral sickness because the heavenly kingdom had a ban on sinners. Even more explicitly, later in Mark, we find: *It is not the healthy that need a doctor, but the sick; I did not come to invite virtuous people but sinners* (Mk 2:17). Jesus tells us the sick are sinners. He was not treating the physical or mental sickness of the people but the sickness in their souls, and this verse proves it. All of the healing miracles need reinterpreting in this light.

Palestinian Jews were dispairing of the fate of the chosen people. Many foes of the Nazarenes openly collaborated with the occupying forces. Others feared reprisals. Both would have been strongly averse to anyone risking further trouble with the authorities. Mark (or Peter) could not put any of this explicitly so it was written allegorically, though the meaning is remarkably transparent. A demon was code for a doubter or opponent of the messianists which had to be driven out with a beating, illnesses were moral and spiritual sickness, helplessness and cowardice. In the scrolls a thanksgiving hymn of the Essenes is explicit, *lying lips shall be dumb*—a diseased spirit is depicted as a physical affliction. Isaiah 35:3–7 expresses it perfectly, and links it unequivocally with messianic expectations:

> Strengthen ye the weak hands, and confirm the feeble knees. Say to them that are of a fearful heart, Be strong, fear not: behold, your God will come with vengeance, even God with a recompense; he will come and save you. Then the eyes of the blind shall be opened, and the ears of the deaf shall be unstopped. Then shall the lame man leap as an hart, and the tongue of the dumb sing. On God's terrible day of vengeance He will save the just. They need fear not. The blind shall see, the dumb shall speak and the lame shall walk.

God will save only the just—the righteous—others had to be cured of their dumbness and blindness—their rejection of the Essene route to the kingdom. All of Jesus's healing miracles are metaphors for removing fear and improving morale so that the children of Israel might be saved—in short recruiting people to the Nazarene cause, the defeat of the oppressors and the proclamation of the kingdom of God.

For those who read on a few verses, the connexion of this part of Isaiah with the Essenes is unmistakeable. We find that in the wilderness waters shall break out, and an high way shall be there called the way of holiness, but the unclean shall not pass over it nor shall any ravenous beast go up thereon, but only the redeemed shall walk there, and they shall return to Zion bringing everlasting joy. This could only be a description of Qumran. The Essenes followed the way of holiness, preparing a high way in the desert that the redeemed could walk, their opponents among the Jews being the unclean, and their gentile opponents being ravenous beasts.

Also relevant here is the passage in 2 Samuel 5:4–10 where king David begins his reign aged 30 years, just as we surmise Jesus had done from his coronation by John the Baptist. David's first trial is to take Jerusalem by defeating the Jebusites who are so defiant that they say to David: *you will have to get rid of us all, even the blind and the lame.* But David was single minded and ordered: *smite the lame and the blind that are hated of David's soul. Then we'll see why they say, There are the lame and blind; he cannot come into the city.* The Essenes could not accept that king David would kill cripples so they read it allegorically. The lame and blind were adversaries, not disabled people.

The Damascus Rule asserts that:

NO MADMAN, LUNATIC, SIMPLETON, OR FOOL; NO BLIND MAN, MAIMED, LAME OR DEAF MAN, AND NO MINOR SHALL ENTER INTO THE COMMUNITY, FOR THE ANGELS OF HOLINESS ARE WITH THEM.

Unfortunately the scroll is damaged and the passage is ambiguous. On the face of it, Essenes believed the physically sick and infirm were already saved and under the protection of the angels of holiness—they did not need special attention. The disabled and afflicted were better off as they are because they are already saved—why then cure them and lead them into temptation? However, if the coded meaning is read then the scroll is simply stating the obvious—that sinners would not be admitted as Essenes because the angels of holiness were with the community. Wrongdoers had to repent sincerely and then they would no longer be afflicted. We can disregard the angels of holiness being with sinners and the remaining possibility is that the community counted the physically afflicted like sinners as not eligible for the kingdom. If this latter were true and Jesus's cures were a deliberate refutation of it, why are Essenes not explicitly mentioned in the gospels to expose their false position as the Sadducees and Pharisees are? And why do they provide rules for the welfare of the old and sick? We have to conclude that Jesus's healings are not what they appear in the gospels. Healing miracles were code. Jesus was intent on winning over people's hearts but both spiritual and physical sickness were caused by demons and they had to be driven out to effect a cure.

The idea that demons were responsible for moral and physical evil, stemmed from Persian Zoroastrianism. It entered deeply into Jewish thought from the time of the Babylonian exile. Azazel, the fallen angel, had corrupted the earth and was responsible for all sin. Mastery over devils depended on mastery of an arcane art known only to a few. Noah and Solomon were two who had mastery over these secrets. The Essenes, for whom Noah and Solomon were counted among the righteous, and the Therapeutae in Egypt were also adepts. Traditions alien to the Christian tradition paint Jesus as a sorcerer and stories like this in Mark do much to confirm that he did indeed use techniques of sorcery.

Before and since the gospel period, not least by Christians, beatings have been used ostensibly to drive out demons but in practice to punish or silence. Evidently it happened here. It works very well. Whether you are outspoken because you have a devil or not, driving it out will make you consider your words more carefully. The clergy say the demons responsible for illness and uncleanness were supernatural enemies of God which Jesus had to drive out. They were the same to the Nazarenes—enemies, albeit not supernatural ones, who tacitly or flagrantly supported the foreign rulers of the land—God's land. They also disapproved of messianists who had caused a lot of trouble over the years by proclaiming a Jewish kingdom—as Jesus wanted to do. Once you accept that Jesus was intent on liberating God's land, it immediately becomes clear why these people had to be silenced—the unclean spirits of opposition had to be driven out.

Jesus's fame as a king, one who spoke with authority, spread. The crowd plainly recognized this but unlike the unclean spirits they were not appalled by the idea. Jesus is not declared a king except by his enemies. His friends use scriptural code—

the circumlocution that he spoke with authority or power, meaning, for those that had ears to hear—not gentiles who did not know the scriptures—that he was a king.

When Mark writes that Jesus was teaching not as the scribes he is virtually admitting that he was an Essene or a Zealot. The scribes were mainly Pharisees. Most of the priests were Sadducees who had little philosophy other than the atoning sacrifices of temple worship and would never have spoken against the status quo with which they were entirely satisfied. Of Josephus's four philosophies of the Jews, only the Essenes and the Zealots are left. From the Qumran literature the Essenes were fanatics for the establishment of the kingdom of God on earth—from Josephus the Zealots also were fanatics for the kingdom of God on earth, and actually fought for it. The gospels tell us that Jesus opposed scribes, Pharisees, priests and Sadducees but taught of the imminence of God's kingdom. He was an Essene and a Zealot.

Though Jesus is often teaching in Mark, the author tells us little about the doctrine. It seems Mark still expected the apocalypse—gentile converts were led to believe that the judgement day was at hand—still! Thus the content of the teaching was unimportant. Furthermore the teaching might have been too Jewish for the gentiles of Rome, AD 70. The earliest gentile converts would generally have known little about the Jewish religion and would not have had the scriptures at hand. The apostle to the gentiles, Paul, was not interested in the work of Jesus, only his death and resurrection. Mark, or his subsequent editors, was a Paulinist despite the tradition which associates him with Peter. Mark had to explain Jewish habits where they inevitably arose but his main object must have been to keep the message simple. A few decades later the very interest created by the earlier Christians in Jewish tradition would have opened up the market for longer and more Jewish accounts like Luke and Matthew respectively.

This incident is better placed later in the narrative because Jesus would have had to have a reliable set of disciples before he could be as bold as this.

Capernaum.

Capernaum is considered to be the town where Jesus did his main work of preaching. Indeed, there are suggestions in the gospels that Capernaum was his home town. It is an important centre in the gospels; a customs post in Matthew 9:9, a garrison town in Matthew 8:5, and a place where noblemen live in John 4:46. Yet Josephus wrote that Capernaum was insignificant.

In a biblical atlas Capernaum is boldly marked near the Sea of Galilee, but the truth is that no one knows where Jesus's Capernaum was. Franciscan monks have excavated a mound and found a third century synagogue which they claim is the one described in 385 AD as being at Capernaum, but the only evidence is that it was approached by many steps. The excavations revealed four steps at one end of a verandah and fourteen at the other. Is that many? In any case was the Capernaum of 385 AD the Capernaum of Jesus? If Josephus was wrong and Capernaum was a town and not just a spring then it was laid waste early enough to be recorded thus in Matthew 11:23. If it existed in 385 AD it must have been rebuilt after Matthew had written his gospel and later destroyed again so thoroughly that it was lost for another 1520 years. It is easier to believes that Josephus was right—Capernaum was always insignificant, Matthew couldn't find it and assumed it had been laid waste and the Capernaum of 385 AD was probably a suitable site newly named, as Nazareth was, when pilgrims found it did not exist.

On examining the meaning of the word Capernaum we find that it does not simply mean village of Nahum as commentators claim but has a suspiciously appropriate meaning.

Kapar occurs frequently in the Jewish scriptures. It relates to kippur meaning atonement, as in the name of the Jewish holiday yom kippur, day of atonement, the only day of the year when the high priest could enter into the presence of God in the holy of holies to make atonement for the people of Israel. Literally it means covering, but figuratively it means covering with the blood of a sacrifice to atone for a sin—from the ritual of sprinkling the sacrificial blood by the priest in atonement for a sin. The physical life of the sacrificial animal was required in exchange for the spritual life of the worshipper—an innocent life given for a guilty life!

Naum is *nahum* denoting a change of the heart or of purpose. It is found in scriptural proper names such as Nehemiah, Nahum, and Menehem. Nahum is often translated as to repent, but meaning God's repentance not man's. God repents—or relents as in Jeremiah 18:8:

> If that nation, against whom I have pronounced, turn from their evil, I will repent
> of the evil that I thought to do unto them.

God often only repented because His chosen had repented or a prophet had interceded on their behalf. Moses (Exod. 32:12) pleaded: *Turn from thy fierce wrath, and repent of this evil against thy people.* Nahum also means to comfort or to be comforted—a word well known to every pious Jew living in exile as he recalled the words of Isaiah 40:1: *Comfort ye, comfort ye my people.* God indicated that He would comfort Jerusalem with the restoration of Israel, as a mother comforts her offspring (Isa. 66:13). As a noun it means compassion.

Thus the connotation of the word Capernaum is that God will repent or show compassion for His people through an atoning sacrifice. John's gospel seems to identify the Jesus of the parousia with a comforter, evidently drawing upon the idea of the atoning sacrifice of Jesus making him a comforter from God. So by one of those miraculous coincidences of the gospels, the man who is a sacrifice to induce God's repentance, carries out his ministry in a place called God will show compassion for His people through an atoning sacrifice! Now if this is intended as evidence of God's plan, one wonders why it is never observed upon. Possibly it is because rational people would see in it not a real place but a poetic choice of name by the gospel writer.

Capernaum has either been given a spiritual or religious name by the evangelists or it is a holy name for some place of special note to the Essenes. If it is the same as the Capernaum described by Josephus as a spring, it seems fairly safe to assume it was a place chosen by Essenes for preaching to the simple of Ephraim and baptizing those who repented. In the Community Rule, the elect had to atone for the land and pay the wicked their due. By so doing they invited God's repentance of the evil Israel suffered.

However since Matthew tells us that Capernaum no longer existed—it had gone down unto Hades—it seems possible that Capernaum was really a coded name for Jerusalem which had been destroyed by the Romans.

Mark 1:21 – 1:28 Restored

And his fame spread abroad throughout all the region. And Jesus went about teaching in synagogues and preaching the gospel of the coming kingdom. Again Jesus came with his disciples to Capernaum and preached in the synagogue. Now there was a man who feared the retribution of the authorities who called out: *Let us alone, Jesus the Nazarene! You will destroy us all. Thou art the messiah, come to drive out the sons of Seth.* But Jesus halted him commanding: *Be silent! The spirit of Belial possesses thee. Let it be driven out.* And the disciples beat him sorely until the perverse spirit left him, and badly torn he cried: *Enough.* And they were all amazed, questioning among themselves: *What thing is this that the perverse spirit called him? For with authority and power he commandeth.* And His fame spread. And great multitudes gathered together unto him. And a large number of people followed him and many came from Judaea and the other side of the Jordan and even from Tyre and Sidon when they heard of his teaching of the kingdom.

Simon's Mother in Law

Mark 1:29 – 1:31

1:29 And forthwith, when they were come out of the synagogue, they entered into the house of Simon and Andrew, with James and John. 1:30 But Simon's wife's mother lay sick of a fever, and anon they tell him of her. 1:31 And he came and took her by the hand, and lifted her up; and immediately the fever left her, and she ministered unto them.

Simon's Mother in Law

The band repare to Simon and Andrew's house where Jesus lifts a fever from Simon's wife's mother. According to Luke 4:39 Jesus rebuked the fever. Though initially skeptical (having a fever) she becomes a convert to the Nazarene cause and she ministered to them. This vignette explains perfectly the code of illness meaning opposition. Plainly the mother in law would have been distraught at her daughter's husband leaving to join a band of militants. She would have opposed the whole

117

scheme vehemently but, like Gorky's mother, she was won over and joined them in the end.

In restoring the passage, we can use the scrolls to explain the Essene code of sickness and its relevance to the coming visitation.

Mark 1:29 to 1:31 Restored

Jesus repared to the house of his new disciple Simon, with Andrew and James and John, to offer the repentant the sacred meal of bread and new wine. But Simon's wife's mother would do naught for them for she was sick out of fear. And speaking to them Jesus said: *When Hezekiah, the king, was sick unto death, he wept and prayed to the Lord: I have walked before thee in truth and with a perfect heart, and have done that which is good in thy sight. And the Lord heard his prayer and said: I will add unto thy days fifteen years. And I will deliver thee and this city out of the hand of the king of Assyria. For God hath created man to govern the world, and has appointed for him two spirits in which to walk until the time of His visitation, the spirits of truth and deceit. For all who walk in the spirit of truth, it shall be healing, a long life and fruitfulness; but for all who walk in the spirit of deceit it shall be blindness of eye and dullness of ear and stubbornness of heart, All who walk in this spirit shall suffer a multitude of plagues and everlasting damnation by the avenging wrath of the fury of God. But God has ordained an end of deceit and at the time of the visitation He shall destroy it forever.* And he came and took her by the hand and rebuked her for her trembling knees, and did tell her privily that the Lord was as a fortified wall and as an iron bar against all destroyers for He would lead His elect in the way of everlasting life and in His paths. And the fever of fear left her; and she arose and ministered unto them.

Making Converts

Mark 1:32 – 1:34

1:32 And at even, when the sun did set, they brought unto him all that were diseased, and them that were possessed with devils. 1:33 And all the city was gathered together at the door. 1:34 And he healed many that were sick of divers diseases, and cast out many devils; and suffered not the devils to speak, because they knew him.

Making Converts

Mark 1:32–39 uses the sickness convention to show that Jesus travelled widely to proclaim his message, meeting however only after sunset so as not to attract the attention of the authorities, and casting out demons—the despair, defeatism and spiritual emptiness of a defeated people. It works! The kingdom is coming! People flock to join the band, and doubters who were ill or possessed by demons are won over. Luke 4:41 reads:

> And devils also came out of many, crying out, and saying, Thou art Christ the Son of God. And he rebuking them suffered them not to speak: for they knew that he was Christ.

The disciples gave those with devils a beating so that they cried out, and subsequently kept quiet about the messianic mission. All are urged to secrecy (Mk 1:34) so as not to arouse the suspicions of the authorities. This remarkable activity all in one evening is Mark's poetic licence. It signifies activity in gaining recruits and silencing opponents over some time. Mark introduces summarizing paragraphs like this occasionally.

Mark 1:32 to 1:34 Restored

> And Jesus travelled through the countryside and villages speaking to them at even, when the sun did set lest the authorities did hear of it. And they that sought the kingdom brought unto him all that dispaired of it, and some that hated it, those blind and dumb and diseased, and those possessed with devils. And all gathered together and he healed many that were sick of divers diseases, and cast out many devils that hated God's kingdom; and suffered not the devils to speak, because they knew him as the prince.

Retreat to a Lonely Place

Mark 1:35 – 1:39

> 1:35 And in the morning, rising up a great while before day, he went out, and departed into a solitary place, and there prayed. 1:36 And Simon and they that were with him followed after him. 1:37 And when they had found him, they said unto him, All men seek for thee. 1:38 And he said unto them, Let us go into the next towns, that I may preach there also: for therefore came I forth. 1:39 And he preached in their synagogues throughout all Galilee, and cast out devils.

Retreat to a Lonely Place

In these verses Jesus gets up in the night and goes to a lonely place—Luke 4:42 calls it a desert place—where his disciples have to find him. In the Greek their following him is not welcomed because the word used implies enmity or harassment. Plainly Jesus is escaping from someone or something and in hiding—we are told: *all men seek for thee*. The word used for seek in verse 37 also implies harassment and is so used elsewhere in Mark. Following as it does the mass healing the impression is that Jesus is in demand because he is popular but his evidently furtive behaviour belies it. Whoever is seeking him does so to persecute him.

119

Also belying it is the detail that Jesus was praying. A Christian might expect God's Son to pray but on the other two occasions when Jesus is described as praying in Mark's gospel, it is because he is under stress. The furtive escape suggests that the pattern is true here also. It is likely that this pericope is misplaced and should follow one in which Jesus is exposed so that Herod's police get on his tail, such as the next one about the leper who betrays him. He decides to move on, in Mark to continue his preaching elsewhere but in fact because discretion is the better part of valour.

Towns here is correctly rendered villages confirming the obvious truth that Jesus is of the barjonim, the outsiders—those who deliberately avoided towns and cities.

Mark 1:35 to 1:39 Restored

And in the night, rising up a great while before day, he went out, and escaped into a solitary place, and there prayed for he was sore afraid. And Simon and they that were with him followed him. And when they found him, they said unto him: *They seek thee everywhere.* And he said unto them: *Let us go away into another part, that I might start afresh: for therefore came I forth.* And they escaped into another part.

A Leper

Mark 1:40 – 1:45

1:40 And there came a leper to him, beseeching him, and kneeling down to him, and saying unto him, If thou wilt, thou canst make me clean. 1:41 And Jesus, moved with pity, put forth his hand, and touched him, and saith unto him, I will; be thou clean. 1:42 And as soon as he had spoken, immediately the leprosy departed from him, and he was cleansed. 1:43 And he straitly charged him, and forthwith sent him away; 1:44 And saith unto him, See thou say nothing to any man: but go thy way, shew thyself to the priest, and offer for thy cleansing those things which Moses commanded, for a testimony unto them. 1:45 But he went out, and began to publish it much, and to blaze abroad the matter, insomuch that Jesus could no more openly enter into the city, but was without in desert places: and they came to him from every quarter.

A Leper

Jesus cures a leper telling him to offer in the temple what Moses prescribed for his cleansing—a strange thing for someone to suggest who, the clergy tell us, abrogated the law of Moses.

Leprosy was a new and most feared illness—it had only arrived in Israel about a hundred years before (the leprosy of the Old Testament being a general term for a variety of ugly skin diseases like ring worm and psoriasis)—and, of course, was incurable making this a remarkable miracle. The corresponding passage to this in

Luke 1:40–45 says it took place in a *certain city* and the passage above from Mark implies it was in a city because afterwards Jesus could no more openly enter the city. But a leper had to avoid human habitation and had to live in the desert, calling out *unclean, unclean* if anyone approached—they were not allowed into cities. This proves that the leper here was no leper in a medical sense or that these cities were not cities.

Luke has leper behaviour right in Luke 17:12 where the ten lepers stay at a distance and call out to Jesus to cure them, but the story of the ten lepers is a Christian invention not Nazarene tradition, the point of it not being the cure but the ingratitude of the nine Jews who were cured compared with the Samaritan—it is another version of the parable of the good Samaritan. Both only appear in Luke and their aim is to discredit Jews while hyping up gentiles (represented by the Samaritans). The myth of Jesus was also growing in stature so the earlier cure of just one leper seemed insufficient for Luke.

The symbolism in Mark's cure is that the man had not been cured. Jesus had warned him you are not to say a word to anybody but the new convert exposes him—he will not be cowed. Consequently Jesus could not enter any town openly but stayed outside in desert (that is, lonely) places (Mk 1:45) hiding not from his own supporters but from Herod's soldiers who came to him from every quarter. In Luke 5:16 Jesus prayed in the lonely place. The occasion is obviously that described previously, but here the behaviour is linked explicitly to Jesus being exposed by the leper.

The towns Jesus frequented are only hamlets and villages anyway so he is obviously seeking refuge in the hills as a guerrilla. He is one of the barjonim. He dared not be known openly making his claims and gaining his recruits. He tells all his recruits to keep quiet, is cautious enough to hide in the hills when needed and has to keep to the hills when one of his converts fails to keep quiet. From the beginning he was a semi-outlaw and Mark makes this absolutely plain. By speaking with authority he was challenging the authorities and even though he did not claim to be the messiah at this stage, those who had ears to hear knew what it was all about. Jesus insists that they keep it to themselves until the time is right.

Many manuscripts say almost the opposite of moved with pity in verse 41— they say moved with anger. All three synoptics follow Mark in having Jesus effect his cure by putting forth his hand and touching him—a euphemism for hitting him. The scriptural usage of putting forth a hand or stretching out a hand frequently means to kill or destroy. And both of the verbs in verse 43 are too weak. The verb for sent away in the Greek is the same as the verb drove out used of demons. Straitly charged is better translated as angrily commanded, matching the codices that describe Jesus as being angry. It seems that the leper is like the first unclean spirit met by Jesus, a fanatical opponent and Jesus and his disciples treat him similarly. The man however takes his revenge by exposing Jesus.

In the light of the later pericope of Simon the leper, it seems that a leper is Nazarene code for a high priest of the unclean Jerusalem temple. It probably stems from the detailed instructions in Leviticus 13:1–14:57 for the diagnosis, treatment and ritual cleansing of leprosy which had to be done by the priests. The Essenes permitted Levites to carry out certain priestly functions but in the Damascus Rule specifically exclude them from applying the law of leprosy. Since only priests could handle leprosy cases and the Jerusalem high priests were as unclean as their polluted temple, priests—particularly high priests—were lepers.

Mark 1:40 to 1:45 Restored

A man came to Jesus calling out and decrying him, for he was a leper, a high priest of the temple. And Jesus, moved with anger, put forth his hand and smote him, and they set their hands upon him, until he was beseeching him, and kneeling down to him. And he was cleansed. And Jesus took him and angrily ordered him: *Go seekest thou God with all thine heart and soul; repent and doest that which is good and right before Him as He commanded by the hand of Moses. And sayest thou nothing to any man, lest thy demon trip thee.* And forthwith he sent him away. But he walketh in the way of deceit, and goeth out and telleth the authorities, and blazeth abroad the matter, insomuch that Jesus could no more openly enter the city for fear of the authorities, for the towns were unsafe, and soldiers sought them; and they were without, in desert places.

A Palsied Man

Mark 2:1 – 1:12

2:1 And again he entered into Capernaum after some days; and it was noised that he was in the house. 2:2 And straightway many were gathered together, insomuch that there was no room to receive them, no, not so much as about the door: and he preached the word unto them. 2:3 And they come unto him, bringing one sick of the palsy, which was borne of four. 2:4 And when they could not come nigh unto him for the press, they uncovered the roof where he was: and when they had broken it up, they let down the bed wherein the sick of the palsy lay. 2:5 When Jesus saw their faith, he said unto the sick of the palsy, Son, thy sins be forgiven thee. 2:6 But there was certain of the scribes sitting there, and reasoning in their hearts, 2:7 Why doth this man thus speak blasphemies? who can forgive sins but God only? 2:8 And immediately when Jesus perceived in his spirit that they so reasoned within themselves, he said unto them, Why reason ye these things in your hearts? 2:9 Whether is it easier to say to the sick of the palsy, Thy sins be forgiven thee; or to say, Arise, and take up thy bed, and walk? 2:10 But that ye may know that the Son of man hath power on earth to forgive sins, he saith to the sick of the palsy, 2:11 I say unto thee, Arise, and take up thy bed, and go thy way into thine house. 2:12 And immediately he arose, took up the bed, and went forth before them all; insomuch that they were all amazed, and glorified God, saying, We never saw it on this fashion.

A Palsied Man

In chapter 2 Mark introduces the conflicts with the Pharisees, casting some doubt on its veracity. Jesus's ministry is entirely peaceful and worthy, filled with healings, miracles and the driving out of demons, yet he finished up crucified. Here is a problem for the gospel writer which Mark begins to solve in Chapter 2 (2:1–3:6) by showing that he was set up by the Pharisees who did not like him, though the ordinary folk did. The alert reader will however have noticed that when Pilate offers to release Barabbas or Jesus at the climax of the story, it is the crowd of ordinary folk who choose the robber for release not Jesus. It is all contrived.

In this chapter Mark puts five anti-Pharisee stories together to make his case. They must be inserted because Jesus is not anxious to keep his messianic secret as he is in chapters 1 and 3, rather assuming the mantle of messiah and the emphasis on unclean spirits in 1 and 3 is missing. Possibly Mark in an earlier draft put the stories together as a later chapter, perhaps preceding the passion narrative, and then he or an editor decided to bring the opposition out early in the story and so moved them forward.

This chapter logically ends at 3:6 with the Pharisees and the Herodians plotting together, an unlikely combination. It opens with another conversion allegorized as a paralysed man on a pallet let down through the roof into Jesus's presence. Plainly this pericope does not logically follow the previous one because Jesus is back in Capernaum, evidently a dangerous place to be. It should perhaps be earlier in the narrative.

The different afflictions might have different political meanings and in this context the palsied man was a bad sinner from the Essene standpoint—like the leper, a Sadducee. This is signified by the pallet which was used to lift the village priest to a roof from which he would offer prayers to God. Essenes, who considered themselves to be priests, prayed at dawn as if in supplication to the rising sun and in Acts 10:9 the apostle Peter goes up onto a housetop at dawn to pray. He is behaving as an Essene and therefore as a priest. In the story in the next two verses of Mark, Levi, suggesting a priest, is recruited—surely the same man.

The Greek words used here are paraluo and paralutikos, compound words made up of the preposition para, meaning near, and words which mean being broken, loosened or enfeebled. I suggest that here the biblical Greek has to be read more literally. Who are those who are breaking or loosening or nearly breaking or loosening and thereby enfeebling the law of Moses? The answer is the Hellenized priests. The metaphor is strengthened by the implication of their nearly breaking down the partition wall in the temple which separated the court of the gentiles from the holy parts of the temple. They were keen to relax age old distinction between Jews and gentiles to bring in more wealth. Since the Essenes were sticklers for this distinction—foreigners had to become Jews before they were accepted into the order—the collaborationist Sadducees could hardly be expected to be welcomed into the Nazarene band of insurrectionists. But Jesus, again demonstrating his authority—all Jews were God's people—forgives his sins, meaning he offered him the chance of repentance thus allowing him into the Nazarene movement. We may assume that the faith spoken of in verse 5 meant genuine belief in the coming kingdom which would allow the palsied man to join the elect upon receiving baptism.

Mark comes to the real point of the story for him. He uses the incident to introduce the dispute between the orthodox Jews (the scribes, lawyers, doctors and Pharisees) and Jesus. Nearby Pharisees say it is blasphemous for a man to forgive sins. It has long been believed that the Jews of the time felt only God could—from Isaiah 43:25—so the dispute, from the orthodox Jewish standpoint is valid. In 2 Samuel 12:13, Nathan forgives David's sin but does so with the authority of God. However in a scroll fragment from Qumran (The Prayer of Nabonidus) we find a gazer, a Jewish healer in captivity in Babylon, forgiving sin. Daniel cures the king, Nabonidus, (Nebuchadnezzar, less correctly in the Book of Daniel, where it is God who does the forgiving) who recalls: *I was afflicted with an evil ulcer for seven years. A gazer pardoned my sins.* This story is important because healing is effected without scandal or blasphemy by forgiveness of sins—among Essenes men could forgive sin. Curing the paralytic, Jesus says: *My son, your sins are forgiven.* Jesus does not blaspheme when he forgives sins because it does not imply that he is divine. Essenes accepted it but not Pharisees though, two centuries later, rabbis agreed that sins had to be forgiven for someone to be cured of an illness.

The forgiveness of sins is on earth because the kingdom expected was to be on earth. If sins could only be forgiven in heaven then there could be no kingdom of God on earth as the Essenes expected. Nevertheless, as Matthew often writes, it would be a kingdom of heaven—a perfect kingdom.

If the anti-Pharisaic verses 6 to 10 are omitted the passage reads better. They have been inserted later to discredit the Pharisees but those who would have been upset by the incident were the man's fellow Sadducees outraged that one of their own should go over. Moreover, the reaction of the scribes to the miracle is not described as would be expected if it were part of the original story. And finally Jesus reads the thoughts of the Pharisees by telepathy in the inserted lines—an editor was giving him god-like abilities.

The expression uncovered the roof is a mistranslation into the Greek of the Aramaic which would have read descended from the roof. Luke 5:19 has, *let him down on his couch.* Uncovered the roof suggests the removal of tiles and Luke states so specifically whereas Palestinian roofs, unless this was a rich man's house, were flat—Jesus was one of the poor and would not have been in a rich man's house. Mark was writing for gentiles who, in the wider Roman Empire, would have been more familiar with tiled roofs. Matthew, writing for Jews, knows that they will connect the scene with a priest praying on a housetop and misses out the lowering from the roof altogether.

In Aramaic son of man either meant man in general, mankind, or it meant I, being a polite circumlocution—this son of man. The clergy took the meaning whenever Jesus used it, as he did often for reasons of modesty, to be the supernatural *one like unto the Son of man* of Daniel's vision (Dan 7:13)—God's redeemer coming on a cloud. The son of man here simply means man in general and not Jesus himself in some supernatural sense. The gospels themselves prove the point. In Mark 8:27 Jesus says: *Who do men say that I am*? In the same passage in Matthew 16:13, we have: *Who do men say that the son of man is*? In Matthew 10:33 the son of man of Luke 9:26 is replaced by I. The expression sons of men occurs in the Master's song of blessing in the Community Rule meaning simply mankind.

Pharisees

The Qumran sectarian documents refer to some of their enemies as Ephraim, builders of the wall and spouters of false things, the latter a play on the words halakhot (religious laws) and halaqot (false things or falsehoods). These are the Pharisees who according to the Talmud held dominance under the Maccabees when they refused to allow the priesthood to return to the Sons of Zadok. The sectarian documents refer to the Sadducees as Manasseh.

Manasseh and Ephraim were the names of the two sons of Joseph blessed by Jacob. Ephraim signifies fertility and Manasseh signifies forgetfulness. The Pharisees' fertility was in creating new, but to the Essene false and spurious, laws and the Sadducees' forgetfulness was over the promise of Solomon to Zadok of the priesthood forever. Furthermore king Manasseh was a reformed idolater and Manasseh in Ezra signified those who had married foreign women, strong hints of Hellenization of the official Priesthood.

The Pharisees were not entirely the men of the people depicted by later rabbinic tradition, though they doubtless had the best interests of the people at heart. The Pharisees had a reputation as surrenderers. In the Qumran writings they were the seekers after smooth things because they took the path of least resistance so that the people would suffer least. Josephus writes that two prominent rabbis, Pollio and Sameas—probably pseudonyms for Hillel and Shammai—convinced the people to surrender to Herod and the Romans in 37 BC. Herod remained forever in the Pharisees' debt. At a later period Josephus says that it was the principal men of the Pharisees, the Chief Priests (Herodian Sadducees) and the men of power (the Herodians) whose intermediary was a mystery man called Saul, who invited the Romans into Jerusalem to put down the uprising in 66 AD. The Pharisees, Josephus himself and Tiberius Alexander, Philo's nephew, supervised the destruction of the city. Pharisees were pragmatists but did not endear themselves to the Essenes who were nationalists, nor most of the people who wanted rid of the invaders.

In religious terms Jesus would not have seen the Pharisees as ultra pious as the gospels make out but as ultra-lax. They sought not to address problems posed by the requirements of the law by building a wall around it to prevent anyone transgressing it inadvertently. (There might be an implication that Essenes considered Pharisees responsible for the partition wall in the temple, which Essenes considered an offence because gentiles should not be there at all unless they came in supplication.) For Jesus this would have been avoiding the issue because he regarded the law itself, being God given, as sacrosanct and not needing protection. The requirements of the law had to be addressed directly and not hidden behind walls to disguise or protect them. God intended them not to be broken but, if He had provided exceptions for special circumstances, His prophets would have written sound precedents in the scriptures to justify it. Pharisees would have seen Jesus as a fundamentalist.

Jesus would certainly have regarded Pharisees as hypocrites—his favourite word for them. Pharisees professed to be against the foreigner but, being pragmatic about it, to a nationalist they seemed hypocritical. Some Pharisees were fed up with madmen claiming to be messianic leaders. Like any other Jew Pharisees hoped for a messiah but too many mountebanks had failed to do anything except stir up trouble with the Romans. Some Pharisees might have thought of Jesus as another madman they should discredit before he caused trouble, but they tended to be cautious, not knowing how God might reveal himself. They dared not take peremptory action for fear of offending God (Acts 5:38–39).

The main enemies of Jesus were the priests and their supporters, the collaborating Sadducees, rather than the Pharisees as the gospels try to make out, though Jesus would have willingly criticized the latter too. It was the High Priest who held the initial hearing into Jesus's crimes; they were the ones who stood to lose if an uprising were successful and they did not like the idea of inviting Roman antagonism even if it were not. After the fall of Jerusalem the temple no longer existed and therefore the Sadducees had lost their raison d'etre. Judaism survived through the Pharisees. The Pharisees therefore became the targets in the Christian gospels.

Mark 2:1 to 2:12 Restored

And as Jesus spake the word to his disciples four men passed down a pallet on which lay an enfeebler of the law, and a profaner of the House of God, for he was Matthew the Levite, a tax collector, a Sadducee, who had been praying on a housetop. Recognizing him Jesus said: *Saith the Lord: if ye turn away from following me then will I cut off Israel out of the land which I have given them and this house, which I have hallowed for my name, will I cast out of my sight; and though this house be never so high yet shall everyone that passeth by it hiss for they forsook the Lord, their God. Yet if my people which are called by my name, shall humble themselves, and pray and seek my face, and turn from their wicked ways then will I hear their prayers in heaven and will forgive their sins and will heal their land. Repent, Levite, discard your pallet and rise.* And the enfeebler of the law was overcome with shame, smiting his breast and calling out: *God be merciful to me, a sinner*; and he was healed of his polluted spirit. He cast aside his pallet and was received by the righteous. At this they were all amazed and glorified God, saying: *We never saw anything like it.* But the

Sadducees were filled with fear for many of their number heard of it also and repented to follow after Matthew.

Levi is Recruited

Mark 2:13 – 2:14

> 2:13 And he went forth again by the sea side; and all the multitude resorted unto him, and he taught them. 2:14 And as he passed by, he saw Levi the son of Alphaeus sitting at the receipt of custom, and said unto him, Follow me. And he arose and followed him.

Levi is Recruited

This two verse pericope tells of the recruitment of Levi, the tax-collector. It mirrors the recruitment of the earlier apostles by the Sea of Galilee, the command by Jesus being obeyed hypnotically by the disciple. We can conclude that it is written thus for harmony and it was not the real recruitment of Levi, which we take to have been the incident of the paralytic. It is added here to provide an explicit link to the next story which is about Jesus dining with sinners because Levi in the previous pericope was depicted as a physical paralytic and so could not have also held down a responsible job. In reality he could well have been a tax collector because his paralysis was metaphorical.

A tax collector here is a customs official collecting duty for Herod Antipas. (If we are in Judaea he is collecting tribute.) Coin was unclean and Levi was therefore a Herodian or a Sadduccee and therefore not well regarded by the Jews in general and the Pharisees and Essenes in particular. Tax collectors were dishonest, keeping a proportion of the taxes collected for themselves and extorting money from people. Someone like Levi must have been regarded as the lowest of the low and certainly, as a collaborator with the foreign ruler, an impossible man to recruit for the Jewish nationalist cause. Whence his paralysis in the previous story.

Each of the three references to tax collectors (or publicans) and sinners in the next story originally read simply sinners but *tax collectors and* has been added to link the two pericopes together.

Mark 2:13 to 2:14 Restored

No restoration is needed. Even if Levi and the paralytic are different men we do not need Levi to be the focus of the next story when we have the converted paralytic, Matthew.

Eating with Publicans and Sinners

Mark 2:15 – 2:17

> 2:15 And it came to pass, that, as Jesus sat at meat in his house, many publicans and sinners sat also together with Jesus and his disciples: for there were many, and they followed him. 2:16 And when the scribes and Pharisees saw him eat with publicans and sinners, they said unto his disciples, How is it that he eateth and drinketh with publicans and sinners? 2:17 When Jesus heard it, he saith unto them, They that are whole have no need of the physician, but they that are sick: I came not to call the righteous, but sinners to repentance.

Eating with Publicans and Sinners

Mark has placed this episode after the recruitment of Levi to make it sound as if Jesus went to dinner with the tax-collector. In fact this is a messianic meal for his converts. Jesus explains: *I have not come to call the righteous but sinners.* In the corresponding part of Matthew 9:13 Jesus adds: *I will have mercy and not sacrifice*, quoting Hosea 6:6: *For I desired mercy, and not sacrifice; and the knowledge of God more than burnt offerings*, as if to demonstrate that he was an Essene for whom this and Proverbs 15:8 express their beliefs: *The sacrifice of the wicked is an abomination to the Lord: but the prayer of the upright is his delight*, a quotation which appears several times in the scrolls. Matthew repeats the quotation from Hosea later (Mt 12:7). Jesus's answer is not given in full making it sound like a non sequitur. Some of the repentant, possibly Sadducees, wanted to know why the sinners were not offering a suitable sacrifice of purification—a sin offering—rather than having a simple meal.

Taxgatherers were agents of the High Priest, supporters of the Sadducee party of collaborators with the Herodians and the Roman rulers of Judaea. They were among the most hated people in the land yet Jesus, the prospective leader of God's revolution was dining with them and evidently urging them to join the Nazarenes. The sinners were ordinary Jews, the men of the land, who were not fastidiously observant of the law of Moses, and perhaps also those who were influenced by Greek culture and fashions.

Pharisees shunned such people. Pious Jews in general did not consort with the impious. Essenes and Pharisees alike felt this way in particular because both regarded themselves as separated out. For Jesus impenitent publicans were just as bad as the gentiles (in Matthew 18:17, he equates the two), but they were still God's chosen and therefore worth saving. When C G Montefiore, a Jewish scholar, wrote: *He did not avoid sinners, but sought them out—they were still children of God*, he expressed the sentiment of the Nazarene militants led by Jesus and before him by John, but these sinners had to repent and be baptized to be accepted by the Nazarenes—they could not continue their sinful work. Levi and the publicans and sinners in this episode *had* repented and *had* been baptized into God's army. The meat they were eating was the bread and wine of the messianic meal of the Essenes which signified acceptance among the elect of God.

Jesus's reply fully and concisely expresses the Nazarene attitude to the sinners of the children of Israel and it is expressed in a way which perfectly explains the healing miracles as metaphors for those who have repented of their sins. They are healed metaphorically and the physical sicknesses which are healed are really spiritual sicknesses. By winning over some of the opposition your foes are weakened and your own cause is strengthened. Jesus's mission was to win over the lost sheep of the house of Israel. He wanted as many people among the elect as he could get both to save the lost sheep and to succeed in establishing God's kingdom. Although it is absent in Mark and placed in different parts of the other gospels (Mt 18:11–14; Lk 15:1–10), the parable of the lost sheep should be placed here: the shepherd rejoices when he finds the one sheep that had strayed of his flock of a hundred. The ninety nine which did not stray are *the righteous*. They are already in the fold. Luke attaches to his version an equivalent parable, that of the woman who lost one of her ten pieces of silver and sought it diligently until it was found.

The righteous are the elect—the Essenes, who are already saved and will enter the kingdom. There is no need to convert them—they already are prepared. Jesus wanted to save some of those—as many as possible—who were heading for the fires of Gehenna. They were children of God and they were potential fighters for the kingdom in the coming struggle. God would win the war but the immediate battle had first to be won and that needed soldiers—Jews who had repented their sins and were ready to fight for God's cause.

Luke elsewhere (19:1–10) tries to indicate that Jesus was forgiving the sins of those who continued in the sinful way of collaboration, with his story about Zacchaeus the head of taxgatherers in Jericho, which interpreted correctly has quite a different meaning from that related. Zacchaeus is observing Jesus from a sycomore, a Pharaoh's fig-tree. The fig-tree in the gospels is a symbol for Rome—Zacchaeus had climbed high in the service of the oppressors. Jesus invites himself to the house of this very rich publican and gives him salvation simply for giving half his goods to the poor and offering reparations to those he has robbed. Yet half was insufficient—it had to be *all* as Luke himself had already told us (18:21)—and so it remained after the crucifixion—that was still the rule in the Acts of the Apostles. The watering down of the ordinances of the original Jerusalem church is demonstrated here clearly in Luke. The aim was to make Jesus seem tolerant of the friends of Rome and to make Christianity acceptable to rich gentiles in the wider Empire. The story is made into a rehash of the recruitment of Levi.

The scribes and the Pharisees could not have been present in the house with these sinners so one looks at this phrase with suspicion. In reality we can see here dissension in the camp of the Nazarenes. Jesus is recruiting lots of Hellenized Jews, people who were despised by more orthodox Jews. Yet some of Jesus's followers were orthodox Jews. It is these who question the attention Jesus is paying to the sinners. Thus the question comes to Jesus from members of his own party not from the Pharisaic party. Later it was changed to conform with Christian vilification of Judaism.

Mark 2:15 to 2:17 Restored

Now when he admitted the Levite to the sacred meal of bread and new wine at his house some of his disciples said: *How is it that he eateth and drinketh with publicans who are the worst sinners?* Hearing this Jesus said: *They that are whole have no need of a doctor, but they that are sick. They that are full have no need of bread, but they that hunger. I come not to call the righteous but sinners to repentance. Saith the Lord: My people have been lost sheep; their shepherds have caused them to go astray.* And he spake unto them a parable, saying: *What man of you, having a hundred sheep, and having lost one of them, doth not leave the ninety and nine in the fold and go after that which is lost, until he find it? And when he hath found it, he layeth it on his shoulders rejoicing. And when he cometh home, he calleth together his friends and neighbours, saying unto them, Rejoice with me, for I have found my sheep which was lost. Likewise there shall be joy in heaven over one sinner that repenteth, more than over ninety and nine of God's righteous which need no repentance. To the lost sheep of the house of Israel this son of man is called and today hath one who was lost been found.*

The Bridegroom and Fasting

Mark 2:18 – 2:20

2:18 And the disciples of John and of the Pharisees used to fast: and they come and say unto him, Why do the disciples of John and of the Pharisees fast, but thy disciples fast not? 2:19 And Jesus said unto them, Can the children of the bridechamber fast, while the bridegroom is with them? as long as they have the bridegroom with them, they cannot fast. 2:20 But the days will come, when the bridegroom shall be taken away from them, and then shall they fast in those days.

The Bridegroom and Fasting

Jesus would not have been so impious as to ignore a fast unless there were a strong reason for it or unless it never happened at all because it was a parable not an actual event. In Jewish tradition the bridegroom is God and the bride or the children of the bridechamber are the children of Israel. God and Israel are betrothed. So Hosea 2:18–20:

And in that day will I make a covenant for them... and I will break the bow and the sword and the battle out of the earth, and will make them to lie down safely. And I will betroth thee unto me for ever; yea, I will betroth thee unto me in righteousness, and in judgment, and in lovingkindness, and in mercies. I will even betroth thee unto me in faithfulness: and thou shalt know the Lord.

And Isaiah (Isa 62:5):

> ...as the bridegroom rejoiceth over the bride, so shall thy God rejoice over thee.

All gospel references to weddings are references to the kingdom to come when God as the bridegroom unites with Israel as the bride. God not Jesus is the bridegroom. The change was effected to make the Son into God.

This is a distorted kingdom parable. In Jewish tradition the bride and bridegroom fast until the solemnizing of their marital promises when the fast is lifted for the wedding feast. In other words the bride (the children) enters the house (the kingdom) of the bridegroom (God). The fast which went before is broken and the joyous wedding feast (messianic meal) begins. In this case Jesus was not recommending that Jews should not fast but giving an analogy between the kingdom and the feast after the wedding fast. Jesus would have used it in this sense implying that there was cause for rejoicing because God was with the elect and they would soon be entering His kingdom. This has been distorted into Jesus feasting when others fasted.

But this and the two mini-parables which follow might also be part of a discussion about the temple related to the promise to raise up the temple in three days. The point is that there is a minor Jewish fast on the 9 Ab mourning the destruction of the temple. The date is that of the end of services in Herod's temple in 70 AD but originally there was a fast mourning the end of Solomon's temple in 586 BC. In the preceding three weeks no marriages are celebrated. When the fast is broken, marriages can again occur and wedding festivities be celebrated.

The Christian interpretation of this mishmash is that Jesus the Christ has stopped the need for absurd duties like fasting, yet immediately he seems to say there will be a time when it is appropriate—when he is killed—even though his death is the very climax of God's plan to redeem mankind. If Jesus died on the cross as part of God's plan to atone for mankind's sins as the clergy would have us believe then the crucifixion was no occasion for fasting! Verse 2:20 has been interpolated. This prediction of the death of Jesus is plainly hindsight. Mark was writing around the time of the Jewish War about 40 years after the events of the gospel so he could put words like this into the mouth of Jesus to make him seem to predict his crucifixion, but the addition is illogical.

In fact the early church found that it was doing what the rest of this distorted passage seemed to forbid—Christians were still fasting because Jesus had issued no such directive. The church therefore had to add this line to justify anew the continuation of the practice.

Disciples of John and of the has been added to the Pharisees in this passage because at an early stage some Nazarenes rejected Jesus to follow John the Baptist and the gospel writer wanted to tar them with the Pharisees' brush.

Mark 2:18 to 2:20 Restored

> And it was the fast of the fifth month when pious Jews mourned the destruction of the temple by Nebuchadnezzar singing lamentations. And his

disciples of the simple of Ephraim come and say unto him: *The Pharisees eat not wine nor meat, and wail and confess and repent. Why doest thou say unto us, brake bread and drink wine?* And Jesus said unto them: *God's righteous will enter into His kingdom and feast. Hearken ye to the word of the Lord: I am returned unto Zion and will dwell in the midst of Jerusalem. The kingdom of God is like a bridegroom who is coming to the wedding feast, for it is written: I will betroth thee unto me for ever; yea, I will betroth thee unto me in righteousness, and in judgment, and in lovingkindness, and in mercies. I will even betroth thee unto me in faithfulness: and thou shalt know the Lord. After the fast the wedding feast begins, and the Lord is even now at the door. Can the children of the bridechamber fast, while the bridegroom is without? This bread and new wine is like unto a wedding feast, for when the bridegroom is without, the fast is ended. Those hypocrites fast for the loss of the temple, when God drove Israel into captivity for her sins. But, on the third day of His visitation, the Lord will raise up to the righteous a new temple not built by hands.*

New and Old

Mark 2:21 – 2:22

2:21 No man also seweth a piece of new cloth on an old garment: else the new piece that filled it up taketh away from the old, and the rent is made worse. 2:22 And no man putteth new wine into old bottles: else the new wine doth burst the bottles, and the wine is spilled, and the bottles will be marred: but new wine must be put into new bottles.

New and Old

Both of these sayings seem to be referring to the newness of the Christian religion compared with the oldness of Judaism and emphasising the need to split cleanly with the old in favour of the new. If so it is something added by Mark and not something that Jesus said.

They have to be given their proper context. The linking of these two mini–parables with the verses about marriage and fasting above suggests that Jesus might have been describing in a parable the nature of the kingdom in the context of the destruction of the temple. He is promising that the kingdom will be accompanied by a new temple, whence the two mini-parables, showing that the old priesthood are incompatible with the new one provided by the Essenes. Elsewhere (Mt 26:61) he is accused of threatening to destroy the temple.

Essenes wore their clothes until they were in tatters. For them there could never be a question of patching old clothes. The reason was the Essene aversion to mixing anything, which in turn reflected their view that Jews and gentiles should remain distinct. Note also that it was the Essenes who used unfermented grape juice in their ceremonies, calling it new wine. Unfermented grape juice would begin to ferment in a skin which had contained wine, thus bursting the skin with the gas pressure generated.

Mark 2:21 to 2:22 Restored

No man seweth a piece of new cloth on an old garment: else the clean will be mixed with the unclean contrary to the commandments of God. Better to wear the old until the tailor delivereth the new. And no man putteth new wine into old bottles: else the new wine doth burst the bottles, and the wine is spilled, and the bottles will be marred: but new wine must be put into new bottles, for only thus may the righteous partake of it. If these be what men do, will God do other wise? The Lord will destroy the polluted temple and in three days will raise up for the righteous a holy temple, as the prophet Ezekiel has written.

Plucking on the Sabbath

Mark 2:23 – 2:28

2:23 And it came to pass, that he went through the corn fields on the sabbath day; and his disciples began, as they went, to pluck the ears of corn. 2:24 And the Pharisees said unto him, Behold, why do they on the sabbath day that which is not lawful? 2:25 And he said unto them, Have ye never read what David did, when he had need, and was an hungred, he, and they that were with him? 2:26 How he went into the house of God in the days of Abiathar the high priest, and did eat the shewbread, which is not lawful to eat but for the priests, and gave also to them which were with him? 2:27 And he said unto them, The sabbath was made for man, and not man for the sabbath: 2:28 Therefore the Son of man is Lord also of the sabbath.

Plucking on the Sabbath

This dispute does not have anything to do with the advent of the kingdom. It is entirely practical and involves nothing that any pious Jew would regard as wrong. Deuteronomy 23:25 allows a hungry man to pluck someone else's corn as long as he does not take a sickle to it, and plucking corn could hardly have been considered harvesting to make the act a violation of Exodus 35:21 which defines the sabbath. The questioners therefore could not have been Pharisees who were familiar with the detail not only of the law but also the supplements to the law which they had devised. Nor would Pharisees have been travelling with Jesus especially on a sabbath when only very short journeys from home were permitted.

The questioners must have been members of his own following, but the author of Mark saw another opportunity to illustrate a dispute with orthodoxy and so introduced some non-existent Pharisees. Really they were either ordinary Jewish converts to the Nazarene cause who had sincerely repented and, as Jews, knew some law, but not the detail of it, and who took it to be a violation of the sabbath when Jesus began to pluck the corn. Or followers who were devout village Essenes, expecting the kingdom of god to be inaugurated imminently. Essenes had very strict rules against breaking the sabbath which they observed with fervent rigour.

An Essene was expressly forbidden by the Damascus Rule to eat anything lying in the fields on a sabbath, and he could not walk more than a thousand cubits away from home. He was not allowed to fill a vessel so could only drink away from home whenever he came to free standing water. He could not even lift a child. Nor could he be near a gentile or indeed willingly mingle with any man on a sabbath. Their aim as Essenes was to be perfect, and perhaps even minor infringements of the sabbath distressed them. But the Damascus Rule allowed an exception when a man was in danger of his life. This is the situation Jesus invokes in the incident of the sabbath plucking.

Jesus explained to them the practical justification for his action using the example of David and his men when he was in need and hungry. David entered the temple and handed out the showbread for his followers to eat, a much worse crime. The implication is that Jesus and his disciples were in a similar predicament. They were on the run from Herod's police and plucked the corn out of sheer hunger.

The parallel passage in Matthew 12:1–8 supports this interpretation. There, having given the speech in Mark, Jesus points out that the priests work in the temple on the sabbath handling the sacrifice of two lambs prescribed in Numbers 28:9–10. Then Jesus says: *If ye had known what this meaneth, I will have mercy and not sacrifice, ye would not have condemned the guiltless.* Again he is paraphrasing Hosea 6:6. This tells us that the act of plucking on the sabbath was an act of mercy. It would not have been an act of mercy if the group were taking a Saturday afternoon stroll—it was an act of mercy because the Nazarenes were hungry. The rest of the quotation from Hosea tells us that the band were Essenes. In the Community Rule we find:

WHEN THE LAND IS HONOURED MORE THAN THE FLESH OF THE WHOLE BURNT OFFERINGS AND THE FATS OF SACRIFICE...

The Essenes were more interested in securing God's country than in the polluted temple worship of the Sadducees.

The verbal formula, *and he said to them*, in Mark is used to link independent sayings. We conclude that the final verses were originally independent of the earlier ones. The Pharisees had a similar teaching to *the sabbath was made for man and not man for the sabbath*, which has come to us in the rabbinical writings: *the sabbath is given unto you and not you to the sabbath*. It was a common Jewish sentiment of the time. This saying is omitted in Matthew and Luke leaving the apparent assertion of the authority of the Son of man over the sabbath. They left out the commonplace saying to leave the emphasis on Jesus's apparent messianic claim.

134

Here the expression the son of man simply means man, but Mark uses it as if it meant Daniel's Son of man. It can only have had the first sense because Jesus gave a legal justification for his action—a justification that a messiah would not have needed. Since the two final verses mean the same thing it is possible that Mark knew of two versions of the story one of which ended with the matter of fact verse 28 whereas the other ended with the more proverbial 27. Mark saw the chance to combine them both with the implication for the ignorant that Jesus was claiming messianic authority. Note that all of these apparent claims to be the messiah belie the theory of the messianic secret proving that these conflicts are at least misplaced.

Have ye never read, is the very way that any Jewish teacher would introduce his answer or argument. He would quote from scripture then comment or interpret it. But Jesus or Mark remembered scripture wrongly for, according to 1 Samuel 21:1, the High Priest was Ahimelech not Abiathar.

The passage in Luke 6:1 begins: *And it came to pass on the second sabbath after the first*, an apparently meaningless expression that has not been explained. The Essenes were careful keepers and recorders of the passage of time, basing it on the solar calendar of Jubilees. This is signified in the scrolls in many ways, one of which is a book of hymns which have been called Songs for the Holocaust of the Sabbath. These have titles like: *For the Master. Song of the holocaust of the seventh sabbath on the sixteenth*. The phraseology is strikingly like that of Luke suggesting its Essene origin.

Mark 2:23 to 2:28 Restored

And it came to pass, as the Nazarenes went before Herod's soldiers that they went through corn fields, and it was the sabbath day; and his disciples hungered and said: *Would that we could enjoy this grain but on the sabbath day we cannot do that which is not lawful.* And Jesus said unto them: *Have ye never read what David did, when he had need, and was an hungred, he, and they that were with him? How he went into the house of God in the days of Ahimelech the high priest, and did eat the shewbread, which is not lawful to eat but for the priests, and gave also to them which were with him? Or how that the priests offer up lambs in sacrifice on the sabbath, thereby profaning it, but are blameless.* And he said unto them: *The sabbath was made for man, and not man for the sabbath: Therefore man, the son of man, is Lord also of the sabbath.*

The Withered Hand

Mark 3:1 – 3:6

3:1 And he entered again into the synagogue; and there was a man there which had a withered hand. 3:2 And they watched him, whether he would heal him on the sabbath day; that they might accuse him. 3:3 And he saith unto the man which had the withered hand, Stand forth. 3:4 And he saith unto them, Is it lawful to do good on the sabbath days, or to do evil? to save life, or to kill? But they held their peace. 3:5 And when he had looked round about on them with anger, being grieved for the hardness of their hearts, he saith unto the man, Stretch forth thine hand. And he stretched it out: and his hand was restored whole as the other. 3:6 And the Pharisees went forth, and straightway took counsel with the Herodians against him, how they might destroy him.

The Withered Hand

The theme of the sabbath continues into the beginning of chapter 3 where Jesus heals a man's withered hand on the sabbath incurring the wrath of the Pharisees who join with the Herodians in a plot against him. Pharisees and Essenes did not dispute that the law had to be broken if it were necessary to save life on the sabbath. Here though there seems to be no life at stake. The conclusion is that the nature of the living and dying in 3:4 was spiritual so the references here are to the coming kingdom and its concomitant judgement when sinners would die and the good be resurrected into the kingdom.

Semites recognize the hand as a symbol of a power and therefore of a ruler. Later in Mark we have the phrase the right hand of power. A man with a withered hand is powerless. In the Master's blessing of God in the Community Rule are the expressions: *He that is everlasting is the support of my right hand...* and *His might is the support of my right hand. Thy right hand* was also to be inscribed on the banners of some of those engaging in the apocalyptic battle described in the War Scroll. Luke 6:6 specifies that it is the man's right hand that is withered! For the Essenes the War Scroll tells us: *Thy mighty hand is with the poor.* Mark's miracle is really a parable in which Jesus is illustrating the return of power to Israel but it has been garbled in the author's determination to make it into a sabbath day healing to invite Pharisaic wrath.

Jerome gives an additional detail about this incident. He quotes from the gospel which the Nazarenes and Ebionites use. The man with the withered hand pleaded: *I was a mason seeking a livelihood with my hands. I pray thee, Jesu, to restore mine health that I may not beg meanly for my food.* The mason is Israel which had lost the power of its right hand and was reduced to begging from the foreigner. If the people repented, God would restore their power through the poor and they would be able to build a new house for the Lord.

One of the Talmudic names used for the Essenes was the banaim, a word derived from the Hebrew for stones (abanim) and which means masons; banim means sons or children—both coming from a word meaning to build. So banim was a pun on banaim and explains the gospel use of the word children to mean the saved—the banaim seek to save the banim. In Mark 6:3 Jesus is described as a carpenter and in Matthew 13:55 his father is so described. S Campbell gives an interesting gloss on the Greek word used in these passages and usually rendered a carpenter. The word is tekton and is found nowhere else in the New Testament. Yet in modern Greek tekton means a mason!

In the scriptures a mason was linked with the building or renewing of the temple. The original context is lost but Jesus's parable could have referred to David hiring masons to build the temple (the task which was carried out after David's death by his son Solomon). Jesus might have told a kingdom parable based on 1 Chronicles 22:2: *and he set masons to hew wrought stones to build the house of God.* David's masons necessarily were foreigners, the nomadic Hebrews knowing nothing of such skills. The Essenes were determined it would not be so this time. Relevant here is the laying of the precious corner stone which for the Essenes meant themselves. The full quotation from Isaiah 28:14–18 puts a whole set of concepts into juxtaposition:

> Wherefore hear the word of the Lord, ye scornful men, that rule this people which is in Jerusalem. Because ye have said: We have made a covenant with death, and with hell are we at agreement. When the overflowing scourge shall pass through, it shall not come unto us, for we have made lies our refuge, and under falsehood have we hid ourselves. Therefore thus saith the Lord God, Behold, I lay in Zion for a foundation a stone, a tried stone, a precious corner stone, a sure foundation. He that believeth shall not make haste. Judgment also will I lay to the line, and righteousness to the plummet. And the hail shall sweep away the refuge of lies, and the waters shall overflow the hiding place. And your covenant with death shall be disannulled, and your agreement with hell shall not stand; when the overflowing scourge shall pass through, then ye shall be trodden down by it.

The meaning of the precious corner stone to the Essenes is explained in the Community Rule:

> THE COUNCIL OF THE COMMUNITY SHALL BE THAT TRIED WALL, THAT PRECIOUS CORNER STONE, WHOSE FOUNDATION SHALL NEITHER ROCK NOR SWAY IN ITS PLACE. IT SHALL BE A MOST HOLY DWELLING FOR AARON, WITH EVERLASTING KNOWLEDGE OF THE COVENANT OF JUSTICE, AND SHALL BE A HOUSE OF PERFECTION AND TRUTH IN ISRAEL THAT THEY MAY ESTABLISH A COVENANT ACCORDING TO THE EVERLASTING PRECEPTS, ATONING FOR THE LAND, AND WITNESSING THE JUDGEMENT OF WICKEDNESS. AND THERE SHALL BE NO MORE INIQUITY.

Essenes were the bridgehead of the kingdom of heaven on earth. The scornful men that rule this people which is in Jerusalem, the Sadducees, are swept away by the scourge of God's vengeance as he introduces His kingdom, founded on the precious corner stone—the Essenes—with judgement the line and righteousness the plummet, and the waters overflowing the hiding place. Here we get both the masonic and the baptismal metaphors rolled into one. It is interesting that when Herod started to rebuild the temple in 19 BC he trained a thousand priests as masons so that they could rebuild the forbidden parts of the building, like the holy of holies, without needing to pollute it with unclean hands. The Essenes might well have seen this as a sign of the times—priest-masons were being called to build the Jerusalem temple. Soon the real priest-masons would get their orders—but not from Herod—from God.

Matthew 12:11–12 introduces an analogy of a sheep falling into a pit which he says the followers of the Pharisees would rescue on the sabbath. It is true that Pharisees but not Essenes would help a stricken animal on the sabbath. For Essenes it was expressly forbidden. Only when the life of a man was in danger did they lift the prohibition. On restoration however the parable has nothing at all to do with the sabbath and the apparent dispute with the Pharisees is revealed as entirely invented including the quoting of a true reference to Pharisaic law.

Nor can the Pharisaic plot (Mk 3:6) have been hatched by the Pharisees, who had little influence in Galilee, if that is where it occurred, and would not have allied with the Herodians It was really hatched by the Sadducees, the party of the priests. The Herodians seem to have been supporters of the Herod family and therefore collaborators since the Herod family were Roman puppets. The natural allies of the Herodians were the Sadducees who were also collaborators and, though the Pharisees were little better in practice because they preferred a path of little resistance, Sadducees makes more sense here.

This verse is the conclusion to the five passages in which Mark invents or magnifies conflicts with the Pharisees.

Mark 3:1 to 3:6 Restored

Again Jesus taught of the kingdom, saying: *A certain mason was stricken and his right hand did wither. He was unable to practise his trade and his children hungered. And he prayed to the Lord, saying: I was a mason seeking my bread with mine hands, and for my sins mine hand hath withered; now my children hunger. Lord, forgive me my sins for I repent my vanity and deceit. And the Lord saw that he was sincere and said to the man: Stand forth and stretch forth thine hand; and it was made whole like as to the other. Then saith the Lord God: Go thou to Zion, and there thou shalt lay for me a stone, a foundation which shall not rock or sway in its place, for thine hand is now whole. And that foundation shall be an house of perfection and truth in Israel forever. And thou shalt inscribe it: who trusts will fear not; for this is my covenant with mine elect. The man did as the Lord commanded, and he did build a house of perfection to the Lord. And the house was the foundation of a great kingdom. In like wise shall the right hand of power be restored to Israel, and God shall build a kingdom, and the scornful men in Jerusalem shall be swept away. And judgement shall be the line and righteousness shall be the plummet.*

Withdrawal to the Sea

Mark 3:7 – 3:12

3:7 But Jesus withdrew himself with his disciples to the sea: and a great multitude from Galilee followed him, and from Judaea, 3:8 And from Jerusalem, and from Idumaea, and from beyond Jordan; and they about Tyre and Sidon, a great multitude, when they had heard what great things he did, came unto him. 3:9 And he spake to his disciples, that a small ship should wait on him because of the multitude, lest they should throng him. 3:10 For he had healed many; insomuch that they pressed upon him for to touch him, as many as had plagues. 3:11 And

unclean spirits, when they saw him, fell down before him, and cried, saying, Thou
art the Son of God. 3:12 And he straitly charged them that they should not make
him known.

Withdrawal to the Sea

Plainly this section continues chapter 1, indicating that chapter 2 was inserted.
Mark seems to be summarising the recruiting which has taken place by the Sea of
Galilee. Mark uses such summaries at intervals to punctuate the text, often using
them to break up a story to create dramatic tension (see Mk 5:25–34;
6:14–29;14:3–9).

Mark's sense is: Jews are arriving from all over Palestine. Some, referred
to as unclean spirits, want to expose him maliciously or overenthusias-
tically wanting to hail him as their king and messiah there and then—but
again Jesus severely commands them to remain silent. Ostensibly he has
done nothing wrong as long as he does not openly claim a kingship that could
disturb the Herodians or the Romans. As yet he was still a sort of John the
Baptist urging people to repent for the kingdom of God was nigh, but the parties
of the collaborators did not like to see the common people gathering together in
large crowds and so Jesus was under suspicion. Wary as ever he has a boat
waiting.

Yet Jesus withdrew—again implying flight. Indeed there is much in the passage
that reads as though Jesus and the disciples were not escaping from an admiring
throng but from a vengeful throng. The Greek translated plagues is literally
scourges which completely changes the sense of the sentence. They were
after him with whips to punish him. The ship had to be provided for them
to escape. Verse 11 perhaps explains why: his enemies the unclean spirits had
revealed him as a Son of God, that is a king and therefore a pretender to the
throne. The spirits did not simply cry out but again screamed possibly in fear as
before but possibly now with anger. The throng were not only from Galilee but
from Judaea, Peraea and Idumaea which confirms that Jesus had been recruiting
further afield than the gospels admit—in the whole of Herod the Great's former
kingdom.

A further oddity is that the sea to which they withdrew was the Mediterranean. The
action takes place in Phoenicia. The Nazarenes seem to have been pursued to
Phoenicia by a vengeful throng. If so it should be placed after Herod became aware
of them forcing them to flee. Presumably Herod's soldiers could not enter Tyre and
Sidon willy nilly but a gang of demons—private citizens forcibly silenced by the
disciples—followed on seeking retribution.

Mark 3:7 to 3:12 Restored

Jesus fled with his disciples to the Great Sea to the north in the land of the
gentiles where Herod could not go; but a vengeful throng followed him, and
about Tyre and Sidon, this multitude came angrily unto him. And he charged

139

his disciples, that a small ship should wait on him because of the multitude, lest they should mob him and harm him. For, though he had straitly charged them not to make him known and they had fallen down before them, unclean spirits had exposed him, saying: *Thou art the Son of God.* And they did scream in anger when they saw him, and pressed upon him for to take hold of him, as many as had scourges to avenge them.

Ordination of the Twelve

Mark 3:13 – 3.19

> 3:13 And he goeth up into a mountain, and calleth unto him whom he would: and they came unto him. 3:14 And he ordained twelve, that they should be with him, and that he might send them forth to preach, 3:15 And to have power to heal sicknesses, and to cast out devils: 3:16 And Simon he surnamed Peter; 3:17 And James the son of Zebedee, and John the brother of James; and he surnamed them Boanerges, which is, The sons of thunder: 3:18 And Andrew, and Philip, and Bartholomew, and Matthew, and Thomas, and James the son of Alphaeus, and Thaddaeus, and Simon the Cananaean, 3:19 And Judas Iscariot, which also betrayed him: and they went into an house.

Ordination of the Twelve

These verses tell of the appointment of the twelve. Jesus has withdrawn into the mountains (strictly into a lonely place), acting again as a guerrilla. The structure of the leadership is that of the Essenes, a council of twelve, and three with special responsibility. Jesus is expecting the kingdom of God which required appointments of leaders for each of the twelve tribes of Israel, whence the number twelve. These men were to be his chief lieutenants in achieving the kingdom. What is revealing is the way Mark describes many of them.

Mark's gospel was written about the time of the Roman triumph in 71 AD when the captured leader of the Jewish Zealots was led in chains through the streets of Rome. Zealots were particularly unpopular but so were Jews generally and Mark was faced with a few problems. Describing the apostle Simon, he deliberately uses the obscure Aramaic expression, the Cananaean, (wrongly Canaanite in the Authorized Version) without explaining it, though Mark normally explains Aramaic words for the benefit of his gentile readers. The Aramaic for Zealots was Canaim. Luke, writing at least ten years later when feelings were running less high, openly uses the Greek equivalent, understood by all—the apostle is Simon the Zealot!

Judas is Iscariot, said to mean of Kerioth but no such place seems to have existed at the time, though there had once been a town Kiriathim in Moab across the Dead Sea. The word sicarii meaning knifemen—those who carried a sica, a dagger or short sword under their cloaks—seems more identifiable with Iscariot. Judas would therefore have been a member of the assassins branch of the Zealots. In Acts 21:38 even Paul is mistaken, by the Roman captain of arms, as the leader of a gang of knifemen: *Art not thou that Egyptian, which before these days madest an uproar, and leddest out into the wilderness four thousand men that were murderers?* The word used for murderer is sikarios, a Greek word derived from the Latin. However, a Syrian word skariot meaning I shall deliver up could be an equally appropriate root. Were the Sikari the deliverers of Israel, a branch of the Essenes—both words meaning the same, deliverers or saviours—or even an alternative name for them?

There was the other Simon called Peter (or, in Aramaic, Cephas), a nickname that today would be rendered as Rocky, another tough sounding name, but one which also resonates with the Essenes' conception of themselves as masons. When Jesus reveals to Simon Peter his messiahship in Matthew 16:17, he calls him Simon Bar-jona as if Bar-jona were Simon's surname. In John 21:15 this is given as bar Jonah, as if it were a patronymic, son of Jonah. It is beyond a coincidence that Judas of Galilee and his followers were called barjonim—we would say guerrillas. Judas the Galilaean was explicitly called Judas Barjona. The Talmud names the leader of the barjonim in Jerusalem during the siege as Abbas Sikari, implying that the barjonim were knifemen or deliverers and were allied to the Zealots—barjonim and Zealots were in effect synonyms. The barjonim avoided the towns, preferring wilderness and mountains, and only visiting towns and villages to commit robberies or political murder. If barjona denotes a guerrilla or bandit, what was originally intended in the gospels? Later in the story Peter slices off a man's ear and in the Acts of the Apostles he seems to murder a man and a woman for holding back money. He seems pretty ruthless.

The two Sons of Thunder, John and James, already sound menacing enough but the expression, Boanerges, a meaningless word, is probably bene reges meaning sons of tumult or bene regaz meaning sons of wrath. Or another reading is bene rehem, sons of the wild ox, which in Job 39:10, where it is wrongly translated unicorn in the King James Bible (*Canst thou bind the unicorn* {wild ox} *with his band in the furrow? or will he harrow the valleys after thee?*)—signifies untameable wildness. Patently these were not boy scouts. One suspects that the word Boanerges only survives because in his original gospel Mark used it without translation like the word Cananaean used of Simon the Zealot. A few years later an editor felt able to explain it and so it comes down to us today—serving no purpose except as a clue to the nature of the Nazarene band. Significantly, in some old manuscripts it seems all of the twelve were called Sons of Thunder!

Bartholomew means Son of Tholomaeus and we know from Josephus in Antiquities that there was a notable Tholomaeus—he was a robber (Josephus's name for a Zealot) chief. If the Nathaniel of John's gospel is identified with Bartholomew as many biblical scholars suggest then the identification looks even more assured. John describes Nathaniel as of Cana meaning he was one of the Canaim, like Simon in Mark 3:18 above—he was a Zealot.

Finally, five of the apostles had previously been with John the Baptist. According to John's disciple, Mark (not the gospel author), John taught that to seek God people had to leave the towns. He was urging them to become barjonim! It has been suggested that the Sadduc who teamed up with Judas of Galilee to form the Zealots was none other than John the Baptist.

141

These men do not sound like pacifists—they sound like what they were, tough insurgents. They were to go out to cast out demons, that is persuade people to join the body of the elect—those who would secure and rule the kingdom of God. Largely from the gospels themselves we learn that more than half of gentle Jesus's twelve leading disciples were tough guys. Is all of this simply to be regarded as coincidence? Can anyone seriously deny that the band of Jesus the Nazarene sound more like the band of Jesus the Zealot?

The list of the twelve is an uncertain list when the various gospels are compared. Even in Mark there is no mention here of Levi who was called earlier. Does this support our contention that he was the same as Matthew? In Luke-Acts we find a Judas of James who is one of the twelve, and are the various Jameses the same or different people? The actual number of disciples is uncertain in view of these discrepancies and the fact that the Essenes had twelve plus three priests. One can guess that altogether there were fifteen as in the Essenes, the twelve plus the three pillar apostles, but that by the time Mark wrote the belief among gentiles was that the twelve covered everyone in the inner circle. Thus Peter, James and John the sons of Zebedee were the priests and the rest, some of whom are lost in Mark, were the twelve—with, as I assume, Jesus standing separately as the prince.

Since we do not have fifteen assured names, in the restoration I use a workaround—cheating perhaps—but accepting that really there were fifteen.

Mark 3:13 to 3:19 Restored

Then Jesus took apart into the hillside twelve men of his disciples that they might be with him until he should ordain them and send them forth as shepherds to gather the lost sheep. There was Simon the brigand whom he called Rocky, for he was immovable; James and John, sons of Zebedaeus, whom he called the sons of tumult and the sons of the wild ox for they were untameable; Andrew, Simon's brother; Philip and Nathanael, his brother, sons of Tholomaeus the Zealot; Matthew the Levite; Thomas the twin; James the son of Alphaeus; Judas Thaddaeus which is broadchest; Simon the Zealot; Judas Iscariot which is the knifeman and the deliverer. And Jesus said: *You shall be twelve apostles as a testimony to Israel, one for each tribe.* And Jesus judged them for qualities and ordained Peter, James and John as pillar apostles who might act as priests when they praised God, and three more he appointed in their place that there were still twelve as a covenant to Israel.

Satan casting out Satan

Mark 3:20 – 3:35

3:19 and they went into an house. 3:20 And the multitude cometh together again, so that they could not so much as eat bread. 3:21 And when his friends heard of it, they went out to lay hold on him: for they said, He is beside himself. 3:22 And the scribes which came down from Jerusalem said, He hath Beelzebub, and by the prince of the devils casteth he out devils. 3:23 And he called them unto him, and said unto them in parables, How can Satan cast out Satan? 3:24 And if a kingdom be divided against itself, that kingdom cannot stand. 3:25 And if a house be divided against itself, that house cannot stand. 3:26 And if Satan rise up against himself, and be divided, he cannot stand, but hath an end. 3:27 No man can enter into a strong man's house, and spoil his goods, except he will first bind the strong man; and then he will spoil his house. 3:28 Verily I say unto you, All sins shall be forgiven unto the sons of men, and blasphemies wherewith soever they shall blaspheme: 3:29 But he that shall blaspheme against the Holy Ghost hath never forgiveness, but is in danger of eternal damnation. 3:30 Because they said, He hath an unclean spirit. 3:31 There came then his brethren and his mother, and, standing without, sent unto him, calling him. 3:32 And the multitude sat about him, and they said unto him, Behold, thy mother and thy brethren without seek for thee. 3:33 And he answered them, saying, Who is my mother, or my brethren? 3:34 And he looked round about on them which sat about him, and said, Behold my mother and my brethren! 3:35 For whosoever shall do the will of God, the same is my brother, and my sister, and mother.

Satan casting out Satan

Again we have garbling of a passage in which disputes with Pharisees have been introduced. Mark's aim is to suggest that they wilfully accused Jesus of being possessed by Satan so focusing attention on the Jews' wilful misunderstanding of his status and intentions.

When his friends heard of what in verse 21? The multitude? Why then should they think he is beside himself because a multitude gathered? The gospel is skating over a great deal here. The truth is that the multitude is not friendly. The word in Greek means a rabble or even a riot. What does it mean that they could not so much as eat bread? It cannot be the mob outside that could not eat bread but the Nazarenes trapped inside with no provisions for the messianic meal!

The discussion was not with Pharisees but among the followers of Jesus themselves. The Greek is not literally friends but *those of his own*. Some of them accuse Jesus of being mad—beside himself means mad—and they try to take hold of him. The Christian Jesus never does anything but good and yet his followers think he is mad. In verse 30 Jesus is accused of being an opponent of the band. They say he has an unclean spirit which hitherto has meant an opponent. Some of them are scared and worried that Jesus's strategy is failing. Those who have repented are perhaps not forming themselves into a very reliable force, and indeed many who have been intimidated are rallying against the Nazarenes. The implication of the criticism is that the many converts have not been sincere—Jesus has not been casting out devils at all!

Beelzebub is the Philistine, Baalzebub, the Lord of the House, disdainfully called the Lord of the Flies, Baalzebul, by the Jews. Jesus defends himself with his stirring speech punning heavily on the house part of Beelzebub's Philistinian name. He denies that Satan can cast out himself and rebukes the dissidents for dividing the band.

The address by Jesus is spoken, the gospel tells us for the first time, in parables. In the first of the three short parables given here Jesus answers those who call him mad and possessed by saying that he has been winning people over to the nationalist cause (casting out devils) which is God's cause. How can it be the work of the devil to cast out devils thus helping God's cause? He then turns the point on to his accusers, pointing out that divisions only weaken and that would be just as true of the devil as it is of those who were seeking the kingdom of God—his own band. The devil, like any divided institution, would have an end, or collapse, if it continues divided. Yet sin still prevails and the devil has not ended. His domain remains united and so too should God's. Jesus is arguing that the band should have an end to its divisions.

From verse 27 the next parable indicates to us the cause of the dispute. Jesus wants to use force against Rome! The strong man (Rome) has to be bound before he can be robbed. The object they wish to rob him of is the kingdom of Israel. Jesus is really saying here that he has come to the conclusion that he has to take what is God's before God will finish the job by bringing in the kingdom. Isaiah 53:12 explains it:

> Therefore will I divide him a portion with the great, and he shall divide the spoil with the strong,

and Isaiah 49:24–26:

> Shall the prey be taken from the mighty, or the lawful captive delivered? But thus saith the Lord, Even the captives of the mighty shall be taken away, and the prey of the terrible shall be delivered: for I will contend with him that contendeth with thee, and I will save thy children. And I will feed them that oppress thee with their own flesh; and they shall be drunken with their own blood.

The strong man of Mark's parable is the mighty, the great and the strong of Isaiah. The strength or might of the oppressor are meant.

At this point in Matthew 12:30 and Luke 11:23 we get: *He that is not with me is against me; and he that gathereth not with me scattereth*, confirming that the speech is a unity speech. Later, in Mark 9:40 the sense appears to be different: *Those who are not against us are for us*. Here Jesus is arguing within the Nazarene band where opposition could be disastrous and mere acceptance would be insufficient. Jesus wanted wholehearted support. In the later context the reference is to those outside the band where only outright opposition could not be tolerated. Jesus would not have used the words me or us but God in these expressions because it was God's will that had to be done.

And indeed the final parable or saying is explicit on this point. Jesus warns those of his opponents who accuse him of madness as deliberately opposing the will of God and therefore blaspheming against the holy spirit. For it is God's will that the kingdom should come and it is Jesus's duty to effect its inauguration on earth. Those who have been baptized into the sect, yet are not with God, will be denied the kingdom. Opponents or even doubters of God's message cannot be saved, cannot be one of the elect, cannot enter the forthcoming kingdom. The Community Rule says:

WHOEVER HAS SLANDERED THE CONGREGATION SHALL BE EXPELLED FROM AMONG THEM AND SHALL RETURN NO MORE. WHOEVER HAS MURMURED AGAINST THE AUTHORITY OF THE COMMUNITY SHALL BE EXPELLED AND SHALL NOT RETURN.

The word used for community is yahad which more strongly embodies the idea of unity and being united than our word community. Unity was essential to success. Jesus's speech is urging unity and strength in preparation for the battle to come.

Quite possibly Jesus concluded this speech with: *For whosoever shall do the will of God, the same is my brother and sister*, emphasising that those of the chosen who do the will of God are united in brotherhood. They are the children of Israel therefore necessarily brothers and sisters in the forthcoming kingdom.

The mention of brother and sister gives Mark or an editor a link with an phony dispute between Jesus and his family (Mk 31–35). The objective is to distance Jesus from the Jews by showing that even his family were against him. Jesus derides his mother and brothers, a most un-Jewish thing to do—the basis of Judaism is the family and respect for parents—and, one would imagine, quite ungodly. If true the story confirms that Jesus had brothers and sisters, contradicting the idea of Mary being a virgin. It makes no mention of Joseph. Now Mark has no nativity narrative as do Matthew and Luke. The myth of virgin birth had yet to arise in the context of Jesus, although it was widespread in other religions. Yet the questioning of him by his family in Mark is carried over into other later gospels contradicting their nativity stories. If Jesus's parents knew from his birth that he was the pre-existent son of God, because of the plethora of angels, kings and wise men that went out of their way to make it clear, why had they forgotten by the time he was actually getting on with the job? The birth narratives can be totally discarded as additions from a later stage when the Christians wanted to impress proselytes with a few of the trappings of orthodox gods and with the realization of a few more prophecies scratched together from the Old Testament.

Note here (Mk 3:28) the use of sons of men to mean men in general not legions of Jesuses.

At this point in Matthew 8:5–13 and Luke 7:1–10 comes the miracle of the healing of the centurion's servant. It is pure propaganda—aimed at a Roman audience—in which Jesus heals at a distance, and the soldier is depicted as one of Jesus's followers—a total absurdity whatever interpretation of the gospels you prefer. Jesus even says: *I have not found such great faith, no, not in Israel.* The servant, like Levi, was paralysed—enfeebled in the law, in our understanding— a backslider, probably a Hellenized Jew. The only way the story could make any sense is if it were the servant really addressing Jesus and expressing his newly found faith, not the centurion. The real mystery is how his pleas get into both gospels in almost the same words without being in Mark. Being narrative it should not have been in the document Q which was a book of sayings.

It seems that an early editor of one of the gospels saw the miracle in the other one and felt it was so important to gentile audiences that he must make use of it. Since it seems as though the story of the curing of a leper has been curtailed in Matthew to fit in the centurion's servant, and because it says the Jews will never enter the kingdom (Mt 8:12) which cannot have been Matthew's original intent in writing the gospel, we conclude that an anti-Jewish gentile editor has transferred the story from Luke into Matthew.

Mark 3:20 to 3:35 Restored

And the multitude cometh together again, besieging them in his house so that they could not so much as bring in bread for the holy meal. And his companions were fearful and went to lay hold on him, for they said: *He is beside himself.* And some of the Nazarenes said: *He hath Beelzebub, and by the prince of the devils casteth he out devils.* And Jesus answered them, saying: *If this son of man hath Beelzebub he could not have cast out a single demon. Yet ye have repented. How can Satan cast out Satan? If a house be divided against itself, that house cannot stand, not even Satan's house. And if a kingdom be divided against itself, that kingdom cannot stand, not even Satan's kingdom. And if Satan rise up against himself, and be divided, he cannot stand, but hath an end. Yet he doth not end. How then can Satan be cast out? When a strong man is armed and defendeth his house, his possessions are in peace; but when a man stronger than he first binds him then takes away his weapons, his possessions are lost. In like wise must we be stronger than Satan and bind him. But if a kingdom be divided against itself, that kingdom cannot stand; and if a house be divided against itself, that house cannot stand. The house of Israel must needs stand as one if Satan is to be bound and cast out. And for this reason all sins shall be forgiven unto the sons of men who repent, save a blasphemy against His holy spirit. He that is not with God is against God; and he that gathereth not with God scattereth. For whosoever shall do the will of God, the same is my brother and sister in God's remnant. But whoever hath slandered the congregation shall be expelled from among them and shall return no more. And whoever hath murmured against the authority of the community shall be expelled and shall not return. Every idle word that men speak, they shall give account of in God's day of vengeance, for by thy words thou shalt be justified and by thy words thou shalt be condemned.* And they murmured no more.

Parable of the Sower

Mark 4:1 – 4:20

4:1 And he began again to teach by the sea side: and there was gathered unto him a great multitude, so that he entered into a ship, and sat in the sea; and the whole multitude was by the sea on the land. 4:2 And he taught them many things by parables and said unto them in his doctrine, 4:3 Hearken; Behold, there went out a sower to sow: 4:4 And it came to pass, as he sowed, some fell by the way side, and the fowls of the air came and devoured it up. 4:5 And some fell on stony ground, where it had not much earth; and immediately it sprang up, because it had no depth of earth: 4:6 But when the sun was up, it was scorched; and because it had no root, it withered away. 4:7 And some fell among thorns, and the thorns grew up, and choked it, and it yielded no fruit. 4:8 And other fell on good ground, and did yield fruit that sprang up and increased; and brought forth, some thirty, and some sixty, and some an hundred. 4:9 And he said unto them, He that hath ears to hear, let him hear. 4:10 And when he was alone, they that were about him with the twelve asked of him the parable. 4:11 And he said unto them, Unto you it is given to know the mystery of the kingdom of God: but unto them that are without, all these things are done in parables: 4:12 That seeing they may see, and not perceive; and hearing they may hear, and not understand; lest at any time they should be converted, and their sins should be forgiven them. 4:13 And he said unto them, Know ye not this parable? and how then will ye know all parables? 4:14 The sower soweth the word. 4:15 And these are they by the way side, where the word is sown; but when they have heard, Satan cometh immediately, and taketh away the word that was sown in their hearts. 4:16 And these are they likewise which are sown on stony ground; who, when they have heard the word, immediately receive it with gladness; 4:17 And have no root in themselves, and so endure but for a time: afterward, when affliction or persecution ariseth for the word's sake, immediately they are offended. 4:18 And these are they which are sown among thorns; such as hear the word, 4:19 And the cares of this world, and the deceitfulness of riches, and the lusts of other things entering in, choke the word, and it becometh unfruitful. 4:20 And these are they which are sown on good ground; such as hear the word, and receive it, and bring forth fruit, some thirtyfold, some sixty, and some an hundred.

Parables

Mark gives a whole chapter largely devoted to the significance of parables and to Jesus's parables of the kingdom, intended to encourage his band.

Mark is convinced that parables are meant to obscure not to clarify but this has been generally ignored by theologians who give long explanations why the parables are actually not obscure. In the rabbinic tradition parables are used to clarify, yet the clergy are not averse to claiming this proves that Jesus, though supposedly repudiating the rabbinic tradition, used them in the same way. All of this fails to look at the question from Mark's own conviction that they were intended to obscure, the reason being that Jesus was in the Essene tradition not the Pharisaic. Since the evangelist is quite explicit that the parables are allegorical— Jesus is saying so in 4:13—it is dishonest for later clergymen to maintain that they are not. But their meaning is not to be sought in the mystical interpretations of the later church but in what we know of the traditions of the Essenes of the time, and what we can deduce of the intentions of the variant sect we call the Nazarenes.

Essenes considered that truth was obscure, drawing on the same passage in Isaiah 6:9–12 where God commanded the prophet to tell the people:

> Hear ye indeed, but understand not; and see ye indeed, but perceive not. Make the heart of this people fat, and make their ears heavy, and shut their eyes; lest they see with their eyes, and hear with their ears, and understand with their heart, and convert, and be healed.

Note the final expression convert and be healed in which healing is equated with conversion. The Essenes took this to mean that people were blind, deaf and hard of heart because they were unrighteous and would not take the trouble to learn the mysteries which God had given them in the scriptures. Taking this literally, they accepted nothing at face value and sought the hidden meaning in the scriptures. Only God's righteous took the trouble to do this and it was against God's will for them to bandy their discoveries about, so they kept them to themselves, in turn couching their own truths in an allegorical language which could be understood by other Essenes but not by anyone else.

In the Community Rule the Master chants in his song of blessings to God:

> MY EYES HAVE GAZED ON THAT WHICH IS EVERLASTING, ON WISDOM CONCEALED FROM MEN, ON KNOWLEDGE AND WISE DESIGN HIDDEN FROM THE SONS OF MEN.

The poem goes on to say that God has given these secrets to His elect as an everlasting possession. The Damascus Rule has similar phrases:

> WITH THE REMNANT WHICH HELD FAST TO THE COMMANDMENTS OF GOD, HE MADE HIS COVENANT WITH ISRAEL FOREVER, REVEALING TO THEM THE HIDDEN THINGS IN WHICH ALL ISRAEL HAD GONE ASTRAY.

In Isaiah 48:6 is God's promise to reveal hidden things (nasar), yet another pun on the word Nazarene—a revealer of hidden things. It was the duty of the Master to instruct the sectaries in these mysteries of amazing truth, that they may walk perfectly together in all that has been revealed to them. Nevertheless, earlier in his song the Master promises: *I will impart knowledge with discretion.* Thus, though the Community Rule prescribes that all novitiates will be taught the things hidden from Israel without fear that he will become an apostate (and reveal them elsewhere), for the men of deceit, the Master was obliged to maintain a spirit of secrecy and to conceal from them the knowledge of the truth and righteous judgement that was required for a proper understanding of the law and the prophets.

In Mark 3.23 the evangelist told us that Jesus spoke in parables, further proof that Jesus was an Essene. For the Nazarenes he was the Master, the Maskil, whose duty was to impart knowledge with discretion and keep it secret from the wicked. We can conclude from this that the parables were allegorical and not, as theologians stoutly maintain, simple stories. If you still do not believe it read Matthew 13:14–15 where Jesus uses the above quotation from Isaiah to explain why he was teaching in parables.

Taking this further we can see that Mark was himself playing the same game, whence our treatment of his gospel. Christians have been happy to recognize that some of the meaning of the parables has been lost because the context has been lost in time. We contend that the context is that of an Essene sect working to help God bring in the Jewish kingdom of God on earth (not the later invention of a mystical kingdom of God in some other dimension). Once this is realized the gospel becomes much more transparent.

Parable of the Sower

The command Hearken! at the beginning might be an echo of the transfiguration, when Jesus becomes *that prophet*, implying that this passage should appear after it. If so, Jesus is now teaching believing himself to be the messiah. The Damascus Rule has sections introduced with the expression Hear Now! reminiscent of God's instruction regarding His prophets and also the ears to hear of the gospels. Indeed in one section we find:

HEAR NOW, ALL YOU WHO ENTER THE COVENANT, AND I WILL UNSTOP YOUR EARS CONCERNING THE WAYS OF THE WICKED;

and in another, further down the same column:

HEAR NOW, MY SONS, AND I WILL UNCOVER YOUR EYES THAT YOU MAY SEE AND UNDERSTAND THE WAYS OF GOD.

Deafness and blindness were Essene ways of describing lack of understanding— and Jesus used the same language. The author of one fragment of the Essene scrolls of Qumran admits he is writing in parables so that only a wise man would understand the deep mysteries that lay behind them. Elsewhere we get expressions like,

GIVE EAR TO ME... THOSE WHO PURSUE RIGHTEOUSNESS: YOU WILL UNDERSTAND MY WORDS AND BE SEEKERS AFTER FAITH AND THE HIDDEN THINGS OF THE TESTIMONY.

Essenes regarded scripture as mysterious. The use of the phrase, *mystery of the kingdom of God,* emphasizes the link between the gospel and the Essene scrolls. Paul often uses the word mystery (sometimes translated as secret) in his epistles. The Essenes used the pesher method whereby old documents were interpreted as prophetic of current events. The Habakkuk Commentary of the Dead Sea Scrolls is of this type. The Essene sages sought to read in the scriptures the hidden things of God and, having discovered them, they sought to conceal them from unrighteous ears. This is the real significance of the parables of Jesus. They look like simple moralistic folk tales but there is more to them than meets the eye... or ear! Those that had ears to hear, those who had been taught and had grasped the method, would understand references intended to baffle the ignorant.

When Jesus says *them that are without* he means those outside the company of the elect who could not understand the method and he gives a scriptural reference to the passage in Isaiah quoted above (Isa 6:10) by way of explanation. Specifically though he meant the foreigners present in the crowd who might understand Aramaic but would not be able to understand Jesus's hidden messages—though they would be transparent to an Essene—and would not be saved if they did.

The first parable is that of the sower much of whose seed goes to waste. It is an allegory, a coded story, which is explained to the twelve—Mark's way of showing that the disciples had to be taught how to understand them. He tells us that the parables are allegories by deciphering this one. The reader realizes that the parables were meant to be obscure but because this one does not seem particularly so, it serves the aim of the followers of Paul, who had gained hold of the church, to denigrate as idiots the original followers of Jesus. The deciphering is bogus because it is done to suit the Christian church and not to interpret the original parable, but the changes are not great.

The parable itself actually is based on several scriptural passages which effectively trace the fortunes of the seed of Abraham—the Jews. It says to Jews that various of their ancestors have been unrighteous in divers ways, and have spiritually died. If they did not repeat their mistakes then they would yield spiritual fruit aplenty and would enter into God's kingdom.

In Mark the seed is the word, possibly a Christian interpolation, but possibly Jesus's original message of the word of God to the children—the need to repent and to prepare for the coming kingdom. Some people reject the message altogether; some believe it but do not have the strength of character to persevere when the going gets rough; some accept the message but fear that they have too much to lose in the world as it is to risk replacing it; finally there are the elect who accept the message and profit a hundredfold in the kingdom of God on earth. The meaning of the allegory is only thinly disguised. Jesus is making a speech of encouragement. Despite the initial interest many recruits were coming up with excuses and leaving the band. Jesus was giving a morale boost to his remaining followers.

The speech would have ended with a quotation from Zechariah 8:12:

> For the seed shall be prosperous; the vine shall give her fruit, and the ground shall give her increase, and the heavens shall give their dew; and I will cause the remnant of this people to possess all these things.

In the kingdom, of course. The remnant is as always the elect of God—the remnant of Israel who are righteous as opposed to all Israel who are wicked. Only they inherit the earth.

Mark 4:1 to 4:20 Restored

> And addressing a multitude, Jesus spoke a parable, saying: *Hearken! A sower went out to sow and as he sowed, some seed fell by the wayside and perished, for it is written: Those who hearken not to the voice of God shall be meat unto the fowls of the air. And some seed fell upon stony ground, and immediately it sprang up, and because it had no depth of earth, when the sun was up, it was scorched because it had no root and it withered away, for it is written: Their stock shall not take root in the earth. And some seed*

fell among thorns and the thorns sprang up and choked them and they yielded no fruit, for it is written: Sow not among thorns. But other seed fell on good ground and did yield fruit that increased and brought forth, some thirty, and some sixty, and some an hundred, for it is written: The seed shall be prosperous and the ground shall give her increase. He that hath ears to hear, let him hear.

A Candlestick under a Bushel

Mark 4:21 – 4:23

4:21 And he said unto them, Is a candle brought to be put under a bushel, or under a bed? and not to be set on a candlestick? 4:22 For there is nothing hid, which shall not be manifested; neither was any thing kept secret, but that it should come abroad. 4:23 If any man have ears to hear, let him hear.

A Candlestick under a Bushel

These verses seem to contradict verses 4:11–12 but they do not. The struggle for the coming kingdom would uncover all secrets. Jesus is explaining that secrecy was an expediency that would become unnecessary. They would soon reveal themselves openly as elite soldiers of God and begin the battle for the kingdom. When they succeeded everything would be clear. The candle conjures up an image of the menorah, the seven branched candlestick, which represents the omniscience of God. God knows everything and when his kingdom is entered, so shall the righteous. It might well have been of some special significance to the Essenes who favoured the number seven, and who favoured bread as an offering to God rather than animal sacrifices. The menorah was set up to illuminate the temple showbread.

Mark 4:21 to 4:23 Restored

And he said unto them: *Is a candle brought to be put under a bushel, or under a bed and not to be set on a candlestick? The Lord hath seven eyes and, from Him, nothing is hid. For there is nothing hid, which shall not be manifested to the elect in God's kingdom; neither was any thing kept secret, but that it should come abroad in God's kingdom. If any man have ears to hear, let him hear.*

Rewards

Mark 4:24 – 4:25

4:24 And he said unto them, Take heed what ye hear: with what measure ye mete, it shall be measured to you: and unto you that hear shall more be given. 4:25 For he that hath, to him shall be given: and he that hath not, from him shall be taken even that which he hath.

Rewards

The gospels give the impression that Jesus never opened his mouth without saying something new, when in fact he must have made the same, or similar speeches repeatedly during his campaigning. This is partly the reason why different gospels have some sayings in different contexts. They were used more than once as proverbs or slogans and were recollected by different people in different contexts. These verses, which Jesus possibly used on several occasions, carry on the theme that the insurgents will be rewarded in the coming kingdom.

Verse 24 is quite crucial for it is saying that the Nazarene band (*you that hear* means they that understand the mysteries of the kingdom—the repentant) have to do something to get the reward. By taking the initial steps the reward of the kingdom will be given by God, but in verse 25 it is made clear that doubters and skeptics will get nothing. They would not enter the kingdom, indeed they would be destroyed. However this saying appears elsewhere and can be omitted here.

Mark 4:24 to 4:25 Restored

And he said unto them: *Take heed what ye hear: with what measure ye mete, it shall be measured to you: and unto you that hear shall more be given. For if what ye mete is God's will then it pleaseth the Lord and ye shall be rewarded with everlasting life.*

The Harvester

Mark 4:26 – 4:29

4:26 And he said, So is the kingdom of God, as if a man should cast seed into the ground; 4:27 And should sleep, and rise night and day, and the seed should spring and grow up, he knoweth not how. 4:28 For the earth bringeth forth fruit of herself; first the blade, then the ear, after that the full corn in the ear. 4:29 But when the fruit is brought forth, immediately he putteth in the sickle, because the harvest is come.

The Harvester

Jesus explains here that their duty is like that of a farmer who has to sow his seed but then can leave it to grow under God's care as if of its own accord. Once the Nazarene band had sowed the seed of rebellion, the growth to fruition of the kingdom would begin under God's care and God would reap the harvest. In short all the hard work is done by God provided that the farmer sows the seed in the first place. The harvest is scriptural code for the kingdom of God and the judgement that accompanies it, and indeed the final verse is a quotation of Joel 3:13. By putting this verse in its context (Joel 3:09–22) the full aims of Jesus and the Nazarenes become clear. It is the day of the vengeance of God and the restoration of His kingdom in Israel—the Lord dwelling in Zion.

> The men of war draw near; let them come up. Beat your plowshares into swords and your pruninghooks into spears. Let the weak say, I am strong. Assemble yourselves, and come, all ye heathen, and gather yourselves together round about. Thither cause thy mighty ones to come down, O Lord. Let the heathen be wakened, and come up to the valley of Jehoshaphat: for there will I sit to judge all the heathen round about. Put ye in the sickle, for the harvest is ripe. Come, get you down, for the press is full, the fats overflow, for their wickedness is great. Multitudes, multitudes in the valley of decision. For the day of the Lord is near in the valley of decision. The sun and the moon shall be darkened, and the stars shall withdraw their shining. The Lord also shall roar out of Zion, and utter his voice from Jerusalem, and the heavens and the earth shall shake, but the Lord will be the hope of his people, and the strength of the children of Israel. So shall ye know that I am the Lord your God dwelling in Zion, my holy mountain. Then shall Jerusalem be holy, and there shall no strangers pass through her any more. And it shall come to pass in that day, that the mountains shall drop down new wine, and the hills shall flow with milk, and all the rivers of Judah shall flow with waters, and a fountain shall come forth of the house of the Lord, and shall water the valley of Shittim. Egypt shall be a desolation, and Edom shall be a desolate wilderness, for the violence against the children of Judah, because they have shed innocent blood in their land. But Judah shall dwell for ever, and Jerusalem from generation to generation. For I will cleanse their blood that I have not cleansed: for the Lord dwelleth in Zion.

God promises to destroy the enemies of Judah. This ought to be sufficient proof that there is more to the parables than clergymen believe and more to Jesus's intentions than persuading people that Christianity was being invented. The quotation ending this parable would have put the whole context of this passage from Joel in the mind of any educated Jew—he that hath ears to hear. His words would have been cryptic above all to gentiles.

Indeed parables do not apply to gentiles as these prove quite explicitly. The seed represents the children of Israel who are the seed of Isaac. These are the seed who are fulfilled an hundredfold and no one else. Thus this short parable says that the sower, Isaac, sowed the seed of the children of Israel then died (slept). The seed brought forth fruit by stages until God reaped the harvest of the righteous. A gentile editor added a couple of helpful phrases which confused the simplicity of the original tale.

Matthew at this point has the parable of the tares and the wheat (Mt 13:24–30), in which the enemy, the devil, sows tares among the wheat of the good farmer, God. The servants are willing to go and pull up the tares but God tells them to wait until the harvest when the tares can be separated and burnt. This is a straightforward apocalyptic parable in which the wicked (the tares) are destroyed at the judgement day while the righteous are saved. This dualist outlook is thoroughly Essene.

Mark 4:26 to 4:29 Restored

And Jesus said: *Hearken ye to this other parable: the kingdom of God is as if a man cast good seed upon the earth, and he slept and went not by night or day and cared not how the seed should spring up and grow. But the earth beareth fruit of herself and when the blade was sprung up so too were tares. And the man's servants said unto him: wilt thou that we go and gather up these tares? But he said: Nay; lest while ye gather up the tares, ye root up also the wheat with them. Let both grow together, first the blade, then the ear, then the full corn in the ear. But when the fruit is ripe, straightway putteth forth the sickle, because the harvest is come. Then separate the wheat from the tares that it be saved for me, and put the tares in a heap that they may be destroyed by fire. For it is written: Put ye in the sickle, for the harvest is ripe, for their wickedness is great. Then shall Jerusalem be holy and there shall no strangers pass through her any more. And the Lord shall roar from Zion; and the heavens and earth shall shake; but the Lord will be a refuge unto his people and a strong hold to the children of Israel. For David said to the Lord: thine hand shall find out all thine enemies; thy right hand shall find out those that hate thee. Thou shalt make them as a fiery furnace in the time of thine anger. Thou shalt swallow them up in thy wrath; and the fire shall devour them. Their fruit shalt thou destroy from the earth, and their seed from among the children of men. And the Lord said to David: My covenant shall stand fast with thee; and thy seed will I make to endure forever.*

The Grain of Mustard Seed

Mark 4:30 – 4:32

4:30 And he said, Whereunto shall we liken the kingdom of God? or with what comparison shall we compare it? 4:31 It is like a grain of mustard seed, which, when it is sown in the earth, is less than all the seeds that be in the earth: 4:32 But when it is sown, it groweth up, and becometh greater than all herbs, and shooteth out great branches; so that the fowls of the air may lodge under the shadow of it.

The Grain of Mustard Seed

Once a seed is planted it can grow into a mighty tree. An insignificant mustard seed will grow so large that even wild birds can roost under its shadow. In like manner the initial effort of the Nazarenes will grow into the kingdom of God. Of course a mustard plant is not a large plant so even the image created by the parable is of an insignificant plant becoming all embracing. Jesus is making no point about growth but about the contrast between the start and the end. From a tiny start God's kingdom on earth will provide peace and protection for all men— some gentiles too in righteous supplication—but under the benevolent rule of the saved Jews, the Nazarenes, themselves led by the elect of God, the Essenes. Once the seed is planted all of the growth is provided by God just as it was in the previous parable.

But what is the seed? It is that remnant of Israel that have adopted righteousness by accepting the soldier's sacramentum of baptism and entered the fray as soldiers of God in the cosmic battle. Jesus is assuring his band of diehards that they are the keys to the kingdom of God.

Mark 4:30 to 4:32 Restored

And Jesus still speaking in parables, said: *Whereunto shall we liken the kingdom of God? It is like a grain of mustard seed, which, when it falleth to earth, is less than all the seeds that be in the earth; but when it groweth up it becometh greater than all the herbs and shooteth out great branches; so that all the fowls of the air may lodge under the shadow of it. For it is written: the Lord will bring down the high tree and will exalt the low tree; and it shall bring forth boughs and bear fruit, and under it shall dwell all fowl of every wing; in the shadow of the branches thereof shall they dwell.*

Parables are Cryptic

Mark 4:33 – 4:34

4:33 And with many such parables spake he the word unto them, as they were able to hear it. 4:34 But without a parable spake he not unto them: and when they were alone, he expounded all things to his disciples.

Parables are Cryptic

These two verses simply point out that the parables were cryptic and needed to be interpreted but those within the circle had been taught how to do it. This is purely Essene.

We group herein the explanations given earlier.

Mark 4:33 to 4:34 Restored

And when he was alone, they that were about him asked of him the parables. And he said unto them: *Know ye not the parable of the sower? and how then will ye know all parables? The parable being interpreted is this. The sower soweth the word of God. And these are they by the way side, who understandeth not the word, and to whom Satan cometh immediately and catcheth away that which was sown in their hearts. And these are they likewise in which the word is sown on stony ground, who immediately receive the word with gladness, but have no root in themselves, and so endure but for a time, and are tempted by hypocrisy.*

155

And these are they in which the word is sown among thorns, and the cares of this world, and the deceitfulness of riches, and the lusts of other things entering in choke the word, and it becometh unfruitful. And these are they in which the word is sown on good ground, such as hear the word, and receive it, and bring forth fruit, some thirtyfold, some sixty, and some an hundred. For it is written in the prophet Zechariah, in the word of the Lord: The seed shall be prosperous; the vine shall give her fruit, and the ground shall give her increase, and the heavens shall give their dew; and I will cause the remnant of this people to inherit all these things. And ye righteous shall receive that inheritance when the kingdom comes. And Jesus expounded all things to his disciples, saying unto them: *This son of man will impart knowledge with discretion for it is written in the prophet Isaiah: Hear ye indeed, but understand not; and see ye indeed, but perceive not. Make the heart of this people fat, and make their ears heavy, and shut their eyes; lest they see with their eyes, and hear with their ears, and understand with their heart, and convert, and be healed. But with the remnant which held fast to the commandments of God, He made His covenant with Israel forever, revealing to them the hidden things in which all Israel had gone astray, the mysteries of amazing truth, that they may walk perfectly together in all that has been revealed to them. Unto you therefore it is given to know the mystery of the kingdom of God: but unto them that are without, all these things are done in parables: That seeing they may see, and not perceive; and hearing they may hear, and not understand.*

A Storm on the Lake

Mark 4:35 – 4:41

4:35 And the same day, when the even was come, he saith unto them, Let us pass over unto the other side. 4:36 And when they had sent away the multitude, they took him even as he was in the ship. And there were also with him other little ships. 4:37 And there arose a great storm of wind, and the waves beat into the ship, so that it was now full. 4:38 And he was in the hinder part of the ship, asleep on a pillow: and they awake him, and say unto him, Master, carest thou not that we perish? 4:39 And he arose, and rebuked the wind, and said unto the sea, Peace, be still. And the wind ceased, and there was a great calm. 4:40 And he said unto them, Why are ye so fearful? how is it that ye have no faith? 4:41 And they feared exceedingly, and said one to another, What manner of man is this, that even the wind and the sea obey him?

A Storm on the Lake

The miracle of the stilling of a storm is related in a different tone to the earlier parables. It is short and coherent. Indeed it looks like an insertion meant to show the Christian god was the equal of others, and of miracle workers like Apollonius of Tyana.

Miracles were either real events which were deliberately disguised by the author or parables rendered as the truth. A storm is scriptural metaphor for hostilities. If this is not a Christian insertion then Mark is distorting a speech by Jesus telling his followers not to fear the coming battle for the kingdom—not to fear the storm—but it has been heavily changed in the telling. The miracle of the walking on water is surely part of the same story which has somehow been split.

Jesus seems to have used in his speech elements from Jonah, Nahum and Psalms 65, 83 and 107. In Nahum God will avenge his people. In Psalms 83 gentile nations surrounding Judaea plotted against the Jews and cut them off from being a nation but, these enemies of Israel, God would pursue with a tempest, and terrify with a storm until they were confounded and perished. On the other hand the Nazarenes need not fear God's storm because in Psalms 107 they need only cry to the Lord in their trouble and God would calm the storm and bring them into a safe haven. In Psalms 65 we find that God stilleth the noise of the seas, the noise of their waves, and the tumult of the people. In Jonah God sends a storm to punish Jonah, but he Jonah sleeps through it when everyone else was fearful. The men rowed hard to get back to the land but they could not. His song from the belly of the fish ends with the name of Jesus! Salvation is of God.

The reason for the speech is that Jesus is starting off with his Nazarenes on their way to Jerusalem. They decide to cross the the Sea of Galilee into the country of the gentiles known as Decapolis which involves making the trip in a flotilla of small boats—the clue that this pericope contains genuine tradition—Mark makes it clear there is more than one boat showing that the Nazarene band was of significant size. Mark cannot report any of this without betraying that the Nazarenes are not a band of peace-loving yokels so rewrites the event as a miracle taking his cues from the speech and the scene of a flotilla of small boats setting off across the sea. Jesus might well have remained calm when others were unsure and excitable.

Why did Jesus want to cross the Sea of Galilee? The practical reasons were to avoid travelling through either Herod's territory of Galilee or the Roman domain of Judaea. More importantly, the scriptures ordained that he should. In Ezekiel 39 we find that God promises to smite all the enemies of Israel represented by the great prince Gog—for the Nazarenes, the Greeks and the Romans. In Ezekiel 39:11 God promises to make a graveyard of Gog's armies in the valley of them that pass through on the east of the sea. In Ezekiel it meant the trade route up the coast, to the east of the Mediterranean Sea, but the Nazarenes in typical Essene fashion would have read this as east of the Sea of Galilee. This was the reason for Jesus's excursion across the water. He felt it was God's will so, for him to succeed, he was destined to enter Judaea by the eastern route, beyond the Jordan. Moreover, Ezekiel prophesies that the weapons left behind by Gog's armies would provide kindling for the children for seven years. In Essene eschatology, this pointed to the first seven years of the forty years of war described in the War Scroll, confirming to Jesus that it was a necessary step in the calling down of the kingdom.

Mark 4:35 to 4:41 Restored

See the restoration of Mark 6:45–52.

The Gadarene Demoniac

Mark 5:1 – 5:20

5:1 And they came over unto the other side of the sea, into the country of the Gadarenes. 5:2 And when he was come out of the ship, immediately there met him out of the tombs a man with an unclean spirit, 5:3 Who had his dwelling among the tombs; and no man could bind him, no, not with chains: 5:4 Because that he had been often bound with fetters and chains, and the chains had been plucked asunder by him, and the fetters broken in pieces: neither could any man tame him. 5:5 And always, night and day, he was in the mountains, and in the tombs, crying, and cutting himself with stones. 5:6 But when he saw Jesus afar off, he ran and worshipped him, 5:7 And cried with a loud voice, and said, What have I to do with thee, Jesus, thou Son of the most high God? I adjure thee by God, that thou torment me not. 5:8 For he said unto him, Come out of the man, thou unclean spirit. 5:9 And he asked him, What is thy name? And he answered, saying, My name is Legion: for we are many. 5:10 And he besought him much that he would not send them away out of the country. 5:11 Now there was there nigh unto the mountains a great herd of swine feeding. 5:12 And all the devils besought him, saying, Send us into the swine, that we may enter into them. 5:13 And forthwith Jesus gave them leave. And the unclean spirits went out, and entered into the swine: and the herd ran violently down a steep place into the sea, (they were about two thousand;) and were choked in the sea. 5:14 And they that fed the swine fled, and told it in the city, and in the country. And they went out to see what it was that was done. 5:15 And they come to Jesus, and see him that was possessed with the devil, and had the legion, sitting, and clothed, and in his right mind: and they were afraid. 5:16 And they that saw it told them how it befell to him that was possessed with the devil, and also concerning the swine. 5:17 And they began to pray him to depart out of their coasts. 5:18 And when he was come into the ship, he that had been possessed with the devil prayed him that he might be with him. 5:19 Howbeit Jesus suffered him not, but saith unto him, Go home to thy friends, and tell them how great things the Lord hath done for thee, and hath had compassion on thee. 5:20 And he departed, and began to publish in Decapolis how great things Jesus had done for him: and all men did marvel.

The Gadarene Demoniac

Next Mark relates the fascinating story of the Gadarene demoniac, a miracle which hides a crucial event. But was the man a Gadarene demoniac, a Gerasene demoniac or even a Gergesene demoniac? All of these names appear in different manuscripts casting doubt on the situation of the miracle which, on the face of it, was Decapolis.

Having performed this miracle Jesus and his men immediately return across the Sea of Galilee, making the whole round trip pointless. Mark had a pericope about a trip in a flotilla across the sea but did not know what happened then so he brought them back.

Nazarene convention is that those who wish to oppose Jesus or expose him as the messiah are called unclean spirits. That applies here—the demoniac is an unclean spirit because he names Jesus as the messiah (Son of God) and, in normal fashion, Jesus drives out the demon but in this story there is a mass of puzzling detail. The lunatic is naked (Lk 8:27); he came from behind tombs; he had often been bound with chains and had broken them; the spirit begs not to be tortured; suddenly there are many of them (there is a host of us) and their name is Legion; indeed there were 2000 unclean spirits; they were driven in the form of swine over a cliff into the sea and were drowned.

The lunatic seems to be a superman who could not be bound by fetters or chains: plainly he is not real but a metaphor for something immensely powerful, uncontrollable and defiled. He is a metaphor for the might of Rome. Jews abhorred nudity, often a euphemism for sexual exposure as Leviticus 18 and 20 makes clear. Essenes felt the same way. The Community Rule prescribes a penance of thirty days for a man who accidentally exposes himself while urinating, and a penance of six months for a man who deliberately goes naked. At the time of the Maccabees, to the prudish Jews such practices as exercising naked in the gymnasium, as the Greeks did, was considered a disgusting violation of the law. Romans were identified with the Greeks—both were from across the Great Sea, the People of the Sea, the Kittim of the scrolls, and had in common the Greek culture. For Jews, tombs and swine are unclean. They signify gentiles—the Romans. Thus many of the identifying features of the demoniac label him a gentile and therefore a Roman.

And why the name Legion which, together with the actual number mentioned, screams out Roman Legion, the equivalent of a modern military regiment. Was it a Roman legion? 2000 seems a peculiar number of devils but a legion was normally 6000 strong. There are, though, reasons and occasions why fighting units might not be up to strength. The 2000 mentioned might have been those killed or captured, the remainder having withdrawn. Or Legion might have just been a way of denoting that the soldiers were Roman—part of a legion—because the governor of Judaea only had 2000 legionaries at his disposal, about three or four cohorts. The biblical scholar J Jeremias has pointed out that the Aramaic word which meant no more than soldier might have been translated Legion, and so we are not bound to be talking about a full legion. Whatever the truth of the number, if the Greek of Mark is based on an Aramaic original we still have the curiosity that the unclean spirits evidently were soldiers.

The Greek used in describing the demoniac and his cure is violent in the extreme though toned down in translation. The words are: dismembered or pulled in pieces, completely crushed or shattered, mangled or chopped down and tortured. On the face of it they refer to actions of the madman but no one so violently lunatic could survive at all, so one can guess that Mark has changed a few subjects and objects.

The steep place that the swine run violently down is really a cliff that they plunged over. The hints here are of a violent event perhaps involving the capture (chains), torture (the legion of demons begged not to be tortured) and death by falling over a cliff, drowning or garroting (the Greek translated drowning means choking in general) of 2000 soldiers.

Graves and Podro in The Nazarene Gospel Restored felt obliged to explain the obvious allusion to Roman soldiers in this miracle and did so by speculating that, by a scribal error, a reader's annotation referring to a Roman defeat had been mistakenly adopted into the text of the gospel at the time of the Jewish War. Perhaps, they were too cautious.

One of the tombs in the Qidron valley, the valley of Jehoshaphat of Joel, a place of apocalyptic significance, which saw the humiliation of the Gadarene swine—the defeat of Jerusalem's Roman garrison. The victory (nasah) convinced Jesus God's miracle was nigh.

Was there really a battle between Nazarenes and Romans in which a Roman Legion was defeated and 2000 prisoners captured, tortured and choked or driven over a cliff? If there were Roman records of this event they would have been destroyed long ago by the Christians when they achieved power in the fourth century. We do know the Roman Tenth Legion (the one called Fretensis—there was another Tenth Legion) was based in Syria, which included Judaea, and its standard carried the image of a boar, a pig. From about the time of the Jewish War this legion seems to have been permanently stationed in Jerusalem with its camp on the site in the Upper City where earlier Herod's palace and the Upper Room of the last supper were believed to have been situated. The Fretensis legion might have been assigned to Judaea before then—as early as 20 AD! The Gadarene swine perhaps referred explicitly to this legion and not just generally to gentiles.

It might seem incredible that Jesus's band should have been strong enough to defeat a Roman legion though remarkable victories occurred only a few decades later during the Jewish War, and had occurred before in the time of Archelaus when the Roman legate of Syria, Quintillus Varus, had to come into Judaea with three legions, four troops of cavalry and Syrian and Arab auxiliaries to put down extensive uprisings. Conceivably the 2000 defeated by the Nazarenes were not Roman professionals but poorly motivated conscripts—raw troops inadequately trained and equipped. Perhaps too they were badly led.

Now if our interpretation is correct and swine was an insulting reference to Romans, the incident need not have been set in a gentile country—it could have been in Judaea, in which case it occurred during the journey to Jerusalem. If it were in Judaea, the reference to the Romans as swine was too transparent because the Jewish aversion to swine was well known, so for credibility's sake the scene had to be set in a gentile country. Mark apparently set the scene deliberately in Decapolis, the gentile country facing Galilee across the lake, using his knowledge that the Nazarenes had crossed the lake at some point. The ten Greek cities of the federation of Decapolis, which included the cities of Gadara and Gerasa, were set up by Pompey in 63 BC as a customs union and as frontier territory, a Roman buffer against the Arabs and the Parthians. Decapolis was under the protection of Rome and was accordingly taxed as a Roman province just as Judaea was. Mark having placed the incident in Decapolis, the Roman demoniac became one of its citizens.

However a mistake made throughout the gospels is to assume that words like Gadarene and Gerasene are Greek names when they are often Greek renderings of Semitic words. Gadarene or Gerasene might be a distortion of an Aramaic word describing the event, to disguise its real meaning. Mark does this elsewhere in his gospel as in the case of Capernaum. If the mention of the cities of Gadara or Gerasa is bogus, it readily explains a problem which has puzzled scholars—neither is by the edge of the lake. Gerasa was forty miles inland!

Gerasene comes from qara which refers to tearing one's garments to bare grievous sorrow of the heart, as at the news of a death or disaster. In the gospels Caiaphas does this when he takes Jesus to be blaspheming. More significantly, when the people had forsaken God, He proved He was the true king of Israel by sending Elisha to perform miracles, after the human claimant to the kingdom had torn his garments in impotent rage. Evidently the Nazarenes had given qara messianic associations from these and other scriptural precedents. In Joel 2:13 God tells his people to repent and rend their hearts rather than their garments. In 1 Samuel 15:28, it is used figuratively of tearing a kingdom from a bad ruler when David was chosen as God's successor to Saul. The sense that comes over is that the Gerasenes are those who have made Israel rend her clothes in sorrow, those who are not God's chosen as ruler of Israel, those whom God will remove if the children of Israel rend their hearts and repent. The Gerasenes are the Roman oppressors!

However Gadarene might be closer to the truth. Gadarene might be a Hellenization of the word, *qidron,* meaning a dark or black place—none other than the brook Qidron which flows in a deep valley between the temple and the Mount of Olives! Another name of this valley is the valley of Jehoshaphat (meaning Jehovah judges), the scene of the final judgement in the passage from Joel quoted above. It was therefore (and still is) lined with the tombs of those hoping to be judged as righteous and resurrected into the kingdom.

Now if Jesus and his band of Nazarenes had destroyed a Roman legion on the way to Jerusalem why would the citizens of the city have wanted him to depart (Mk 8:17). The Jews who had been eager for a saviour messiah should have been delighted, yet they were not grateful that Legion had been driven out—they were frightened and begged the Nazarenes to leave. The answer is given by a more careful reading of Mark. He says: *they that fed the swine fled, and told it in the city* (Mk 8:14). He is speaking about the Jews who made a comfortable living out of providing for the Roman soldiers—the collaborators, and we can be sure it was the chief collaborators, the Sadducees, that came back with them from the city and begged Jesus to depart. They were the ones who stood to lose. That is just the behaviour you might expect of collaborators in a dependency faced with the possibility of retribution against themselves by the dominant power. The Pharisees would have had the same attitude. They would have been glad to be permanently liberated but distrusted Jewish princes, realized it could not last and feared the consequences, especially if the guerrilla army remained in the area.

Jesus refused to accept the cured maniac as a follower, implying that some soldiers had offered to change sides and support him. This might suggest that some at least of the Legion were allies, not native Romans but opportunists ready to fight for whoever was likely to win, and not soldiers of the highest morale. If Jesus released any and sent them on their way, to proclaim the great things the Lord hath done, it could only be because they had offered to support him. But Jesus wanted only Jews. These were gentiles and there was no time for them to be circumcised as proselytes, recover and join God's soldiers. With this victory the gates of the kingdom had begun to open! However the last three verses are in the unmistakeable style of Mark the editor and have been composed by him for his gentile readers.

The conclusion to all this is that here we have the Nazarene victory over the Romans which made them withdraw from Jerusalem to get reinforcements from Caesarea on the coast or even from Syria. The skeptic might wonder, if our reconstruction is correct and the incident was so embarassing to the first gentile Christians, why the passage should have been included in the gospels at all. The answer is that it is genuine tradition. Those who knew the truth were repeating the story and it could not be ignored. Instead it was re-written and reinterpreted, as other difficult instances were. The bishops told the gentile converts who had been hearing stories from Palestinian Jews: "It wasn't quite like that. This is what really happened..." What we have in the gospels is the attempt of the bishops to render acceptable stories of an astonishing military victory by their God over their rulers, the Romans.

Mark 5:1 to 5:20 Restored

And the ruler of Judaea had sent out soldiers to punish the Jews. And Jesus taught, saying: *Israel did rend her clothes in sorrow, for God choseth not the stranger as ruler of Israel. The stranger was like unto a man with an unclean spirit, desireth of destroying the Son of God, and was mighty, such that no man could bind him, no, not with fetters or with chains, neither could any man tame him, save God alone. But, God will tame them, because the children of Israel have rent their hearts and repented.* And they took arms and went out to confront those whom they hated. And coming nigh unto a mountain, there was there a great herd of swine feeding in the valley of the Qidron. There were about 2000 of them for they were a legion. And they came at them from the mountain, by surprise, cutting them with stones and darts hurled from high, and others caught those who tried to shelter from the stones and cut them down with swords. And ran them down, pulled them in pieces, mangled them, and chopped them down. And some were put in chains, and they besought in loud voices for them to torture them not, to spare them. But they heard them not, and some were choked to death in the waters of the brook, and others besought him that they might be with him, and others escaped to Caesarea. And they that fed the swine fled, and told it in the city, and told what was befallen. And the Sadducees and Pharisees said: *What manner of man is this?* And, behold, they came out and besought him to depart from them; for they were taken with great fear. And Jesus said: *Sing ye unto the Lord a new song in the assembly of all the saints: Praise ye the Lord. Let the children of Zion be joyful in their king; for the Lord taketh pleasure in His people; He will beautify the meek with salvation. Let the saints exult in His glory with two edged swords in their hands; to execute vengeance on the nations; to bind their kings with chains, and their nobles with fetters of iron; to execute upon them the judgement written: this honour have His saints. Praise the Lord.*

A Dead Girl and a Menstrual Woman

Mark 5:21 – 5:43

5:21 And when Jesus was passed over again by ship unto the other side, much people gathered unto him: and he was nigh unto the sea. 5:22 And, behold, there cometh one of the rulers of the synagogue, Jairus by name; and when he saw him, he fell at his feet, 5:23 And besought him greatly, saying, My little daughter lieth at the point of death: I pray thee, come and lay thy hands on her, that she may be healed; and she shall live. 5:24 And Jesus went with him; and much people followed him, and thronged him. 5:25 And a certain woman, which had an issue of blood twelve years, 5:26 And had suffered many things of many physicians, and had spent all that she had, and was nothing bettered, but rather grew worse, 5:27 When she had heard of Jesus, came in the press behind, and touched his garment. 5:28 For she said, If I may touch but his clothes, I shall be whole. 5:29 And straightway the fountain of her blood was dried up; and she felt in her body that she was healed of that plague. 5:30 And Jesus, immediately knowing in himself that virtue had gone out of him, turned him about in the press, and said, Who touched my clothes? 5:31 And his disciples said unto him, Thou seest the multitude thronging thee, and sayest thou, Who touched me? 5:32 And he looked round about to see her that had done this thing. 5:33 But the woman fearing and trembling, knowing what was done in her, came and fell down before him, and told him all the truth. 5:34 And he said unto her, Daughter, thy faith hath made thee whole; go in peace, and be whole of thy plague. 5:35 While he yet spake, there came from the ruler of the synagogue's house certain which said, Thy daughter is dead: why troublest thou the Master any further? 5:36 As soon as

Jesus heard the word that was spoken, he saith unto the ruler of the synagogue, Be not afraid, only believe. 5:37 And he suffered no man to follow him, save Peter, and James, and John the brother of James. 5:38 And he cometh to the house of the ruler of the synagogue, and seeth the tumult, and them that wept and wailed greatly. 5:39 And when he was come in, he saith unto them, Why make ye this ado, and weep? the damsel is not dead, but sleepeth. 5:40 And they laughed him to scorn. But when he had put them all out, he taketh the father and the mother of the damsel, and them that were with him, and entereth in where the damsel was lying. 5:41 And he took the damsel by the hand, and said unto her, Talitha cumi; which is, being interpreted, Damsel, I say unto thee, arise. 5:42 And straightway the damsel arose, and walked; for she was of the age of twelve years. And they were astonished with a great astonishment. 5:43 And he charged them straitly that no man should know it; and commanded that something should be given her to eat.

A Dead Girl and a Menstrual Woman

More miracles. Two stories are presented, one surrounding the other. A woman touches the fringe of Jesus's robe and is cured of a haemorrhage she has had for twelve years. The fringe referred to is the four tassels required by the law of Moses, showing again that Jesus followed Jewish orthodoxy. More amazingly the daughter, aged twelve, of a president of a synagogue—a Pharisee!—is raised from the dead. Peter and the Sons of Thunder as well as the parents are present. The two stories are written in different styles so must have come from different sources originally but Mark had reason to present them together. If the two stories were originally together but Mark got two versions of them he might have preferred one from each of his two versions. If the two stories occurred separately Mark has seen their connexion and linked them.

The period of twelve years is the link. A woman ill for twelve years is cured and a girl at the beginning of womanhood dies but is resurrected. Two healing miracles, one of them apparently truly miraculous. The clue that the story of the older woman was a parable and not a real event is that no Jewish woman with such a haemorrhage would have been in a crowd. She would have been unwelcome—menstrual discharges were unclean. If she had touched Jesus then he would also have been unclean. And this poor woman had been ritually unclean for twelve years continuously!

There was a point about the touching for gentile readers of the time of Mark. They believed that holy men exuded their power or dynamis involuntarily. Believers could tap it just as the menstruating woman did. Mark has to make Jesus different however and, at the same time, get over a Pauline message. Mark makes Jesus immediately aware that his power is being drained from him and demands to know who had stolen it from him. Nevertheless he forgives her and assures her, and the Christian proselytes reading the story, that faith is the essence of salvation. All of which makes it clear that none of it is genuine Nazarene tradition and can be ignored.

In the story about the raising of the little girl, besides forgetting about the mutual antagonism between Jesus and the Pharisees, Mark forgets that the crowd must still have been outside even though he had forbidden them to see the cure itself. Thus they would all have known about it as soon as the little girl chose to appear in public and his strait charge that no man should know is absurd. This too is a parable.

Here we have two bold speeches or declarations of Jesus in which he uses the two metaphors to show that the time to liberate Judaea is right. Naive Christians or the evangelist transmute them into innocent healing miracles.

The woman and the girl are personifications of Israel. Sickness and death, as ever, represent spiritual sickness—defeatism, lack of morale, fear. Judaea has been unclean for twelve years, suffered for twelve years, from her occupation by the Romans in 6 AD. Now she would be cleansed or cured—the word for healed used in the parables really means saved or delivered. In another sense Israel has been like a little girl growing up for twelve years. She is God's betrothed. Now, though she is on the verge of maturity and soon will be able to marry, she has been sentenced to death. For the Essenes, according to a scroll fragment, a betrothed girl who committed adultery had committed a capital crime. Israel had committed adultery because she had allowed herself to be abducted and ravished by the Romans. For that she should die but Jesus intended to save her from death so that the intended marriage could go ahead.

Jesus reassures his followers that she is not dead but only sleeping and tells her to rise using the expression, Talitha cumi, Maiden arise, a possible pun on words like, *lambs rise up* or *poor ones rise up*. The audience are amazed in just the sense that they were amazed in other parts of the gospel—Jesus was boldly declaring UDI. Finally he tells them to be discreet and not to tell anyone, for obvious reasons. Jesus could not have even imagined that he would be able to keep quiet the miracle of bringing a physically dead person to life. The correct interpretation makes it possible and necessary.

There is yet more to the raising of the young girl. The clue here is that Jesus takes with him the three priests in the leadership of the Nazarenes, Peter, James and John. They always accompany Jesus on solemn occasions, like the transfiguration and the expected miracle in Gethsemene. The raising of the girl is therefore actually a Nazarene ritual, an acted parable. It seems that Jesus with his high priests ritually raises Israel from her death with the slogan or war cry, Talitha Cumi. The ruler of the synagogue would have been a mistranslation of the guardian of the congregation or assembly, an Essene camp rather than the synagogue—the Hebrew can be translated as either according to context. The name of the guardian, Jair, means God's enlightened.

The evangelist adds that the maiden should be given something to eat, seemingly to add realism to his rewriting of the ritual as a miracle, but probably that part of the ritual when the Nazarenes were given a morsel of the holy bread of life. In other words, the Essene messianic meal concluded the ceremony, but the gospel writer cannot say so because he is reserving the institution of the Eucharist for the last supper, later in the narrative.

This explanation of the interval of twelve years would put the activity of Jesus at the time that Caiaphas was appointed High Priest (18 AD). Pilate might also have been appointed prefect at about this time and not eight years later as Josephus appears to write in Antiquities of the Jews. It is possible that the two intervals that Josephus mentions that provide our only information about the extent of Pilate's prefecture have been altered,

Control of Judaea was vested by the Emperor of Rome in prefects and later procurators who he appointed to govern the province on his behalf. They had to report to him all significant events that occurred. Imperial policy centred on raising revenue through taxation and, to do so effectively, maintaining peace, the pax romani. So a governor's duties included keeping law and order and raising taxes. Since they were unpaid, governors had to obtain their own income out of local revenue. By milking the province to get rich they created another source of unrest. They had a small garrison of about 3000 soldiers based at Caesarea on the coast but some were deployed in Jerusalem especially when it was crowded with pilgrims at the Passover.

The first three prefects served a tour of duty of three years each (four years in ancient reckoning because they counted inclusively—they counted the part year at the beginning and end of a period of office as a year). The Emperor was Augustus. The next prefect, Gratus, according to extant works of Josephus, served for eleven years and then Pilate served for ten. The Emperor these two served under was Tiberius.

The High Priest under the first three prefects was Annas, but Gratus introduced regular changes of High Priest. Josephus tells us that he immediately replaced Annas, and successively appointed Ismael, Eleazar, Simon and finally Joseph Caiaphas. Caiaphas was, of course, the villain of the gospel stories and we know from Josephus that he served as High Priest for the entire time of Pilate's prefecture. Curiously though, the fourth gospel speaks of Caiaphas being High Priest of the year, implying that when he was appointed the tenure was only for a year. That would fit in with what Josephus told us about the system introduced by Gratus. If Gratus changed the High priest annually and he appointed four in all, then he served a three year tour like his three predecessors. Caiaphas had been appointed just as Gratus left and was therefore the incumbent when Pilate arrived. Pilate found he could work with Caiaphas, reverted to the procedure which preceded Gratus and left Caiaphas in post.

If this reasoning is correct Caiaphas was appointed in 18 AD and Pilate later the same year. Pilate was withdrawn in the year before Tiberius died, 36 AD, so that he served 18 years. Why, you might ask did Pilate get such a long tour of duty? The answer is that Tiberius knew that governors bled their provinces to get rich, but he had the express philosophy that a bloated fly fell off the corpse. Tiberius let his governors have long tours of duty so that the people of the provinces would get some peace once the governor had made his fortune. When he became Emperor he inherited Augustus's system of short tours of duty and so Gratus served his allotted three years. Once Tiberius had formulated his bloated fly philosophy, the governor was in post for an indefinite period.

Mark 5:21 to 5:43 Restored

And many people gathered unto Jesus, who stood with Peter, and James, and John the brother of James. And behold, there cometh from the crowd one of the rulers of the council, Jair, which is God's enlightened. And he announced: *The bridegroom is without, but woe to us all; for His betrothed, a damsel coming to the age of marriage hath been ravished by the stranger, and must die.* While he yet spake, a voice said: *The damsel is dead: why troublest thou the Master any further?* And the people wept and wailed. And Jesus saith unto them: *Why make ye this ado, and weep? She shall live, and find favour once more with the bridegroom. Be not afraid, only believe; the damsel is not dead, but sleepeth.* And a voice, which was Satan, laughed him to scorn. And Jesus looked up, praying: *Lord, forgive thy children their trespasses, hear them repent and enter the sacred water. If it be thy will, let Israel be restored in thy sight. Talitha cumi, Damsel, I say unto thee, arise.* And a voice announced: *the damsel is arisen, and walketh.* And Jesus said unto them: *the bridegroom awaiteth.* And they were astonished with a great astonishment. And he charged them straitly that no man should know it. And he commanded that they should partake of the holy meal of the just. And Jesus said to them a parable. *A certain woman had an issue of blood twelve years, and had suffered many things of many physicians, but none could heal her. And eventually she had spent all that she had, and was still nothing bettered, but rather grew worse. And a gazer came to her, and said: Doest thou know, and believe in your whole heart that thou hast only one Lord, the Lord thy God? And the woman wept and confessed her sins, and begged forgiveness, and repented. And the gazer forgave her sins. And when she stepped from the holy water, straightway the fountain of her blood was dried up; and she felt in her body that she was healed of that plague and cleansed. And this son of man says unto you, truly Israel shall be healed of her plague.*

A Prophet without Honour

Mark 6:1 – 6:6

6:1 And he went out from thence, and came into his own country; and his disciples follow him. 6:2 And when the sabbath day was come, he began to teach in the synagogue: and many hearing him were astonished, saying, From whence hath this man these things? and what wisdom is this which is given unto him, that even such mighty works are wrought by his hands? 6:3 Is not this the carpenter, the son of Mary, the brother of James, and Joses, and of Juda, and Simon? and are not his sisters here with us? And they were offended at him. 6:4 But Jesus, said unto them, A prophet is not without honour, but in his own country, and among his own kin, and in his own house. 6:5 And he could there do no mighty work, save that he laid his hands upon a few sick folk, and healed them. 6:6 And he marvelled because of their unbelief. And he went round about the villages, teaching.

A Prophet without Honour

Why is Jesus at this point coming back into his own country when we did not even know he had left it. This pericope must belong after Jesus returns from his trip to Phoenicia. He has crowned himself messiah—the transfiguration—adding prophet to his previous titles.

His family are explicitly described but with no mention of Joseph—he is found nowhere in Mark—and it is not Jewish custom to refer to lineage through the mother, as here. The dogma of the perpetual virginity of the Mother of Christ had not arisen at the time of Mark so he jollily lists Mary and his brothers, James, Joses, Judas and Simon, and some sisters too.

They and others are offended by Jesus's teaching, leading Jesus to comment that a prophet is not without honour save in his own country and among his own kin. Yet if Jesus were teaching simple honest truths why should anyone have been offended. Nor is it because he was preaching insurgency and anyone contemplating rebellion against the Romans and their Herodian puppets must be mad—it was because he now claimed to be the messiah.

Luke 4:16 – 30—A Speech in Nazareth

The corresponding passage in Luke 4:16–24 gives much more detail. He tells us that Jesus taught in the synagogue at Nazareth, and quoted a passage from Isaiah 61:1–2:

> The spirit of the Lord God is upon me, because the Lord hath anointed me to preach good tidings unto the meek; he hath sent me to bind up the brokenhearted, to proclaim liberty to the captives, and the opening of the prison to them that are bound; to proclaim the acceptable year of the Lord, and the day of vengeance of our God; to comfort all that mourn.

The passage is from the late parts of Isaiah which were probably written by Essenes or their predecessors, the Hasidim. The language is purely Essene and messianic—just what we would have expected a nasi like John the Baptist and now Jesus to be proclaiming. He is proclaiming an insurrection which will change the hearts of the oppressed children of Israel. Captives and prisoners will be released. He even announces the day of vengeance of our God also calling it the acceptable year of the Lord. The acceptable year of the Lord is not as the clergy maintain the era of salvation following the messiah but is the appointed time of the Lord as the Essenes would put it. This is plain because it is when God takes his vengeance. Luke does not include the final line of Isaiah's verse 61:2—his quotation ends at acceptable year of the Lord. Clergymen argue that Jesus deliberately ended there because his message was not one of vengeance, but that is nonsense. The author of Luke or an editor ended there because he wanted to suppress the real Nazarene message!

The quotation is altered as well as curtailed. The *meek* of Isaiah is changed to the *poor* of Luke and Luke inserts after captives, *and recovering of sight to the blind*. The Essenes knew themselves as the meek and the poor, so Jesus was not preaching good tidings to any meek or poor people but only those who were righteous, those who had repented and accepted baptism. The Nazarenes understood doubt, unbelief, opposition and apostasy in terms of metaphors of physical affliction. Offering to recover the sight of the blind, Jesus is saying that he will persuade doubters to repent and join God's army.

Jesus boldly declares: *This day is this scripture fulfilled in your ears*, announcing himself as *that prophet* of Moses, he who will fulfil the prophecy of Isaiah. He symbolically proclaims it by choosing the passage where Isaiah movingly says that the spirit of the Lord was upon him, and in Luke 4:24 specifically uses the word prophet of himself. Now he is prophet, priest and prince—the messiah, the Lord hath anointed me. The age of prophecy was considered to have ended, so for Jesus to claim to be a prophet was as bold as his other claims. People were now very skeptical of him and he could not persuade any (or not many) people to join his crusade.

Mark 6:1 to 6:6 Restored

And he came into his own country, and his disciples follow him. And when the sabbath day was come he began to teach in the synagogue. There came thither his brethren and his kinfolk. And he read from the book of the prophet Isaiah: *The spirit of the Lord God is upon me, because the Lord hath anointed me to preach good tidings to the poor; he hath sent me to bind up the brokenhearted, to proclaim liberty to the captives, and the recovering of sight to the blind, and the opening of the prison to them that are bound; to proclaim the acceptable year of the Lord, and the day of vengeance of our God. This day is the scripture fulfilled in your ears.* And he told them of the kingdom to come calling for their repentance. And many hearing him were astonished saying: *Whence hath this man this authority? Is not this the mason; and his brethren and sisters, are they not with us?* And Jesus said unto them: *Who are my brethren? For the sons of Levi slew their brethren which trespassed against the Lord. My brethren are these which hear the word of God and slayeth the deceiver.* And Jesus could do no mighty works because of their unbelief, and he said: *A prophet is not without honour, save in his own country and among his own kin; nor is a physician able to cure those who know him.* And they were offended at him. They went out to lay hold on him, for they said: *He has gone mad to preach such things.*

The Mission of the Disciples

Mark 6:7 – 6:13

6:7 And he called unto him the twelve, and began to send them forth by two and two; and gave them power over unclean spirits; 6:8 And commanded them that they should take nothing for their journey, save a staff only; no scrip, no bread, no money in their purse: 6:9 But be shod with sandals; and not put on two coats. 6:10 And he said unto them, In what place soever ye enter into an house, there abide till ye depart from that place. 6:11 And whosoever shall not receive you, nor hear you, when ye depart thence, shake off the dust under your feet for a testimony against them. Verily I say unto you, It shall be more tolerable for Sodom and Gomorrha in the day of judgment, than for that city. 6:12 And they went out, and preached that men should repent. 6:13 And they cast out many devils, and anointed with oil many that were sick, and healed them.

The Mission of the Disciples

Jesus gets concerned that many Jews will not hear his message before the kingdom dawns. The signs of the times tell him it is imminent and he would have no chance of reaching all Jews before judgement day. He therefore hopes to speed up the recruitment process by sending out disciples.

The fashion in which the disciples were sent out is revealing. They followed the practice of the Essenes who always succoured brother travellers passing by. Jesus tells them to carry only the minimum with them (though they were allowed a staff, as were the Essenes largely for defensive and hygienic reasons) and to depend upon voluntary assistance. Josephus in The Jewish War writes: *They carry nothing with them on a journey except arms as a protection against brigands. In every city there is one of their order expressly appointed to attend strangers, who provides them with clothing and other necessities.*

The message in Mark 6:12 is the urgency of repentance for the coming of the kingdom and Matthew 10:7 states it explicitly: *And as ye go, preach, saying, The kingdom of heaven is at hand.* The message in Luke 10:9, repeated in 10:11, is: *The kingdom of God is come nigh unto you.* In Matthew 8:22 and Luke 9:60 the urgency is such that Jesus says: *Let the dead bury the dead.* It was too late for funereal nostalgia, too late for the physically dead to repent. The living had to be persuaded to repent. Then as the righteous, they would be resurrected into everlasting life. Jesus expected the kingdom of God to come with a vengeance at almost any time soon. His message was urgent! That people can still be waiting 2000 years later proves their gullibility and the power of the priesthood to control people's thoughts. As an Essene, Jesus knew the signs of the times—those times! They told him that the day of judgement was nigh! Then! He was wrong but is still believed now!

The warning to those who did not welcome or listen to the messengers, even whole households or cities, was severe: *It shall be more tolerable for Sodom and*

Gomorrha in the day of judgement, than for that city. Jesus is saying that at the appointed time of God's vengeance the judgement on cities which reject the disciples will be worse than the Old Testament judgement on Sodom and Gomorrha. If they did not listen and repent, then that was their punishment.

Jesus's message was specifically for Jews and not gentiles. Jesus's command (Mt 10:5–6) was not to go into the way of the gentiles or into any city of the Samaritans but go rather to the lost sheep of the house of Israel. Luke's creation (Lk 10:1–16) of the mission of the seventy—which he bases on the mission of the twelve in Mark—is a Christian invention to retrieve the situation and include gentiles. Luke was writing for gentiles and finishes up cursing Jewish cities because of their failure to repent and praising gentile cities like Tyre and Sidon. In Matthew 11:20–24 this cursing happens in a different context casting doubt on it.

However comparing Mark 6:11 and Matthew 10:15 with Matthew 11:22 and Luke 10:14 shows that Tyre and Sidon should really be Sodom and Gomorrha. Indeed it is clear even within Luke (Lk 10:12 and Lk 10:14). A gentile has altered the original comparison in Mark of the faithless cities with Sodom and Gomorrha to one with the gentile cities Tyre and Sidon to make it sound as though Jews were less worthy than gentiles. It is patently nonsense because the Jewish yardstick for sinning was the law of Moses. How could a gentile repent of sins of which he was not aware? So the woes on the cities seem like edited Nazarene tradition—a bewailing of hard-hearted towns that had rejected the disciples. It therefore all belongs when they return.

Matthew glaringly contradicts himself in verses 10:8 and 10:10. In verse 8 the disciples were to deliver their message freely as it was received, but in 10 the implication is that they should be paid. Jesus as an Essene would have expected no payment, nor accepted it, but only food and shelter. He was an Ebionite, one of the poor. Paul it was who taught that missionaries should expect to be paid. It has been the justification of every evangelical quack ever since—and don't they get rich!

The anointing with oil in verse 6:13 is probably wrong. Essenes did not use oil which they considered defiling, though they would have used ointments to cure physical ailments. These people were not physically sick but spiritually sick, though Mark thinks or pretends they were physically sick. Spiritual sickness is cured by repentance and baptism not by oil. The evangelist changed the sacrament by baptism into anointing with oil to maintain the pretence that physical ilnesses were being cured.

Mark has Jesus dispatching the twelve to preach when elsewhere in his account they show little understanding of Jesus's message. Either they are not as stupid as Mark depicts them or they were not sent out in this way. The twelve is Mark's convenient way of indicating the selected twelve but it does not come from the original tradition where it would have been simply disciples. Disciples, not the twelve, were sent out to the surrounding villages to garner support.

In Matthew, Jesus's mission speech goes on for another 26 verses after it ends in Mark, but some of it turns up in Mark's mini-apocalypse in his chapter 13. Mostly it is not genuine Nazarene tradition but Christian additions. However we find (Mt 10:23): *Ye shall not have gone over the cities of Israel, till the Son of man be come*, which—if the Son of man meant Daniel's one like unto a Son of man—means the appointed time of the Lord was due soon. And then we find (Mt 10:34): *Think not that I am come to send peace on earth: I came not to send peace, but a sword*, which can only be interpreted in a non-peaceful sense since Jesus plainly says so! In Luke 12:51 it is toned down to a division, but Luke says also: *I am come to send fire on the earth; and what will I if it be already kindled.* Freely rendered Jesus is saying: I didn't start the trouble, it had already started.

Mark 6:7 to 6:13 Restored

And he resolved to baptize many of the simple of Ephraim. and he called unto him disciples and began to send them forth by two and two. Nor would they need take anything for their journey, no scrip, no bread, no money in their purse, neither two pairs of sandals, nor two coats, save only a staff; for the elect would provide. And Jesus commanded them: *Go not into the way of the gentiles and into any city of the Samaritans enter ye not: but go rather to the lost sheep of the house of Israel. And when ye stand before them, take no thought beforehand what ye shall speak, neither do ye premeditate: but whatsoever shall be given you in that hour, that speak ye: for it is not ye that speak, but the holy ghost. And as ye go preach, saying: The kingdom of God is at hand, repent that God might heal thee that thou might join the elect of God. Ye shall not have gone over the cities of Israel, till the kingdom be come.* And thereby gained they power over sickness and unclean spirits. So they went out and preached repentance; and they cast out demons and cured sick people admitting them into the new covenant by the sacrament of baptism.

Herod is Informed

Mark 6:14 – 6:16

6:14 And king Herod heard of it; for his name was spread abroad: and he said, That John the Baptist was risen from the dead, and therefore mighty works do shew forth themselves in him. 6:15 Others said, That it is Elias. And others said, That it is a prophet, or as one of the prophets. 6:16 But when Herod heard thereof, he said, It is John, whom I beheaded: he is risen from the dead.

Herod is Informed

All this recruitment activity had got through to Herod who believed that John the Baptist had returned from the dead, although we have not yet been told that he had died. The implication of this is that Jesus was John's successor but John did not, in fact, die until after Jesus. Jesus had to take the mantle prematurely because John was imprisoned by Herod for the latter part of his life. This in turn indicates that John the Baptist was more than just a desert hermit forgiving sins in the Jordan. He too had been recruiting supporters to the cause of national rebellion. Indeed in 6:20 John is described as a zaddik and a saint (a just man and an holy), one of the righteous, an Essene.

Mark 6:14 to 6:16 Restored

And king Herod heard of it, for his name was spread abroad. And he asked: *is John the Baptist burst free from prison and again preaching sedition?* They replied: *No, it is Elias or that prophet.* But Herod said: *if it cannot be John, whom I imprisoned, then his successor is risen.*

The Death of John the Baptist

Mark 6:17 – 6:29

6:17 For Herod himself had sent forth and laid hold upon John, and bound him in prison for Herodias' sake, his brother Philip's wife: for he had married her. 6:18 For John had said unto Herod, It is not lawful for thee to have thy brother's wife. 6:19 Therefore Herodias had a quarrel against him, and would have killed him; but she could not: 6:20 For Herod feared John, knowing that he was a just man and an holy, and observed him; and when he heard him, he did many things, and heard him gladly. 6:21 And when a convenient day was come, that Herod on his birthday made a supper to his lords, high captains, and chief estates of Galilee; 6:22 And when the daughter of the said Herodias came in, and danced, and pleased Herod and them that sat with him, the king said unto the damsel, Ask of me whatsoever thou wilt, and I will give it thee. 6:23 And he sware unto her, Whatsoever thou shalt ask of me, I will give it thee, unto the half of my kingdom. 6:24 And she went forth, and said unto her mother, What shall I ask? And she said, The head of John the Baptist. 6:25 And she came in straightway with haste unto the king, and asked, saying, I will that thou give me by and by in a charger the head of John the Baptist. 6:26 And the king was exceeding sorry; yet for his oath's sake, and for their sakes which sat with him, he would not reject her. 6:27 And immediately the king sent an executioner, and commanded his head to be brought: and he went and beheaded him in the prison, 6:28 And brought his head in a charger, and gave it to the damsel: and the damsel gave it to her mother. 6:29 And when his disciples heard of it, they came and took up his corpse, and laid it in a tomb.

The Death of John the Baptist

Only now do we get the death of John the Baptist. In Matthew 11:2–19 and Luke 7:18–25 we were told of messengers coming from John in prison to ask of Jesus: *Art thou he that should come, or do we look for another?* The implication is that John the Baptist is impatient with Jesus's work. As an Essene leader he knows just as well as Jesus that the signs of the times are prophesying the day of the vengeance of the Lord. Yet Jesus does not seem to be preparing for it adequately as the nasi. These gospels tell us Jesus gratuitously demonstrates his healing powers to prove to John's disciples that he is doing his job.

In Matthew 11:7 and Luke 7:24 John's disciples depart, to report Jesus's reply back to their master. It is quite apparent however that the verses in Matthew 11:7–15 and in Luke 7:24–30 are out of sequence. This is transparently clear in Matthew because his verse 15 contains Jesus's formula for ending a parabolic speech: *He that hath ears to hear, let him hear*, but the speech continues. Matthew 11:16–19 and Luke 7:31–35 are part of the reply to John's messengers, although tampered with by Christian editors at the end. Jesus is complaining to the messengers of John: *we can mourn before people but they will not lament; we can pipe for people but they will not dance*. The proverb we are familiar with is: *you can take a horse to water but you cannot make it drink*. He is complaining about the response from the simple of Ephraim.

Only after this should follow the misplaced verses. The messengers go, and Jesus turns to those observing and berates them: *What did they think John was doing in the desert? Dressing as a king or waving a reed in the wind?* He was a great prophet sent to prepare the way for the coming kingdom, not a namby-pamby. John is the herald of the kingdom. With him it begins but it has suffered violence under the oppressors and has to be taken by force. This little speech probably belongs elsewhere but has been placed here because it refers to John the Baptist.

The story about Herodias, Herod's wife plotting to have the Baptist killed contrary to Herod's wishes has characteristically Essene features. The scrolls show that the Essenes disagreed with the lax marital practices of the Herodians. Antipas had married his half-brother Philip's divorced wife, Herodias, who were their niece and already had four children. Philip was not the tetrarch of Iturea who married Herodias's daughter, Salome, but a brother who lived in Rome as a private citizen. Marrying a sister-in-law was illegal according to Leviticus 18:16 unless the woman had had no children when it was obliged (Deut 25:5). However John would also have objected to Herod marrying his niece. Jewish law allowed this but not the Essenes.

The story is romanticized here using scriptural precedents. There are echoes of Jezebel from 1 Kings and the fairy-tale formula of Esther 5:3 is used by Herod in verse 23. Incidentally this latter tends to show this passage is not genuine Nazarene tradition because it seems the Essenes did not regard Esther as being canonical, no copies being found in their library, though possibly the copies they had have all decayed. The fairy-tale elements are added as a distraction from the truth that, though respecting him as a saint, Herod feared John as a rebel. After all, John the Baptist had apparently done nothing worse than baptize a few multitudes in the Jordan river. Why should that worry a potentate like Herod Antipas to the extent of having him beheaded? Of course it could not but the Baptist was a dangerous barjona recruiting people to join the army of God, just like Jesus. Josephus is more honest in Antiquities of the Jews where John is described as *a disturber of the people, who seemed ready to do anything he should advise*. Mark cannot allow this to be known and so the original Essene complaint against the Herodians was expanded to cover up the truth.

The reason why the story appears at all is to mark the death of John the Baptist and the succession of Jesus. In Matthew 14:13 the connexion is explicit. The aim was to show to followers of the Baptist that they should have transferred their allegiance to Jesus on his death. Hitherto Jesus had been the crown prince but now he had become the mebaqqer of the Nazarenes. But all of Mark 6:14 to 6:29 interrupts the dispatching of the disciples on their mission and their return, serving only as a literary device to signify the passage of time. Indeed it could have been omitted and no one would have noticed, except that the disciples would have seemed to have returned immediately. The passage is a Christian elaboration, for Jesus became the leader in practice when John was captured not when John was murdered—though he was not the titular leader. The gospels succeed in suggesting the passage of time between John's capture and death, and Matthew gives just the right flavour when John sends a message from prison to Jesus in verses 11:2–3. Almost half way through the gospel, John the Baptist is still alive in jail, and able to get messages to the outside! Only half way through Matthew in 14:2 are we told indirectly that John is dead. Gospel truth is a powerful concept and because the gospels tell us that John died first we all believe it even though Josephus contradicts it. Jesus must have died first.

Antipas's previous wife was the daughter of Aretas (Harith) IV, the Arabian king of Nabataea, who Josephus tells us began a war with Herod when he divorced his daughter. Herod rapidly lost a large army against the Arabs and according to rumour the Jews believed it was his punishment for murdering the Baptist. That the rumour should have been important enough for Josephus to record shows that John left a deep impression in Palestine at that time. The war did not begin until 36 AD whereas on gospel dating Jesus died not later than 33 AD and possibly a decade earlier.

Now Antipas married Herodias about the time that Tiberius succeeded Augustus to the Imperial Throne in 14 AD. If John really complained about Herod's marital affairs then he must have complained immediately and Herod must have had to put up with John's criticism. John must have been an important person in Judaea when Tiberius came to the throne. John the Baptist's long career has been compressed in the gospels to make it seem insignificant compared with Jesus's. In fact John started long before Jesus and was not murdered until some time after Jesus was. The early church had to counter the impression that John was the more important person, so they compressed his life, made him acknowledge Jesus as the messiah, gave him the role of compere and made him die first so that Jesus became the message—not John as many thought at the time—not the messenger.

Why then did it take Harith so long to avenge his daughter? The reason probably was that Harith was scared of the consequences—scared of Rome— because Antipas was well considered by the imperial court. He had to bide his time. Tiberius began as a vigorous Emperor, a good administrator, an active soldier supporting effective military campaigns and a successful statesman annexing Commagene and Cappadocia. Harith thought it too risky to take on a Roman favourite. Later Tiberius became morose and reclusive, eventually retiring to Capri where he ruled by diktat. From 32 AD until his death in 37 AD he did not budge from his island home. Plainly the lack of vigour of the Emperor, combined with Harith's awareness that time was no longer on his side, for he too was an old man, and a border dispute with Antipas, impelled him to strike. Thus it was that it took him twenty years to avenge his daughter's dishonour. In fact his judgement was pretty shrewd, because Tiberius was enraged by the attack on Antipas and ordered Vitellius, legate of Syria, to march with a large army to punish him, but Tiberius died before the command could be carried through.

John was active in the south by the Jordan and Josephus tells us that he was put to death in the fortress of Machaerus to the east of the Dead Sea, a place that can be seen across the lake from Qumran. If there were any truth in the gospel story it all occurred at Machaerus, where Herod had his southern palace, but his capital was at Tiberias where it seems more likely that he would celebrate a birthday. John must have been murdered during the hostilities—which would have been in the south where Nabataea and Peraea adjoined—because Herod feared the Nazarenes as potential fifth columnists. That explains why Josephus associates John's death and Herod's defeat which must have followed soon afterwards.

The Three Snares of Belial

The Damascus Rule in an interpretation of Isaiah 24:17: *Fear, and the pit, and the net, are upon thee, O inhabitant of the earth*, refers to three particular sins which concerned the community. Fear, the pit and the net are the three snares of Belial: fornication, riches and profanation of the temple. Isaiah 24:18 says everyone will be caught in one or another of these three snares.

Fornication included improper marriages such as taking more than one wife or marrying a niece. The Damascus Rule speaks of a spouter who married again while his first wife still lived, whereas the principle of creation is: *Male and female created He them* (Gen 1:27). This is the same principle expounded by Jesus and yet it is quite alien to normal Jewish law which bases itself on the commandments brought down by Moses and not on Genesis.

The Damascus Rule continues by forbidding marriage between uncles and nieces on the grounds that the law of Moses prescribes only that: *You shall not approach your mother's sister; she is your mother's own near kin*. The law quoted here forbids nephews and their maternal aunt marrying (Lev 18:13), so that there is no specific

Mosaic law against uncles marrying nieces, and the Pharisees even took it to be worthy. The Essenes asserted that laws of incest true for men were true for women also. If an aunt could not marry her nephew neither could an uncle marry his niece. Another complete scroll, the Temple Scroll, echoes the Damascus Rule in forbidding a king of Israel from marrying his niece. Since the only dynasty for which this was common practice was that of the Herodians, the scroll must refer to them. If so these scrolls must date from the time of Herod, the period of the gospels. This is the sin which Herod Antipas committed and which John the Baptist condemned. It must also negate the good terms Josephus said were shared by the community and the Herodians.

Though fornication is one of the three snares of Belial, the early characters of the Old Testament were unabashed fornicators—king David had many wives. How was this to be justified? The Qumran Community did so by arguing that the law had not yet been revealed to them or had not yet been fully revealed. They could not live according to standards that God had not yet provided. Paul, showing familiarity with Essene reasoning, uses a similar argument in Galatians 3 and Romans 4 to back up his rejection of the law. Abraham could not have been restricted by a law which did not exist yet he remained good because of his faith. Paul cunningly and deliberately uses the Essenes' own argument to maintain that faith is superior to the law. The evidence is that Paul had been trained as an Essene.

Finally for the sectaries the temple was polluted. Those in charge of it, the Sadducees, profaned it with their wealth, their disregard for the Mosaic law against sleeping with a woman who was menstruating and their acceptance of gifts from foreigners. Acts 15 and 21:25 depict James, the leader of the Jerusalem Church, as objecting to people indulging in blood, fornication and food or things sacrificed to idols—expressing concern at the pollution of the temple.

The three snares of Belial help us to understand Jesus's outlook. He also identified wealth with sin, raged at the pollution of the temple and refused to accept divorce.

Mark 6:17 to 6:29 Restored

Now when John had heard in the prison these works of Jesus, he was troubled, and sent two of his disciples, And said unto him: *Art thou he that should come, or do we look for another?* Jesus answered and said unto them: *Go and shew John the blind receive their sight, and the lame walk, the lepers are cleansed, and the deaf hear, the dead are raised up, and the poor have the glad tidings preached to them. But whereunto shall I liken this generation? It is like unto children sitting in the markets, and calling unto their fellows, and saying: We have piped unto you, and ye have not danced; we have mourned unto you, and ye have not lamented. For John came offering the bread and wine, and they say, He is mad. And this son of man came offering the bread and wine, and they say, Behold a friend of publicans and sinners. Is the wisdom of the just of her children?*

And they departed. And Jesus began to say unto the multitudes: *What went ye out into the wilderness to see? A reed shaken with the wind? A man clothed in soft raiment? They that wear soft clothing are in kings' houses. A prophet? Yea, and more than a prophet. For this is he, of whom it is written, Behold, I send my messenger, which shall prepare the way before me. Truly, among them that are born of women there hath not risen a greater than John the Baptist. Notwithstanding he that is least in the kingdom of heaven is greater than he. And the signs are that from the days of John the Baptist until now the kingdom of heaven suffereth violence, and the violent take it by force.*

The Mass Feedings and the Sermon

Mark 6:30 – 6:44

6:30 And the apostles gathered themselves together unto Jesus, and told him all things, both what they had done, and what they had taught. 6:31 And he said unto them, Come ye yourselves apart into a desert place, and rest a while: for there were many coming and going, and they had no leisure so much as to eat. 6:32 And they departed into a desert place by ship privately. 6:33 And the people saw them departing, and many knew him, and ran afoot thither out of all cities, and outwent them, and came together unto him. 6:34 And Jesus, when he came out, saw much people, and was moved with compassion toward them, because they were as sheep not having a shepherd: and he began to teach them many things. 6:35 And when the day was now far spent, his disciples came unto him, and said, This is a desert place, and now the time is far passed: 6:36 Send them away, that they may go into the country round about, and into the villages, and buy themselves bread: for they have nothing to eat. 6:37 He answered and said unto them, Give ye them to eat. And they say unto him, Shall we go and buy two hundred pennyworth of bread, and give them to eat? 6:38 He saith unto them, How many loaves have ye? go and see. And when they knew, they say, Five, and two fishes. 6:39 And he commanded them to make all sit down by companies upon the green grass. 6:40 And they sat down in ranks, by hundreds, and by fifties. 6:41 And when he had taken the five loaves and the two fishes, he looked up to heaven, and blessed, and brake the loaves, and gave them to his disciples to set before them; and the two fishes divided he among them all. 6:42 And they did all eat, and were filled. 6:43 And they took up twelve baskets full of the fragments, and of the fishes. 6:44 And they that did eat of the loaves were about five thousand men.

Mark 8:1 – 8:10

8:1 In those days the multitude being very great, and having nothing to eat, Jesus called his disciples unto him, and saith unto them, 8:2 I have compassion on the multitude, because they have now been with me three days, and have nothing to eat: 8:3 And if I send them away fasting to their own houses, they will faint by the way: for divers of them came from far. 8:4 And his disciples answered him, From whence can a man satisfy these men with bread here in the wilderness? 8:5 And he asked them, How many loaves have ye? And they said, Seven. 8:6 And he commanded the people to sit down on the ground: and he took the seven loaves, and gave thanks, and brake, and gave to his disciples to set before them; and they did set them before the people. 8:7 And they had a few small fishes: and he blessed, and commanded to set them also before them. 8:8 So they did eat, and were filled: and they took up of the broken meat that was left seven baskets. 8:9 And they that had eaten were about four thousand: and he sent them away. 8:10 And straightway he entered into a ship with his disciples...

Mass Feedings

In Mark the return of the disciples from their mission is dismissed in a single verse. In fact the woes to the unrepentant cities belong here.

Mark also tells us that Jesus becomes one of the barjonim, having escaped hurriedly to the desert in a boat. To get to the desert by boat from Galilee implies crossing the Sea of Galilee to Decapolis as he had done earlier to cure the Demoniac of Gerasa. But the word used for a lonely or desert place is used in the Septuagint to mean the wilderness which usually meant the Judaean wilderness. If it is considered that the gospel sets the story in Galilee to account for Jesus and his followers being called Galilaeans—rebel followers of the philosophy of Judas the Galilaean—then we can conclude that some of the Galilaean ministry probably happened elsewhere. As an Essene Jesus would have trained his new volunteers at Qumran.

Many people, the simple of Ephraim, had responded to the appeal of the Nazarenes—they had repented and accepted baptism. In the feeding of the five thousand we are told they came out to the desert, probably the wilderness of Judaea, to join his band—they had to be introduced to Essene disciplines. The miracle of the loaves and fishes, an explicit allegory of a training camp, follows. The crowd assemble in companies, they sit down in ranks by hundreds and by fifties an expression reminiscent of the Essenes who, following Exodus 18:21,25, spoke of their ranks as: *by thousands, hundreds, fifties and tens*. The Greek implies they look like a well tended vegetable patch, in other words neatly paraded in rows according to military discipline. There is nothing symbolic here—the crowd is explicitly drawn up in military order.

Later, in Mark 8:1–10, is the feeding of the four thousand. There are too many similarities in the two stories to be accidental, not just with the action described but with the whole arrangement of their respective sections—Mark 8:1 to 26 is an almost exact reflexion of Mark 6:35 to 7:37. It is just as if some pages of an earlier draft by mishap had been gathered with a later one and have remained there ever since because no one felt able to change the holy book.

These two feeding incidents look like the same one slightly distorted in the telling, especially since the disciples on the second occasion behave as if it had never happened before. In Christian tradition, they are so stupid that even though they had just taken part in an identical miracle, they had forgotten all about it—struck with collective amnesia. Only the stupid could believe such stupidity.

The second account has no mention of assembling in military-like ranks as the other did suggesting deliberate editing. Writing around the time of the Jewish War,

Mark would not have wanted to implicate Jesus in soldiering and the edited version was circulated. A few years later after the Jewish capital had been destroyed feelings were not running so high and the fuller version could be reintroduced with no concern about the implication of soldiering because the first Christians had established Jesus's character as pacific. An editor of Mark found himself with both accounts of a mass messianic meal in the desert, and by intention or error both were bound into the gospel. The authors of the later gospels found mustering in ranks too explicitly military and out of character for their Jesus, so again they omitted it, except in the vestigial form of Luke 9:14.

Once introduced, the second miraculous feeding had to be given a meaning and subsequent editors made sense out of the two by introducing minor symbolic differences, and adding a spurious quizzing—which must be an invention if the two accounts are of the same incident—of the disciples about them by Jesus (Mk 8:14–21). They were made to indicate that Israel, the party to God's old covenant, had been superseded. In its place was the Christian church, party to God's new covenant—later translated as New Testament—represented by the seven churches of Asia. The numbers of hampers filled were written in explicitly, and a different Greek word was used for the hamper in each miracle, to imply a qualitative as well as a quantitative difference. After the five thousand were fed twelve hampers of crumbs were gathered. In the parallel feeding of the four thousand seven hampers of crumbs were gathered. The reading was that the five loaves were the five books of the Torah and the twelve baskets were the twelve tribes of Israel. In the second miracle, theologians deliberately changed both to the number seven symbolically representing the seven churches of Asia and the seventy gentile nations of earth.

The result of the feedings is that more bread remained than they began with. How did Jesus do it? He did not—they weren't miracles. Though it is something of a convention to denote miracles or other remarkable events with expressions of astonishment, the gospel gives us none—Mark does not explicitly tag the feedings as miraculous. On completion of the muster, Jesus conducted a mass communion. The massed volunteers were received into the company of Essenes with their sacred meal—the messianic meal in which everyone received a small portion of bread and the 4000 or 5000 were spiritually filled. The original incident has been adapted along the lines of 2 Kings 4:43–44 where Elisha carries out a miracle in which small quantities of food suffice for many, with some remaining.

Mark is describing the Pentecostal Essene festival of the renewal of the covenant. This occurred on the feast of weeks, the feast of the new wheat, the Jewish Shavuot, which for Essenes was held on Sunday on the fifteenth day of the third month, Sivan (about the end of May). It celebrated the ingathering of the wheat harvest and naturally would be symbolized by ceremonies involving loaves. The two feedings in the gospel just might represent two separate annual Pentecostal festivals of the renewal of the covenant, suggesting that Jesus campaigned for over one year but less than three years. There is no mention of wine—unless the fish were originally jars of wine—possibly because Christians suppressed it as being too allied in characteristics to the Eucharist. However, the vine harvest was not yet due for several more weeks which might account for the absence of wine—Essenes using only grape juice. When unfermented wine was out of season the Essenes, who had immense faith in the purifying power of water, will have used water instead of wine.

The Essenes treated wine with some disdain as a Nazirite sect would. When they made their scriptural interpretations, the Essenes read *hyyn* which is wine as *hwn* which is wealth. As they were the poor, they rejected wine as having connotations of wealth, substituting water normally or grape juice in season. The miracle of Cana, given only in John, is a trace of this—because grape juice was unseasonal, water was ritually converted into new wine for ceremonial purposes (the wedding was the eschatological symbol of the uniting of God with Israel). For most of its first four centuries the Christian Eucharist was celebrated with bread and water not wine! In 140 AD, Justin Martyr relates how the deacons administer the Eucharist to the faithful, giving them bread and water representing the body and blood of Christ! The early Christians were continuing the traditions of of the Essenes whose new wine often meant water.

The association of the Essenes and bread is clear in their choice of this festival as their principle one. Bread symbolizes life and we can be certain that it is a metaphor for the new life to come in God's kingdom. John repeatedly (Jn 6:33;35;48;51) has Jesus calling himself the bread of life. The people gathered were being fed in a purely spiritual way as a sacrament. It is identical to the last supper but written large—both are descriptions of a symbolic Essene messianic meal. A tiny fragment of bread would serve for a symbolic spiritual feeding, just as it does in the Christian Eucharist, and the recipients would have been satisfied because they had been spiritually filled—received into the company of the Nazarenes and the elect of God. The spiritual nature of the feeding is even clear in one of the Christian gospels. Matthew has: *Blessed are they which do hunger and thirst after righteousness* (Mt 5:6). The mass feeding was to fill the Nazarenes' hunger for righteousness, not to fill their bellies. The clergy have known this for at least a hundred years (since Albert Schweitzer) but they are not keen to tell it to their flock—it would spoil the miracle.

In feeding the five thousand there are two fish. The feeding of the four thousand merely says some fish implying that the number is unimportant, and, since legendary information accumulates with time, confirming that the feeding of the 4000 is the earlier tradition. Nor does Jesus mention fish in the parabolic passage (Mk 8:17–21). He mentions only the five loaves, five thousand and twelve hampers, and the seven loaves, four thousand and seven hampers: *Having eyes, see ye not; having ears, hear ye not?* Jesus asks them—but does not explain. Apparently the fish do not matter. The symbol of the fish became important to Christians later and is being imported anachronistically into Mark's gospel. At some stage in the tradition the original seven loaves are varied into five loaves and two fish possibly because someone who saw no symbolism in the feeding felt it inconceivable that fishermen in Galilee would have no fish. Curiously fish and grain in Hebrew are closely related words, possibly inviting confusion. John

6:9 adds the detail that the loaves were of barley, the grain of the poor, tying in with the Ebionim, though the festival was that of wheat.

The twelve baskets of crumbs (morsels of bread, akin to the wafers of the Eucharist) were present at the start of the feeding. God had divided His people into twelve tribes and Jesus reflected this in his choice of twelve apostles. It signifies the children of Israel, the original chosen of God—the old covenant. Jesus, conducting the ritual, brandishes seven loaves, representing the perfect of God—the new covenant. The loaves and baskets were explained by Jesus in terms of the end of the world, and using the analogy of Elisha. The twelve tribes of Israel reach the kingdom of God (everlasting life) portrayed as bread provided in twelve baskets, by the action of the remnant of Israel, the elect of God, the Essenes, indicated by the seven loaves. Seven is the Old Testament number of perfection and so represents the Essenes, who attempted to be perfect like God—the new covenant. They would have noticed that $5 + 7 = 12$ meaning that the Pentateuch and the perfect of God— the law and the prophets (it seems Essenes also thought of themselves as prophets)—added up to the saving of the children of Israel in the kingdom to come. At some stage the perfect number seven became implicit and the Pentateuch explicit leading to the variant tradition which is recorded in the earlier feeding. Soon afterwards the Nazarenes had appointed seven deacons (Acts 6:3), and later the Christians had seven churches.

Note, though they were supposed to be at a lonely place in the desert to the east of the lake, people were able to walk there quicker than Jesus could get there by boat, and they were sufficiently near some adequate source of food because the disciples offered to go buy some. These are Mark's way of decorating the story. He had no knowledge of the area or assumed his readers had none.

Among the scrolls the rules of the festival of the renewal of the covenant have not survived, and so we do not know what the proceedings were in detail. But we know the elect were mustered and had to account for themselves, finally being assessed and regraded. It must have taken several days. Here there is the suggestion that the ritual feeding takes place after three days (Mk 8:2), not a long time for assessing 4000 people, assuming that the feeding was the termination of the proceedings, unless the assessment was perfunctory for most. Since the kingdom was imminent, the grading *will* have become perfunctory, sincere repentance being acceptable to the Master and to God. If people were not sincere, God would judge them accordingly.

Matthew 5:1 – 7:27—The Sermon

Matthew and Luke in the sermon on the mount (Mt 5:1–7:27; Lk 6:20–49) are drawing a picture of this spectacle—whether Essene or proselyte, they must have seen it.

The Rule of the Congregation directs that, in the last days, when all the congregation of Israel joins the community to walk according to the law of the sons of Zadok, the priests and the men of their covenant who have turned aside from the way of the people, then the men of His council keeping His covenant and offering expiation for the land amidst iniquity shall summon them all when they come, the little children and the women also and they shall read into their ears the precepts of the covenant and shall expound to them all their statutes, that they may no longer stray in their errors. This is precisely what Jesus is doing in the sermon on the mount. He is reading to the simple of Ephraim, who have repented and joined the new covenant, the precepts and statutes that they have to obey until the appointed day of the Lord.

There seems no obstacle to restoring the speech here, but we shall be content merely to indicate points of similarity between the sermon and the disciplines of the Essenes. Even though most of the original words are lost, it has much in common with the books of rules of the Essenes, as would be expected if the newly baptized Nazarene followers were being read the rules. Matthew's sermon is much fuller than Luke's, possibly because Matthew was an Essene. It begins with nine blessings, but originally there were probably only seven. The reward of the poor in spirit in verse 3 and the persecuted in verse 10 is the same because verse 10 has been added, and the slightly different blessing in verse 11 has also been added. Luke adds woes to his blessings and is more likely to be authentic, Matthew having omitted the woes to try to keep Jesus in character.

> 5:3 Blessed are the poor in spirit: for theirs is the kingdom of heaven. 5:4 Blessed are they that mourn: for they shall be comforted. 5:5 Blessed are the meek: for they shall inherit the earth. 5:6 Blessed are they which do hunger and thirst after righteousness: for they shall be filled. 5:7 Blessed are the merciful: for they shall obtain mercy. 5:8 Blessed are the pure in heart: for they shall see God. 5:9 Blessed are the peacemakers: for they shall be called the children of God. 5:10 Blessed are they which are persecuted for righteousness' sake: for theirs is the kingdom of heaven.

Blessings in the scrolls are quite common though usually the elect are blessing God, but one of the scrolls has a set of beatitudes similar in form to these. The words used in Matthew are purely Essene even to the use of poor in spirit which occurs for example in the War Scroll but otherwise is unknown in old scriptures. We find the poor, the meek, those hungering and thirsting for righteousness, the merciful, the pure in heart. The reward of those who are blessed is to inherit the earth or to enter the kingdom of God—the very expectations of the apocalyptic Essenes. Note also that in verse 5:9 Jesus is calling his followers, the children of God. When he talks about children in the gospels, he means—as here—the repentant, or the children of Israel. The Essenes were fond of calling themselves children also, though the word is usually translated in the masculine making them sons. No one can deny the common origin of these verses and the Dead Sea writings.

Suddenly the next two verses (Mt 5:11–12) are directed at the audience when previously they had been impersonal blessings, and Jesus loses his normal modesty, blessing those who suffer for *my sake* when the real Jesus would only have spoken of *God's sake*. They have been Christianized, emphasisng persecution—a later phase of the development of the religion. Verse 5:12 was probably: *Rejoice, and be exceeding glad: for great is your reward in heaven: for so rewarded were the prophets which were before you.* The next verses (Mt 5:13–16) have been taken

183

from a different context in Mark. However the expression: *Ye are the light of the world*, must be genuinely Nazarene.

This liturgy was probably followed by the Essene creed given in Matthew 25:31–36 in the form of a final judgement. The judge is introduced as the Son of man who comes with the angels in glory and judges all nations, dividing them into sheep and goats. The king announces to the sheep, the righteous at his right hand:

> Come, ye blessed of my Father, inherit the kingdom prepared for you from the foundation of the world: For I was an hungred, and ye gave me meat: I was thirsty, and ye gave me drink: I was a stranger, and ye took me in: Naked, and ye clothed me: I was sick, and ye visited me: I was in prison, and ye came unto me.

The righteous do not understand but the king tells them: *inasmuch as ye have done it unto one of the least of these my brethren, ye have done it unto me*. Then in typically Essene fashion the wicked on the left hand are cursed and sent into everlasting punishment, but the righteous are sent into everlasting life. This passage is singularly Essene in words and form, matching the litanies of the Community Rule in the initial part when the novice was being introduced to the order! This passage should be restored to here.

It is relevant to note that very similar phraseology to this in Matthew appears in the Testament of Joseph in the Testaments of the Twelve Patriarchs, where we find: *I was beset by hunger and the Lord himself nourished me. I was sick and the Lord visited me. I was alone and the Lord comforted me*. The Testaments of the Twelve Patriarchs, though Christianized, are considered to have been adapted from Essene originals dating from about 100 BC. It seems likely that Matthew draws upon an Essene tradition for this litany.

In the next verses of the sermon (Mt 5:17–20) Jesus explains why he is not come to destroy the law. But why should anyone think that Jesus had come to destroy the law? Either this passage is out of context or part of the speech has been omitted. In the Damascus Rule the price of departing from the law is death, which means everlasting death—no admission into God's kingdom. Jesus tells the simple of Ephraim that they need not think that because they have repented and been baptized that they were absolved from God's laws, saying: *Ye are forgiven and baptized as repentant sinners but think not that the gates of the kingdom are wide open to you all; think not that the glory of God's kingdom meaneth an end to the law. This son of man is come not to destroy the law but to fulfil it*. Later (Mt 5:19) those who break the law or cause others to break it are merely called the least in the kingdom of heaven—the work of a Christian editor. Such people would not enter the kingdom! The Essenes (Damascus Rule) said anyone teaching apostasy will be treated as if they are possessed—the punishment (Lev 20:27) was death. Having vowed to keep the law, anyone who broke it was punished by death, and anyone who vowed to break the law was punished by death. For the Essenes, everlasting death was meant—they would be turned away from God's kingdom.

Now follows a set of assertions introduced by *You have heard that it was said* and linked to their rebuttal by *but I say to you*. This form of argument is paralleled in the scrolls. One Qumran document, apparently a letter, lays out a set of 22 false interpretations of law and their rebuttal. A series of assertions are prefaced *You say* and are answered by arguments preceded by *but we think*—in essence the same as Jesus does in his sermon.

The first proclaims that no one should bear malice against a brother but should be reconciled with him as quickly as possible. Matthew also handles this elsewhere (Mt 18:15–20) laying out rules for handling disputes.

> Moreover if thy brother shall trespass against thee, go and tell him his fault between thee and him alone: if he shall hear thee, thou hast gained thy brother. But if he will not hear thee, then take with thee one or two more, that in the mouth of two or three witnesses every word may be established. And if he shall neglect to hear them, tell it unto the church: but if he neglect to hear the church, let him be unto thee as an heathen man and a publican.

The Essene rule books are equally concerned that those in the order should not bear malice but settle disputes. They were to follow Leviticus 19:17: *Thou shalt not hate thy brother in thine heart: thou shalt in any wise rebuke thy neighbour, and not suffer sin upon him.* In both the Community Rule and the Damascus Document they are commanded to bring bad feelings into the open by telling the elect to rebuke one another in truth, humility and charity. In other words, rather than letting a grievance fester, it should be brought out.

> LET HIM REBUKE HIM ON THE VERY SAME DAY LEST HE INCUR SIN BECAUSE OF HIM. AND LET NO MAN ACCUSE HIS COMPANION BEFORE THE CONGREGATION WITHOUT HAVING FIRST ADMONISHED HIM IN THE PRESENCE OF WITNESSES.

The aggrieved person must rebuke his brother before witnesses, and not, through anger, take the law into his own hands, or even think evil. If a grievance is confronted, witnesses being present, and there not being satisfaction, the problem could then be taken to higher authorities, and ultimately to the council of the community. The procedure in Matthew is practically identical. In Hebrew the word congregation here is the word which was habitually translated into Greek as ecclesia and thence church in English. It literally means the called. Thus the two passages are directly equivalent.

Note that in the sermon on the mount (Mt 5:22) a hierarchy is mentioned one step of which was the council. This was not the Great Sanhedrin but the Essene council of the community. Finally Jesus seems to regard bearing malice as equivalent to murder, the punishment being the ultimate sanction of death and hell-fire. The Damascus Rule tells us that to speak against another in the heat of anger is a capital matter. Now it is true that the whole question must have been more complicated, certainly for the monastic sectaries who had lesser punishments prescribed for various violations of this rule. But the ultimate sanction was everlasting death, and Jesus and the Nazarenes must have felt that a punishment such as exclusion from the sacred meal for a year was superfluous and could never atone for the sin because the kingdom would have arrived within a year.

185

Verses 5:23 to 5:26 in Matthew have been added for the benefit of orthodox Jews and gentiles.

Verses 5:27 to 5:32 on adultery appear in a different context in Mark and are dealt with there. It is not to say that Matthew added them out of context here—perhaps Mark did—but that Jesus must have warned against adultery on different occasions.

Next Jesus teaches that oaths are unnecessary because no one should ever tell lies (Mt 5:33–37). We have seen the concern of the community for truth. The Community Rule calls the group the community of truth; they rail against the lie. Josephus says they refused to swear on oath and were excused from taking the oath of loyalty to Herod. The sermon on the mount includes the duty to turn the other cheek towards an aggressor and this too is an Essene precept. The Essenes hated their enemies without compunction, an apparent significant difference with what Jesus was teaching. But the Essenes had to love each other, and the Nazarenes had to show mercy to any Jew willing to repent. Matthew has lost something in the speech that would have put the statement in context. If Jesus were really telling the Jews to love their Roman oppressors, it would be equivalent to a German Jew in 1944 telling his fellows to love the Nazis, or a Palestinian Arab today being told to love the Jews. It is absolutely incredible! Jesus wanted Jews to love Jews not the foreign tyrants. The proof is that he does not say: *Even Romans do the same*, but: *Even publicans do the same*. He is talking only about Jews.

In verse 5:48 Jesus says: *Be ye therefore perfect, even as your Father which is in heaven is perfect*. This is purely Essene! Some fragmentary texts convey to us that perfection language is important to the community. Thus the scrolls and fragments have the perfect of the way, perfection of the way, walking in perfection and perfect holiness (cf. 2 Cor 7:1). *The way* terminology also illustrated in these expressions and very common in the scrolls is similarly echoed in Acts (see 16:16, 18:24f, 24:22).

The whole feeling of Essene writings is one of immense—perhaps excessive—modesty. In verses 6:1 to 6:8 Jesus tells the recruits that they should not offer alms or pray flamboyantly but do these things quietly—even secretly. The sentiments of 6:16 to 6:19 on fasting are the same. Essenes did not believe in self-praise. They were the poor, the meek and the downtrodden—they believed in being humble. They dressed in simple clothes which they wore to rags. Grandeur and conceit were the opposite of their ideals. So Jesus's homily against flamboyant prayer and alms-giving was quite in character, though nothing explicitly seems to match them among the Qumran writings. The warning about vain repetitions might seem odd in the context of the Qumran material where it is clear that the litany therein was repeatedly used, but Jesus was speaking of private prayer. Ceremonial necessarily involves repeated procedures and prayers, otherwise it is another of the many injunctions of Jesus that the Christians happily flout.

The prayer which Jesus offers in verses 6:9 to 6:13, known as the Lord's prayer, is thoroughly Essene—a prayer for God's kingdom to come on earth as it was in heaven, and for the righteous to keep righteous until it came. In verses 6:19 to 6:21 and 6:24 we can hear the words of the Ebionim. Treasure on earth is worthless but the righteous store up treasure in heaven. Verses 6:22 and 6:23 are about the dualistic theory of light and dark being metaphors for good and evil—thoroughly Essene, who call themselves the sons of light and their enemies the sons of darkness. Christians were ever after fond of the same imagery. The Epistle of Barnabas is a second century Christian but non-canonical work full of Qumran expressions such as the way of light, the way of darkness, the way of holiness, the way of death, the last judgement, uncircumcised heart, dark Lord and such.

Verse 6:25 to 6:31 are again saying that Essenes have no care for personal adornment, adding to it the idea that God will provide food for the righteous. The kingdom would shortly be here and so there was no need to have to store up anything. But Christian editors have seen the opportunity to introduce apparent rejection of the food taboos once more. Jesus could never have expected Jews to eat anything.

Next Matthew adds in a battery of proverbs, some of which might have been Essene but will probably not have been part of the original speech, at any rate in this simplistic form. Then at verses 7:24 to 7:27 Jesus concludes with more plainly Essene material, talking of building houses with sound foundations. The Essenes regarded themselves as masons and were fond of building metaphors. The council of the community was the foundation of the kingdom of heaven on earth.

There are simply too many metaphorical allusions of the sermon on the mount which match the Essenes' philosophy to be merely serendipitous.

Mark 6:30 to 6:44 and 8:1 to 8:10 Restored

And the apostles gathered themselves together unto Jesus, and told him all things, both what they had done, and what they had taught. And they told Jesus of the cities at which they had to shake off the dust of their feet. And Jesus said: *Woe unto thee, Chorazin! It shall be more tolerable at the day of God's vengeance for Sodom and Gomorrha than for you. Woe unto thee, Bethsaida! It shall be more tolerable at the day of God's vengeance for Sodom and Gomorrha than for you. For if God's mighty works had been done even in Sodom and Gomorrha, they would have repented long ago in sackcloth and ashes. But ye reject God's message.* And he took the multitude of repentant apart into a desert place, for it was Pentecost, the festival for the renewal of the new covenant. And many ran afoot thither out of the camps, and came together unto him. And Jesus, when he came out, saw much people, and was moved with compassion toward them, because they were as sheep not having a shepherd. And he commanded them to make all sit down by companies upon the green grass. And they sat down in ranks, by hundreds, and by fifties, and by tens. And he stood on a high place, and began to teach them many things, blessing the men of the lot of God, saying: *Blessed are the poor and humble in spirit: for theirs is the kingdom of heaven. Blessed are the meek: for they shall inherit the earth. Blessed are they which do hunger and thirst after righteousness: for they shall be filled with everlasting life. Blessed are they merciful unto the poor: for they shall obtain God's mercy. Blessed are the pure in heart: for they shall see the face of God. Blessed are the peacemakers: for they shall be called the children of God. Blessed are they that mourn: for they shall be comforted in everlasting light. Ye are the light of the world. Come, ye blessed, inherit the kingdom prepared for you from the foundation of the world: For I was an hungred, and ye gave me meat: I was thirsty, and ye gave me drink: I was a stranger, and ye took me in: Naked, and ye clothed me: I was sick, and ye visited me: I was in prison, and ye came unto me.* Then a voice calleth him, saying: *Master, when saw we thee an hungred, and fed thee? or thirsty, and gave thee drink? When saw we thee a stranger, and took thee in? or naked, and clothed thee? Or when saw we thee sick, or in prison, and came unto thee?* And Jesus answered, saying unto them: *Truly, inasmuch as ye have done it unto one of the least of these my brethren, ye have done it unto me.* Then he cursed them of the lot of Satan, saying: *Depart from me, ye cursed, into everlasting fire, prepared for the devil and his angels: For I was an hungred, and ye gave me no meat: I was thirsty, and ye gave me no drink: I was a stranger, and ye took me not in: naked, and ye clothed me not: sick, and in prison, and ye visited me not.* Then Satan led other voices answering him, saying: *Lord, when saw we thee an hungred, or athirst, or a stranger, or naked, or sick, or in prison, and did not minister unto thee?* Then Jesus answered them, saying: *Truly, inasmuch as ye did it not to one of the least of these, ye did it not to me. And these shall go away into everlasting punishment: but the righteous into life eternal. Rejoice, and be exceeding glad, ye righteous: for great is your reward in heaven: for so rewarded were the prophets which were before you. Be ye therefore perfect, even as your Father which is in heaven is perfect. After this manner therefore pray ye: Our Father which art in heaven, hallowed be thy name. Thy kingdom come, thy will be done in earth, as it is in heaven. Give us this day our daily bread. And forgive us our sins, as we forgive those that sin against us. And lead us not into temptation, but deliver us from evil: For thine is the kingdom, and the power, and the glory, for ever. Truly. For if ye forgive men their trespasses, your heavenly Father will also forgive ye: But if ye forgive not men their trespasses, neither will your Father forgive your trespasses, and ye shall find the gates of the kingdom closed. Ye are forgiven and baptized as repentant sinners but think not that the gates of the kingdom are wide open to you all; think not that the glory of God's kingdom meaneth an end to the law. This son of man is come not to destroy the law, or the prophets: this son of man cometh not to destroy, but to fulfil. For till heaven and earth pass, one jot or one tittle shall in no wise pass from the law, till all be fulfilled. Whosoever therefore shall break one of these least commandments, and shall teach men so, he shall suffer everlasting death: but whosoever shall do and teach them, the same shall be called into the kingdom of heaven, and have everlasting life. For except that ye hunger for righteousness, ye shall not enter into the kingdom of heaven.* And the day was now far spent, and he called out: *O ye poor ones! be ye ordained that God shall save you! The children shall have bread and be filled.* And a voice answered him: *Whence can a man in the wilderness be satisfied?* And he asked: *How many loaves have ye?* And the disciples called out: *Seven.* And he said: *This is the bread of life. If ye be repentant, ye who partake of it shall be filled and have everlasting life.* And he commanded the people to sit down on the ground. And when he had taken the seven loaves, he looked up to heaven, and blessed, and brake the loaves, and gave morsels to his disciples that they might eat. And his disciples then took up, and blessed, and set before them twelve baskets of morsels of bread, full. And they did all eat, and were filled of the bread of life. And they that did eat of the loaves were about four thousand.

Walking on Water

Mark 6:45 – 6:52

6:45 And straightway he constrained his disciples to get into the ship, and to go to the other side before unto Bethsaida, while he sent away the people. 6:46 And when he had sent them away, he departed into a mountain to pray. 6:47 And when even was come, the ship was in the midst of the sea, and he alone on the land. 6:48 And he saw them toiling in rowing; for the wind was contrary unto them: and about the fourth watch of the night he cometh unto them, walking upon the sea, and would have passed by them. 6:49 But when they saw him walking upon the sea, they supposed it had been a spirit, and cried out: 6:50 For they all saw him, and were troubled. And immediately he talked with them, and saith unto them, Be of good cheer: it is I; be not afraid. 6:51 And he went up unto them into the ship; and the wind ceased: and they were sore amazed in themselves beyond measure, and wondered. 6:52 For they considered not the miracle of the loaves: for their heart was hardened.

Walking on Water

Typically this pericope, the miracle of walking on water, is unrelated to the previous one as is clear from the confused timings. The feeding miracle took place in the evening then Jesus straightway sent off the disciples and dispersed the crowd and yet still had time to go into a mountain before evening. It looks a plain interpolation.

The disciples thought Jesus was an apparition which hints that it is a misplaced post-crucifixion appearance. However, though the passage has been layered over with Christian values, it is a brief and straightforward miracle, like the miracle of the stilling of the storm. Its situation and wording is so similar to the earlier miracle it is tempting to believe that the two are really one.

The implication could be that Jesus's speech of encouragement also drew upon Job 9:5–8 where God moves mountains, shakes the earth, stops the sun from rising and treads on water, and Psalms 77:16–20 where he leads his people through his paths in the great waters out of a fearful storm guided by Moses and Aaron. Moses and Aaron as king and priest represented the titles that Jesus had as the nasi. So he was using the psalm to assure his followers that he would lead them successfully under God's guidance in the coming battle. Somehow in the oral tradition the two parts of the speech got separated and we finished up with two consequent miracles.

The reference to the fourth watch sounds Roman, and is possibly Mark's translation of an expression denoting the period just before dawn. Verse 6:52, a Pauline denigration of the poor stupid apostles, is misplaced from the feeding miracles.

Mark 6:45 to 6:52 Restored

And Jesus told them to prepare boats that they might cross the sea into Decapolis. And he said unto them: *They that hate you have said to the Lord: Let us cut off thy people from being a nation. But God is a jealous God and taketh vengeance against His adversaries. He pursueth them with His tempest and terrifieth them with His storm. For the Lord hath His way in the whirlwind and the storm; He rebuketh the sea and dries it up. The sea is the people of the waters, and though they be mighty and likewise many, even so shall they be cut down and shall pass away. For of them it is written: the waters saw thee, O God, the waters saw thee; they were afraid: the depths also were troubled. The clouds poured out water: the skies sent out a sound: thine arrows also went abroad. The voice of thy thunder was in the heaven: the lightnings lightened the world: the earth trembled and shook. Thy way is in the sea, and thy path in the great waters, and thy footsteps are not known. Thou leddest thy people by the hand of Moses and Aaron. Thou alone spreadeth out the heavens, and treadeth upon the waves of the sea. Know ye then that ye shall have no fear of the storm, for when God sent to Jonah a great wind into the sea, and there was a mighty tempest in the sea, so that the ship was like to be broken, and the mariners were afraid, Jonah was gone down into the ship, and he lay, and was fast asleep, and the men roweth hard to bring it to the land, but they could not, for the sea wrought, and was tempestuous against them. When ye are pressed by your enemies, let not your cry be: The Lord sleepeth. Lord carest thou not that we perish? It is written: The Lord of Hosts shall defend them, for as they draw near unto the gates of death, they cry unto the Lord in their trouble, and He cometh and bringeth them out of their distresses. He stilleth the noise of the seas, the noise of their waves. He rebuketh the sea and maketh the storm calm, so the waves thereof are still. And He bringeth them into the haven where they wouldst be, and stilleth the tumult of the people. The haven is the kingdom of God. Be ye of good spirits; be ye of good cheer; for the dawn soon breaketh and the storm will calm, and the kingdom come with everlasting light.* And Jesus bound his disciples to get into boats, saying: *Pass over to the other side.* And when morning came they were at the other side.

A Summary of Healing

Mark 6:53 – 6:56

6:53 And when they had passed over, they came into the land of Gennesaret, and drew to the shore. 6:54 And when they were come out of the ship, straightway they knew him, 6:55 And ran through that whole region round about, and began to carry about in beds those that were sick, where they heard he was. 6:56 And whithersoever he entered, into villages, or cities, or country, they laid the sick in the streets, and besought him that they might touch if it were but the border of his garment: and as many as touched him were made whole.

A Summary of Healing

This is not Nazarene tradition but a literary bridge by Mark bringing the band back to Galilee, and continuing the theme of recruitment, the intention being to suggest it was a continuing process—as it evidently was for some time. It says nothing specific and seems to link only with the miracle of the woman with the haemorhage because she too touched his tassel. Here though there is no suggestion that Jesus responded. Gennesaret, the word from which Mark obtained Nazareth, is Galilee.

Mark 6:53 to 6:56 Restored

There is nothing here to restore. It can be omitted.

Cleanliness and Food Taboos

Mark 7:1 – 7:8

7:1 Then came together unto him the Pharisees, and certain of the scribes, which came from Jerusalem. 7:2 And when they saw some of his disciples eat bread with defiled, that is to say, with unwashen, hands, they found fault. 7:3 For the Pharisees, and all the Jews, except they wash their hands oft, eat not, holding the tradition of the elders. 7:4 And when they come from the market, except they wash, they eat not. And many other things there be, which they have received to hold, as the washing of cups, and pots, brasen vessels, and of tables. 7:5 Then the Pharisees and scribes asked him, Why walk not thy disciples according to the tradition of the elders, but eat bread with unwashen hands? 7:6 He answered and said unto them, Well hath Esaias prophesied of you hypocrites, as it is written, This people honoureth me with their lips, but their heart is far from me. 7:7 Howbeit in vain do they worship me, teaching

191

for doctrines the commandments of men. 7:8 For laying aside the commandment
of God, ye hold the tradition of men, as the washing of pots and cups: and many
other such like things ye do.

Mark 7:14 – 7:23

7:14 And when he had called all the people unto him, he said unto them,
Hearken unto me every one of you, and understand: 7:15 There is nothing from
without a man, that entering into him can defile him: but the things which come
out of him, those are they that defile the man. 7:16 If any man have ears to
hear, let him hear. 7:17 And when he was entered into the house from the people,
his disciples asked him concerning the parable. 7:18 And he saith unto them,
Are ye so without understanding also? Do ye not perceive, that whatsoever thing
from without entereth into the man, it cannot defile him; 7:19 Because it entereth
not into his heart, but into the belly, and goeth out into the draught, purging
all meats? This he said making all meats clean. 7:20 And he said, That
which cometh out of the man, that defileth the man. 7:21 For from within, out of
the heart of men, proceed evil thoughts, adulteries, fornications, murders, 7:22
Thefts, covetousness, wickedness, deceit, lasciviousness, an evil eye, blasphemy,
pride, foolishness: 7:23 All these evil things come from within, and defile the
man.

Cleanliness

Mark does not let us go far without a dose of anti-Jewish material. In verses 7:1
to 7:23 we get a compilation of anti-Pharisaic material much of which might
be genuine but written out of context. Mark's indication that he is starting an
extract from a new source is, *And he said to them...* so the first pericope ends
at verse 9. Verses 9 to 13 are inserted and the discussion on cleanliness then
continues.

The whole up to verse 5 is a free composition by the author to introduce the
discussion. Only verses 6, 7 and the first part of 8 are genuine.

Jesus was seeking to save the Jews not the gentiles. He was not abrogating
any of the Mosaic laws to allow gentiles easier access to the kingdom. Pious
Jews were meticulous about ritual cleanliness but Mark was wrong in asserting
that the Pharisees and all the Jews washed before every meal. Only Essenes did
that. Jesus would not have willingly condoned eating defiled bread. A quotation
from Isaiah is given which would certainly have accurately expressed the
difference in religious outlook between an Essene and a Pharisee. The Essenes
were more fundamental and rejected the oral law of the Pharisees, the
commandments of men referred to. The reason then for the rejection of the
Pharisees would have been the exact opposite of that assumed by later Christians.
It was because the oral law of the Pharisees was too lax, not that it was too
strict. The last part of verse 8 is therefore Mark's clarification for his gentile
readership.

If there is any truth in the sense and circumstances of this incident, it must be
placed with the discussion, ostensibly with the Pharisees, about the sabbath. There
were no Pharisees. The questioners were pious Nazarenes who felt guilt toward God

that they had to remain unwashed in their difficult circumstances. The quotation is more accurately:

> Wherefore the Lord said, Forasmuch as this people draw near me with their mouth, and with their lips do honour me, but have removed their heart far from me, and their fear toward me is taught by the precept of men.

Jesus is saying that the questioners are pious in prayer but not in their hearts. They have been taught to fear God by men. In adverse circumstances in which ritual cleanliness is impossible, as long as they honour God in their hearts, they need not fear Him. God will forgive them this necessary infringement of the law—but it is not a permanent abrogation of it.

Food Taboos

These verses follow verse 7:8 quite nicely indicating that the intervening verses are inserted. Jesus is continuing to reassure his pious followers that they did no wrong in appearing to defile themselves when they had no option. The Nazarenes would not have ignored the law of Moses unnecessarily—the second part of verse 19 (*This he said making all meats clean*) is patently a Christian afterthought—but there were practical matters to address. The problem of guerrillas maintaining strictly Mosaic laws were insuperable and Jesus urged his followers that for soldiers of God in practice it did not matter—they had been ritually purified by baptism—as long as they kept themselves spiritually pure.

He continues the teaching began with the quotation from Isaiah in verse 7:6. With the kingdom due at any time, his followers had to be spiritually pure rather than bodily pure. So a man is defiled by what is in his heart not what is in his stomach— by lack of righteousness not wrong food or dirty habits. The point was not that food taboos were wrong, but that they were irrelevant in the circumstances. The Nazarenes had taken their sacramentum of baptism and had repented their sins. Those provided true purity. If it were necessary to dirty their hands to trigger the new kingdom then so be it. Assuming that the Nazarene barjonim accepted this, it is easy to see that Nazarene missionaries—who continued to believe the kingdom was due after Jesus's death and felt they were struggling for it in adverse circumstances—could in practice have used it as an abrogation of the law. The accusation that Jesus superseded the law is based entirely on this misunderstanding, legitimized by Paul.

As usual, the Pauline church cannot resist showing the original followers as idiots in verse 18, apparently taking to be in code what was innocuous practical guidance. It is a caricature.

Mark 7:1 to 7:8 and 7:14 to 7:23 Restored

> And his disciples understood and began, as they went, to pluck the ears of corn. But then yet others among them found fault saying, Master: *Howbeit that we can do that which is not lawful for we eat with unwashen hands that which is unclean and pleaseth not the Lord?* And he said

unto them: *Hearken every one of you, and understand. It is written in the book of Isaiah, Wherefore the Lord said, Forasmuch as this people draw near me with their mouth, and with their lips do honour me, but have removed their heart far from me, and their fear toward me is taught by the precept of men. There is nothing from without a man, that entering into him can defile him: but the things which come out of him, those are they that defile the man. If any man have ears to hear, let him hear. And they looked one to the other, and Jesus said: Are ye yet without understanding? Ye are cleansed by the holy waters, for ye have repented that ye be received into the kingdom. Do ye not then perceive, that whatsoever thing from without entereth into God's perfect, it cannot defile him because it entereth not into his heart, but into the belly, and goeth out into the draught, purging all meats? And he said, That which cometh out of the man, that defileth the man. For from within, out of the heart of men, proceed evil thoughts, adulteries, fornications, murders, thefts, covetousness, wickedness, deceit, lasciviousness, an evil eye, blasphemy, pride, foolishness: All these evil things come from within, and defile the man. If a man be truly repentant his heart is pure. If a man be not perfect in his heart then he shall not be cleansed whether he be washed by rivers, yea and even by seas.*

Corban

Mark 7:9 - 7:13

7:9 And he said unto them, Full well ye reject the commandment of God, that ye may keep your own tradition. 7:10 For Moses said, Honour thy father and thy mother; and, Whoso curseth father or mother, let him die the death: 7:11 But ye say, If a man shall say to his father or mother, It is Corban, that is to say, a gift, by whatsoever thou mightest be profited by me; he shall be free. 7:12 And ye suffer him no more to do ought for his father or his mother; 7:13 Making the word of God of none effect through your tradition, which ye have delivered: and many such like things do ye.

Corban

This section has been inserted by Mark from another context. Jesus's choice of example here—honouring parents or corban—betrays the dispute as one with Sadducees or even village Essenes in his own band not with Pharisees. Corban was the temple treasury and Jesus was saying that offering as a gift to the temple the money needed to keep your parents was wrong because Moses had taught honour your father and your mother. Applied to Pharisees the passage is nonsensical because, whatever else they might have been, they strictly adhered to the sanctity of the family which is the reason rabbinic Judaism has survived so many tribulations.

The sect which really had an interest in the temple funds were the Sadducees. We know little about their precepts because they died out with the destruction of the temple in 70 AD but, since it was the basis of their good living, we can guess that they urged devout Jews to place the temple ahead of all else including their parents. Indeed the implication seems to be that they persuaded people to take a vow to give money to the temple which they then felt unable to break even at the cost of leaving their parents destitute, because of the commandments of Numbers 30:2 and Deuteronomy 23:21–23.

However the Essenes had a rule in the Damascus Rule that breaking a binding oath was punished by death and it seems possible that this is another tutorial given by Jesus to his own recruits. It is conditioned by a rule that a man shall die if he swears to depart from the law. This explains verse 7:10. Furthermore the Essene was specifically forbidden in the Damascus Rule from consecrating the staples of his house to God. Village Essenes were not to vow to the temple food needed for the wellbeing of their household, and elderly parents obviously depended on their children. If his audience were Nazarene recruits, Jesus is seen to be explaining priority in the sect's ordinances. It is easy to understand Jesus's attitude and arguments once it is realized that he is an Essene.

Essenes habitually expressed their rules in a practical way. Rather than giving a precise measure of water for ritual purification with the danger that the pious come to believe that the precise quantity is important, they simply say it must be sufficient for a man to fully immerse himself. Here, the link with the previous dispute is that in both Jesus is recommending the adoption of the practical principle when laws conflict.

Mark 7:9 to 7:13 Restored

And he said unto those who had repented: *Your baptism is a binding oath, which dedicates you to god until ye shall enter His kingdom. Yet ye might not say to thy father or mother: I have vowed myself to God, therefore that which I wouldst provide for thee is corban (which is a gift to the temple) and thou must go destitute, for my vows to God are binding to me unto death. For corban is merely a tradition whereas Moses said, Honour thy father and thy mother; and, Whoso curseth his father or mother, let him die the death. Make not the word of God of none effect, for no man on pain of everlasting death might swear to depart from God's law. If ye wouldst please God, your tradition must be to reserve for your household that which it needs, then give your surplus to God.* For there were those of Israel who would seek atonement from God by vowing the money of their family to the temple treasury.

The Syro-Phoenician Woman

Mark 7:24 – 7:30

> 7:24 And from thence he arose, and went into the borders of Tyre and Sidon, and entered into an house, and would have no man know it: but he could not be hid. 7:25 For a certain woman, whose young daughter had an unclean spirit, heard of him, and came and fell at his feet: 7:26 The woman was a Greek, a Syrophoenician by nation; and she besought him that he would cast forth the devil out of her daughter. 7:27 But Jesus said unto her, Let the children first be filled: for it is not meet to take the children's bread, and to cast it unto the dogs. 7:28 And she answered and said unto him, Yes, Lord: yet the dogs under the table eat of the children's crumbs. 7:29 And he said unto her, For this saying go thy way; the devil is gone out of thy daughter. 7:30 And when she was come to her house, she found the devil gone out, and her daughter laid upon the bed.

The Syro-Phoenician Woman

For once Mark indicates a major change of scene. Jesus has gone to the next country, gentile Phoenicia. Many pious Jews of Palestine considered gentile countries unclean in themselves but since the Essenes in the Damascus Rule provide for life among gentiles we can deduce that Jesus would have been comfortable living in such a country because Essene ordinances ruled how it should be done.

He does no teaching and addresses no multitudes. In Mark there is no mention even of the disciples though Matthew tells us some were with him. Jesus is in hiding. Mark says so explicitly, writing: *he entered into a house, and would have no man know it; but he could not be hid.* Even when he returns to Galilee in verse 9:30 he does so in secret. There can be no misunderstanding this. He has plainly been forced to flee with only a few companions presumably to escape Herod's soldiers as Luke tells us (Lk 13:31 where the warning comes from a Pharisee). Mark is keen to depict this as a missionary journey to preach to gentiles but he has very little to work with because it was untrue. Biblical Greek scholars note these sections as unusually opaque even for Mark.

Why cannot Jesus be hid? Because a certain woman heard of him. Jesus is in hiding but the woman has easily found him, a strange contradiction which even Mark appreciates—the woman cannot have been a stranger. Yet she is described as a Greek woman, specifically she is a Syro-Phoenician by nation—apparently a gentile—and wants Jesus to cure her daughter of an unclean spirit!

Matthew 15:22 peculiarly calls her a woman of Canaan, an absurdly anachronistic description—Canaan had not existed for centuries. Earlier in Mark, Canaanite (or properly, Cananaean) meant one of the Canaim—she is a supporter of the Zealots, a Jewish nationalist. Indeed the woman is a Nazarene herself—that is why she knew where Jesus was though he was supposed to be hiding—as is evident from the story but explicit in Matthew where she addresses Jesus as the son of David, acknowledging him as king of the Jews. In Mark this declaration in public would have made her, as well as her daughter, an unclean spirit, but, because Jesus was hiding, speaking to her privately in a safe house, she was publicly betraying no secrets.

If she was a Nazarene, she must have been Jewish—a proselyte, a gentile convert to Judaism, which is why Mark says she is Syro-Phoenician *by nation*. Her daughter however, who was not a child, remained antagonistic to the Jewish religion and particularly to the Nazarene cause, and perhaps threatened to expose Jesus. The woman was distressed that her daughter's opposition risked Jesus's safety. The disciples in Matthew want her sent away (Mt 15:23) because she crieth after us, apparently meaning the woman, but really meaning that the daughter was betraying them.

Unmoved Jesus makes his views of gentiles crystal clear: *Let the children first be filled: for it is not meet to take the children's bread and cast it to the dogs.* Dogs were unclean flesh eaters banned from the temple. The Essenes called gentiles dogs, code for their enemies like the deaf and the blind. Jesus also uses his bread metaphor again—it is the staff of life and therefore the symbol of the kingdom to come. But only the children of Israel can partake of it. It is too precious to cast to the dogs—an outrageous insult still—gentiles like her daughter.

However verse 27 says: *let the children first be filled*, implying that at some stage gentiles will receive the bread of life. This reflects the view among the Essenes that some gentiles would be saved and would be ruled in peace by God's children in the kingdom. Other early writings of the New Testament such as Acts 13:46; 18:5–6 still retain the view that the gentiles are called only after the Jews. Even Paul writes: *To the Jew first, and then to the Greek* (Rom 1:16). Knowing this, the woman impresses Jesus with her understanding and her humility when she rejoins: *yet the dogs under the table eat of the children's crumbs*. Note that Mark refers to the children of Israel simply as the children. He concludes that she finds her daughter laid upon a bed with no more devil in her. Like the others she would have been silenced with a beating and threatened with everlasting death. Jesus thinks it sensible to move on quickly!

Jesus said, in the sermon on the mount (Mt 5:45): *God made the sun rise on good and bad alike and the rain to fall on the just and the unjust*, which means everyone deserves equal treatment by each other and should love each other, just as God does—and so the church has taught until today though few take any notice. Jesus's teaching was to love everyone—but only as long as they were Jews!

In interpreting the gospels, we apply the rule that a statement which contradicts the later teaching of the church is a fossil of the original Nazarene doctrine. Conversely a statement which supports the later church but contradicts the doctrines of Judaism at the time is safer considered a Christian editor's improvement. When Jesus says his work is for the children of Israel alone we can accept it as the truth, for why should a Christian editor want to insert something so contrary to the message of a church trying to get gentile converts. It could only be there because it was there in the first place—it would not have been added. When he says his message is for gentiles also, we incline to the view that an editor of the later gentile church has thought it important to insert this message.

Glimpses such as these show that the real Jesus was a Jewish nationalist. He did not believe that God had abandoned the Jews in favour of Roman hoi polloi. He gave his life believing that God was about to establish a new Jewish kingdom which would rule the earth. The sermon on the mount was addressed to repentant Jews being admitted to the Nazarene order—the elect of God's kingdom. In it Jesus says (Mt 7:6): *Give not that which is holy to the dogs, neither cast ye your pearls before swine, lest they trample them under their feet and turn and rend you.* The dogs and swine of this proverb are unclean animals—they signify gentiles. Historically Jews had been badly treated by gentiles and had no reason to trust them. Essenes hated them, and this expression is an expression of that hatred. Here he unequivocally states that gentiles, described as swine and dogs, are not fit for the holy.

Elsewhere, on the same theme, he told his apostles (Mt 10:5): *Do not go among the gentiles, and do not enter a Samaritan town, rather make your way to the lost sheep of the house of Israel.* That these commands go against the church's later teaching suggests that they are genuine and indeed the Acts of the Apostles confirms them in the case of the family of Cornelius. Cornelius was a gentile godfearer who sought an audience with Peter. Peter replies that Cornelius, as a godfearer, knew it was against the law of Moses for a Jew to mix with gentiles. In this case, though, God had told Peter, in a dream, it was all right (Acts 10:28). So, though Jesus supposedly taught that Jews and gentiles were equal, Peter apparently did not accept it until God told him in person! In Acts 11:19 even the Hellenizing faction of the Nazarenes had no intention of preaching to the gentiles, proving that Jesus could never have directed his message to gentiles: *Now they which were scattered abroad upon the persecution that arose about Stephen travelled as far as Phoenice, and Cyprus, and Antioch, preaching the word to none but unto the Jews only.* The clergy have tried to make out that it was the fictitious tribe of Judaizers who tried to forbid the Christian message back to gentiles but here in Acts we have proof that even the Hellenizing Nazarenes preached only to Jews.

The whole episode of the Syro-Phoenician woman is curiously similar to that related in 2 Kings 17:1–24 when Elijah, also fleeing into Phoenicia to escape the ire of king Ahab, cures a widow's son.

It seems odd that Luke, who is keen to depict gentiles as being acceptable to Jesus's ministry, does not use this incident. The reason is that it appears in the sections of Mark accompanying the second feeding which Luke evidently rejected as being a spurious reflexion of the first.

Mark 7:24 to 7:30 Restored

And thence he fled into the borders of Tyre and Sidon, and entered into an house, and would have no man know it; but he could not be hid. For a certain woman, whose daughter had an unclean spirit, heard of him, and came and fell at his feet. The woman was a Greek, a Syro-Phoenician by nation, but she had sought the kingdom of God, and had become a proselyte of the Nazarenes. And she besought him privately that he would cast forth the devil out of her daughter, and prepare her for the kingdom. But Jesus said unto her: *Let the children first be filled: for it is not meet to take the children's bread, and to cast it unto the dogs. For I am come to save the children of Israel alone.* And she answered and said unto him: *Yes, Master, yet the dogs under the table eat of the children's crumbs,* for she knew there was a time to come when the gentiles would be called. And he said unto her: *For this saying, so be it; the devil is gone out of thy daughter.* And he sent disciples to heal her. And when she was come to her house, she found the devil gone out, and her daughter laying bruised upon the bed.

A Dumb Man

Mark 7:31 – 7:37

7:31 And again, departing from the coasts of Tyre and Sidon, he came unto the sea of Galilee, through the midst of the region of Decapolis. 7:32 And they bring unto him one that was deaf, and had an impediment in his speech; and they beseech him to put his hand upon him. 7:33 And he took him aside from the multitude, and put his fingers into his ears, and he spit, and touched his tongue; 7:34 And looking up to heaven, he sighed, and saith unto him, Ephphatha, that is, Be opened. 7:35 And straightway his ears were opened, and the string of his tongue was loosed, and he spake plain. 7:36 And he charged them that they should tell no man: but the more he charged them, so much the more a great deal they published it; 7:37 And were beyond measure astonished, saying, He hath done all things well: he maketh both the deaf to hear, and the dumb to speak.

A Dumb Man

Jesus's returns from Tyre to Galilee by way of Decapolis a route which required him going also through, Iturea, the country of Herod Philip, the half brother of Herod Antipas of Galilee. He is travelling the long way round, going down the east side of the Lake and entering Galilee from the south. In Decapolis he cures a deaf-mute. Though the man is described as deaf and dumb which would suggest opposition to the band in Jewish territory we cannot accept it is simply this because in gentile country support could hardly have been expected.

Evidently the man was refusing to give the Nazarene band information but they forced it out of him. That is why he was taken away from the crowd privately. The War Scroll has a line in a victory hymn: *He has lifted up in judgement the fearful of heart and has opened the mouth of the dumb that they might praise the mighty works of God.* In the scrolls judgement usually means of the wicked and therefore meant punishment. This captive, was deaf because he refused to help them and would not respond to their questions except in an uninformative way—the Greek word translated impediment means speaking very little. The disciples were determined to open his mouth in pursuit of the mighty works of God.

They tortured him into talking. They spat upon him and held his tongue somehow, the gospel says with string, though the Greek actually means fetter—this was not merely metaphorical. Translators of the gospels from Greek into English, faced with words which cannot be accepted in context at their face value, adopt figurative meanings for them however unlikely they might be semantically, when a literal meaning would be correct. Much of the so-called New Testament Greek is distorted Greek—distorted to fit the meanings Christian translators have determined to find.

Almost a trivial example occurs in John where the marriage at Cana is introduced with the phrase, *And the third day*. Theologians seem determined to mistranslate this simple phrase. A frequent reading is, *three days later*. The immensely popular Today's English Version of the New Testament, Good News for Modern Man, translates it as, *two days later*. There is no excuse for this except to mislead. The correct translation is, *And on Tuesday*, the Jews and the Greeks alike giving numbers to their days of the week not names (except the sabbath). Tuesday is also for Jews a traditional day for marriage because in the story of the creation God twice notes that what he did on Tuesday was good. The refusal to translate it correctly is virtually unintelligible—certainly in the TEV—but seems to be to preserve a spurious reference to the resurrection on the third day. There are more serious examples.

To put your hands upon someone is taken to be a gesture of healing but when you put your hands on someone you are more likely to be manhandling them. The earlier incident of the demoniac suggested that torture occurred. This confirms it. He would not talk so he had a string tied to his tongue and no doubt pulled vigorously with the threat of cutting it out, and his ears poked. Jesus commands in Aramaic: *Be opened*! but cognate words in Hebrew mean *draw out* or *break*. Mark disguised it all by making it appear like a magic exorcism and adding the final two verses to match other miracles.

The other gospel writers do not like this miracle. It is too blatantly violent so they omit it. Matthew 15:29–31 substitutes a general description of healing which includes dumb people.

Mark 7:31 to 7:37 Restored

And he went through the midst of the region of Decapolis. And they found a man who would betray them, and sought the reason, but he was deaf to their questions and would hardly speak. And they took him aside from the multitude, and they laid hands upon him, and put fingers into his ears, and spat upon him, and fastened his tongue with string. And looking up to heaven, Jesus sighed, and saith unto them: *Ephphatha!* that is: *draw it out!* And straightway he begged them to cease, his ears were opened, and the string of his tongue was loosed, and he spake plain. And Jesus charged him that he should tell no man of them. And they were beyond measure astonished, saying: *He hath done all things well: he maketh both the deaf to hear, and the dumb to speak.*

No Signs will be Given

Mark 8:11 – 8:13

...and came into the parts of Dalmanutha. 8:11 And the Pharisees came forth, and began to question with him, seeking of him a sign from heaven, tempting him. 8:12 And he sighed deeply in his spirit, and saith, Why doth this generation seek after a sign? verily I say unto you, There shall no sign be given unto this generation. 8:13 And he left them, and entering into the ship again departed to the other side.

No Signs will be Given

Dalmanutha is an unknown place. However dallim, like ebionim means the poor (ones) and manath means count or ordain so we seem to have an Aramaic reference to the counting or ordaining of the poor ones—it must be the ritual feeding at the feast of the renewal of the covenant. It might signify: *O ye Poor Ones, Be ordained!* Since we have just experienced a mass feeding it seems that the reference has been slightly misplaced and was part of the Pentecostal ritual. In Matthew 15:39 the place is called Magdala, considered by New Testament authorities to be the home of Mary Magdalene, and has been used deliberately to replace Dalmanutha by the evangelist. Neither Dalmanutha nor Magdala has been convincingly identified because they never existed.

Mark now records an incident which proves that all the miracles and cures in the gospel are misinterpretations, distortions or concoctions—Jesus is adamant there will be no sign for this generation, meaning the offspring of the wicked. Most of Mark so far has been a parade of Jesus's signs, yet he apparently refused to give one! There are two reasons for this. First, the coming of the kingdom itself would be sign enough, and Jesus sighs with exasperation (Mk 8:12) that he had not managed to impress upon them the imminence of the kingdom. Second, the interpretation of signs was one of God's mysteries—the scrolls prove it to be an essential Essene skill—that the Master had to reveal with discretion. In Matthew 16:3 he says to his inquisitors: *can ye not discern the signs of the times?* As an Essene he could discern them but he was not ready to explain them to those who had not sincerely repented and joined the elect.

In a more complete version of the same incident in Matthew 12:38–42 the evangelist in fact says the sign shall be the sign of the prophet Jonah. The sign turns out to be a hindsight prophecy of Jesus rising after three days because Jonah was three days and three nights in the whale's belly (Mt 12:40; Jonah 1:17). For those for whom the Bible is infallible, here is a problem—Jesus was only three days and two nights in the metaphorical whale's belly, even counting part days as days—

Campbell builds an intriguing but far-fetched theory on this. Luke mentions Jonah but omits the analogy between sojourns in bellies and in tombs, either realizing that they did not match, or because he had no knowledge of the passage in Matthew, it having been added later. Justin Martyr, discussing the parallel of Jonah and Jesus does not mention this reference in Matthew, suggesting it did not exist in about 140 AD.

Jesus did not give signs like some sort of conjurer, he read them like an augurer. A healing miracle would be a plain enough sign, but he did not perform any such tricks—he was never a faith healer but a politico-religious leader. All the apparent signs are—as we have shown—parables recorded as true stories or deliberate distortions of brutal events which would outrage the faithful. He healed people of their spiritual malaise, the result of hopeless submission, and drove out his opponents—devils—with sticks.

Jesus was a pious man and upholder of the law. He knew that God was loath to give miraculous signs to any generation. He had however told His people in Deuteronomy 18:21–22 how to distinguish a true prophet from a false prophet. It was simple—if the pronouncements of the prophet turned out to be false, then the Lord hath not spoken it and the prophet is a fake. Only when pronouncements come true are they spoken in the name of the Lord. And fake prophets shall die (Deut 18:20). Sadly on these criteria Jesus, as he himself came to realize, is unmistakably a false prophet. His most important prediction—that the kingdom of God would be seen within a generation—is still untrue 50 generations later. And Jesus was himself crucified. The significance of a generation—to a Jew 40 years—relates to the 40 years of conflict before the general resurrection of the righteous on the third day of the kingdom.

If the questioner was a Pharisee the incident is misplaced from the earlier stage of recruiting in synagogues, but in his version Luke (11:29–32) does not suggest that the questioner was a Pharisee as he surely would have done if he had firm grounds for it. Matthew has two versions of the same incident (Mt 12:38–42 and 16:1–4). The second one says the questioners were Pharisees and Sadducees and the first one says scribes and Pharisees. There seems no reason to suppose that the request came from anyone other than the simple of Ephraim who wanted to be convinced that the kingdom was indeed nigh before they signed up to a tough discipline.

Mark 8:11 to 8:13 Restored

And some of the simple of Ephraim came forth, and began to question with him, seeking of him a sign from heaven that the kingdom was indeed nigh. And he sighed deeply in his spirit, and saith: *Why doth this generation seek after a sign? Truly, no further sign shall be given unto this generation save the day of God's vengeance.* And he left them.

Interpreting the Feedings

Mark 8:14 - 8:21

> 8:14 Now the disciples had forgotten to take bread, neither had they in the ship with them more than one loaf. 8:15 And he charged them, saying, Take heed, beware of the leaven of the Pharisees, and of the leaven of Herod. 8:16 And they reasoned among themselves, saying, It is because we have no bread. 8:17 And when Jesus knew it, he saith unto them, Why reason ye, because ye have no bread? perceive ye not yet, neither understand? have ye your heart yet hardened? 8:18 Having eyes, see ye not? and having ears, hear ye not? and do ye not remember? 8:19 When I brake the five loaves among five thousand, how many baskets full of fragments took ye up? They say unto him, Twelve. 8:20 And when the seven among four thousand, how many baskets full of fragments took ye up? And they said, Seven. 8:21 And he said unto them, How is it that ye do not understand?

Interpreting the Feedings

A speech of Jesus in which he likens the kingdom of God to bread is used by the evangelist as another occasion to denigrate the chosen disciples as idiots. Inserted as it is here, it seems to occur on a boat but of course it did not.

Disciples who supposedly have just witnessed two miraculous mass feedings squabble because they have only one loaf of bread with them. You have to admit that this is laying it on a bit thick. Jesus spoke about leaven as part of the mass registration of the Nazarenes. Many of these people would have been Hellenized Jews—Jews who had largely lapsed in Jewish practice under the influence of Romano-Greek culture—but, in view of the coming kingdom, glad to be accepted back into the chosen. These were the sinners and tax collectors. They could not be expected necessarily to understand common scriptural symbolism let alone the arcane speeches of the Nazarene. (Where genuine misunderstandings are recorded in Mark they are not the misunderstandings of the apostles but of ordinary disciples.)

Note that Mark expressly says that an underlying meaning is to be perceived here— Jesus tells us so—proving once again that allegorical meanings have to be sought in the parables. Mark records a trace of Jesus's parabolic speech. It is about the kingdom of God expressed as baskets of the life giving bread and the tiny remnant of God, the elect or perfect, the seven loaves which will trigger its introduction. First he warns against Pharisaism and Sadducaism, inevitably using a bread and growth metaphor.

Leaven is a small piece of dough used to prove the new bread—to make it rise. It has not been baked so is corruptible—it can ferment or become fusty. (Leaven therefore represents evil in the surviving Jewish tradition—the rabbinic.) The leaven of the Pharisees and the Herodians (Sadducees) is corrupt and can yield no bread of life—no entry to the kingdom of God. So it is with their teaching of the kingdom. Matthew gives the correct interpretation in 16:12. By mentioning two of

Josephus's philosophies of the Jews, Mark implies that Jesus belongs to the third main philosophy, the Essenes.

Whereas Mark has been keen to explain parables for his readers, he fails to do so here because to do so would remove the miraculous elements from the feeding miracles. It is because the true interpretation is so much at variance with the Marcan illusion that Christian scholars label this as a particularly difficult passage. Being interpreted, this means they can make no sense of it as scholars that does not impinge upon their beliefs as Christians.

Mark 8:14 to 8:21 Restored

> And he charged them, saying: *Take heed, beware of the leaven of the Pharisees, and of the leaven of the Sadducees, for leaven can be sour, and yield foul bread; or it can be sweet, and yield choice bread. If ye would have the bread of everlasting life, hearken ye not to these others, for they know not the kingdom of God.*

A Blind Man

Mark 8:22 – 8:26

> 8:22 And he cometh to Bethsaida; and they bring a blind man unto him, and besought him to touch him. 8:23 And he took the blind man by the hand, and led him out of the village; and when he had spit on his eyes, and put his hands upon him, he asked him if he saw ought. 8:24 And he looked up, and said, I see men as trees, walking. 8:25 After that he put his hands again upon his eyes, and made him look up: and he was restored, and saw every man clearly. 8:26 And he sent him away to his house, saying, Neither go into the village, nor tell it to any in the village.

A Blind Man

This seems to be a straightforward healing miracle but there are several reasons to distrust it.

Is it misplaced from the recruitment phase earlier? It is unlikely, though it did not take place in Bethsaida, a city not a village, the word used in the Greek. Furthermore Herod Philip had renovated it and renamed it Julias in honour of Augustus's daughter, Tiberius's estranged wife, Julia. The Nazarenes were, of course, barjonim and avoided the main towns. Possibly there was another Bethsaida, but, if so, no one now knows where it was. Most probably it simply means the place where the messianic meal would be held—the house (beth) of food (sayid).

There is no suggestion of repentance, no hint at the coming kingdom.

This miracle is, in the Greek, worded so similarly to the miracle of the deaf and dumb man that it is beyond coincidence. Essentially it is a copy of the earlier miracle except that the first saw a deaf man cured—here it is a blind man. Both are depicted as magic healings. If the editors of Mark have composed around a single feeding incident which they thought was two, then this miracle is probably imaginary. Matthew and Luke both recognize it as compositional and omit it, and indeed also the earlier parallel miracle of the dumb man, perceiving the second as a copy of the first and the first one as too distasteful to include.

It was added simply as a literary reflexion of the earlier miracle, which completed the first feeding cycle, to complete the second, and provide a link with the next four verses where the disciples are metaphorically made to see the truth about Jesus. So this is no miracle of the master but a linking bridge carefully composed by an editor drawing upon Hellenistic not Jewish tradition. There is an identical miracle attributed to the Greek god Asclepius who cures a man of blindness and the first things he sees are trees. The editors place it here to signify that Jesus has hitherto been unrecognized but now will begin to reveal himself.

Mark 8:22 to 8:26 Restored

This passage is omitted as not genuine Nazarene tradition.

The Revelation

Mark 8:27 – 8:33

8:27 And Jesus went out, and his disciples, into the towns of Caesarea Philippi: and by the way he asked his disciples, saying unto them, Whom do men say that I am? 8:28 And they answered, John the Baptist; but some say, Elias; and others, One of the prophets. 8:29 And he saith unto them, But whom say ye that I am? And Peter answereth and saith unto him, Thou art the Christ. 8:30 And he charged them that they should tell no man of him. 8:31 And he began to teach them, that the Son of man must suffer many things, and be rejected of the elders, and of the chief priests, and scribes, and be killed, and after three days rise again. 8:32 And he spake that saying openly. And Peter took him, and began to rebuke him. 8:33 But when he had turned about and looked on his disciples, he rebuked Peter, saying, Get thee behind me, Satan: for thou savourest not the things that be of God, but the things that be of men.

The Revelation

A pericope which came to Mark has been almost entirely rewritten. Much of verses 8:27 to 8:33 are transparently not parts of the Nazarene gospel but are Christian additions. Mark continues the bridge from the previous section. In the first four verses there is a repeat of the section where Herod believes Jesus is John reincarnated which is the beginning of Jesus's ministry. As such it is a literary closing bracket marking the conclusion of the first phase of the gospel.

The scene is set in the region of Caesarea Philippi, in the shadow of Mount Hermon. Jesus as ever does not go into the town itself. Evidently the leadership of the

Nazarenes are still barjonim, keeping out of towns and cities. They are still on the run, staying out of Herod Antipas's kingdom, in the kingdom of Antipas's more tolerant brother Philip, in Iturea, north of Galilee, suggesting that the event occurs on the journey back from Tyre.

The prominence of Peter, his apparent insistence on saying that Jesus was the messiah, and the sternness of the charging in verse 30 (in the Greek it is the same word as the rebuke of Peter in verse 32) and Jesus's response in verse 33 suggest that the two were having a row. There might well have been such a row when Jesus declared his conviction that he was the messiah and had to capture Jerusalem. The difference with the gospel record was that Peter thought that Jesus was not the messiah. He probably thought he was mad to suggest it.

Jesus would have seen in the row a further fulfilment of prophecy because the coronation described in Zechariah 3:1–10 involves a staged row between Satan and the messiah which has already appeared after the baptism of Jesus as the temptation. The High Priest, said to Satan: *the Lord rebuke thee, O Satan; yea the Lord that hath chosen Jerusalem rebuke thee: is not this a brand plucked out of the fire?* This passage perfectly described Jesus's aim and so would have taken Peter's objections to his revelation as evidence that God had willed him the role of Satan. Later, when Peter had been convinced of the plan, Jesus required him to play the role of Satan at the transfiguration. Whence the words spoken here by Jesus. So the row which is recorded was a ritual one, part of the crowning ceremony, the transfiguration. The ritual given in Zechariah was performed with Peter in the role of Satan and he was rebuked. The Greek translated *savourest not* implies disagreeing with another's opinion or taking sides against.

The way Matthew has Jesus posing the question about his messiahship (Mt 16:13) allows for only one answer. He asks: *Whom do men say that I, the Son of man, am?* using a title which clergymen consider as messianic, and therefore giving away the answer. But only Peter gets it! If the question were not part of a coronation ritual, then Jesus would have said: *Who do men say that this son of man is?* Here *this son of man* simply means I, spoken thus to affect modesty. The gospel account shows that the question and answer were formal ones. Only Peter answered because he had to answer in his role as Satan. Satan had to recognize the messiah, God's messenger, and then be rebuked according to the ritual.

In his brief account, written much later (Jn 6:66–71), John can see no merits in including any of this Essene ritual and makes Judas Iscariot, not Peter, into Satan.

In Matthew's version (Mt 16:13–23) Jesus is so pleased that Peter got the answer to his inquiry right, having told him the answer, that he gives him the keys of the kingdom of God and, using the masonic analogy, tells him he will be the rock upon which the church is built, punning on his nickname, Rocky. This is all fictional nonsense which did not exist in the second century, as we know because it does not appear in the first gospel harmony, the Diatessaron. It was added quite late to puff the church of Rome, whose founder was supposed to have been Peter, in its ambition to be top church. The only significance in it is that Matthew calls Peter by the name barjona, admitting that he is an outlaw.

Verse 31 is such a categorical prediction of the events which are later described that, if genuine, it could not have been mistaken especially if there was a row about it. Yet no one was the wiser after it, even when the predicted events occurred. The prediction is hindsight. This conclusion is confirmed when the passage has Jesus *rising* and not *being raised* by God. The former is the later concept—God and Jesus being equated. Beforehand God took the credit for all miracles.

Mark 8:27 to 8:33 Restored

And Jesus goeth out, and his disciples, into the region of Caesarea Philippi. And he saith unto them: *Whom say ye that this son of man is?* And Peter answereth and saith unto him: *Thou art the nasi, the prince of the many.* And Jesus said: *Blessed art thou Simon barjona, for is not the prince the messiah at the holy meal of the saints? And saith the Lord: Is not this a brand that must be plucked from the fire? This son of man must lead you upon Jerusalem.* And Peter was perplexed, saying he was beside himself. And Jesus taught them that, at God's appointed time, Israel would have a prince, and a priest, and a prophet; and, like Moses, the prince, and the priest, and the prophet would lead them into a promised land. And they heard him and wondered. And he charged them that they should tell no man. And from that time forth he began to teach them that they must go unto Jerusalem, and must suffer many things in the coming battle, even death but, on the third day would rise again in God's kingdom, with God's elect; for God had sent His messiah. And he spake that saying privily. And Peter took him, and began to rebuke him but when he had turned about and looked on his disciples, he rebuked Peter.

A Speech for the Kingdom

Mark 8:34 – 8:38

8:34 And when he had called the people unto him with his disciples also, he said unto them, Whosoever will come after me, let him deny himself, and take up his cross, and follow me. 8:35 For whosoever will save his life shall lose it; but whosoever shall lose his life for my sake and the gospel's, the same shall save it. 8:36 For what shall it profit a man, if he shall gain the whole world, and lose his own soul? 8:37 Or what shall a man give in exchange for his soul? 8:38 Whosoever therefore shall be ashamed of me and of my words in this adulterous and sinful generation; of him also shall the Son of man be ashamed, when he cometh in the glory of his Father with the holy angels.

A Speech for the Kingdom

This is heavily Christianized. If the cross of the command, *take up his cross*, meant a cross of a crucifixion, then the expression must have come into common usage after the crucifixion. Who would have understood it beforehand? None of the moronic disciples say at this point: *Er, what is this 'take up your cross' boss?* What is more likely is that Jesus spoke of the baptismal cross mark made in sanctified water upon the forehead of the righteous according to Ezekiel's prescription (Ezek 9:4). Interestingly, Luke says: *take up his cross daily* supporting the link with the Essenes and baptism because the Essenes believed in daily lustrations. Jesus must have said: *take the cross of repentance and be baptized.*

The expression, *and the gospel's*, is omitted in all three other gospels and must be a late addition to Mark. Moreover Jesus would never have put himself in the foreground by using my and I. Such passages are Christianized. Jesus the Essene would have considered everything God's, even the words in his own mouth. The euphemism son of man was intended to avoid I and we can be sure too that my would also have been avoided. At stake was the everlasting life of the kingdom. A man saving his physical life would lose everlasting life, but those willing to give up his life for God would gain everlasting life.

If it reflects Christian experience rather than the original tradition, it implies that Christians had lost their lives for their faith even at the early date at which Mark wrote and, though many Nazarenes probably died during the Jewish War, it seems unlikely that Jewish Christians were meant.

If the passage has any basis in Nazarene tradition, it seems to be a rallying speech in Essenic language urging the Nazarenes not to fear for their lives in the coming battles, since the kingdom was nigh and their reward would be everlasting life. *Adulterous and sinful generation* is an Essene expression. Here Jesus unmistakably uses Son of man in the messianic sense of Daniel. In Mark though it is not absolutely clear that he means himself, though the other synoptics leave no room for doubt. Jesus might have believed that the Daniel figure was the heavenly messiah, the archangel Michael, leading in his heavenly hosts, as the Essenes believed. The role of the earthly messiah, himself, was to capture the city of God from the heathen.

The use of *his Father* implies that Jesus expected to become the archangel Michael, the one like unto Son of man, but it is possibly a Christianization. Originally it was probably simply God, though the Essenes might have understood that the earthly and heavenly messiahs became the same when heaven and earth joined.

Mark 8:34 to 8:38 Restored

And when he had called the people unto him with his disciples also, he said unto them: *Whosoever would be saved, let him take the cross of repentance in baptism, obey God and fear not. For whosoever will save his life shall lose it; but whosoever shall lose his life for God's sake, the same will save it. For what shall it profit a man, if he shall gain the whole world, and lose his own soul? Or what shall a man give in exchange for his soul? Whosoever therefore shall be ashamed to take the cross of repentance in this adulterous and sinful generation, of him also shall the Son of man be ashamed, when he cometh in the glory of God with the holy angels.*

The Imminence of the Kingdom

Mark 9:1

9:1 And he said unto them, Verily I say unto you, That there be some of them that stand here, which shall not taste of death, till they have seen the kingdom of God come with power.

The Imminence of the Kingdom

Mark concludes Jesus's speech with a pericope from elsewhere betrayed by his introductory, *And he said unto them.* Jesus's most important prediction—that the kingdom of God would be seen by this generation—is still untrue today. Christian scholars have fought with this difficult verse but for the impartial observer the meaning is clear.

When Jesus repeatedly says that the kingdom of God is nigh, he means exactly that—it was due at any time. And the kingdom of God was assuredly not some fourth dimensional kingdom or mysterious kingdom only entered by faith in the resurrection. He meant that the kingdom would be here on earth within the lifetime of a mature adult. It is clearer in Mark 13:30: *I say unto you, that this generation shall not pass, till all these things be done.* The other two synoptic gospels also contain this formula (Mt 24:34; Lk 21:32). The Essenes believed the battle would take forty years, a Jewish generation, so Jesus felt sure that some of his followers, repentant and baptized as they were, would not have died before the appearance of the kingdom.

If the kingdom means everlasting life for the righteous, then those who do not die physically before it comes, never die at all, but Jesus actually says: *they shall not taste of death, till they have seen the kingdom of God come*, implying that the coming of the kingdom will kill them. The day of God's vengeance meant that everyone would physically die, but the righteous would be resurrected on the third day of the kingdom to live for ever after. In this case Jesus is actually saying to everyone: *The kingdom is due within a generation, so some of you will be still alive when the kingdom comes, but like everyone else, sinner and righteous, will die on its arrival in the terrible day of God's vengeance, but only the righteous will be resurrected in the general resurrection on the third day.* Admittedly the author of 1 Thessalonians 4:16–17 does not mention the deadly effect of the coming of the kingdom: *For the Lord himself shall descend from heaven with a shout, with the voice of the archangel, and with the trump of God: and the dead in Christ shall rise first: Then we which are alive and remain shall be caught up together with them in the clouds, to meet the Lord in the air: and so shall we ever be with the Lord*; but nor does he exactly deny it. He would not have wanted to scare off potential converts, and this seems to show that Christians had forgotten the idea of the general resurrection on the third day.

If Jesus expected, like everyone else to die before the general resurrection on the third day, then all of his prophecies of rising on the third day are explained as a general belief and not a singular prediction.

Mark 9:1 Restored

And he said unto them: *Truly, there be some of them that stand here, which shall not taste of death, till they have seen the kingdom of God come with power. For the kingdom of God is at hand unto this generation, and they might be still live when the kingdom comes. And both sinner and righteous shall depart in the terrible day of God's vengeance, but the righteous alone will be resurrected on the third day.*

The Transfiguration

Mark 9:2 – 9:8

9:2 And after six days Jesus taketh with him Peter, and James, and John, and leadeth them up into an high mountain apart by themselves: and he was transfigured before them. 9:3 And his raiment became shining, exceeding white as snow; so as no fuller on earth can white them. 9:4 And there appeared unto them Elias with Moses: and they were talking with Jesus. 9:5 And Peter answered and said to Jesus, Master, it is good for us to be here: and let us make three tabernacles; one for thee, and one for Moses, and one for Elias. 9:6 For he wist not what to say; for they were sore afraid. 9:7 And there was a cloud that overshadowed them: and a voice came out of the cloud, saying, This is my beloved Son: hear him. 9:8 And suddenly, when they had looked round about, they saw no man any more, save Jesus only with themselves.

The Transfiguration

Jesus goes up to a high mountain and is transfigured. The incident is extremely terse suggesting that much is omitted. The meaning of transfigured in verse 9:2 is also unclear. The Greek verb is to metamorphose which literally means to be transformed or to change one's form.

White robes signify a priest and the Essenes, who regarded themselves as a priestly sect, wore white as the sign of righteousness. We find early Christians accepting the same symbolism in Revelation 19:8: *And to her was granted that she should be arrayed in fine linen, clean and white: for the fine linen is the righteousness of saints* (Rev 19:8). And in Revelation 3:4–5 Jesus speaks of the significance of white garments for those who are worthy.

Jesus emerges not merely white but dazzlingly white, even radiant. Josephus described the sight of Herod's temple as it was approached in the sunlight, saying that onlookers had to turn away from the blaze of fire reflected from the temple rooftops. The roofs were gilded and the structure faced with white marble. This fiery brilliance of the golden roofs reflecting the sun atop the marble columns of the porticoes is the impression Jewish writers try to suggest of the effect of God's presence—supernatural whiteness and brilliance became a convention applied to those who had entered the sight of God. Only the high priest was allowed to enter the Holy of Holies into the presence of God, and only at Yom Kippur when he was also allowed to utter the divine name. Normally he wore elaborate coloured garments decorated with a cosmic motif but to enter into the presence of God, he wore pure white robes. Ben Sira describes him as emerging radiant with God's aura just like the description of the reflexion of the sun from the gilded roof of the temple in Josephus, though Ben Sira was writing at the time of the high priest Simon the Just, Onias II, father of Onias III who lost the Jerusalem priesthood for the zadokites.

The shining whiteness also echoes 1 Enoch 62:13–16 which says: *the elect will be clothed with garments of glory from the Lord of spirits, and their glory shall never fade away*; and 2 Enoch 22:8: *Take Enoch from his earthly garments and clothe him in garments of glory.* Fiery brilliance was also the garb of the glorious messiah and the archangel Michael.

Jesus is again announced as *my beloved Son* by a voice described as God's. We have noted that this is the liturgy for crowning a king or ordaining a priest. It seems that the transfiguration is another coronation making Jesus a priest or a king. But Jesus as an Essene is already a priest and his baptism seemed to make him a king or nasi. What then is this coronation?

The two supernatural figures attending the coronation were Moses and Elijah, both prophets who, like Jesus, fasted for forty days. Jews believed that some scriptural figures would reappear at the end time (see Mt 8:11; Lk 13:28f). Moses was the first prophet and Elijah the last—not because he was the last in sequence but because he was prophesied in Malachi 4:5 to be the last to appear before the final visitation to turn men's hearts back to the purity of their fathers. Moses and Elijah represent the law and the prophets, and as such appear to testify, in an age of false prophets, to the authenticity of Jesus as a prophet—here was one of their own! Jesus was being acknowledged as a true prophet! The priestly liturgy of the transfiguration adds the words, *listen to him*, confirming that Jesus was now the prophet—the prophet promised by Moses (Deut 18:15,18), called by Jews *that prophet*. The transfiguration therefore ritually proclaims Jesus as the prophet, priest and king of the Essenes—and this translates into the messiah. By being crowned as that prophet as well as the priest and the king, Jesus was crowned messiah. Jesus realized that should he prove wrong and not be *that prophet* then he would have been crowned falsely—he would be a false prophet. The punishment was death (Deut 18:20).

211

From the Epistle to the Hebrews he also becomes Melchizedek, the priest-king of Genesis 14:18–20. Its author asserts Jesus's superiority to the temple by showing him to be Melchizedek—the king of righteousness and the king of peace—and because he was immortal, a priest forever. Hebrews expressly says he had no father and no mother and therefore no genealogy. He sounds like an Essene waif. The Essenes were particularly interested in Melchizedek because he was the legendary priest who preceded the Zadokite line. He was considered an immortal being, like the angels and the sons of God in Genesis. He had supernatural powers, raised up the righteous for judgement and punished the wicked.

The Essenes seem to identify Melchizedek with the archangel Michael but in the Essene text Songs of the Sabbath Sacrifice, Melchizedek officiates as the High Priest in heaven just as Jesus does according to the author of Hebrews. Melchizedek was the heavenly messiah, the one unto the Son of man of Daniel. Jesus came to believe he was the earthly messiah, then his followers identified him with the Son of man and thence with Melchizedek.

Jesus has prepared for the ceremony for six days, ritually purifying himself to appear before God as the scriptures prescribe—in Exodus 24:16 God calls Moses after six days on Mount Sinai. The appearance of a cloud through which God speaks is a normal scriptural device occurring frequently in Exodus. A vigorous fire covered in green leaves would suffice.

Apparently only Jesus's three principle lieutenants, Peter, John and James, were present besides the supernatural figures. Though Mark gives no clues in the passage itself as to when it occurred, from the previous passage, he places it when the party are supposed to be in Iturea. Jesus was travelling back from Tyre where he had been accompanied only by a few disciples, perhaps only by these three. At the ceremony, one of them played the role of Elijah, one the role of Moses and one the role of Satan. One of the prophetic figures would have spoken the part of God. Jesus is crowned messiah and then the four participants find themselves alone!

Mark puts the transfiguration here as an indication that the coming in power of verse 9:1 was arriving. The curious and inappropriate proposal of Peter is perhaps a device by the author to distinguish the apostles from the supernatural figures they played. If there is any significance in it, it might be a hint that the occasion was the feast of booths or tabernacles, the Jewish feast commemorating the period in the desert, when God dwelt in the midst of them as he would again at the coming of the kingdom. Note though that Peter does not offer to make a booth for God which would have been more appropriate, possibly implying that they had already prepared a booth for God and Peter is saying: *Let's make one each for the other two as well.* Perhaps Peter said this ineptly but his crassness is probably part of Mark's theme of making the apostles seem like idiots. Probably the ritual required booths for them all. There would have been more detail in the original tradition that Mark has omitted.

Christians like to think that the mountain on which all this occurred was Mount Tabor, though it seems that there were people living on the domed top of this mountain at that time. Another, more likely candidate is Mount Hermon, though possibly not at the summit of the mountain itself but one of its lesser peaks. The ridge of high land of which Hermon is a part is extensive, extending south through the Golan Heights as the eastern scarp of the rift valley. The event probably occurred on this ridge somewhere near Caesarea Philippi.

Mark 9:2 to 9:8 Restored

And after six days of purification in readiness Jesus taketh with him Peter, and James, and John, and leadeth them up into an high mountain apart by themselves. And Peter said to Jesus: *Master, this is a good place. Let us make here three tabernacles; one for thee, and one for Moses, and one for Elias.* And they built a smoky fire, and he appeared, transfigured, before them, in raiment, shining exceeding white. And there appeared the prophets Elias and Moses: and they were talking with Jesus. And there was a cloud that overshadowed them: and a voice came out of the cloud, saying: *This is my beloved Son: hear him,* as it is written that the prophet must be heard. And Satan came and he rebuked him, saying: *Get thee behind me, Satan: for thou savourest not the things that be of God, but the things that be of men.* And, suddenly, when they had looked round about, they saw no man any more, save Jesus only with themselves.

The Objectives Remain Secret

Mark 9:9 – 9:10

9:9 And as they came down from the mountain, he charged them that they should tell no man what things they had seen, till the Son of man were risen from the dead. 9:10 And they kept that saying with themselves, questioning one with another what the rising from the dead should mean.

The Objectives Remain Secret

Mindful of Jesus now being officially a prophet Mark immediately makes him prophesy his own resurrection which the disciples do not understand—naturally—despite the detailed explanation earlier in Mark 8:31. Jesus had the same reasons as before, if not better ones, for keeping his titles secret.

It seems that Jesus had thoughts of dying himself before the kingdom was inaugurated. He would have seen himself dying in the battle against the dark forces to allow the kingdom to begin—not on the cross. In Mark's chronology Jesus had just been urging his men not to fear for their own lives because the righteous would nonetheless see God's kingdom. The thought that he too would die in battle must therefore have crossed his mind but like all the righteous people in Hosea's prophecy (Hos 6:2) he would be resurrected by God to inherit the kingdom. If references to resurrection at this early stage are genuine, they do not mean the later gospel story but the resurrection of the righteous who have fallen in the battle for the kingdom.

Hence the original context would have been Jesus explaining that he and indeed they might fall in battle but they need not fear because the righteous would be resurrected by God in the kingdom to come.

Mark 9:9 to 9:10 Restored

And as they came down from the mountain, he charged them that they should tell no man what things they had seen, for first they must go up to Jerusalem. And there they would commence the battle for the kingdom in which they would die; but God would resurrect them all, the righteous, on the third day, as it is written in the prophet Hosea. And they kept it close, with themselves.

Elijah has been

Mark 9:11 – 9:13

9:11 And they asked him, saying, Why say the scribes that Elias must first come? 9:12 And he answered and told them, Elias verily cometh first, and restoreth all things; and how it is written of the Son of man, that he must suffer many things, and be set at nought. 9:13 But I say unto you, That Elias is indeed come, and they have done unto him whatsoever they listed, as it is written of him.

Elijah has been

The second line of command of the Nazarenes are again depicted as dolts. Peter, James and John are puzzled that Elijah had apparently not come as he was supposed to, according to scripture. Jesus seems to tell them that Elijah had already come, in the person of John the Baptist who was imprisoned.

The text is garbled but this must refer back to the row between Jesus and the apostles, especially Peter. That is possibly why it has been so badly distorted. When Jesus announces that he must be crowned messiah the disciples quarrel with him. One of their arguments would have been: *If you're the messiah, what happened to Elijah?* because Elijah was to appear before the messiah. Jesus answers: *John the Baptist is Elijah.* The identification here is parabolic: *they did with him what they pleased*, which applies to John the Baptist—Matthew 17:13 says so explicitly.

Unfortunately the scriptures do not, as Jesus asserts, say this of Elijah at his second coming. Malachi 4:6 says Elijah will restore the hearts of the fathers and the children, thereby restoring all things, as Jesus says. You might contend that John began to restore all things, with his hugely successful call for repentance, but was prevented when they did to him whatsoever they wanted. And that seems to have been Jesus's argument.

Further confusion has occurred here with the justification for Elijah's presence at the coronation ceremony. Moses plainly had a right to be there but some of the disciples might not have known the reason for Elijah being present. Isaiah might have had an equal or better claim for Essenes. Jesus has therefore explained to his converts that Elijah was the last prophet according to Malachi. Whereupon some might have asked the gospel question. We do not have to believe that the question came from Jesus's High Priesthood, who must have known Malachi.

Mark 9:11 to 9:13 Restored

And they stood before him, saying: *Before the messiah cometh, it is written, Elias must first come.* And he told them: *Elias truly cometh first, and restoreth all things; but, that Elias is indeed come, and they have done unto him whatsoever they listed, as it is written of him. For he was imprisoned.*

Back from the Mountain

Mark 9:14 – 9:16

9:14 And when he came to his disciples, he saw a great multitude about them, and the scribes questioning with them. 9:15 And straightway all the people, when they beheld him, were greatly amazed, and running to him saluted him. 9:16 And he asked the scribes, What question ye with them?

Back from the Mountain

Mark gives the impression that we are still near Caesarea Philippi but the passage holds no clue to its location so the reappearance could be in the land of Antipas. Jesus returns from the mountain to meet a multitude who are amazed. No reason for this amazement is given and clergymen are wont to think it is because Jesus was still radiant after the transfiguration. The real reason is that Jesus had reappeared in public in Galilee after his period of hiding, a bold thing to do. Mark sees a parallel with Moses in Exodus 32–33 and plays it up.

The debate between the scribes and the disciples, which Jesus fails to overhear supernaturally as he does elsewhere, is not explained. It disappears for a time and an epileptic boy appears instead. It becomes clear later that the disciples are debating among themselves and the subject is precedence. Mark is simply using Jesus's question as a way of introducing a discussion about precedence which belongs with the feeding of the 5000.

Mark 9:14 to 9:16 Restored

And returning thence to Galilee he came to some of his disciples with a great multitude about them, and the disciples questioning with each other. And straightway all the people, when they beheld him, were greatly amazed that he had appeared again in Galilee, for Herod would imprison him, and running to him saluted him.

A Dumb Spirit

Mark 9:17 – 9:29

9:17 And one of the multitude answered and said, Master, I have brought unto thee my son, which hath a dumb spirit; 9:18 And wheresoever he taketh him, he teareth him: and he foameth, and gnasheth with his teeth, and pineth away: and I spake to thy disciples that they should cast him out; and they could not. 9:19 He answereth him, and saith, O faithless generation, how long shall I be with you? how long shall I suffer you? bring him unto me. 9:20 And they brought him unto him: and when he saw him, straightway the spirit tare him; and he fell on the ground, and wallowed foaming. 9:21 And he asked his father, How long is it ago since this came unto him? And he said, Of a child. 9:22 And ofttimes it hath cast him into the fire, and into the waters, to destroy him: but if thou canst do any thing, have compassion on us, and help us. 9:23 Jesus said unto him, If thou canst believe, all things are possible to him that believeth. 9:24 And straightway the father of the child cried out, and said with tears, Lord, I believe; help thou mine unbelief. 9:25 When Jesus saw that the people came running together, he rebuked the foul spirit, saying unto him, Thou dumb and deaf spirit, I charge thee, come out of him, and enter no more into him. 9:26 And the spirit cried, and rent him sore, and came out of him: and he was as one dead; insomuch that many said, He is dead. 9:27 But Jesus took him by the hand, and lifted him up; and he arose. 9:28 And when he was come into the house, his disciples asked him privately, Why could not we cast him out? 9:29 And he said unto them, This kind can come forth by nothing, but by prayer and fasting.

A Dumb Spirit

Verse 17 begins a healing miracle, differing from earlier ones in that it gives remarkable detail of the symptoms, that the disciples had tried and failed and that the devil could only be cast out by prayer. *How long shall I be with you?* is plainly hindsight and, indeed, verses 18 to 24 look to be overblown compared with other verses and comparable stories, with symptoms unnecessarily repeated, suggesting Christian elaboration and that they contain little of the original. Both Matthew and Luke concur and eliminate the father's speech which looks added. Both of the final two verses 28–29 are considered by scholars also to be late additions to the original story. The point of the reference (Mk 9:18) to the disciples' inability to cure is to contrast their lack of faith with the messiah—in Acts they can cure anything that appears before them. It too is added.

In verse 22 appears the detail that the spirit cast the young man into the fire and into the waters. Of course, fire and water are the very elements that purify, implying what is perhaps obvious—that we have a very intractable unclean spirit!

When insertions have been removed an exorcism miracle remains. These are cases of strong arm tactics by the band and the symptoms here are the same. The story turns out to be similar to that of the Syro-Phoenician woman and her daughter with the sex of the suppliants changed. The epileptic is described as a child but he is more likely to have been a young man over the age of thirteen since in verse 21 the father says he has had the affliction since childhood. He and his father are at loggerheads about the Nazarenes and the father complains about him. The disciples beat the son unconscious so that people think he is dead.

Mark's dominant theme from now on is the resurrection of Jesus and here is a hint of it—the messiah raising the boy from apparent death just as God would raise the messiah from death itself. The same words are used here in the Greek. Thus the pious addendum of verses 28 and 29 probably included verse 27 so that in the original incident the man's son was left for dead. The other two synoptic gospels mention nothing about the youth being as one dead—their authors considering it too transparently savage—and also leave out much more of Mark's account, because of its barely disguised violence.

Mark 9:17 to 9:29 Restored

And one of the multitude said: *Master, I have brought unto thee my son, a man which hath a dumb spirit, for he denieth the kingdom of God.* And Jesus would have him brought unto him. And when they brought him unto them, Jesus said unto him: *If thou canst believe, all things are possible to him that believeth. The kingdom of God cometh.* But he raged and foamed at them, saying: you will bring us all trouble; we have no king but Caesar. Straightway they did tare him, until he fell on the ground. And he cried, and they rent him sore; and he was as one dead, insomuch that many said: *He is dead.*

Return to Galilee

Mark 9:30 – 9:32

9:30 And they departed thence, and passed through Galilee; and he would not that any man should know it. 9:31 For he taught his disciples, and said unto them, The Son of man is delivered into the hands of men, and they shall kill him; and after that he is killed, he shall rise the third day. 9:32 But they understood not that saying, and were afraid to ask him.

Return to Galilee

Mark adds a couple of verses to allow Jesus to get back to Galilee but still indicates that he is travelling incognito, adds a future reference to Jesus's death and resurrection, and again depicts the disciples as idiots. The only points of historical interest are that Jesus has completed his round trip and is still in hiding. The rest is to fulfil Mark's intentions.

Jesus predicts his death and resurrection quite explicitly for the second time. He will do it yet again to complete the set of three. If these were genuine prophecies of his own death by Jesus as theologians believe then the stupidity of the people being told, the disciples, is beyond credibility. The alternative is more credible— Jesus did not make any such explicit predictions. They were added with hindsight by Mark. As we saw above, Jesus will have noted the likelihood that he among others would die before the arrival of kingdom which he anticipated. But that is a far cry from Mark's predictions.

Mark 9:30 to 9:32 Restored

And they departed thence, and passed through Galilee; and he would not that any man should know it, lest Herod should send soldiers. For he taught his disciples, and said unto them: *It pleaseth the Lord that Jerusalem, the brand, is plucked from the fire, and the battle for the kingdom shall then be fierce. If this son of man is delivered into the hands of men, and they kill him, fear ye not; for he shall rise with you all on the third day, for so it is written.*

Precedence

Mark 9:33 – 9:35

9:33 And he came to Capernaum: and being in the house he asked them, What was it that ye disputed among yourselves by the way? 9:34 But they held their peace: for by the way they had disputed among themselves, who should be the greatest. 9:35 And he sat down, and called the twelve, and saith unto them, If any man desire to be first, the same shall be last of all, and servant of all.

Precedence

The reference to the dispute en route (*by the way*) in the beginning of this passage would appear to be that in verse 9:14 where no further details of the disagreement are given but scribes are mentioned. As we have surmised several times disputes said to have been with Pharisees were actually among the disciples themselves. This seems an explicit case because the scribes are mentioned no further and here it states the dispute is among themselves.

This time Jesus knows by telepathy what they have been discussing, although Matthew (18:1) records it as a direct question. The disciples wants to know who is superior among them. No one seems to have any idea who was first among them implying that they have all been treated as equals. Jesus answers by denying the apparently strict rules of precedence of the Essenes. In the scrolls the Essenes seem to be obsessed by their ranks but things are not always what they seem to us. For the Essenes precedence seemed to mean exactly what Jesus was teaching, whereas outside the Essene movement precedence was much as we take it to be. The key was humility. Humility was an important virtue to the Essenes. They called themselves the meek and the poor. Precedence for them depended on each Essene's fulfilment of their ordinances and these were heavily weighted in favour of humility. First in order for them did not imply standing above but standing below, putting service to God and his brethren before anything else and especially personal ambitions, as it did to Jesus. Ambition and pride were sins which were punished by relegation to the bottom of the hierarchy. Thus the first were last and the last first. Matthew 23:11–12 has the Essene idea of precedent perfectly expressed:

> He that is greatest among you shall be your servant. And whosoever shall exalt himself shall be abased; and he that shall humble himself shall be exalted.

Mark knew of the Essene rules of precedence based on the dictum of verse 9:35 and wanted to get it into his narrative. The rest of it is probably made up. Its proper place is in the mass feeding.

Mark 9:33 to 9:35 Restored

If any man desire to be first, the same shall be last of all, and servant of all; for even he that is greatest among you shall be your servant, and whosoever shall exalt himself shall be abased and he that shall humble himself shall be exalted.

Receiving the Children

Mark 9:36 – 9:37 and 9:41 – 9:42

9:36 And he took a child, and set him in the midst of them: and when he had taken him in his arms, he said unto them, 9:37 Whosoever shall receive one of such children in my name, receiveth me: and whosoever shall receive me, receiveth not me, but him that sent me.

9:41 For whosoever shall give you a cup of water to drink in my name, because ye belong to Christ, verily I say unto you, he shall not lose his reward. 9:42 And whosoever shall offend one of these little ones that believe in me, it is better for him that a millstone were hanged about his neck, and he were cast into the sea.

Receiving the Children

Jesus might have dramatized this parable by using a child as a prop or the evangelist might have written a purely verbal parable as partly acted. The little child is simply a personification of the children of Israel. The child was not a gentile child—Jesus was not sent for gentiles. Jesus is simply pointing out that any one of the children of Israel can receive God. The conditions were that they should repent sincerely and be baptized. Mark sees that it ties in with the rejection of precedent and includes it here though it might not have been here originally but in his instructions to the disciples departing on their mission of recruitment. This is where Matthew puts it (Mt 10:40–42).

Verse 37 has been Christianized by placing Jesus and his name central. Originally it was more modest. He was deliberately playing down his role as Nazarene leader: *Whosoever shall receive one of such children receiveth not this son of man but God alone.* And since he was giving the disciples instructions for their mission, he was really saying to them: *When you recruit someone, make sure they understand that God is leader of the Nazarenes not me.*

The narrative here is interrupted by the insertion of verses 38 to 40 but continues in verse 41. Verse 9:41 has been changed because originally it referred to baptism, and Mark wanted to distinguish Jesus from John the Baptist. Originally it read: *For whosoever shall mark them in baptism with the cross of water in God's name, because they belong to Him, they shall not lose their reward.* But anyone abusing a Nazarene convert (these little ones who believe in me) will be lost to the coming kingdom. Nonetheless the vigorous words used seem to be threatening. In other words he is saying to the disciples: *you don't have to wait any longer to mete out appropriate treatment. The end time is now. If you punish those who are attacking you then it is God's will.*

Mark 9:36 to 9:37 and 9:41 to 9:42 Restored

And he took a child, and set him in the midst of them, and he said unto them: *Whosoever shall receive one of these children, the children of Israel, receiveth not this son of man but Him that sent him. For it is not for this son of man to receive the children into God's kingdom, but God alone. But whosoever shall mark them in baptism with the cross of water in God's name, because they belong to Him, truly, they shall not lose their reward when the kingdom comes. And whosoever shall offend any one of these little ones that believe that God cometh, yea, any one of these simple of Ephraim that have repented and entered the pure water of baptism, it is better for him that a millstone were hanged about his neck, and he were cast into the sea; for his punishment at God's appointed time will be an hundred fold.*

An Exorcist

Mark 9:38 – 9:40

9:38 And John answered him, saying, Master, we saw one casting out devils in thy name, and he followeth not us: and we forbade him, because he followeth not us. 9:39 But Jesus said, Forbid him not: for there is no man which shall do a miracle in my name, that can lightly speak evil of me. 9:40 For he that is not against us is on our part.

An Exorcist

John has seen someone, though not a Nazarene himself, apparently punishing a vocal opponent of the Nazarenes. The disciples were concerned. Perhaps the man had a reputation as criminal or a thug—who knows? He is casting out devils not in God's name but in Jesus's, whereas Jesus would have cast out devils in God's name—it was God's will that the kingdom would come. Jesus is not bothered because he says (quoting a well known maxim even at that time): *he that is not against us is for us*, a perfectly pragmatic attitude to take in a rebellion. Unlike the apparently contradictory earlier instance the question is not one of internal unity. Any help from outside was helping to fulfil God's will which was the objective. (Note that *do a miracle* was originally simply *speak*.) Indeed the very act of supporting God's warriors will reap its own reward.

Of course the man was not an exorcist as Christians believe. If he were then Jesus's response as the Son of God would be incomprehensible to a Christian. Would he seriously have allowed a quack to use his Father's name, or even his own, for his quackery? Does God condone confidence tricksters?

Note the pericope begins with an answer to no apparent question suggesting that the start of the passage has been suppressed. It probably made the meaning of the exorcisms too plain.

Mark 9:38 to 9:40 Restored

And Jesus saw John and some disciples beating a man, and asked: *Has this man an unclean spirit? Is he an enemy of the kingdom of God?* And John answered him, saying: *Master, we saw him punishing one who decried you, and we forbade him because he followeth not us.* But Jesus said: *Forbid him not. For if this man shall speak for God, though he be not repentant, he speaketh not evil of God's kingdom. For he that is not against us is on our part.*

Offending Limbs

Mark 9:43 – 9:49

9:43 And if thy hand offend thee, cut it off: it is better for thee to enter into life maimed, than having two hands to go into hell, into the fire that never shall be quenched: 9:44 Where their worm dieth not, and the fire is not quenched. 9:45 And if thy foot offend thee, cut it off: it is better for thee to enter halt into life, than having two feet to be cast into hell, into the fire that never shall be quenched: 9:46 Where their worm dieth not, and the fire is not quenched. 9:47 And if thine eye offend thee, pluck it out: it is better for thee to enter into the kingdom of God with one eye, than having two eyes to be cast into hell fire: 9:48 Where their worm dieth not, and the fire is not quenched. 9:49 For every one shall be salted with fire,

Offending Limbs

Christian commentaries on Mark suggest that this passage is a compilation by the author because in other gospels many of its elements are scattered. It is, though, quite coherent, and it is presented as a call and response litany, suggesting it was part of a ritual. It could preserve a genuine tradition of the Essenes who were fond of this sort of service, and takes the line to be expected of an apocalyptic sect.

Here we have an apocalyptic speech with nothing to put it in context, except that similar sentiments appear in Matthew in the sermon on the mount (Mt 5:27–30) concerning adultery. For Essenes the ideal state was chastity and members of the monastic order were celibate.

Jesus is tirading against carnal sin, not against various bits of the body in a material sense. He did not expect people to go about castrating themselves because they might be lustful as Origen did—and he was not alone—making himself a Christian equivalent of the Galli of the Great Mother Goddess Cybele, foot being a euphemism for the penis. The three sins highlighted are plainly masturbation, unlawful sex and even looking upon someone lustfully. Jesus's point as ever was that the kingdom might arrive at any moment. No one should be tempted to do anything sexual, using any part of their body to commit a sin, lest they be left with no time to repent anew before the salting with fire. Entry into God's kingdom requires spiritual wholeness not physical wholeness.

The speech concludes with a reference to seasoning with fire, the judgement which accompanies the kingdom and which is only unpleasant for the unrighteous—an echo of John the Baptist's announcement of one who will baptize with fire.

Mark 9:43 to 9:49 Restored

And Jesus led a service of dedication of the repentant to God. And he said: *God's judgement will be as a refiners fire, and the wicked shall be burned as stubble; but for the righteous it shall be as warm milk; for the wicked will be punished in a fire that never shall be quenched: but the righteous shall be rewarded in everlasting life. Ye repentant, remain chaste and think not adulterous thoughts, so that ye be not tempted into sin, for the kingdom is nigh, and every one shall be salted with fire.* And he called out, chanting: *If thine hand offend thee, cut it off. It is better for thee to enter into life maimed, than having two hands to go into hell.* And they all sang: *Into the fire that never shall be quenched: Where their worm dieth not, and the fire is not quenched.* And again he called out, chanting: *And if thy foot offend thee, cut it off. It is better for thee to enter halt into life, than having two feet to be cast into hell.* And they all sang: *Into the fire that never shall be quenched: Where their worm dieth not, and the fire is not quenched.* And again he called out, chanting: *And if thine eye offend thee, pluck it out. It is better for thee to enter into the kingdom of God with one eye, than having two eyes to be cast into hell fire.* And they all sang: *Into the fire that never shall be quenched: Where their worm dieth not, and the fire is not quenched.* And Jesus said: *Lord, let thy will be done; we are ready; salt us with thy fire...*

Salt

Mark 9:50

and every sacrifice shall be salted with salt. 9:50 Salt is good: but if the salt have lost his saltness, wherewith will ye season it? Have salt in yourselves, and have peace one with another.

Salt

The apparent ending of the speech seems incoherent and one might assume must come from elsewhere. It looks as if it has been added to the end of the speech only because the word salt is repeated, but the sense has changed from a metaphorical purification to something else. Salt cannot mean salt because salt does not lose its saltiness, and prelates' appeals to the interesting but irrelevant properties of the Dead Sea deposits are desperate. However, In the final sentence something like restraint seems to be called for, apparently to end the earlier dispute.

The end of verse 9:49 is missing in many old manuscripts. It refers to temple sacrifice from Leviticus 2:13 though many Christians will assume it is some sort of reference to Jesus's death. It seems to have been included in some codices because it explains what salt is in verse 9:50, an explanation that the followers of Jesus would not have needed. The verse in Leviticus uses the metaphor *the salt of the covenant of thy God.* Using this clue to interpretation we can see that these few lines probably *do* belong with the rest of the salt related speech, and the speech is a continuation of Jesus's settlement of the dispute over precedence.

The sense which emerges from the argument over precedence is: The new covenant ordains that no one is first. The duty of the chosen is to serve and no one is superior. All are judged equally in the fire of judgement. You would cut off a hateful limb or pluck out a lustful eye, if necessary, to enter the kingdom. So it is with those who do not uphold God's covenant. God's covenant is good but if no one upholds it then what other good is there? The implication is that they must put the covenant in their hearts and have peace with each other.

The only trouble then is to explain the litany. Why is it presented in this way? It serves no obvious purpose for the early church and we must conclude that it is presented in that way because that is how it came to Mark. It must therefore have been part of a Nazarene ritual. If it was, then the argument about precedence must also have been part of the ritual. All of it must be a recollection of the festival of the renewal of the covenant, the mass feedings. We know from the scrolls that this was the main festival of the Essene year, the one when the membership were regraded. It involves the determination of precedence, and all the reference to precedence must have come from the annual regrading.

At one time, in rational explanation of the gospel story, the theory was proposed that it was not a real event but consisted of recollections of a religious drama, a sort of mystery play. It now seems that the idea was not far off the mark. Chunks of the gospels seem to be memories of Essene liturgy and ritual, parts of which might have been dramatized. The source of them will largely have been the annual renewal festival.

Mark 9:50 Restored

> *...for every sacrifice shall be salted with salt. Salt is good: but if the salt have lost His saltness, wherewith will ye season it? Have salt in yourselves, and have peace one with another.* And being interpreted this is the meaning of the parable: Ye shall be salted with the salt of the covenant of thy God. Ye would not suffer thy lustful eye, or thy grasping hand, to tempt you into sin. Howbeit then that God would admit you into His kingdom, who do not hold to His covenant with His chosen? Know ye then that ye must honour God's covenant with His elect for it is good, for if no one honoureth it then what other good is there? And last of all he said: *Ye of His new covenant! for ye, God hath ordained that the first is last and the last first. Ye who are most humble, ye who serve God, and his brothers, ye shall be first. And ye who would be first, ye vainglorious and ye who love esteem above all else, ye shall be last. For, all are judged in the fire of God's judgement. Put the covenant in your hearts and have peace with each other.*

Divorce

Mark 10:1 – 10:12

> 10:1 And he arose from thence, and cometh into the coasts of Judaea by the farther side of Jordan: and the people resort unto him again; and, as he was wont, he taught them again. 10:2 And the Pharisees came to him, and asked him, Is it lawful for a man to put away his wife? tempting him. 10:3 And he answered and said unto them, What did Moses command you? 10:4 And they said, Moses suffered to write a bill of divorcement, and to put her away. 10:5 And Jesus answered and said unto them, For the hardness of your heart he wrote you this precept. 10:6 But from the beginning of the creation God made them male and female. 10:7 For this cause shall a man leave his father and mother, and cleave to his wife; 10:8 And they twain shall be one flesh: so then they are no more twain, but one flesh. 10:9 What therefore God hath joined together, let not man put asunder. 10:10 And in the house his disciples

asked him again of the same matter. 10:11 And he saith unto them, Whosoever shall put away his wife, and marry another, committeth adultery against her. 10:12 And if a woman shall put away her husband, and be married to another, she committeth adultery.

Divorce

The Nazarene band head for Judaea travelling apparently on the eastern side of the Jordan river—which in the north was part of Decapolis and, in the south, part of Herod Antipas's kingdom—possibly so as not to attract premature attention from the Romans in Judaea. Pharisees appear to be there again but many early manuscripts make no mention of them, the question simply being put abstractly. This is one case in which it is manifest that a reference to Pharisees is not genuine. That is generally the case.

A dispute over divorce arises and Jesus's answer, fleshed out in Matthew 19:1–12, is purely Essene—divorce by either party is adultery. The Damascus Rule prescribes that marriage is permanent! An Essene could not remarry even if his wife had died. Justification is that Genesis 1:27 states God's intent in creating man and woman. Both Jesus and the Essenes considered it more fundamental than Deuteronomy 24:1–4, the Mosaic statement of the law of divorce. The Essenes also quoted the pairing of creatures in Noah's Ark and Deuteronomy 17:17: *He shall not multiply wives unto himself.* Similarly Jesus quoted another verse—Genesis 2:24—that *a man shall cleave unto his wife and they shall be of one flesh.* This has been considered the only direct pronouncement on law made by Jesus in the gospels.

Nonetheless it is parabolic as ever. Jesus is not merely teaching what the Essenes accepted as the law in respect of divorce. He is using it to justify his incursion against the Roman province of Judaea, the heart of the promised land. The reason why the discussion about divorce comes at this point is precisely that Jesus is intent on dispatching the Roman usurper of God's rightful position as bridegroom of Israel. God was the bridegroom of Israel—divorce is not allowed under any circumstances, so God would not divorce his bride, Israel. As in the miracle of the raising of Jair's daughter, the problem is that the bride has been illegally taken by another, Rome! Jesus saw it as the duty of the Nazarenes to recover the virtue of Israel by liberating Jerusalem. When it had been done, the marriage could go ahead, and the gates of the kingdom would open.

Israel is personified as an unfaithful or forsaken wife in the scriptures. In Isaiah 54:5–8 the Jews are described as a forsaken wife. The husband who forsook her? God! But he promises it was only for a moment. In Jeremiah 3:20 God speaks to the children of Israel who had become idolatrous: *Surely as a wife treacherously departeth from her husband, so have ye dealt treacherously with me.*

The disciples ask Jesus for an explanation of the parable but either Mark cannot see, or does not want to suggest, that this is a parable. Mark therefore writes of the same matter changing the original of the parable. Neither is Mark's explanation genuine. Proof is that, in Judaic law, a wife could not divorce her husband and adultery could

225

only be committed against a man not a woman. Mark's answer is fitted to gentile not Jewish practices of the time. Mark's false answer has been substituted for Jesus's explanation of the foregoing passage.

Jesus argues that God and Israel are as a groom and a bride. If divorce were possible then God could notionally divorce Israel, but He has decreed that once married the twain are one flesh—divorce is not lawful and He will never divorce His bride. So far Jesus is just restating that Israel is God's forever but he does not conclude in such a simple fashion. He asserts: *What God has joined together, let no man put asunder.* His point is not simply that divorce is illegal but that, in addition, no one can forcibly separate a married couple. Yet the married couple have been separated because the bride was no longer God's but Rome's. Remember that the Jews were theocrats—the metaphor of God as Israel's groom meant God was Israel's king. Rome had usurped God's position as ruler of Israel.

The suppressed conclusion is, of course, that God simply awaits a sign from his people that the illegal marriage is rejected. That sign is that Jerusalem, symbolic of Israel as a whole, should be freed from the Romans. God would then respond appropriately. Thus the dispute about divorce is Jesus's parabolic explanation of his purpose in heading for Jerusalem with his band of Nazarenes.

We find confirmation in Revelation 19 where the marriage is between the lamb and his wife after the destruction of Rome. The marriage still requires the destruction of Rome who had usurped God's position. The change that has been made in Revelation is that the lamb has been substituted for God who was the true bridegroom and the only logical one in Jewish tradition. The wife was arrayed in clean white linen, the righteousness of the saints. And we also find: *Blessed are they who are called to the marriage supper of the lamb.* It seems clear that the Essenes had a ceremonial marriage of God to Israel—the marriage that is recorded in John 2:1–11 as the miracle at Cana—the marriage supper of which was the messianic meal.

Mark 10:1 to 10:12 Restored

And he arose from thence, and cometh into the coasts of Judaea by the farther side of Jordan. And he taught his followers what he was about. And he asketh them: *Is it lawful for a man to put away his wife?* And they said: *Moses suffered to write a bill of divorcement, and to put her away.* And Jesus answered and said unto them: *For the hardness of your heart he wrote you that precept. But, if ye wouldst be perfect, know ye from the beginning of the creation God made them male and female. For this cause shall a man leave his father and mother, and cleave to his wife; and they twain shall be one flesh: so then they are no more twain, but one flesh. What therefore God hath joined together, let not man put asunder. Let us go up to Jerusalem, that the bride might be freed, and the bridegroom enter in. He that hath ears to hear, let him hear.* Being interpreted, Jesus spoke of the marriage of God and Israel. For God hath made a covenant with His people, Israel; and they shall be like unto a bridegroom and a bride. They are joined together by God, and might not be put asunder by another.

Forbid the Children Not

Mark 10:13 – 10:16

10:13 And they brought young children to him, that he should touch them: and his disciples rebuked those that brought them. 10:14 But when Jesus saw it, he was much displeased, and said unto them, Suffer the little children to come unto me, and forbid them not: for of such is the kingdom of God. 10:15 Verily I say unto you, Whosoever shall not receive the kingdom of God as a little child, he shall not enter therein. 10:16 And he took them up in his arms, put his hands upon them, and blessed them.

Forbid the Children Not

This is the famous passage much loved by Christian illustrators in which Jesus says: *suffer the little children to come unto me.* Unfortunately the children referred to by Jesus are the children of Israel not kiddy-winkies, though the saying might have arisen from an occasion when little children were present.

The original reference was too explicit for Mark who had made the Jews the enemy of Jesus and he changed it into a homely little episode. Luke 18:15 eliminates any possible confusion by turning the children into infants. But the meaning is transparent—it is a re-wording of Jesus's perennial message that he had come only for the children of Israel. As we have seen the kingdom was of this earth, and included righteous gentiles coming in supplication to the Jews. But only righteous Jews could bring it about. This is crystal clear in Matthew 18:10–14 where a warning not to despise these little ones is followed by the parable of the lost sheep. The little ones and the lost sheep are the simple of Ephraim of the scrolls—lapsed and sinful Jews, but Jews nonetheless and entitled to the chance of God's mercy as His chosen of the covenant with Abraham.

The original would have read: *Suffer all the children to come; forbid them not; for of such is the kingdom of God. Verily: Whosoever is not one of the children shall not enter therein, save who the Lord taketh unto him and blesseth.* Jesus was not excluding gentiles from the kingdom, if they were righteous, but they came in the second phase to pay tribute to the Most High in Jerusalem when the kingdom was set up. In the Talmud the same idea is expressed: *into the Jerusalem of the world to come they only may enter who are appointed thereto.*

Thus the little children of this passage were not children but children of Isarael—adult Jews wanting baptism into the sect. The baptismal litany of the primitive church included the call: *What forbids?* prior to the baptism echoing Jesus's injunction: *Forbid them not*, confirming that the passage concerns entry into the kingdom via baptism.

If the beginning is not simply composed by Mark to fit his interpretation that the children are children and to suit his persistent blackening of the lieutenants of Jesus, then the implication is that Jesus rebuked the disciples for turning away potential converts. This in turn suggests that it happened early on in the ministry when the disciples might have regarded certain Hellenized Jews as personae non gratae. Jesus tells them otherwise. The sense of the passage is that of verse 9:38–40 and it might have originally linked in there. They both hark back to the period before the departure of the disciples on their mission to gather recruits.

Mark 10:13 to 10:16 Restored

And they brought backsliders to him, children of Israel who had turned away from God to the gods of the Greeks, for they now sought the kingdom of God. And his disciples rebuked those that brought them. But when Jesus saw it, he was much displeased, and said unto them: *Suffer all the children to come; forbid them not; for of such is the kingdom of God. Truly: Whosoever is not one of the children shall not enter therein, save who the Lord taketh unto him and blesseth.*

A Rich Young Man

Mark 10:17 – 10:25

10:17 And when he was gone forth into the way, there came one running, and kneeled to him, and asked him, Good Master, what shall I do that I may inherit eternal life? 10:18 And Jesus said unto him, Why callest thou me good? there is none good but one, that is, God. 10:19 Thou knowest the commandments, Do not commit adultery, Do not kill, Do not steal, Do not bear false witness, Defraud not, Honour thy father and mother. 10:20 And he answered and said unto him, Master, all these have I observed from my youth. 10:21 Then Jesus beholding him loved him, and said unto him, One thing thou lackest: go thy way, sell whatsoever thou hast, and give to the poor, and thou shalt have treasure in heaven: and come, take up the cross, and follow me. 10:22 And he was sad at that saying, and went away grieved: for he had great possessions. 10:23 And Jesus looked round about, and saith unto his disciples, How hardly shall they that have riches enter into the kingdom of God! 10:24 And the disciples were astonished at his words. But Jesus answereth again, and saith unto them, children, how hard is it for them that trust in riches to enter into the kingdom of God! 10:25 It is easier for a camel to go through the eye of a needle, than for a rich man to enter into the kingdom of God.

A Rich Young Man

These passages, though quite explicit, have been traditionally totally ignored by the clergy. Jesus has no doubt that wealth corrupts—his view being that of a poor one but quite different from mainstream Jews who took wealth to be a blessing of God.

A man wants to know how to inherit eternal life. He wants to be sure of entering the coming kingdom. Jesus tells him that those who have followed God's commandments—the law of Moses—will be saved. The man says he has followed them since his youth—if we are to believe Luke 18:18 who calls him a certain ruler, he is a Sadducee—and appears thoroughly complacent. Jesus is about to burst this particular bubble. To become a Nazarene he must give all he had to the poor (the Essenes) then he would gain treasure in heaven. The man cannot do it— he is rich—proving that he did not believe in the imminence of God's kingdom as Jesus and the Nazarenes did. For the sake of the story the other requirements which Jesus would have stated, repentance and baptism, are omitted by Mark as irrelevant since the man would not give up his wealth. Mark is also constantly at pains to edit out references to baptism which would make Jesus sound like John the Baptist.

This little nugget shows that the Nazarenes, even when Jesus was alive, had the same requirement of forgoing material possessions as the Essenes. In Acts of the Apostles this rule is explicitly stated. As if to emphasize it—and, since Mark reports this emphasis, it was obviously still held by the early church—Jesus says (in some manuscripts twice): *How hardly shall they that have riches enter the kingdom of God*; adding: *It is easier for a camel to go through the eye of a needle, than for a rich man to enter the kingdom of God.* Jesus's attitude is not surprising. For Essenes wealth was one of the three snares of Belial—the three major sins. The corresponding passage in Matthew makes the Essene connexion more explicit still. He writes (Mt 18:21): *If thou wouldst be perfect, go, sell that thou hast.* Essenes called themselves the perfect so Matthew is precisely saying: *To be an Essene you must sell...* etc.

In Luke 12:15–21 there is even a little parable. A man is very smug and wealthy, and considers building bigger barns to hold his burgeoning produce to set himself up for the rest of his life, but little did he know that God was about to call in his soul rendering his accumulation of riches worthless to him. The conclusion is: *If you lay up treasure on earth but neglect your duties to God, you shall not enjoy everlasting life.* Though the sentiment is undoubtedly of the poor ones, the Essenes, the composition sounds like Luke's.

It was a requirement rapidly abandoned by all Christians except certain monks and ascetics. Nowadays if you are wealthy you are courted by Christian churches or even found your own with an associated TV station! Even in Mark's time it was being watered for the sake of wealthy Romans. Mark puts, *they that trust in riches*, when Luke 18:24 puts the more obvious and certainly original, for it matches Mark 10:23, *they that have riches.* In Luke's day for some the Essene poverty principle still held as an ideal and, as if to show there is no mistake Luke 16:19–31 gives the parable of the rich young man and Lazarus the beggar, in which Lazarus goes to heaven and the rich man to Hades. Curiously the parable concludes by refuting the basis of Christianity, saying that a man who will not obey the law will not repent even if *one rise from the dead!*

Christian churches are amongst the wealthiest institutions on earth but still gladly accept the mites of widows. Their defence of wealth is that it does not matter as

229

long as you trust in God rather than trust in riches. Well, they should read the story again! Jesus's parable is unmistakably clear, and he says it is impossible for the rich to enter the kingdom of God. Who are the hypocrites now? The only reason Jesus does not say it is easier for a rich man to fly or walk on water is that there is a tiny hole in a needle which offers for the rich sinner the chance of God's forgiveness once he has given away his wealth, repented sincerely and accepted baptism. The young man's reaction shows how difficult it is.

Without any evidence at all from early manuscripts, some Christian apologists have argued that *for a rich* in verse 25 is an interpolation. Perhaps that suits them because it then reads that it is impossible for any man to enter the kingdom! Other attempts to discredit the passage persist but there is absolutely no scholarly basis for the camel being a cable or the eye of a needle a narrow gate in Jerusalem.

The Western Text manuscripts of Mark place verse 24, with *trust in riches* removed, after verse 25 removing the curious repetition and adding to the sense of the passage. The disciples in verse 26 are then responding to Jesus in 24 saying: *It's hard to enter the kingdom of God!*

Christians, in particular, might also note that, in Mark 10.18 and in Luke 18:19 but not in Matthew, Jesus denies that he is God, for only God is good—Jesus does not claim to be. Neither Essenes nor Pharisees would have made a claim to perfection, especially Essenes whose goal it was! For an Essene to claim perfection would be so lacking in humility that he would be dropped right to the back of the queue for the kingdom.

The list of commandments must have not been needed by any but the most uncouth Jew. Mark wants to avoid saying the law of Moses and yet provide a basic moral code for Christian converts. Books of the scriptures in Greek would have been rare among gentiles in the earliest days of the gentile church so the list fills a gap.

The expression treasure in heaven occurs in the Psalms of Solomon 9:9 which is decidedly Essenic in tone. We observed in a previous passage above that to take up the cross looks all the world like a Christian interpolation but could be genuine Essene tradition for, following the example of the first visitation, they were certainly marked with an invisible cross at baptism, just as Christians still are. Thus the reference is really to baptism and not to crucifixion. Matthew and Luke seem to realize that before the crucifixion the reference looks oddly anachronistic and omit it here.

Observe Jesus's mode of address to his adult audience—children!

Mark 10:17 to 10:25 Restored

> And when he was gone forth into the way, there came running, a Sadducee, and kneeled to him, and asked him: *Good Master, what shall I do that I may inherit eternal life?* And Jesus said unto him: *Why callest thou me good? there is none good but one, that is, God. Thou knowest the law of Moses;*

obey God's commandments. And he answered and said unto him: *Master, all these have I observed from my youth.* Then Jesus beholding him loved him, and said unto him: *One thing thou lackest: go thy way, sell whatsoever thou hast, and give to the poor, and thou shalt have treasure in heaven: and come, take up the cross of baptism, and be of God's elect.* And he was sad at that saying, and went away grieved: for he had great possessions. And Jesus looked round about, and saith unto his disciples: *How hardly shall they that have riches enter into the kingdom of God! It is easier for a camel to go through the eye of a needle, than for a rich man to enter into the kingdom of God.*

Rewards for the Loyal

Mark 10:26 – 10:31

10:26 And they were astonished out of measure, saying among themselves, Who then can be saved? 10:27 And Jesus looking upon them saith, With men it is impossible, but not with God: for with God all things are possible. 10:28 Then Peter began to say unto him, Lo, we have left all, and have followed thee. 10:29 And Jesus answered and said, Verily I say unto you, There is no man that hath left house, or brethren, or sisters, or father, or mother, or wife, or children, or lands, for my sake, and the gospel's, 10:30 But he shall receive an hundredfold now in this time, houses, and brethren, and sisters, and mothers, and children, and lands, with persecutions; and in the world to come eternal life. 10:31 But many that are first shall be last; and the last first.

Rewards for the Loyal

Mark has had to include what were surely extremely popular stories among the slaves and poor citizens of the Roman Empire who were such fertile soil for the growth of Christianity. But he, or an editor, sees the problem introduced by his inclusion of Jesus's categorical denunciation of wealth. He has an undoubtedly genuine saying which came to him in isolation—*with God all things are possible*—and wants to use it as an escape clause—a let out for wealthy Christians who would not give up their wealth. So he has the disciples, who are patently aware that righteousness is the way to get into the kingdom, absurdly saying: *Gosh! How do you get into the kingdom then?* To which the answer is the saying Mark wishes to use, a paraphrase of Job 42:2 and Jeremiah 32:17, respectively: *Lord, Thou canst do all things* and *Lord, There is nothing too hard for thee.* His problem is solved—God can find a way to get the wealthy into His kingdom, after all, but it is plainly contrived, and must be omitted from the restoration.

Mark concludes with the equally patently genuine speech of Jesus telling the repentant followers who abandon everything for the battle for the kingdom that they will be rewarded a hundred times over. The words after hundredfold to the end of verse 30 are Mark's pious construction, as few scholars will disagree.

Verse 31 also evidently circulated as an isolated saying because it appears in various settings in the different gospels. In its previous setting it seemed a possible rejection of Essene rules of precedence but it is not. If it circulated as a separate saying, whatever its origins, it seems to have been taken to mean that the normal hierarchies of earth would be reversed in the kingdom. That seems to be the sense of it used as a conclusion to these tales. Here it did not refer to individuals but to the Essene order as a whole, the poor and the meek who expected to be honoured in God's kingdom.

Mark 10:26 to 10:31 Restored

And Jesus said: *There is no man, that hath brethren, or sisters, or father, or mother, or wife, or children, and hath left them and house or lands, for God, but he shall receive an hundredfold; and in the world to come, everlasting life. The poor, who are last in earth shall be first in heaven.*

Another Prediction of Suffering

Mark 10:32 – 10:34

10:32 And they were in the way going up to Jerusalem; and Jesus went before them: and they were amazed; and as they followed, they were afraid. And he took again the twelve, and began to tell them what things should happen unto him, 10:33 Saying, Behold, we go up to Jerusalem; and the Son of man shall be delivered unto the chief priests, and unto the scribes; and they shall condemn him to death, and shall deliver him to the Gentiles: 10:34 And they shall mock him, and shall scourge him, and shall spit upon him, and shall kill him: and the third day he shall rise again.

Another Prediction of Suffering

Mark introduces the most detailed prediction yet of the passion of Jesus and mentions Jerusalem as the destination for the first time. It is a purely literary composition summarising the action to follow. It has been written by Mark who knew what happened, and that is plain to see.

The followers are afraid. If theologians are to be believed it could only be because, after the two specific prophecies so far and several strong hints, the message has penetrated—they will all be in danger when Jesus is arrested and killed. But they are dolts and poltroons; they will always be cowards and will never understand. To achieve Mark's normal purpose they should have been amazed and afraid after prophecies not before, so the second part of 32 should go logically after verse 34.

The truth is that they were afraid because they were entering upon a dubious adventure. They were to seize Jerusalem and the temple from the authorities and then await the start of the cosmic battle. Each of the three prophecies of the passion in Mark do not mention the crucifixion suggesting that Mark had something apparently prophetic to base his prophecies on, but it did not include the crucifixion. If this passage records anything of the Nazarene leader's thoughts it is that he, and others, knew they would die in the battle for the kingdom—but they would be resurrected when it arrived. Matthew (20:19) is the only gospel writer to add the detail of the resurrection.

Mark 10:32 to 10:34 Restored

And they were in the way going up to Jerusalem, and Jesus took to one side the apostles and said: *Behold, we go up to Jerusalem; and ye shall confront the gentiles: ye will suffer hardships and even death in the battle for the kingdom; but yet, if ye be killed, on the third day ye shall rise again in God's kingdom.* And they were amazed. And Jesus went before them; and they followed, afraid.

Precedence

Mark 10:35 – 10:45

10:35 And James and John, the sons of Zebedee, come unto him, saying, Master, we would that thou shouldest do for us whatsoever we shall desire. 10:36 And he said unto them, What would ye that I should do for you? 10:37 They said unto him, Grant unto us that we may sit, one on thy right hand, and the other on thy left hand, in thy glory. 10:38 But Jesus said unto them, Ye know not what ye ask: can ye drink of the cup that I drink of? and be baptized with the baptism that I am baptized with? 10:39 And they said unto him, We can. And Jesus said unto them, Ye shall indeed drink of the cup that I drink of; and with the baptism that I am baptized withal shall ye be baptized: 10:40 But to sit on my right hand and on my left hand is not mine to give; but it shall be given to them for whom it is prepared. 10:41 And when the ten heard it, they began to be much displeased with James and John. 10:42 But Jesus called them to him, and saith unto them, Ye know that they which wish to rule over the Gentiles exercise lordship over them; and their great ones exercise authority upon them. 10:43 But so shall it not be among you: but whosoever will be great among you, shall be your minister: 10:44 And whosoever of you will be the chiefest, shall be servant of all. 10:45 For even the Son of man came not to be ministered unto, but to minister, and to give his life a ransom for many.

Precedence

Did this happen? Mainly, no! Mark has a clear purpose here—to justify the fact that neither of these two apostles became prominent in the post-resurrection church even though they were two of Jesus's three right hand men in the Nazarene movement. He shows them demanding prominence, and for their presumption they do not get any.

These verses seem to belong with the calling of John and James, when Jesus apparently gives them a mini-tutorial on precedence. After *you do not know what you are asking* which is verifying their determination to join the group, verses 38 and 39 are simply instructions on the seriousness of Essene initiation—baptism and the messianic meal (the cup is the wine—breaking bread has been omitted to disguise it from the last supper which has no precedents in Christian tradition). In the context of the approach to Jerusalem these words look prophetic but this is the skill of the compiler not anything intrinsic in the words, which are quite innocuous. For the rest Jesus gives an apparently non-rebuking answer to the brothers' request to be alongside him in the kingdom. The simple answer is: *It is not for Jesus to decide.* In the final judgement all rankings will be God's decision, but a sentence which has been conjoined suggests that he will have already made his choice. This ties in well with Essene fatalism.

The rest is the mini-lesson on precedence. In the coming kingdom hierarchies, like gentile kings lording it over their administrators and these over their subjects will not apply. For the Nazarenes, greatness is service—and so it will be in God's kingdom. The communism of the Essenes will extend into the kingdom, not surprisingly since they considered that they had already started to build it on earth. The evangelist adds the final phrase of verse 45.

However, this story is probably not remembered as the actual calling of the two but because, as Jesus's pillar apostles, John and James had significant roles at the Pentecostal festival of the renewal of the covenant. John and James were two of Jesus's priestly assistants who always seemed to be present on ritual occasions. They must have participated in the ceremony of precedence at the festival—possibly as antagonists, like Peter in his ceremonial role as Satan. The tradition came to Mark in the form of their seeking some advantage, and he has used bits of it in several different places as it suited him. They are participating in a ritualized drama showing to the simple of Ephraim that in the Essene way of things precedence depends on service.

Mark 10:35 to 10:45 Restored

And James and John, the priestly apostles, come unto him, saying: *Master, we would that we may sit, one on thy right hand, and the other on thy left hand, in the glory of God's kingdom.* But Jesus said unto them: *Ye know not what ye ask. Can ye drink of the cup of righteousness? and be baptized with the baptism of repentance?* And they said unto him: *We can.* And Jesus said unto them: *So be it. Withal shall ye be baptized, but to sit on my right hand and on my left hand in the kingdom is not mine to give. God only knowest what He hath prepared, seeing your works. Ye know that they which wish to rule over the gentiles exercise lordship over them; and their great ones exercise authority upon them. But so shall it not be among you: but whosoever will be great among ye, shall be your servant. And whosoever of ye will be the chiefest, shall be servant of all. For ye come not to be served, but to serve.*

Blind Bartimaeus

Mark 10:46 – 10:52

10:46 And they came to Jericho: and as he went out of Jericho with his disciples and a great number of people, blind Bartimaeus, the son of Timaeus, sat by the highway side begging. 10:47 And when he heard that it was Jesus of Nazareth, he began to cry out, and say, Jesus, thou son of David, have mercy on me. 10:48 And many charged him that he should hold his peace: but he cried the more a great deal, Thou son of David, have mercy on me. 10:49 And Jesus stood still, and commanded him to be called. And they call the blind man, saying unto him, Be of good comfort, rise; he calleth thee. 10:50 And he, casting away his garment, rose, and came to Jesus. 10:51 And Jesus answered and said unto him, What wilt thou that I should do unto thee? The blind man said unto him, Lord, that I might receive my sight. 10:52 And Jesus said unto him, Go thy way; thy faith hath made thee whole. And immediately he received his sight, and followed Jesus in the way.

Blind Bartimaeus

This is the final healing of the gospel. Jesus cures the blind man, Bartimaeus. For Mark the symbolism of this is that Jesus no longer hides his position and objectives. He has come out and is openly the heir of David—the messiah.

Now blindness is one of the Nazarene code words for a skeptic or opponent of the Nazarenes, but he is more than blind. He identifies Jesus as the king of the Jews, an action that hitherto has been coded as an unclean spirit which has to be battered to release it. Here the disciples sternly tell him to be silent but Jesus intervenes and cures him—converts him into a follower. No unclean spirit is mentioned.

Or is it? Mark gives Aramaic words when he wants to disguise something from the uncomprehending gentile Christians, though later an editor sometimes adds a translation. This is the only cured man whose name is recorded in the gospel but here it is not a real name. Mark gives it as Bartimaeus and explains that it means Son of Timaeus, but by the strangest coincidence Timaeus is the Greek rendering of a word which in Aramaic means unclean!

This remarkable clue shows that this was originally another story of an unclean spirit being driven out of one of the Nazarenes' opponents by a beating—the blind man begs for mercy. But Mark, anticipating the triumphal entry into Jerusalem, wants Jesus to acknowledge his kingship openly. So he has changed a cleansing into an acceptance by Jesus of his messiahship. Mark chose the affliction of blindness, rather than leprosy or palsy, to symbolize, through its cure, visibility or openness, and to punctuate the end of this section which began immediately after the previous curing of a blind man.

Note that the cured blind man followed Jesus in *the way*, the word that the Essenes had used for their movement long before Jesus appeared on the scene. Such apparently small correspondences prove Christianity's debt to the Essenes.

235

The event is recorded at Jericho, only twelve miles from Qumran and 17 from Jerusalem. It is quite likely that fellow Essenes from the tented city at Qumran joined the Nazarenes on the final few miles to Jerusalem. On leaving Jericho two things happen in Luke's gospel, Jesus calls the head taxgatherer Zacchaeus and then he tells a parable about a man who receives a kingdom. Both stories contain genuine tradition.

The eccentric naming of Jericho twice in the opening sentence suggests that a passage has been moved or excised at an early stage. The most obvious events to insert here are those which refer to payment of tribute or custom because there was a custom post at Jericho as Luke implies with his story about Zacchaeus, the tax collector. Zacchaeus is a collaborator, a man who shelters in a sycomore tree—a fig tree. In the Zacchaeus story there seems to be an allusion to the fourfold division of the kingdom of Herod, with the assurance that half shall be returned and then the fourfold parts. The Romans had taken half of the Jewish kingdom and now they would be made to restore it to its rightful owners, the poor, God's righteous.

Judaea was formerly the kingdom of Herod Archelaus, the son of Herod the Great. Archelaus had been ethnarch, a title meaning a king of a half of a kingdom. His two brothers had been given the other two quarters of the kingdom—they were tetrarchs. In a speech Jesus refers to all this and it has appeared in Luke as the promise of Zacchaeus to yield up half his possessions (two parts of the kingdom—Judaea) and then to restore fourfold—in other words the whole kingdom—all four parts. The reference to Archelaus is confirmed in the next parable of Luke when he appears again.

At this point the Greek cleverly uses for defrauded the word, *sukophanteo*, which gives us the word, sycophant, meaning a toady or flatterer but which literally means *one who shows figs*. Unless there was a similar pun in the Aramaic it is doubtful that Jesus could have put it the way the gospel writer did, but Luke puts the meaning over clearly. The ones who showed figs, those who pandered and toadied to the Romans, were the two Herods, Antipas and Philip, who would soon be passing over their respective quarters of the kingdom to make up the fourfold restoration.

Luke, but not the other gospel writers, adds another parable here. Christians think it is a reference to Jesus's impending death because it is about a nobleman who goes to a far country to receive a kingdom. Their interpretation is that his servants left in charge are Christian disciples who will be punished if they do not use all their abilities to make the kingdom grow in the absence in death of the king, the Christ. Yet the man who would be a king is a tyrant in every respect, and could not be identified with God or gentle Jesus under any circumstances.

Jesus the Essene could not have preached either this parable or the equivalent one in Matthew 25:14–30, the parable of the talents, both of which seem to praise the garnering of riches. Jesus was one of the poor. He despised wealth and considered the wealthy as men of the pit. He could not have advocated rewarding extortioners even parabolically. He could only have preached it as a warning or as an acknowledgement of a wrong to be righted.

The speech is in two related parts which the author has intermixed. One part harks back to the Zacchaeus parable, adding a clue to its interpretation. Extracted it is this. A certain nobleman went into a far country to receive for himself a kingdom, and to return. And he called servants and said unto them: Occupy till I come. But his citizens hated him, and sent a message after him, saying: We will not have this man to reign over us. And it came to pass, that when he was returned, having received the kingdom, then he commanded these servants to be called unto him, those mine enemies, which would not that I should reign over them, bring hither, and slay them before me.

This short tale is simply a piece of history. If it is Jesus's and not Luke's, it is part of the explanation of the half and the fourfold of Zacchaeus because it tells the story of how the ethnarch, Archelaus, came by his half of the Jewish kingdom, and his relations with his subjects. We know that Archelaus went to Rome to plead for the kingdom of his father Herod from Augustus, the Roman Emperor. The leaders of the Jews sent a delegation begging Augustus to refuse the supplications of Archelaus. Augustus decided to split the kingdom

Behold, thy king cometh unto thee. He is just, and having salvation, lowly and riding on an ass (Zech 9:9). By entering Jerusalem in this way, Jesus, which means salvation, the title of the High priest in Zechariah, an Essene, the significance of "just", openly declares himself king, as all watching Jews recognized. For Essenes, the priest who is king is Melchizedek, Jesus's name in the Epistle to the Hebrews.

and gave half to Archelaus and the other two quarters to his brothers. According to Josephus, at the first Passover of Archelaus's inheritance of Judaea on his father's death he called in a Roman legion to kill 3000 of his subjects. Jesus the Essene had no interest in turning the other cheek to Romans or collaborators like the Herodians. So doubtless the final line of this tale was meant as a reminder of retribution outstanding.

The other tale is a modified version of Matthew's parable of the talents. Evidently Luke or an editor saw fit to merge them into one. Jesus comments from an Essene view of justice on the treatment meted out by the tyrants notably the taxation system.

The money given by the wicked king to his servants was the total wealth of a peasant—the servants therefore represent ordinary people. While the king is away, some succeeded through extortion to multiply many fold the money they had initially received. Where else but extortion would their profits come from? Pilate, the high priests and the wealthy puppet kings all got their wealth by exploitation. The wicked king returns and rewards the most successful extortioner with a proportionate number of cities to exploit permanently—he makes him a publican. The next one gets a lesser reward but is also made a publican. The last one representing the remainder of the ten—the majority of the people— struggled to earn a living. He was only able to return the original sum, and says to the king: *I feared thee, because thou art an austere man: thou takest up that thou layedst not down, and reapest that thou didst not sow*, and the king agrees with him. This tyrant and robber is the man clergymen think is Jesus. The cautious man's reward was to be impoverished to the benefit of one of the rich publicans. The remaining seven protest to the king that the rich man already has wealth: *Lord, he hath ten pounds*, but to no avail. The king tells them: *Unto every one which hath shall be given; and from him that hath not, even that he hath shall be taken away from him.*

The parable was obviously directed at the tax collector, Zacchaeus, possibly meant to be the High Priest (Zacchaeus meaning *cleansed*—the temple would soon be cleansed) or even the Roman governor (his position is unique in the Greek). Jesus was commenting on the injustice of the system that rewarded the dishonest few—the tax collectors—while penalizing the many. He was saying that Zacchaeus and his type had become rich by extortion—otherwise they were no different from anyone else. Now the exploitation would end. It is not coinci- dence that the same expression summarizes the respective rewards of the righteous and the wicked—the wicked are rewarded in the polluted kingdom of Israel in just the same way as the righteous are rewarded in God's kingdom on earth. Jesus will have finished with some mention of the reward for the righteous poor in the kingdom. It is the origin of the pie in the sky that Christians have accepted ever since.

In Luke 19:11 the expectation of the multitude surging upon Jerusalem was that the kingdom would appear immediately when they reached the city. One has only to reject the later Christian concept of a suffering messiah coming in peace and realize that the Jewish prospect was of a Davidic messiah, a warrior who would retake the city and set up a kingdom, to grasp that the entry into Jerusalem would be frightening to the administrators and garrison of the city.

Mark 10:46 to 10:52 Restored

And as he went out of Jericho with his disciples and a great number of people, an unclean spirit, one of those blind to the kingdom of God, heard that it was Jesus, the Nazarene, and began to cry out, and say: *Jesus, thou wouldst be a king, a son of David*. And many took hold of him, and charged him that he should hold his peace. And he lost his garment in the commotion, and he cried the more a great deal:

thou wouldst be a son of David, the messiah. And Jesus stopped, and commanded him to be called. And they took the blind man, saying unto him: *Get up, he calleth thee.* And they raised him and pulled him to Jesus, and beat him, and by and by he said: *Have mercy on me, Master.* And Jesus said unto him: *By thy works shalt thou be justified. If thou wouldst be saved, repent and be baptized, for the kingdom is entered only by those who follow the way.* And coming unto Jerusalem, Jesus looked up to the city, and spake: *Ye princes of strangers make haste and come down out of the city; for today shall be prepared a pure house for the Lord, and He shall abide therein.* And the people of Jerusalem came out to welcome Jesus joyfully. And Jesus said unto them: *This day is salvation come to this house; for God's chosen are come to seek and to save that which had perished, the lost House of the children of Israel. It shall be cleansed of the name of the strangers, and that half which is the twofold part shall be returned, but the fourfold part shall the Lord redeem from those foreign flatterers. For Herod received not his twofold part from God but went into a far country to receive for himself this kingdom, and to return. But his citizens hated him, and sent a message after him, saying: We will not have this man to reign over us. And it came to pass, that when he was returned, having received the two parts of the kingdom, that he commanded these servants to be called unto him, saying: Those mine enemies, which would not that I should reign over them, bring hither, and slay them before me. And he did slay them. And his two brothers similarly received a single part each, making the four parts of the kingdom. And the half shall be returned to the Lord, and then the fourfold parts, while they as a recompense shall suffer everlasting torment.* And they clamoured that he overthrow the strangers, for they expected the kingdom immediately to appear. And as they heard these things, he added and spake a parable, because he was nigh to Jerusalem. Saith he: *And when that nobleman went to the far country he called his ten servants and said unto them: Occupy till I come, for on my return I shall be a king and shall collect my taxes from you and ye shalt collect them for me. No man shall yield less than a pound, for all men can earn this, but those who yield up more will I reward as my tax-collector. And it came to pass, that when he was returned, having received the kingdom, then he commanded these servants to be called unto him, to whom he would collect taxes, that he might know how much every man had yielded. Then came the first, saying: Lord, thy servant hath raised ten pounds; for he had bullied and extorted money as his master's servant. And he said unto him: Well, thou good servant: have thou now authority over ten cities. And the second came, saying: Lord, thy servant hath raised five pounds; for he had extorted also. And he said likewise to him: Be thou over five cities. And another came, saying: Lord, behold, here is one pound, which your servant yieldeth; for he was a just man. And the king was much annoyed for he was an austere man, taking up that he laid not down, and reaping that he did not sow, and he said: You deliver up to me only that which any man yieldeth. And he said unto them that stood by: Take from him all that he hath, and give it to him that hath the ten cities. And the seven other servants also had failed to raise a surplus, and said unto him: Lord, he already hath ten cities. And the king answered, saying: So be it, for unto every one which hath shall be given; and from him that hath not, even that he hath shall be taken away from him.* And Jesus said: *But God hath decreed that at His appointed time, when He comes in judgement, the wicked shall receive their just recompense, and the poor and downtrodden will receive their just reward, for unto every one which hath shall be given; and from him that hath not, even that he hath shall be taken away from him.* Being interpreted, he meant in the kingdom of God. And when he had thus spoken, he went before, ascending up to Jerusalem.

The Entry into Jerusalem

Mark 11:1 – 11:11

11:1 And when they came nigh to Jerusalem, unto Bethphage and Bethany, at the mount of Olives, he sendeth forth two of his disciples, 11:2 And saith unto them, Go your way into the village over against you: and as soon as ye be entered into it, ye shall find a colt tied, whereon never man sat; loose him, and bring him. 11:3 And if any man say unto you, Why do ye this? say ye that the Lord hath need of him; and straightway he will send him hither. 11:4 And they went their way, and found the colt tied by the door without in a place where two ways met; and they loose him. 11:5 And certain of them that stood there said unto them, What do ye, loosing the colt? 11:6 And they said unto them even as Jesus had commanded: and they let them go. 11:7 And they brought the colt to Jesus, and cast their garments on him; and he sat upon him. 11:8 And many spread their garments in the way: and others cut down branches off the trees, and strawed them in the way. 11:9 And they that went before, and they that followed, cried, saying, Hosanna; Blessed is he that cometh in the name of the Lord: 11:10 Blessed be the kingdom of our father David, that cometh in the name of the Lord: Hosanna in the highest. 11:11 And Jesus entered into Jerusalem, and into the temple: and when he had looked round about upon all things, and now the eventide was come, he went out unto Bethany with the twelve.

The Entry into Jerusalem

Verses 2 to 7 are considered by Christian scholars difficult. The reason is that they do not want to accept the obvious—Jesus had already arranged for a suitable ass to be available. Jesus looks to be devious, the miraculous is removed, and the implication is that he had other followers in or around Jerusalem—they were of course the Essenes. Christians also like to think that the colt of the ass signifies humbleness, but unless they are really stubborn they cannot deny that Jesus was deliberately fulfilling the prophecy of Zechariah 9:9 (which in turn stems from Jacob's testament to Judah in Genesis 49:11):

> Rejoice greatly, O daughter of Zion; shout, O daughter of Jerusalem: behold, thy king cometh unto thee: he is just, and having salvation; lowly and riding upon an ass, even upon a colt, the foal of an ass... And he shall speak peace unto the nations: and his dominion shall be from sea to sea, and from the river to the ends of the earth.

This passage is purely messianic. It states unequivocally that the king will ride into Jerusalem on a foal. For what purpose? It is worth quoting succeeding passages in Zechariah (Zech 9:13 and 10:5):

> When I have bent Judah for me, filled the bow with Ephraim, and raised up thy sons, O Zion, against thy sons, O Greece, and made thee as the sword of a mighty man.

> And they shall be as mighty men, which tread down their enemies in the mire of the streets in the battle: and they shall fight, because the Lord is with them, and the riders on horses shall be confounded.

These two passages prove that Jesus's intentions were not peaceful when he ordered a foal of an ass to enter Jerusalem. He intended to destroy the enemies of Israel and institute a Jewish kingdom—only then would he bring peace to the world. When Jesus enters Jerusalem on a colt, the foal of an ass, he is stating: *I am the king!*

Zechariah is thoroughly apocalyptic, and indeed the second part of Zechariah is purely Essene in its sentiments. It goes on at length about God fighting the nations and restoring Judah and Jerusalem to introduce the kingdom of God. In Zechariah 14:4 the miracle on the Mount of Olives which will precede the coming of the Lord of hosts is predicted. It is followed by the nations of the earth being punished. Peace is spoken unto nations only when the kingdom is established. Note that Zechariah declares the king a just man and one having salvation. A just man is a righteous one, a zaddik, a name used by the Essenes of themselves. And having salvation is the very meaning of Jesus, suggesting that Jesus was a messianic title rather than a name.

In verse 3 the instruction was really: *Say: The nasi has need of it; and he will send it straight away.* Jesus would have called no one Lord but God and Matthew 21:3 supports the rest of the reading. One could speculate that the Essenes of Qumran permanently kept a foal ready for the messiah.

By deliberately entering Jerusalem on a foal, Jesus publicly declared himself king of the Jews, and declared his intention of following the prophecy of Zechariah. No Jew could have mistaken the symbolism and the crowd call out: *Hosanna and Blessed is he that cometh in the name of the Lord: Blessed be the kingdom of our father David, that cometh in the name of the Lord: Hosanna in the highest.* Mark also says the crowd waved branches as he entered the city, more symbolism—in Zechariah 6:12–13 the messiah is the branch—but possibly also hiding the fact that the crowd was armed. The branches were staves and swords.

Lest anyone should accuse me of being too free with Mark in my interpretations, when it comes to justifying the unjustifiable, the clergy do not hesitate to throw Mark out of the window. By one Christian explanation of the branches, the entry was not at Passover but at the festival of booths when branches were waved. So Jesus was teaching in the temple for a period of fully six months before the Jews got rid of him!

Remarkably, in view of the sequel, one can read in Christian commentaries discussions of why the authorities took no action against this messianic demonstration! The Christian is so blinded to the blazingly obvious, it defies understanding. The authorities did indeed take action for this and other violations of the civil law and the result was that their instigator paid a felon's price for them. Perhaps they mean, why did they not take immediate action? Exactly! If they could have taken immediate action they would have done. The reason they did not is that Jesus and his Nazarenes were de facto in control of the city, because the Romans had withdrawn.

Verses 9 and 10 have been garbled somewhat. The first cry is from Psalms 118:26 but the second and third would seem nonsensical to a Jew. The hand of the censor might have been at work because Mark's original account was too obviously revolutionary. Mark, scared of offending his Roman audience, does not want to say that Jesus was literally acclaimed king, merely admitting: *Blessed be the kingdom of our father, David*. He tries to remove anything suggesting a challenge to Caesar whilst making the entry suitably triumphal and messianic. Matthew puts simply: *Blessed be the Son of David*, which, to a Jew, identifies Jesus as a king, though a gentile would not know it. Later writers were less concerned because the Jewish War was now in the past and because Christianity was now better known, not as a revolutionary, but as a mystical movement or superstition, as Roman historians called it. Luke and John therefore had no qualms about it, writing respectively: *Blessed be the king that cometh in the name of the Lord*, and *Blessed is the king of Israel that cometh in the name of the Lord*.

Luke adds a revealing detail in his gospel (Lk 19:39–40). Some Pharisees in the crowd tell him to rebuke his followers for acclaiming him a king. Jesus replies with a reference to Habakkuk 2:10–11, saying: *the stones would cry out*. The subject of the Habakkuk quotation is the priesthood, as the Commentary on Habakkuk makes clear. The Essenes' interpretation of this passage is that the priests will be judged by God and found guilty in the midst of many people, and would be chastised with brimstone. If the reply was to be appropriate, the inquisitor was not a Pharisee but a Sadducee. To get the correct assonances in the Aramaic, Jesus's reply must have been: *Should not these children proclaim, then would these stones cry out (banim, abanim with za'ak, to proclaim or cry out)*. Again his followers are children.

Now hosanna in the highest means nothing. Christians have come to believe that hosanna means something like *hurrah* or *greetings* so that the crowd are saying, *sincere greetings, Jesus* or *three cheers for Jesus*. The crowd actually shouted *osanna*, an Aramaic word which means *save us* or *deliver us*, meaning from the Roman oppressors, and perhaps best rendered in this context, *free us*. Jeremiah 2:27 indicates, logically enough, that it is shouted in times of trouble, and the Jews had long been held captive in their own homeland by the Romans. The crowd are calling to the man who signals he has come as their king: *Free us, Son of David, Free us, Son of the Most High.* The correct expression was used in the Gospel of the Hebrews, an Aramaic version of Matthew, and in the Nazarene Gospel as Jerome writing in the latter part of the fourth century tells us.

Verse 11 and the following passage are added by the author to separate the entry from later events in the temple to give an impression that the entry into Jerusalem was peaceful. Like tourists sightseeing, they have a brief look round then go back to their digs for the night. Matthew and Luke, writing later, are more honest—the cleansing occurs immediately.

On entering Jerusalem, the gospels tell us, Jesus is immensely popular. The Pharisees observe (Jn 12:19): *Look, the world has gone after him.* He is widely acclaimed as a king, the heir to the throne of David and now Jesus does not refute these acclamations according to the gospel writers. Beginning the descent from the Mount of Olives we find people shouting (Lk 19:38): *Blessed is the king that cometh in the name of the Lord!* Even after the crucifixion the disciples express (Lk 24:21) their former hopes in the same terms: *We had hoped that it was he who would deliver Israel,* and meeting the resurrected Jesus they still believe it, asking (Acts 1:6): *Lord, will you at this time restore the kingdom of Israel?* All of the expectations of the Jerusalem crowds were of a restored Jewish kingdom, a new kingdom of David and Solomon on earth, a Jewish state strong enough to expel the invaders and establish a new world order.

But the clergy tell us that the disciples were mistaken. It was never Jesus's intention to introduce a Jewish kingdom of God on earth. Of course they ignore that Jesus himself, explaining to the apostles how they should pray, tells them in Matthew and Luke to say the Lord's prayer: *Thy kingdom come. Thy will be done in earth, as it is in heaven.* The prayer was for God to inaugurate the messianic age of God's kingdom on earth. It clearly says *in earth* yet the argument of the gospel writers is that the kingdom referred to is not of this world but in heaven, and John has Jesus himself saying so (Jn 18:36). Jesus's followers did not understand this because they were certifiably stupid and, following Mark's lead, the gospel writers go to some trouble to depict the apostles as complete morons even though they had been personally selected by Jesus. This is manifest rubbish. We can be sure that the apostles, as well as the Jerusalem throng, knew exactly what kingdom Jesus meant. And the deceitful Christian interpretation is plainly refuted in the principal prayer of Christendom.

Luke concludes his version (Lk 19:41–44) with Jesus weeping over the city because it would be sieged and razed—prophesying with hindsight the Jewish War. That Jesus wept on entering the city seems quite likely. No doubt most of the multitude did too.

Mark 11:1 to 11:11 Restored

And when they came nigh to Jerusalem, unto Bethphage and Bethany, at the mount of Olives, he sendeth forth two of his disciples, and saith unto them: *Go your way into the village over against you: and as soon as ye be entered into it, ye shall find a colt tied, whereon never man sat; loose him, and bring him. And if any man say unto you: Why do ye this? say ye that the nasi hath need of him; and straightway he will send him hither.* And they went their way, and found the colt tied by the door without in a place where two ways met; and they loose him. And certain of them that stood there said unto them: *What do ye, loosing the colt?* And they said unto them even as Jesus had commanded: and they let them go. And they brought the colt to Jesus, and cast their garments on him; and he sat upon him. And many spread their garments in the way: and others cut down branches off the trees, and strawed them in the way. And they that went before, and they that followed, cried, saying: *Osanna, Free us, Son of David; Blessed be the king that cometh in the name of the Lord.* And some Sadducees standing by said unto him: Master rebuke thy disciples. And Jesus replied: *Should not these children proclaim, then would these stones cry out;* for children are banim and stones are abanim. And Jesus entered weeping into Jerusalem.

The Fig Tree Cursed

Mark 11:12 – 11:14, 11:20–11:26 and 13:28 – 13:29

13:28 Now learn a parable of the fig tree; When her branch is yet tender, and putteth forth leaves, ye know that summer is near: 13:29 So ye in like manner, when ye shall see these things come to pass, know that it is nigh, even at the doors.

11:12 And on the morrow, when they were come from Bethany, he was hungry: 11:13 And seeing a fig tree afar off having leaves, he came, if haply he might find any thing thereon: and when he came to it, he found nothing but leaves; for the time of figs was not yet. 11:14 And Jesus answered and said unto it, No man eat fruit of thee hereafter for ever. And his disciples heard it.

11:20 And in the morning, as they passed by, they saw the fig tree dried up from the roots. 11:21 And Peter calling to remembrance saith unto him, Master, behold, the fig tree which thou cursedst is withered away. 11:22 And Jesus answering saith unto them, Have faith in God. 11:23 For verily I say unto you, That whosoever shall say unto this mountain, Be thou removed, and be thou cast into the sea; and shall not doubt in his heart, but shall believe that those things which he saith shall come to pass; he shall have whatsoever he saith. 11:24 Therefore I say unto you, What things soever ye desire, when ye pray, believe that ye receive them, and ye shall have them. 11:25 And when ye stand praying, forgive, if ye have ought against any: that your Father also which is in heaven may forgive you your trespasses. 11:26 But if ye do not forgive, neither will your Father which is in heaven forgive your trespasses.

The Fig Tree Cursed

To avoid the impression that Jesus entered Jerusalem as anything other than a pilgrim, Mark has inserted the innocuous verse 11 and put the cleansing of the temple in the middle of the miracle of the fig tree. Really the cleansing of the temple happened immediately, as the other two synoptic gospels make clear. The miracle of the fig tree possibly preceded the cleansing of the temple as Mark indicates—indeed might have preceded the entry into the city—but it was not a miracle. The gospel itself tells us it was not the season for figs so why should Jesus expect to find sustenance on it? For those with ears to hear it shouts out that the story is a parable.

Jesus seems to be acting in an un-Christian way in cursing the fig tree but it is understandable when he is seen as a Jewish nationalist. The fig tree represented the Romans. In this mosaic Romulus and Remus are sheltered by a she-wolf and a fig tree.

Elsewhere (Mt 24:32; Mk 13:28) we get a little analogy of the signs of the times, graced with the description parable because the Nazarene oral tradition knew of a fig tree parable, but Mark had turned it into a miracle and so had to introduce this to cover the missing parable. Plainly the original parable was re-written as a miracle, and Mark took a portion of the original as the parable. That Jesus theatrically ring barked an actual fig tree, thus killing it, is possible.

What really happened was that Jesus had entered or was about to enter Jerusalem as a king. Jesus makes a speech using a fig tree as a metaphor for Rome. The problem is that some Old Testament passages use the fig tree as an alternative to the vine as a metaphor for Israel, though elsewhere it seems to mean gentiles so that vine and fig tree cover all mankind. The fig tree was the symbol of Rome because, in the myth of the foundation of the city, the abandoned twins Romulus and Remus are sheltered by a fig tree while being suckled by a she-wolf and tended by a woodpecker. When the gentile enemy's city arms include a fig tree, there is no mistaking gospel references here and in Luke 13:6–9. Those who had ears to hear would have recognized the fig-tree as Rome. Ever since the fig tree, like the sycomore and the carob in Middle Eastern mythology, have been considered unholy trees which offer perches for demons.

Jesus says the fig-tree would be barren forever—he would render Rome impotent. Jeremiah 28:10–14 uses a similar metaphor. Jesus goes on to say that they could throw this mountain into the sea if they had faith. What was this mountain other than the might of Rome? It is a common metaphor for an empire and is so used in Revelation. Jesus was reassuring his followers that they would succeed through their faith in defeating the might of the gentile. Then with the coming of the kingdom God makes them world leaders with His miracle.

In John 1:48 Jesus sees Nathanael under a fig tree, meaning that he accepted the power of Rome. Jesus wins him over to the cause of the revolution. Zacchaeus climbed into a Pharaoh's fig tree, a sycamore, in Luke, meaning he too was high in the service of Rome.

Jesus concludes the speech by drawing lessons from the parable, but this part has been transferred until after the cleansing of the temple because Mark has dramatized it and has to allow time to pass for the tree to wither.

Those with God in their hearts can cast a mountain—meaning Rome—into the sea. Luke 17:5–6 makes an alteration—it is a mulberry tree which is uprooted and dropped into the sea. Luke actually writes a sycamine tree which is a mulberry, but since the mulberry is a small tree no more than 30 feet high whereas the sycamore tree is a large tree, giant in girth, with widespreading branches and huge roots, Luke plainly meant the latter. Without doubt the tree thrown into the sea, like the mountain, represented Roman power so it would have been a large fig tree rather than a modest mulberry bush.

Mark 11:12 - 11:14 Restored

And seeing a fig tree afar off having leaves, but no fruit, for the time of figs was not yet, Jesus said: *See ye this fig tree, it beareth no fruit, for it is not the season for figs; but as her branch is yet tender, and putteth forth leaves, ye know that summer is near, and the harvest time of fruit is nigh. So ye in like manner, when ye shall see the signs, know ye that the end time is nigh, even at the doors. This fig tree hath oppressed the children, and it shall not bear fruit, Nay, not ever; for God cometh to establish a new order in which the vine shall be fruitful and the fig barren. Have faith in God. For whosoever shall say unto this mountain: Be thou removed, and be thou cast into the sea; and shall not doubt in his heart, but shall believe that those things which he saith shall come to pass; he shall have whatsoever he saith. Therefore this son of man telleth you, What things soever ye desire, when ye pray, believe that ye receive them, and ye shall have them. And when ye stand praying, forgive, if ye have ought against any: that your Father also which is in heaven may forgive ye your trespasses. But if ye do not forgive, neither will your Father which is in heaven forgive your trespasses.* And he took a knife and stripped it of its bark. And his disciples saw it.

The Cleansing of the Temple

Mark 11:15 - 11:19

11:15 And they come to Jerusalem: and Jesus went into the temple, and began to cast out them that sold and bought in the temple, and overthrew the tables of the moneychangers, and the seats of them that sold doves; 11:16 And would not suffer that any man should carry any vessel through the temple. 11:17 And he taught, saying unto them, Is it not written, My house shall be called of all nations the house of prayer? but ye have made it a den of thieves. 11:18 And the scribes and chief priests heard it, and sought how they might destroy him: for they feared him, because all the people was astonished at his doctrine. 11:19 And when even was come, he went out of the city.

The Cleansing of the Temple

Mark gives us in verses 15 to 19 a taste of violence when Jesus—according to John, fatuously armed only with a home made whip of knotted cords—overturns the tables in the temple and refuses to let anyone through. Why did the tradesmen themselves not stop him if a piece of string were his only weapon? Why did the temple guard, the civil police of Jerusalem, or Roman legionaries not stop him? Roman soldiers were housed in the Antonia fortress adjacent to the temple and had easy access to the temple and the city. The answer can only be that the Jerusalem garrison had been overpowered, or had withdrawn,

The cleansing of the temple was the minimum any apocalyptic leader was expected to do. Ezekiel 40–48 prescribes the renovation of the temple in detail. An Essene like Jesus had a special hatred of the corrupt temple priesthood and would have been intent on purifying the temple at the first opportunity. Essenes could see only corruption in the way the Sadducees conducted temple business and scriptural passages dear to the Essenes prescribed the cleansing of Jerusalem of strangers and visitors. Zechariah 14:21 concludes with: *In that day there shall be no more a Canaanite in the house of the Lord of Hosts*. In the scriptures a Canaanite is a non–Jew—a gentile!

The cleansing was not merely to stop the temple being used as a market place. The market which Jesus wrecked was in the court of the gentiles, separated by an inviolable wall from the sacred parts of the temple, the two inner courts. But pollution is not contained by walls! Jesus at the transfiguration had undertaken to cleanse the courts as the ritual in Zechariah 3:7, which Jesus followed at the transfiguration, tells us: *Thou shalt keep my courts*.

Jesus makes a speech to explain his action to those remaining but it has been partly suppressed. A hint of its content is preserved in verse 17 which has been introduced by Mark's formula indicating a new source. Here he quotes Isaiah 56:7 which seems to oppose his action, and Jeremiah 7:11 which supports it. Plainly Jesus has been confronted by the temple authorities who ask him why he has cleared out the court of the gentiles contrary to the teaching of Isaiah. From Mark's clues, his answer would have been: *Holdeth these strangers to the covenant of the Lord? It is indeed written, My house shall be called of all nations the house of prayer, but ye have made it a den of thieves. Saith the Lord: I will cast you out of my sight.* God's condition in Isaiah for gentiles (strangers) to enter the temple was that they should join themselves to the Lord—become Jewish proselytes. These gentiles had not done so and were unclean. Since God's holy house was unclean it was unfit for God to step into, and yet his kingdom was nigh. It answered Jeremiah's description; it was a den of thieves which God would cast out of his sight. And so Jesus had done, following God's will.

Naturally the Sadducees were annoyed. The evangelist has emphasized this to deflect attention from the rebellion. In Matthew 21:15–16 we get a detail missing in Mark. it reads:

> And when the chief priests and scribes saw the wonderful things that he did, and the children crying in the temple, and saying, Hosanna to the Son of David; they were sore displeased, And said unto him, Hearest thou what these say? And Jesus saith unto them, Yea; have ye never read, Out of the mouth of babes and sucklings thou hast perfected praise?

Of course the children crying Hosannas in the temple were not young children as theologians infer from the subsequent quotation from Psalms 8:2. Who could believe anything other than that they were the children of Israel weeping in gratitude and praising their king who had just purified the defiled temple? That is what they were and the meaning of the psalm proves it. The quotation in Matthew, intended for gentiles, is a misrepresentation. The psalm properly reads:

> Out of the mouth of babes and sucklings hast thou ordained strength because of thine enemies, that thou mightest still the enemy and the avenger.

Jesus is saying that God ordained these children weeping in gratitude like babies to provide the strength to subdue Israel's enemies. And that they had done.

These passages end with the barren fig tree withering away. The story of the fig tree need not interrupt the cleansing of the temple and has been told in one piece above.

Did Jesus do it alone? That was the idea Mark wanted to give but it is manifestly nonsense unless Jesus wore blue leotards. He did it with his disciples. And not just those noted as the twelve or even the pious invention, the seventy, but the whole of his army—four or five thousand, if the gospels are to be believed, a hundred to nine hundred if profane sources are accepted. The gospels imply there was little resistance but the misplaced story of the legion of devils disguised as swine must really tell of the defeat of the Jerusalem garrison in the valley of the brook Qidron. The surviving soldiers judiciously withdrew to await reinforcements.

Could Roman legionaries really have been defeated by Jesus's gang? There is no denying even from the gospels that the Nazarenes assumed civil power even though only temporarily. If Jesus had been a lone demonstrator, as the gospels suggest, he would have been instantly arrested by the temple guards. The only reason nothing seems to have happened is that the Nazarenes were in control. Though we have few clues about the Nazarenes' arms or their skills in warfare, they were evidently determined and strengthened by the power of religious conviction—they were fanatics. And the Romans will have found that there was more to worry about than the Nazarene militia—they and their cause were popular. Jerusalem at Passover time, according to Josephus, was packed with almost three million pilgrims. These are the babes and sucklings whom

Jesus acknowledges as having given the strength for the Nazarenes to still their enemies. The Roman commander of the Antonia Fortress, with only two thousand infantrymen, could not contain such numbers and, having suffered a defeat beneath the Mount of Olives, must have chosen to withdraw until additional soldiers came up to Jerusalem from Caesarea on the coast. That would have taken a few days. And according to Mark, it is a few days that Jesus had in control of the city.

D E Nineham naively or dishonestly asks: If Jesus was assisted by his followers why did the temple police or the Roman garrison do nothing? and Why was the matter not raised at Jesus's trial? Answers respectively: they bowed to a superior force, and it was. Luke 23:2 gives perverting our nation as one of Jesus's crimes. It means the crime of Laesae Majestatis, assuming the power of government illegally. Can a single demonstrator do this?

Verses 25 and 26 seem a bit over elaborate, and might have been inserted by Mark from elsewhere (they echo the Lord's Prayer) simply to end, literally, on a forgiving note thus detracting from the violence and hints of insurrection which preceded. Matthew is shorter. But they do sound Essene, so might be reasonably retained.

Mark 11:15 to 11:19 Restored

And they surrounded the temple and Jesus, going in, forbade the priests to do ought; and they began to cast out them that sold and bought in court the temple, and overthrew the tables of the money changers, and the seats of them that sold doves. And would not suffer that any man should pass through the temple. And he said unto them: *Is it not written, Behold, a day of the Lord cometh. In that day there shall be no more a Canaanite in the house of the Lord of Hosts.* And the chief priests heard it, and said: *Yet it is written in Isaiah: Mine house shall be called an house of prayer for all peoples?* And Jesus answereth, saying: *Hold ye these strangers to the covenant of the Lord? It is indeed written: My house shall be called of all nations the house of prayer? but the Lord also saith: Ye have made it a den of thieves.* Therefore will I cast ye out of my sight. And the chief priests were sore displeased, and when they saw the children of Israel crying in gratitude in the temple, and saying: *Osanna, Son of David*, they said unto him: *Hearest thou what these say?* And Jesus saith unto them: *Yea; have ye never read: Out of the mouth of babes and sucklings hast thou ordained strength because of thine enemies, that thou mightest still the enemy and the avenger.* And they knew not how to answer.

Authority

Mark 11:27 – 11:33

11:27 And they come again to Jerusalem: and as he was walking in the temple, there come to him the chief priests, and the scribes, and the elders, 11:28 And say unto him, By what authority doest thou these things? and who gave thee this authority to do these things? 11:29 And Jesus answered and said unto them, I will also ask of you one question, and answer me, and I will tell you by what authority I do these things. 11:30 The baptism of John, was it from heaven, or of men? answer me. 11:31 And they reasoned with themselves, saying, If we shall say, From heaven; he will say, Why then did ye not believe him? 11:32 But if we shall say, Of men; they feared the people: for all men counted John, that he was a prophet indeed. 11:33 And they answered and said unto Jesus, We cannot tell. And Jesus answering saith unto them, Neither do I tell you by what authority I do these things.

Authority

Mark implies the events recounted next occurred on a later visit to Jerusalem but obviously they did not. The question in verse 28 shows it was on the occasion of the cleansing. The priests in the temple ask Jesus by whose authority he had overthrown the tables, inviting him to admit he is a king. Authority, sometimes translated as power, is code for a king.

They are saying: *You have to be the king to do this. Who made you a king?* Jesus is unperturbed. His answer really means: *What's it to you? You can do nothing about it.* Mark explains why. If the temple officials agreed that John had God's authority, that was sufficient because Jesus was his successor. If they denied it, he had the de facto authority of the crowd and the Nazarenes. Jesus was in charge, either way, and when they declined to answer there was nothing more to be said.

People recognized Jesus as having the authority or power of a king according to the scriptures. Those that had ears to hear would understand!

From this point on in Mark we have several debates between Jesus and the Sadducees and perhaps some Pharisees. So far as it is possible to tell previous disputes in Mark have not been with Jesus's opponents but with his converts—the simple of Ephraim. In the Community Rule we learn that the Master shall not rebuke the men of the pit, or dispute with them, and will not grapple with the men of perdition until the day of vengeance. The Damascus Rule explains that the men of the pit are the rich—primarily the Sadducees. It seems that the capture of Jerusalem and the temple for Jesus freed him to grapple with and rebuke the men of the pit. It must have signified the day of God's vengeance—Jesus felt free to argue with the priesthood but also he must now have expected God or the archangel Michael to act.

Mark 11:27 to 11:33 Restored

And the chief priests say unto him: *By what authority doest thou these things? and who gave thee this authority to do these things?* And Jesus answered and said unto them: *I will also ask of you one question, and answer me, and I will tell you by what authority I do these things. The baptism of John, was it from heaven, or of men? answer me.* And they reasoned with themselves: If we shall say, From heaven; he will say, Why then did ye not believe him? But if we shall say, Of men; they feared the many thronging about: for all men counted Jesus, that he was a king indeed. And they answered and said unto Jesus: *We cannot tell.* And Jesus answering saith unto them: *Then ye need not me to tell you by what authority I do these things.*

The Wicked Husbandmen

Mark 12:1 – 12:12

12:1 And he began to speak unto them by parables. A certain man planted a vineyard, and set an hedge about it, and digged a place for the winefat, and built a tower, and let it out to husbandmen, and went into a far country. 12:2 And at the season he sent to the husbandmen a servant, that he might receive from the husbandmen of the fruit of the vineyard. 12:3 And they caught him, and beat him, and sent him away empty. 12:4 And again he sent unto them another servant; and at him they cast stones, and wounded him in the head, and sent him away shamefully handled. 12:5 And again he sent another; and him they killed, and many others; beating some, and killing some. 12:6 Having yet therefore one son, his wellbeloved, he sent him also last unto them, saying, They will reverence my son. 12:7 But those husbandmen said among themselves, This is the heir; come, let us kill him, and the inheritance shall be our's. 12:8 And they took him, and killed him, and cast him out of the vineyard. 12:9 What shall therefore the lord of the vineyard do? he will come and destroy the husbandmen, and will give the vineyard unto others. 12:10 And have ye not read this scripture; The stone which the builders rejected is become the head of the corner: 12:11 This was the Lord's doing, and it is marvellous in our eyes? 12:12 And they sought to lay hold on him, but feared the people: for they knew that he had spoken the parable against them: and they left him, and went their way.

The Wicked Husbandmen

Mark relates the parable of the wicked husbandmen, a parable which was spoken against the temple authorities (Mk 12:12). The gate of the temple sanctuary was decorated with a magnificent solid gold vine representing Israel and meant to remind the priesthood that God had given them charge of Israel as its husbandmen. There can be no argument but that the description of the vineyard is an allegorical description of Israel. The metaphor is used in Isaiah 5:1–7 and the beginning of this parable uses the same imagery. Yet commentaries on the

251

gospels swear black and blue that this is not an allegory because parables are not allegories. Well parables are, and this plainly is.

If the vineyard is Israel and the man is God, then the wicked husbandmen are the temple priesthood who want to keep the fruits of the vineyard for themselves. They kill or maim the messengers, meaning the prophets, sent by God. Only the Sadducees rejected the prophets as a point of principle—Sadducees were concerned only with the Torah not the later books of the scriptures— further proof that the story was directed at the priesthood. Finally God sends his wellbeloved son, wellbeloved signifying that he is a king. The parable would have continued from 12:7: *and the son evicted the wicked husbandmen and returned the vineyard to the hands of his father*. The parable justified Jesus's eviction of the corrupt temple priesthood, and the return of Israel to its proper owner, God.

Unfortunately this happy ending was later spoiled by the son himself being crucified. Mark therefore had to alter it. From 12:7 onwards the son was also killed, the tenants killed by the father and the vineyard handed to others—the gentile church. If Mark's ending were genuine it would have been another prediction by Jesus of his death, a prediction of the destruction of the temple and a prediction of the gentile church. To a rational person this cries out that it was added after 70 AD.

In verse 1, *went into another country* signifies the feeling that God no longer dwelt with his people as he had at the time of Moses in the desert. Conventional commentators, immune to the idea of allegory, create for themselves even more problems. They say the story, to be the sort of parable they want, must be realistic and it is unrealistic to have a landlord with such patience that he sent many servants. Does it make them begin to think it is an allegory in which the landlord is God? No! The story has been altered! There were only three servants.

The quotation which follows is from Psalms 118:22–23, a song which cries for the day which the Lord hath made, meaning the day of the restoration of the kingdom. It is the psalm which the crowd sang at the entry of Jesus into Jerusalem. The humble stone rejected by the builders became the head of the corner, a corner stone, the basis of the temple. The Christian interpretation is that the humble stone was Jesus, a humble man, but that is only partly true. In the psalm it is Israel that is the humble stone—compassed about by all nations, its gentile enemies. The prayer in the song is that Israel will cut off these enemies. Many of the psalms have much in them to suggest an Essene origin and the Essenes would read as Israel in this context, not the whole nation which was all Israel but the remnant of Israel that was righteous, namely, themselves. The humble stone elevated to the greatest was meant to be the replacement of the official priesthood by the humblest of men, the poor men, the Essenes. In the sense that Jesus was their leader, the Christian reading is correct.

In Matthew 21:28–32 the parable of the wicked husbandmen is preceded by another parable about a vineyard—the parable of the two sons.

But what think ye? A certain man had two sons; and he came to the first, and said, Son, go work to day in my vineyard. He answered and said, I will not: but afterward he repented, and went. And he came to the second, and said likewise. And he answered and said, I go, sir: and went not. Whether of them twain did the will of his father? They say unto him, The first. Jesus saith unto them, Verily I say unto you, That the publicans and the harlots go into the kingdom of God before you. For John came unto you in the way of righteousness, and ye believed him not: but the publicans and the harlots believed him: and ye, when ye had seen it, repented not afterward, that ye might believe him.

The parable is quite appropriate, except that it possibly followed the one about the husbandmen rather than preceded it. The second son portrays the rulers of Israel who undertook to do God's work but did not. The first son portrays the repentant sinners—the publicans and harlots—who believed John the Baptist and were baptized. Interesting here is that Matthew acknowledges that most of the Nazarene converts came from the efforts of John the Baptist not Jesus or his disciples. Matthew also says: *John came unto you in the way of righteousness*, using the Essene expression, *the way of righteousness*. John and Jesus were Essenes.

After Jesus had finished the parable of the wicked husbandmen, the chief priests were surely outraged. They believed they were doing God's work, and they took the fact that they were so rich to be God's approval. They were impotent to do anything but would have expressed their outrage to Jesus. Jesus replied with his second parable.

Mark 12:1 to 12:12 Restored

And Jesus said: *And have ye not read this scripture: The stone which the builders rejected is become the head of the corner. This is the Lord's doing; it is marvellous in our eyes. This is the day which the Lord hath made; We will rejoice and be glad in it.* And the stone stands for God's righteous who are poor and downtrodden. And Jesus began to speak to the chief priests by parables, saying: *A certain man planted a vineyard, and set an hedge about it, and digged a place for the winefat, and built a tower, and let it out to husbandmen, and went into a far country. And at the season he sent to the husbandmen a servant, that he might receive from the husbandmen of the fruit of the vineyard. And they caught him, and beat him, and sent him away empty. And again he sent unto them another servant; and at him they cast stones, and wounded him in the head, and sent him away shamefully handled. And again he sent another; and him they killed, and many others; beating some, and killing some. Having yet therefore one son, his wellbeloved, he sent him also last unto them, saying: They will reverence my son. And the son evicted the wicked husbandmen and returned the vineyard to the hands of his father.* And they knew that he had spoken the parable against them. And the priests were outraged, and they said unto Jesus: *We do God's works according to Moses and God rewards us. How are we wicked?* And Jesus answered: *What think ye? A certain man had two sons; and he came to the first, and said, Son, go work today in my vineyard. He answered and said, I will not: but afterward he repented, and went. And he came to the second, and said likewise. And he answered and said, I go, sir: and went not. Whether of them twain did the will of his father?* They say unto him: *The first.* Jesus saith unto them: *Truly, that the publicans and the harlots go into the kingdom of God before you. For God trusted his works to you but ye did it not. And when John came unto you in the way of righteousness, and ye believed him not. But they that had refused God's works, the publicans and the harlots, believed him and repented with baptism: and ye, when ye had seen it afterward, believed him not, that ye might repent.* And the priests understood and would have laid hold on him, but feared to for many people reverenced him.

Tribute

Mark 12:13 – 12:17

12:13 And they send unto him certain of the Pharisees and of the Herodians, to catch him in his words. 12:14 And when they were come, they say unto him, Master, we know that thou art true, and carest for no man: for thou regardest not the person of men, but teachest the way of God in truth: Is it lawful to give tribute to Caesar, or not? 12:15 Shall we give, or shall we not give? But he, knowing their hypocrisy, said unto them, Why tempt ye me? bring me a penny, that I may see it. 12:16 And they brought it. And he saith unto them, Whose is this image and superscription? And they said unto him, Caesar's. 12:17 And Jesus answering said unto them, Render to Caesar the things that are Caesar's, and to God the things that are God's. And they marvelled at him.

Tribute

The gospel story seems to refute the idea that Jesus was a nationalist because his answer seems to acknowledge Caesar's political power and imply that Jesus would have paid the tribute. Yet in Luke 23:2 he was accused of refusing to pay! Even for Alfred Loisy, the biblical scholar, who was excommunicated by the Pope for his intellectual honesty, this declaration meant the kingdom of God was not to be established by violence. Loisy's prejudice for the Christian image of gentle Jesus had distorted his judgement. Jesus is asserting clearly that Caesar had no authority over God's country and people.

The question was a trick. Whatever reply he gave would have discredited him. To have denied the tribute money would have suited Jewish nationalists but would have been treasonable to the Romans; to have recognized Caesar's right to tribute would have pleased the Romans but lost support from most Jews. Commentators on the gospels try to find in Jesus's audience both collaborators and nationalists so that one or the other would be offended by Jesus's answer. Taking the Pharisees to be collaborators, they identify Mark's Herodians with Jewish nationalists—people of the philosophy of the real Jesus. Yet the Herods were Roman puppets! It is true that Josephus tells us that the Essenes were favoured by Herod the Great but the discoveries at Qumran suggest quite the opposite. Nobody is certain who the Herodians were, but their name must imply associations with the detested puppet kings. They were allies of the Romans and allies of the Sadducees and might have been the Sadducees by another name. There is no need to look for explicit mention of nationalists and collaborators—they were there. The band accompanying Jesus were nationalists—the inquisitors were collaborators.

Jesus's answer in the gospels: *Render to Caesar the things that are Caesar's and to God the things that are God's*, is considered by clergymen to be very clever, implying that the tribute money is merely this-worldly whereas God was interested only in other-worldly matters.

This interpretation is nonsense. If the reported words were those of Jesus, he was openly defying Caesar and the Romans. He was telling Romans they had no right to be there and he had no intention of paying them tribute. When Jesus spoke of the things that are God's no Jew could mistake his meaning—Israel and the children of Israel! There could be no mistake in the context in which it is spoken—what is God's is contrasted with what is Caesar's. He is saying: *Judaea is God's land; the Jews are God's chosen people. Caesar is welcome to what is his, the rest of the Roman Empire, but he can have no claim to what is God's.* That this is the correct interpretation explains the charge in Luke of refusing to pay the tribute money.

Depicted as part of Jesus's confrontation with the Jewish authorities—Mark places this episode in the temple—the questioners have, nonetheless, become Pharisees. In the same episode related in Luke 20:19–26 it was the Chief Priests who instigated the question, which was put via their spies. Unless the incident has been transposed from elsewhere this seems more likely. The Sadducees were out and out collaborators, kept wealthy out of the temple tax, paid by all Jews, and the sale of sacrificial animals. As agents of the occupying power they were the real enemies of Jesus. But really the incident must have happened elsewhere. Jesus would not have discussed money in the temple after cleansing it and, having disposed of the Jerusalem garrison, he would not have been bothered about tribute anyway.

Its real setting was on entering Judaea at the customs post of Jericho. Its absence there explains the curious double reference to Jericho in Mark 10:46. Then Herodians and Sadducees is the original tradition—they were the border officials and customs men. Mark replaced Sadducees with Pharisees and an editor moved the incident into the temple. Luke then changed Mark's text because he realized that in the temple the inquisitors should have been the priests, but seemed to hedge his bets in that he implies that the question was put at another time at the instigation of the Sadducees.

The people marvelled or were amazed. Why! These are words used of daring deeds or remarkable events like miracles. Interpreted the Christian way, the answer was clever but not amazing. Interpreted properly it was amazing because it was so bold. Jesus was openly defying Caesar.

Note that the priests address Jesus as one who teaches *the way of God in truth*. They state categorically that he is an Essene.

Matthew 17:24–27—The Tribute Money

> 17:24 And when they were come to Capernaum, they that received tribute money came to Peter, and said, Doth not your master pay tribute? 17:25 He saith, Yes. And when he was come into the house, Jesus prevented him, saying, What thinkest thou, Simon? of whom do the kings of the earth take custom or tribute? of their own children, or of strangers? 17:26 Peter saith unto him, Of strangers. Jesus saith unto him, Then are the children free. 17:27 Notwithstanding, lest we should offend them, go thou to the sea, and cast an hook, and take up the fish that first cometh up; and when thou hast opened his mouth, thou shalt find a piece of money: that take, and give unto them for me and thee.

The story of Caesar's tribute money does not appear in Matthew. Instead we get what seems to be an entirely different tribute—the annual temple tax of half a shekel. There is no Christian who will not read this episode as a miracle—the precise coin to pay the tax for Jesus and Peter is found in the mouth of a fish—but you will note that no miracle is recounted. We are not told that such a marvellous fish is caught!

Jesus's direct speech has become nonsense through pious editing, and yet the original meaning shines through—for anyone not blinkered! Jesus is not telling Peter to pay the tax, he is telling him not to pay it. And the tax he meant must have been the tribute money to Caesar not the temple tax. The miracle is not recorded because Jesus was being heavily sarcastic in saying: *go to the sea, cast a hook, open the mouth of the first fish that you catch, and if you find the money for the tax, take it to them and pay it*. He was really saying: it will take a miracle for me pay this tax.

Now Jesus would not have paid either the temple tax or the tribute to Caesar. Essenes had no respect for the polluted temple and, as the scrolls indicate, would have fulfilled only the strictest requirements of the law by paying the tax once in their lifetime—Jesus would already have paid it at his age. The tone of the tax collector in verse 24 is menacing, and the implication is that Peter agreed with him to avoid trouble. Temple Levites would have bullied many people into paying the tax, though they could not afford it, but they would not have wasted their efforts on any as committed as Essenes, who had a vow of poverty, besides their disdain for the temple. Peter, who was a rock, would not have been intimidated by a temple bully. He would, however, have been scared of anyone collecting the Roman tribute levied by Caesar.

Though the text, by using in the Greek the word didrachmon, implies that the tax is the temple tax, it also uses words which mean custom and poll tax. The temple tax is a Jewish matter but the poll tax is the tribute owed to the Romans. Though the evangelist has tried to confuse the issue, there is no doubt in Matthew that Jesus is talking about the Roman tax. Jesus asks Peter: *of whom do the kings of the earth take tribute?* The kings of the earth cannot be priests in the temple of Jerusalem but must be gentile kings—the emperors of Rome, the rulers of almost the whole known world. He is referring to Tiberius Caesar.

Jesus's question has been slightly altered by an editor. The question was originally: *Of whom do the kings of the earth take tribute, of God's children or of strangers?* Peter gives the correct answer—of strangers. God's children paid tribute only to God. The kings of the earth take tribute from those they have conquered—as long as they are not God's children! Jesus then says: *Then are the children free.* When Jesus says the children he does not mean immature adults he means the children of Israel, establishing the original question. Jesus reaffirms the principle that God's children do not pay tribute to foreigners— he is refusing tribute just as he did in Luke—and just as Judas of Galilee a few years earlier had refused to pay tribute. He concludes with his heavily ironical: By all means pay the tribute—if you can catch a fish with the money in its mouth.

Interestingly there must have been a census in 20–21 AD because there was one in 6–7 AD and they were every fourteen years. This numbering of the people was the sad calamity of Josephus in Antiquities of the Jews that led to Jesus's uprising, but has been suppressed. Luke's reference to the census at the time of the birth of Jesus was perhaps a transference of the fact that a census led to his death! Jesus plainly saw the census as yet another sign of the times.

We are told the incident in Matthew occurs in Capernaum in Galilee but Matthew probably knows less about Jesus's itinerary than Mark. He has set it in Capernaum because it refers to catching fish, and Matthew has to make that possible. If it corresponds with Mark it occurred in Judaea, where it would have been collected when Jesus entered the country on his way to Jerusalem. The oasis of Jericho is only five miles from the river Jordan.

Matthew 17:24 to 17:27 Restored

And when they were come to Judaea to Jericho, they that received tribute money came to Peter, and said: *Doth not your master pay tribute?* And when he was come to tell his master, Jesus asked: *What thinkest thou, Simon? of whom do the kings of the earth take custom or tribute? of God's children, or of strangers?* Peter saith unto him: *Of strangers.* Jesus saith unto him: *Then are the children free. Notwithstanding, shouldst thou go to the river, and cast an hook, and take up the fish that first cometh up; and when thou hast opened his mouth, shouldst thou find a piece of money, that take, and give unto them for tribute.* For he knew no man would catch such a fish and the tribute would go unpaid.

Mark 12:13 to 12:17 Restored

And the Sadducees tried to incriminate him, and they say unto him: *Master, we know that thou art true, and carest for no man: for thou regardest not the person of men, but teachest the way of God in truth: Is it lawful to give tribute to Caesar, or not? Shall we give, or shall we not give?* But he, knowing their hypocrisy, said unto them: *Why tempt ye me? The answer is not a secret. Bring me a penny, that I may see it.* And they brought it. And he saith unto them: *Whose is this image and superscription?* And they said unto him: *Caesar's.* And Jesus answering said unto them: *Render to Caesar the things that are Caesar's, and to God the things that are God's.* And they marvelled at him, for he meant that God had appointed a covenant with the people of His land. Though Caesar was a mighty king, he could make no claim to what is God's.

Resurrection

Mark 12:18 – 12:27

12:18 Then come unto him the Sadducees, which say there is no resurrection; and they asked him, saying, 12:19 Master, Moses wrote unto us, If a man's brother die, and leave his wife behind him, and leave no children, that his brother should take his wife, and raise up seed unto his brother. 12:20 Now there were seven brethren: and the first took a wife, and dying left no seed. 12:21 And the second took her, and died, neither left he any seed: and the third likewise. 12:22 And the seven had her, and left no seed: last of all the woman died also. 12:23 In the resurrection therefore, when they shall rise, whose wife shall she be of them? for the seven had her to wife. 12:24 And Jesus answering said unto them, Do ye not therefore err, because ye know not the scriptures, neither the power of God? 12:25 For when they shall rise from the dead, they neither marry, nor are given in marriage; but are as the angels which are in heaven. 12:26 And as touching the dead, that they rise: have ye not read in the book of Moses, how in the bush God spake unto him, saying, I am the God of Abraham, and the God of Isaac, and the God of Jacob? 12:27 He is not the God of the dead, but the God of the living: ye therefore do greatly err.

Resurrection

The debate in the temple continued. Mark tells us here that the interrogators were Sadducees as they must have been as the temple authorities but it is the first time in the gospel that they are mentioned. Jesus had explained that the kingdom of God was at hand. The children of Israel had to be repentant, then the righteous would be resurrected and would rule in God's kingdom. The Sadducees did not accept such Persian introductions as angels and resurrection and their delegation posed an extreme instance to Jesus which they thought would refute him. Jesus however was an Essene and believed in resurrection, angels, demons and all the Persian innovations and is shown answering them in his terms with ease.

The first answer Jesus gives is likely to be Essene because it draws on the apocryphal book 1 Enoch which the Essenes revered. The Essenes believed that God's kingdom was an everlasting kingdom in which the righteous would have everlasting life. In God's kingdom the righteous became immortal, one of the main attractions of Christianity to the gentile Romans and indeed to people today. Now the creatures which were already immortal were angels and demons. In 1 Enoch God tells the angels, *because they are immortal for all the generations of the world, therefore have I not appointed wives for you*—immortal beings had no need of procreation. The Essenes deduced that, in God's kingdom, the righteous would have no wives. And indeed the most pious Essenes, those of the Qumran monastery, who were beginning to build God's kingdom on earth, took no wives, partly for this reason. They seemed to believe the kingdom was contiguous with life on earth but nevertheless different, because it was perfect, and so marriage was superseded.

Since Essenes would have regarded Enoch as scripture there was no need to add the second answer simply to complete Jesus's declaration that his inquisitors did not know the scriptures. But, since Jesus must have known his first answer would not satisfy a Sadducee—for whom scripture was only the five books of Moses, an answer which would satisfy them was needed. Unfortunately, it is not an answer to the question—it simply tells them from their own holy books that the dead live, supposedly explaining resurrection. However the additional answer contradicts what went before, casting doubt on one or the other. If the patriarchs are not dead but somehow still live, then they cannot rise from the dead, and verses 25 and 26 should not speak of such rising.

If the second part of the answer is genuine tradition, it seems that the Essenes actually did not believe in death of the righteous at all! The scriptures refer to the righteous dead as sleeping and so, it seems, the Essenes thought of them. Resurrection from the dead was possible because, for God, the righteous never died but slept and resurrection became simply an awakening into everlasting life. They certainly were not alive and in heaven, because only Enoch himself dwelt with God. However Josephus asserts that the Essenes believed in an immortal soul which was overjoyed to be freed from the prison of a corruptible body. It seems the Essenes must have believed the souls of the dead remained as free spirits until the general resurrection on the third day of the kingdom when they were resurrected into perfect and therefore uncorruptible bodies.

Mark 12:18 to 12:27 Restored

The Sadducees, which say there is no resurrection, tried to confound Jesus, saying: *Master, Moses wrote unto us, If a man's brother die, and leave his wife behind him, and leave no children, that his brother should take his wife, and raise up seed unto his brother. Now there were seven brethren: and the first took a wife, and dying left no seed. And the second took her, and died, neither left he any seed: and the third likewise. And the seven had her, and left no seed: last of all the woman died also. In the resurrection therefore, when they shall rise, whose wife shall she be of them? for the seven had her to wife.* And Jesus answering said unto them: *Ye err because ye know not the power of God. For when they shall rise from the dead, they neither marry, nor are given in marriage; but, as it is written in Enoch, they are as the angels which are in heaven. Nor know ye the book of Moses, else ye would have read how in the bush God spake unto him, saying, I am the God of Abraham, and the God of Isaac, and the God of Jacob? He is not the God of the dead, but the God of the living. Their rising up on the third day is like one who awakens from sleep. Ye therefore do greatly err.*

The First Commandment of them All

Mark 12.28 – 12:34

12:28 And one of the scribes came, and having heard them reasoning together, and perceiving that he had answered them well, asked him, Which is the first commandment of all? 12:29 And Jesus answered him, The first of all the commandments is, Hear, O Israel; The Lord our God is one Lord: 12:30 And thou shalt love the Lord thy God with all thy heart, and with all thy soul, and with all thy mind, and with all thy strength: this is the first commandment. 12:31 And the second is like, namely this, Thou shalt love thy neighbour as thyself. There is none other commandment greater than these. 12:32 And the scribe said unto him, Well, Master, thou hast said the truth: for there is one God; and there is none other but he: 12:33 And to love him with all the heart, and with all the understanding, and with all the soul, and with all the strength, and to love his neighbour as himself, is more than all whole burnt offerings and sacrifices. 12:34 And when Jesus saw that he answered discreetly, he said unto him, Thou art not far from the kingdom of God. And no man after that durst ask him any question.

The First Commandment of them All

Then Mark depicts a scribe asking Jesus to say what was the greatest commandment. For all Jews the greatest commandment is to love God, and verses 29–30 are in the Shemah (Deut 6:4–5) which pious Jews recite every day.

Since he was asked for one only, Jesus curiously gives a second commandment, to love your neighbour, from Leviticus 19:18. It is an Essene's answer but one which a Pharisee, certainly of the school of Hillel, the noted Pharisee teacher and leader, could accept. The Damascus Rule has: *They shall love each man his brother as himself; they shall succour the poor, the sick and the needy.* And Rabbi Hillel, when challenged to teach the Torah as succinctly as possible, offers it in the form: *What is hateful to thee, do not unto thy fellow: this is the whole law.* Hillel called it the great practical principle.

Jesus gives both commandments together as if they were one. Josephus in Antiquities says John the Baptist taught righteousness toward men and piety towards God, bracketing the two together and also notes this as Essene practice. In the scroll fragments we find that the community's notion of piety meant loving God's name—piety towards God is another way of saying loving God. Essene teaching, the teaching of the Baptist and the teaching of Jesus are the same. Both the Epistle of James and the Qumran texts associate piety with poorness and meekness and they and the gospels declare that wealth is not compatible with righteousness.

Verses 32–33 are unusual in allowing the scribe a response and one which Jesus agrees with. Jesus's Pharisaic inquisitor comments that these principles are more important than burnt offerings, an expression of Pharisaic opposition to the Sadducees whose emphasis was on ritual rather than piety. Pharisees accepted sacrifice only as a token of sincere repentance. The Damascus Rule quotes Proverbs 15:8 as Essene belief: *The sacrifice of the wicked is an abomination, but the prayer of the just is as an agreeable offering.* The agreement over the burnt offerings is significant in that both Pharisees and Essenes consider temple ritual alone is insufficient for entry to God's kingdom. Pharisee and Essene have united against the Sadducees.

Jesus concludes by telling the scribe that he is not far from the kingdom of God. The scribe was righteous but not an Essene. He had to repent sincerely and be baptized to be one of the elect. Mark normally runs down Pharisees yet here he leaves a good impression. It all leads you to think it must come from genuine tradition. Because Mark was the first gospel, written while the church was still evolving, the treatment of the story is liberal. It was edited in later gospels to temper this praise and leave no credit to the Pharisee.

However the way it is presented in Luke 10:25–28 sounds more authentic in that it is all in the mouth of the Pharisee. The Pharisee does not ask Jesus what the first commandment is, but asked him how he could inherit eternal life—meaning enter the kingdom. Jesus did not tell him but asked the scribe to explain what was written in the law. It is the scribe that answers Jesus's question in the rabbinic fashion to be expected and Jesus compliments him. It all fits in better, which might be Luke's literary skill, but the original question is better in this context than Mark's rather phony sounding one. Thus it avoids the problem of getting two answers from one question, because the question was not simply what was the first commandment, the answer to which any Jew would know, as we noted above.

In Luke the phrase about burnt offerings is missing, possibly because Luke is not using the incident to run down the Sadducees but as a link to the likable but bogus parable of the good Samaritan which continues the theme of neighbourliness. The parable is bogus because the hero is made into a Samaritan to represent gentiles, fulfilling one of Luke's aims—to render Jewish teaching suitable for non-Jews. The original story might have been a genuine parable but we shall dismiss it as uncertain. The logic of the sequence of priest then Levite is that the next along the road should be an Israelite, a lay Jew, not a Samaritan, the castes of society in the Jewish theocracy below Levite being Israelites and proselytes. In this context, the lay Jew implies an unpious Jew, a publican, a man of the land, a backslider. The parable depicted the layman, the simple of Ephraim as more neighbourly to the downtrodden and more righteous than the priesthood, the acknowledged rulers of God's kingdom. It could have been a Nazarene parable directed at the Jewish nobility, the Sadducees.

The quotation from Leviticus 19:18 in full reads: *Thou shalt not take vengeance nor bear any grudge against the children of thy people but shalt love thy neighbour as thyself.* I give the full quotation to show that it applies to Jews specifically. The *children of thy people* are the Jews. Neighbour is not used in the sense of any neighbour and once it is recognized that Jesus was an Essene it is plain that he could only have meant a Jewish neighbour. Thus it is that Luke's extension of the story into the tale of the good Samaritan, beautiful as it is, could not have been original, but is a distortion of the evangelist who had to prove somehow that one's best neighbour need not be a Jew for Christianity to prosper.

Note that it quotes the commandment and then repeats: *The Lord is one*, denying the Trinity.

Mark 12:28 to 12:34 Restored

> And one of the scribes came, and hearing them reasoning together, and perceiving that he had answered them well, asked him: *What shall I do to inherit eternal life?* And Jesus said: *What is written in the law?* And he answering said: *The Lord our God is one Lord, and thou shalt love the Lord thy God with all thy heart, and with all thy soul, and with all thy strength, and with all thy mind, and, thou shalt love thy neighbour as thyself.* And Jesus said: *Thou hast answered right; for this is more than all whole burnt offerings and sacrifices. Thou art not far from the kingdom of God.*

Who is David's Lord?

Mark 12:35 – 12:37

> 12:35 And Jesus answered and said, while he taught in the temple, How say the scribes that Christ is the son of David? 12:36 For David himself said by the Holy Ghost, The LORD said to my Lord, Sit thou on my right hand, till I make thine enemies thy footstool. 12:37 David therefore himself calleth him Lord; and whence is he then his son? And the common people heard him gladly.

Who is David's Lord?

Several other lessons appear now in a speech which must have been an attempt to challenge Jesus's authority. At verses 35–37 appears an apparent denial that the messiah could be of the house of David. Why should he want to do this? Is it because he was not, or could not show that he was a son of David himself?

Mark has nothing to say about Jesus's father. Though Jesus is described as a carpenter, his father is nowhere mentioned either as the carpenter or as Joseph. This suggests that, in the earliest tradition, Jesus was an orphan. The Qumran Essene monks took in waifs and strays and so they could have placed no importance on lineage. Though they considered themselves Zadokites, they considered themselves priestly from practice not by descent. They were interested in Melchizedek, the priest of Genesis 14:18–20 who preceded the Zadokite line. The Essenes probably had arrived at symbolic ways of fulfilling scripture just as, it seems, they had ritual coronations to confer titles on to their chosen candidates. Jesus was not necessarily a claimant to the throne of Israel by lineage but a star, a man whose destiny it was. Like Son of Zadok, Son of David was a position to be attained or granted by God not one that came by birth.

Here we find Jesus replying to a question which has been crudely omitted because the editor has already written that no one dared ask any more questions. Carelessly he writes that Jesus is answering it. It is: *How can you be a son of David when you haven't got a father?* Note that Jesus seems to consider himself messiah. Jesus quotes the beginning of Psalms 110. The elder is the Lord of the younger in Jewish lineages. The point is that David (who traditionally was the author of Psalms) as head of the line is its Lord. So, if the messiah were his son (meaning a descendant) then the messiah should call David, Lord, not the other way around. Therefore David in the psalm cannot regard the messiah as his son—ergo, the messiah is not literally David's descendant.

And the common people heard him gladly. The mass of the people accepted that the Son of David was a man in the mould of David and not necessarily of his stock. Jesus had persuaded them that the Essene view was the correct one.

Conceivably the passage could be misplaced from elsewhere and Jesus is arguing in the abstract, but Mark can have had no reason for including any passage in which Jesus seems to deny what was already accepted by the church unless it was genuine tradition and he felt obliged to put it in this particular spot.

Mark 12:35 to 12:37 Restored

And they hoped they might turn the multitude against him, who believed the messiah was the son of David; and, knowing he was an orphan, they asked him: *How canst thou be a son of David when thou hast not a father?* And Jesus answered and said: *Why do the scribes say that the messiah is the son of David? For David, the psalmist, himself said by the holy ghost, in the scriptures: The LORD said to my Lord: Sit thou on my right hand, till I make thine enemies thy footstool. David therefore himself calleth the messiah his Lord; and whence is he then his son?* And the common people heard him gladly, for they understood that the messiah was not of the line of David.

Poor Widows

Mark 12:38 – 12:44

12:38 And he said unto them in his doctrine, Beware of the scribes, which love to go in long clothing, and love salutations in the marketplaces, 12:39 And the chief seats in the synagogues, and the uppermost rooms at feasts: 12:40 Which devour widows' houses, and for a pretence make long prayers: these shall receive greater damnation. 12:41 And Jesus sat over against the treasury, and beheld how the people cast money into the treasury: and many that were rich cast in much. 12:42 And there came a certain poor widow, and she threw in two mites, which make a farthing. 12:43 And he called unto him his disciples, and saith unto them, Verily I say unto you, That this poor widow hath cast more in, than all they which have cast into the treasury: 12:44 For all they did cast in of their abundance; but she of her want did cast in all that she had, even all her living.

Poor Widows

In verse 12:18 we had Sadducees since when it has been scribes. If this is a genuine sequence then Sadducees it would have been all along, because they were the caretakers of the temple which Jesus had occupied. Though that is not always obvious, it is here. The characteristics are more applicable to the priests than to the Pharisees. There were local priests in every village and it is they rather than the Pharisees who would behave in the way described. It would be unwise to argue that some Pharisees did not have an exaggerated idea of their own piety but many did not, despite the impression Mark tries to force upon his readers.

The families of priests took it in turns in serving in the temple and would have expected the men of the land to recognize and admire their close practical contact with God. The best clue, though, is the implication that they robbed widows. Pharisees could not be accused of so doing but the priesthood could. The priests were known to have been ready to turn to extortion to add to the temple's coffers and it must be to this that Mark is alluding, widows then as now being particularly open to emotional pressure, especially religious pressure. As if to prove the point Mark moves on to the next part of the story.

The reference to scribes is shown now to mean Sadducees. The treasury was the temple treasury and because it was the feast of unleavened bread it was obligatory according to Deuteronomy 16:16–17 for everyone to give a sum to the temple. Originally it was only men but the law had been extended to both sexes.

Jesus has just said that those who devour widow's houses will be damned meaning they will not be admitted into the kingdom of eternal life, God's kingdom. Mark shows Jesus as demonstrating in reality what he means. They observe people casting their gifts into the temple treasury and it is the poor widow who puts in her entire livelihood. Widows were inclined to make gifts they could ill-afford in memory of their deceased husbands. The extension to women of the ordinance of Moses in Deuteronomy had made it almost an obligation. The beneficiaries were the already wealthy priesthood.

The point of the demonstration is twofold: a condemnation of the Sadducees who accept the last farthing from a poor woman; a further condemnation of the rich for whom an abundance meant little. Jesus was one of the poor, an Essene.

Jesus next leaves the temple but it is worth noting that some fragments of an unknown gospel and of Josephus say that Jesus officiated as a priest, entering the holy place, implying both that Jesus had the role of an alternative priest and that he was in a position to play it because the temple had been captured. The only people who maintained a priestly tradition outside the temple priesthood were the community at Qumran, the Essene guardians of the Dead Sea Scrolls.

Mark 12:38 to 12:44 Restored

And he said unto them, for he was a Zadokite: *Beware of these priests, which love to go in long clothing, and love salutations in the marketplaces, and the chief seats in the synagogues, and the uppermost rooms at feasts; which devour widows' houses as corban as a petition to God, and for a pretence make long prayers. They honour wealth and esteem above the Lord. They shall be damned.* And Jesus went over against the treasury, and watched the people cast money into the treasury. And many that were rich cast in much. And there came a certain poor widow, and she threw in two mites, which make a farthing. And he called unto those assembled: *Truly, this poor widow hath cast more in than all they which have cast into the treasury, for all they did cast in of their abundance; but she of her want did cast in all that she had, even all her living. This woman honoureth God above wealth; the gates of the kingdom are open to her.*

Destroying the Temple

Mark 13:1 – 13:2

13:1 And as he went out of the temple, one of his disciples saith unto him, Master, see what manner of stones and what buildings are here! 13:2 And Jesus answering said unto him, Seest thou these great buildings? there shall not be left one stone upon another, that shall not be thrown down.

Destroying the Temple

Mark introduces us to the little apocalypse of chapter 13 with a prediction of the destruction of the temple, an event which actually occurred after the Jewish War in 70 AD. He probably wrote at about the time of Titus's Triumph in Rome and could include this prophecy knowing it to be true. It was a heavy defeat of the Jews by Roman military might, and it stands here in Mark's account because the same happened in the story he is narrating—but a generation earlier!

Curiously though, the prediction of the destruction of the temple was just what the Jews would have liked to hear from their messiah because the Sadducees who administered the temple and the building itself were hated. They had been imposed by the unpopular foreign king, Herod the Great. Jews expected nothing less than the destruction of the unclean temple and the restoration of Solomon's temple according to Ezekiel's blueprint at the coming of the kingdom. According to the Enoch literature—so much loved by the Essenes that multiple copies were found in the caves of Qumran—God would restore the temple on the third day after His appointed time, the great day of the Lord.

So it is quite possible that Jesus did prophecy the polluted temple's destruction because of his conviction that the great day had arrived. He was certainly accused of it later. Its apparent fulfilment in 70 AD gave the new religion a useful boost, if not to membership, to the morale of those who were still waiting for Jesus to return on a cloud.

The third day of the kingdom was also the day on which all the dead of the righteous would be resurrected. Hosea 6:2 declares: *on the third day he shall raise us up and we shall live before him*. All of Jesus's prophecies of rising on the third day are really his statement that the dead of the elect would rise then. If he were to die in the battles for the kingdom, as he expected, then it would be on the third day of the kingdom that he would arise and rejoin his fellows.

Mark is fond of having Jesus answer questions or reply to his critics, but in reality much of what is recorded in the gospels probably came from discourses or speeches that Jesus made. Here the disciples gape at the stones of the temple as though they had never seen them and made inane observations. That suits Mark who wanted them to look like imbeciles. Luke, however, has Jesus commenting on generally admiring remarks around him. It really came in a discourse on the kingdom to come.

Mark 13:1 to 13:2 Restored

And Jesus observed on the grandeur of the temple and the manner of stones of which it was built, and he said: *And yet these great buildings will be destroyed, for they are unclean, and not a stone will rest upon another, for it is as nothing to the temple which God will raise up on the third day of His kingdom, for so it is written in Hosea and Ezekiel.*

The Mount of Olives

Mark 13:3 – 13:4

13:3 And as he sat upon the mount of Olives over against the temple, Peter and James and John and Andrew asked him privately, 13:4 Tell us, when shall these things be? and what shall be the sign when all these things shall be fulfilled?

The Mount of Olives

The disciples are beginning to get anxious. Having taken the city and cleansed the temple they—and Jesus too—were expecting God to begin to act. So far nothing. Mark uses their anxiety to give Jesus an excuse for making his long apocalyptic speech to hide the tragedy of the defeat of the Nazarene guerrillas. Mark makes the reason for this his prediction that the temple would be destroyed, but it must really have been an explanation of the signs of the end time. The disciples were not concerned about the temple but that the day of the Lord had arrived with no appearance of God's miracle. They were impatient and asked Jesus to review the signs for them. They wanted reasons to feel encouraged. Jesus would have been explaining why he had come to the conclusion that the day of the Lord was due.

The association of the mount of Olives with the speech describing the apocalypse is not coincidental. In Zechariah 14:4 the prophecy is that the miracle of God inaugurating the kingdom will occur on the Mount of Olives. Jesus and his band would have spent time each day waiting and watching there. Indeed that is what they are doing when Jesus is arrested. At some point, probably the first occasion, the band arrived at the Mount of Olives and Jesus made a speech describing what was expected to happen in the cosmic conflict for the kingdom. On another occasion, the final trip to Olivet, with the Romans back in control of the city, it was an impassioned speech appealing to God to respond to their act of faith in capturing Jerusalem. Mark uses bits of both and also possibly bits of the speech made when Jesus first took the city because there is a further reference to the fig tree.

The Mount of Olives is of apocalyptic importance to the Essenes because it lies in direct line between Jerusalem and Qumran. The prophet Ezekiel saw God leave the polluted city of Jerusalem (Ezek 10:19) and hurry away to the east directly over the Mount of Olives (Ezek 11:23). Later God returned along the same route (Ezek 43:2). The Essenes, who seemed to regard this as history not prophecy, deduced that the New Jerusalem must be to the east, beyond the Mount and they founded it at Qumran, as far east as you could get without crossing the Dead Sea, and conveniently close to several springs in the limestone that bubbled out into the Dead Sea allowing plants to grow. On God's return, the Mount of Olives would split asunder as Zechariah describes, God sending his power along the east-west axis of the New Jerusalem to the Old Jerusalem.

Olives of the Mount of Olives seems to be a misunderstanding and mistranslation of an Aramaic proper noun meaning the Most High—Elion, the same root as Allah. Because it was a proper noun, it was not translated into Greek but some readers nevertheless took it to be a Greek word—elaion, an olive, and so thought that was the name of the mountain (Olivet). Now the Mount of Olives is not very high. The name Elion therefore does not refer to the height of the place itself. It is obviously called the Most High because of its association with the Most High God.

Mark 13:3 to 13:4 Restored

And Jesus took his priestly disciples, Peter, James and John, up to the Mount of Olives to watch for God's miracle, and as they sat there over against the temple, Peter, James and John came to him privately, for they were anxious, and said: *Thou hast said it was the day of the Lord, but yet the mountain trembleth not. Tell us, when shall these things be, and what shall be the sign when all these things shall be fulfilled?*

Signs of the Apocalypse

Mark 13:5 - 13:27

13:5 And Jesus answering them began to say, Take heed lest any man deceive you: 13:6 For many shall come in my name, saying, I am Christ; and shall deceive many. 13:7 And when ye shall hear of wars and rumours of wars, be ye not troubled: for such things must needs be; but the end shall not be yet. 13:8 For nation shall rise against nation, and kingdom against kingdom: and there shall be earthquakes in divers places, and there shall be famines and troubles: these are the beginnings of sorrows. 13:9 But take heed to yourselves: for they shall deliver you up to councils; and in the synagogues ye shall be beaten: and ye shall be brought before rulers and kings for my sake, for a testimony against them. 13:10 And the gospel must first be published among all nations. 13:11 But when they shall lead you, and deliver you up, take no thought beforehand what ye shall speak, neither do ye premeditate: but whatsoever shall be given you in that hour, that speak ye: for it is not ye that speak, but the Holy Ghost. 13:12 Now the brother shall betray the brother to death, and the father the son; and children shall rise up against their parents, and shall cause them to be put to death. 13:13 And ye shall be hated of all men for my name's sake: but he that shall endure unto the end, the same shall be saved. 13:14 But when ye shall see the abomination of desolation, spoken of by Daniel the prophet, standing where it ought not, (let him that readeth understand,) then let them that be in Judaea flee to the mountains: 13:15 And let him that is on the housetop not go down into the house, neither enter therein, to take any thing out of his house: 13:16 And let him that is in the field not turn back again for to take up his garment. 13:17 But woe to them that are with child, and to them that give suck in those days! 13:18 And pray ye that your flight be not in the winter. 13:19 For in those days shall be affliction, such as was not from the beginning of the creation which God created unto this time, neither shall be. 13:20 And except that the Lord had shortened those days, no flesh should be saved: but for the elect's sake, whom he hath chosen, he hath shortened the days. 13:21 And then if any man shall say to you, Lo, here is Christ; or, lo, he is there; believe him not: 13:22 For false Christs and false prophets shall rise, and shall shew signs and wonders, to seduce, if it were possible, even the elect. 13:23 But take ye heed: behold, I have foretold you all things. 13:24 But in those days, after that tribulation, the sun shall be darkened, and the moon shall not give her light, 13:25 And the stars of heaven shall fall, and the powers that are in heaven shall be shaken. 13:26 And then shall they see the Son of man coming in the clouds with great power and glory. 13:27 And then shall he send his angels, and shall gather together his elect from the four winds, from the uttermost part of the earth to the uttermost part of heaven.

The Mini-Apocalypse

Chapter 13 is one long, long discourse by Jesus known as the little apocalypse. To understand the purpose of Mark's little apocalypse, it is necessary to grasp the mood of it. It is unbearably gloomy. It has been put here to pull a veil over a tragic event which cannot be told—the Roman counter attack on Jerusalem in which the legionaries from Caesarea on the coast arrive and savage the Nazarenes and their admiring throng into submission in a few hours. Mark hints at the counter attack but no more. He obviously could not be explicit. He either has to omit it altogether or disguise it as something else.

An apocalypse is a prophecy of the end. Often it is disguised history written to encourage oppressed people who could not write openly for fear of further persecution from their oppressors. It is coded history with a moral message—the encouragement that God would bring them through their crises. The historical prophecies of the prophet proved true—naturally, they were actually history—so then should their victory and their salvation at the hand of God with which the apocalypse ended. The Book of Daniel is the best biblical example. It is a history of the Jews from the exile until the time of the Seleucid Greek king Antiochus Epiphanes in the second century BC.

The author of an apocalypse writes history as if it were a prophecy by pretending to be from an earlier time. Here Mark writes the apocalypse as if he were Jesus. Even then the imagery is necessarily obscure. It is not surprising that an apocalyptic sect like the Essenes took to believing that all scripture was coded and that they began to use code among themselves in everyday life, as Jesus did with his parables. The parables therefore are an extension of the idea of apocalyptic writing—both apocalypses and parables are allegories, both might get slightly garbled in transcript making them harder to decipher, but both are unmistakable in form.

Mark must have had an Essene explanation of the signs of the end time possibly Peter's, and he combined it with snippets of the history of the years between the death of Jesus and the time when he was writing. In reconstructing the Essene discourse, the history has to be omitted and what remains checked against Essene teaching.

Since Jesus's expectation of the arrival of the kingdom was never fulfilled Mark had to improvise with what he knew had happened while cutting out what he knew had not happened. Mark begins the serious business of apocalypse writing by issuing warnings in the name of the Christ that Christians will be persecuted and divided. Dissension in the Christian camp, we know from the Epistles, occurred. The famine, which scourged Palestine in the forties, and the Jewish War are similarly prophesied. But such is the stuff of apocalypses—it could have been said by Jesus in the general sense that the approaching day of the Lord is preceded by such happenings.

Jesus expected God's miracle at any moment because he had cleansed the Jerusalem temple. Quite what he expected to happen afterwards is not clear, but the miracle would have followed the prophecy of Zechariah. He expected the cosmic battle to begin and continue for forty years reflected in warfare and tribulations on earth. Then the sons of light would have their victory and the gates of the kingdom would open. If he was writing less than forty years later, Mark might still have believed this. In any case he would surely have begun Jesus's discourse with him explaining the Essene idea of the cosmic battle as we find in the War Scroll. It would act as a suitable veil for the unacceptable truth that the Romans fought the Nazarenes as insurgents, and defeated them.

The bulk of 13:9 to 13:13 is late but there are elements here such as the idea of strife within families that might have come from Jesus's speech based on scriptural ideas of the end time. Parts of it are poetic and hint at a hymn of encouragement during Roman official oppression. Verses 9 and 10 are definitely late additions. In other gospels verse 11 is part of Jesus's speech to the disciples beginning their mission and perhaps that is where it belongs, Mark having plucked it out and used it here because he needed material. Betray in verse 12 should be deliver.

The Abomination of Desolation. Did Pilate's soldiers erect their standards in the Jerusalem temple, the definitive sign of the end time according to Daniel, and so noted by the Essenes who were keen to divine the portents of the coming of the kingdom of God?

The second half of verse 13 is clearly genuine Essene tradition provided that some qualification in terms of righteousness is introduced. Verses 14, 15, 16, 19, 20 and 24–27 reflect Jesus's speech. Verses 21–23 might be another indication of early divisions in the gentile church but might also be a reference to other false messiahs like Simon Magus, known by Mark, and particularly Bar Kosiba who claimed to be the messiah in 132 AD and was followed by Jews and Nazarenes alike, an insertion by a later editor.

In verse 14 the abomination of desolation spoken of in Daniel 9:27 was the pollution of the temple with an image of a pagan god (Zeus) under Antiochus Epiphanes. The Emperor Caligula almost repeated the crime when he ordered his own image to be erected in the temple in about 40 AD. King Herod Agrippa I persuaded him to change his mind. Mark and his readers would have known this and interpreted it nevertheless as fulfilment of Jesus's prophecy.

Jesus himself had witnessed the abomination of desolation. It was a similar misdeed by Pontius Pilate who allowed the legions to display their standards in Jerusalem at the start of his prefecture. Josephus does not say they went into the temple, but the relevant parts of Josephus's works have been censored by clerics. Pilate was certainly being provocative because he brought in his troops by night, so when the citizens found out in the morning it was a fait accompli. For the legionaries, their standards bearing Caesar's effigy were gods, and, if it was the tenth legion, they carried banners depicting swine—an even viler depravity. Any graven image in God's house was an abomination to a Jew, especially if it stood for another god. The Essenes must without doubt have regarded this provocation as a sign of the times.

Mark uses the circumlocution *where it ought not* when he meant temple. He refrained from using the word temple as being too vexatious since he was writing about the time when the destruction of the temple was a bone of contention, but adds a note to draw the reader's attention to it. (It was not Jesus's aside because he was not expecting what he said to be read.)

Mark has no obvious reference to a provocative act but in Luke 17:37 in a passage that ends another apocalyptic speech by Jesus (or the same one misplaced) Jesus says: *Wheresoever the body is, thither will the eagles be gathered together.* Though a paraphrase of Job 39:29–30 Jesus is plainly meaning the standards of the Roman legions which were called eagles. The eagles here and in Job are plainly not eagles but vultures, which is just how the Nazarenes, indeed most Jews, will have seen the Romans.

It was probably Pilate's profane act which led the Essenes to conclude that the appointed time had come, and everyone had to flee to the mountains to become barjonim. In Matthew 24:28 the quotation about the eagles seems totally misplaced being apparently bizarrely associated with the coming of Daniel's one unto the Son of man, the glorious messiah. In fact however it is used as a closing bracket, effectively referring back to the abomination of desolation which is the opening bracket (Mt 24:15) of his lengthy description of the day of the Lord.

Verse 15 and 16 seem cryptic but are fully reconstituted in Luke 17:26–32 and are apparently part of Jesus's speech. The reference is to the flood of Noah and the destruction of Sodom when God rained judgement on the people, only the elect being spared. In one case, the flood, it was sensible to take refuge on the roof and in the other, fire and brimstone, it was sensible to take refuge in the mountains and not to look back! Verses 17 and 18 seem to be historic, referring to famine and war in Judaea.

Verse 19 is anticipating the end of the world. It echoes Daniel 12:1 where appears the archangel Michael who the Essenes associated with Melchizedek and perhaps the messiah. Verse 20 is obviously Essene—note Mark's use of the Essenes' name for themselves, the elect, with the explanation *those he had chosen.* Verse 21 to 23 are Mark's composition, though the Essenes must themselves have been concerned with false prophets and messiahs.

The remainder becomes purely apocalyptic with few appended phrases or historical material. Verse 26 recalls Daniel 7:13:

> Behold there came with the clouds of heaven one like unto the Son of man, and he came even unto the ancient of days, and they brought him near before him. And there was given him dominion, and glory and a kingdom, that all the nations, peoples and languages should serve him: his dominion is an everlasting dominion which shall not pass away, and his kingdom that which shall not be destroyed.

In Daniel the one like unto the Son of man receives the kingdom to replace a world crushed by a mighty and cruel king depicted as a beast with iron teeth. This expresses perfectly the core of Jesus's message—a Jewish kingdom of God would replace Rome as the world power forever. The rulers of the new kingdom are the saints of the Most High which means the elect, the Essenes. Mark goes on to explain this in verse 27. The clouds of this passage might well be translated princes (nesiim).

Mark 13:1 to 13:27 Restored

And Jesus answering them began to say: *Ye shall know that the day of the Lord is nigh by these signs, for such things must needs be: when ye hear of wars and rumours of wars, for nation shall rise against nation, and kingdom against kingdom: and there shall be earthquakes in divers places, and there shall be famines and troubles: but the end shall not be yet, these are the beginnings of the birth pangs, which endure forty years. Now the brother shall deliver the brother to death, and the father the son; and children shall rise up against their parents, and shall cause them to be put to death. And ye that shall endure in righteousness unto the end time shall be saved. And, wheresoever the body is, thither will the eagles be gathered together, for ye shall see the abomination of desolation, spoken of by Daniel the prophet, standing in the temple, and ye shall know that the appointed time cometh. As it was in the days of Noah, so shall it be also in the last days. They did eat, they drank, they married wives, they were given in marriage, until the day that Noah entered into the ark, and the flood came, and destroyed them all. Likewise also as it was in the days of Lot; they did eat, they drank, they bought, they sold, they planted, they builded; But the same day that Lot went out of Sodom it rained fire and brimstone from heaven, and destroyed them all. Even thus shall it be in the day of the Lord. In that day, he which shall be upon the housetop, and his stuff in the house, let him not come down to take it away: and he that is in the field, let him likewise not return back. Remember Lot's wife. Whosoever shall seek to save his life shall lose it; and whosoever shall lose his life shall preserve it. In that night there shall be two men in one bed; the one shall be taken, and the other shall be left. Two women shall be grinding together; the one shall be taken, and the other left. Two men shall be in the field; the one shall be taken, and the other left. For in those days shall be affliction, such as was not from the beginning of the creation which God created unto this time, neither shall be. And except that the Lord had shortened those days, no flesh should be saved: but for the elect's sake, whom he hath chosen, he hath shortened the days. But in those days, after that tribulation, the sun shall be darkened, and the moon shall not give her light, And the stars of heaven shall fall, and the powers that are in heaven shall be shaken. And then shall they see coming with great power and glory Michael with his host of angels, the Son of man with the princes of heaven, Melchizedek and the sons of light, to justify the holy ones of God. And then shall he gather together his elect from the four winds, from the uttermost part of the earth to the uttermost part of heaven.*

Watch for the Coming

Mark 13:30 – 13:37

13:30 Verily I say unto you, that this generation shall not pass, till all these things be done. 13:31 Heaven and earth shall pass away: but my words shall not pass away. 13:32 But of that day and that hour knoweth no man, no, not the angels which are in heaven, neither the Son, but the Father. 13:33 Take ye heed, watch and pray: for ye know not when the time is. 13:34 For the Son of Man is as a man taking a far journey, who left his house, and gave authority to his servants, and to every man his work, and commanded the porter to watch. 13:35 Watch ye therefore: for ye know not when the master of the house cometh, at even, or at midnight, or at the cockcrowing, or in the morning: 13:36 Lest coming suddenly he find you sleeping. 13:37 And what I say unto you I say unto all, Watch.

Watch for the Coming

Jesus concludes his speech with a promise that the kingdom will be here within a generation, the forty years of the cosmic battle.

Bible commentators have seen a contrast between the first part of the speech and the end. Initially certain, Jesus finishes not sure, but the two halves are perfectly compatible. The first part answers the question: *What shall be the sign when all these things shall be fulfilled?* Jesus, as an Essene has read the signs of the times and is certain that the kingdom is imminent. *Tell us, when shall these things be?* the disciples had also asked. As depicted by Mark, having taken some time listing the signs, Jesus finally gives his answer. It consists of verses 30 to 37: the kingdom will have arrived fully within the present generation but no one except God knows precisely when it will all begin. It could be anytime— everyone should be vigilant—everyone should Watch—should keep alert—it will not be long!

Jesus makes it plain that he is not talking about an unlimited time, the interpretation the clergy use, because he gives a little story to explain it. The master of the house may come in the evening, or at midnight, or at cockcrow, or in the morning— but not next year or in 2000 years time! While one can grant that the times in the illustrative tale are metaphorical up to a point, they have been chosen to show that he was not talking about long. In Luke 12:35–40 the story is modified, but significantly the man is attending a wedding—again the metaphor of Israel being reunited with her husband God (the necessary preliminary being the defeat of the Romans who had usurped God's position). One of the names of the Essenes was the watchers for the kingdom—plainly these verses of Mark are reflecting that.

At this point Luke 21:37–38 tells us that Jesus taught in the temple by day but, at night, he did not go to Bethany or lodgings anywhere else but he went to the Mount of Olives! The reason for this strange behaviour was to watch for the coming of the archangel Michael, which Zechariah 14:4 had prophesied would be when the Mount of Olives split east and west.

Matthew 25:1–13 gives us the parable of the wise and foolish virgins, the message of which is the same: be alert for the coming of the kingdom. Do not relax. The foolish virgins were not prepared—they had not brought oil for their lamps. When the message came that the bridegroom was arriving, their sisters, the wise virgins, would not share their oil with them. The foolish virgins departed to buy oil for their lamps and while they were gone the bridegroom arrived. On their return the door was shut and they were forever excluded. As always the bridegroom is God—not Jesus—and his arrival is for the marriage with His people, Israel. Those who are prepared—the righteous—are admitted to the wedding but not those who are unprepared. The parable makes it clear that the watchers for the kingdom are not merely look-outs. The point of their alertness is not to see the miracle, but to be sure not to transgress in the slightest way. The kingdom might arrive that very instant, and a transgression would mean you are locked out.

Those unsure of the later pagan elaborations of Christianity should note that in verse 32 Jesus again distinguishes himself from his father, God. If Jesus and his father were one and the same Jesus must, like his father, have known the precise time of the apocalypse. The Trinity concept leads one to conclude that if the gospels are true then Jesus (and therefore God) is a liar! But the reference to the Son in verse 32 does not sound genuine. It has probably been added by the early church.

Mark, because he is hiding it, says nothing unequivocal about the Roman counter attack, though broader hints of it appear (misplaced) in Luke's gospel. The Romans had made a strategic withdrawal to await reinforcements. When they arrived a few days later, they counter-attacked. The success enjoyed by the irregular in the countryside cannot be enjoyed in set battles. The Nazarenes were beaten—probably relatively easily—by the well drilled and disciplined Romans. Mark's gloomy apocalypse records trials and tribulations to stand for something which could not be related—defeat! From this point on Jesus is a dead man.

Mark 13:30 to 13:37 Restored

This generation shall not pass, till all these things be done. But of that day and that hour knoweth no man, no, not the angels which are in heaven, but only the Lord God. Watch and pray, for ye know not when the time is. For it is as a man taking a far journey to attend a wedding, who left his house, and gave authority to his servants, and to every man his work, and commanded the porter to watch. Watch ye therefore, for ye know not when the master of the house cometh, at even, or at midnight, or at the cockcrowing, or in the morning: lest coming suddenly he find you sleeping.

Then shall the kingdom of heaven be likened unto ten virgins, which took their lamps, and went forth to meet the bridegroom. And five of them were wise, and five were foolish. They that were foolish took their lamps, and took no oil with them: But the wise took oil in their vessels with their lamps. While the bridegroom tarried, they all slumbered and slept. And at midnight there was a cry made, Behold, the bridegroom cometh; go ye out to meet him. Then all those virgins arose, and trimmed their lamps. And the foolish said unto the wise, Give us of your oil; for our lamps are gone out. But the wise answered, saying, Not so; lest there be not enough for us and you: but go ye rather to them that sell, and buy for yourselves. And while they went to buy, the bridegroom came; and they that were ready went in with him to the marriage: and the door was shut. Afterward came also the other virgins, saying, Lord, Lord, open to us. But he answered and said, Truly, I know you not. Watch therefore, for ye know neither the day nor the hour wherein the kingdom cometh. If ye would be watchers for the kingdom, then Watch!

The Roman Counter Attack

The gospels admit that Jesus was not as peaceful as the clergy like to make out but do so as quietly as possible. In Matthew 10:34 Jesus tells his followers that he had not come to send peace on the earth but a sword, plainly meaning conflict in the struggle for the coming kingdom and subsequently the judgement of God. In Luke, Jesus says he would cast fire on the earth and the kingdom of God had to be entered violently. This was certainly not a pacifist talking but Luke or an editor realized that sword did not match the desired image and toned it down.

Luke 22:36 also has biblical commentators thrashing around in discomfort because gentle Jesus, the pacifist Son of God, urges his followers to buy arms— though two swords turn out to be enough! This looks like a prime example of a difficult passage for theologians being toned down by Christian editors. Luke tries to make out that Jesus wants the weapons so that he will deliberately be breaking the law to fulfil prophecy (Isa 53:12), but since he had repeatedly broken the law, this is quite fatuous. It is an evangelical attempt to account for the band being armed, as Peter's assault on a temple guard proved. Both instances belie the gentle Jesus image revealing instead some of the truth hovering beneath the extant text.

Elsewhere in Luke 11:50 Jesus preaches in an impassioned speech that the blood of all the prophets which was shed from the foundation of the world, will be required of this generation. This sounds like Shakespeare's Henry V rallying his troops, though as usual supposedly spoken to Pharisees. Is it coincidence that Luke is soon writing (Lk 13:1) of news arriving of Pilate's troops mixing Galilaeans' blood with their sacrifices, and then of the death of eighteen men when the Tower of Siloam collapsed (Lk 13:4)? Though misleadingly placed in the gospel, these sounds like tantalizing references to a battle—a battle in progress, about which Jesus was receiving reports. Note that the men were Galilaeans. Why should Pilate have especially committed an atrocity on a group of pilgrims from Galilee? The meaning has to be that they were of the militant sect of Judas of Galilee.

Romans were military masters and it is likely that they would have deliberately attacked on the sabbath, guessing that Jews would be thrown into confusion. Had Pilate's troops counter attacked and slaughtered Galilaeans in the temple while they were offering sacrifices? It had happened before. Pompey had seiged the Jerusalem temple in 63 BC and had been astonished that the priestly supporters of Aristobulus, probably Essenes, continued with their temple duties even while they were being cut down by the legionaries. Were those killed when the Tower of Siloam fell on them defending themselves by the pool on one of the aqueduct piers or in a tower of the city wall against an attack by Pilate's soldiers using battering rams? Had the insurgents been attacked by a stronger force sent from Caesarea on the coast? None of this is mentioned in the extant works of contemporary historians—but the clergy had plenty of time to expurgate them.

If anyone should doubt that the followers of Jesus had been involved in bloody rebellion in which many had died, let them turn to Acts 6:1-3 where the surviving Nazarenes have to appoint as many as seven men to ensure that no widows were neglected in the daily ministration. The Nazarenes had to make special provision for widows just after Jesus's crucifixion because many women were left destitute when their husbands died fighting for the kingdom.

The Roman Counter Attack Restored

And word came to Jesus that the Romans had returned, and soldiers were bloodletting in the city, and eighteen men had died when they took refuge on the Tower of Siloam, and it collapsed before the might of Rome. And Jesus turning unto his disciples, said: *Saith the wisdom of God, I will send them prophets and apostles, and some of them they shall slay and persecute. The blood of all the prophets, which was shed from the foundation of the world, may be required of this generation, from the blood of Abel unto the blood of Zacharias which perished between the altar and the temple. Truly, it shall be required of this generation. Be not afraid of them that kill the body, and after that have no more that they can do. But I will forewarn you whom ye shall fear: Fear him, which after he hath killed hath power to cast into hell. Yea, Fear him! Are not five sparrows sold for two farthings, and not one of them is forgotten before God? But even the very hairs of your head are all numbered. Ye are of more value than many sparrows, therefore, Fear not! Take no thought for your life, for life is more than meat, and the body is more than raiment.* And some arriving told him of Galilaeans, whose blood Pilate had mingled with their sacrifices. And Jesus answering said unto them: *Suppose ye that these Galilaeans were sinners above all the Galilaeans, because they suffered such things? I tell you, Nay. Or those eighteen, upon whom the tower in Siloam fell, and slew them, think ye that they were sinners above all men that dwelt in Jerusalem? I tell you, Nay: but, except ye avow God before men, ye shall all perish in everlasting death. But whosoever shall avow God before men, him shall the angels of God avow before God: But he that denieth God before men shall the angels of God deny before God. And whosoever shall speak a word against this son of man, it shall be forgiven him: but unto him that blasphemeth against the holy ghost it shall not be forgiven.* And they went out in God's name, but there was naught to be done for the soldiers were many, and many were killed and many held captive. And Jesus and some disciples went into hiding in the city.

A Plan of Capture

Mark 14:1 – 14:2

14:1 After two days was the feast of the Passover, and of unleavened bread: and the chief priests and the scribes sought how they might take him by craft, and put him to death. 14:2 But they said, Not on the feast day, lest there be an uproar of the people.

A Plan of Capture

The final two chapters of Mark contain the events which had most impressed the early Christians. All four gospels agree substantially on the passion narrative showing that it had become accepted by the gentile church at an early stage and had been worked and reworked to suit one objective from the earliest time: it had to prove that the Jewish bandit was innocent, and that, as the Son of God, he must have suffered because God wanted him to—it was God's will and had been so prophesied! With such strong motives for distortion the final parts are less reliable than some of the more casually related passages earlier in the gospel.

Here Nazarene tradition is much more overlaid with later doctrine, so the original allusions are harder to recover. Post crucifixion Nazarenes and Christians looked in the scriptures to find anything relevant to the death of the Christ, and whenever they found a suitable instance alluded to it in their passion story. Very quickly we had a story that was centred on an almost obliterated core of truth and a mass of Old Testament prophecy. But though believers saw the Son of God as a holy sacrifice for the sins of men to atone for the sins of Adam, the prime villains could not be Romans. They had to be Jews if the religion was to prosper in the Roman Empire.

Mark seems to have the Chief Priests (Sadducees but not scribes most of whom were Pharisees) deciding not to seek Jesus's arrest during the Passover festival. But according to the plot as it unravels that is precisely what they do. The truth is that there was no scheme to set Jesus up. It was unnecessary because he had already committed serious crimes in the eyes of the Roman governor. This is indisputably true even by Mark's own evidence, so it is idle for anyone to deny it.

The Roman prefects left non-political matters to a council of senior Jews called the Sanhedrin. The principle force in it was the High Priest and his party of Sadducees and they controlled the temple guard which had the powers of a police force. The death sentence for purely civil matters could only be declared by the Roman Governor. The Sanhedrin could possibly have declared a sentence of stoning for a religious misdemeanor, but, if so, it rarely did. The Romans would have disapproved of and, most probably never allowed, a concession which might have been used against collaborators.

Some of the Sanhedrin shared with the Romans a distaste for rebel movements—they posed a threat to the whole Jewish nation from Roman reprisals. Centuries before the Romans had razed under the plough the great city of Carthage, an enemy of Rome. Later they were to raze Jerusalem. There was reason for Jews to worry if Rome became incensed. Josephus says that Herod Antipas killed John the Baptist, not because of the plottings of his wife, but because he saw a threat of an uprising in the large crowds that John was attracting. Herod's fear of the multitude is declared in Matthew 14:5 but as a reason for not killing John, though this fear did not deter him from killing John when Herodias requested it. Repeatedly in Mark, Luke and Acts the fear of the authorities for the people is expressed.

After the brief counter-attack, the Roman commander, probably Pilate himself, was back in charge, and he it was, not scribes, who discussed with the Chief Priest, as Chief of Police, how to apprehend the leader of the Nazarene gang who was still at large, and put him to death. Pilate was an ogre. Contemporaries, Agrippa I, the Jewish king, and Philo of Alexandria describe him as corrupt, violent, dishonest, cruel, tyrannical, inflexible, merciless, obstinate and an illegal executioner. In retaking the city he had killed and captured many of the Nazarenes, and many pilgrims too. The gospels mention two unknown men who were crucified with Jesus for their part in the uprising—there would have been many, many more, but the extent of the insurrection has to be played down. Pilate would willingly have butchered half of Jerusalem, but did not want to lose his job, so he first puts the burden of catching the leader of the insurrection on to the Jewish authorities. If they failed he would then have a carte-blanche to proceed in his own way.

Jesus in hiding was not easy to find because of the millions of pilgrims thronging the city. Caiaphas foresees riots and more innocent blood shed, if the Romans carry out a house-to-house search using the military. *Not on the feast day, lest there be an uproar of the people. We must take him by craft*, he advises Pilate. To avoid a bloody massacre, Caiaphas promises to use his network of informers to seek out the miscreants, and bring them in using the temple guard.

In John 11:49–51 and 18:14, Caiaphas, directly expressing the fears of the Jewish rulers, sums up his policy: *It is expedient for us, that one man should die for the people, and that the whole nation perish not.* If the Romans murdered hundreds in a day, there was nothing to do about it, but the Pharisees had established a tradition that, in Jewish law, no more than one man should be condemned on one day. Even the Sadducee High Priests felt obliged to follow Pharisaic law in the courts, and preferred that only the Nazarene leader should die rather than the whole band and an unknown number of pilgrims for good measure. A general outbreak of rebellion would bring retribution on the whole nation by the Romans. If it could be nipped in the bud by disposing of the leader of the insurgents, the state would be preserved. They succeeded but a few decades later it happened anyway.

Note that *after two days*, if the Romans attacked on the sabbath, puts the Passover on a Tuesday. It might be a mistranslation of *on the second day* which would put the Passover on a Monday, but if Mark is using gentile or Essene days rather than Jewish ones, the seder of a Tuesday Passover is eaten on a Monday evening.

Mark 14:1 to 14:2 Restored

After two days was the feast of the Passover, and of unleavened bread. And Joseph Caiaphas and the chief priests came unto Pilate that they might take Jesus the Nazarene by craft, and put him to death; for they said to each other: *It is expedient for us, that one man should die for the people, and that the whole nation perish not.* And they said unto Pilate: *Search not for him on the feast day, lest there be an uproar of the people.* And Pilate, who feared the Emperor should learn he was an illegal executioner, gave them leave to take hold of the Nazarene by craft.

An Anointing

Mark 14:3 – 14:9

14:3 And being in Bethany in the house of Simon the leper, as he sat at meat, there came a woman having an alabaster box of ointment of spikenard very precious; and she brake the box, and poured it on his head. 14:4 And there were some that had indignation within themselves, and said, Why was this waste of the ointment made? 14:5 For it might have been sold for more than three hundred pence, and have been given to the poor. And they murmured against her. 14:6 And Jesus said, Let her alone; why trouble ye her? she hath wrought a good work on me. 14:7 For ye have the poor with you always, and whensoever ye will ye may do them good: but me ye have not always. 14:8 She hath done what she could: she is come aforehand to anoint my body to the burying. 14:9 Verily I say unto you, Wheresoever this gospel shall be preached throughout the whole world, this also that she hath done shall be spoken of for a memorial of her.

An Anointing

Mark offers us here an absurdly artificial scene. As it stands, this story is mostly a fabrication of the early church, as Jesus's lack of modesty proves. It is designed to predict once more the death of Jesus, the Son of God and to symbolize his messiahship. Nevertheless that the poor are mentioned implies that the story might have a genuine Essene root—the expression: *For ye have the poor with you always*, sounds traditional. What Jesus obviously meant was that the poor would be the ones accepted into the kingdom which was, of course, an everlasting kingdom. The poor, the Ebionim, would last for ever: no one else would. Jesus was not expecting anyone to be around this world for long so *always* had to pertain to the coming kingdom.

The anointing seems pointless except to provide a basis for verse 8. It is easy to see how the story was developed. Dead bodies in those times would be laid out, anointed with oil or perfume. Jesus rose from the dead before the women were able to lay out his body properly. Some pious Christians might have been upset to think this, and this story filled a non-existent gap. Jesus is anointed as a dead man while he is still alive. If it were intended as an anointment for burial, it confirms that Jesus had lost control—proving the Romans had retaken the city. Also the messiah was one who is anointed as a king and, hitherto in Mark's account, Jesus had not been— it had to be done symbolically before he died. Lastly the analogy of the breaking of the vessel with the breaking of Jesus's body was added. The expression *preached throughout the whole world* betrays a gentile Christian outlook. The main other giveaway, apart from the obviously prophetic references, is the use of oil. Josephus tells us that Essenes did not use oil and we have seen that their coronations were aqueous ceremonies not unctuous ones.

Christians always regard the spikenard as a perfume, even though it is described correctly as an ointment, and so fail to realize that it is for the leper not for Jesus. In fact nard is an oil from the plant Nardostachys jatamansi which is a member of the valerian family. Its active constituents include camphor and patchouli. Certainly it is used as a deodorant but is also used medicinally and in aromatherapy. It was used as a vapour for depression and as a sedative, and externally for skin conditions—rashes, boils, abscesses, fungal skin infections like ringworm, acne, weeping eczema, cold sores and impetigo—in other words the conditions considered in those days to be leprosy!

What then is at the core of the story? Clues are the leper, the very expensive oil and Jesus's statement about the poor. Unless Bethany was a leper colony, Jesus could not have been dining with a leper. Nor would he anyway—leprosy was unclean. Either leper is a code word or the event did not happen in reality. If Simon was a leper, it was because he had been a vigorous opponent of the Nazarenes but had converted. He might have converted secretly so that he was a sort of double agent. Perhaps he was the man who procured the upper room or the foal and the ass. It is not unusual for clandestine organizations to use code to cover their operations. Perhaps Simon's code name leper gave Jesus the cue for a story. We have noted that Essenes disdained the use of oil, and since they were the poor they would not have wasted their money on this expensive stuff. The conclusion of the story is that the poor will have everlasting life. Plainly it is another kingdom parable that Mark has used for his own purposes.

Only someone who was very wealthy could afford a box of nard. It would take a day labourer a year to earn enough money even if he saved everything he earned. The woman was therefore the wife of a rich man and the leper was the rich man. Note that the beginning of the story is ambiguous—it is not clear whose head received the ointment. Having been diagnosed with the disease the rich leper was ordered from the city according to the law expressed in Leviticus 13:46. If the rich man was a High Priest he would also according to Leviticus 21:21 have lost his job. His wife buys nard and visits him in the leper colony to anoint him with the expensive ointment hoping to effect a cure. The poor lepers murmur against her, saying the money could have been put to better use on behalf of them all. Jesus's conclusion is that the money is unimportant: the poor (the lepers) would live forever but the rich man (the High Priest) would not live forever despite his expensive treatment.

In Luke's overelaborated version (Lk 7:36–50) the leper disappears but Luke adds a non-cryptic mini-parable about two debtors being forgiven. The message is that the one forgiven the greater debt had more reason to be grateful. The link with the parable of the rich leper is that he had every reason to be immensely grateful if, through repentance, he were accepted into the kingdom.

In verse 7 Jesus says he will not always be with them, an apparent contradiction of everything that a Christian believes. Mark was, of course, reminding his readers of Jesus's forthcoming physical death but forgot his everlasting spiritual life which is supposed to be far more important.

Mark 14:3 to 14:9 Restored

And being in Bethany Jesus sat at meat in the house of Simon the leper, which is a nobleman which opposed them but was baptized as repentant. And Jesus told a parable, saying: *A priest declared a certain rich man as a leper, and, according to the law, he had to leave the city and live with the lepers. And there cometh unto him a woman, his wife, having an alabaster box of ointment of spikenard very precious; and she braketh the box, and poureth it on his head, praying to the Lord that he be cured. And there were poor lepers standing by, and they had indignation within themselves. And they murmured against her, saying: Why was this waste of the ointment made? For it might have been sold for more than three hundred pence, and used for us all. But the lepers knew not that the poor shall live forever. And the rich man gaineth nought from his expensive unction, for perchance he saveth his skin but surely he loseth his soul.* And he turned to Simon saying*: Yet this leper hath gained everlasting life for he hath given all he hath to the poor and taken his cross of baptism in repentance.*

Judas

Mark 14:10 – 14:11

14:10 And Judas Iscariot, one of the twelve, went unto the chief priests, to betray him unto them. 14:11 And when they heard it, they were glad, and promised to give him money. And he sought how he might conveniently betray him.

Judas

If Jesus were really a simple mendicant preacher, during the period when he taught in the temple, the priesthood could have ordered the temple guards to take him with no more ado, as the gospel admits when Jesus eventually is arrested. There must have been more to it and it was that Jesus had control of the temple and the city. Mark says the priests were afraid of the crowds but the manner in which they arrested Jesus, immediately through force or later through betrayal, would not have affected the way the crowds responded. However, if by now the Romans had retaken the city and Jesus was in hiding, he could not have simply been arrested and a betrayal would make more sense.

If Jesus and his disciples were dressed like ordinary pilgrims, among so many people, it might have been difficult to find them—this presumably was the point of the betrayal—but there are huge difficulties about the whole story. The betrayer was taking an immense risk. He could easily have been captured and tortured by the guards into yielding his information at no cost to the priests. Moreover, are we to believe that Jesus's teaching was so ineffective that Judas did not believe that God's kingdom was nigh? Or did he only take this view since the Roman counter attack? Such a betrayal could only make sense after the miracle failed to appear on Passover night which had only just started.

Mark simply says the chief priests gave money. Matthew tells us that the sum involved was thirty pieces of silver, in Exodus 21:32 the price of a slave—a word which also means son in Greek! In the gospels a piece of silver is a Roman denarius, a silver penny—the pay of a day labourer in Palestine. A navvy's monthly pay was not worth taking the risk of being captured and tortured. The falseness of the betrayal is indicated by the accord of the sum with the scriptural reference in Zechariah 11:12 where it is the price of the worthless shepherd. It symbolizes Jesus as a false prophet—a worthless shepherd—to be punished accordingly.

That a man whose calling was to the Jewish philosophy which treasured poverty should betray the group for money is absurd. But Judas was not only an Essene, we are told in the gospels that he was the bursar of the Nazarenes, a responsible and honorable position. That he should be seeking paltry sums of money when, if he so chose, he had the accumulated possessions of the Nazarenes at his disposal is multiply absurd. Like the Essenes, Nazarenes were poor ones but each man's individual wealth was given to the community—the bursar must have had money in the communal purse had he wanted to steal it. What is more the Damascus Rule has a rule that forbids anyone to vow another to destruction by the law of the gentiles. The punishment was death, meaning excommunication—eternal death. If Judas betrayed Jesus he broke this rule of the community also. It is impossible to believe that anyone believing he was on the edge of eternal life would risk eternal death.

The word Iscariot is considered by some to mean that the alleged traitor was one of the sicarii or knifemen. In fact, this is what all the Nazarenes were. They carried swords under their robes, as the gospels admit, just as the knifemen did. But Iscariot could be related to the word sikari—deliverer. Now all the Nazarenes were deliverers—their duty was to deliver Israel from the hands of their enemies. That Judas is the only one for whom the appellative is retained suggests he is a paper character. The name Judas means Jew and it is not too much to believe that the name was deliberately chosen from among the main disciples by the gentile Christians to state unequivocally, as far as they were concerned, it was the Jews who sold out the Son of God. Judas Sikari is the Jew, the Deliverer, the Jew who delivered up the messiah. There is the further possibility that Jesus chose Judas to deliver him to his maker.

Considering the vital role he has in the drama, we know nothing about him even though he is one of the twelve. As a betrayer, he was plainly an afterthought. In the Greek, Jesus was not betrayed he was *handed over*. The word is the same one as that used of John the Baptist when he was captured by Herod. The truth is that Jesus's habit of waiting for the miracle at the Garden of Gethsemane, where he would have had a good view of the Mount of Olives, must have been well known among the Nazarenes, and probably among a large number of the pilgrims in Jerusalem, after Jesus had been preaching there for several days. It is noteworthy that Jesus was not arrested in the safe house or anywhere that could have been construed as secret, as one would have expected of a betrayal.

Though the episode is briefly told in all four gospels, it nevertheless grows in detail with time. Mark gives no detail simply making money the apparent motive. Matthew tells us exactly how much money was involved. Luke doesn't know the sum but adds that Satan had entered into Judas. John knows all these things and more.

Mark 14:10 to 14:11 Restored

And the chief priests questioned some of those who had heard Jesus, and persuaded them to reveal his habits unto them, that they might know where he dwelt. And they promised to give them money in gratitude.

A Water Carrier

Mark 14:12 – 14:16

14:12 And the first day of unleavened bread, when they killed the Passover, his disciples said unto him, Where wilt thou that we go and prepare that thou mayest eat the Passover? 14:13 And he sendeth forth two of his disciples, and saith unto them, Go ye into the city, and there shall meet you a man bearing a pitcher of water: follow him. 14:14 And wheresoever he shall go in, say ye to the goodman of the house, The Master saith, Where is the guestchamber, where I shall eat the Passover with my disciples? 14:15 And he will shew you a large upper room furnished and prepared: there make ready for us. 14:16 And his disciples went forth, and came into the city, and found as he had said unto them: and they made ready the Passover.

A Water Carrier

This is genuine tradition. One small factor here showing that it is genuine tradition is that the references are to the disciples not to the twelve, the latter being a later construct. Everywhere the expression the twelve occurs is in a connecting passage obviously composed by Mark just as it is at the start of the next pericope (verse 17).

Verses 13 to 16 prove that Jesus and the Nazarenes were in hiding, and Jesus feared he might be arrested. It is all cloak and dagger stuff. Elaborate precautions are taken to keep secure the location of the safe house—even the disciples did not know where it would be. Unknown to them Jesus has arranged for a room to be ready for the messianic meal. They are led to it in classic manner through a mysterious liaison—with an anonymous water carrier in the street. The man must have been disguised as a temple Levite because carrying water was a woman's work except when it was for temple use. When they get there they have passwords. It all proves that Jesus had an organization behind him that went beyond that known to the disciples. It was the Essenes.

The date given here is wrong. The first day of the unleavened bread is the Passover itself, not the day before it. If this is not a glaring mistake it must reflect differences in the reckoning of time by Mark and the Jewish priesthood. The temple priesthood are thought to have used the same calendar then as the rabbis still use, and which reckons days from sunset to sunset, and normal Jewish practice was that a new day started at sunset. But for the Essenes who prayed to the rising sun, a new day might have started at daybreak and the gospel writers must have used sunrise to sunrise reckoning. For the Essenes the Jewish Passover meal must have been eaten on the day that the temple sacrifices were killed. The sacrifices were prepared in the afternoon and eaten in the evening of—to us and Mark—the same day, but to Jews, on different days, a new one having started at sunset.

This is understandable if the gospel writers, as we might expect, are using the reckoning of the gentiles—sunrise to sunrise—but if this reckoning was used also by the sect of the Nazarenes, it becomes quite important. It is further proof that they were Essenes, but it also shows, accepting Thiering's assertion that Christians used what she calls the Northern Solar calendar, that the crucifixion happened before 29 AD but after 15 AD. Thiering's chronological hypotheses might support 21 AD as the date of the crucifixion.

If the man carrying a pitcher of water, apparently a detail, delivered it to the safe house when he led the disciples there, it might be further circumstantial evidence that the Essenes used water in their ritual meal, not wine, when fresh grape juice, new wine, was out of season, as it was at Passover. Christian wine was originally Essene new wine, which in practice was water for most of the year.

Mark 14:12 to 14:16 Restored

And in the morning before the first day of unleavened bread, when they killed the Passover, his disciples said unto him: *Where wilt thou that we go and prepare that thou mayest eat the Passover?* And he sendeth forth two of his disciples, and saith unto them: *Go ye into the city, and there shall meet you a man bearing a pitcher of water: follow him. And wheresoever he shall go in, say ye to the goodman of the house: The Master saith: Where is the guestchamber, where I shall eat the Passover with my disciples? And he will shew you a large upper room furnished and prepared: there make ready for us.* And his disciples went forth, and came into the city, and found as he had said unto them: and they made ready the Passover.

A Prophecy of Betrayal

Mark 14:17 – 14:21

14:17 And in the evening he cometh with the twelve. 14:18 And as they sat and did eat, Jesus said, Verily I say unto you, One of you which eateth with me shall betray me. 14:19 And they began to be sorrowful, and to say unto him one by one, Is it I? and another said, Is it I? 14:20 And he answered and said unto them, It is one of the twelve, that dippeth with me in the dish. 14:21 The Son of man indeed goeth, as it is written of him: but woe to that man by whom the Son of man is betrayed! good were it for that man if he had never been born.

A Prophecy of Betrayal

The surviving senior officers of the sect had come together in secret to eat the messianic meal because Jesus had done his job of capturing Jerusalem, albeit temporarily, and cleansing the temple, and still expected the miracle at any moment. But this passage is unlikely to be genuine Nazarene tradition. Verse 21, with its hindsight prophecy, looks unhistoric. Indeed the repetition in verses 18 and 22— *And as they did eat, Jesus*—suggests all these verses are added.

The passage is typically primitively Christian, the curse of Judas being directed at all Jews, its purpose being to place the guilt of Christ's death on the Jews. Jesus is made to say, *It is one of the twelve*, using Mark's expression, the twelve, showing that it is composed rather than tradition.

If Jesus knew of the betrayal because it was part of God's plan then the curse on Judas in 21 is ungodlike. Clergymen seem able to accept that a man following God's plan to the letter can also be a traitor. If it were simply God's purpose to sacrifice an innocent man, Jesus could have given himself up to the authorities making himself look even more innocent and humble. In reality many people had seen Jesus preaching and anyone of them could have pointed the authorities to the Garden of Gethsemene and the Mount of Olives where Jesus had been in the habit of watching for the miracle for the last week. The chief priests had argued with him face to face and knew Jesus in person so, having found the gang's hideout, they could have identified Jesus themselves but Judas theatrically and unnecessarily kisses Jesus on the cheek to betray him. The betrayal has no purpose except to incriminate the perfidious Jew.

Though the Chief Priest promised to deliver only Jesus to Pilate for punishment, we can hardly believe that the Sadducees and the temple guard would not have arrested others of the gang even if they intended to release them only with a flogging. If the soldiers were Romans they would not have been satisfied with only the leader, whatever the deal, since they had been put to some trouble by the Nazarenes, and had probably lost some of their colleagues. They would willingly have arrested and crucified the whole gang using whatever force was needed. Yet if Jesus was merely a pacifist wonder worker and travelling preacher he could have been no threat.

In verse 21 there seems to be an allusion to Psalms 41:9. Psalm 41 is Essene as its first line shows: *Blessed is He that considereth the poor*. The Essene Teacher of Righteousness had an enemy called the Wicked Priest or the Liar who had been one of the elect but split away. This psalm perhaps refers to this and it is this betrayal which has been echoed by Christians in the Judas story. Nowhere in the scriptures is there a son of man who is betrayed as verse 21 seems to say. If anything like this was spoken by Jesus it must have been when he was actually arrested in the Garden.

In verses 18 to 20 Jesus does not seem to be making a prophecy but seems to be telling the disciples—commanding them—that one of them has to betray him. They understand this and in turn ask: *Is it I?* They are allowing Jesus to indicate who has to do the evil deed, but Jesus does not say. Mark reports it all in a matter of fact way with no expressions of amazement. If this is genuine Nazarene tradition, and yet Jesus was not expecting to be captured, what can it mean? Was he now beginning to doubt he own prophecies, and preparing to submit as the worthless shepherd of Zechariah, the punishment of the false prophet?

Essenes apparently understood that if the archangel Michael failed to appear as the nasi prophesied then the false prophet would have to suffer. The reason for this comes from Zechariah 13, which significantly enough, Mark soon has Jesus quoting. It prescribes the punishment for false prophets!

Essenes were convinced they could read the runes but must have realized from experience that they could be wrong. God would not fool them—His signs were there—but they might misread them and get the calculation wrong, so they kept adjusting their arcane theories and trying again. This must imply that Jesus was only one nasi of many that went forth to test whether the appointed time was nigh. If they decided it was, but led people falsely because they were mistaken and it never arrived, then each had to be prepared to take on the role of the worthless shepherd—they had prophesied falsely and had to suffer according to Zechariah 13.

If no miracle appeared, there was no future for Jesus—he had lost all credibility, leading his band to capture Jerusalem and to expect a miracle, which never came. Jesus therefore had to become the worthless shepherd. Graves and Podro believe Jesus always intended to force God's hand by enacting the prophecies of Zechariah—becoming the worthless shepherd. Later the first Christians, loath to have their God depicted as worthless, claimed that he was in fact the noble figure of the suffering servant of Isaiah. Steuart Campbell believes that Jesus plotted a bogus fulfilment of the suffering messiah prophecy, accepting the basic gospel story with opium replacing God. In fact, Jesus never expected to be either stabbed as a worthless shepherd or crucified as a suffering servant. He sincerely expected God's miracle inaugurating the kingdom of God, but the command to the Master in the Community Rule was: *He shall freely delight in all that befalls him and nothing shall please him but God's will.* When Jesus prophesied God's will wrongly he had to delight in his punishment—to be stabbed in the chest.

Now all of this throws a fresh light on the story of Judas and the thirty pieces of silver, which is the price of the worthless shepherd. Judas's reward is merely a literary device to show that Jesus became Zechariah's worthless shepherd because the prophesied miracle on the Mount of Olives never happened. That Jesus prepared for this eventuality might explain the apparent lottery at the last supper. One of the disciples had to be chosen to be the executioner! The man chosen was Judas. Here we find one of those unexplained coincidences of the gospels. We have noted that Judas Iscariot was really Judas Sikari meaning Judas the Deliverer. The Greek word translated *betray*, paradidomi, really means *deliver* as in *deliver in judgement*! Judas was not a betrayer but was chosen by Jesus to deliver him in judgement to God—to kill him!—as the worthless shepherd. When Jesus realizes there is to be no miracle, in the morning of Passover, he says: *Rise up, let us go; lo, he that betrayeth me is at hand.* But it should read: *Rise up, let us go; lo, he that delivereth me is at hand.* Jesus was ready to suffer his fate as the worthless shepherd at the hand of Judas.

Why then didn't he? It seems the arresting party arrived first. The next sentence is: *And immediately, while he yet spake, cometh a great multitude with swords and staves, from the chief priests and the scribes and the elders.* All I have omitted in this sentence is what was inserted by Mark: *Judas, one of the twelve, and with him.* Judas had been chosen as a reliable man to do the horrible deed but Mark labels him a traitor and so has western culture seen him since.

Matthew 27:3-10 describes how Judas tries to return the money in return for Jesus's release, fails and hangs himself. The priests, not wishing to taint the temple treasury with blood money instead buy the potter's field in which to bury foreigners. This field was therefore called the field of blood. In Acts 1:15-20 Peter gives quite a different explanation of the tradition of a field of blood. He says it was so called because Judas, who was not remorseful, bought it with the money and in it he fell down and burst asunder, spilling his bowels everywhere. These explanations are incompatible attempts to explain a mysterious legend among the early Christians of a field of blood—or perhaps of sleep, a euphemism for death—in which foreigners lie dead. Bishops attempting to explain this came up with various answers, two of which we have preserved. Peter's is quite false, being an adaptation of the death of Nadhan, the wicked nephew of Ahikar, from the Book of Ahikar which circulated amongst the semitic races since the fifth century BC, and was popular among the eastern Christians.

Matthew contains more of the truth in calling the field the potter's field and that foreigners were buried in it. Furthermore the field was considered from at least the fourth century AD to have overlooked the junction of the valleys of Hinnom and the brook Qidron.

The field of blood or sleep reserved for foreigners is obviously the site of the Nazarene victory over the Jerusalem garrison in the Qidron valley. The reference to the potter reflects the already quoted passage in the second psalm in which the foreigners are to be broken with with a rod of iron and dashed in pieces like a potter's vessel. It would have been quite natural after the victory for the Nazarenes to have called the field of victory the potters field, referring to this psalm.

Mark 14:17 to 14:21 Restored

And Jesus said: *It is written, I will smite the shepherd, and the sheep shall be scattered. If ye are offended by me this night, truly, one of you which eateth with this son of man shall deliver him.* And they began to be sorrowful, and to say unto him one by one: *Is it I?* and another said: *Is it I?* And he came to Judas, and he said: *Is it I?* And Jesus said unto him: *That thou doest, do quickly.*

The Last Supper

Mark 14:22 – 14:25

14:22 And as they did eat, Jesus took bread, and blessed, and brake it, and gave to them, and said, Take, eat: this is my body. 14:23 And he took the cup, and when he had given thanks, he gave it to them: and they all drank of it. 14:24 And he said unto them, This is my blood of the New Testament, which is shed for many. 14:25 Verily I say unto you, I will drink no more of the fruit of the vine, until that day that I drink it new in the kingdom of God.

The Last Supper

The Romans had counter attacked, the temple was lost, Galilaeans were killed and the Tower of Siloam had collapsed. The Nazarenes had been beaten but Jesus was not about to surrender. He had done all he thought was necessary and now expected God's miracle, prophesied in Zechariah 14:4. It was likely to happen on the anniversary of the previous visitation—Passover night. Shortly they would go armed to the Mount of Olives overlooking the city to wait for it. The Nazarenes had temporarily freed the Holy City from its enemies. Now it was up to God to complete the task as he had promised. Jesus wants his men to wait and watch for the signs of the miracle.

The basic tradition here is genuine. Jesus withdrew to take a meal with his closest associates. We know it as the *last supper*. If the meal was a Passover meal, it was an unusual one. There is no mention of lamb being served, and, indeed, how would fugitives have got the lamb sacrificed by the Levites at the temple ready for a Passover supper in a secret location. Nor is there mention of bitter herbs or the dip called *the haroseth*, though this might be implied (Mk 14:20). These problems do not arise in both John's gospel and the Talmud because they say that Jesus was hanged on the day before the Passover.

The Essene ritual meal was for only the pure and Jesus believed that God would intervene only if they were all sufficiently pure of spirit. The community whether in the monastery or the camps was bonded by this common meal. Only the perfect were allowed to partake of it and in particular to partake of the new wine which is to say the unfermented grape juice of the congregation. The Community Rule says that whenever as many as ten members of the community gathered for a meal they took their seats in the order of their rank, and the priest presided. No one could touch the bread or new wine until the priest had stretched out his hand to bless the new wine.

But in the Rule of the Congregation at a meeting of ten or more *men of renown*, leaders of the council of the community, the messiah is present and takes bread and wine after the priest but before the others did according to their seniority. Since the sacred meal anticipates the banquet in the kingdom at the end of days, they assume the participation of the messiah to be symbolic—he was present only in spirit. But, from the description, it sounds as if the messiah were really there—the nasi, on ceremonial occasions playing the role of the messiah.

Jesus, the prophet, priest and prince, treats the last supper as a messianic meal not a Passover meal, though for an Essene it was both. It was the last chance and the best one for a miracle, and so he was sure that God's appointed time for the visitation had come and pledges to his disciples: *Verily, I say unto you, I will no more drink of the fruit of the vine, until that day when I drink it new in the kingdom of God.* The statement Luke puts in the mouth of Jesus on the cross belongs here: *Today shalt thou be with me in paradise.* The day began at sunset or sunrise, not at midnight, so a miracle which happened in the early hours of the morning, as Jesus expected, would have been on the same day. Jesus would not partake of another ritual meal before the miracle happened. His next meal would be the messianic meal in the kingdom, after the general resurrection.

The messianic meal comes from *Isaiah* 25:6 where only two items of the menu are mentioned: fat things full of marrow and wine on the lees. As a priest in the service of God, Jesus was not allowed wine (Lev 10:9) and prophets could drink no wine according to *Amos* 2:12 because they were Nazirites, dedicated to God. Jesus was both priest and prophet. In Mark, the fruit of the vine is unfermented grape juice not alcoholic wine and one suspects that is what *wine on the lees* means. It is unracked and probably unfermented wine. Essenes were a priestly order and were Nazirites: they did not drink wine.

Now if the Nazarene leadership were to accept the prophet's description of the messianic meal, lamb would have been included as a fat thing full of marrow but in fact the Essenes went by Hosea's dictum (Hos 6:6): *I desire mercy not sacrifice, and the knowledge of God more than burnt offerings.* This is echoed several times in the Dead Sea literature. For the Nazarenes the Passover meal probably did not include the fat thing anyway and the Passover meal and the messianic meal on this occasion were one and the same thing, but governed by Essene observances not rabbinic.

The last supper is not the Passover meal of rabbinic Judaism but an Essene messianic meal dressed up later by Christians according to Paul's prescription in 1 Corinthians 11:23–26:

> The Lord Jesus the same night in which he was betrayed took bread and when he had given thanks, he break it and said: Take, Eat: This is my body which is broken for you: This do in remembrance of me. After the same manner he also took the cup when he had supped, saying, This cup is the New Testament in my blood: this do ye, as oft as ye drink, in remembrance of me.

Paul was writing about 20 years before Mark so the symbolism of the tradition came from Paul—who had never known Jesus when he was alive—though not the idea of the meal itself. Paul gives no clue that the meal was originally the Passover meal whereas it's close affinity with the Essene messianic meal is undeniable. Jesus could have had no purpose in devising such a ritual because, for him, the miracle inaugurating the kingdom was due within hours.

Paul's liturgy seems to follow Essene ritual quite closely, which would suggest that Paul knew it well. It is quite likely Paul trained as an Essene himself. His New Testament is not the collection of books that Christians revere but the *new covenant* that God made with his *elect*, the Essenes. The word *testament* is the same as *covenant* in Greek. The blood of the new covenant in the liturgy of the Eucharist must go back to the messianic meal. The old covenant was that of God with the Israelites and was sanctified with a sprinkling of blood (Exod 24:8). Jeremiah 31:32 introduces the new covenant. New covenanters will not need to be taught because they have the law written in their hearts and their iniquities would be forgiven. In Jeremiah 31:30–31, sour grapes, which set your teeth on edge, are used as a metaphor for sin. That might be why the new covenanters drank unfermented grape juice. It symbolized their sin and reminded them that they had to strive for perfection.

Essenes before Jesus sanctified the new covenant with the new wine symbolizing the blood of the old covenant, not the blood of Jesus. It is doubltful though that this blood, even symbolically, would have been drunk by Jews for whom such a thought would have been abhorrent. Some wine would simply have been sprinkled to symbolize the covenant, but it would have been drunk simply as wine.

The Development of the Eucharist

So the faithful of the newly founded Christian religion met to eat a meal together in anticipation of the return of their god. This was the messianic meal of the apocalyptic Essenes transferred into the wider Empire by the apocalyptic Christians. The Didache or Teaching of the Apostles written before 90 AD and based on an Essene original gives instructions for the meal which was held, it says, on sundays. A cup of the holy wine of David was passed round, no reference being made to Christ's blood. Then the bread described as the life and knowledge made known to us by Jesus was handed out. Then the group ate heartily, giving thanks at the end.

But Paul, in 1 Corinthians 11:21, complains that some regarded it as a free meal and an opportunity to get drunk. Even so early it had degenerated into an unruly occasion—you could not expect Romans to stick to *new wine*. The simple truth is that years after the last supper no miracle had occurred and the messianic meal of the Essenes had degenerated into a free for all among the gentile Christians. Paul had to give them a deeply venerable way of thinking about it. Urging decorum, he tells them it is a sacred meal involving the body of Christ and explains its origins at the last supper when, he gives his new interpretation of Essene liturgy.

Indeed Paul did more than that. The messianic meal was a brotherly communion for the Essenes, who considered themselves the *new covenant* with God, and a celebration of the expectation of the coming life with God in the kingdom. But the popular religions among the gentiles of the Roman Empire at that time were the mystery religions which all involved some sort of communion rite whereby the mystae partook of something symbolizing the body of a sacrificed god and thereby became a part of him. Paul simply introduces exactly the same rite into Christianity using the, already established, messianic meal as its basis. He uses the word communion (1 Cor 10:16) of the blood and the body of Christ and warns against similar ceremonies for pagan gods whom he calls devils. The concept of eating human flesh and blood, even symbolically, is disgustingly primitive, a huge step back from the celebration of future rewards for the righteous. For Jews consuming blood was taboo, even symbolically. A devout Jew like Jesus could not possibly have said such things. He did not—it was Paul, who, if he was Jewish as he claimed, was a proselyte.

Paul knew that pagans as well as Essenes had ritual meals, and he calls it (Cor 10:16) a communion:

> The cup of blessing which we bless, is it not the communion of the blood of Christ? The bread which we break, is it not the communion of the body of Christ?

Initiates of the mystery religions sought communion with their god to achieve immortality. That was the purpose of the pagan meal—a communion—food symbolizing the body of the god was eaten to unite the god with the worshipper. Primitive societies believe that cannibalism can be used to confer the qualities of the person eaten to the person eating. It is a slight step to eating a person assumed to be a god incarnate to get the qualities of the god himself. If cannibalism had died out in the Roman Empire by the time of Christ, rites that imitated it were very common. In the mysteries of Dionysus the baked image of a child was eaten. The first Christians must have been quite familiar with such cannibalistic rituals. Words like John 6:53:

> Except ye eat the flesh of the Son of man and drink his blood, ye have not life in yourselves. He that eateth my flesh and drinketh my blood shall have eternal life,

were written by someone who regarded eating human flesh as normal, at least symbolically—an initiate into the mysteries of Dionysus who ate raw flesh as a communion?

The aspect of the Eucharist of a rehearsal for a messianic banquet shortly to be held diminished when the end of the world did not come, and the idea of mystic communion gained importance as Christianity developed in its pagan environment. As a mystic communion it did not need to be a meal, it needed only to symbolize the sacrifice of the dead god, and so the bread and new wine of the original meal came to symbolize the body and blood of the god as Paul had instructed. From this the idea of transubstantiation developed so that real bread and wine became actual flesh and blood. Loaves were even made in the image of a man and the faithful had different parts depending on their social rank, a practice eventually forbidden. Of course the reason why the bread always looked and tasted like bread was because God realized how awful it would be for humans to eat human flesh so he successfully hid its real nature from the communicants. This whole nonsense came of the adoption by Christianity of pagan sacraments.

Paul's instructions were written into the gospels as if they had come from Jesus. And the legend grows with time. The references to Jesus's blood are slight in Mark and Luke, have for the remission of sins added in Matthew, and are extensive in John. Around 100 AD the meal of remembrance was a sacramental rite in which water was used not wine. Pliny speaks of the meal in 112 AD saying that it was quite innocent. In 140 AD Justin Martyr describes how the faithful receive bread and water representing the body and blood of Christ from the deacons. The use of water reflected the Essene use of water as new wine, but at the suppression of paganism at the end of the fourth century, water was forbidden because of its pagan associations.

Mark 14:22 to 14:25 Restored

In the evening he cometh with the disciples. And as they did eat, Jesus took bread, and blessed, and brake it, and gave to them, and said: *Take, eat! this is the bread of everlasting life.* And he took the cup, and when he had given thanks, he gave it to them, and they all drank of it. And sprinkling it upon them, he said unto them: *This is the blood of the new covenant, which God hath made with His chosen. Truly this son of man will drink no more of the fruit of the vine, until that day that he drinks it new in the kingdom of God.*

A Prophecy of Denial

Mark 14:26 – 14:31

14:26 And when they had sung an hymn, they went out into the mount of Olives. 14:27 And Jesus saith unto them, All ye shall be offended because of me this night: for it is written, I will smite the shepherd, and the sheep shall be scattered. 14:28 But after that I am risen, I will go before you into Galilee. 14:29 But Peter said unto him, Although all shall be offended, yet will not I. 14:30 And Jesus saith unto him, Verily I say unto thee, That this day, even in this night, before the cock crow twice, thou shalt deny me thrice. 14:31 But he spake the more vehemently, If I should die with thee, I will not deny thee in any wise. Likewise also said they all.

A Prophecy of Denial

This is a Christianized passage containing very little Nazarene tradition.

They went out to the Mount of Olives to wait for the miracle which would take place there as prophesied in Zechariah 14:4. The evangelist knows this but chooses to have Jesus quoting from an earlier verse in Zechariah 13:7. As we noted above, the Essenes were aware that if they misinterpreted the signs of the times and their predictions turned out to be wrong then they were false prophets. At this point Jesus was still convinced he was correct, so would have been turning to Zechariah 14:4 for his text. The quotation of Zechariah 13:7 would have occurred in the morning when he realized he had been wrong, and turned to Judas expecting his deserts.

At this point Mark has Jesus predicting that he will be denied by Peter. The fairy tale formulae show it to be false, though the tradition of the denial is most likely true and has been used by Mark to let Jesus prophesy again. The personal detail both here and in its fulfilment is unusual but the moral of the story is the perennial one in Mark, that Jews are no good, even Jesus's best mates. Now, of course, this could not be taken too far in case the evangelists who founded the church should lose respect so the quotation of Zechariah 13:7 is given to show that it is all God's will. Jesus used the quotation from Zechariah 13:7 when he had given up hope of

God's miracle but here it justifies for theologians the behaviour of the disciples after the arrest and crucifixion.

Jesus is also made to say he will go before them into Galilee. The remnant of the Nazarenes escaped after the crucifixion to Galilee and there was a tradition of sightings of the risen Christ there. Mark takes the opportunity of explaining their flight there in a mystical way.

In Luke 22:36–38 Jesus tells his disciples to buy swords, but two turn out to be enough. This is a passage that belongs earlier but after the mission of the disciples, to which it refers. Sensibly it belongs to the period just after the transfiguration when Jesus decides to march on Jerusalem. His earlier band had been scattered when he went into Phoenicia, but on re-entering Galilee he must have drawn the ones remaining loyal together again. At this point he would have told them to sell whatever they could to buy swords. The fact that two is sufficient is obviously a Christian dilution. To die as a false prophet, only one was needed.

Mark 14:26 to 14:31 Restored

And when they had sung an hymn, they went out into the mount of Olives. And Jesus saith unto them: *It is written: the Mount of Olives shall cleave in the midst thereof and the Lord my God shall come and all the holy ones with thee, and the Lord shall be king over all the earth.* And Jesus said: *Let us go to the garden that we might watch for the coming of the Lord.*

Watching for the Miracle

Mark 14:32 – 14:42

14:32 And they came to a place which was named Gethsemane: and he saith to his disciples, Sit ye here, while I shall pray. 14:33 And he taketh with him Peter and James and John, and began to be sore amazed, and to be very heavy; 14:34 And saith unto them, My soul is exceeding sorrowful unto death: tarry ye here, and watch. 14:35 And he went forward a little, and fell on the ground, and prayed that, if it were possible, the hour might pass from him. 14:36 And he said, Abba, Father, all things are possible unto thee; take away this cup from me: nevertheless not what I will, but what thou wilt. 14:37 And he cometh, and findeth them sleeping, and saith unto Peter, Simon, sleepest thou? couldest not thou watch one hour? 14:38 Watch ye and pray, lest ye enter into temptation. The spirit truly is ready, but the flesh is weak. 14:39 And again he went away, and prayed, and spake the same words. 14:40 And when he returned, he found them asleep again, (for their eyes were heavy,) neither wist they what to answer him. 14:41 And he cometh the third time, and saith unto them, Sleep on now, and take your rest: it is enough, the hour is come; behold, the Son of man is betrayed into the hands of sinners. 14:42 Rise up, let us go; lo, he that betrayeth me is at hand.

Watching for the Miracle

Here we have a tremendously moving scene. Christians hate it because Jesus is manifestly distraught and appears to be weak—in other words, human. This suggests the tradition is genuine.

The remnants of the Nazarene band are at the end of their tether. They are exhausted and fearing capture at any time. Jesus selects his three high priests, Peter, James and John as he always did for ritual occasions. He is expecting God to split open the Mount of Olives, to take him up, to call in *the elect* and send forth the archangel Michael with the hosts of heavenly angels. Matthew and Luke have fossils of this in their parallel accounts. In Matthew 26:53 Jesus boasts that should he wish it his prayer would call down more than twelve legions of angels. In Luke 22:43 a single angel actually *does* appear. Luke also has Jesus apparently sweating blood, another possible allusion to the cosmic battle that was expected at this juncture. The idea was probably to imply to those converts who had some knowledge of Essene philosophy, that the cosmic battle actually mystically occurred within Jesus. In Revelation 12:7–9 Michael and the angels *did* fight a battle against Rome—the dragon—and Michael prevailed, the archangel Michael taking on the role of the messiah. Plainly this is a Christian expression of the brief victory that Jesus and the Nazarenes *did* experience against the Romans in capturing Jerusalem.

Jesus becomes sore troubled, an expression which is not too strong, the Greek having connotations of indescribable anguish. Nothing is happening. Could he have been wrong all along? He hopes desperately for a miracle but is beginning to lose faith himself. *My soul is exceeding sorrowful even unto death*, he says meaning he is wondering whether his destiny might be eternal death rather than eternal life. There must be a sign somewhere. *Watch!* he tells Peter, James and John, echoing his advice in verse 13:37.

He prays that the miracle will come because God can do anything: *If it were possible the hour might come for me. Father, Abba, all things are possible unto thee.* Conventionally translators write the hour might pass away from me and remove this cup from me both constructions of the later church. For clergymen the hour came to mean the hour of Jesus's suffering, atoning for the sins of mankind. The cup similarly became a church term for suffering. But Jesus could only have used *the hour* in an absolute way like this in the sense to which he was accustomed—the sense in which it was so used before the church invented new meanings. For Jesus it meant the hour of fate—the hour at which the miracle to open up the kingdom was to occur. The proper sense is *the appointed time. Pass* is properly *arrive* or simply *come* and *from him* should be *for them*, meaning the children of Israel.

Returning from prayer to see whether the disciples have seen any signs of the miracle he finds them asleep. He comments on the weakness of their flesh—the fact that they have collapsed exhausted—though this is possibly a statement meant to be of himself when he realizes his fate is that of the worthless shepherd not the glorious messiah. Interestingly Jesus calls Peter by his proper name, Simon. Talking tough was no longer appropriate. He rouses them; urges them to watch again and repeats his prayers. The same happens—they are again asleep.

Jesus's prayers are heartwrenching, pleading and tearful prayers of supplication, as *Hebrews* 5:7 clearly reveals if it is not clear enough here, but not for his own life— for the kingdom to come. After a third prayer Jesus gives up, saying to God: *Not what I will but what thou wilt*. The glow of the dawn sun can be seen. His prayers have not been answered. He has misinterpreted the signs of God's will. The disciples are again asleep. *Sleep on now; take your rest. The hour has come; the end is yet far*, he says admitting his error, the phrase *it is enough* being properly translated *the end is yet far*. The kingdom is not imminent. Verse 41 should be omitted. It adds nothing that is not instantly clear and has been retained only because it has been read as a supernatural perception. It looks as if a marginal note, serving as a title or signpost for some diligent bishop has been mistakenly incorporated into the text by a copyist.

The story has been stylized into a typical threefold tale but it probably signifies that they waited in the Garden overnight. In that time Jesus could have found the exhausted disciples asleep several times, as the story indicates. Eventually Passover night came to an end, and with it Jesus's hopes of a miracle—the new visitation would have corresponded in time to the previous one. Once dawn had come, once the hour had come—the prophesied hour—with no result, the Essene has to return to his calculations and interpretations. But Jesus had committed himself. He was now a false prophet and had to submit himself to the false prophet's punishment, to offer himself as the worthless shepherd in atonement for his presumption of knowing God's will.

Notice that Jesus seemed to consider the day to have ended at dawn whereas a Jewish day normally ends in the evening. This suggests that Jesus was reckoning on the basis of the Essene solar calendar.

Mark 14:32 to 14:42 Restored

And they came to a place which was named Gethsemane: and he saith to his disciples: *Sit ye here, while I shall pray*. And he taketh with him Peter and James and John, to greet the archangel Michael; but late in the night he began to be sore troubled, and to be very heavy. And saith unto them: *My soul is exceeding sorrowful unto death: tarry ye here, and watch*. And he went forward a little, and fell on the ground, and prayed: *Abba, Father, all things are possible unto thee: if it were possible, thy appointed time might come for them; nevertheless not what I will, but what thou wilt*. And he cometh, and findeth them sleeping, and saith unto Peter: *Simon, sleepest thou? couldest not thou watch one hour? Watch ye and pray, lest ye enter into temptation*. And again he went away, and prayed, and spake the same words. And when he returned, he found them asleep again, for their eyes were heavy, neither wist they what to answer him. And he cometh the third time, and saith unto them: *Sleep on*

*now; take your rest. The hour has come; the end is yet far. It is written, I
will smite the shepherd, and the sheep shall be scattered. Rise up, let us go;
he that delivereth me is at hand; the spirit truly is ready, but the flesh is
weak.*

The Arrest

Mark 14:43 – 14:52

14:43 And immediately, while he yet spake, cometh Judas, one of the twelve, and
with him a great multitude with swords and staves, from the chief priests and the
scribes and the elders. 14:44 And he that betrayed him had given them a token,
saying, Whomsoever I shall kiss, that same is he; take him, and lead him away
safely. 14:45 And as soon as he was come, he goeth straightway to him, and saith,
Master, master; and kissed him. 14:46 And they laid their hands on him, and took
him. 14:47 And one of them that stood by drew a sword, and smote a servant of
the high priest, and cut off his ear. 14:48 And Jesus answered and said unto them,
Are ye come out, as against a thief, with swords and with staves to take me?
14:49 I was daily with you in the temple teaching, and ye took me not: but the
scriptures must be fulfilled. 14:50 And they all forsook him, and fled. 14:51 And
there followed him a certain young man, having a linen cloth cast about his naked
body; and the young men laid hold on him: 14:52 And he left the linen cloth, and
fled from them naked.

The Arrest

The text reads perfectly well without verses 44 and 45 which must be
considered as additions to the tradition to further the treachery of Judas. Indeed the
introduction of Judas as one of the twelve again, having been so introduced already
in verse 10, cries out that he has been added to the arresting party as an
afterthought. In John 18:5,8 Jesus freely admits who he is, proving that the kiss was
unnecessary.

There is a skirmish which must have been the immediate response to the arresting
party, belying the fiction of the kiss. In John 18:6 the reaction of the arresting
party on seeing the Nazarenes is that they retreated, and fell to the ground, virtually
admitting the fight. Mark does not say explicitly that the guards coming to
arrest him are Roman soldiers or temple guards. However chief priests, scribes
and elders are mentioned, meaning the Sanhedrin, and in the clash someone
described as a servant of the High Priest loses an ear. In John the smiter is Peter,
but oddly the servant's name is Malchus which means king, possibly a veiling of a
tradition that Jesus was wounded in the skirmish—a blemish that might have
prevented him being the paschal lamb. The arrest must have been effected by
temple guards. That of course is what we expect because Caiaphas assured Pilate
that he would arrest the criminal by stealth, in other words not with a great show
of Roman overkill.

When a disciple cut off the ear of the priests' servant in the garden, why was he
carrying a sword if the pacific nature of the Nazarenes propagated by the Christians

is true? It was illegal to carry arms. Luke 22:35–36 tries to offer the explanation that Jesus told his disciples to carry arms—two swords suffice—deliberately to break the law so that he would fulfil prophecy and be numbered among the transgressors. Jesus already was a transgressor—it is transparently an attempt to explain that the gang were armed.

Mark answers a couple more objections that opponents of the Christians were raising by giving Jesus a short speech:

> Are ye come out, as against a thief, with swords and with staves to take me? I was daily with you in the temple teaching, and ye took me not: but the scriptures must be fulfilled.

One objection was that Jesus could have been arrested in the temple. Jesus answers: *the scriptures must be fulfilled*, meaning for Jesus that he must become the worthless shepherd or for Mark the suffering servant of Isaiah which is how the immediate successors of Jesus had reinterpreted his death. The other was to counter critics who remembered that he led an armed band of insurrectionists, and were reminded of it by the striking off of the guard's ear. Thief in this context is a deliberate mistranslation—the word is insurrectionist. Today if we were opposed to the Nazarenes we would write terrorist; if we were in favour of them we would write freedom fighter. By showing Jesus indignant that he should be arrested as an insurrectionist, Mark hoped to suggest otherwise.

In verse 49 Mark suggests that Jesus had control of the temple longer than you might think—he taught there daily. Finally verses 51 and 52 seem very mysterious but they are an unhistorical addition by Mark using Amos 2:16 where God punishes the Israelites for their iniquities so severely that even the courageous among the mighty shall flee away naked. It follows the fleeing of the disciples in verse 50 and is another amelioration passage. Disciples had to be denigrated as Jews but, as founders of Christianity they had to be respected. Here they are pictured as cowardly Jews, which is fine, but they had to be excused as Christians. Didn't God say in Amos 2:16 that even their bravest would be made cowards by God's will? For Mark the disciples behaved just as you'd expect as Jews, but they couldn't help it and the image of the youth fleeing naked conjured up the appropriate scriptural reference to excuse them.

Mark 14:43 to 14:52 Restored

> And immediately, while he yet spake, cometh a detachment of guards with swords and the chief priests with staves. And they that stood by drew swords, and smote the servants of the high priest, but they saw all was lost, and forsook him, and fled. And they laid their hands on him, and took him.

The Committal Hearing

Mark 14:53 – 14:65

14:53 And they led Jesus away to the high priest: and with him were assembled all the chief priests and the elders and the scribes. 14:54 And Peter followed him afar off, even into the palace of the high priest: and he sat with the servants, and warmed himself at the fire. 14:55 And the chief priests and all the council sought for witness against Jesus to put him to death; and found none. 14:56 For many bare false witness against him, but their witness agreed not together. 14:57 And there arose certain, and bare false witness against him, saying, 14:58 We heard him say, I will destroy this temple that is made with hands, and within three days I will build another made without hands. 14:59 But neither so did their witness agree together. 14:60 And the high priest stood up in the midst, and asked Jesus, saying, Answerest thou nothing? what is it which these witness against thee? 14:61 But he held his peace, and answered nothing. Again the high priest asked him, and said unto him, Art thou the Christ, the Son of the Blessed? 14:62 And Jesus said, I am: and ye shall see the Son of man sitting on the right hand of power, and coming in the clouds of heaven. 14:63 Then the high priest rent his clothes, and saith, What need we any further witnesses? 14:64 Ye have heard the blasphemy: what think ye? And they all condemned him to be guilty of death. 14:65 And some began to spit on him, and to cover his face, and to buffet him, and to say unto him, Prophesy: and the servants did strike him with the palms of their hands.

The Committal Hearing

Many respectable Christian commentators think this section is fictional with mere elements of tradition. The intentions are the usual Marcan ones of denigrating the Jews and painting Jesus as a pacifist innocent. It should be treated with suspicion especially as the chief priests had to put the manifest crimes of Jesus before Pilate anyway. Three of them cannot be denied even on the facts in this gospel: he allowed his followers to carry swords in the streets and wound a man; he led a messianic demonstration in which he was hailed a king; he committed the crime of Laesae Majestatis by taking over the temple. The punishment for such crimes in Roman law was death. Whether he blasphemed or not was irrelevant and scenes of the trial before the Sanhedrin, the council of 70 Jewish elders, in the gospels are purely to incriminate the Jews.

Imperial policy was to leave local matters in the hands of local chiefs—in Judaea, the Sanhedrin. In the Sanhedrin's handling of civil matters though not religious ones, Sadducees, who were collaborators, dominated and knew they had to denounce a man claiming kingship or be tried as traitors themselves. Mark states in verse 55 the first trial is before the full Sanhedrin but, the gospel maintains it was still the Passover and at night, so it could not have been—for religious reasons the Sanhedrin never met at night and most certainly would not meet during a festival or on a sabbath in any circumstances. No Pharisee would have broken the law to attend. If Jesus had seen the night of the Passover through, as seems likely from his final resigned attitude, then the hearing was in the day time which is Luke's contention (Lk 22:66).

Furthermore the Sanhedrin met within the temple precincts yet, as the first part of 53 and verse 54 imply, this hearing is held in the house of the High Priest (according to Matthew and John, Joseph Caiaphas, who John admits was the High Priest that same year—implying the position was changed annually). The insurgents of the Nazarene band were not taken back into the city. The palace of the Annas family of High Priests was outside the city walls, not far away from the Garden of Gethsemane on the Mount of Olives, as we know from Josephus because later rebels burnt it down. Since the High Priest was also the local policeman and magistrate, he was responsible for public order. He had promised Pilate that he could capture Jesus by stealth to avoid excessive bloodshed of innocent pilgrims, and having done so he had to hold a committal hearing. He had to be seen to be doing his duty to satisfy the Romans, and the Romans, having set up a judicial system, would not gratuitously sidestep it. So Jesus appeared before the High Priest in the equivalent of what we used to call Police Courts. That is how John's gospel records it, for Caiaphas simply passes Jesus straight on to Pilate for civil trial, omitting all pretence of a trial for blasphemy. The High Priest could do nothing other than refer Jesus to the Governor for sentencing. He had obviously committed capital offences.

In the fictional committal hearing in Mark, charges are brought, but witnesses did not agree—an essential criterion of Jewish justice. The pious aim here however is to realize prophecies from Psalms; Ps 27:12, *False witnesses are risen up against me*; Ps 35:11, *Unrighteous witnesses arise up*; Ps 109:2, *The mouth of the wicked and the mouth of deceit have they opened against me*. The message was that the Christian God had done no wrong and the perfidious Jews were having difficulty setting him up.

A charge was brought that Jesus had threatened to destroy the temple, the house of God. That sounds fairly blasphemous. In verse 57 Mark declares that verse 58, *We heard him say, I will destroy this temple that is made with hands, and within three days I will build another made without hands*, was a false accusation yet Jesus said it in essence in 13:2 of this gospel. Other New Testament books (Jn 2:19 and Acts 6:14) repeat the threat. It is entirely messianic so surely true.

The temple was built by Herod the Great, the hated foreign king. Though most Jews continued to accept the ritual of Herod's temple they did not approve of it or its functionaries, the collaborating priestly caste. The temple of Herod would not have been tolerated by any credible messiah, nor would the Jews have expected it to continue to exist in the messianic age. To destroy it and rebuild it is what any messiah would promise, and such a threat was just what messianic Jews would have liked to hear. Since it implied defiance of the state it was the view of the nationalists.

The temple made without hands was the temple of the kingdom of God. It was raised up on the third day of the everlasting kingdom, on the same day that the righteous were resurrected. Jesus could not have failed to have said this, whatever sort of messiahship he claimed. Even if he did not it was implicit in the theory of the kingdom and so would have been understood by any Jew.

John records that Jesus had said: *Destroy this temple and in three days I will raise it up*, meaning, John maintains, the temple of his body which he would raise up after three days—a prediction of his resurrection. This is John being ingenious but he betrays an Essene way of thinking for Essenes regarded the community as a living temple as John does here. But Jesus would have spoken only of God carrying out a resurrection and he would have meant on the third day of the kingdom. If he really did say it, he must have meant he could replace the collaborationist temple organization controlled by the Boethusians and the Sadducees and not the bricks and mortar of the temple. He was simply saying that he could replace the unpopular priesthood with an acceptable alternative in a few days, because he had an alternative priesthood at the ready. The priests Jesus had in mind must surely have been members of the Qumran community, guardians of the Dead Sea Scrolls, who maintained themselves specifically as an alternative priesthood and a living temple. The implication is that Jesus had links with the Essenes. If he had, then the threat to the chief priests would be even more transparent and their attitude toward Jesus thoroughly explicable.

Though most Pharisees would not have objected to Jesus's words, the Sadducaean priesthood could not have been expected to take them lying down. They feared a direct threat to their position of power—and with justification. At a later date the sicarii murdered a High Priest and, during the Jewish War, the rebels actually appointed their own.

The charge of making the threat to the temple was therefore again a political threat—this time to the ruling Jewish caste. No blasphemy was incurred. The High Priest knows what the claim about the raising of the temple means and In 60 to 61 Mark has him making a dramatic intervention, but Jesus remains silent in fulfilment of Psalms 38:13–14 and Isaiah 53:7. He is depicted as being mainly silent in front of Pilate as well, but this would have been genuine tradition. The Essenes were not allowed to condemn each other in the courts of the gentiles, and that would also have ruled out self-condemnation. Effectively Jesus was refusing to recognize the Roman court.

Finally the High Priest asks Jesus directly if he is the messiah, Son of God. Jesus seems to reply *I am* apparently uttering the name of God. The Greek words actually mean *as you say* or *so you say*. In view of his failure, the latter seems more likely. The High Priest takes this for blasphemy and he rents his clothes. If Jesus claimed to be the messiah, was he committing a blasphemy? The answer is no because only a claim to be God was blasphemous and the Jews did not regard the messiah as an aspect or a title of God. It is no blasphemy in Judaism to claim to be a son of God who is merely a man not God. Later, Christians thought Christ was a divine title and that Jesus was claiming divinity. That would have been blasphemous—but Jesus made no claim to divinity. That Jesus kept his claim to divinity secret, the messianic secret, is a later idea, but knowing what the Roman attitude was to royal claimants, Jesus preferred not to attract premature attention from the authorities.

A son of God, though, is a king, so when Jesus apparently replies *I am* he is admitting to treason against the Emperor. That is the real crime. The messiah was a king of Israel and was, therefore, a political threat to the Romans—the claim was a political crime not a religious one, especially in view of the Jews' reputation as rebels constantly hankering after a warrior messiah to save them from their oppressors. Other claimants to messiahship—such as Bar Kosiba, a militant rebel, or Theudas, mentioned in the New Testament, who also expected a miracle—were not accused of blasphemy.

Why then did the High Priest rend his clothes if no blasphemy had been spoken. There are only two other reasons for doing it besides blasphemy, tragedy to a close relative or friend and when the whole nation has sinned. It seems that either Jesus was a member of Caiaphas's family or that Caiaphas considered that Jesus's admission of treason incriminated the whole nation. The latter ties in with Caiaphas statement that it was better for one to suffer for all.

Mark has added, *Ye shall see the Son of man sitting on the right hand of power*. The appointed time had passed. Jesus could not have said this. He no longer regarded himself as the messiah because God's miracle had not occurred. Jesus was an Essene well versed in biblical interpretation. Since he was wrong he must now have been resigned to his punishment which, having failed also to sacrifice himself as the worthless shepherd, he must have seen as God's will. His surviving followers must have been bemused, everything went wrong so quickly. God had not responded to the liberation of Jerusalem with the expected miracle, and they had been unable to bring themselves to despatch Jesus as a worthless shepherd, as he had ordered them, and now they realized he was to be crucified alongside the other rebels captured in the counter attack. Yet within a few years they were expounding in the New Testament books that it had been his intention all along to die as the suffering messiah.

Verse 65 is in pure fulfilment of prophecy (Isa 50:6; 53:3–4) and since the allusions match the Greek versions of the scriptures better than the Hebrew versions it must be a gentile improvement. If the idea came for it from something in the original tradition then it must have been the temple guards after the arrest, as Luke 22:63–65 maintains. The High Priest, whatever his faults, was not a lout.

Jesus does not seem to protest and elsewhere (Mt 5:39: Lk 6:29) is shown rejecting the old Hammurabi principle of an-eye-for-an-eye, which the Pharisees accepted, and replacing it with that of turning the other cheek. In fact the Pharisees did not literally approve of an-eye-for-an-eye. Pharisees did not believe in fundamentalism but interpretation—they made no virtue of tearing out eyes. They took an-eye-for-an-eye to be a law of equivalence for compensation of wrongs. It gave a measure of the recompense needed when someone had suffered an injury but whatever rights the principle gave anyone, the Pharisees favoured a merciful response. Effectively they also advocated the principle of turning the other cheek. A man who had suffered a theft by a desperate man might, in mercy, wish to waive the compensation to which he was entitled under the law. He could turn the other cheek by refusing compensation to which he was entitled. But he would defend another man's right to insist upon such recompense before the law. To turn the other cheek as a manifestation of God's love invited others to do the same but it did not require them to do so. Essenes positively believed in turning the other cheek.

If, as the gospels make out, Pharisees opposed Jesus on sabbath healing, why did they not bring this charge at the hearing? Indeed why were no charges brought specifically by the Pharisees? Precisely because the hearing was not before the Sanhedrin but before the court of the High Priest acting as a Roman stooge in his capacity as chief of police. Pharisees would not have been present. Elsewhere in the New Testament, the Sanhedrin seems to concur with the High Priest's persecution yet the Pharisees on the Sanhedrin oppose the priestly faction. The Pharisaic opposition to the High Priests, under the leadership of Gamaliel, even succeed in defeating the Sadducaic faction intent on persecuting the Nazarenes. In the trial of Peter which was before the Sanhedrin because the grounds were religious, Gamaliel, the leading Pharisee, defended Peter. The Acts of the Apostles quite often favours the Pharisees by depicting them as being liberal about religious differences and factions. If parts of Acts were written before the Jewish war, the later need to discredit the Jews would not have been so intense and many remnants of the original sympathy of the Pharisees for the Nazarenes would remain.

Other gospels add further charges to those expressed clearly in Mark. One is that Jesus abrogated the laws of Moses. Scholars accept that the declaration of all food as clean in Mark 7:19 is a later addition, and it is contradicted by the New Testament itself in other books. In Matthew 5:17-19 Jesus is emphatic that he had not come to destroy the law but to fulfil it, and not just its general principles but each jot and tittle. It is certain that Jesus is referring to the laws of Moses because he mentions it in conjunction with the prophets showing that he meant all the teachings of the Old Testament—of the Jewish sects it was the Essenes who counted the prophets as equal to the law of Moses. If not a jot or tittle could be omitted, then the food laws too had to be obeyed. In the later gospel of Luke 16:16-17, the contradiction had been realized and the editor pretends it is sarcasm.

Inasmuch as theologians considered rejection of the law of Moses a crucial issue, Jesus's supposed teaching on it was remarkably slow to sink in. That was because the disciples were stupid, the clergy say. Peter for example was totally confused. In *Acts* 10:14 some time after the death of Jesus, Peter says he had never eaten anything that was unclean. It is a vision from God that tells him that formerly unclean items are now clean, not the teaching of Jesus, but according to the New Testament he changes his mind more than once. James the Just, the brother of Jesus and leader of the church after Jesus's death never accepted the law had been rejected. He rebuked Paul for ignoring the law and made him do penance.

Jesus might have made a genuine point about the relative merits of purity of spirit and ritual purity but he did not reject the law of Moses. The truth is that the abrogation of the Mosaic law was not a novelty of Jesus but of the evangelist, Paul, so that he could recruit gentiles.

Mark 14:53 to 14:65 Restored

And they led Jesus away to the high priest, that he might commit him for trial before Pilate; and Peter was taken too, even into the palace of the high priest. And the high priest asked Jesus, and said unto him: *Art thou the messiah, the Son of the Blessed?* And Jesus answered: *Thou sayest.* Then the high priest rent his clothes, for the nation had followed him, a false prophet, and saith: *What need we of witnesses? he is a false prophet who says he is the messiah, a king. It is sedition; what think ye?* And they all condemned him to be guilty. And the guards began to spit on him, and to cover his face, and to buffet him, and to say unto him: *Prophesy, thou false prophet,* and the servants did strike him with the palms of their hands.

Denying Thrice

Mark 14:66 – 14:72

14:66 And as Peter was beneath in the palace, there cometh one of the maids of the high priest: 14:67 And when she saw Peter warming himself, she looked upon him, and said, And thou also wast with Jesus of Nazareth. 14:68 But he denied, saying, I know not, neither understand I what thou sayest. And he went out into the porch; and the cock crew. 14:69 And a maid saw him again, and began to say to them that stood by, This is one of them. 14:70 And he denied it again. And a little after, they that stood by said again to Peter, Surely thou art one of them: for thou art a Galilaean, and thy speech agreeth thereto. 14:71 But he began to curse and to swear, saying, I know not this man of whom ye speak. 14:72 And the second time the cock crew. And Peter called to mind the word that Jesus said unto him, Before the cock crow twice, thou shalt deny me thrice. And when he thought thereon, he wept.

Denying Thrice

Meanwhile in the courtyard below, Peter who, the gospel implies, has furtively followed the arresting party back to the court of the High Priest, denies his master thrice, fulfilling Mark's contrived prophecy of verse 14:30.

Fowl were not allowed in Jerusalem, creating an immediate difficulty for the legend, but the legionaries in the Antonia fortress had a morning bugle call at cock crow and for that reason called it the Gallicinium after the Roman word for cockerels. If true the story proves that the soldiers were back in command in Jerusalem and this might be its subtle message. It is based on a genuine reminiscence of Peter who uses it indirectly to indicate that the occupation of Jerusalem by the Nazarenes was over. Mark makes it into a prophecy and works it up in legendary fashion.

If the gospels are true, it is incredible that Peter was not also seized in the garden. In reality he must have been arrested, together with some of the other disciples and taken with Jesus for committal. The little fairy tale published here would therefore be a cover up for Peter's own hearing in which he denies that he is a Nazarene. Graves and Podro argue that Luke has actually given Peter's trial in the Acts of the Apostles 23:1–5 as part of a trial of Paul. Paul is appearing before a High Priest called Ananias, just as Jesus appeared briefly before a previous Ananias (or Annas) in John. This earlier Ananias, who was Caiaphas's father in law, had been High Priest himself and was still a powerful man. Five of his sons became High Priests. In Acts 23:5 Paul is shown apologizing to the court for verbally abusing the High Priest, saying: *I wist not that he was the High Priest for it is written: Thou shalt not speak evil of the ruler of thy people*, yet it is incredible that Paul would not know who such a prominent official as the High Priest was. But if the incident was misplaced and Paul were really Peter then the remark would be apt. Peter did not know he was speaking to the High Priest because Ananias was only acting for Caiaphas in a lower court. However, the ruler Peter spoke of was Jesus not the priest.

It seems then that, because Caiaphas thought there had already been enough bloodshed from the Romans and the priesthood feared further uprisings, that they decided to send only Jesus, the leader of the gang, for trial. In Jewish custom (not Roman!) only one man each day could be condemned and Caiaphas was happy that it should be Jesus. Peter and any other captured disciples would be released with a whipping once they had admitted that Jesus was a fraud, but Peter, loyal to Jesus as he'd promised to be, put himself in danger of his life, at first refusing to deny his king. Invited by Annas to condemn the leader of the Nazarenes to save his own skin, he quoted the line in *Exodus* 22:28 forbidding the cursing of the ruler of the people—not the priest, as the passage in Acts implies, but Jesus. Then, threatened by Annas with crucifixion under Roman justice or the alternative of freedom with a whipping, he succumbed, but still would not vow before God that Jesus was not the king, chosing instead to deny his leader three times according to the formula of an old semitic abjuration. This satisfied Annas who then turned him over to the guards for scourging. At that moment the trumpets sounded the Gallicinium from the Antonia fortress.

Mark 14:66 to 14:72 Restored

And Peter was brought before Annas, in the lower court, and the priest said: *Thou also wast with Jesus the Nazarene. Vow that he is a false prophet and thou shalt go free with a whipping.* But Peter replied, saying: *I know not, neither understand I what thou sayest, for it is written: Thou shalt not speak evil of the ruler of thy people.* And the priest said: *Thou shalt be crucified by the Romans if thou deniest him not. If thou wilt not sware then deny him thrice and save thyself, for it is not lawful for us to condemn two men on the same day.* And Peter feared to be hung on a tree, and he denied him thrice; and Annas ordered him to be whipped. And as he went out the bugles sounded the Cockcrow from the Antonia fortress. And when he thought thereon, he wept.

The Trial

Mark 15:1 – 15:5

> 15:1 And straightway in the morning the chief priests held a consultation with the elders and scribes and the whole council, and bound Jesus, and carried him away, and delivered him to Pilate. 15:2 And Pilate asked him, Art thou the king of the Jews? And he answering said unto them, Thou sayest it. 15:3 And the chief priests accused him of many things: but he answered nothing. 15:4 And Pilate asked him again, saying, Answerest thou nothing? behold how many things they witness against thee. 15:5 But Jesus yet answered nothing; so that Pilate marvelled.

The Trial

Is this the same morning or has another day gone by in Mark? It is ambiguous. The consultation mentioned might have really been the hearing already described which, as we saw, it is difficult to believe was held at night. But conceivably the priests wanted to report to the full Sanhedrin their decision. Now in fact, Jewish law required a court to meet twice on separate days to convict a man legally of a capital crime. As we have noted these courts were formalities because Pilate was not going to let a seditionist free whatever the Jews decided but we have no reason to believe that the formalities would have been omitted, except that it suits the Christian myth. Mark is not clear, but he seems to be saying that a second meeting was held in the morning, thereby inserting another day into the story. If the Passover was over and the next day was not a sabbath, the Sanhedrin could have met. Bearing in mind that the solar calendar of the Essenes, which would have been the one used for relating the original Nazarene tradition, was different from the priests', it becomes possible for Jesus to have completed his Passover before the lunarists, the priests, had celebrated theirs.

The gospels record the trials of Jesus as if there were a visitors' gallery in each of the courtrooms. Ordinary Jews or supporters of Jesus could not have been present at either of the two hearings. It is not clear therefore how accurate records of the proceedings of the Roman Court or the Court of the High Priest could have reached us. If the story were related at second hand by others who were present then distortions are more likely. A brief report of the trial by Pilate must have been posted and could have formed the basis of subsequent romanticized versions by the disciples.

Jesus is delivered up to Pilate. Mark speaks of no evidence offered. Only Luke 23:2 tells us the charges brought before Pilate against Jesus. They are precisely those of an insurrectionist and they exactly match the crimes described in the gospels:

> We found this fellow perverting the nation, and forbidding to give tribute to Caesar, saying that he himself is Christ a king.

Pilate then directly asks: *Are you the king of the Jews?* Here the Greek implies an emphasis on the *you* suggesting disbelief or contempt. Jesus replies as before, *That's what you say,* or *So you say* or *As you say*—it is not clear which (the Greek is simply *you say*). Though Jesus might have been convinced he was God's king until the night of the Passover, he was now the worthless shepherd, and as an Essene unable to recognize Roman justice he would neither affirm nor deny the charge. Jesus was acclaimed a king—there is no denying that crime. Guilty!

When Luke speaks of perverting the nation he is referring to the Roman law of *Laesae Majestatis* whereby the assumption of the power of the government without authority was punishable by death. The gospels state clearly that Jesus defied the civic authorities. He overthrows the tables in the temple court and controls access into it because he refuses, in Mark, to allow anyone to carry anything through it. Yet the High Priests had absolute power in the temple precinct and would have set the temple police on to anyone disrupting temple activities in such a manner. Instead they merely asked Jesus on whose authority he carried out these acts. Of course they might well have asked this question to get Jesus to incriminate himself, but whatever his reply he would have been swiftly arrested. Why did they not do it? The only explanation is that Jesus and his followers had forcibly occupied the temple and almost certainly the city as well. Under his regime Jesus taught daily in the temple implying a continuous period of occupation of at least several days. These are crimes of Laesae Majestatis. Guilty!

What of Jesus's attitude to the money required as tribute to Caesar (Mt 22:15–22). In Luke 23:2 Jesus is accused of refusing to pay it and we have seen that the gospel story means exactly that. His answer does not acknowledge Caesar's political power, it denies it, and implies therefore that Jesus would not have paid the tribute. That explains Luke's charge. Guilty!

The gospel of John, the last gospel written, blatantly seeks to dissociate the events in the temple from Jesus's arrest. It puts them at the start of a four year ministry instead of at the end of a shorter one as do the other gospels. The raising of Lazarus is unconvincingly substituted as the reason for Jesus's arrest. It also has the defendant agreeing (Jn 18:36) he is the king but explaining that his kingdom was not of this world, a later addition because the idea of an other-worldly kingdom of God was developed by Christianity, the Jews believing firmly that the kingdom of God would be here on earth. However, in John that explanation is sufficient for Pilate to find Jesus innocent.

Yet even if John's defence of Jesus were true history and even if Pilate had been a humane person, and he was not, he would himself have invited a charge of treason to have ignored a challenge to the authority of the Emperor. Pilate undoubtedly knew this but John 19:12 has the Jews reminding him of his duty:

> If you release this man you are not Caesar's friend: everyone that maketh himself a king speaketh against Caesar.

Here the gospel writer puts the indefensible case against Jesus in a nutshell. It is absurd to imagine that the Roman prefect of Judaea needed reminding of Roman law, or of his own duty. That this line should be included proves that the gospel writer knew that Pilate had no option but to crucify the defendant. The elaborate story of the Jewish trials was pure fiction composed to absolve Romans of the guilt of murdering a god.

John 18:36 is a very telling little verse because Jesus also says to Pilate:

> If my kingdom were of this world then my men would fight to prevent me from being captured.

The author hoped to show that rumours of Jesus being an armed rebel were nonsense by making Jesus himself say: *we could have fought if we had wanted to— but we didn't.* In fact he gives the game away, admitting that Jesus and his men were a capable fighting force, sufficient in numbers, armed and willing to fight at Jesus's command!

Jesus's subsequent silence in the three following awkwardly placed verses in Mark 15:3–5 is explained by his Essene principles. The Damascus Rule forbids anyone from vowing a man to destruction by the laws of the gentiles—Essenes could not recognize gentile justice. Jesus must have remained silent throughout. If he answered Pilate with, *You say* then he was really sneering at himself, saying: *That's what I thought too.* But the three verses also serve to picture the Jews in their usual role. They have no basis in fact. Pilate had enough evidence. Jesus was guilty!

The gospel picture of Pilate as a kindly man is nonsense. The Emperor Tiberius wanted to keep peace and order in a sensitive but politically important area of the empire. To get the confidence of some at least of the population he allowed the Jews religious privileges: they were free to pursue their own religion; they were exempt from military service; Roman soldiers were not allowed to insult the Jewish religion on pain of death and were subject to the Jewish penalty of death if they stepped beyond the court of the gentiles in the temple.

But Pontius Pilate was singularly crass in his treatment of the Jews, offending them repeatedly. He was spiteful, unjust, greedy and indiscreet. As soon as he was appointed he carried Roman standards bearing the image of Caesar into Jerusalem knowing the Jews would have been incensed. He took the temple treasure to build an aqueduct into the city, an action that one might have thought would be welcomed—but the Jews put God before any beneficent actions of the foreigner. He strongly favoured the priestly party of the Sadducees—disliked by the masses—and its leaders, the Annas family.

Such obduracy led to a series of uprisings. After savagely putting down an uprising in Samaria the complaints of the Samaritans to the Roman Legate in Syria, Vitellius, led to Pilate's recall to Rome where he disappears from history.

Now this is still happening on the *day of the unleavened bread*, Passover day, if we are to accept the timings of Mark, on 15 Nisan, but according to John it all happened a day before the Passover on 14 Nisan, the favoured view of theologians even though Mark's is the first gospel written.

Mark 15:1 to 15:5 Restored

And in the morning the chief priests held a consultation with the elders and scribes and the whole council, to confirm the committal, for they had no other authority, and then carried Jesus away bound, and delivered him to Pilate. And Pilate asked him: *Art thou the king of the Jews?* And Jesus answered him nothing, for it was not lawful in his philosophy for him to vow a man to destruction in the courts of the gentile.

Barabbas

Mark 15:6 – 15:15

15:6 Now at that feast he released unto them one prisoner, whomsoever they desired. 15:7 And there was one named Barabbas, which lay bound with them that had made insurrection with him, who had committed murder in the insurrection. 15:8 And the multitude crying aloud began to desire him to do as he had ever done unto them. 15:9 But Pilate answered them, saying, Will ye that I release unto you the king of the Jews? 15:10 For he knew that the chief priests had delivered him for envy. 15:11 But the chief priests moved the people, that he should rather release Barabbas unto them. 15:12 And Pilate answered and said again unto them, What will ye then that I shall do unto him whom ye call the king of the Jews? 15:13 And they cried out again, Crucify him. 15:14 Then Pilate said unto them, Why, what evil hath he done? And they cried out the more exceedingly, Crucify him. 15:15 And so Pilate, willing to content the people, released Barabbas unto them, and delivered Jesus, when he had scourged him, to be crucified.

Barabbas

Mark next records the incident of Barabbas. Pilate is ready to release a condemned prisoner, either Jesus or a rebel and murderer called Barabbas. Note that the implication is that Jesus is a condemned prisoner—he had already been found guilty though the gospel at this point does not say so. Mark gives the impression the trial is outdoors answering the criticism: How do you know what happened? It would not have been outdoors. Nor would Pilate have debated with the crowd.

Jesus, as a king, was a Son of God, and so he had been named at his baptism and the transfiguration. Consequently Jesus always called God, my Father, using an affectionate Aramaic word for father, Abba. If God is my Father then the Son of God is the Son of my Father. Now Mark tells us the name of the rebel Pilate offered to the crowd for release instead of Jesus was Barabbas. By coincidence Barabbas, in Aramaic, means the Son of my Father. So the bandit's name is a name which is singularly appropriate for Jesus. Some old manuscripts of Matthew, confirmed by the writings of the church father, Origen, reveal the full name of the criminal—it is Jesus Barabbas, and so it is written in modern versions of Matthew's gospel.

If we follow Matthew 27:17, Pilate asks the multitude: *Which Jesus will ye that I release unto you? Barabbas or bar Abbas?* The crowd replied, bar Abbas—or, as the clergy would have it, Barabbas. Now the thesis presented here is that Jesus the Son of God was Jesus, the king of the Jews, a man who believed that by capturing Jerusalem from the Romans and cleansing the temple, God would be induced to send a miracle to free his chosen people, the Jews. So both Barabbas and bar Abbas are revolutionaries! In Roman law, a man who is acclaimed king is a seditionist, so Barabbas and bar Abbas are both revolutionists even in Christian terms! Can we really accept that Pilate offers the crowd the choice of Jesus Barabbas, a seditionist, or Jesus Bar Abbas, the son of his father, God, a different seditionist? Is this really historical as clergymen would have us believe?

It is also remarkable that the Jewish throng, which had hailed and hosannahed Jesus as a king only a few days before, turned against him so completely that they now wanted him crucified. A man, who is a king leading his ecstatic people one day, does not suddenly become hated when the next day he is captured. His disciples and supporters, we are invited to believe, thought he was the Son of God. Would they have summoned God's wrath by turning against his son in his hour of need? Surely, as long as Jesus were alive, they would have expected God to intervene with a miracle, and they would have clamoured for their leader.

The habit of the Governor at festival time of releasing the prisoner begged for by the crowd is not recorded outside the New Testament and was unknown anywhere in the Roman Empire, let alone in Judaea which was at the time a hotbed of unrest. Even granted that there had been until then such a custom, it again stretches credibility that Pilate would release one such as Barabbas—he would have committed treason against the Emperor if he had! Pilate knew his duty, if only—according to John 19:12—because the priests had reminded him. Roman law could tolerate no rivals to Caesar.

By fomenting an insurrection Jesus had committed a political crime against the Emperor and against the Roman state. Pilate would have had to report such a serious crime, and his response to it, to the Emperor himself. He could have found no excuse for letting such a man off—he had no say in the matter. Rebellion was a capital crime requiring the lowest form of death—crucifixion. Yet the Holy Book of Christianity tells us it was gentle Jesus of Nazareth who was unjustly crucified while Pilate himself committed treason against the Emperor by releasing the leader of a revolution.

Mark would have got his idea for the nonexistent custom from the genuine Jewish custom that only one man could be condemned on one day. The disciples captured with Jesus owed their own lives to this rule and the fact that it was administered by the Jews not the Romans—it was a Jewish not a Roman rule. Pilate would have had no compunction at all about condemning and crucifying half of Jerusalem in one day, if he could justify it to the Emperor.

In the battle to retake the city the Romans had captured Nazarenes and other Jews who had joined in its defence and they were crucified alongside Jesus as the gospels tell us.

The gospels confirm that an insurrection with popular support had occurred in Jerusalem at the Passover festival. Its instigator, Jesus the Nazarene, nicknamed Barabbas by the crowd from his habit of referring to God in heaven as his father, had been caught by the authorities and promptly taken to Pilate with the Jewish crowds still milling around in a religious and nationalist fervour, expecting a miracle. They called out, Barabbas, Barabbas, asking for the release of the Nazarene, their leader, using their nickname for him. Pilate, who despised the Jews, realized the only way to curb the unrest was to dispatch the Jewish leader with no further ado... and that is what he did.

If, as the gospels say, Pilate did agree to release Jesus Barabbas, later known as Jesus Christ, then he deliberately duped the crowd. But that sounds more like the real Pilate, the rapacious, two-faced Pilate of history, and less like the kindly Pilate of the gospels. Faced with the excited and rebellious crowd, Pilate cunningly decides to give them their miracle—he agrees to release Jesus if the crowd would only disperse. Pilate has such a vile reputation that this really does seem like a miracle to the crowd—they disperse in wonder. Then Pilate crucifies Jesus as he always intended.

Later, when Christians passed on the story by word of mouth, it included the scene of the crowd assembled outside the official building calling, Barabbas, Barabbas. When the oral tradition of the first Christians was being recorded by the gospel writers this was one of the many difficulties that they had to hide or explain.

Reimarus pointed out two hundred years ago, there was one Jesus only, a freedom fighter leading a revolution against the Roman occupiers of Judaea. That is why Jesus was arrested by the authorities. The evidence of the gospels in summary is this:

- Jesus invited suspicion by gathering large crowds which the authorities considered potentially subversive;

- he was described as a Galilaean, like Judas the Galilaean—a rebel;

- many of Jesus's followers sound, from their nicknames, more like men of violence than men of peace;

- Jesus deliberately depicted himself as a king as he entered Jerusalem and his supporters greeted him thus openly;

- Jesus had committed the crime in Roman law of Laesae Majestatis by assuming the power of civic authorities to permit passage through the temple;

- an insurrection had occurred in which men had died and Jesus's supporters had been armed and resisted arrest with violence, cutting off a man's ear;

- when Jesus was charged as a rival to Caesar's rule in Palestine, claiming to be the king of the Jews, he chose not to deny it unequivocally at his trial.

Jesus was Barabbas, the nasi, one of the holy ones of God but a failed rebel. Christians wanted their incarnated god to be remembered only as a saintly man. Jesus was condemned and crucified by Romans yet, for Christianity to prosper, it had to seek respectability within the Roman Empire. But tradition showed Jesus, himself a Jew, being hailed by Jews, a race which was widely scorned within the Roman world when they rebelled in 66 AD. They were trouble makers or even terrorists.

So the gospel writers pretended Barabbas was not Jesus and invented the story of the Passover custom to explain why the crowd called for the release of Barabbas. The just Roman prefect, Pilate, offered to let the mob have their choice of prisoner but the treacherous Jews picked the murderer Barabbas. The gospel writers could use the Aramaic word *Barabbas* knowing that few of their Latin or Greek speaking gentile converts would know its meaning and question the coincidence. The Romans were depicted as fair and just; the Jewish supporters of the Jew, Jesus, were shown as treacherous villains. A Jewish incident was de-Judaized and the Jewish religion simultaneously discredited within the Roman Empire as a rival religion to Christianity.

Mark 15:6 to 15:15 Restored

And after his condemnation, Jesus lay bound with them that had made insurrection with him, who had committed murder in the insurrection. And the multitude came to the palace, crying aloud to Pilate, and began to beseech him, as he was wont to make them, calling: *Barabbas, Barabbas*, for this was their name for Jesus. And Pilate said unto them: *Will ye that I release unto you the king of the Jews? Then take ye to your homes, and I shall release him.* And they dispersed in wonder that Pilate had heard them. And Pilate, when the people had gone, delivered Jesus, when he had scourged him, to be crucified, for he was deceiving them.

The Mockery

Mark 15:16 – 15:20

15:16 And the soldiers led him away into the hall, called Praetorium; and they call together the cohort. 15:17 And they clothed him with purple, and platted a crown of thorns, and put it about his head, 15:18 And began to salute him, Hail, king of the Jews! 15:19 And they smote him on the head with a reed, and did spit

upon him, and bowing their knees worshipped him. 15:20 And when they had
mocked him, they took off the purple from him, and put his own clothes on him,
and led him out to crucify him.

The Mockery

The Roman legionaries cannot have been too pleased to have had a forced march
of 60 miles uphill with their heavy packs, then to have had to fight a band of
religious fanatics. Pilate turns over the leader of the gang of rebels to the soldiers
for them to have their bit of fun.

In the Roman Saturnalia slaves are freed and are treated as Lords by their
masters. Here the soldiers mock Jesus with this sort of treatment. He is elevated
to the mock position of a king to ridicule what, to Roman eyes, seemed his
pretentious claims. The Saturnalia probably involved some such ceremony (or
play) because it is reminiscent of a similar ceremony from Babylonia called the
Sacaea which might have entered Roman culture along with the eastern mystery
religions.

Could the time of year have been Saturnalia when the soldiers mocked Jesus?
The festival of Saturnalia began on December 19 and lasted a week. Since the
events depicted in Mark take place in spring there seems no connexion. But
the Roman new year originally fell in spring, and Saturnalia would then have
been held at about the same time as the Jewish Passover. Some communities
retained, at least partially, the earlier festival, and the period of celebration of
Saturnalia eventually extended over the whole period from December to March.
The modern day relic of the Saturnalia, Christmas aside, is the European tradition
of the Carnival (Fasching in Germany) which begins at Epiphany and ends
at Easter. Christianity, as was its wont, took over the extended Saturnalia and
made it into Carnival. Thus for the Roman soldiers the mockery of Jesus might have
been their bit of Saturnalia fun, allowing them to get their own back on the man
who had caused them some trouble. Alternatively they might have simply used
Saturnalian practices to mock the man as a false king whether or not it was actually
Saturnalia.

However, the scene as described by Mark and echoed in Matthew is a private scene.
Jesus is turned over to the soldiers who lead him away to some part of the palace—
probably meaning the Antonia fortress. There they abuse him but who would have
seen it to report it. It is highly unlikely that the soldiers would have told Jews. They
simply would not have been on good enough terms with the Jews—they treated
them with contempt, as Josephus shows us on another occasion, describing one
legionary as peeing onto the Jews below from the height of the temple portico. After
a forced march and a battle they would certainly not have been friendly.
Furthermore it is at least doubtful that the paraphernalia of the mocking—the thorns
for the crown and the reed—would be readily at hand in a fortress in the centre of
a city.

Much scholarly opinion is that the passage is an insertion and Luke choses to omit it, but it is hard to believe that Mark, who is careful to put Romans in a generally good light, will have a cohort of them mistreating a god—even if he felt soldiers were louts—unless it represented some sort of standard practice that no Roman would be surprised at. It seems it was! Exactly the same is recorded of the legionaries stationed at the frontier post of Durostorum in the Balkans who at Saturnalia treated another mock king to identical indignities. One has to conclude that it is genuine tradition which Mark could not leave out; and since the scourging and mockery recalls the treatment of the suffering servant in Isaiah, he had good reason to put it in. It could not therefore have been a private affair. There seems no reason why it should have been—the Romans were trying to make an example of Jesus and his followers and had every reason for mocking him publicly.

Ecce Homo is Latin for Behold the Man. It refers to: Behold, the man whose name is the Branch (Zech 6:12), part of the coronation liturgy of Joshua (Jesus). To the Essenes, the branch was neser, a title of Jesus and a source of the word, Nazarene.

In John, Jesus is publicly paraded in his mock regal attire and Pilate, behaving in character, jeeringly declares: *Ecce homo! Behold the man!* If this is genuine Pilate had an unusual interest in Jewish beliefs because he is quoting Zechariah 6:12–13 where God's message is: *Behold the man whose name is The Branch; and he shall grow up out of his place, and he shall build the temple of the Lord: Even he shall build the temple of the Lord; and he shall bear the glory, and shall sit and rule upon his throne; and he shall be a priest upon his throne: and the counsel of peace shall be between them both.* Possibly Pilate had been advised of this passage by the priests and was being appropriately sarcastic.

This bit of Roman fun seems to have become quickly well known because a few years later in 40 AD Philo reports the Jews of Alexandria, a town with a large expatriate Jewish population, mocking the Roman puppet Agrippa I who had just been appointed king of the Jews by the mad Emperor Caligula. They dressed up a Jewish simpleton in mock finery, gave him a sceptre and pretended to make obeisance to him as the king of the Jews. The interesting thing is that they called the mock Agrippa, Karabbas, possibly a badly remembered version of Barabbas, or a deliberate pun on Barabbas—the Jews also censuring the growing cult of the false god, Jesus Barabbas, the Christ. The Hebrew word *gur*, transliterated here as *kar*, pertains to a stranger or foreigner, with connotations of fear or dislike, but another word pronounced similarly means a fatted ram—probably the semitic word behind that used by John when he speaks of the lamb of God, a sacrificial lamb—and therefore means simply fat. It is easy to see how all of these could have been applied to Agrippa, a descendant of the hated Herod. They were saying: *Barabbas, Karabbas; son of my father, fat foreigner of my father, more like*.

Note that the number of troops mentioned is a cohort which is about 500. Whether this implies that the number of troops in Jerusalem was a cohort or whether this cohort guarded the Palace or whether this cohort was off-duty is anybody's guess. More than a cohort will have come from Caesarea.

Finally, it seems unlikely that after the mockery they would have bothered clothing Jesus in his own clothes—such as they were—Essenes wore their clothes completely to rags. Part of the indignity of the punishment was to be hung up naked. Later in the story, when Jesus hangs on the cross, the soldiers divide his garments among themselves. They would surely have done so at the mockery when they stripped him to mock him showing that the scene is included to fulfil prophecy.

Mark 15:16 to 15:20 Restored

And the soldiers led him away into a public place that all might see him, and they called together the legionaries. And, after the fashion of the Roman festival of Saturnalia, they dressed him as the fool who would be king; they clothed him with purple, and platted a crown of thorns, and put it about his head, and began to salute him: *Hail, king of the Jews*! And they smote him on the head with a reed, and did spit upon him, and bowing their knees worshipped him. And when they had mocked him, they took the purple from him, and led him out naked to crucify him.

The Crucifixion

Mark 15:21 – 15:32

15:21 And they compel one Simon a Cyrenian, who passed by, coming out of the country, the father of Alexander and Rufus, to bear his cross. 15:22 And they bring him unto the place Golgotha, which is, being interpreted, The place of a skull. 15:23 And they gave him to drink wine mingled with myrrh: but he received it not. 15:24 And when they had crucified him, they parted his garments, casting lots upon them, what every man should take. 15:25 And it was the third hour, and they crucified him. 15:26 And the superscription of his accusation was written over, THE KING OF THE JEWS. 15:27 And with him they crucify two thieves; the one on his right hand, and the other on his left. 15:28 And the scripture was fulfilled, which saith, And he was numbered with the transgressors. 15:29 And they that passed by railed on him, wagging their heads, and saying, Ah, thou that destroyest the temple, and buildest it in three days, 15:30 Save thyself, and come down from the cross. 15:31 Likewise also the chief priests mocking said among themselves with the scribes, He saved others; himself he cannot save. 15:32 Let Christ the king of Israel descend now from the cross, that we may see and believe. And they that were crucified with him reviled him.

The Crucifixion

It was a capital offence to act against the Empire or Caesar; it was a capital offence to assume the actions of an official without authority; it was a capital offence to join an armed body in capturing a public place—indeed simply to carry arms. The gospels are clear that Jesus was guilty of each of these offences. Pilate had no discretion in the matter of sentencing. Under the laws of Rome Jesus was guilty of treason. Simply being acclaimed a king without an insurrection was sufficient for the Roman authorities to find him guilty. There is no argument about this! The punishment for these crimes could only be crucifixion. Jesus is crucified at the third hour—about 9 o'clock in the morning—a curious detail to find in Mark when the other synoptists omit it, suggesting it is an addition, but not an unreasonable one.

Mark's connecting paragraph is peculiar. Why is this man Simon, a Cyrenian, introduced? Why indeed would the Romans compel a man to carry the cross for Jesus, making him miss part of his punishment? Simon's Christian purpose seems to be to act as a witness, and his sons are mentioned to prove it, implying that they were known in Christian circles, though the other gospels omit them. But does Cyrenian really mean *of Cyrene*, a place in Libya? There must surely be an Aramaic word behind it, which Mark has not explained, and it has been rendered as something the Romans could understand. Some say it means a man who works with lime, or in the cornfields, or is a fowler, or comes from the city. Perhaps the reference is not to words meaning lime or grain but to the root *qara* yielding a word meaning a planned encounter, deliberate and arranged for a purpose. It is used of an intentional meeting with God. The Cyrenian was a man who had to make a prearranged rendezvous with Jesus as he carried the cross—but if the encounter with this Simon was planned, what was its purpose and who planned it? It begins to look as though Jesus was indeed substituted before his crucifixion—by the Essenes?

Mark *does* translate an Aramaic word for us here. Golgotha is interpreted as *the place of the skull*—the word, properly *golgoltha*, simply means skull or head. Christians have always believed it meant a rock or hillock shaped like a skull as Gordon of Khartoum did but *golgoltha* is used of counting heads, as in a census or poll-tax. There would have been a census in 20–21 AD—when the Acta Pilati say that Jesus died—if the Augustan cycle of censuses was followed. Perhaps all those pious pilgrims who imagined it to refer to a feature of the landscape were quite wrong—it was a place near the tax office.

More probably the heads counted would have been those of the dead in the recent counter attack. The Romans might have used decapitated heads to count dead Jews giving us the precise meaning of *golgoltha*, and perhaps they left the pile of them as a warning. Christians usually discount this argument—after 2000 years the evangelists' aim of whitewashing the Romans still carries clout—because the considerate Romans could not possibly have done such an offensive thing to the Jews. Hacked up corpses lying about for days on end was against Jewish law so the kindly Romans tidied them up. It is true that the Romans normally *did* bend over backwards to defer to Jewish demands—but not when faced with rebellion! Even the gospel accounts declare there had been an insurrection so the arguments that *golgoltha* cannot have had anything to do with actual skulls is nonsense. The place of the skull was where a pile of skulls had been made when the insurrection was put down. As an admonition it would have been near the site of the recent battle between the Nazarenes and the Jerusalem garrison described in the story of the Gadarene swine—overlooking the Qidron valley to the east of the city.

The rest of this pericope is tradition buttressed with scriptural fulfilments. The drink offered in verse 23 fulfils Proverbs 31:6; parting his garments in verse 24 was inserted to fulfil Psalms 22:18; verse 27, as verse 28 explains, fulfils Isaiah 53:12; the beginning of verse 29 fulfils Psalms 22:7. Mark composes these prophecies for the informed reader to note, but in verse 28 he expressly points out the scriptural reference, *And he was numbered with the transgressors*, namely the crucified rebels alongside him. He does so because it was the only one of these *prophecies* that had really been fulfilled. But some copyists thought it said too honestly that Jesus was a transgressor, effectively labelling him as the rebel he was, and omitted it. Hence it is missing in some early manuscripts.

The transgressors, two thieves—the Greek word is again *lestai* meaning insurrectionists—defenders of the city against the Romans, were crucified with Jesus, one on either side and they reviled him. It is quite unlike Essenes to break under torture, as we know from Josephus, so we can be sure that these men are not lifelong Essenes but either Jesus's converts, accepted into the movement on the basis of repentance and baptism, or bystanders who undertook to help the Nazarenes against the legionaries. Luke 23:39–43 gives us their conversation in detail. One man demands that Jesus save them to prove his claims but *the other* tells him off, saying:

> Dost thou not fear God, seeing thou art in the same condemnation? And we indeed justly; for we receive the due reward of our deeds. But this man hath done nothing amiss.

The other who answers is Jesus himself not the other anonymous man—it was Jesus who was addressed, and he it should be who answers. The implication is that the third of the trio, *this man*, was an onlooker arrested and condemned in error. Luke's ambiguity suggests it is Jesus but allows that it was the third man.

If the purpose of the dialogue is to distinguish Jesus from the rebels, Luke fails miserably when he tells us the rebuked bandit and Jesus were in the same condemnation. He is evidently not raising the question of whether Jesus was in the same condemnation or not, but simply whether it was just or not—for one of them, *this man*, it was unjust. If this were not genuine tradition, it would never have been included. Jesus was named as an insurrectionist like the others. The *denouement* is that one of the two men, again it is not clear whether it is the rebuked man suitably chastened or the defended one suitably grateful, asks to be remembered in the kingdom and Jesus responds favourably. Since Jesus no longer expected the kingdom to be coming, these last verses are added, implying as they do that the kingdom would follow the suffering of the servant—a later idea.

Jesus's attendants on the cross had their legs broken to shorten their lives (Jn 19:31–32) but Jesus was already dead. The object of crucifixion was to provide a slow death. The victims were usually tied to the cross or branches, and sometimes nailed too. Their feet rested on a ledge on the upright or trunk, or they were nailed laterally through their heels with a huge nail, providing support to allow them to press upward from time to time and relieve the strain on the chest and lungs. Once the legs were broken, the strain would soon lead to death. Since Jesus was already dead without any broken bones and, according to John, on the eve of the Passover, he became the perfect sacrifice. The paschal lamb had to be perfect—it could have none of its bones broken! It also had to be sacrificed on 14 Nisan and this became the early Christian tradition of the actual date of the crucifixion.

The sacrifice of the lamb or kid at Passover symbolized human sacrifice. The substitution of a ram for Isaac when Abraham intended to sacrifice his son Isaac represented the change over from human to animal sacrifice and provided the authority for it which was formalized in the laws of Moses. Making Jesus the paschal lamb is substituting a human sacrifice for that of a sheep—the crucifixion is a barbarous throw back to the ancient custom. Eusebius tells us, quoting Philo of Byblus, the Jewish king traditionally gave his beloved son as a sacrificial offering for the nation as a ransom to avenging devils. Besides Abraham, David attempted to stop a famine by sacrificing seven royal princes, hanging them before the Lord, at the beginning of the barley harvest, about the time of the Passover; Mesha of Moab sacrificed his eldest son; king Hiel sacrificed his sons when Jericho was founded; Kings Ahaz and Manassah burnt their children in sacrifice; Ishmael was nearly sacrificed by his father, like Isaac, according to Arab legend.

The king personified the tribal god and as such was the father of the people; the son therefore represented the people themselves. The actual son of the king was sacrificed as the symbolic Son of the Father (bar Abbas) representing the unworthy tribe. The victims of the sacrifices were normally hanged on a tree until dusk as the Old Testament repeatedly indicates and in the Greek language hanging from a tree and crucifixion are synonymous. With time this rite became more symbolic, a condemned criminal being substituted for the prince. Jesus ben Pandira in the reign of Alexander Jannaeus (105–76 BC) was stoned and hanged from a tree on the eve of the Passover, an indication perhaps that the people in cruel mockery sometimes sacrifced a human even as late this. As in the Babylonian Sacaea the substitute was dressed in fine robes to represent the prince, a crown was put on his head, he was scourged and finally hanged or crucified—just as Jesus was! The two others hanged with Jesus would, on this hypothesis, represent the king's attendants, one being on his right hand and one on his left.

Though human sacrifice was made illegal in the Roman republic in 196 BC, it seems to have continued till later, particularly associated with the military. In many places in Roman Britain for example human skulls or skeletons are found with the bones of sacrificed animals at the sites of temples or shrines. They might have been people who died naturally though it seems unlikely that a ready made corpse would be thought to propitiate the god rather than a sacrificial victim. More probably they were criminals who had been sentenced to capital punishment and so were used to double up as a human sacrifice. The mockery of Jesus by the Roman soldiers who dressed him in robes and crowned him with thorns prior to his crucifixion was plainly some such ritual—Jesus might well have been a human sacrifice in fact.

Even if the Romans did not intend the crucifixion as a human sacrifice, anyone who knew of the old custom must have seen it as just that. Thus, following ancient and largely superseded traditions, early Christians thought of Jesus's crucifixion as sacrificial (1 Cor 15:3: *Christ died for our sins*). Paul's teaching of Christ crucified was central to the success of the evangelist in the world of the gentiles. The followers of Jesus were able to convince themselves that their hero had died as a human sacrifice. He had become the paschal Lamb—it was God's will. The dead Christ became more important than the live one almost as soon as the death occurred and certainly by the time Paul had taken it to the gentiles.

In Matthew and Mark the drink of wine mingled with myrrh is offered to Jesus before he is crucified and also another bitter drink on the cross. Proverbs 31:6 forbids strong drink to princes and wine to kings but Mosaic law allows a man about to perish a drink *that he remember his misery no more*. The wine and myrrh mixture was offered to Jesus to dull the pain of the crucifixion, but he was priest, prophet and prince and refused to break his Nazirite vow even to ease his pain on the cross.

Verse 31 says that the Chief Priests, meaning the Sadducees, mocked him, then *with the scribes* was added for Mark's usual reason. The direct speech is a Marcan summary of what they said and must be true in essence—the Sadducees were glad to be rid of him.

Pilate did not imagine that Jesus was innocent as the gospels make out. He insisted that the inscription on the cross should read *the king of the Jews* rather than *He said: I am king of the Jews* (Jn 19:21). Pilate intended the execution and the inscription to serve as a lesson to all Jews never to harbour nationalistic ideas. Crucifixion would be the fate, not only of false kings, but also of genuine kings should they emerge—Caesar alone had power. It did not have the desired effect. After Pilate's disgrace in 36 AD Roman prefects came and went until Agrippa, the grandson of Herod the Great, was instated for a few years until 44 AD when Roman rule resumed under the procurators. Immediately there was an uprising under a messiah called Theudas who was slain. A High Priest was murdered by the sicarii.

Simon Magus assembled a crowd at the Mount of Olives to see a miracle. The revolt of Eleazar continued for twenty years until he was captured by the procurator Felix and sent to Rome. James the Just, brother of Jesus, was stoned to death in 62 AD, instigating the war, Josephus implies.

The Jewish War began in 66 AD with astonishing successes. The leader of the Zealots, Menehem, a son of Judas of Galilee, and Eleazar, the captain of the Temple Guard, revolted at the same time. The Zealots captured the fortress of Masada and murdered the Roman garrison; the captain of the Temple Guard refused to allow a daily sacrifice for the Emperor, a blatant outrage to the Romans; the Roman garrison in Jerusalem surrendered and was butchered. The Legate of Syria had to send an army of twenty thousand men which the rebels promptly defeated. It all proves that Jews were more than capable of defeating the legions unless they came in overpowering might.

But, as Jesus realized decades before, the Jews lacked unity—the rebels began to quarrel among themselves. Menehem declared himself king only to be murdered by the Sadducees. John of Gischala, another Galilaean, leader of the Zealots, then murdered the High Priest, Annas, and overthrew the Sadducees.

It took a large force from Rome under the generalship of Vespasian, soon to be Emperor, and his son Titus to put down the rising, taking advantage of the disunity of the Jewish factions. With the fall of Jerusalem after a siege of five months, the Jewish state was crushed. The temple was shattered and with it the party of the Sadducees; Jews were taken captive to Rome; Jewish wealth was plundered; the Sanhedrin was disbanded; the Rabbis and the Pharisees were scattered to re-establish Judaism centred on the synagogue; most important of all from the viewpoint of Christianity, the Jewish followers of Jesus in Jerusalem were also dispersed, a few remnants taking to the desert, traditionally via Pella. Even after Jerusalem and the temple had been razed, Jewish spirit was not destroyed. There were to be further messianic uprisings in 116 AD and 136 AD when, with the slaying of Bar Kosiba, the flame of revolt was finally extinguished.

The cross was significant in itself—it was an object of worship in its own right long before the Christian era. The cross was a stylized tree and trees and groves had been sacred to some of the earliest gods. The worship of the crucifix carried on where pagan cross worship left off and that in turn was a continuation of tree worship.

Mark 15:21 to 15:32 Restored

And as they passed by, one Simon, encountered them and took his cross. And they bring him unto the place Golgoltha, which is, being interpreted: The skull. And, to ease his pain, they gave him to drink wine mingled with myrrh: but he received it not, for he would not break his vow of consecration to God. And it was the third hour, and they crucified him. And the superscription of his accusation was written over: THE KING OF THE JEWS. And with him they crucify many more seditionists; and one was on his right hand, and another on his left. And the scripture was fulfilled, which saith: *And he was numbered with the transgressors.* And they that were crucified with him reviled him saying: *Ah, thou that destroyest the temple, and buildest it in three days, Save thyself, and us, and come down from the cross.* And Jesus answered, saying: *Doest thou no longer fear God, since thou art in the same condemnation. And we indeed justly, for we receive punishment for what we have done. But this other, hath done nothing amiss.* For one hanging near them was an innocent pilgrim. And they that passed by railed on him, wagging their heads, and likewise also the chief priests mocking said among themselves: *He saved others; himself he cannot save. If he be the messiah, the king of Israel let him now descend from the cross, that we may see and believe. Let God deliver him now, if he will have him, for he said: I am the Son of God.*

The Finish

Mark 15:33 – 15:41

15:33 And when the sixth hour was come, there was darkness over the whole land until the ninth hour. 15:34 And at the ninth hour Jesus cried with a loud voice, saying, Eloi, Eloi, lama sabachthani? which is, being interpreted, My God, my God, why hast thou forsaken me? 15:35 And some of them that stood by, when they heard it, said, Behold, he calleth Elias. 15:36 And one ran and filled a spunge full of vinegar, and put it on a reed, and gave him to drink, saying, Let alone; let us see whether Elias will come to take him down. 15:37 And Jesus cried with a loud voice, and gave up the ghost. 15:38 And the veil of the temple was rent in twain from the top to the bottom. 15:39 And when the centurion, which stood over against him, saw that he so cried out, and gave up the ghost, he said, Truly this man was the Son of God. 15:40 There were also women looking on afar off: among whom was Mary Magdalene, and Mary the mother of James the less and of Joses, and Salome; 15:41 (Who also, when he was in Galilee, followed him, and ministered unto him;) and many other women which came up with him unto Jerusalem.

The Finish

The darkening mentioned by Mark is not an eclipse but simply what Mark expected from scripture (Isa 50:3; Amos 8:9). After six hours on the cross Jesus cries: *My God, my God, why hast thou forsaken me?* Mark records it in Aramaic and translates it for his gentile audience. That this is the first line of psalm 22 leads one to think it is a false but pious conclusion to Jesus's life. Psalm 22 is really two psalms, one a cry of despair and one a messianic response. Commentators say that the cry of despair invites the response, and perhaps that is so, but a cry of despair is a strange choice for the gospel writer given that psalm 22 was unfamiliar to gentiles without access to the Septuagint. The other gospel writers omit it as inappropriate for a God.

Yet a hundred years ago, it was pointed out that the earliest Christians would never have accepted a cry of despair from their God, even if it was a quotation from scripture, unless it was unequivocally vouchsafed by history. That must be true, and a clue that it is genuine is the next line in which some of the observers think he is saying *Elias* when he is saying *Eloi*. This is almost like a sick joke and it is difficult to believe it is other than genuine. Verse 36 is a fulfilment of prophecy and completion of the joke.

Jesus was steeped in interpretations of the scriptures and his final appeal to God in his agony might well have been couched in a scriptural quotation. He did not have to rack his brain to come up with it—it was simply the way he thought. Many pious Jews, perhaps most, would have been similarly conditioned but none more so than the Essenes. He was in agony and despair. Inadvertently his cry to God is psalm 22. Now once this is accepted it becomes clear why so much more of the psalm is then added to the account of Jesus's suffering. Much of the detail of the passion is taken directly from psalm 22 because it provided Jesus's last words and so seemed particularly holy.

After only a short time on the cross Jesus is offered a sponge of vinegar whereupon he cries out and dies. A Roman soldier, not a Jew, first recognizes Jesus as the Son of God. Mark is sucking up to the Romans again—a gentile first recognizes Jesus as the messiah. Mark concludes this section by pointing out that many women followers look on from afar, a sop to the early membership of the gentile church— women. Gentile women were much more ready to become Jewish proselytes than men because they did not have to undergo the painful and dangerous operation for adults of circumcision. Christianity found a ready basis for recruiting in the Roman Empire in the women who had already adopted Judaism. The relationships given in verse 40 are not clear.

When Jesus died, John gives no miracles. Mark and Luke mention the darkness of the sky for three hours and the tearing of the veil in the temple. The grosser effects—the earthquake, the bursting open of graves and the dead (described as *saints* meaning Essenes) walking—are the product of the fervid imagination of Matthew. If any one of these spectacular events really happened, on an occasion as memorable anyway as the death of a god, surely they would have been widely remembered and would have appeared in the other accounts. Besides their inconsistent use in the gospels, Seneca and Pliny who compiled records of such events had never heard of them.

Mark 15:33 to 15:41 Restored

And after three days Jesus cried with a loud voice, saying: *Eloi, Eloi, lama sabachthani?* which is, being interpreted: *My God, my God, why hast thou forsaken me?* And some of them that stood by, when they heard it, said: *Behold, he calleth Elias.* And one ran and filled a sponge full of vinegar, and put it on a reed, and gave him to drink, saying: *Let alone; let us see whether Elias will come to take him down.* And Jesus again cried with a loud voice, and gave up the ghost.

The Burial

Mark 15:42 – 15:47

15:42 And now when the even was come, because it was the preparation, that is, · the day before the sabbath, 15:43 Joseph of Arimathaea, an honourable counsellor, which also waited for the kingdom of God, came, and went in boldly unto Pilate, and craved the body of Jesus. 15:44 And Pilate marvelled if he were already dead: and calling unto him the centurion, he asked him whether he had been any while dead. 15:45 And when he knew it of the centurion, he gave the corpse to Joseph. 15:46 And he bought fine linen, and took him down, and wrapped him in the linen, and laid him in a sepulchre which was hewn out of a rock, and rolled a stone unto the door of the sepulchre. 15:47 And Mary Magdalene and Mary the mother of Joses beheld where he was laid.

The Burial

In verses 42 to 47, Joseph of Arimathea, Mark tells us a member of the Sanhedrin, asked Pilate's permission to take him from the cross. He had to do it boldly and Pilate was astonished that Jesus was already dead. Pilate asked the centurion to confirm it, which he did, and permission was given. Normally crucifixion was a slow death. That was why it was used for the most heinous crimes. It was possible for a crucified man to take five days to die. The gospels have Jesus dying after only six hours. Joseph and Nicodemus (in John's gospel), both behaving as if they had an interest in the body, wrapped it in linen and put it in a new tomb cut out of rock in a private garden. The tomb was sealed by a large rock pushed against the entrance.

Much is made of the command in Deuteronomy 21:23 that a hanged man should not be allowed to hang on a tree overnight. Joseph seems to be making sure that Jesus does not. But what of the so called criminals who were hanging with him? According to John 19:32–33 they had their legs broken to bring on a quick death so that they did not have to hang on the cross overnight. Would the Romans, for whom crucifixion was meant to be an exemplary punishment which is why it was public and devised to be slow, be willing to allow terrorists to hang only for twelve hours, whether they were Jews or not? Usually they would be left to rot unless the corpse were claimed by relatives, and we can guess that is what Pilate would have preferred. Sources like Josephus suggest that, for the Jews, the Romans were accommodating, but facing an ogre like Pilate after an uprising, the courage Joseph has to gather denotes an uncertain response.

In John, Joseph of Arimathea is described as a disciple of Jesus—he is apparently a Nazarene. Arimathea never existed. Ramathea from Ramah is probably meant. It was the birthplace of Samuel, the prophet who was a priest because he anointed the kings David and Saul and also a king because previously he had ruled Israel as a Judge. Samuel was also a Nazirite dedicated by his mother before his birth to God, and like Isaac was a child of God's promise. He wore the priestly ephod of white linen. In short, he was the epitome of the ideal Essene. Doubtless the significance of the mysterious word Arimathea of Mark is that Joseph was in fact an Essene, and we might have inferred it from Mark who wrote he *waited for the kingdom of God*. Luke virtually confirms this by adding that he was *a good man and just, just* being the same word as *righteous*, the word used by the Essenes of themselves. Jesus's brother, James who became leader of the Nazarenes after the crucifixion was called, James the Just. Incidentally Joseph in Greek is Joses, and a Joses was one of Mary's sons and therefore a brother of Jesus. Though it was a common name it offers the possibility that Joseph of Arimathea was one of Jesus's brothers, and that is why he was claiming the body. In Roman law the corpse of a crucified criminal belonged to the next of kin.

Could an Essene be a member of the Sanhedrin? An alternative translation would be simply an honourable man respected in the community. Indeed Matthew takes him to be a rich man (to fulfil *Isaiah* 53:9), which an Essene could not be. Either Essenes were represented on the Sanhedrin (which seems unlikely) or Joseph was an Essene of some status in the community but not a member of the Sanhedrin. Possibly the council mentioned did not mean the Sanhedrin but the Essenes' *council of the community*.

In the Copper Scroll there is a reference to the *Tomb of Zadok* and the *Garden of Zadok* next to it. They are under the southern corner of Solomon's Portico on the east side of the temple and, like the Garden of Gethsemane, beneath the Mount of Olives. It is the only reference to a garden near the Mount of Olives outside the gospels. The Garden of Zadok *was* the Garden of Gethsemane. The name Zadok might imply it was owned by the Essenes and so its association with Joseph of Arimathea is understandable.

When Herod was reconstructing Jerusalem and the temple, there was a concern that the newly built town should not be desecrated by the dead and many tombs were built just beyond the walls notably in the Qidron valley where even then there were tombs. Jewish tombs already present in Jesus's time are still there, cut out of the rock. Among the prominent ones are the tomb of the Bene Hezir, the family tomb of a dynasty of Hasmonean priests and dated last century BC. It has distinctly Hellenistic influences. Another is the tomb of the kings, a large mausoleum outside the walls of Jerusalem built by the Adiabene, a Parthian royal family from the upper Tigris who had converted to Judaism, according to Josephus, in the time of the procurator Fadus, the tomb being built where tombs traditionally were built. The pillar of Absalom, is a monument associated with the tomb of Jehoshaphat, also in the Qidron valley not far from the mausoleum of the sons of Hezir. Very many less imposing tombs must have existed and evidently Jesus was laid in one—in the Essenes' garden of rest.

This valley of tombs, the valley of Jehoshaphat of Joel's prophecy, was surely the site of the defeat of the legionaries in the battle with the Nazarenes for Jerusalem—possible the battle described in code as the Gadarene swine and the Gerasene demoniac. The demoniac came out of the tombs. The Nazarenes engaged the Jerusalem garrison there to fulfil the prophecies of Joel and Zechariah which might have been explicit in the War Scroll but have been lost, and because it offered practical advantages, the Nazarenes and the multitudes accompanying them being able to hurl rocks from high vantage points behind the tombs. The captain of the garrison would not have wished to move far from the city, fearing that in his absence it would be taken by fifth columnists infiltrating as pilgrims or even by the citizens of Jerusalem themselves in an uprising.

The last verse was added later to answer the objection that the women did not know where Jesus was placed by Joseph and the resurrection was a case of a mistaken tomb.

The Year of the Crucifixion

When exactly did the crucifixion occur? Surprisingly no one knows and it is impossible to deduce with certainty. We know it occurred near the time of the Passover in spring in the prefecture of Pilate and the reign of Tiberius, 14 AD to 37 AD. By the time the gospels were written, no one could remember for sure on what day or even in what year the crucifixion occurred. It was not considered important because judgement day was still expected. Nevertheless the gospels record the earliest tradition—the tomb was found empty on the day after the sabbath, the first day of the week, a Sunday. If Jesus's body had been left unattended because of the sabbath then he had been placed there before sunset on the preceding Friday, a period of three days if the days were counted inclusively. The disappearance of the body and the apparent agreement with Hosea's prophecy led the Nazarene converts of the simple of Ephraim into believing that the general resurrection had started—the failed warrior messiah had turned out to be the suffering servant, the kingdom had come, at least in embryo, and would be introduced fully fledged when the messiah returned in glory—Christianity in principle if not yet in name had been born.

In Josephus's Antiquities, although Pilate does not start his term as prefect of Judaea until 26 AD, the sense of chapter 18:3, which narrates tumults, demands that the third of the tumults occurring under Pilate was that of Jesus the messiah, and an association of it with events in Rome datable from other sources seems to place these around 18 or 19 AD, near the crucifixion date of 21 AD given in the allegedly forged Acta Pilati of 311 AD. Pilate's inaugural act of sneaking the standards into Jerusalem, to the Jews fulfilled Daniel's prophecy of the *Abomination of Desolation* which heralded the final days. Origen in the third century considered it so. Such an offensive incident would be more likely to trigger a rebellion than merely invite the petitions for their removal recorded.

The event of the standards was probably that which stimulated Jesus to begin his mission to invest God's kingdom on earth. Pilate therefore began his term in 18 AD not in 26 AD. This ties in with the number twelve in the miracles of Jairus's daughter and the woman with a haemorrhage, it being the twelfth year of Roman rule, the twelfth year since Judas the Galilaean rebelled against the numbering of the people. If Jesus began his ministry in 18 AD it was 21 years after John the Baptist began his according to Mandaean tradition in 4 BC agreeing with the idea that the Baptist was Jesus's predecessor as the *nasi*. They were not exact contemporaries as Luke makes out unless Jesus also was much older in which case he could have been Judas the Galilaean! Christians must have altered Josephus to make Pilate's rule seem shorter than it really was. They wanted to discredit the Acta Pilati which were not forged but the genuine Acts of Pilate.

The synoptic gospels have Jesus crucified on the morning of 15 Nisan, the day after the Passover on 14 Nisan when the passover meal, the seder, is eaten in the evening. John's gospel makes it on the morning of 14 Nisan. The Talmud agrees with accepted Christian tradition that Jesus was crucified on a Friday and rose on a Sunday. It says the crucifixion was on the day before the Passover which that year fell on a sabbath. The Talmud however will be recording Nazarene tradition and not be an independent record.

The gospels admit there had been an insurrection. Pilate could not have been in a pretty mood, and certainly not if the Nazarenes had captured Jerusalem. In such circumstances he could not have honoured Jewish religious sentiments. Jesus was crucified on Passover day.

As a rule of thumb Passover occurs at the first full moon in the Jewish year, but in theory it is more complicated. The first month in the year is Nisan and the start of it is declared when a new moon is first observed. That day is therefore 1 Nisan and fourteen days later is Passover, on the evening of 14 Nisan, which is really 15 Nisan since the Jewish day begins at sunset. The trouble is that the new moon might not be visible for up to three days after it is astronomically new, depending upon alignments and circulations of the planetary orbs, so it is impossible to say when the priests will have declared 1 Nisan in the feasible years of the crucixion.

Worse still, the new year notionally began near the spring equinox and the paschal full moon was therefore the first after the equinox, but confusingly the Jewish equinox seems not to have matched the astronomical one but came earlier. Third century clergymen protested that Jews sometimes declared Nisan such that the paschal full moon fell before the equinox. In seeking suitable dates, if the expected paschal full moon falls late in April, it is likely that the previous full moon in March should be considered as marking Passover that year even if it falls before the equinox.

In the year 21 AD astronomically Passover should have been Wednesday 16 April, but this is late and it could have fallen Monday 17–18 March. That year 15 Nisan was therefore Tuesday 18 March and that was the day that Jesus was crucified. Now according to Epiphanius, the *Acta Pilati* gives the date of the crucifixion as 18 March but in all later copies it had been altered to 25 March, and that date became traditional in the early imperial church. The change was made for several reasons. First 18 March was before the equinox which the clergy considered must have been an error. Second many pagan festivals—most notably the date of the conception of the sun god whose birth was 25 December— fell on 25 March and it was convenient for the church to emulate popular pagan festivals. Third, when 25 December was also adopted as Christmas, then the day of the annunciation of the blessed virgin, the day of Jesus's conception by God, also fell on 25 March. If that was the day he was conceived it was also the day a perfect being should die.

Verily, Jesus was crucified on 15 Nisan, Tuesday 18 March, 21 AD.

What then of the gospels, which say that Jesus entered the tomb on a Friday and had left it by Sunday morning? The simple explanation is that Jesus did not die on the cross within six hours but hung on it for three days! Three days is much more like the normal time it takes a man to die when crucified, unless his legs are broken. Jesus did not have his legs broken according to John 19:32. We have seen that from Deuteronomy 21:23 a man hung on a tree, though accursed of God, should not be left hanging there all night. The Romans were normally very patient about Jewish sensitivities and the gospels depict Pilate as happy to defer to the Jews' desire that the malefactors should be taken down. Not only did Jews not want them hanging overnight, but traditionally the next day was the sabbath and that is the reason for their request to remove the bodies given in John. The gospels, keen to depict Pilate as a good man, say he readily agreed.

Pilate was not a nice man at all—he hated the Jews and would certainly have not been lenient to a seditionist of any sort. Furthermore the Romans were not so kindly disposed to Jews that they still honoured their customs in times of war. The Nazarenes had just fought two battles with the legionaries and the latter would not have felt well-disposed towards Jews. For these reasons Pilate would have been happy to leave Jesus hanging on the cross as the exemplary punishment that he was intended to be. In John the element of tradition is that, after the bodies had been hanging for three days, the Jews came in supplication to Pilate on the Friday asking for them to be cut down so as not to desecrate the sabbath. Satisfied that order had been restored and the malefactors were now dead, Pilate concurred with this request and sent out soldiers to despatch any that were still lingering before cutting them down. John says that Jesus was stabbed with a spear to make sure, and then handed to Joseph of Arimathea.

Why then did the gospels pretend that Jesus was dead after only six hours? The object of the gospel writers was to show the Jews as the villains and the Romans as kindly but crucifixion was a Roman punishment. There was no gainsaying that, but the evangelists wanted it to seem that the Son of God had not suffered unduly from this cruel Roman punishment. So they argued that the Son was crucified only a few hours before he died and was laid to rest in a rock tomb.

Finally why was the early Christian tradition, beginning with Paul, that Jesus had been crucified on 14 Nisan not 15 Nisan? And why is it confirmed by the Jewish

Talmud? The three synoptic gospels put the crucifixion on 15 Nisan and only John's gospels plumps for 14 Nisan. Paul in 1 Cor 5:7 chooses 14 Nisan and in 1 Cor 15:20 he implies 14 Nisan in his reference to his resurrection as the *first fruits* meaning it happened on 16 Nisan, when the sheaf of barleycorn was being offered in the temple. Early Christians honoured the date 14 Nisan, later translated as 25 March, as the date of the crucifixion irrespective of what day it fell on—there was no Good Friday in those days. The answer must be that the myth of the paschal lamb was one of the first Christian myths— Nazarenes directly saw Jesus as the perfect sacrifice. Still expecting judgement they remembered the image of Jesus as the paschal lamb not precise dates. A paschal lamb could only be sacrificed on the 14 Nisan and so the image conditioned the memory of the event. The Nazarene memory entered the Jewish tradition partly because the Nazarenes were a Jewish sect before they became gentile and partly through transference from Christianity. However the synoptic tradition came from Peter who had a first hand experience of the events and transmitted it through Mark.

The accepted year of the crucifixion is 33 AD but Paul the apostle visited Jerusalem for the Apostolic Council of 49 AD and he tells us that 17 years had elapsed since his conversion, which must therefore have been in 32 AD. Paul converted before the official year of the crucifixion! The previous accepted date of 29 AD gives Paul time to be converted but both of these dates are wrong simply because scholars have erroneously accepted that Jesus was crucified on a Friday. Once this assumption is discarded the tradition of the Acta Pilati is found to be true.

Mark 15:42 to 15:47 Restored

And now when the even was come, because it was the preparation, that is, the day before the sabbath, Joseph of Arimathaea, which also waiteth for the kingdom of God, being an Essene, an honourable counsellor of the council of the congregation, came and went in boldly unto Pilate, and craved the body of Jesus, since he was the next of kin. And Pilate, satisfied with the punishment, called unto him the centurion, asking him whether he had been any while dead, and the centurion avowed he was dead, for he had pierced him with his spear. When Pilate knew it of the centurion, he yieldeth the corpse to Joseph, and he bought white linen, and took him down, and wrapped him in the linen, and laid him in a sepulchre which was hewn out of a rock in the Garden of Zadok, and rolled a stone unto the door of the sepulchre.

The Empty Tomb

Mark 16:1 – 16:8

16:1 And when the sabbath was past, Mary Magdalene, and Mary the mother of James, and Salome, had bought sweet spices, that they might come and anoint him. 16:2 And very early in the morning the first day of the week, they came unto the sepulchre at the rising of the sun. 16:3 And they said among themselves, Who shall roll us away the stone from the door of the sepulchre? 16:4 And when they looked, they saw that the stone was rolled away: for it was very great. 16:5 And entering into the sepulchre, they saw a young man sitting on the right side, clothed in a long white garment; and they were affrighted. 16:6 And he saith unto them, Be not affrighted: Ye seek Jesus of Nazareth, which was crucified: he is risen; he is not here: behold the place where they laid him. 16:7 But go your way, tell his disciples and Peter that he goeth before you into Galilee: there shall ye see him, as he said unto you. 16:8 And they went out quickly, and fled from the sepulchre; for they trembled and were amazed: neither said they any thing to any man; for they were afraid.

The Empty Tomb

The end of the gospel is freely rendered by Mark. Verse 1 is Mark's introduction. The women are listed again because the previous verse was an insertion. The two Marys and Salome (or Mary Magdalene alone, according to John) visit the tomb early on the Sunday morning the day after the sabbath ostensibly to wash and prepare the body. It seems unlikely that the women would really be going to anoint a body that might have already started to decompose in the hot climate. Friends and family might wish to visit a tomb for a few days after burial to grieve but surely not to anoint the corpse. They could have gone on the previous night after the stars came out when the sabbath was over, and indeed it is strange that someone so revered as Jesus should have unnecessarily been left another twelve hours if they really wanted to embalm the body. For what it is worth, John 19:39–40 tells us the corpse had already been embalmed by Joseph and Nicodemus.

They found the stone had been rolled away and the tomb was empty. A young man (or two men) in pure white garments tells them that Jesus is risen and has gone ahead to Galilee as he promised. The direct speech is all made up by Mark. It is not in the language of tradition but in Mark's language. Mark wishes to assure the reader that the women saw the very place where Jesus had been laid. The women fled trembling and amazed and, at this point, the earliest gospel ends (ignoring the final twelve verses which were added later).

The white robe and youth are conventional characteristics of an angel, but the significance of the pure white garments is not that these men are angels of God but that they are messengers of the Essenes. Jesus the nasi had an important position in the Essene order. He alone had not misread the signs of the times but the whole order. The readings and prophecies had been wrong but Jesus had carried out his duties as John the Baptist had before him, and had suffered for it. His body was removed so that he could be given a proper burial in a place approved by the community. The messengers from the sect give orders to the disciples that they were to escape to Galilee, out of Roman jurisdiction. Matthew says temple guards had been placed outside the tomb to prevent the disciples from stealing the body but no other gospel mentions this and it is transparently an editorial addition to overcome the criticism that the body had been stolen by Jesus's followers. It was!

According to the other gospels, immediately after the crucifixion, the disciples had despaired and were incredulous to hear that the tomb was empty. This proves that Jesus cannot have taught his disciples to expect his bodily resurrection on the third day as the gospels maintain since otherwise they would have been expecting Jesus to rise, would not have despaired at his death and would have rejoiced to hear of the empty tomb. The five occasions Jesus spoke of his death and resurrection in the gospel stories are interpolations based on hindsight.

The church's attempt at accounting for the inconsistency of the apostles' behaviour was to accuse them of stupidity. They were not stupid. If they were, Jesus must have been stupid to have chosen them. It is interesting to realize how the early church got away with labelling the Jewish followers of Jesus as stupid. Once it is appreciated that Jesus was an Essene sent to recruit the wayward children of Israel in the last days, it is obvious. Jesus went out to recruit the *simple of Ephraim*. His converts were therefore *the simple*! Once the church had escaped into the gentile world, it was a short and easy progression from *the simple* to being simple. That suited the gentile leaders of the gentile church just fine. Jesus was a god but his simple followers thought he was a king.

Since the Nazarene leaders at least were not simple, if they really did not understand when Jesus told them what to expect, then his prophecies must have been far more obscure than they are in the New Testament—or they never occurred! The plausible explanation, since the disciples were completely surprised by the news of the empty tomb, was that Jesus had made no prophecies about his personal resurrection. Their behaviour was therefore perfectly understandable. Their leader was dead, their rebellion had failed, God had not intervened—they despaired. Then someone had the temerity to steal the corpse!

According to the fictitious verses added to Mark, it is Mary Magdalene who first sees the risen Jesus. As if to provide an explanation the author immediately tells us that Jesus had cast seven devils from her. The writer of these late verses was not likely to have been using Nazarene convention and must have understood devils to signify madness, not opposition or apostasy. Both Matthew 12:43–45 and Luke 11:24–26 using Nazarene code speak of unclean spirits, having been driven out, returning to their host accompanied by seven other, even more wicked spirits. They were saying that some converts were utter doubters who had to be repeatedly reassured. But it seems Mary Magdalen was unreliable and unstable—she was badly neurotic. Still, if Jesus had made numerous prophecies of his resurrection, the disciples should have received her news cautiously perhaps but ready to accept it with joy. He had done no such thing and, not surprisingly, the neurotic woman was ignored.

Christian belief depends mainly on Jesus's appearances rather than the empty tomb. Writing long before the gospels were written, in the earliest Christian works we have, the apostle Paul never attempts to convince skeptics about the resurrection by quoting witnesses to the empty tomb. His evidence is Jesus's appearances: to the women, to two disciples on the way to Emmaus, to Peter and others in Jerusalem, to the apostles on a Galilaean mountain. Paul was not interested in the living Jesus but only in the resurrection and, as the first Christian writer, having possibly heard of a hysterical woman's reaction to Jesus's crucifixion and abduction, he could have invented additional appearances to confirm it. He adds a remarkable appearance to a throng of 500 which even the gospel writers must have found stretched credulity too far.

If, as some suggest, Jesus did survive the crucifixion he could hardly have been making appearances all over the place within days. He had been horribly wounded in arms, feet and side. He must have been kept in a safe house for months to recover, moved only if absolutely necessary, and when sufficiently fit would have been taken out of the Roman Emperor's reach to Parthia.

Yet the disciples in the gospels are certain that Jesus was alive and not just a vision—at an early stage critics had said that Jesus was not human. The author of Luke is at pains to demonstrate that Jesus was truly alive. In Acts he tarries for as long as forty days but he was not recognized by Mary Magdalene nor by two disciples on the road to Emmaus. In his final appearance in John by the Sea of Galilee, the disciples again do not recognize him. If all this were true and not elaborations of a Pauline invention then it implies that Jesus was heavily disguised—or it was someone else! These people knew him extremely well, so why otherwise couldn't they recognize him?

If in disguise, he must have been hiding from the authorities! At his final appearance he behaves like a man about to depart quickly—to Parthia rather than heaven—repeatedly urging his disciples to take care of my sheep—plainly meaning the lost sheep of the house of Israel. If the Jesus who appeared was someone else, the inference is that Jesus the Nazarene was an Essene title and, from the crucifixion, someone else had assumed the position, just as Jesus had taken over from John the Baptist.

The Quran says that Jesus survived because a substitute was crucified in his stead. According to the Basilidians, the substitute was Simon of Cyrene. Mark's and Matthew's gospels, from the point when Simon is mysteriously introduced into the account (Mt 27:32–44; Mk 15:21–32), are completely ambiguous about who was crucified. They could read that Simon was. Only at the point of death when they report that Jesus cries out is the doubt settled.

Only Luke mentions the public ascension into heaven (Luke 24:51; Acts 1:9–11). The words in Mark are simply that he was received up into heaven and even these are in the final twelve sham verses. We are faced with an astonishing event, reputedly seen by many but recorded only by one. It simply is not credible that people seeing such an astonishing occurrence would not report it later. Plainly it is a fiction.

Mark 16:1 to 16:8 Restored

And when the sabbath was past, Mary Magdalene, and Mary the mother of James, and Salome came to mourn him. And very early in the morning the first day of the week, they came unto the sepulchre at the rising of the sun. And they said among themselves: *Who shall roll us away the stone from the door of the sepulchre?* And when they looked, they saw that the stone was rolled away: for it was very great. And entering into the sepulchre, they saw a young man sitting on the right side, clothed in a long white garment; and they were affrighted. And he saith unto them: *Be not affrighted: Ye seek Jesus the Nazarene, which was crucified: he is not here: behold the place where they laid him. But go your way, tell his disciples that they must go into Galilee to be safe.* And they went out quickly, and fled from the sepulchre; for they trembled and were amazed: neither said they any thing to any man; for they were afraid.

The False Ending

Mark 16.9 – 16.20

The remaining verses of Mark (Mk 9–20) were added a long time later. The reason why scholars know the last verses are false are:

- many manuscripts end at verse 8; many have just two sentences added to the end of verse 8; some have both the two sentences and the twelve verses:

- Eusebius and Jerome in the fourth century did not know of the added twelve verses:

- the style and vocabulary cannot possibly be first century.

Some who admit this say they replace Mark's original ending which was lost. That is not true. The gospel ends perfectly well in the middle of verse 8 before anyone knew of appearances. But, without the appearances, the resurrection has no basis, and so theologians have to claim that they are accidentally missing.

Nothing more need be said. The earliest gospel is unable to testify to the appearances. The reason is that it was written before Paul or some early editor of his epistles had invented them. Hence we end this commentary on Mark's gospel at verse 16:8.

CHRISTIANITY

The Early Church

The Jerusalem Church

The converts of the simple of Ephraim thought that the righteous would be raised from the dead on God's day of vengeance. When rumours circulated that the tomb of Jesus was empty, they jumped to the conclusion that Jesus had been resurrected as the first of the righteous. The early Christian writers prove this. In Revelation 1:5 Jesus is: *the first begotten of the dead, and the prince of the kings of the earth.* Here the author of Revelation also declares Jesus to be the nasi. Paul writes in 1 Cor 15:20: He is *risen from the dead, and become the firstfruits of them that slept.* Both quotations show that the first Christians thought that with Jesus the general resurrection had begun. In a religious hysteria maybe some of them thought they had seen the risen Jesus.

Undoubtedly the post-crucifixion followers of Jesus continued to believe what Jesus had believed when he was alive—the kingdom of God was about to start. When, in the beginning of Acts (1:6) the apostles ask the risen Jesus: *Lord, is this the time you are going to restore the realm to Israel?* they indicate that even after the death of Jesus they expected his mission to be that of a Jewish Messiah—to retrieve the Jewish kingdom from the enemy as a national saviour. The views of the Nazarenes are given explicitly in Acts 15:16 which reports James quoting Amos 9:11 on the restoration of the kingdom, to show that such a restoration was still expected. This was no other-worldly kingdom and James argues that there is no need to convert gentiles because they would be judged on entry to the kingdom. James was still expecting a Jewish superstate ruling the world.

Eusebius in his history of the church tells us that the Jerusalem Church continued to sacrifice in the temple and to keep the law even after the gentile churches had split away. Even in Acts 5:34–40 the Sanhedrin continues to accept the activities of the apostles. They were still Jews. The only difference in the two sets of beliefs was that the Nazarenes had put in an extra stage, that of the suffering and sacrifice of the Son of God before he returned on a cloud to inaugurate the kingdom.

Shortly after the crucifixion, as Acts 6:1,7 describes, the number of disciples in Jerusalem greatly increased. Few of these would have been gentiles though many were Hellenized Jews, considered as apostates or backsliders by the orthodox. Even a great company of priests joined the Nazarene sect. Orthodox Jews feared that the whole population would be converted. What was the reason for this astonishing success?

After the disciples' intial disappointment at Jesus's death, they convinced themselves that Jesus was not a warrior Messiah but was the suffering servant of Isaiah. Like Jesus, this scorned man was sentenced to a dishonourable death, remaining silent in his defence, and was killed but was rewarded with victory after death. Jesus had spread the word that the day of judgement was at hand, indeed twice in Matthew (Mt 16:28 and Mt 24:34) Jesus promised the kingdom in their lifetime to his disciples. The message that had evidently been fitfully received in his lifetime became compelling upon his death and the church benefited in apocalyptic hysteria.

The word Christianity was not used until about 50 AD in Antioch (Acts 11:26), a town which had a large Jewish population and must surely have had a substantial Essene community, accessible as it was to the new covenanters of Parthia as well as those of Palestine. In the move from Palestine into the Roman Empire the Nazarene movement began to mutate into the Christianity we now know, but its foundations in the manuscripts of Qumran seem clear. Christianity grew from a Palestinian mystic cult who knew they were elected by God to fight a holy war against the forces of darkness. Their leader led them into the holy war, they lost it and the leader was crucified.

Paul the Apostle to the Gentiles

No doubt there were several strands, such as Gnosticism, to the ultimate success of Christianity as a world religion but one of them recognized by the Christian churches was the evangelist, Paul who began his career as Saul, a brownshirt beating up Jesus's followers. Temple thugs, apparently led by Saul (Paul's name before his conversion), were employed by the Saducees to make havoc of the church, to arrest Nazarenes and to cast them into jail. But, though Saul was the leader, Luke says he merely watched the coats of Stephen's killers. The Sanhedrin, normally a tolerant and civilized body in spite of the New Testament picture, seems unlikely to have commissioned such action. They had no power over the temple guard, effectively agents of the Romans who saw the community of Nazarenes as revolutionaries.

Acts but not Paul says he was born in Tarsus—Paul wanted to be thought of as a full Jew. Only Acts, not Paul himself, speaks of the dramatic experience on the road to Damascus, Paul implying his conversion occurred in Damascus. In Acts 9:18–19 is told the story of how the scales fell from Paul's eyes giving him his sight, how he arose and was baptized and took food and was strengthened. He receives his sight because he has seen the errors of his ways—the miracle is a metaphor. He repents and is baptized and he receives the bread and wine—the messianic meal which spiritually strengthens him. Eschew miracles and think in Essenic terms and all is clear.

The coded significance of Paul's conversion is that Paul was a sinner—a man of darkness, metaphorically blind—and was converted. It is a parable expressed in Essenic terms invented by Luke. Paul does not mention the Ananias of Acts and Acts makes no mention of a visit to Arabia even though it must have been important because in his own account he goes there directly after his conversion without even visiting Jerusalem—according to Galatians 1:11 Paul started his ministry in Damascus stating (Gal 1:17–18) he had already been there but his visit to Jerusalem three years later was his first—directly contradicting the story given three times in Acts 9:1–28; 21:6ff; 26:12ff.

After three years in Damascus learning the new teaching (Gal 1:18), Paul escaped (2 Cor 11:32–33) apparently from the Arab governor of the king, Aretas (Harith), but really from Qumran where he had spent three years as a novice but failed to complete the novitiate because he lacked Essene humility—he goes to Jerusalem. After only 15 days there in which time he saw James and Peter but no other apostles he leaves and does not return for another 14 years (Gal 2:1). The true apostles really want nothing to do with him.

Paul says Arabia was governed by Aretas of Petra but on the face of it neither the Damascus in Syria nor Qumran, if that was meant, could have been governed by Aretas. We have it only from Paul, unconfirmed by other historians, that Aretas ever ruled the Syrian city of Damascus. Syria was a major Roman centre and the base of several Roman legions. It could never have been ruled, at this time, by Aretas.

Paul seems to say Damascus was in Arabia. The Arabia ruled by Aretas was not Syria north east of Judaea but Nabataea whose capital was Petra, the Rose Red City, south of the Dead Sea. The area west of the Dead Sea, extending to the plain of Jericho, was called Arabah even in Deuteronomy 1:7. Aretas possibly laid claim to this land. Nabataea was a Roman client state and since Arabah was mainly wilderness, the Romans probably did not care whether it was formally part of Judaea or Nabataea. We know that Aretas had a dispute with Herod Antipas over borders to the east of the Dead Sea and, when he attacked Peraea in 36 AD to punish Antipas, Aretas might have occupied most of the Dead Sea area. Vitellius, who had been sent to punish Aretas for attacking Herod Antipas, withdrew his army when Tiberius died just as Aretas had expected. Thereafter, the Romans would have been more likely to mollify Aretas than to sympathize with Antipas. Both were Roman puppets but Aretas was the more important as a buffer with Parthia, and controlling important trade routes through Petra to the east—the supply of perfumes, spices and drugs from the Arabian peninsula. Paul was converted sometime in the thirties. Paul's Damascus must have been Qumran, and it must have been briefly under the jurisdiction of Aretas, king of Petra.

So Paul was trained as an Essene—he claims for three years—but failed to complete the course. Nevertheless his training shows. Paul uses many Essene expressions including the word Belial, the Essene word for the devil which is used nowhere in the New Testament except in 2 Corinthians 6:14–15, a purely Essene passage: *What fellowship hath righteousness with unrighteousness? and what communion hath light with darkness? And what concord hath Christ with Belial?* Paul writes of a mystery and hidden wisdom in 1 Corinthians 2:7: *But we speak the wisdom of God in a mystery, even the hidden wisdom, which God ordained before the world unto our glory*, language we can see precisely in the scrolls. Nevertheless Paul wanted to be known as a Pharisee because they were better known as the philosophers of

Judaism, and not as an Essene who, if known at all were considered terrorists or—at the least—mad.

Paul left no stone unturned in deriding the true apostles. He boasts of his superiority to the apostles (2 Cor 11:5). They were merely Nazarenes, mostly converts of the simple of Ephraim, whereas he had been trained as an Essene. He denigrates them as false apostles (2 Cor 12–23), discredited them (Gal 2:6), ran down their speaking in tongues (1 Cor 13:1) and curses them (Gal 1:8–9). He declares the only authentic gospel is not of human origin and had not been taught him by anyone—the dead Jesus had himself supernaturally revealed it to Paul (Gal 1:11–12).

Knowing nothing about Jesus, Paul can say nothing about him, and confesses (2 Cor 12:1–4) what he does know comes from his visions. He confirms that Jesus was a descendant of David and was human (Rom 1:3) but he does not mention Jesus's father, nor does he name Jesus's mother in the only place he mentions her (Gal 4:4). Since Paul's epistles are the earliest surviving Christian writings, Paul's attestation (1 Cor 15:3–8) to the death, the resurrection and the appearances are the earliest we have. The only teaching of Jesus that Paul speaks of is that of the Eucharist (1 Cor 11:23–25), so this too is the earliest we have. Though Paul claims to be a Jew and Jews have one God only, he virtually deifies Jesus (Col 1:15–22) and he blames the Jews for Jesus Christ's death (Thess 2:14), if this epistle is Paul's. In other disputed epistles he describes the teachings of the true apostles about Jesus as fables (1 Tim 1:4;4:7; Tit 1:14) which are unimportant because faith is all that matters. The Jerusalem Church's answer to Paul's teaching might have been the Epistle of James as it was addressed to the twelve tribes of the dispersion—all Jews in the wider empire.

The Ebionites or poor men, were suppressed by the church as heretical but fragments of their believes remain in Heresies by Epiphanius. They say that Paul was not a Pharisee, his parents were gentile converts to Judaism, he went to Jerusalem as an adult, became a henchman of the High Priest and eventually sought fame by creating a new religion. Ebionites did not accept Paul's view that Jesus was divine but saw him as a human sent to begin the new era. They accepted the Torah, obeyed the Law of Moses and regarded themselves still as Jews. As the true successors to the Nazarenes it was they, not Paul, who transmitted the pure teaching of Jesus for their founders, Peter and James, had known Jesus in life. All of it sounds credible.

Paul was evidently not a Pharisee and his parents were godfearers, but he saw the advantages of being thought a pious Jew and he adjusted his biography accordingly. He taught that the Torah had been superseded by the death on the cross of a divine being, Jesus, in atonement of men's sins. Faith in this was the only way to be saved. These were the ideas of the mystery religions and Gnosticism. Paul reached this synthesis of ideas from paganism, the Essenes and from the Jewish scriptures. Paul could usurp the history of the Jews to use its long tradition as prophetic of his concept of Christianity with its dying and resurrected god of the mystery religions and its heaven descended redeemer of the Gnostics. Paul's stories were incredible—except to people influenced by paganism. And the Nazarenes had a lot of such people among them—the publicans and sinners—Jewish backsliders and apostates receptive to Hellenistic culture. They had flocked to John the Baptist and Jesus contrite and repentant as sinning Jews when they were expecting God's kingdom at any moment. When the kingdom failed to appear they were easily persuaded that their dead leader was the latest of the dying and resurrected gods of the mystery religions. Such thoughts, represented by Stephen and Philip, were anathema to orthodox Jews but were eagerly grasped by Paul.

There are signs in the New Testament that Paul was disliked by the Nazarenes. In Revelation 2:9 we find: *I know the blasphemy of those who say they are Jews and are not, but the synagogue of Satan.* The author possibly means Paul explicitly but certainly means those like him who had altered Jewish beliefs to suit pagans. Elsewhere in Revelation 13:1 the heads of the great beast which is Rome, have the name of blasphemy written on them. Revelations has been compiled from writings of different times. The implication here is that one of the earlier works was actually directed at the Hellenizers who were paganizing Nazarene beliefs.

The Roman Church

Less than 30 years after the crucifixion the Pauline gentile churches of Italy, Greece and Asia Minor, and the Gnostic churches of Libya and Egypt split from the Nazarene church in Jerusalem. The latter led by James the Just remained under the authority of the Sanhedrin and followed Judaic conventions. Only a few years before the Jewish War, the teachings of Paul had been rejected by James, but the Jerusalem Church lost most of its influence with the destruction of the holy city, and Paul's heretical teachings suddenly found themselves unopposed. The propagators of Christian beliefs became those who followed Paul and not those who had known Jesus and his original teaching. Indeed the main enemies of Jesus, the Herodians and the froward priests of Jerusalem, probably sought and found a new career after the destruction of the temple in the new Hellenized Judaism that was spreading into the empire. The Church directly associated with Jesus and his followers had so soon been disregarded.

For a long time there was no centre of Christianity at all, each of the churches founded in the world of the gentiles going its own way, but Romans were ready to try out religious novelties and the door was open for a metamorphosis into a new religion of a Jewish sect which revered a failed Jewish pretender. The centre of Christianity could now only be Rome where it developed as a gentile religion.

Views at variance with Paul's, like the Ebionites', were declared heretical by the gentile church though originally they had been orthodox. Were the works of the apostles Peter, James and John also suppressed? Why are the twelve apostles almost ignored in the gospels and in Acts, or treated as if they were complete idiots when they are mentioned? James, Jesus's brother, must have known his brother better than Paul. On the few brief instances when the gospels mention him they imply he thinks Jesus mad yet he succeeded Jesus as the leader of the

Nazarenes after the crucifixion. The church's answer to this oddity is that he was miraculously converted by the resurrected Jesus. One would have thought that he would therefore have been in great demand as a preacher of the power of the new faith like that other convert, Paul, but, apart from one epistle which seems to be genuine, his testimony did not suit the Pauline church so he was virtually erased from history.

A third century work the Recognitions of Clementine speaks of a tradition that Peter tells followers at Tripolis to believe only those who bring from Jerusalem the testimonial of Jesus's brother, James. Here it is Peter who warns of false prophets, and false apostles and false teachers, who indeed speak in the name of Christ but do the work of the devil. He could only have meant the Hellenizers who followed Paul.

The Acts of the Apostles is of course really the Acts of the Apostle Paul because other than an initial description of the period just after the crucifixion and although churches are mentioned, including that at Rome, that were not founded by Paul, there is little account of the work of the other apostles. Nothing is said about the fate of the Jerusalem Church. Indeed nothing is said about the fate of Paul himself, the story being left unfinished with Paul waiting for an Imperial decision.

The subsequent history of the Jerusalem Church is given by Eusebius quoting Hegesippus, the second century historian. Jesus was followed as leader by James, then Simeon (Jesus's cousin by Mary and Clopas), and finally by two grandsons of Jude, Jesus's brother, until the dispersion of the Jerusalem Church by Hadrian in 135 AD. Hegesippus tells how the Emperor Diocletian, concerned about possible pretenders to the Jewish throne, questioned the grandsons of Jude about their Davidic descent. Their poverty and their starving, calloused bodies convinced the Emperor they were no threat and they were released.

Some of the earliest Christian documents such as the Epistles of John tell us that even in those days many people did not believe that Jesus had come in the flesh— he was an apparition or a ghost. And there were those who doubted the divinity of Jesus. Heretics who denied it were persecuted by the Christians into extinction and, after the Christian triumph, all pagan religions were also rigorously driven into oblivion.

On the other hand, despite Christian mythology, persecution of Christians by the Romans only became serious in the third and fourth centuries, curiously enough on the eve of the Christian triumph. Origen, the respected father of the Church who only missed canonization because of his enthusiasm for chastity, declared that the number of martyrs was very inconsiderable. Many martyrs were Jewish martyrs—messianic Jews, some of whom might have been Christians. Christian martyrs like Maximilianus of Theveste were not executed because the Roman state particularly objected to Christians but because they refused to do military service or carry out military duties. Whether you were a Christian or not, the penalty was death!

In the Shadow of Darkness

From the Maccabees to the intertestamental period two powerful, opposing forces wrenched Judaism—Hellenization and Apocalypticism. The future for the Hellenizers was in the Graeco-Roman world but the future for the Apocalypticists was in the day of judgement and the kingdom of God. Hellenization was loosening the ties of the Laws of Moses to permit Jews more freedom within the Empire whereas Apocalyticism was cleaving rigidly to the Jewish Law, separating from the gentiles and the unholy, and preparing for the coming kingdom.

The pragmatic Pharisees restricted the spread of Hellenization within the Jewish community leading to modern Rabbinic Judaism. Apocalyptic Jews meanwhile prepared for the kingdom, fighting and dying until the Romans felt they had to destroy the temple and with it the priestly parties to punish their rebellious clients. The outcome was paradoxical. The converts of one apocalyptic sect—the Nazarenes—were to factionalize, break loose from the bounds of Judaism, adapt to the Hellenistic culture and eventually form a new world religion based on Jewish tradition and using the Jewish Holy Books. All of this was done in the name of Jesus, the Prince of the Nazarenes, a man who thought he would see perfectly holy and sincerely repentant Jews ruling the world in the kingdom of God. Instead Jews were sidelined and persecuted as deicides, while Christianity—Judaism for gentiles—was to conquer, and through wanton destruction of ancient knowledge, inaugurate a thousand year dark age which still leaves its shadow.

The Real Gospel Message

If Jesus was not the Son of God then is Christianity totally written off? Is there nothing in the death of Jesus on the cross? There is but Jesus's real message has been lost in the mysticism of organized Christianity.

Jesus died expecting a supernatural external power to act on his behalf. When nothing happened he died feeling forsaken. The lesson is that *there are no external supernatural powers whether for good or for evil.* Jesus died on the cross as a warning to everyone not to fear or put faith in such external powers. His death is a perennial warning against the folly of passing the buck of wrongdoing to agents beyond ourselves. It is folly because it absolves us of reponsibility for what we do and allows men—many of them unscrupulous—to use God to control our lives.

If there are no supernatural powers there is no God. What then of the conviction of many people that their prayers are answered? They are! Prayer is answered from within. People pray for strength and often they feel that they get it, but no external god miraculously puts additional strength within them because they prayed. The strength was there all the time waiting to be tapped. Prayer untaps it. Other people feel an urge to commit murder or burn down public buildings and claim they are commanded or controlled from outside. It is a cop out! God—or the devil—is within.

If the story of Jesus had any meaning it was meant to redeem us from the belief that help—or evil—comes from beyond. The lesson was never heard. It was immediately lost by the rush of those convinced that the external power was still coming but now led by the resurrected Son. After 2000 years and increasingly sophisticated savagery to each other and the world we live in, we are in a position to address the truth. No external powers impel people to evil or to good. No external power makes us destroy. We do good or evil ourselves. *For from within, out of the heart of men, proceed evil thoughts, adulteries, fornications, murders, thefts, covetousness, wickedness, deceit, lasciviousness, an evil eye, blasphemy, pride, foolishness: All these evil things come from within, and defile the man. If a man be truly repentant his heart is pure. If a man be not perfect in his heart then he shall not be cleansed whether he be washed by rivers, yea and even by seas.*

Our gods and devils are within us and that is where we must seek them and confront them.

THE SECRET TESTAMENT REVEALED

The beginning of the gospel of Jesus, which is God's saviour, whom they called Barabbas, which is the son of my father, for he was the Son of God, the messiah, a prince of Israel.

Even as it is written in the prophets: *The voice of one crying: in the wilderness prepare ye the way of the Lord, make straight a high way in the desert for our God. For the glory of God shall be revealed and all flesh shall see it together. Saith the Lord: Behold, I send my messenger, which shall prepare the way before me, and the Lord whom ye seek shall suddenly come to His temple.*

John appeared baptizing and preaching a baptism of repentance for the remission of sins, saying: *Ye shall not enter the water to be cleansed unless ye turn from your wickedness, obeying the law, as He commanded you through Moses to do by His holy spirit; for all who transgress His word are unclean.*

John was the nasi, which is prince of the congregation, the Master of the Nazarenes, the successor of the nasi Zacharias, but, being humble, called himself Enosh, which is man; and he was great in the sight of the Lord drinking neither wine nor strong drink for he was also nazir, which is consecrated to God. He went before God to make ready a righteous people ready for the day of the Lord. And multitudes from Judaea and from Jerusalem went out to him and were baptized in the river Jordan, confessing their sins.

And John announced: *After me one who is mightier than me will come, and I am not fit to stoop and untie the latchet of his sandals. I have baptized you with water but he will baptize you with the holy spirit for it is written: Who may abide the day of His coming? For he is like a refiner's fire. And I will come near to you in judgement. When the day cometh it burneth as a furnace, and all the proud and all that work wickedness shall be stubble, and the day that cometh shall burn them up; but ye that fear my name shall gambol as calves of the stall and ye shall tread down the wicked, for they shall be ashes under the souls of your feet.* Being interpreted, the angel Michael cometh to judge the world.

Now it came to pass in those days that a man of repute, a Nazarene, being thirty years old, was baptized by John in the Jordan, and Zadokite priests came from Damascus by the Dead Sea. One was the Angel of the Lord and one was the Satan and John was Joshua, the High Priest. And the Angel spake: *Be silent, all ye flesh, before the Lord, for he is raised up out of his holy habitation.*

And the Zadokites asked: *Where is he who shall be the prince of the congregation, a sceptre who shall smite all the children of Seth, for it is written: a star shall come out of Jacob and a sceptre shall rise out of Israel.* And straightway the Nazarene rose up from the water. And the Angel said: *Saith the Lord of hosts: If thou wilt walk in my ways, and if thou wilt keep my charge, then thou shalt also judge my house, and shalt also keep my courts, and I will give thee places to walk among these that stand by. Hear now, behold, I bring forth my servant the branch; and I will remove the iniquity of that land in one day.*

And Joshua, the High Priest spake: *Saith the Lord of Hosts: I have set my king upon my holy hill of Zion. Thou art my son. This day have I begotten thee. Ask of me and I will give thee the nations for thine inheritance, and the uttermost parts of the earth for thy possession. Thou shalt break them with a rod of iron. Thou shalt dash them in pieces like a potter's vessel. Thou shalt be called the Son of the Highest, for thou shalt go before the face of the Lord to prepare His ways, to give knowledge of salvation unto His people by the remission of their sins, through the tender mercy of our God, whereby the branch from on high hath visited us, to give light to them that sit in darkness and in the shadow of death, to guide our feet into the way of peace.*

Joshua, the High Priest, sprinkled him with water, making the sign of the cross on his forehead so that he would be among the saved, as in the previous visitation. They named him Joshua, the salvation of God, which is Jesus.

And Joshua, the High Priest, spake unto Jesus: *The Lord saith: Behold, I have caused thine iniquity to pass from thee, and I will clothe thee in pure apparel.* And they gave him holy objects and clothed him in clean white garments, and the spirit of the Lord settled on him.

And Joshua said unto Jesus: *Master, now lettest thou thy servant depart in peace, according to thy word, for mine eyes hath seen salvation which thou hast prepared before the face of the people, a light to lighten the darkness and the glory of thy people Israel.*

And Jesus replied saying: *My soul doth magnify the Lord, And my spirit hath rejoiced in God my saviour. For He hath regarded the low estate of His servant: and from henceforth all generations shall bless Him. For He that is mighty hath done great things; and holy is His name. And His mercy is on them that fear Him from generation to generation. He hath shewed strength with his arm; He hath scattered the proud in the imagination of their hearts. He hath put down the mighty from their seats, and exalted them of low degree. He hath filled the hungry with good things; and the rich He hath sent empty away. He hath holpen his servant Israel, in remembrance of His mercy, as He spake to our fathers, to Abraham, and to His seed for ever.*

And Jesus blessed God, saying: *Blessed be the Lord God of Israel; for He hath visited and redeemed His people, And hath raised up an horn of salvation for us in the house of His servant David, as He spake by the mouth of His holy prophets which have been since the world began, that we should be saved from our enemies, and from the hand of all that hate us, to perform the mercy promised to our fathers, and to remember His holy covenant, the oath which He sware to our father Abraham, that He would grant unto us that we, being delivered out of the hand of our enemies, might serve Him without fear, in holiness and righteousness before Him, all the days of our life.*

And the Satan tested him with promises of finery and glory. And they all called out: *The Lord bless Jesus, the salvation of God, and all the men of the lot of God who walked perfectly in His ways*; and they all called: *Truly, Truly.* And they called out: *The Lord rebuke thee Satan, and all the men of the lot of Satan for their wickedness and the darkness of their deeds; yea, the Lord that hath chosen Jerusalem rebuke thee Satan, for is not this brand now plucked out of the fire?* And they all called: *Truly, Truly.*

And he was tested by the Satan that he should stumble on the path to the kingdom of God. But Jesus was not tempted, rejecting all that Satan offered. And he said: *Get thee behind me, Satan; for it is written, Thou shalt worship the Lord thy God, and Him only shall thou serve.* And when the devil had ended all the temptation, he departed from him for a season.

Immediately the spirit driveth him into the wilderness; for the battle for the kingdom would be forty years and for every year a day and a night he fell down before the Lord in the wilderness lest Belial should triumph and the Lord look upon the stubbornness of His people, or on their wickedness, or sin, and destroy them. And the Lord hearkened to him that His people should enter the kingdom which He had promised. And the Angel and God's elect ministered to him.

Now Herod the tetrarch feared John as a disturber of the multitudes, which counted him a prophet and were ready to do anything he should advise, and went out to lay hold on him, and would have him killed. He took him and bound him, and held him in prison in the fortress of Machaerus. But Herod feared John knowing he was a righteous one and an holy one for he was an Essene, and kept him safe. And when he heard him, he heard him gladly.

And this is what became of John. Herod sought to divorce his wife, the daughter of the king of Petra, that he might marry a niece, his brother Philip's wife, Herodias. And John said unto him: *It is not lawful that a man should marry his niece, nor even the mother of his brother's children; yet thou wouldst uncover her nakedness though she hath four children, thy brother's.* And when he heard him Herod was sore perplexed, and Herodias had a quarrel against him; and Herod resolved to rid himself of John. And a day came that Herod on his birthday, made a supper to his lords, high captains, and chief estates of Galilee, for he was at war with the king of Petra who would avenge the wrong done to his daughter, and he said unto Herodias: *Whatsoever thou shalt ask of me, I will give it thee.* And straightway she came in with haste unto the king, saying: *I will that thou give me by and by the head of John the Baptist.* And the king sent an executioner, and commanded his head to be brought for Herodias's sake. And he went and beheaded him in the prison, and brought his head unto Herod. And he gave it to Herodias in a charger. And when his disciples heard of it, they came and took up his corpse, and laid it in a tomb.

After that John was handed over in Peraea, Jesus took up his mantle that had fallen from him, and he came thence into Galilee, by the sea that he might baptize, preaching the gospel of the kingdom of God. saying: *The time is now come; the kingdom of God is at hand; hear this gospel; repent and be saved by God's mercy.*

And many heard, and Jesus spake unto them saying: *As the fishes that are caught in an evil net even so are the sons of men snared in an evil time. But, saith the Lord: I shall send for many fishers, and they shall fish them and I will bring them again unto their land that I gave unto their fathers. If thou wilt, follow me and thou shalt be fishers of men.*

For the day of judgement is like a net cast into the sea which drew in fishes of every kind, clean and unclean. The fisher gathered the clean into baskets but cast away the unclean. In like wise shall the wicked be separated from the righteous in the end time. For the prophet Enoch said: The Most High will deliver the evil ones to His angels for punishment for they have oppressed His children but the righteous and elect shall be saved.

Cast ye nets on the wrong side and ye will gather in empty but cast ye nets on the right side and ye will gather in full, for every nation on earth will yield to the good net. And they were astounded by his teaching, for he taught them with authority; and only a king's word hath authority.

And he saw Simon and Andrew his brother, and Jesus said unto each of them: *Wilt thou repent and be a fisher of men?* And they followed him and were baptized. And he saw James the son of Zebedee, and John his brother; and Jesus said unto each of them: *Wilt thou repent and be a fisher of men?* And they left their father Zebedee with the hired servants, and went after him and were baptized.

Jesus repared to the house of his disciple Simon, with Andrew and James and John, to offer the repentant the sacred meal of bread and new wine. But Simon's wife's mother would do naught for them for she was sick out of fear.

And speaking to them Jesus said: *When Hezekiah, the king, was sick unto death, he wept and prayed to the Lord: I have walked before thee in truth and with a perfect heart, and have done that which is good in thy sight. And the Lord heard his prayer and said: I will add unto thy days fifteen years. And I will deliver thee and this city out of the hand of the king of Assyria.*

For God hath created man to govern the world, and has appointed for him two spirits in which to walk until the time of His visitation, the spirits of truth and deceit. For all who walk in the spirit of truth, it shall be healing, a long life and fruitfulness; but for all who walk in the spirit of deceit it shall be blindness of eye and dullness of ear and stubbornness of heart, All who walk in this spirit shall suffer a multitude of plagues and everlasting damnation by the avenging wrath of the fury of God. But God has ordained an end of deceit and at the time of the visitation He shall destroy it forever.

And he came and took her by the hand and rebuked her for her trembling knees, and did tell her privily that the Lord was as a fortified wall and as an iron bar against all destroyers for He would lead His elect in the way of everlasting life and in His paths. And the fever of fear left her; and she arose and ministered unto them.

Again Jesus taught of the kingdom, saying: *A certain mason was stricken and his right hand did wither. He was unable to practise his trade and his children hungered. And he prayed to the Lord, saying: I was a mason seeking my bread with mine hands, and for my sins mine hand hath withered; now my children hunger. Lord, forgive me my sins for I repent my vanity and deceit. And the Lord saw that he was sincere and said to the man: Stand forth and stretch forth thine hand; and it was made whole like as to the other. Then saith the Lord God: Go thou to Zion, and there thou shalt lay for me a stone, a foundation which shall not rock or sway in its place, for thine hand is now whole. And that foundation shall be an house of perfection and truth in Israel forever. And thou shalt inscribe it: who trusts will fear not; for this is my covenant with mine elect. The man did as the Lord commanded, and he did build a house of perfection to the Lord. And the house was the foundation of a great kingdom. In like wise shall the right hand of power be restored to Israel, and God shall build a kingdom, and the scornful men in Jerusalem shall be swept away. And judgement shall be the line and righteousness shall be the plummet.*

And his fame spread abroad throughout all the region. And Jesus went about teaching in synagogues and preaching the gospel of the coming kingdom. Again Jesus came with his disciples to Capernaum and preached in the synagogue. Now there was a man who feared the retribution of the authorities who called out: *Let us alone, Jesus the Nazarene! You will destroy us all. Thou art the messiah, come to drive out the sons of Seth.* But Jesus halted him commanding: *Be silent! The spirit of Belial possesses thee. Let it be driven out.* And the disciples beat him sorely until the perverse spirit left him, and badly torn he cried: *Enough.* And they were all amazed, questioning among themselves: *What thing is this that the perverse spirit called him? For with authority and power he commandeth.* And His fame spread. And great multitudes gathered together unto him. And a large number of people followed him and many came from Judaea and the other side of the Jordan and even from Tyre and Sidon when they heard of his teaching of the kingdom.

And as Jesus spake the word to his disciples four men passed down a pallet on which lay an enfeebler of the law, and a profaner of the House of God, for he was Matthew the Levite, a tax collector, a Sadducee, who had been praying on a housetop. Recognizing him Jesus said: *Saith the Lord: if ye turn away from following me then will I cut off Israel out of the land which I have given them and this house, which I have hallowed for my name, will I cast out of my sight; and though this house be never so high yet shall everyone that passeth by it hiss for they forsook the Lord, their God. Yet if my people which are called by my name, shall humble themselves, and pray and seek my face, and turn from their wicked ways then will I hear their prayers in heaven and will forgive their sins and will heal their land. Repent, Levite, discard your pallet and rise.* And the enfeebler of the law was overcome with shame, smiting his breast and calling out: *God be merciful to me, a sinner*; and he was healed of his polluted spirit. He cast aside his pallet and was received by the righteous. At this they were all amazed and glorified God, saying: *We never saw anything like it.* But the Sadducees were filled with fear for many of their number heard of it also and repented to follow after Matthew.

Now when he admitted the Levite to the sacred meal of bread and new wine at his house some of his disciples said: *How is it that he eateth and drinketh with publicans who are the worst sinners?* Hearing this Jesus said: *They that are whole have no need of a doctor, but they that are sick. They that are full have no need of bread, but they that hunger. I come not to call the righteous but sinners to repentance. Saith the Lord: My people have been lost sheep; their shepherds have caused them to go astray.*

And he spake unto them a parable, saying: *What man of you, having a hundred sheep, and having lost one of them, doth not leave the ninety and nine in the fold and go after that which is lost, until he find it? And when he hath found it, he layeth it on his shoulders rejoicing. And when he cometh home, he calleth together his friends and neighbours, saying unto them, Rejoice with me, for I have found my sheep which was lost. Likewise there shall be joy in heaven over one sinner that repenteth, more than over ninety and nine of God's righteous which need no repentance. To the lost sheep of the house of Israel this son of man is called and today hath one who was lost been found.*

And Jesus expounded all things to his disciples, saying unto them: *This son of man will impart knowledge with discretion for it is written in the prophet Isaiah: Hear ye indeed, but understand not; and see ye indeed, but perceive not. Make the heart of this people fat, and make their ears heavy, and shut their eyes; lest they see with their eyes, and hear with their ears, and understand with their heart, and convert, and be healed. But with the remnant which held fast to the commandments of God, He made His covenant with Israel forever, revealing to them the hidden things in which all Israel had gone astray, the mysteries of amazing truth, that they may walk perfectly together in all that has been revealed to them. Unto you therefore it is given to know the mystery of the kingdom of God: but unto them that are without, all these things are done in parables: That seeing they may see, and not perceive; and hearing they may hear, and not understand.*

And it was the fast of the fifth month when pious Jews mourned the destruction of the temple by Nebuchadnezzar singing lamentations. And his disciples of the simple of Ephraim come and say unto him: *The Pharisees eat not wine nor meat, and wail and confess and repent. Why doest thou say unto us, brake bread and drink wine?* And Jesus said unto them: *God's righteous will enter into His kingdom and feast. Hearken ye to the word of the Lord: I am returned unto Zion and will dwell in the midst of Jerusalem.*

The kingdom of God is like a bridegroom who is coming to the wedding feast, for it is written: I will betroth thee unto me for ever; yea, I will betroth thee unto me in righteousness, and in judgment, and in lovingkindness, and in mercies. I will even betroth thee unto me in faithfulness: and thou shalt know the Lord. After the fast the wedding feast begins, and the Lord is even now at the door. Can the children of the bridechamber fast, while the bridegroom is without? This bread and new wine is like unto a wedding feast, for when the bridegroom is without, the fast is ended. Those hypocrites fast for the loss of the temple, when God drove Israel into captivity for her sins. But, on the third day of His visitation, the Lord will raise up to the righteous a new temple not built by hands.

No man seweth a piece of new cloth on an old garment: else the clean will be mixed with the unclean contrary to the commandments of God. Better to wear the old until the tailor delivereth the new. And no man putteth new wine into old bottles: else the new wine doth burst the bottles, and the wine is spilled, and the bottles will be marred: but new wine must be put into new bottles, for only thus may the righteous partake of it. If these be what men do, will God do other wise? The Lord will destroy the polluted temple and in three days will raise up for the righteous a holy temple, as the prophet Ezekiel has written.

And they brought backsliders to him, children of Israel who had turned away from God to the gods of the Greeks, for they now sought the kingdom of God. And his disciples rebuked those that brought them. But when Jesus saw it, he was much displeased, and said unto them: *Suffer all the children to come; forbid them not; for of such is the kingdom of God. Truly, Whosoever is not one of the children shall not enter therein, save who the Lord taketh unto him and blesseth.*

And some of the simple of Ephraim came forth, and began to question with him, seeking of him a sign from heaven that the kingdom was indeed nigh. And he sighed deeply in his spirit, and saith: *Why doth this generation seek after a sign? Truly, no further sign shall be given unto this generation save the day of God's vengeance.* And he left them.

Then Jesus took apart into the hillside twelve men of his disciples that they might be with him until he should ordain them and send them forth as shepherds to gather the lost sheep. There was Simon the brigand whom he called Rocky, for he was immovable; James and John, sons of Zebedaeus, whom he called the sons of tumult and the sons of the wild ox for they were untameable; Andrew, Simon's brother, Philip and Nathanael, his brother, sons of Tholomaeus, the Zealot; Matthew, the Levite; Thomas the twin; James the son of Alphaeus, Judas Thaddaeus which is broadchest; Simon the Zealot; Judas Iscariot which is the knifeman and the deliverer. And Jesus said: *You shall be twelve apostles as a covenant to Israel, one for each tribe.* And Jesus judged them for qualities and ordained Peter, James and John as pillar apostles who might act as priests when they praised God, and three more he appointed in their place that there were still twelve as a covenant to Israel.

And he resolved to baptize many of the simple of Ephraim. and he called unto him disciples and began to send them forth by two and two. Nor would they need take anything for their journey, no scrip, no bread, no money in their purse, neither two pairs of sandals, nor two coats, save only a staff; for the elect would provide. And Jesus commanded them: *Go not into the way of the gentiles and into any city of the Samaritans enter ye not: but go rather to the lost sheep of the house of Israel. And when ye stand before them, take no thought beforehand what ye shall speak, neither do ye premeditate: but whatsoever shall be given you in that hour, that speak ye: for it is not ye that speak, but the holy ghost. And as ye go preach, saying: The kingdom of God is at hand, repent that God might heal thee that thou might join the elect of God. Ye shall not have gone over the cities of Israel, till the kingdom be come.* And thereby gained they power over sickness and unclean spirits.

And he took a child, and set him in the midst of them, and he said unto them: *Whosoever shall receive one of these children, the children of Israel, receiveth not this son of man but Him that sent him. For it is not for this son of man to receive the children into God's kingdom, but God alone. But whosoever shall mark them in baptism with the cross of water in God's name, because they belong to Him, truly, they shall not lose their reward when the kingdom comes. And whosoever shall offend any one of these little ones that believe that God cometh, yea, any one of these simple of Ephraim that have repented and entered the pure water of baptism, it is better for him that a millstone were hanged about his neck, and he were cast into the sea; for his punishment at God's appointed time will be an hundred fold.*

So they went out and preached repentance; and they cast out demons and cured sick people admitting them into the new covenant by the sacrament of baptism.

And Jesus travelled through the countryside and villages speaking to them at even, when the sun did set lest the authorities did hear of it. And they that sought the kingdom brought unto him all that dispaired of it, and some that hated it, those blind and dumb and diseased, and those possessed with devils. And all gathered together and he healed many that were sick of divers diseases, and cast out many devils that hated God's kingdom; and suffered not the devils to speak, because they knew him as the prince.

And he took the multitude of repentant apart into a desert place, for it was Pentecost, the festival for the renewal of the new covenant. And many ran afoot thither out of the camps, and came together unto him. And Jesus, when he came out, saw much people, and was moved with compassion toward them, because they were as sheep not having a shepherd. And he commanded them to make all sit down by companies upon the green grass. And they sat down in ranks, by hundreds, and by fifties, and by tens.

And James and John, the priestly apostles, come unto him, saying: *Master, we would that we may sit, one on thy right hand, and the other on thy left hand, in the glory of God's kingdom.* But Jesus said unto them: *Ye know not what ye ask. Can ye drink of the cup of righteousness? and be baptized with the baptism of repentance?* And they said unto him: *We can.* And Jesus said unto them: *So be it. Withal shall ye be baptized, but to sit on my right hand and on my left hand in the kingdom is not mine to give. God only knowest what He hath prepared, seeing your works. Ye know that they which wish to* rule over the gentiles exercise lordship over them; and their great ones exercise authority upon them. But so shall it not be among you: but whosoever will be great among ye, shall be your servant. And whosoever of ye will be the chiefest, shall be servant of all. If any man desire to be first, the same shall be last of all, and servant of all; for even he that is greatest among ye shall be your servant, and whosoever shall exalt himself shall be abased and he that shall humble himself shall be exalted. For ye come not to be served, but to serve.

And he said unto those who had repented: *Your baptism is a binding oath, which dedicates you to god until ye shall enter His kingdom. Yet ye might not say to your father or mother: I have vowed myself to God, therefore that which I wouldst provide for thee is corban (which is a gift to the temple), and thou must go destitute, for my vows to God are binding to me unto death. For corban is merely a tradition whereas Moses said, Honour thy father and thy mother; and, Whoso curseth his father or mother, let him die the death. Make not the word of God of none effect, for no man on pain of everlasting death might swear to depart from God's law. If ye wouldst please God, your tradition must be to reserve for your household that which it needs, then give your surplus to God.* For there were those of Israel who would seek atonement from God by vowing the money of their family to the temple treasury.

And he stood on a high place, and began to teach them many things, blessing the men of the lot of God, saying: *Blessed are the poor and humble in spirit: for theirs is the kingdom of heaven. Blessed are the meek: for they shall inherit the earth. Blessed are they which do hunger and thirst after righteousness: for they shall be filled with everlasting life. Blessed are they merciful unto the poor: for they shall obtain God's mercy. Blessed are the pure in heart: for they shall see the face of God. Blessed are the peacemakers: for they shall be called the children of God. Blessed are they that mourn: for they shall be comforted in everlasting light.*

Ye are the light of the world. Come, ye blessed, inherit the kingdom prepared for you from the foundation of the world: For I was an hungred, and ye gave me meat: I was thirsty, and ye gave me drink: I was a stranger, and ye took me in: Naked, and ye clothed me: I was sick, and ye visited me: I was in prison, and ye came unto me. Then the righteous answered him, saying: *Master, when saw we thee an hungred, and fed thee? or thirsty, and gave thee drink? When saw we thee a stranger, and took thee in? or naked, and clothed thee? Or when saw we thee sick, or in prison, and came unto thee?* And Jesus in turn answered, saying unto them: *Truly, inasmuch as ye have done it unto one of the least of these my brethren, ye have done it unto me.*

Then he cursed them of the lot of Satan, saying: *Depart from me, ye cursed, into everlasting fire, prepared for the devil and his angels: For I was an hungred, and ye gave me no meat: I was thirsty, and ye gave me no drink: I was a stranger, and ye took me not in: naked, and ye clothed me not: sick, and in prison, and ye visited me not.* Then Satan led other voices answering him, saying: *Lord, when saw we thee an hungred, or athirst, or a stranger, or naked, or sick, or in prison, and did not minister unto thee?* Then Jesus answered them, saying: *Truly, inasmuch as ye did it not to one of the least of these, ye did it not to me. And these shall go away into everlasting punishment: but the righteous into life eternal.*

Rejoice, and be exceeding glad, ye righteous: for great is your reward in heaven: for so rewarded were the prophets which were before you. Be ye therefore perfect, even as your Father which is in heaven is perfect. After this manner therefore pray ye: Our Father which art in heaven, hallowed be thy name. Thy kingdom come, thy will be done in earth, as it is in heaven. Give us this day our daily bread. And forgive us our sins, as we forgive those that sin against us. And lead us not into temptation, but deliver us from evil: For thine is the kingdom, and the power, and the glory, for ever. Truly. For if ye forgive men their trespasses, your heavenly Father will also forgive you: But if ye forgive not men their trespasses, neither will your Father forgive your trespasses, and ye shall find the gates of the kingdom closed.

Ye are forgiven and baptized as repentant sinners but think not that the gates of the kingdom are wide open to ye all; think not that the glory of God's kingdom meaneth an end to the law. This son of man is come not to destroy the law, or the prophets: this son of man cometh not to destroy, but to fulfil. For till heaven and earth pass, one jot or one tittle shall in no wise pass from the law, till all be fulfilled. Whosoever therefore shall break one of these least commandments, and shall teach men so, he shall suffer everlasting death: but whosoever shall do and teach them, the same shall be called into the kingdom of heaven, and have everlasting life. For except that ye hunger for righteousness, ye shall not enter into the kingdom of heaven.

And many people gathered unto Jesus, who stood with Peter, and James, and John the brother of James. And behold, there cometh from the crowd one of the rulers of the council, Jair, which is God's enlightened. And he announced: *The bridegroom is without, but woe to us all; for His betrothed, a damsel coming to the age of marriage hath been ravished by the stranger, and must die.* While he yet spake, a voice said: *The damsel is dead: why troublest thou the Master any further?* And the people wept and wailed. And Jesus saith unto them: *Why make ye this ado, and weep? She shall live, and find favour once more with the bridegroom. Be not afraid, only believe; the damsel is not dead, but sleepeth.* And a voice, which was Satan, laughed him to scorn. And Jesus looked up, praying: *Lord, forgive thy children their trespasses, hear them repent and enter the sacred water. If it be thy will, let Israel be restored in thy sight. Talitha cumi, Damsel, I say unto thee, arise.* And a voice announced: *the damsel is arisen, and walketh.* And Jesus said unto them: *the bridegroom awaiteth.* And they were astonished with a great astonishment. And he charged them straitly that no man should know it. And he commanded that they should partake of the holy meal of the just.

And the day was now far spent, and he called out: *O ye poor ones! be ye ordained that God shall save you! The children shall have bread and be filled.* And a voice answered him: *Whence can a man in the wilderness be satisfied?* And he asked: *How many loaves have ye?* And the disciples called out: *Seven.* And he said: *This is the bread of life. If ye be repentant, ye who partake of it shall be filled and have everlasting life.* And he commanded the people to sit down on the ground. And when he had taken the seven loaves, he looked up to heaven, and blessed, and brake the loaves, and gave morsels to his disciples that they might eat. And his disciples then took up, and blessed, and set before them twelve baskets of morsels of bread, full. And they did all eat, and were filled of the bread of life. And they that did eat of the loaves were about four thousand.

And he charged them, saying: *Take heed, beware of the leaven of the Pharisees, and of the leaven of the Sadducees, for leaven can be sour, and yield foul bread; or it can be sweet, and yield choice bread. If ye would have the bread of everlasting life, hearken ye not to these others, for they know not the kingdom of God.*

And Jesus said to them a parable. *A certain woman had an issue of blood twelve years, and had suffered many things of many physicians, but none could heal her. And eventually she had spent all that she had, and was still nothing bettered, but rather grew worse. And a gazer came to her, and said: Doest thou know, and believe in your whole heart that thou hast only one Lord, the Lord thy God? And the woman wept and confessed her sins, and begged forgiveness, and repented. And the gazer forgave her sins. And when she stepped from the holy water, straightway the fountain of her blood was dried up; and she felt in her body that she was healed of that plague and cleansed. And this son of man says unto you, truly Israel shall be healed of her plague.*

And Jesus led a service of dedication of the repentant to God. And he said: *God's judgement will be as a refiners fire, and the wicked shall be burned as stubble; but for the righteous it shall be as warm milk; for the wicked will be punished in a fire that never shall be quenched: but the righteous shall be rewarded in everlasting life. Ye repentant, remain chaste and think not adulterous thoughts, so that ye be not tempted into sin, for the kingdom is nigh, and every one shall be salted with fire.*

And he called out, chanting: *If thine hand offend thee, cut it off. It is better for thee to enter into life maimed, than having two hands to go into hell.* And they all sang: *Into the fire that never shall be quenched: Where their worm dieth not, and the fire is not quenched.*

And again he called out, chanting: *And if thy foot offend thee, cut it off. It is better for thee to enter halt into life, than having two feet to be cast into hell.* And they all sang: *Into the fire that never shall be quenched: Where their worm dieth not, and the fire is not quenched.*

And again he called out, chanting: *And if thine eye offend thee, pluck it out. It is better for thee to enter into the kingdom of God with one eye, than having two eyes to be cast into hell fire.* And they all sang: *Into the fire that never shall be quenched: Where their worm dieth not, and the fire is not quenched.*

And Jesus said: *Lord, let thy will be done; we are ready; salt us with thy fire, for every sacrifice shall be salted with salt. Salt is good: but if the salt have lost His saltness, wherewith will ye season it? Have salt in yourselves, and have peace one with another.* And being interpreted this is the meaning of the parable: Ye shall be salted with the salt of the covenant of thy God. Ye would not suffer thy lustful eye, or thy grasping hand, to tempt you into sin. Howbeit then that God would admit you into His kingdom, who do not hold to His covenant with His chosen? Know ye then that ye must honour God's covenant with His elect for it is good, for if no one honoureth it then what other good is there? And last of all he said: *Ye of His new covenant! for ye, God hath ordained that the first is last and the last first. Ye who are most humble, ye who serve God, and his brothers, ye shall be first. And ye who would be first, ye vainglorious and ye who love esteem above all else, ye shall be last. For, all are judged in the fire of God's judgement. Put the covenant in your hearts and have peace with each other.*

And the apostles gathered themselves together unto Jesus, and told him all things, both what they had done, and what they had taught. And they told Jesus of the cities at which they had to shake off the dust of their feet. And Jesus said: *Woe unto thee, Chorazin! It shall be more tolerable at the day of God's vengeance for Sodom and Gomorrha than for you. Woe unto thee, Bethsaida! It shall be more tolerable at the day of God's vengeance for Sodom and Gomorrha than for you. For if God's mighty works had been done even in Sodom and Gomorrha, they would have repented long ago in sackcloth and ashes. But ye reject God's message.*

And when he was gone forth into the way, there came running, a Sadducee, and kneeled to him, and asked him: *Good Master, what shall I do that I may inherit eternal life? And Jesus said unto him: Why callest thou me good? there is none good but one, that is, God. Thou knowest the law of Moses; obey God's commandments.* And he answered and said unto him: *Master, all these have I observed from my youth.* Then Jesus beholding him loved him, and said unto him: *One thing thou lackest: go thy way, sell whatsoever thou hast, and give to the poor, and thou shalt have treasure in heaven: and come, take up the cross of baptism, and be of God's elect.* And he was sad at that saying, and went away grieved: for he had great possessions. And Jesus looked round about, and saith unto his disciples: *How hardly shall they that have riches enter into the kingdom of God! It is easier for a camel to go through the eye of a needle, than for a rich man to enter into the kingdom of God.*

And one of the scribes came, and hearing them reasoning together, and perceiving that he answered them well, asked him: *What shall I do to inherit eternal life?* And Jesus said: *What is written in the law?* And he answering said: *The Lord our God is one Lord, and thou shalt love the Lord thy God with all thy heart, and with all thy soul, and with all thy strength, and with all thy mind, and, thou shalt love thy neighbour as thyself.* And Jesus said: *Thou hast answered right; for this is more than all whole burnt offerings and sacrifices. Thou art not far from the kingdom of God.*

And one of the multitude said: *Master, I have brought unto thee my son, a man which hath a dumb spirit, for he denieth the kingdom of God.* And Jesus would have him brought unto him. And when they brought him unto them, Jesus said unto him: *If thou canst believe, all things are possible to him that believeth. The kingdom of God cometh.* But he raged and foamed at them, saying: *You will bring us all trouble; we have no king but Caesar.* Straightway they did tare him, until he fell on the ground. And he cried, and they rent him sore; and he was as one dead, insomuch that many said: *He is dead.*

A man came to Jesus calling out and decrying him, for he was a leper, a high priest of the temple. And Jesus, moved with anger, put forth his hand and smote him, and they set their hands upon him, until he was beseeching him, and kneeling down to him. And he was cleansed. And Jesus took him and angrily ordered him: *Go seekest thou God with all thine heart and soul; repent and doest that which is good and right before Him as He commanded by the hand of Moses. And sayest thou nothing to any man, lest thy demon trip thee.* And forthwith he sent him away. But he walketh in the way of deceit, and goeth out and telleth the authorities, and blazeth abroad the matter, insomuch that Jesus could no more openly enter the city for fear of the authorities, for the towns were unsafe, and soldiers sought them; and they were without, in desert places.

Now when John had heard in the prison these works of Jesus, he was troubled, and sent two of his disciples, And said unto him: *Art thou he that should come, or do we look for another?* Jesus answered and said unto them: *Go and shew John the blind receive their sight, and the lame walk, the lepers are cleansed, and the deaf hear, the dead are raised up, and the poor have the glad tidings preached to them. But whereunto shall I liken this generation? It is like unto children sitting in the markets, and calling unto their fellows, and saying: We have piped unto you, and ye have not danced; we have mourned unto you, and ye have not lamented. For John came offering the bread and wine, and they say, He is mad. And this son of man came offering the bread and wine, and they say, Behold a friend of publicans and sinners. Is the wisdom of the just of her children?* And they departed.

And Jesus began to say unto the multitudes: *What went ye out into the wilderness to see? A reed shaken with the wind? A man clothed in soft raiment? They that wear soft clothing are in kings' houses. A prophet? Yea, and more than a prophet. For this is he, of whom it is written, Behold, I send my messenger, which shall prepare the way before me. Truly, among them that are born of women there hath not risen a greater than John the Baptist. Notwithstanding he that is least in the kingdom of heaven is greater than he. And the signs are that from the days of John the Baptist until now the kingdom of heaven suffereth violence, and the violent take it by force.*

And king Herod heard of it, for his name was spread abroad. And he asked: *is John the Baptist burst free from prison and again preaching sedition?* They replied: *No, it is Elias or that prophet.* But Herod said: *if it cannot be John, whom I imprisoned, then his successor is risen.*

And in the night, rising up a great while before day, he went out, and escaped into a solitary place, and there prayed for he was sore afraid. And Simon and they that were with him followed him. And when they found him, they said unto him: *They seek thee everywhere.* And he said unto them: *Let us go away into another part, that I might start afresh: for therefore came I forth.* And they escaped into another part.

And it came to pass, as the Nazarenes went before Herod's soldiers that they went through corn fields, and it was the sabbath day; and his disciples hungered and said: *Would that we could enjoy this grain but on the sabbath day we cannot do that which is not lawful.* And Jesus said unto them: *Have ye never read what David did, when he had need, and was an hungred, he, and they that were with him? How he went into the house of God in the days of Ahimelech the high priest, and did eat the shewbread, which is not lawful to eat but for the priests, and gave also to them which were with him? Or how that the priests offer up lambs in sacrifice on the sabbath, thereby profaning it, but are blameless.* And he said unto them: *The sabbath was made for man, and not man for the sabbath: Therefore man, the son of man, is Lord also of the sabbath.*

And his disciples understood and began, as they went, to pluck the ears of corn. But then yet others among them found fault saying, Master: *Howbeit that we can do that which is not lawful for we eat with unwashen hands that which is unclean and pleaseth not the Lord?* And he said unto them: *Hearken every one of you, and understand. It is written in the book of Isaiah, Wherefore the Lord said, Forasmuch as this people draw near me with their mouth, and with their lips do honour me, but have removed their heart far from me, and their fear toward me is taught by the precept of men. There is nothing from without a man, that entering into him can defile him: but the things which come out of him, those are they that defile the man. If any man have ears to hear, let him hear.*

And they looked one to the other, and Jesus said: *Are ye yet without understanding? Ye are cleansed by the holy waters, for ye have repented that ye be received into the kingdom. Do ye not then perceive, that whatsoever thing from without entereth into God's perfect, it cannot defile him because it entereth not into his heart, but into the belly, and goeth out into the draught, purging all meats?* And he said, *That which cometh out of the man, that defileth the man. For from within, out of the heart of men, proceed evil thoughts, adulteries, fornications, murders, thefts, covetousness, wickedness, deceit, lasciviousness, an evil eye, blasphemy, pride, foolishness: All these evil things come from within, and defile the man. If a man be truly repentant his heart is pure. If a man be not perfect in his heart then he shall not be cleansed whether he be washed by rivers, yea and even by seas.*

And thence he fled into the borders of Tyre and Sidon, and entered into an house, and would have no man know it; but he could not be hid. For a certain woman, whose daughter had an unclean spirit, heard of him, and came and fell at his feet. The woman was a Greek, a Syro-Phoenician by nation, but she had sought the kingdom of God, and had become a proselyte of the Nazarenes. And she besought him privately that he would cast forth the devil out of her daughter, and prepare her for the kingdom. But Jesus said unto her: *Let the children first be filled: for it is not meet to take the children's bread, and to cast it unto the dogs. For I am come to save the children of Israel alone.* And she answered and said unto him: *Yes, Master, yet the dogs under the table eat of the children's crumbs*, for she knew there was a time to come when the gentiles would be called. And he said unto her: *For this saying, so be it; the devil is gone out of thy daughter.* And he sent disciples to heal her. And when she was come to her house, she found the devil gone out, and her daughter laying bruised upon the bed.

Jesus fled with his disciples to the Great Sea to the north in the land of the gentiles where Herod could not go; but a vengeful throng followed him, and about Tyre and Sidon, this multitude came angrily unto him. And he charged his disciples, that a small ship should wait on him because of the multitude, lest they should mob him and harm him. For, though he had straitly charged them not to make him known and they had fallen down before them, unclean spirits had exposed him, saying: *Thou art the Son of God.* And they did scream in anger when they saw him, and pressed upon him for to take hold of him, as many as had scourges to avenge them.

And the multitude cometh together again, besieging them in his house so that they could not so much as bring in bread for the holy meal. And his companions were fearful and went to lay hold on him, for they said: *He is beside himself.* And some of the Nazarenes said: *He hath Beelzebub, and by the prince of the devils casteth he out devils.* And Jesus answered them, saying: *If this son of man hath Beelzebub he could not have cast out a single demon. Yet ye have repented. How can Satan cast out Satan? If a house be divided against itself, that house cannot stand, not even Satan's house. And if a kingdom be divided against itself, that kingdom cannot stand, not even Satan's kingdom. And if Satan rise up against himself, and be divided, he cannot stand, but hath an end. Yet he doth not end. How then can Satan be cast out? When a strong man is armed and defendeth his house, his possessions are in peace; but when a man stronger than he first binds him then takes away his weapons, his possessions are lost. In like wise must we be stronger than Satan and bind him. But if a kingdom be divided against itself, that kingdom cannot stand; and if a house be divided against itself, that house cannot stand. The house of Israel must needs stand as one if Satan is to be bound and cast out. And for this reason all sins shall be forgiven unto the sons of men who repent, save a blasphemy against His holy spirit.*

He that is not with God is against God; and he that gathereth not with God scattereth. For whosoever shall do the will of God, the same is my brother and sister in God's remnant. But whoever hath slandered the congregation shall be expelled from among them and shall return no more. And whoever hath murmured against the authority of the community shall be expelled and shall not return. Every idle word that men speak, they shall give account of in God's day of vengeance, for by thy words thou shalt be justified and by thy words thou shalt be condemned. And they murmured no more.

And Jesus goeth out, and his disciples, into the region of Caesarea Philippi. And he saith unto them: *Whom say ye that this son of man is?* And Peter answereth and saith unto him: *Thou art the nasi, the prince of the many.* And Jesus said: *Blessed art thou Simon barjona, for is not the prince the messiah at the holy meal of the saints? And saith the Lord: Is not this a brand that must be plucked from the fire? This son of man must lead you upon Jerusalem.* And Peter was perplexed, saying he was beside himself. And Jesus taught them that, at God's appointed time, Israel would have a prince, and a priest, and a prophet; and, like Moses, the prince, and the priest, and the prophet would lead them into a promised land. And they heard him and wondered. And he charged them that they should tell no man. And from that time forth he began to teach them that they must go unto Jerusalem, and must suffer many things in the coming battle, even death but, on the third day would rise again in God's kingdom, with God's elect; for God had sent His messiah. And he spake that saying privily.

And they stood before him, saying: *Before the messiah cometh, it is written, Elias must first come.* And he told them: *Elias truly cometh first, and restoreth all things; but, that Elias is indeed come, and they have done unto him whatsoever they listed, as it is written of him.* For he was imprisoned. And Peter took him, and began to rebuke him but when he had turned about and looked on his disciples, he rebuked Peter.

And after six days of purification in readiness Jesus taketh with him Peter, and James, and John, and leadeth them up into an high mountain apart by themselves. And Peter said to Jesus: *Master, this is a good place. Let us make here three tabernacles; one for thee, and one for Moses, and one for Elias.* And they built a smoky fire, and he appeared, transfigured, before them, in raiment, shining exceeding white. And there appeared the prophets Elias and Moses: and they were talking with Jesus. And there was a cloud that overshadowed them: and a voice came out of the cloud, saying: *This is my beloved Son: hear him,* as it is written that the prophet must be heard. And Satan came and he rebuked him, saying: *Get thee behind me, Satan: for thou savourest not the things that be of God, but the things that be of men.* And, suddenly, when they had looked round about, they saw no man any more, save Jesus only with themselves.

And as they came down from the mountain, he charged them that they should tell no man what things they had seen, for first they must go up to Jerusalem. And there they would commence the battle for the kingdom in which they would die; but God would resurrect them all, the righteous, on the third day, as it is written in the prophet Hosea. And they kept it close, with themselves.

And returning thence to Galilee he came to some of his disciples with a great multitude about them, and the disciples questioning with each other. And straightway all the people, when they beheld him, were greatly amazed that he had appeared again in Galilee, for Herod would imprison him, and running to him saluted him.

And when he had called the people unto him with his disciples also, he said unto them: *Whosoever would be saved, let him take the cross of repentance in baptism, obey God and fear not. For whosoever will save his life shall lose it; but whosoever shall lose his life for God's sake, the same will save it. For what shall it profit a man, if he shall gain the whole world, and lose his own soul? Or what shall a man give in exchange for his soul? Whosoever therefore shall be ashamed* to take the cross of repentance in this adulterous and sinful generation, of him also shall the Son of man be ashamed, when he cometh in the glory of God with the holy angels.

And addressing a multitude, Jesus spoke a parable, saying: *Hearken! A sower went out to sow and as he sowed, some seed fell by the wayside and perished, for it is written: Those who hearken not to the voice of God shall be meat unto the fowls of the air. And some seed fell upon stony ground, and immediately it sprang up, and because it had no depth of earth, when the sun was up, it was scorched because it had no root and it withered away, for it is written: Their stock shall not take root in the earth. And some seed fell among thorns and the thorns sprang up and choked them and they yielded no fruit, for it is written: Sow not among thorns. But other seed fell on good ground and did yield fruit that increased and brought forth, some thirty, and some sixty, and some an hundred, for it is written: The seed shall be prosperous and the ground shall give her increase. He that hath ears to hear, let him hear.*

And he said unto them: *Is a candle brought to be put under a bushel, or under a bed and not to be set on a candlestick? The Lord hath seven eyes and, from Him, nothing is hid. For there is nothing hid, which shall not be manifested to the elect in God's kingdom; neither was any thing kept secret, but that it should come abroad in God's kingdom. If any man have ears to hear, let him hear.*

And he said unto them: *Take heed what ye hear: with what measure ye mete, it shall be measured to you: and unto you that hear shall more be given. For if what ye mete is God's will then it pleaseth the Lord and ye shall be rewarded with everlasting life.*

And Jesus said: *Hearken ye to this other parable: the kingdom of God is as if a man cast good seed upon the earth, and he slept and went not by night or day and cared not how the seed should spring up and grow. But the earth beareth fruit of herself and when the blade was sprung up so too were tares. And the man's servants said unto him: wilt thou that we go and gather up these tares? But he said: Nay; lest while ye gather up the tares, ye root up also the wheat with them. Let both grow together, first the blade, then the ear, then the full corn in the ear. But when the fruit is ripe, straightway putteth forth the sickle, because the harvest is come. Then separate the wheat from the tares that it be saved for me, and put the tares in a heap that they may be destroyed by fire. For it is written: Put ye in the sickle, for the harvest is ripe, for their wickedness is great.*

Then shall Jerusalem be holy and there shall no strangers pass through her any more. And the Lord shall roar from Zion; and the heavens and earth shall shake; but the Lord will be a refuge unto his people and a strong hold to the children of Israel. For David said to the Lord: thine hand shall find out all thine enemies; thy right hand shall find out those that hate thee. Thou shalt make them as a fiery furnace in the time of thine anger. Thou shalt swallow them up in thy wrath; and the fire shall devour them. Their fruit shalt thou destroy from the earth, and their seed from among the children of men. And the Lord said to David: My covenant shall stand fast with thee; and thy seed will I make to endure forever.

And Jesus still speaking in parables, said: *Whereunto shall we liken the kingdom of God? It is like a grain of mustard seed, which, when it falleth to earth, is less than all the seeds that be in the earth; but when it groweth up it becometh greater than all the herbs and shooteth out great branches; so that all the fowls of the air may lodge under the shadow of it. For it is written: the Lord will bring down the high tree and will exalt the low tree; and it shall bring forth boughs and bear fruit, and under it shall dwell all fowl of every wing; in the shadow of the branches thereof shall they dwell.*

And when he was alone, they that were about him asked of him the parables. And he said unto them: *Know ye not the parable of the sower? and how then will ye know all parables? The parable being interpreted is this. The sower soweth the word of God. And these are they by the way side, who understandeth not the word, and to whom Satan cometh immediately and catcheth away that which was sown in their hearts. And these are they likewise in which the word is sown on stony ground, who immediately receive the word with gladness, but have no root in themselves, and so endure but for a time, and are tempted by hypocrisy. And these are they in which the word is sown among thorns, and the cares of this world, and the deceitfulness of riches, and the lusts of other things entering in choke the word, and it becometh unfruitful. And these are they in which the word is sown on good ground, such as hear the word, and receive it, and bring forth fruit, some thirtyfold, some sixty, and some an hundred. For it is written in the prophet Zechariah, in the word of the Lord: The seed shall be prosperous; the vine shall give her fruit, and the ground shall give her increase, and the heavens shall give their dew; and I will cause the remnant of this people to inherit all these things. And ye righteous shall receive that inheritance when the kingdom comes.*

And Jesus said: *There is no man, that hath left brethren, or sisters, or father, or mother, or wife, or children, and hath left them and house or lands, for God, but he shall receive an hundredfold; and in the world to come, everlasting life. The poor, who are last in earth shall be first in heaven.*

And he came into his own country, and his disciples follow him. And when the sabbath day was come he began to teach in the synagogue. There came thither his brethren and his kinfolk. And he read from the book of the prophet Isaiah: *The spirit of the Lord God is upon me, because the Lord hath anointed me to preach good tidings to the poor; he hath sent me to bind up the brokenhearted, to proclaim liberty to the captives, and the recovering of sight to the blind, and the opening of the prison to them that are bound; to proclaim the acceptable year of the Lord, and the day of vengeance of our God. This day is the scripture fulfilled in your ears.* And he told them of the kingdom to come calling for their repentance. And many hearing him were astonished saying: *Whence hath this man this authority? Is not this the mason; and his brethren and sisters, are they not with us?* And Jesus said unto them: *Who are my brethren? For the sons of Levi slew their brethren which trespassed against the Lord. My brethren are these which hear the word of God and slayeth the deceiver.* And Jesus could do no mighty works because of their unbelief, and he said: *A prophet is not without honour, save in his own country and among his own kin; nor is a physician able to cure those who know him.* And they were offended at him. They went out to lay hold on him, for they said: *He has gone mad to preach such things.*

And they departed thence, and passed through Galilee; and he would not that any man should know it, lest Herod should send soldiers. For he taught his disciples, and said unto them: *It pleaseth the Lord that Jerusalem, the brand, is plucked from the fire, and the battle for the kingdom shall then be fierce. If this son of man is delivered into the hands of men, and they kill him, fear ye not; for he shall rise with you all on the third day, for so it is written.*

And Jesus told them to prepare boats that they might cross the sea into Decapolis. And he said unto them: *They that hate you have said to the Lord: Let us cut off thy people from being a nation. But God is a jealous God and taketh vengeance against his adversaries. He pursueth them with His tempest and terrifieth them with His storm. For the Lord hath His way in the whirlwind and the storm; He rebuketh the sea and dries it up. The sea is the people of the waters, and though they be mighty and likewise many, even so shall they be cut down and shall pass away. For of them it is written: the waters saw thee, O God, the waters saw thee; they were afraid: the depths also were troubled. The clouds poured out water: the skies sent out a sound: thine arrows also went abroad. The voice of thy thunder was in the heaven: the lightnings lightened the world: the earth trembled and shook. Thy way is in the sea, and thy path in the great waters, and thy footsteps are not known. Thou leddest thy people by the hand of Moses and Aaron. Thou alone spreadest out the heavens, and treadest upon the waves of the sea. Know ye then that ye shall have no fear of the storm, for when God sent to Jonah a great wind into the sea, and there was a mighty tempest in the sea, so that the ship was like to be broken, and the mariners were afraid, Jonah was gone down into the ship, and he lay, and was fast asleep, and the men roweth hard to bring it to the land, but they could not, for the sea wrought, and was tempestuous against them.*

Even so, when ye are pressed by your enemies, let not your cry be: The Lord sleepeth. Lord carest thou not that we perish? It is written: The Lord of Hosts shall defend them, for as they draw near unto the gates of death, they cry unto the Lord in their trouble, and He cometh and bringeth them out of their distresses. He stilleth the noise of the seas, the noise of their waves. He rebuketh the sea and maketh the storm calm, so the waves thereof are still. And He bringeth them into the haven where they wouldst be, and stilleth the tumult of the people. The haven is the kingdom of God. Be ye of good spirits; be ye of good cheer; for the dawn soon breaketh and the storm will calm, and the kingdom come with everlasting light. And Jesus bound his disciples to get into boats, saying: *Pass over to the other side.* And when morning came they were at the other side.

And he went through the midst of the region of Decapolis. And they found a man who would betray them, and sought the reason, but he was deaf to their questions and would hardly speak. And they took him aside from the multitude, and they laid hands upon him, and put fingers into his ears, and spat upon him, and fastened his tongue with string. And looking up to heaven, Jesus sighed, and saith unto them: *Ephphatha!* that is: *draw it out!* And straightway he begged them to cease, his ears were opened, and the string of his tongue was loosed, and he spake plain. And Jesus charged him that he should tell no man of them. And they were beyond measure astonished, saying: *He hath done all things well: he maketh both the deaf to hear, and the dumb to speak.*

And they were in the way going up to Jerusalem, and Jesus took to one side the apostles and said: *Behold, we go up to Jerusalem; and ye shall confront the gentiles: ye will suffer hardships and even death in the battle for the kingdom; but yet, if ye be killed, on the third day ye shall rise again in God's kingdom.* And they were amazed. And Jesus went before them; and they followed, afraid.

And he said unto them: *Truly, there be some of them that stand here, which shall not taste of death, till they have seen the kingdom of God come with power. For the kingdom of God is at hand unto this generation, and they might be still live when the kingdom comes. And both sinner and righteous shall depart in the terrible day of God's vengeance, but the righteous alone will be resurrected on the third day.*

And Jesus saw John and some disciples beating a man, and asked: *Has this man an unclean spirit? Is he an enemy of the kingdom of God?* And John answered him, saying: *Master, we saw him punishing one who decried you, and we forbade him because he followeth not us.* But Jesus said: *Forbid him not. For if this man shall speak for God, though he be not repentant, he speaketh not evil of God's kingdom. For he that is not against us is on our part.*

And he arose from thence, and cometh into the coasts of Judaea by the farther side of Jordan. And he taught his followers what he was about. And he asketh them: *Is it lawful for a man to put away his wife?* And they said: *Moses suffered to write a bill of divorcement, and to put her away.* And Jesus answered and said unto them: *For the hardness of your heart he wrote you that precept. But, if ye wouldst be perfect, know ye from the beginning of the creation God made them male and female. For this cause shall a man leave his father and mother, and cleave to his wife; and they twain shall be one flesh: so then they are no more twain, but one flesh. What therefore God hath joined together, let not man put asunder. Let us go up to Jerusalem, that the bride might be freed, and the bridegroom enter in. He that hath ears to hear, let him hear.* Being interpreted, Jesus spoke of the marriage of God and Israel. For God hath made a covenant with His people, Israel; and they shall be like unto a bridegroom and a bride. They are joined together by God, and might not be put asunder by another.

And when they were come to Judaea to Jericho, they that received tribute money came to Peter, and said: *Doth not your master pay tribute?* And when he was come to tell his master, Jesus asked: *What thinkest thou, Simon? of whom do the kings of the earth take custom or tribute? of God's children, or of strangers?* Peter saith unto him: *Of strangers.* Jesus saith unto him: *Then are the children free. Notwithstanding, shouldst thou go to the river, and cast an hook, and take up the fish that first cometh up; and when thou hast opened his mouth, shouldst thou find a piece of money, that take, and give unto them for tribute.* For he knew no man would catch such a fish and the tribute would go unpaid.

And the Sadducees tried to incriminate him, and they say unto him: *Master, we know that thou art true, and carest for no man: for thou regardest not the person of men, but teachest the way of God in truth: Is it lawful to give tribute to Caesar, or not? Shall we give, or shall we not give?* But he, knowing their hypocrisy, said unto them: *Why tempt ye me? The answer is not a secret. Bring me a penny, that I may see it.* And they brought it. And he saith unto them: *Whose is this image and superscription?* And they said unto him: *Caesar's.* And Jesus answering said unto them: *Render to Caesar the things that are Caesar's, and to God the things that are God's.* And they marvelled at him, for he meant that God had appointed a covenant with the people of His land. Though Caesar was a mighty king, he could make no claim to what is God's.

And seeing a fig tree afar off having leaves, but no fruit, for the time of figs was not yet, Jesus said: *See ye this fig tree, it beareth no fruit, for it is not the season for figs; but as her branch is yet tender, and putteth forth leaves, ye know that summer is near, and the harvest time of fruit is nigh. So ye in like manner, when ye shall see the signs, know ye that the end time is nigh, even at the doors. This fig tree hath oppressed the children, and it shall not bear fruit, Nay, not ever; for God cometh to establish a new order in which the vine shall be fruitful and the fig barren. Have faith in God. For whosoever shall say unto this mountain: Be thou removed, and be thou cast into the sea; and shall not doubt in his heart, but shall believe that those things which he saith shall come to pass; he shall have whatsoever he saith. Therefore this son of man telleth ye, What things soever ye desire, when ye pray, believe that ye receive them, and ye shall have them. And when ye stand praying, forgive, if ye have ought against any: that your Father also which is in heaven may forgive ye your trespasses. But if ye do not forgive, neither will your Father which is in heaven forgive your trespasses.* And he took a knife and stripped it of its bark. And his disciples saw it.

And as he went out of Jericho with his disciples and a great number of people, an unclean spirit, one of those blind to the the kingdom of God, heard that it was Jesus, the Nazarene, and began to cry out, and say: *Jesus, thou wouldst be a king, a son of David.* And many took hold of him, and charged him that he should hold his peace. And he lost his garment in the commotion, and he cried the more a great deal: *thou wouldst be a son of David, the messiah.* And Jesus stopped, and commanded him to be called. And they took the blind man, saying unto him: *Get up, he calleth thee.* And they raised him and pulled him to Jesus, and beat him, and by and by he said: *Have mercy on me, Master.* And Jesus said unto him: *By thy works shalt thou be justified. If thou wouldst be saved, repent and be baptized, for the kingdom is entered only by those who follow the way.*

And coming unto Jerusalem, Jesus looked up to the city, and spake: *Ye princes of strangers make haste and come down out of the city; for today shall be prepared a pure house for the Lord, and He shall abide therein.* And the people of Jerusalem came out to welcome Jesus joyfully. And Jesus said unto them: *This day is salvation come to this house; for God's chosen are come to seek and to save that which had perished, the lost House of the children of Israel. It shall be cleansed of the name of the strangers, and that half which is the twofold part shall be returned, but the fourfold part shall the Lord redeem from those foreign flatterers.*

For Herod received not his twofold part from God but went into a far country to receive for himself this kingdom, and to return. But his citizens hated him, and sent a message after him, saying: We will not have this man to reign over us. And it came to pass, that when he was returned, having received the two parts of the kingdom, that he commanded these servants to be called unto him, saying: Those mine enemies, which would not that I should reign over them, bring hither, and slay them before me. And he did slay them. And his two brothers similarly received a single part each, making the four parts of the kingdom. And the half shall be returned to the Lord, and then the fourfold parts, while they as a recompense shall suffer everlasting torment.

And they clamoured that he overthrow the strangers, for they expected the kingdom immediately to appear. And as they heard these things, he added and spake a parable, because he was nigh to Jerusalem. Saith he: *And when that nobleman went to the far country he called his ten servants and said unto them: Occupy till I come, for on my return I shall be a king and shall collect my taxes from ye and ye shalt collect them for me. No man shall yield less than a pound, for all men can earn this, but those who yield up more will I reward as my tax-collector. And it came to pass, that when he was returned, having received the kingdom, then he commanded these servants to be called unto him, to whom he would collect taxes, that he might know how much every man had yielded. Then came the first, saying: Lord, thy servant hath raised ten pounds; for he had bullied and extorted money as his master's servant. And he said unto him: Well, thou good servant: have thou now authority over ten cities. And the second came, saying: Lord, thy servant hath raised five pounds; for he had extorted also. And he said likewise to him: Be thou over five cities. And another came, saying: Lord, behold, here is one pound, which your servant yieldeth; for he was a just man. And the king was much annoyed for he was an austere man, taking up that he laid not down,* and reaping that he did not sow, and he said: *You deliver up to me only that which any man yieldeth. And he said unto them that stood by: Take from him all that he hath, and give it to him that hath the ten cities. And the seven other servants also had failed to raise a surplus, and said unto him: Lord, he already hath ten cities. And the king answered, saying: So be it, for unto every one which hath shall be given; and from him that hath not, even that he hath shall be taken away from him.*

And Jesus said: *But God hath decreed that at His appointed time, when He comes in judgement, the wicked shall receive their just recompense, and the poor and downtrodden will receive their just reward, for unto every one which hath shall be given; and from him that hath not, even that he hath shall be taken away from him.* Being interpreted, he meant in the kingdom of God. And when he had thus spoken, he went before, ascending up to Jerusalem.

And when they came nigh to Jerusalem, unto Bethphage and Bethany, at the mount of Olives, he sendeth forth two of his disciples, and saith unto them: *Go your way into the village over against you: and as soon as ye be entered into it, ye shall find a colt tied, whereon never man sat; loose him, and bring him. And if any man say unto you: Why do ye this? say ye that the nasi hath need of him; and straightway he will send him hither.* And they went their way, and found the colt tied by the door without in a place where two ways met; and they loose him. And certain of them that stood there said unto them: *What do ye, loosing the colt?* And they said unto them even as Jesus had commanded: and they let them go.

And being in Bethany Jesus sat at meat in the house of Simon the leper, which is a nobleman which opposed them but was baptized as repentant. And Jesus told a parable, saying: *A priest declared a certain rich man as a leper, and, according to the law, he had to leave the city and live with the lepers. And there cometh unto him a woman, his wife, having an alabaster box of ointment of spikenard very precious; and she brake the box, and poureth it on his head, praying to the Lord that he be cured. And there were poor lepers standing by, and they had indignation within themselves. And they murmured against her, saying: Why was this waste of the ointment made? For it might have been sold for more than three hundred pence, and used for us all. But the lepers knew not that the poor shall live forever. And the rich man gaineth nought from his expensive unction, for perchance he saveth his skin but surely he loseth his soul.* And he turned to Simon saying: *Yet this leper hath gained everlasting life for he hath given all he hath to the poor and taken his cross of baptism in repentance.*

And the ruler of Judaea had sent out soldiers to punish the Jews. And Jesus taught, saying: *Israel did rend her clothes in sorrow, for God choseth not the stranger as ruler of Israel. The stranger was like unto a man with an unclean spirit, desireth of destroying the Son of God, and was mighty, such that no man could bind him, no, not with fetters or with chains, neither could any man tame him, save God alone. But, God will tame them, because the children of Israel have rent their hearts and repented.* And they took arms and went out to confront those whom they hated. And coming nigh unto a mountain, there was there a great herd of swine feeding in the valley of the Qidron. There were about 2000 of them for they were a legion. And they came at them from the mountain, by surprise, cutting them with stones and darts hurled from high, and others caught those who tried to shelter from the stones and cut them down with swords. And ran them down, pulled them in pieces, mangled them, and chopped them down. And some were put in chains, and they besought in loud voices for them to torture them not, to spare them. But they heard them not, and some were choked to death in the waters of the brook, and others besought him that they might be with him and others escaped to Caesarea. And they that fed the swine fled, and told it in the city, and told what was befallen.

And the Sadducees and Pharisees said: *What manner of man is this?* And, behold, they came out and besought him to depart from them; for they were taken with great fear. And Jesus said: *Sing ye unto the Lord a new song in the assembly of all the saints: Praise ye the Lord. Let the children of Zion be joyful in their king; for the Lord taketh pleasure in His people; He will beautify the meek with salvation. Let the saints exult in His glory with two edged swords in their hands; to execute vengeance on the nations; to bind their kings with chains, and their nobles with fetters of iron; to execute upon them the judgement written: this honour have His saints. Praise the Lord.*

And they brought the colt to Jesus, and cast their garments on him; and he sat upon him. And many spread their garments in the way: and others cut down branches off the trees, and strawed them in the way. And they that went before, and they that followed, cried, saying: *Osanna, Free us, Son of David; Blessed be the king that cometh in the name of the Lord.* And some Sadducees standing by said unto him: Master rebuke thy disciples. And Jesus replied: *Should not these children proclaim, then would these stones cry out;* for children are banim and stones are abanim. And Jesus entered weeping into Jerusalem.

And they surrounded the temple and Jesus, going in, forbade the priests to do ought; and they began to cast out them that sold and bought in court the temple, and overthrew the tables of the money changers, and the seats of them that sold doves. And would not suffer that any man should pass through the temple. And he said unto them: *Is it not written, Behold, a day of the Lord cometh. In that day there shall be no more a Canaanite in the house of the Lord of Hosts.* And the chief priests heard it, and said: *Yet it is written in Isaiah: Mine house shall be called an house of prayer for all peoples?* And Jesus answereth, saying: *Hold ye these strangers to the covenant of the Lord? It is indeed written: My house shall be called of all nations the house of prayer? but the Lord also saith: Ye have made it a den of thieves. Therefore will I cast you out of my sight.* And the chief priests were sore displeased, and when they saw the children of Israel crying in gratitude in the temple, and saying: *Osanna, Son of David,* they said unto him: *Hearest thou what these say?* And Jesus saith unto them: *Yea; have ye never read: Out of the mouth of babes and sucklings hast thou ordained strength because of thine enemies, that thou mightest still the enemy and the avenger.* And they knew not how to answer.

And the chief priests say unto him: *By what authority doest thou these things? and who gave thee this authority to do these things?* And Jesus answered and said unto them: *I will also ask of you one question, and answer me, and I will tell you by what authority I do these things. The baptism of John, was it from heaven, or of men? answer me.* And they reasoned with themselves: If we shall say, From heaven; he will say, Why then did ye not believe him? But if we shall say, Of men; they feared the many thronging about: for all men counted Jesus, that he was a king indeed. And they answered and said unto Jesus: *We cannot tell.* And Jesus answering saith unto them: *Then ye need not me to tell you by what authority I do these things.*

And Jesus said: *And have ye not read this scripture: The stone which the builders rejected is become the head of the corner. This is the Lord's doing; it is marvellous in our eyes. This is the day which the Lord hath made; We will rejoice and be glad in it.* And the stone stands for God's righteous who are poor and downtrodden.

And Jesus began to speak to the chief priests by parables, saying: *A certain man planted a vineyard, and set an hedge about it, and digged a place for the winefat, and built a tower, and let it out to husbandmen, and went into a far country. And at the season he sent to the husbandmen a servant, that he might receive from the husbandmen of the fruit of the vineyard. And they caught him, and beat him, and sent him away empty. And again he sent unto them another servant; and at him they cast stones, and wounded him in the head, and sent him away shamefully handled. And again he sent another; and him they killed, and many others; beating some, and killing some. Having yet therefore one son, his wellbeloved, he sent him also last unto them, saying: They will reverence my son. And the son evicted the wicked husbandmen and returned the vineyard to the hands of his father.*

And they knew that he had spoken the parable against them. And the priests were outraged, and they said unto Jesus: *We do God's works according to Moses and God rewards us. How are we wicked?*

And Jesus answered: *What think ye? A certain man had two sons; and he came to the first, and said, Son, go work today in my vineyard. He answered and said, I will not: but afterward he repented, and went. And he came to the second, and said likewise. And he answered and said, I go, sir: and went not. Whether of them twain did the will of his father?* They say unto him: *The first.* Jesus saith unto them: *Truly, that the publicans and the harlots go into the kingdom of God before you. For God trusted his works to you but ye did it not. And when John came unto you in the way of righteousness, and ye believed him not. But they that had refused God's works, the publicans and the harlots, believed him and repented with baptism: and ye, when ye had seen it afterward, believed him not, that ye might repent.* And the priests understood and would have laid hold on him, but feared to for many people reverenced him.

The Sadducees, which say there is no resurrection, tried to confound Jesus, saying: *Master, Moses wrote unto us, If a man's brother die, and leave his wife behind him, and leave no children, that his brother should take his wife, and raise up seed unto his brother. Now there were seven brethren: and the first took a wife, and dying left no seed. And the second took her, and died, neither left he any seed: and the third likewise. And the seven had her, and left no seed: last of all the woman died also. In the resurrection therefore, when they shall rise, whose wife shall she be of them? for the seven had her to wife.* And Jesus answering said unto them: *Ye err because ye know not the power of God. For when they shall rise from the dead, they neither marry, nor are given in marriage; but, as it is written in Enoch, they are as the angels which are in heaven. Nor know ye the book of Moses, else ye would have read how in the bush God spake unto him, saying, I am the God of Abraham, and the God of Isaac, and the God of Jacob? He is not the God of the dead, but the God of the living. Their rising up on the third day is like one who awakens from sleep. Ye therefore do greatly err.*

And they hoped they might turn the multitude against him, who believed the messiah was the son of David; and, knowing he was an orphan, they asked him: *How canst thou be a son of David when thou hast not a father?* And Jesus answered and said: *Why do the scribes say that the messiah is the son of David? For David, the psalmist, himself said by the holy ghost, in the scriptures: The LORD said to my Lord: Sit thou on my right hand, till I make thine enemies thy footstool. David therefore himself calleth the messiah his Lord; and whence is he then his son?* And the common people heard him gladly, for they understood that the messiah was not of the line of David.

And he said unto them, for he was a Zadokite: *Beware of these priests, which love to go in long clothing, and love salutations in the marketplaces, and the chief seats in the synagogues, and the uppermost rooms at feasts; which devour widows' houses as corban as a petition to God, and for a pretence make long prayers. They honour wealth and esteem above the Lord. They shall be damned.* And Jesus went over against the treasury, and watched the people cast money into the treasury. And many that were rich cast in much. And there came a certain poor widow, and she threw in two mites, which make a farthing. And he called unto those assembled: *Truly, this poor widow hath cast more in than all they which have cast into the treasury, for all they did cast in of their abundance; but she of her want did cast in all that she had, even all her living. This woman honoureth God above wealth; the gates of the kingdom are open to her.*

And Jesus observed on the grandeur of the temple and the manner of stones of which it was built, and he said: *And yet these great buildings will be destroyed, for they are unclean, and not a stone will rest upon another, for it is as nothing to the temple which God will raise up on the third day of His kingdom, for so it is written in Hosea and Ezekiel.*

And Jesus took his priestly disciples, Peter, James and John, up to the Mount of Olives to watch for God's miracle, and as they sat there over against the temple, Peter, James and John came to him privately, for they were anxious, and said: *Thou hast said it was the day of the Lord, but yet the mountain trembleth not. Tell us, when shall these things be, and what shall be the sign when all these things shall be fulfilled?*

And Jesus answering them began to say: *Ye shall know that the day of the Lord is nigh by these signs, for such things must needs be: when ye hear of wars and rumours of wars, for nation shall rise against nation, and kingdom against kingdom: and there shall be earthquakes in divers places, and there shall be famines and troubles: but the end shall not be yet, these are the beginnings of the birth pangs, which endure forty years. Now the brother shall deliver the brother to death, and the father the son; and children shall rise up against their parents, and shall cause them to be put to death. And ye that shall endure in righteousness unto the end time shall be saved. And, wheresoever the body is, thither will the eagles be gathered together, for ye shall see the abomination of desolation, spoken of by Daniel the prophet, standing in the temple, and ye shall know that the appointed time cometh.*

As it was in the days of Noah, so shall it be also in the last days. They did eat, they drank, they married wives, they were given in marriage, until the day that Noah entered into the ark, and the flood came, and destroyed them all. Likewise also as it was in the days of Lot; they did eat, they drank, they bought, they sold, they planted, they builded; But the same day that Lot went out of Sodom it rained fire and brimstone from heaven, and destroyed them all. Even thus shall it be in the day of the Lord. In that day, he which shall be upon the housetop, and his stuff in the house, let him not come down to take it away: and he that is in the field, let him likewise not return back. Remember Lot's wife.

Whosoever shall seek to save his life shall lose it; and whosoever shall lose his life shall preserve it. In that night there shall be two men in one bed; the one shall be taken, and the other shall be left. Two women shall be grinding together; the one shall be taken, and the other left. Two men shall be in the field; the one shall be taken, and the other left. For in those days shall be affliction, such as was not from the beginning of the creation which God created unto this time, neither shall be. And except that the Lord had shortened those days, no flesh should be saved: but for the elect's sake, whom he hath chosen, he hath shortened the days.

But in those days, after that tribulation, the sun shall be darkened, and the moon shall not give her light, And the stars of heaven shall fall, and the powers that are in heaven shall be shaken. And then shall they see coming with great power and glory Michael with his host of angels, the Son of man with the princes of heaven, Melchizedek and the sons of light, to justify the holy ones of God. And then shall he gather together his elect from the four winds, from the uttermost part of the earth to the uttermost part of heaven.

This generation shall not pass, till all these things be done. But of that day and that hour knoweth no man, no, not the angels which are in heaven, but only the Lord God. Watch and pray, for ye know not when the time is. For it is as a man taking a far journey to attend a wedding, who left his house, and gave authority to his servants, and to every man his work, and commanded the porter to watch. Watch ye therefore, for ye know not when the master of the house cometh, at even, or at midnight, or at the cockcrowing, or in the morning: lest coming suddenly he find you sleeping.

Then shall the kingdom of heaven be likened unto ten virgins, which took their lamps, and went forth to meet the bridegroom. And five of them were wise, and five were foolish. They that were foolish took their lamps, and took no oil with them: But the wise took oil in their vessels with their lamps. While the bridegroom tarried, they all slumbered and slept. And at midnight there was a cry made, Behold, the bridegroom cometh; go ye out to meet him. Then all those virgins arose, and trimmed their lamps. And the foolish said unto the wise, Give us of your oil; for our lamps are gone out. But the wise answered, saying, Not so; lest there be not enough for us and you: but go ye rather to them that sell, and buy for yourselves. And while they went to buy, the bridegroom came; and they that were ready went in with him to the marriage: and the door was shut. Afterward came also the other virgins, saying, Lord, Lord, open to us. But he answered and said, Truly, I know you not. Watch therefore, for ye know neither the day nor the hour wherein the kingdom cometh. If ye would be watchers for the kingdom, then Watch!

And word came to Jesus that the Romans had returned, and soldiers were bloodletting in the city, and eighteen men had died when they took refuge on the Tower of Siloam, and it collapsed before the might of Rome. And Jesus turning unto his disciples, said: *Saith the wisdom of God, I will send them prophets and apostles, and some of them they shall slay and persecute. The blood of all the prophets, which was shed from the foundation of the world, may be required of this generation, from the blood of Abel unto the blood of Zacharias which perished between the altar and the temple. Truly, it shall be required of this generation. Be not afraid of them that kill the body, and after that have no more that they can do. But I will forewarn you whom ye shall fear: Fear him, which after he hath killed hath power to cast into hell. Yea: Fear him! Are not five sparrows sold for two farthings, and not one of them is forgotten before God? But even the very hairs of your head are all numbered. Ye are of more value than many sparrows, therefore, Fear not! Take no thought for your life, for life is more than meat, and the body is more than raiment.*

And some arriving told him of Galilaeans, whose blood Pilate had mingled with their sacrifices. And Jesus answering said unto them: *Suppose ye that these*

Galilaeans were sinners above all the Galilaeans, because they suffered such things? I tell you, Nay. Or those eighteen, upon whom the tower in Siloam fell, and slew them, think ye that they were sinners above all men that dwelt in Jerusalem? I tell you, Nay: but, except ye avow God before men, ye shall all perish in everlasting death. But whosoever shall avow God before men, him shall the angels of God avow before God: But he that denieth God before men shall the angels of God deny before God. And whosoever shall speak a word against this son of man, it shall be forgiven him: but unto him that blasphemeth against the holy ghost it shall not be forgiven. And they went out in God's name, but there was naught to be done for the soldiers were many, and many were killed and many held captive. And Jesus and some disciples went into hiding in the city.

After two days was the feast of the Passover, and of unleavened bread. And Joseph Caiaphas and the chief priests came unto Pilate that they might take Jesus the Nazarene by craft, and put him to death; for they said to each other: It is expedient for us, that one man should die for the people, and that the whole nation perish not. And they said unto Pilate: Search not for him on the feast day, lest there be an uproar of the people. And Pilate, who feared the Emperor should learn he was an illegal executioner, gave them leave to take hold of the Nazarene by craft.

And the chief priests questioned some of those who had heard Jesus, and persuaded them to reveal his habits unto them, that they might know where he dwelt. And they promised to give them money in gratitude.

And in the morning before the first day of unleavened bread, when they killed the Passover, his disciples said unto him: Where wilt thou that we go and prepare that thou mayest eat the Passover? And he sendeth forth two of his disciples, and saith unto them: Go ye into the city, and there shall meet you a man bearing a pitcher of water: follow him. And wheresoever he shall go in, say ye to the goodman of the house: The Master saith, Where is the guestchamber, where I shall eat the Passover with my disciples? And he will shew you a large upper room furnished and prepared: there make ready for us. And his disciples went forth, and came into the city, and found as he had said unto them: and they made ready the Passover.

In the evening he cometh with the disciples. And as they did eat, Jesus took bread, and blessed, and brake it, and gave to them, and said: Take, eat! this is the bread of everlasting life. And he took the cup, and when he had given thanks, he gave it to them, and they all drank of it. And sprinkling it upon them, he said unto them: This is the blood of the new covenant, which God hath made with His chosen. Truly, this son of man will drink no more of the fruit of the vine, until that day that he drinks it new in the kingdom of God.

And Jesus said: It is written, I will smite the shepherd, and the sheep shall be scattered. If ye are offended by me this night, truly, one of you which eateth with this son of man shall deliver him. And they began to be sorrowful, and to say unto him one by one: Is it I? and another said: Is it I? And he came to Judas, and he said: Is it I? And Jesus said unto him: That thou doest, do quickly.

And when they had sung an hymn, they went out into the mount of Olives. And Jesus saith unto them: It is written: the Mount of Olives shall cleave in the midst thereof and the Lord my God shall come and all the holy ones with thee, and the Lord shall be king over all the earth. And Jesus said: Let us go to the garden that we might watch for the coming of the Lord.

And they came to a place which was named Gethsemane: and he saith to his disciples: *Sit ye here, while I shall pray.* And he taketh with him Peter and James and John, to greet the archangel Michael; but late in the night he began to be sore troubled, and to be very heavy. And saith unto them: *My soul is exceeding sorrowful unto death: tarry ye here, and watch.* And he went forward a little, and fell on the ground, and prayed: *Abba, Father, all things are possible unto thee: if it were possible, thy appointed time might come for them; nevertheless not what I will, but what thou wilt.* And he cometh, and findeth them sleeping, and saith unto Peter: *Simon, sleepest thou? couldest not thou watch one hour? Watch ye and pray, lest ye enter into temptation.* And again he went away, and prayed, and spake the same words. And when he returned, he found them asleep again, for their eyes were heavy, neither wist they what to answer him. And he cometh the third time, and saith unto them: *Sleep on now; take your rest. The hour has come; the end is yet far. It is written, I will smite the shepherd, and the sheep shall be scattered. Rise up, let us go; he that delivereth me is at hand; the spirit truly is ready, but the flesh is weak.*

And immediately, while he yet spake, cometh a detachment of guards with swords and the chief priests with staves. And they that stood by drew swords, and smote the servants of the high priest, but they saw all was lost, and forsook him, and fled. And they laid their hands on him, and took him.

And they led Jesus away to the high priest, that he might commit him for trial before Pilate; and Peter was taken too, even into the palace of the high priest. And the high priest asked Jesus, and said unto him: *Art thou the messiah, the Son of the Blessed?* And Jesus answered: *Thou sayest.* Then the high priest rent his clothes, for the nation had followed him, a false prophet, and saith: *What need we of witnesses? he is a false prophet who says he is the messiah, a king. It is sedition; what think ye?* And they all condemned him to be guilty. And the guards began to spit on him, and to cover his face, and to buffet him, and to say unto him: *Prophesy, thou false prophet,* and the servants did strike him with the palms of their hands.

And Peter was brought before Annas, in the lower court, and the priest said: *Thou also wast with Jesus the Nazarene. Vow that he is a false prophet and thou shalt go free with a whipping.* But Peter replied, saying: *I know not, neither understand I what thou sayest, for it is written: Thou shalt not speak evil of the ruler of thy people.* And the priest said: *Thou shalt be crucified by the Romans if thou deniest him not. If thou wilt not sware then deny him thrice and save thyself, for it is not lawful for us to condemn two men on the same day.* And Peter feared to be hung on a tree, and he denied him thrice; and Annas ordered him to be whipped. And as he went out the bugles sounded the Cockcrow from the Antonia fortress. And when he thought thereon, he wept.

And in the morning the chief priests held a consultation with the elders and scribes and the whole council, to confirm the committal, for they had no other authority, and then carried Jesus away bound, and delivered him to Pilate. And Pilate asked him: *Art thou the king of the Jews?* And Jesus answered him nothing, for it was not lawful in his philosophy for him to vow a man to destruction in the courts of the gentile.

And after his condemnation, Jesus lay bound with them that had made insurrection with him, who had committed murder in the insurrection. And the multitude came to the palace, crying aloud to Pilate, and began to beseech him, as he was wont to make them, calling: *Barabbas, Barabbas*, for this was their name for Jesus. And Pilate said unto them: *Will ye that I release unto you the king of the Jews? Then take ye to your homes, and I shall release him.* And they dispersed in wonder that Pilate had heard them. And Pilate, when the people had gone, delivered Jesus, when he had scourged him, to be crucified, for he was deceiving them.

And the soldiers led him away into a public place that all might see him, and they called together the legionaries. And, after the fashion of the Roman festival of Saturnalia, they dressed him as the fool who would be king; they clothed him with purple, and platted a crown of thorns, and put it about his head, and began to salute him: *Hail, king of the Jews!* And they smote him on the head with a reed, and did spit upon him, and bowing their knees worshipped him. And when they had mocked him, they took the purple from him, and led him out naked to crucify him.

And as they passed by, one Simon, encountered them and took his cross. And they bring him unto the place Golgoltha, which is, being interpreted: The skull. And, to ease his pain, they gave him to drink wine mingled with myrrh: but he received it not, for he would not break his vow of consecration to God. And it was the third hour, and they crucified him. And the superscription of his accusation was written over: THE KING OF THE JEWS. And with him they crucify many more seditionists; and one was on his right hand, and another on his left. And the scripture was fulfilled, which saith: *And he was numbered with the transgressors.* And they that were crucified with him reviled him saying: *Ah, thou that destroyest the temple, and buildest it in three days, Save thyself, and us, and come down from the cross.* And Jesus answered, saying: *Doest thou no longer fear God, since thou art in the same condemnation. And we indeed justly, for we receive punishment for what we have done. But this other, hath done nothing amiss.* For one hanging near them was an innocent pilgrim. And they that passed by railed on him, wagging their heads, and likewise also the chief priests mocking said among themselves: *He saved others; himself he cannot save. If he be the messiah, the king of Israel let him now descend from the cross, that we may see and believe. Let God deliver him now, if he will have him, for he said: I am the Son of God.*

And after three days Jesus cried with a loud voice, saying: *Eloi, Eloi, lama sabachthani?* which is, being interpreted: *My God, my God, why hast thou forsaken me?* And some of them that stood by, when they heard it, said: *Behold, he calleth Elias.* And one ran and filled a sponge full of vinegar, and put it on a reed, and gave him to drink, saying: *Let alone; let us see whether Elias will come to take him down.* And Jesus again cried with a loud voice, and gave up the ghost.

And now when the even was come, because it was the preparation, that is, the day before the sabbath, Joseph of Arimathaea, which also waiteth for the kingdom of God, being an Essene, an honourable counsellor of the council of the congregation, came and went in boldly unto Pilate, and craved the body of Jesus, since he was the next of kin. And Pilate, satisfied with the punishment, called unto him the centurion, asking him whether he had been any while dead, and the centurion avowed he was dead, for he had pierced him with his spear. When Pilate knew it of the centurion, he yieldeth the corpse to Joseph, and he bought white linen, and took him down, and wrapped him in the linen, and laid him in a sepulchre which was hewn out of a rock in the Garden of Zadok, and rolled a stone unto the door of the sepulchre.

And when the sabbath was past, Mary Magdalene, and Mary the mother of James, and Salome came to mourn him. And very early in the morning the first day of the week, they came unto the sepulchre at the rising of the sun. And they said among themselves: *Who shall roll us away the stone from the door of the sepulchre?* And when they looked, they saw that the stone was rolled away: for it was very great. And entering into the sepulchre, they saw a young man sitting on the right side, clothed in a long white garment; and they were affrighted. And he saith unto them: *Be not affrighted: Ye seek Jesus the Nazarene, which was crucified: he is not here: behold the place where they laid him. But go your way, tell his disciples that they must go into Galilee to be safe.* And they went out quickly, and fled from the sepulchre; for they trembled and were amazed: neither said they any thing to any man; for they were afraid.

BIBLIOGRAPHY

Many readers like to see extensive notes and references in a book of this kind while others are put off by numbers in the text, and pages of discontinuous prose and lists of books at the end. Writing about Christianity has been a mass industry for 1700 years and the listable books are uncountable. There have even been hundreds of critical books in the last 200 years. The following selection of books are the ones that have been stimulating or useful in some particular respect. Those who want long bibliographies will have to turn to academic works, although Campbell's *The Rise and Fall of Jesus*, otherwise bizarre, has a concise summary of critical work on the foundation of Christianity and over six dense pages of references to the critical literature.

Allegro J, *The Dead Sea Scrolls*, London 1964
Armstrong K, *A History of Jerusalem*, London, 1996
Baigent M & Leigh R, *The Dead Sea Scrolls Deception*, London 1991
Barnes E W, *The Rise of Christianity*, London 1948
Black M & Rowley H H, (Eds), *Peake's Commentary on the Bible*, London 1962
Campbell S, *The Rise and Fall of Jesus*, Explicit Books, Edinburgh, 1996
Cruden A, *Cruden's Complete Concordance*, London 1963
Dodd C H, *The Founder of Christianity*, London 1971
Douglas J D (Ed), *New Bible Dictionary*, Leicester 1982
Eisenman R & Wise M, *The Dead Sea Scrolls Uncovered*, Shaftesbury, 1992
Ellis Enterprises Inc, *The Bible Library CD-ROM v 1.1a*, Oklahoma, 1994
Forster W, *Palestinian Judaism in New Testament Times*, London, 1964
Furneaux R, *The Other Side of the Story*, London 1953
Graves R and Podro, J, *The Nazarene Gospel Restored*, London 1953
Grollenburg L H, *Shorter Atlas of the Bible*, Edinburgh, 1959
Lehmann J, *The Jesus Report*, London, 1972
Maccoby Hyam, *The Mythmaker: Paul and the Invention of Christianity*, London 1986
Manson T W, *The Teaching of Jesus*, Cambridge 1951
Nineham D E, *Pelican Commentaries: Saint Mark*, Middlesex, 1969
Renan E, *The Life of Jesus*, London 1935
Shanks H (Ed), *Understanding the Dead Sea Scrolls*, London 1993
Taylor V, *The Formation of the Gospel Tradition*, London 1933
Thiering B, *Jesus the Man*, London 1992
Vermes Geza, *Jesus the Jew*, London 1973
Vermes Geza, *The Dead Sea Scrolls in English*, London 1990
Wells G A, *The Jesus of the Early Christians*, London 1971
Whiston W. (Trans), *The Works of Josephus*, London, undated
Wilson E, *The Scrolls from the Dead Sea*, New York, 1955

Books by

DR MICHAEL D MAGEE

published by AskWhy! Publications

The Mystery Of Barabbas
Exploring the Origins of a Pagan Religion

From time to time we read of churchmen scaring us with accounts of the spread of paganism, by which they usually mean worshipping satan. Pagan religions were really the religions which preceded Christianity in the lives of the citizens of the Roman empire. When Christianity became the state religion all pagan religions were banned and pagans were persecuted. So it has been ever since, only in the last few hundred years has Christianity adopted a mask of liberality. The author decided to explore the origins of Christianity, an exploration that eventually took him into the present book, *The Hidden Jesus*, and he found that there is very little that can be identified in Christianity that did not have its origin elsewhere. Christianity is itself pagan insomuch that it has adapted its ceremonies and liturgies from the pagan precursors that it professes to decry as the work of the devil. *The Mystery of Barabbas* can be thought of as the companion of *The Hidden Jesus*.

ISBN 0-9521913-1-8 £9.99 Add £1.00 p&p UK ($19.00 inc shipping US)

Who Lies Sleeping?
The Dinosaur Heritage and the Extinction of Man

Mankind seems to suffer from an inability to recognize and understand what it is doing to its own environment. In this book Dr Magee considers the extinction of the dinosaurs 65 million years ago and shows that its symptoms were just the symptoms of the mass extinction which is occuring at present. Is it possible that the dinosaurs developed intelligence and destroyed themselves just as present day humans seem to be doing? The author examines the evidence in detail and shows that the dinosaurs gave every indication of being ready to become intelligent. Some species of dinosaur somewhere had all the attributes considered necessary for intelligence in the intelligent mammal. The latter has used its gift to begin the destruction of the world within 200 years of inventing technology. If the intelligent dinosaur had done the same, all that would remain of it in the fossil record would be an oily smear, polluted with heavy metals and exotic compounds. That is just what we find when the dinosaurs died.

ISBN 0-9521913-0-X £7.99 pbk. Add £1.00 p&p UK ($16.00 inc shipping US)

"**A book to savour... Deserves all the hype it can get.**" UFO Magazine.

"**A terrific writer... Compelling as any first rate thriller**." Bath Evening Chronicle.

About the author

Michael D Magee was brought up by Christian parents but was never indoctrinated into one dogma and was able from an early age to make his own judgements about the Christian religion.

He was born in Hunslet, an industrial suburb of Leeds, Yorkshire, in 1941.

He attended Cockburn High School in South Leeds. He won a studentship to the Royal Military College of Science, Shrivenham, where he graduated with an honours degree in natural science in 1963. He went on to obtain a Ph.D. degree from the University of Aston in Birmingham in 1967 and a teaching qualification, a PGCE, from Huddersfield before it was a university.

He carried out research at the Universities of Aston and Bradford, and at the Wool Industries Research Association, taught in a Further Education College in Devon for seven years and for ten years was an advisor to the UK government at the National Economic Development Office in London.

This is his third book. *Who Lies Sleeping? The Dinosaur Heritage and the Extinction of Man* and *The Mystery of Barabbas: Exploring the Origins of a Pagan Religion*, available from AskWhy! Publications, being the others. He has also written over a dozen scientific papers on the structure and interactions of small molecules investigated using microwave radiation, and he has written or edited some forty publications on microeconomic issues for the government.

Now living in Somerset, he spends his time drinking the fermented juice of the apple and solving the mysteries of the universe, like why anybody would buy designer beer when such wonderful stuff as traditional cider is available at a fraction the price. He writes as a hobby but hopes his observations will interest others.